SHORES OF REFUGE

· RONALD SANDERS ·

SHORES
OF REFUGE

A HUNDRED YEARS
OF JEWISH EMIGRATION

SCHOCKEN BOOKS · NEW YORK

Library of Congress Cataloging-in-Publication Data

Sanders, Ronald.
Shores of refuge.

Bibliography: p.
Includes index.
1. Jews—Migrations. 2. Jews—Soviet Union—
Persecutions. 3. Soviet Union—Emigration and
immigration. 4. United States—Emigration and
immigration. 5. Jews, East European—United States.
6. Immigrants—United States. 7. Holocaust, Jewish
(1939-1945). 8. Hebrew Sheltering and Immigrant Aid
Society of America. 9. Soviet Union—Ethnic relations.
10. United States—Ethnic relations. I. Title.
DS125.S284 1989   304.8'08992404   88-43131
ISBN 0-8052-0916-6

Book Design by Victoria Hartman
Manufactured in the United States of America
Photographs have been provided through the courtesy of HIAS, the
YIVO Institute for Jewish Research, and the Leo Baeck Institute.

This book is gratefully dedicated to:
George Jaffin
Joseph and Ida Liskin
Edwin Shapiro
and
The People of HIAS

Contents

Contents

Photographs appear on pages 203–212 and 401–410.

Preface

In 1880, the Jews of Central and Eastern Europe—of the three empires of Germany, Austria-Hungary, and Russia, and of the Balkan countries—numbered more than six million, or about 80 percent of the Jewish population of the world. About three million were in the Russian Empire alone. Their forebears had, for the most part, lived in these regions for centuries. On the other hand, there were only about twenty-five thousand Jews in Palestine and three hundred thousand in the United States, the great majority of them in these countries for not more than a generation. There were about two hundred thousand Jews altogether in Western Europe and Great Britain, and mere handfuls in the British Empire and Latin America.

By the 1980s, about half the world's Jewish population of thirteen million lived in the Western Hemisphere, more than five million of them in the United States. Another 3.5 million were in Israel, and more than a million in Western Europe, mainly in Britain and France. In Eastern Europe, there were still possibly two million Jews in the Soviet Union, but otherwise the Jewish populations had become negligible in their ancient centers. In Poland, where there had been more than three million Jews on the eve of World War II, there now were considerably fewer than ten thousand.

Much of this enormous shift in the worldwide balance of Jewish population was due to the Nazi slaughter of six million Jews. But, for the rest, what had occurred was perhaps the largest exodus of a single people in history—larger, and scarcely less resolute, than the ancestral one of the Old Testament. It had taken a hundred years rather than forty; but it had been directed at more than one Promised Land.

· · ·

xi

The beginnings of the exodus can be traced to the year 1881 in Russia, when the assassination of Tsar Alexander II by a terrorist organization was followed by a wave of anti-Jewish rioting. There had been a small emigration from the fringes of the Russian Empire before this; but now the heartlands of its Jewish population were struck with a passion to depart. Jewish immigration into the United States—the principal destination of the movement from the outset—suddenly leaped from an unprecedented 5,692 arrivals in 1881 to more than thirteen thousand the following year. In another two years, this spurt had turned into a steadily increasing outflow, not only to the United States but to other destinations as well—Britain and its Empire, Latin America, and Palestine, where modern agricultural settlement began in 1882. By 1900, Jews of the other East European countries, mainly Rumania, had joined the movement. A constant stream came from Austrian Galicia.

This classic era of Jewish emigration was characterized as much by the rise of agencies to help them as by the wanderers themselves. That very first spurt of refugees from the disturbances of 1881 had stimulated the growth of a network of rescue, from the Brody office of the Alliance Israélite Universelle just across the Austro-Russian border, to the Mansion House Fund in London and the Hebrew Emigrant Aid Society in New York. Some of these organizations did not last very long, but others replaced them, and a few became permanent institutions. Foremost among these was the Hebrew Immigrant Aid Society, or HIAS. The special place of HIAS in that classic emigration is due not only to its having preeminently served it, as this book will show, but to its being a product of it: for HIAS was the first such organization to be founded and led by people who were themselves immigrants from Eastern Europe.

World War I, the Russian Revolution and civil wars, and U.S. immigration legislation of 1921 and 1924 brought an end to that classic era. There were more than four million Jews in the United States, but now its gates were all but closed to the rest. Jewish emigrants, the bulk of them from the newly independent Poland (few were able to leave Soviet Russia), turned for the most part to Germany, France, and Palestine.

Then, in 1933, the entire Jewish situation in Europe changed drastically, and so did the character of the emigration. The mass exodus that had begun in 1881 was almost exclusively East European in provenance. But, from 1933 to 1940, German and Austro-German Jews fleeing Hitler's oppressions became Europe's preeminent refugees. They went where they could in a world that had become largely unreceptive: even immigration into Palestine was severely restricted by 1937. About half of the seven hundred thousand Jews of Germany and Austria were able to find refuge before it was too late.

Of the small numbers of Jews who survived the campaign of extermination waged upon them, only a tiny few were able to get out of
Nazi-ruled Europe between 1941 and 1945. It was not until the war's
end—and especially the creation of the Jewish State—that rescue again
became fully practicable, and the hundred-year exodus was resumed. In
the displaced-persons crisis that lasted into the 1950s, an organization
like HIAS, with a fully developed international network of its own, could
see to the emigration and placement of tens of thousands of European
Jews, into the United States and other countries of settlement. And
when new upheavals occurred—the uprisings in Poland and Hungary in
1956, the East European campaign against "Zionists" in 1968—bringing
new outpourings of emigrants, there were new efforts at assistance and
rescue. Finally, we have witnessed the great emigration of Soviet Jews
in the 1970s—a return, as it were, to the original sources of that hundred-
year history that had now come full circle.

It is the task of the pages that follow to tell that story in full.

—Ronald Sanders

PART ONE

Upheaval
in Russia

· 1881 ·

·1·

A PROLOGUE IN ODESSA

The terrorist bombs had found their target. "And it was on March 1, 1881," lamented a Russian-Jewish memoirist,

> that the sun which had risen over Jewish life in the eighteen-fifties was suddenly eclipsed. Alexander II was assassinated on the bank of the Catherine Canal in Saint Petersburg. The hand that had signed the edict freeing sixty million serfs had become motionless. The mouth that had uttered the great word "Emancipation" was silenced forever. And the salvation hoped for by the people receded far into the distance.

It had been little in the end, yet Alexander II had let more of the currents of liberalism seep into Russia than had any other tsar. There had been the historic edict of Emancipation in 1861, and other reforms as well—in the military and judiciary, and in local government, for which a system of representative institutions had been established that seemed to presage an eventual all-Russian parliament. Alexander's Minister of the Interior, General M. T. Loris-Melikov, had even been preparing a modest program that caused eager spirits to believe they saw a constitution in the offing.

As for his Jewish subjects, Alexander had been as cautiously benevolent toward them as he had been toward the country at large. In 1856, he had abolished his father's cruel cantonist system, whereby annual quotas of Jewish boys of twelve and younger had been conscripted for more than twenty-five years of military service. And although Russia's academic institutions had always been open to Jews in principle, he had instigated reforms making them less forbidding. Above all, he had relaxed some of the restrictions applying to the Pale of Settlement, that sprawling network of provinces in the west and southwest of his Empire outside which the vast majority of its three million Jews were not allowed to reside.

To be sure, that colossal ghetto remained, and poverty was still widespread among Jews, yet there had been considerable advances. "Toward the end of the seventies of the nineteenth century," another memoirist could say,

> the Jews of Russia felt quite happy. This was particularly true of those Jews who were more enlightened and came in contact with the outside world. The high schools and universities were open to the Jew; everywhere he was welcomed, and he was successful in every field of human endeavour.

Genuine grief interrupted Purim festivities throughout the land at the news of Alexander's death, and the leaders of the Jewish community of Saint Petersburg—a bastion of wealth and privilege far outside the Pale—attended the funeral, laying "a silver wreath, surrounded with palm branches and roses, on the bier of the murdered Czar. Verses from Lamentations and from I Samuel were worked on the bands which were tied to the wreath."

And what now? Despite the murder, there was some hope for the future. On the day of the funeral, prominent Jewish mourners were received by the new Tsar, Alexander III. "This," according to the news report, "is stated to be the first time that a Jewish deputation has been admitted to the presence of a Russian Emperor." There were, nonetheless, good reasons for apprehension as well. "It is, we fear," ruminated the *Jewish Chronicle* of London,

> unfortunately to be dreaded that in the reaction which is sure to come on the murder of the Czar, the Jews will lose some of the privileges gained during the reign of Alexander II. Such fear is augmented when we remember how persistently the Russian officials contend that the Nihilist movement is supported by Jews. God help them if but the faintest shadow of suspicion rests upon any Jews for complicity in the regicide conspiracy.

A Jewish woman, Hessia Helfman, was among the six conspirators rounded up in the next few days.

By then the signs were coming quickly that the liberalism of the father had died with him. The new Tsar's closest adviser was his boyhood teacher Konstantin Pobedonostsev, a writer and scholar who held the post of procurator of the Holy Synod, or official lay leader of the Russian Orthodox Church. A translator of Ralph Waldo Emerson, Thomas Carlyle, Herbert Spencer, and Saint Augustine, this clean-shaven intellectual had emerged from his life's spiritual journey in passionate reaffirmation of his Byzantine roots. Although he continued to admire the "Anglo-Saxons," he had concluded that their "peculiar institutions" did not suit Holy Russia, where an indissoluble union of state and orthodoxy, embodied in the Tsar and uncorrupted by parliaments, was needed for the redemption of its vast, ignorant, and impoverished peasantry. "For God's sake, Your Majesty," he had written to Alexander III a few days after the succession, warning him against Loris-Melikov's wisp of constitutional reform, "do not believe and do not listen. This will be ruin, the ruin of Russia and of you."

Alexander III did not believe, and had begun listening to his own entourage instead. This soon included the conservative Count N. P. Ignatiev, who was to replace Loris-Melikov in the Cabinet at the end of that April. It also included a secret organization called the Holy Brotherhood, a shock troop of members of the privileged classes ready to act on their own initiative and use any tactics they thought necessary for stamping out the revolutionary movement. They also had surrogates: suddenly in April, bands of young ruffians—soon popularly known as "barefoot brigades," though they were mainly from the middle classes—were to appear in various towns of southern Russia, spoiling for a fight. There is little reason to doubt that the Holy Brotherhood was behind them.

But with whom were they to do battle? Five of the conspirators against Alexander II—Hessia Helfman was spared because she turned out to be pregnant—were publicly hanged on April 3. Hadn't this checked the revolutionary momentum of Narodnaya Volya (People's Will), the organization they led? Or was an uprising only now to follow? The government was taking no chances. "The authorities appear to have feared some kind of reprisal on the part of the friends and fellow-conspirators of the executed [persons]," cabled the Saint Petersburg correspondent of *The Times* of London on April 8,

> for on the evening of the execution all the small restaurants and drinking shops were suddenly closed by the police at 6 o'clock, and numerous Cossacks patrolled the streets. A large number of important arrests have been made, about which it is forbidden to telegraph a word.

The Russian Easter, a season of revelry hard to control, was approaching that Sunday, April 12, and the government issued an official postponement of the holiday celebration for a week, offering the late Tsar's forthcoming birthday as an excuse.

But this deferral of festivities only caused the tension to mount.

"Advices from St. Petersburg," reported *The Times* for Friday, April 17,

> represent all business as at a momentary standstill owing to the Easter solemnities, and the season seems to be passing without bringing the reform *Ukase* expected about this time. This was the birthday, too, of the deceased Emperor, which it was confidently hoped his successor would commemorate by some concession to the popular demands, but disappointment seems to have again taken the place of hope; and much anxiety is being created by the continued silence and apparent inactivity of the new Czar, who has hitherto given no clear sign of his ruling intentions.

Surely something was about to burst; the gentlemen of the foreign press thought so, at any rate. "The New York *Herald*," Abraham Cahan, then a member of the Vilna cell of Narodnaya Volya, was to recall, "had even sent a special correspondent to St. Petersburg, to be on the spot when the revolution broke out."

Yet the chill north remained quiet.

Hundreds of miles to the south, Prince A. M. Dondukov-Korsakov, the provisional Governor-General of Odessa, and M. Levkovich, the city's commandant, had confined the soldiers of the local garrison to the barracks under arms for three days beginning Sunday, April 12. They well knew what they were doing. What they were taking precaution against was not some dimly anticipated revolutionary uprising, but the clear threat of rioting against Odessa's Jews. This would have been far from the first time such an incident had occurred.

The Black Sea port city of Odessa, rough-hewn but sophisticated, European to a degree rare in Russia at the time, was a kind of Chicago of the steppes: Ukrainian grain was its meat, sent out in ships to all over the Near East and beyond, bringing prosperity to those who dealt in it. At the beginning of the century it had still been a sleepy village, a former Turkish fort inherited by Russia through war and treaty; but the lure of its sunlight and commercially advantageous location had caused it to grow into a lively metropolis of more than three hundred thousand by 1881. In some ways it was hardly Russian at all: Frenchmen had designed and developed it, Englishmen had joined in exploiting it, Greek and Italian businessmen had become its dominating class—Odessa's Italian opera was the best in the land—and Turks, Armenians, and Jews flourished and loomed large there. Yet this ethnic complexity, and the proximity of a rural peasantry that was more Ukrainian and Moldavian than anything else, made Russianness all the more a universal ideal to live up to in Odessa, especially among its Jews.

In a sense, their Odessa—located well within the Pale—was something the Jews had had to invent, since Moscow and Petersburg were all but completely closed to them. It was as much an immigrant center as any overseas city, and Jews swarmed into it not only from the impoverished townlets and villages of the Pale, but also from other countries—from Turkey, from Germany, and, in particularly large numbers, from Austrian Galicia. Cosmopolitan and ethnocentric all at once, the Jews of Odessa had made their city the capital of Russian-Jewish literature—in Hebrew, in Yiddish, and in Russian at the same time—and of a certain folk-vision of the good life. "Like God in Odessa" was to be the popular Yiddish expression denoting ease, contentment, and prosperity, and by 1881 some seventy-five thousand Jews—one-quarter of the city's population—were there seeking this quasi-divine status.

Latecomers, the Jews of Odessa were making rapid advances in its economy and had recently displaced the Greeks as the majority owners of grain export businesses. And it was between Greeks and Jews in particular that tensions had grown over the years—especially among their youth, two participating groups in the raucous street life of the city. The main synagogue and the Greek church were near each other, and brawling among younger members of the crowds spilling from them during the Passover-Easter season had become virtually an annual occurrence.

Indeed, ten years earlier—during Easter week of 1871—a few months after the city had emerged from the ravages of a cholera epidemic, there had been something much worse.

The *Jewish Chronicle* had conveyed the unhappy news to the English-speaking world at that time, reporting on April 21, 1871, that

> during the Russian Easter holidays the mob pillaged the houses of the Jewish inhabitants at Odessa, forcibly entering counting houses and shops, and causing great devastation. There is a panic also amongst Christians. The damage is enormous. The authorities could not do anything to protect the population.

Noting that anti-Jewish riots took place in Odessa every Easter, the *Chronicle* stressed that they had nevertheless "not assumed such dimensions for the last 12 years." What had happened this time?

The *Chronicle* was able to put the story together in the ensuing weeks. "It was rumored," the paper reported in June,

> that some Jewish students had thrown a dead cat upon the altar of the Greek church; others circulated a report that a holy image had

been pelted with stones by them. Nothing more was wanted to incite the mob to give a beating to the Jews on Easter Sunday, and no importance was attached to this fact, because it constitutes a regular feature of the annual program of the Easter amusements of the Russian populace. But the administration of blows increased, and took place simultaneously in several localities.

Suddenly the lid had blown off this exercise in conventional ruffianism. "Then would have been the proper moment to take energetic measures," the *Chronicle* chides; "the arrest of a few young rowdies would have nipped the riot in the bud." But this was not done.

Instead, the city was taken over by a hellish anarchy. "Odessa was in the hands of about twenty-five or thirty bands," according to the *Chronicle*, "forming a complete force of robbers. Nothing escaped their violence." Homes and shops "where no signs of Christianity, such as images of saints or Easter loaves, were displayed, were bombarded with stones and plundered; and doors and windows broken in." But destruction rather than looting was the principal goal. "Banknotes were torn to pieces; the most costly furniture was wantonly destroyed. Beds were ripped up, the feathers strewn through the streets so that for several days some portions of the city looked quite white, as if a heavy fall of snow had taken place." Whole families were stripped of their clothing. "The cries of women and children were fearful. Brutal outrages on women, and the most horrible scenes took place." As for the bystanders, not all of them were innocent. "Russian ladies in carriages were noticed driving in the streets, and even pointing out to the bandits the houses occupied by Jews."

Night fell on that brutal Sunday at last, but the mob's fury had not died; it reawoke and grew worse the next day. "On Monday afternoon the work of destruction was resumed on a larger scale," the *Chronicle* relates. The rioters now gathered in the main Jewish residential street and went from house to house, smashing windows and doors. "Scarcely a pane of glass remained entire in the Jewish quarter. Even the highest windows of the Temple were broken with a dexterity worthy of a better cause. The popular fury increased hourly." On Italian Street in the commercial center, a large Jewish banking establishment was broken into:

The large panes of glass of the superb building were destroyed, without exception. The multitude penetrated into the house and into the office; the heavy business books, accounts, copies, everything, was thrown out of the windows, picked up among loud hurrahs by those on the street below, and torn into small fragments. The whole street was literally strewn with account currents, bills and documents of all kinds.

Another type of business establishment in which Jewish owners were prominent was also not forgotten: "One liquor store after another was taken by storm, and the audacity of the rioters increased with the consciousness of their impunity." The methods of destruction became more severe with evening. "What could not be destroyed by hand and stones was burnt, and many houses fell a prey to the flames."

The scene was prolonged into yet another day. "On Tuesday there was hardly one street left where some houses were not demolished or pillaged." Disorder reigned and authority had disintegrated:

> Cossacks were dragged out of their saddles; like an avalanche the mania of destruction was hurled onward from quarter to quarter, and finally human life was no more respected. A Cossack was stabbed and the multitude cried out: "Hurrah, it is but a Cossack!" The feathers of the destroyed beds lay from 3 to 6 inches high on the street, and about thirty soldiers were silent spectators when a ruffian, encouraged by the cheering of the populace, dragged a piano toward a balcony for the purpose of hurling it down into the street, in spite of the officer who was standing below.

In the end, about a thousand homes had been destroyed. "Four thousand Jewish families are in utter destitution, through the pillage of three whole days," the *Chronicle* reported;

> sixteen persons have been murdered; sixty seriously wounded; females have been brutally violated; a mother, who was trying to prevent her daughter from being outraged, had her ears cut off and died from loss of blood; Jewish synagogues have been pillaged; the books of the Law torn and trodden upon.

Entire sections of the city lay in ruins.

What, indeed, had happened to the enforcers of law and order? "The part the authorities have played in the affair is highly exasperating," the *Chronicle* observed. "It has been asserted that the governor ... forbade on the first day of the outrage the despatch of any other communications than commercial intelligence to St. Petersburg." The *Chronicle* subsequently relayed a report from the St. Petersburg correspondent of the *Neue Freie Presse* of Vienna

> which states that great irritation is manifested in Odessa against the officials who, if they did not connive at the outrages, permitted them. ... The judicial investigation amply demonstrates that the people were convinced that the Government permitted the outrages, for some persons said, "If such were not the case, would the authorities have let us go on three days with the work without hindrance?" Such logic gravely compromises the officials.

Clearly, it was the local authorities who were compromised. Saint Petersburg was far away and had been ill-informed. "When Prince [S. G.] Stroganoff was Governor of Odessa similar excesses were never committed," the *Jewish Chronicle* pointed out with regard to a well-known Russian liberal; "he prevented them, but the present Governor took no notice of them, nor did the police interfere." With all due propriety, Governor Kotzebue was in fact promptly removed from his post; but he was soon to be Governor of Warsaw, and the incident seems to have done no harm to his career. The initial ignorance of Saint Petersburg—and the government of the Tsar Liberator, Alexander II—regarding what had been done to the Jews of Odessa in Easter week of 1871 was followed by indifference. This did not bode well for the future.

But now, at any rate, at Eastertime ten years later, and in a moment of grave national crisis, the Governor-General of Odessa was prepared.

·2·

A SEASON OF DEVASTATIONS

"If a statement made by the St. Petersburg *Exchange Gazette* is correct," the *Jewish Chronicle* had written just after the riots in 1871,

> the population of Southern Russia is hopefully looking forward to some fresh sport in the way of Jew-baiting. "The account of the deeds of the Greeks and inhabitants of Odessa," writes the *Gazette*, "arouses wild instincts in the South Russian people, and especially in the Cossacks. A new outrage on the Jews is spoken of as imminent. Our population is not remarkable for mildness of temper, and there is hardly an atrocity that it may be expected to shrink from."

There had been no further trouble at the time, perhaps because of the appointment of a new governor for the region. But these words were a grim reminder that attacking Jews had once been a major southern Russian pastime: there had been the slaughters waged by the Zaporogian Cossacks during their uprising under the Hetman Bogdan Khmelnitsky in 1648, and the depredations of the unruly *haidamak* Cossack bands through the first half and more of the eighteenth century. Much had changed, of course, since those primitive times; the Ukraine, now in the forefront of Russian economic progress, was in the first stages of a surge of industrialization that would startle the world with its rapidity. But the Jews, forcibly confined there, remained a prominent and, for many, irritating presence, whose economic gifts often enabled them to outstrip the efforts of the Christian populations among which they lived. And this was even truer in the hinterland towns than amid the fiercely competitive atmosphere of Odessa.

Such a town was Yelizavetgrad, about 150 miles northeast of Odessa, midway along the road to Poltava. Yelizavetgrad had fully enjoyed

11

its share in the fortunate history of the region. Like Odessa, it had been
a Turkish village at the beginning of the century and had grown dramatically. By 1881, it was a prosperous community of about fifty thousand that not only figured prominently in the region's grain commerce
and milling of flour, but also had some substantial industries all its own,
notably tobacco. In the eyes of a small Jewish farm boy, Lev Davidovich
Bronstein—the future Trotsky—arriving there on a visit with his father
just four years later, it was a lovely metropolis. "Not a single capital in
the world," he was to recall, "neither Paris nor New York, made in
after years such an impression on me as Yelizavetgrad with its side-
walks, green roofs, balconies, shops, policemen and red balloons. For
several hours, with my eyes wide open, I gaped at the face of civilization."

This civilization, like the one in Odessa, had a large Jewish component. The crucial parts of its economy were mainly in Jewish hands—
the grain brokerages, the flour mills, the tobacco industry, and the
liquor trade, which had been a predominantly Jewish activity in Poland
and Russia since time immemorial. Moreover, the fifteen thousand or
so Jews of Yelizavetgrad—forming almost a third of the population—
were strongly drawn to the Russian culture and had a "modern" rabbi,
trained in one of the government seminaries, who dressed in the European manner and spoke the language well. This, after all, was the new
frontier, far from the ancient and often impoverished Jewish centers to
the northwest, where the Yiddish language and narrow religious tradi-
tionalism formed barriers against the wide world.

A good example of the bright younger generation of Yelizavetgrad
Jewry in 1881 was the editor of *Yuzhni Krai (Southern Frontier)*, one
of the town's Russian newspapers. Born near Poltava in 1853, Jacob
Gordin was eventually to settle in New York and become the first major
playwright in the Yiddish language; but at this time his grasp of the
ancestral mother tongue had become shaky (in later years some of his
critics were to say he never quite recovered it). He was utterly Russian
now, something of a socialist, like so many of the acculturated intellectuals of his generation, and a Tolstoyan, largely preoccupied with a
quasi-religious sect of his own making, the Duchovno-Bibleyiskoye
Bratsvo (Spiritual-Biblical Brotherhood), which preached a life of Old
Testament simplicity and rejected Talmudic orthodoxy. His criticism of
the Jewish life of his time was once summed up by him in *Yuzhni Krai*
like this:

> Brother Jews . . . why do all elements of the Russian society
> hate you? Is this only a religious hatred? . . . Our love of money,
> . . . stinginess and rush for profits, our arrogance, quarrelsomeness,
> our silly and slavish aping of the inflated and dissolute Russian

nobility, our usury, saloon-keeping, and tactlessness . . . turn the
Russian people against us.

He was to write these words two years after the disaster had struck in
Yelizavetgrad.

It began that tense Easter week of 1881 at one of the inevitable sites
of Jewish-Christian confrontation in Russia—a tavern. Since those ancient days when Polish landlords had favored them in the granting of
rights to distill and sell liquor in the villages, Jews had remained—in
the lands that Russia had taken over from the Poles—prominent in the
risky business of catering to the drinking habits of the rural and small-
town populations. It was a situation disliked not only by Jews who were
more fortunate than to have to sell liquor to live, but also by the Russian
government, which usually blamed Jews for the chronic drunkenness of
the peasantry and had spent the better part of the century trying to
force them out of the villages and the liquor trade. Jews had indeed left
the villages for the most part, usually in great distress, but in the towns
and cities of the Pale they went right on being the chief purveyors of
vodka and brandy. "The drunkenness of Ivan" was a conception in Jewish folklore to serve attitudes of prim and invidious self-satisfaction; but
for the Jewish tavernkeeper it also was a grim and occasionally violent
fact of life.

In the perturbed atmosphere following the assassination of the Tsar,
other elements now were added to this traditionally hazardous situation. On Saturday, April 11, bands of young strangers began appearing
at the Yelizavetgrad railroad station and circulating through the streets
and public places of the town. The next day, Easter Sunday, the members of these "barefoot brigades" organized street-corner conversations, claiming that the Tsar had issued his long-awaited ukase, and that
it commanded Orthodox Russians to beat up the Zhids and take their
property.

Jewish leaders promptly appealed to the municipality for protection. The local police responded with concern and called in a detachment
of soldiers from some distance away to help maintain public order. Their
vigil lasted three days, and nothing untoward occurred during that time.
Then, on Wednesday afternoon, April 15, the troops withdrew, and in
virtually the next moment, trouble began.

At four o'clock, a fight broke out in a tavern between its Jewish
proprietor and a gentile customer who had smashed a drinking glass
and refused to pay for it. Pushing the customer into the street, the
proprietor found a hostile crowd gathered there, as if the incident had
been prearranged. Immediately the cry went up: "The Zhids are beating up our people!" A scuffle ensued, during which some members of

the mob flung themselves upon Jewish passers-by and others forced their way into the tavern. "Inflamed by the drink thus obtained," according to one contemporary account, "the rioters proceeded to the Jewish quarter, and commenced a systematic destruction of the Jewish shops and warehouses. At first some attempt was made by the Jews to protect their property"—a few of the sterner defenders fired at their assailants with revolvers—"but this only served to increase the violence of the mob, which proceeded to attack the dwellings of the Jews and to wreck the synagogues."

The attacks subsided as darkness fell and the police reassembled; but the latter were now without the aid of troops, and, as on a similar night in Odessa ten years before, the mob's excitement proved to be only temporarily damped. At seven the next morning, the rioting resumed, "spreading with extraordinary violence all over the city," according to an official inquiry that was later to be held. "Clerks, saloon and hotel waiters, artisans, drivers, flunkeys, day laborers in the employ of the Government, and soldiers on furlough—all these joined the movement." Houses with Easter loaves in their windows or crosses on their doors were once again avoided by the mob. Soon this lovely city of balconies and green roofs

> presented an extraordinary sight: streets covered with feathers and obstructed with broken furniture which had been thrown out of the residences; houses with broken doors and windows; a raging mob, running about yelling and whistling in all directions and continuing its work of destruction without let or hindrance.

Troops had been summoned again, but when they arrived, according to the official report, they "were without definite instructions, and at each attack of the mob on another house, would wait for orders of the military or police authorities, without knowing what to do." This, after all, was not Odessa, with its well-organized system of public security and large garrison of its own. "The authorities were wholly unprepared," according to Madame Zinaida Ragozin, a contemporary Russian observer not at all unsympathetic toward the rioters. "The ordinary police force was far too small to be of any use, and of the military, only four squadrons of cavalry were on hand—a force particularly ill-suited for action in narrow, crowded streets—not quite five hundred men in all against a mob of many thousands." More severe critics were to accuse the troops called in of acting "at first as spectators and afterwards as active participators." At any rate, the troops were ineffectual, with the further result, according to the official inquiry, that the mob "was bound to arrive at the conclusion that the excesses in

which it indulged were not an illegal undertaking but rather a work
which had the approval of the Government."

Toward evening, the report continues,

> the disorders increased in intensity, owing to the arrival of a large
> number of peasants from the adjacent villages, who were anxious
> to secure part of the Jewish loot. There was no one to check these
> crowds; the troops and police were helpless. They had lost all heart,
> and were convinced that it was impossible to suppress the disorders
> with the means at hand.

At 8:00 P.M., a merciful downpour, accompanied by a cold wind, dispersed the crowd. At eleven, fresh troops arrived, and the next morning
a full battalion of infantry was in place. Order was restored to the town.

Hundreds of shops and homes had been demolished, one Jewish
man was dead, and there had been a number of rapes; but few were
seriously wounded and, miraculously, there had been no fires. In short,
it was not another Odessa. But was this the end of the rioting?

After order had been restored in Yelizavetgrad, more than a week went
by quietly, and many must have felt the threat of public disturbance
had passed. But the "barefoot brigades" had not had enough. The first
new outbreak occurred on Saturday, April 25, at Smela, a town about a
hundred miles southeast of the provincial capital of Kiev. It took on a
ferocity unknown at Yelizavetgrad. So also did the riot that broke out
the following day in Kiev itself.

This ancient and beautiful city, the first seat of Russia's monarchy
and cradle of its Christianity, was in some ways an anomaly. The natural
capital of the Ukraine, Kiev was an island of Great Russian culture amid
a countryside that was increasingly claiming the status of separate na-
tionhood. By tradition the chief city of southern Russia—even though
Odessa had grown larger—it was excluded by law from the Pale of Settlement surrounding it. Jews were not supposed to live there unless, as
in Moscow or Saint Petersburg, they were rich or belonged to certain
other privileged categories. Yet Jews, beating as an ocean on all sides
against the crumbling walls of this fortress, were everywhere to be seen
in Kiev. By 1881, the official Jewish population of the city, confined by
law to residence in the suburbs of Lyebed and Podol, was about fifteen
thousand, or some 10 percent of the whole; but this figure does not
include the untold numbers who had settled there illegally, or the many
who streamed in daily on temporary permits for the purpose of conducting their affairs. With its important Stock Exchange and its air of
higher civilization, Kiev had by now become, in spite of everything, a
main center of Russian-Jewish life.

It may therefore have been deliberately chosen as the best place for an object lesson by the "barefoot brigades," who had gone there and established a secret printing press from which to issue fake tsarist proclamations against the Jews. But there had also been another good reason for them to set up there. The Governor-General of Kiev and of the entire province—including unhappy Smela—was General Adjutant A. P. Drenteln, a man who, according to one of his colleagues, "hated the Jews from the bottom of his heart."

Jewish community leaders got a foretaste of this attitude on Saturday, the 25th, when, hearing rumors of an impending riot in Kiev—and perhaps news of what was happening in Smela that very day—they asked for police protection. In response, they were told not to leave their homes or open their shops the following day—even though Sunday was the main business day of the week for Russian-Jewish merchants. Stunned by this evident capitulation to unlawfulness, the Jews of Kiev nonetheless complied.

But the precaution was of no use. On Sunday morning, bands of ruffians began to assemble in the streets of the Podol district. Then, at noon, as if a signal had been given, "the air suddenly resounded with wild shouts, whistling, jeering, hooting and laughing," according to an eyewitness:

> An immense crowd of young boys, artisans, and laborers was on the march. The whole city was obstructed by the "bare-footed brigade." The destruction of Jewish houses began. Window panes and doors began to fly about, and shortly thereafter the mob, having gained access to the houses and stores, began to throw upon the streets absolutely everything that fell into their hands. Clouds of feathers began to whirl in the air.

The mob soon found its way to the synagogue, "which, despite its strong bars, locks and shutters, was wrecked in a moment. . . . The scrolls were torn to shreds, trampled in the dirt, and destroyed with incredible passion." The streets filled rapidly with "the trophies of destruction. Everywhere fragments of desks, furniture, household utensils, and other articles lay scattered about."

By about two o'clock, the rioters had inundated the Jewish markets and bazaars, shut up for the day and all the more ripe for looting. "Barely two hours after the beginning" of the riot, according to the eyewitness,

> the majority of the "bare-footed brigade" was transformed into well-dressed gentlemen, many of them having grown excessively stout in the meantime. The reason for this sudden change was sim-

ple enough. Those that had looted the stores of ready-made clothing put on three or four suits, and, not yet satisfied, took under their arms all they could lay their hands on. Others drove off in vehicles, carrying with them bags filled with loot.

"When I reached the grain bazaar," wrote a reporter for a Kiev newspaper,

the Jewish shops were already demolished and plundered; the mob was just attacking the taverns. Having broken in doors and windows, they rolled the barrels out on the street and broke them to pieces. Vodka flowed in streams. The rioters waded—they bathed—in vodka. The marauding women carried it away by the pailfuls.

A correspondent for *The Times* also saw the market district. "The streets," he wrote, "were littered with all imaginable kinds of wares, including groceries, drapery, mercery, confectionery, etc., and flooded with wines and spirits. The mob even tore up the paper money and scattered the pieces to the wind." With all that alcohol and paper lying about, it was no wonder that, as he wrote, "a quantity of matches which were thrown out of a shop caused a fire."

The scene had taken on, as even Madame Ragozin was to concede, "a rather more malignant character" than the one at Yelizavetgrad a week and a half before. "Through the uproar," the Kiev reporter writes,

I could clearly distinguish the shouts coming from all sides: "The Jews have lorded it over us long enough!" "It is our turn now." "They have got everything into their own hands!" ... "They grind us to death!" etc. Some well-intentioned persons went about amongst groups of idlers, who were evidently anxious to begin operations ... and tried to dissuade them. "How can you be so foolish?" they would say. "Don't you know that you will be punished?" The reply in almost every case amounted to this: "No matter; we will take our punishment—it will be only *once*. The Jews torture us all our lives."

This was the mood carried later that day into the Jewish slum quarter of Demiovka—whose inhabitants had little in their hands—where several persons, including at least one small child, were beaten to death, and where there were numerous rapes. More fires were started, with the depredations continuing until about three o'clock the following morning.

That Monday, another Kiev journalist wandered into "an enclosure that serves as an ammunition store for the arsenal," and beheld a truly heartrending sight. Packed together like ants in an anthill were more than eighteen hundred Jews, with their wives and children—many of them mere infants. They were clad in rags and barefooted. Many of them bore traces of ill-treatment, and a number of them had bandaged heads. All were ghastly pale and terror-stricken. As I approached them I saw a boy of ten dying in terrible agony. His mother sat by him, tearless, as if too deeply afflicted to weep.

These were the homeless.

Throughout the Kiev riots, General Drenteln and his entourage made their way through the crowds, stopping now and then to deliver a speech of admonition, only to move on so the lawlessness could resume. As for the police, the Austrian consul in Kiev wrote to his Foreign Ministry, "The entire behavior of the police leads one rightfully to the conclusion that the disturbances are abetted by the authorities." General V. D. Novitsky, chief of police for the province, laid the blame squarely on Drenteln and complained to the government in Saint Petersburg. He was able to prove his point a few days later, when rioting again broke out in Kiev, and he took charge and quickly put a stop to it.

But the anti-Jewish fever that had spread through southern Russia could not be quenched so easily. In the ensuing week, it struck in several more towns and villages, as well as in the small city of Berditchev, where a Jewish self-defense group succeeded in halting the attacks. On the following Sunday, May 3, it came full circle and hit Odessa, where Governor-General Dondukov-Korsakov was caught off guard, having dispatched troops to put down riots in other towns and villages. He nevertheless acted swiftly, and though there were two deaths, the disturbances in Odessa were brought to an end after only six hours.

Still, the rioting continued to spread.

·3·

DISILLUSIONMENT AND FLIGHT

How had it all come about? "Bigotry, envy, ignorance and excitement combine to make the mind of the Russian peasant particularly inflammable just now," reasoned the *Jewish Chronicle,*

> after the remarkable tragedy recently enacted at St. Petersburg. It is intensely to be regretted that, in addition to this source of evil, a further and more potent instrument is at work in the general official distrust of the Jews in Russia. When . . . the peasant is aware that the object of his persecution is unfavorably regarded by the police and official authorities, all checks to license are removed and scenes of violation, like that which occurred at Kiev this week, become only too common.

This much was understood right away—and something else as well before the wave of rioting had passed. A government inquiry was begun at Smela after the outbreak there, which had left thirteen dead, and a dispatch sent abroad from Kiev on May 5 could announce as a result:

> It is officially stated that the investigation instituted by the authorities shows that the ringleaders were persons not belonging to the place, and that the population were only induced to take part in the riots by false representations made to them by evil-disposed persons, who even circulated proclamations calling upon the people to commence an anti-Jewish agitation, which it was alleged would accord with the wishes of the Government.

"There is evidence to show," read another report, this time dealing with Kiev itself, "that the ringleaders were strangers who came from the North."

19

Beyond this, however, there was some confusion as to the political identity of these mysterious "barefoot" agitators—usually young men of some education, who often dressed as peasants or workers and even, on at least one occasion, as police. Eventually there was to be little doubt among those who understood the Russian scene that these young men represented forces opposed to social and political progress. "Ever since the German anti-Semites had raised an outcry against their Jewish fellow-citizens," a writer in *The Times* would be able to observe the following winter, "it had been feared that the movement would spread to Russia, and there take a form more adapted to the less civilized state of the country." Indeed, it was the rise of a new political anti-Semitism in Germany that had been commanding worldwide attention in the preceding few years and had raised fears of popular reprisals against the Jews there.* Pastor Adolf Stoecker of Berlin and his Christian Social Workers' Party had been demonstrating how Jew-hatred could be used as an instrument to arouse the masses to the side of reaction. German anti-Semitism had now come to perceive the Jew—at all times considered by it to be the enemy of Christian values—not only as the usurer and capitalist of old, but as the new socialist and revolutionary as well. For the true modern anti-Semite, the seeming opposition between a Rothschild and a Karl Marx was only a cover for a Jewish conspiracy to subvert the Christian world.

In Russia, this notion—endorsed by no less a figure than Fyodor Dostoevsky—was bound to take on a special potency. Russia's enormous Jewish population was both a constant source of resentment among the peasantry and a constant object of suspicion for the ruling classes. Anti-Semitism allied the two disparate groups, even if the one saw Jews mainly as rapacious merchants and the other, increasingly, as "nihilists." "Everyone knows," the conservative Saint Petersburg daily *Novoye Vremya (New Times)* had written even before the assassination, "that these Jews, since time immemorial the representatives of the revolutionary spirit, now stand at the head of the nihilists." Since then, the "barefoot brigades" could, according to a correspondent of the London *Daily Telegraph*, hold up the Jews "to popular reprobation as the assassins of the late Czar, and Jessie [Hessia] Helfman, the Jewess, who was implicated, as having been the soul of the whole plot." The hooligans were thus achieving two goals at once for their princes—diverting the potentially revolutionary excitement of the masses into the politically harmless channel of Jew-baiting, and trouncing Jewish "nihilists" at the same time.

Yet, in those first weeks of rioting, the feeling had persisted among

---

*The very term "anti-Semitism" originated in Germany in this period, said to have been invented by one of its literary exponents, Wilhelm Marr.

many that the "barefoot brigades" themselves were nihilists, stirring
up the first stages of a more radical revolt. The *Daily Telegraph* correspondent relayed the assurances of Russian informants that "the anti-
Jewish movement in Russia is entirely the work of the revolutionarists.
They understand," he continued,

> that it would be of no avail to appeal to an ignorant and bigotedly
> loyal peasantry on the grounds of political emancipation. . . . The
> revolutionists have, consequently, touched another chord, and have
> excited [the peasant's] religious fanaticism. They have represented
> the Jews as the source of all the evils with which Russia is af-
> fected. . . . The object of the revolutionists is to create a popular
> rising, in which the troops would be called upon to defend the Jews
> against the Christians.

Since the troops, according to this theory, would ultimately refuse such
a call, a general collapse of government authority would ensue. Even
the Tsar and some members of the government accepted this notion of
what was going on. "The persecution of the Jews in Southern Russia,"
said the new Minister of the Interior, Count Ignatiev, "shows how people otherwise devoted to the throne yield to the influence of evil-dis-
posed persons and unsuspectingly serve their rebellious plans."

The revolutionaries themselves vehemently denied the charge. Late
in May, *The Times* conveyed an announcement by the Narodnaya Volya
leadership "that the assertion of the Emperor and the Government at-
tributing the attacks upon the Jews to [revolutionary] political propa-
gandists is altogether untrue." Then, not hesitating to pour some fat
into the fire, the statement added that it was not the organization's
policy "to incite the people against the Jews, because the latter are too
numerous and too useful in the ranks of the party, many of the most
intelligent and redoubtable of the Revolutionists having been Jews."

In general, their responses in this moment indicate that the radicals
were, in their own way, as confused by what was happening as many
members of the government and of the press. They knew that their
people were not implicated in the riots, but this did not stop them from
believing that these events might indeed be the first signs of oncoming
revolution. A well-known Ukrainian socialist, M. Dragomanov, had concluded in the immediate wake of the Yelizavetgrad and Kiev outbursts
that these were

> the beginning of a social war long foreseen by those familiar with
> the condition of the Ukraine. . . . Through [the Jews'] hereditary
> vocation as usurers, spirit dealers, traders, etc., they have made
> themselves masters alike of the indebted landlords and of the un-

fortunate peasants. It is the deep-rooted detestation of the peasant for the money-lender which is breaking out in the Ukraine.

Perhaps, then, the radicals reasoned, this "deep-rooted detestation" was the momentum of revolution and should be encouraged. A growing enthusiasm for this notion soon caused the Executive Committee of Narodnaya Volya to abandon its own principles; at the end of August, it issued this proclamation:

> Good people, honest Ukrainian people! Life has become hard in the Ukraine, and it keeps getting harder. The damned police beat you, the landowners devour you, the Zhids, the dirty Judases, rob you. People in the Ukraine suffer most of all from the Zhids. Who has seized the lands, the woodlands, the taverns? The Zhids. Whom does the peasant beg with tears in his eyes to let him near his own land? The Zhids. Wherever you look, whatever you touch, everywhere the Zhids. The Zhid curses the peasant, cheats him, drinks his blood. The Zhid makes life unbearable.

Surely, the peasants would now move more quickly through the preliminary task of assaulting Jews and on to the main one of stamping out the tsarist regime.

But some Jewish revolutionaries were beginning to wonder.

How great a presence in fact were Jews in the Russian revolutionary movement at this time? One authoritative estimate has given their proportion among its adherents as about 4 percent, or roughly the same as the proportion of Jews in the general population. But since large areas of the country had few Jews or none, their proportion in the radical movement must have been much higher in areas where Jews actually were settled. There can be no doubt that radicalism was by this time exercising a powerful attraction among a younger generation of secularly educated Russian Jews. And, indeed, how could it have been otherwise? Awakening to a regime of oppression in which they were themselves prominent among the insulted and the injured, they were responding to it in a way befitting the inheritors of a great moral tradition. "The enthusiasm for an idea, so characteristic of the Jewish nation," conceded even the bourgeois, antiregicide *Jewish Chronicle*, "has led some more ardent members of the race to cast their lot with the fanatical apostles of liberty, equality and fraternity, who possess only the 'patriotism of dynamite.' "

In these early years of the Russian revolutionary movement, however, a Jew who chose to participate was understood to be abandoning his or her Jewish commitments. As one was to say in summing up his outlook, "We are *Narodniki,* the muzhiks are our natural brothers." There was to be no difference between a Jew and a Russian, least of all a peasant. "I still remember, when I first read [Ferdinand] Lassalle," said Paul Axelrod, later to be one of the founders of Russian Marxism,

> how ashamed I became because I was interested in Jewish affairs. What significance can the interests of a handful of Jews have, I thought, compared with the interests and the "idea of a working class," with which socialism was imbued? For there is actually no Jewish problem, but only the general question of liberating the working masses of all nations, including also the Jewish masses. With the victory of socialism, this so-called Jewish question will be solved.

Some Jewish radicals of relatively privileged background went beyond this, concurring, as Jacob Gordin did, in the view that Jews were mainly a class of exploiters. "I will never forget those evenings," wrote Chaim Zhitlovsky of his bourgeois childhood in the 1870s,

> when our handyman, a Russian peasant, sat in a corner of our dining room, his plate on his knees, while my father regaled himself at table with jokes about Jews outwitting the stupid Russian peasants. Who would have thought then that I would regard our Russian servant as the symbol of the whole Russian people? That I would feel we all lived and enjoyed ourselves at his expense and thought ourselves toweringly superior to him, whereas in truth we owed him so much—this indebtedness of ours rested most heavily on me.

Such ardent young spirits had yet to discover the depth and extent of poverty among the Jews of Russia and Poland, or foresee the misfortune that now came in the spring of 1881.

Even news of the riots was at first met by many of them with indifference or worse. "I must admit," Abraham Cahan later wrote, "this matter was of little interest to me and to the other Jewish members of our cell. We considered ourselves to be 'human beings, not Jews.' Jewish matters had no special appeal for us." Another young Jewish radical, recalling shortly afterward the "whooping and howling" of the mob in Yelizavetgrad, and the "groans and screams" of the Jews, declared: "We, of the Populist circle, were joyful. We thought these were the signs of the Russian revolution, expressing itself first on the Jews; but then it would develop in length and breadth." To be sure, he noticed, the mob was "not making distinctions, not excepting the poor, nor the women"; but, as one of his comrades put it even after witnessing with horror the grislier riots in Kiev, "We were convinced that all Jews

were swindlers and that we ought to stand on the sidelines and not
interfere."

Time and unrelenting violence would cause many of these attitudes
to yield to dismay. "How comical we were," the young Kiev observer
was soon to admit, "how childishly naive." "The blood runs cold in the
veins," another young *Narodnik* would say, "when we look at the insulted and humiliated [Jewish victims]. . . . At all levels of society, from
the university intelligentsia to the ignorant peasant, a savage attitude
toward Jews can be observed." Paul Axelrod was to concede that the
Jewish radicals had made a mistake not to realize "that the Jews as a
people are in a unique situation in Russia, hated by the most diverse
segments of the Christian population." They should not "in the name
of cosmopolitanism have forsaken the Jewish masses," who were themselves impoverished, he wrote.

But for Axelrod, whose overriding loyalty was to remain the Russian Revolution, it had been above all a problem of tactics. A properly
organized Jewish leadership might have been able "to divert the mobs
from attacking the poor and direct them toward the rich Jews, if they
could not be directed against all exploiters in general." In Kiev, for
example,

> it was only necessary . . . to direct the crowd to the quarter of the
> Jewish capitalists, to the banks, where the capital of the upper
> classes of all nationalities is concentrated. Of course, if the "disor-
> der" had received this sort of direction the further course of the
> movement would inevitably have been such as to lead the rebellious
> masses into direct clashes with the wealthy elements in general and
> with their natural ally, the government.

Others were not so sanguine. Abraham Cahan writes of a group of
radical students in Kiev who walked into a synagogue "filled with weeping, mourning Jews." One of them, a slim young man named Nicholas
Aleinikoff, went before the congregation, prostrated himself, and said:

> "We are your brothers. We are Jews just like you. We repent
> of having considered ourselves Russians and not Jews. The events
> of the last few weeks—the rioting in Yelizavetgrad, in Smela, here
> in Kiev, and in other towns, has shown us what a grievous mistake
> we were making. Yes, we are Jews."

Another kind of revolution was beginning. Masses of Jews were
fleeing their old homes, while significant numbers of the Jewish radical
and student intelligentsia began finding ways to recover their origins in
secular terms. The repentant Aleinikoff, for example, was soon to become leader of the Kiev branch of a new Jewish movement formed in

Odessa after the riot. There a group of young *maskilim* (disciples of the Haskalah, or Hebrew secular "Enlightenment") had conceived a plan "to found in America cooperative colonies in the spirit of Robert Owen, Fourier, and Tolstoy." The idea of agricultural colonies was not really new among Russian Jews. For many years the government had sought to aid and encourage the settlement of Jews as farmers on the frontier lands of southern Russia, and, despite considerable ineptitude in the administration of the program, had enjoyed a modest degree of success: David Leontievich Bronstein, for one, the father of the future Trotsky, had grown up in one of these colonies and was now a prospering farmer on his own. Agriculture had not been prominent among Jewish occupations since ancient times, but the ideal of a return to the soil—championed by the Narodniki, by Turgenev and Tolstoy—was fervently held in Russia, not least among those secular Hebraists who longed for the pastoral world of Bible and Talmud, and for whom such an endeavor would mean a recovery of Jewish dignity.

The idea was now reviving in a mood of awakened Jewish national feeling. The new movement was given the Hebrew name Am Olam (Eternal People), a term originated shortly after the Odessa riot of 1871 by the Haskalah writer and editor Peretz Smolenskin, as the title of an article in which he argued vigorously against Jewish assimilation. Smolenskin himself, in fact, like the Am Olam group he had inspired, was now also moving from a strong ethnocentrism to an outright Jewish nationalism under the impact of the 1881 riots; otherwise, there was a significant parting of the ways between them. Noting that large numbers of the victims were beginning to leave the country, he wrote:

> There is no doubt that it would be best for people who are leaving one country to migrate together to the same new land, for they could then understand and help one another. If the wave of emigration is to direct itself to one place, surely no other country in the world is conceivable except Eretz Israel.

Some were soon to begin heeding this call to Palestine. But the leaders of Am Olam were among the many who regarded another country as conceivable. America was already becoming the Zion toward which the greatest numbers of the newly uprooted were turning their eyes as they fled.

By the beginning of May, the *Daily Telegraph* reported:

> The Jews are removing from the disturbed districts as fast as they can, but they are even molested in their flight. Yesterday a train conveying a large number of Jewish families from Kiev to Fastov was stoned and obliged to pull up half-way along the route.

The passengers fled to a neighboring village. They were attacked by the inhabitants, and the huts where some of them had taken refuge were set fire to and burnt. Several rich Jewish families, coming from Kiev, have arrived at the Austrian frontier.

Austria was increasingly the goal: "Crowds of refugees," according to an April 30 dispatch from Vienna, "are crossing the Austrian frontier at Volochisk." And again, from Cracow on May 4: "Many refugee Jews crossed the frontier in consequence of the anti-Jewish outbreak on Saturday at Kamenetz-Podolsk." Two days later, Vienna reported: "All the available space at the Austrian railway station on the frontier is occupied by Jewish refugees."

The adjacent Austrian province of Galicia was fast becoming a magnet. Its border poorly patrolled, so that one could easily cross without a passport, it was, in its eastern sector, virtually a part of southwestern Russia ethnically and historically. In its large Yiddish-speaking communities, a Russian Jew would not feel like a stranger and might hope to be welcome, at least in times of distress. Collections were already being made in Lemberg, the capital of Galicia, and a few of the refugees were making their way to it. But for the tired fugitive it required a little extra energy to get to Lemberg, which was not the first stop in one's flight. Rather, by the beginning of the summer, the place where hundreds of fleeing Russian Jews had gathered was the ancient Galician city of Brody, just across the border.

PART TWO

The First Russian Refugees

·1881-1882·

·4·

THE BRODY REFUGE

When, at the end of the eighteenth century, Poland was divided among
Russia, Prussia, and Austria, so that it ceased to exist as a separate
political entity, the Austrians named their part of it Galicia. This geo-
graphically ill-defined province formed a right-angled triangle whose
base and side, to the east and to the north, backed onto the Russian
Empire, and whose hypotenuse was a northwest-to-southeast line of
some five hundred miles running from Cracow to Bukovina along the
foothills of the Carpathian Mountains. Beyond the Carpathians, to the
south and west, was all the rest of the Habsburg Empire, to which this
forlorn province, its largest and its poorest, remained a kind of step-
child. Retarded in industrial development, Galicia in 1881 had a population of about six million that was still at least 80 percent peasants,
most of them illiterate. This peasantry was about evenly divided between Poles, who predominated in the west, and Ruthenians—or West
Ukrainians—in the east. But in the cities, east as well as west, the Poles
were more numerous, and—having obtained political and cultural privileges under the Austro-Hungarian constitution of 1867—tended to be
better educated, a bit more socially and economically advantaged, and
more assertive of their ethnic prerogatives than the Ruthenians.

The other ethnic groups in Galicia were far smaller but of no less
significance. Czechs and Germans made up the ruling bureaucracy, and
there was a small but prominent Armenian business class. But in 1881,
the largest and most pervasive minority were the Jews, who made up
11 percent of the population.

In strict legality, the Jews of Galicia were, unlike their Russian
coreligionists across the border, free and equal citizens of the country
in which they lived: this was another legacy of the Austro-Hungarian
constitution of 1867. They could purchase land without restrictions, for

example, and for this reason a number of Jews had in recent years emigrated from Russia to form part of the Galician landholding class. Furthermore, they no longer were confined to a Pale of Settlement, so that many of the more ambitious Jewish sons and daughters of Galicia went off to Vienna and other cities of opportunity whenever they wished. To be sure, there were still problems. Poverty was great enough so that Galicia was at this time the principal area in Europe from which Jews were emigrating to America in search of better opportunities. Jewish representation in both the Galician and the Imperial diets was, in spite of the constitution, manipulated to well below its proper proportion. An anti-Semitic revival was under way in Austria as in Germany, and group relations were particularly tense in a city such as Lemberg, where Jews formed one-quarter of the population and where they had been legally confined to a ghetto until as recently as 1858. Yet Austria was a land of the free in the eyes of most Russian Jews, and their cousins just across the border—the *Galitzianer*, with their strange Yiddish accent and irksome quality of seeming coarseness combined with Germanic airs of cultural superiority—were inclined to agree.

Brody was a Galician phenomenon unto itself. At the beginning of 1881, its Jewish population was fully fifteen thousand out of a total of twenty-five thousand, yet this represented both a relative and an absolute decline since the early decades of the century, when the town had been a flourishing center of commerce and of Jewish culture. Immediately after the Polish partitions, the Jewish merchants of Brody, enjoying a special relationship with their colleagues in trade and religion on the other side of the Russian border, had been able to supersede the Armenians as the commercially preponderant class. That also was the moment when Brody had been recognized as one of the preeminent centers of the Haskalah in Eastern Europe. But in the meantime, the failure of Galicia to industrialize had contributed to a decline in commerce, and by mid-century many of the region's best Jewish talents had left, going chiefly to Odessa, where the "Brody Synagogue" became one of the most imposing edifices in town. More recently, the Polish nationalist revival in Galicia had produced a campaign to replace Jewish with Polish merchants as much as possible, and restrictive trade laws passed by the provincial diet had caused a further exodus of wealthier Jews. "Failed in Brody" had become a standard saying among businessmen by 1880, when, to make matters far worse, a fire broke out and destroyed a good part of the town. By 1881, Brody was largely impoverished.

"In many places," Abraham Cahan was to observe upon entering Brody as a refugee, "stood ruins of houses or bare chimneys and their ovens." The lodging he and several others shared with a family "consisted of a single room, which had survived the collapse of the building's outer wall. Next to it, under the same roof, the floor and foundation had been completely destroyed. There only remained a large hole in the ground, filled with pieces of fallen brick." He was struck by the presence of poverty everywhere. "Everything was squalid and run-down, poor as the poorest little street back home in Vilna." When he arrived in Brody to aid the refugees in October 1881, Moritz Friedländer, secretary of Vienna's Israelitische Allianz, found himself sinking knee-deep in mud as he tried to walk to his hotel. Abandoning the attempt, he rode in a "moth-eaten" old fiacre that he had turned down at the station, though he had been assured that it was the best in town.

Not that the original home of the "Brody Singers"—stars of the cabarets of Galicia and Rumania, and participants in the founding of the fledgling Yiddish theater—had lost all its old debonair charm. In his first moments of arrival there, Cahan also noticed "a water carrier in a high hat," and a "barefoot boy of about thirteen running around with a large basket of bagels, also wearing a high hat." This Dickensian sight caused him to recall that, where he had come from, "only a Jew of social standing would have worn such a hat, and then only on the Sabbath. In Vilna, only rabbis wore high hats on weekdays." George Price, another young Russian-Jewish refugee, had come knowing four outstanding things about Brody through Jewish folklore: "the synagogue, the cantor, the rumors and the unpleasant odor." He found all these things upon arrival and thought the Jews of the town were "indeed comical," but he also admired their women. "In entire Galicia including Brody (so they say) one cannot find a homely girl," he noted. "And if you meet one, she must be a Russian Jewess."

This, then, was the refuge into which the Russian-Jewish victims staggered after the riots of 1881, at first by the hundreds and then by the thousands, in a constantly renewing stream as the months went by. "God! What Pandemonium!" George Price wrote in his diary at the sight of it. Whole families wandered through the streets, often sleeping outdoors while the weather still was warm. Others found shelter in such places as "a factory in the city which lodges about three thousand emigrants and a stable which accommodates three hundred," according to Price, writing in the spring of 1882. "In both dwellings, the condition of the emigrants is unbearable. They sit on the floor, huddled together, hungry and thirsty." Luckier ones—those with a little money in their pockets—found accommodations in Jewish homes, sometimes even a little better than where Cahan put up.

In the summer and fall of 1881, during the first rush, many of the refugees had simply camped out at the railway station. The Austrian authorities, moderately sympathetic at first—and not unmindful of the moral triumph they were thereby enjoying over the Russian regime— even allowed the refugees to stay there, on the assumption that they would soon move on. Friedländer was not to forget the scene that met his eyes as he stepped off his train that wet morning in October. "Here squats a young mother," he would write,

> with her frail, scantily dressed children by her side, pressing a suckling infant against her breast and handing to the other little ones a dry crust of bread. There a father limps along, held up by his children, a large tattered bundle dragging behind him, in which the pathetic remnants of the family's clothing is visible. And over there an old woman, panting in exhaustion, helped along by two grandchildren who have themselves lost their sources of sustenance. Here a woman with despairing eyes pushes through the crowd in search of her children who have strayed off; there a whole family whispers, racked with hunger and cold.... Everywhere, misery, confusion and want.

It was a situation that called for an emergency effort—the very task for which Herr Friedländer had been summoned from Vienna.

Jewish philanthropic groups throughout the world had been stirred by the riots and the plight of the victims, but none more decisively so than the Alliance Israélite Universelle. Founded in Paris in 1860, the Alliance was a wholly new form of an ancient phenomenon. Philanthropy was nothing new in Judaism; but a secular organization poised to give aid or relief to distressed Jews anywhere in the world could only have come out of the Western liberal democracies of the nineteenth century. It is significant that this organization was created in France, where Jewish traditions tended to be weak, and by a group of distinguished public figures—including the Senator and former Minister of Justice Adolphe Crémieux—for whom religious observance was not a prominent part of their lives. Concerned not only with charitable work and the defense of Jewish rights, the Alliance also had addressed itself to the lately burgeoning ideal of returning Jews to the soil—in Morocco, which had become the principal area of its activities, and in Palestine, where the organization had founded the Mikveh Israel agricultural school near Jaffa in 1870.

After issuing a worldwide appeal for the Russian-Jewish victims in May, the Alliance called a conference of European Jewish philanthropic organizations, which was held in Vienna the following month. The aims of the conference were to provide relief for the victims, to rebuild their homes, and, as swiftly as possible, to *repatriate* those who had fled the country—for at this stage, none of the Jewish leaders in Europe were yet thinking of emigration. Certainly not Baron Horace Günzburg, wealthiest of Russian Jews and their spokesman in the opinion of many, who feared any mass flight as a surrender in the generations-long struggle for Jewish rights in Russia. Nor could the substantial number of Jews in Germany, Austria, France, and Great Britain who had risen high against all odds contemplate with equanimity the arrival into their midst of masses of destitute coreligionists—least of all from Russia, that land of bomb-throwing nihilists, not a few of whom were known to be Jews. Indeed, if emigration were to prove to be the only choice for many, most of these august Hebrew gentlemen were determined to send them on to the faraway United States, none of whose Jewish leaders were present at the conference.

The Alliance was entirely in accord with this general view. Emigration work had never been among its purposes, and had been avoided in the past, with one notable exception. In 1868 and 1869, an outbreak of cholera and famine in Russia's northwestern provinces had caused large numbers of Jews to flee across the border into East Prussia, where many of them expressed their unwillingness to return and their desire to go to America instead. In the ensuing year, the Alliance had arranged for their emigration, with the cooperation of the Board of Delegates of American Israelites in New York, who hoped to settle them on the land and in the small towns of hinterland America, rather than let them gather in New York and other cities. In the sequel, the American Jewish leaders had not been particularly satisfied with the result. But for the Alliance the experience had clarified a twofold reality: it was preferable to send destitute and nonrepatriable Russian Jews to America rather than let them settle in Western Europe; and America was, in any case, where most of them wanted to go.

The fact that the situation of 1870 was now more than repeating itself does not seem to have dawned upon the Alliance leaders through most of that summer of 1881. As they sought entry into Russia for their representatives—which was slow to be granted—in order to survey the damage, they prepared to resettle as many of the refugees as possible in agricultural colonies in the Ukraine, for which Baron Günzburg had contributed 16,000 rubles. Then, at the end of August, visa in hand at last, an Alliance representative headed by train for southern Russia and stopped off in Brody on the way. The representative, Dr. H. Schafier, a physician and by origin a Russian Jew, thought he would spend two days in the Galician town to deal with the two or three hundred refugees he expected to find there. He found nearly six hundred families instead, and new ones coming in all the time. Schafier was not to leave Brody for seventeen weeks.

Setting up office at the Hotel Rainer, where he was staying, Schafier had no trouble organizing a small staff from among the local bureaucracy, who were eager to do what they could to speed the new arrivals on their way. The problem was where to send them. The official policy represented by Schafier still was repatriation; but one did not have to be long among the refugees of Brody to know that few of them would even consider such a prospect. "They would rather suffer here," Schafier wrote to Paris, "than return to their old homes." And, above all, they would rather go to America—in proof of which, some who were a little behind in their American history told Schafier they were prepared to sell themselves into slavery in order to do so.

Gradually the Alliance leadership, in correspondence with Schafier, arrived at a furtive policy: to start sending across the Atlantic as many as they could until the inevitable American-Jewish protest came. Perhaps the Americans would even understand. "Emigration may continue yet for a long time," ruminated the oracular author of an Alliance report, "perhaps for many years. Through our efforts we shall succeed in establishing a systematic emigration from Russia [to the United States]. . . . Every immigrant capable of work will become a force that will attract relatives and friends." The way to start this historic movement, then, was to be through the time-honored French principle of *fait accompli*.

Under instructions from Paris, Schafier proceeded to try as much as he could to weed out all but the young and able-bodied, capable—it was hoped—of becoming farmers or artisans, and send the latter to the United States. There were moments when this was fairly easy to do, as when the Am Olam groups started arriving in force early the following year. But in his first weeks, Schafier found that he rarely was able to follow the prescription without breaking up families—in particular, separating the young from parents and grandparents who had become enfeebled by their suffering. Once when he tried to do this, the offended group put together what money they had and wired Alliance headquarters in Paris: "Impossible accept. Spirits broken, hope lost. Even more unhappy than in Russia. Would rather starve than leave families." Schafier had to relent, at least a little. Moreover, Baron Maurice de Hirsch, the eminent Jewish philanthropist of Paris, who had contributed a good deal to refugee relief, now issued his own insistence that families not be broken up.

It was a dilemma, especially when the inevitable protests from the American-Jewish organizations began to arrive.

·5·

AMERICAN ISRAELITES

"It is very philanthropic to desire the Jews of Russia to leave that Empire, now that riots have broken out in the Ukraine," said an editorial in the New York *Jewish Messenger* on May 20, 1881,

> but to suggest that three million of them settle in America evidences more enthusiasm than common sense. A better way, perhaps, would be to send American Jewish missionaries to Russia to civilize them there, rather than give them an opportunity to Russianize us in the event of such a colossal emigration. The Russian Jewish population in New York, Chicago, or elsewhere, has doubled within the past five years, and the task of Americanizing them is too difficult for one to view the advent of three million more with anything but trepidation.

Isaac Mayer Wise, the founder of the Hebrew Union College in Cincinnati and by this time the preeminent leader of American Reform Judaism—indeed, of institutional American Jewry in general—had been a little more circumspect a few weeks earlier, when he wrote in his own weekly newspaper, the *American Israelite*, of the Russian Jews already in the United States:

> It is high time for them to understand that they live in America, and that the American Hebrews are naturally their friends; that they wish to be recognized as men and Israelites, consequently that they must show their willingness to have friends and assist in bearing the burden.

> There can be no doubt that the approximately three hundred thousand Jews of the United States in 1881 had become almost as deeply

integrated into American life in general as they believed themselves to be. With the prominent exception of early Massachusetts and Connecticut—the Puritans, after all, had been the new Israelites and could brook no rivals in the role—there had scarcely been a phase of American history in which a significant Jewish presence could not be perceived. From the predominantly Sephardic Jews of the mercantile classes of colonial Newport, New York, Philadelphia, Charleston, and Savannah, to the mainly German-born Jewish retailing pioneers of the expanding Middle and Far West, the people of Israel had woven themselves into the fabric from which America was being created. As for the highest ideals that had inspired the Republic, no other group held them more ardently: "A free country, and a young people," wrote Wise jubilantly of his mood as a youthful immigrant from Bohemia—which he spoke of by contrast as a "monarchical country with its inherited prejudices and stereotyped habits," and in which he believed the Jewish tradition could no longer thrive.

In order that it should thrive in the New World, Rabbi Wise and his fellow American Israelites—a term he preferred with increasing fervor to "Jews"—had re-created that tradition, to such an extent that its critics saw Reform Judaism as the merest variation on some American Protestant denomination. Indeed, in dispensing with the Talmudic restrictions on dress, diet, and Sabbath behavior, Wise was as zealously beating down barriers between Jews and the life around them as the tsars were maintaining them with the Pale of Settlement. In the new Promised Land, an Israelite was to be as American as any Christian living there—a situation that seemed no problem at all to most American Jews by 1881, not even to those who spoke in a foreign accent, as Wise did. In fact, in that era when two hundred thousand German Americans, both Christians and Jews, had fought in the Union Army (and a few in the Confederate one as well), and when some of the greatest cities in the country—notably Saint Louis, Cincinnati, Milwaukee, Chicago, and, above all, New York—throbbed with the life and cultural activities of their large German-speaking populations, it often seemed as natural to be an American with a living German heritage as with an English one.

But Russian, Polish—or Yiddish: "a jargon," Wise was to write, "without alphabet (they use the Hebrew) and without grammar, an obsolete and corrupt German-Hebrew-Slavonic excuse for a language"— these represented cultures that were not viewed in the same light. Nor was language the only disagreeable trait of the East European Jews in the eyes of their German-American coreligionists. They tended, if they remained religious at all, to be resolutely Orthodox. They were disconcertingly ethnocentric. And, perhaps worst of all, they tended to be poor. In 1881, there still were few restrictions upon immigrant entry into the United States—this was to start changing dramatically the following year—and any Jews who arrived unable to support themselves simply became, as had been true since time immemorial, a matter for the Jewish charities. And it was natural for American Jewish communal leaders to want to prevent as much as possible the arrival of potential charity cases—though there were very few ways of judging who these might assuredly be.

In the old days, when immigration had still been mainly an accumulation of individual histories, there had been no good way of controlling who came, anyway; but a mass exodus—wherein a great many destinies, from departure through passage to arrival and placement in homes and jobs, had to be watched over all at once—was an entirely different matter. When such a case involved Jews, the organized Jewish community could function, in effect, as its own immigration authority. The first opportunity to demonstrate this had come in 1870.

The cholera epidemic of 1868 in northwestern Russia, followed by a famine in 1869, had caused about five thousand Polish and Lithuanian Jews to flee the provinces of Suwalki and Kovno and gather in the nearby Prussian port cities of Königsberg, Memel, and Stettin. Fed up with a Russian regime whose anti-Polish policies had been hitting their districts with severity, they refused to return home and sought to emigrate. Many of them wanted to go to the United States, which, on account of recent great improvements in transatlantic shipping, no longer seemed very far from the Baltic and North Sea ports. A few already had relatives there.

The organized Jewish communities of Germany, who had rallied to provide these refugees with charitable assistance, were perfectly ready to help them move on. In July 1869, the Union of German Jewish Communities held an initial meeting in Leipzig to discuss the situation, and this was followed in October by a conference in Berlin between its leaders and those of the Alliance Israélite Universelle. The immediate result was the creation of a Central Frontier Committee in Königsberg, whose task was to watch over the welfare of the refugees, organize their emigration, and aid in the purchase of their steamship tickets—in time, whole ships were to be chartered for the purpose. The principal aim continued to be getting as many as possible to the United States.

They could not simply be dumped there, however; the success of the operation depended upon the good will of the organized American Jewish community, who had to be ready to receive the emigrants and guide them into their new lives. Specifically, the mantle of responsibility fell as a matter of course upon the Jewish community of New York, America's main port of entry and its largest Jewish population center. New York was in general a city that felt its European roots more strongly than most others in the country, and its Jewish leaders tended to be more involved in the affairs of their coreligionists across the Atlantic than were their fellow Israelites in the West. Their spirit of relative independence from Rabbi Wise and Cincinnati had been demonstrated in 1859, when, in direct response to Jewish problems in Europe, they had created an organization called the Board of Delegates of American Israelites. Inspired by the Old World example of the Board of Deputies of British Jews, this New York organization was part of the religious community rather than secular like the Alliance Israélite Universelle, created the following year. But, like the Alliance, it concerned itself mainly with international Jewish problems. In this way, it was not much to the liking of Rabbi Wise, who resisted such tendencies to treat Jews as a worldwide people rather than an American religious denomination. What was going on, in effect, was a quiet Jewish-American cultural war between New York and Cincinnati.

Yet, for all its spirit, the New York Board of Delegates balked at first when it was asked by the Alliance at the end of 1869 if it would take in the Kovno and Suwalki refugees. With its Jewish population of well over a hundred thousand, New York already seemed—in the eyes of its Jewish bourgeoisie in particular—to have too many of them; and the task of getting poor Jewish immigrants to settle in small towns and rural communities to the west was not an easy one. Even a newly created branch of the Alliance in Philadelphia shared the Board of Delegates' hesitation. Rather, the most ardent opinions in favor of receiving the refugees came at first from non-Jewish sources. "Let our rich Israelites bring their oppressed brethren to this new land of promise," the New York *Herald* had editorialized in September. "Here at least, they will be free men, and milk and honey will not be found wholly wanting."

Sentiments like these certainly had their effect, as did the continuing blandishments from the Alliance in France, culminating in a letter to American-Jewish leaders from Adolphe Crémieux himself, in which he gave assurance that there was "no thought of sending over beggars and people who are not capable of making a living." The result was that, by the beginning of 1870, the Board of Delegates had been persuaded to accept a limited number of healthy immigrants of good character, and soon raised $7,000 for the task. The first group of 250 refugees arrived in New York on April 19.

It was immediately clear that the Königsberg Committee had not been tuned to the delicate requirements of the New York Jewish leadership. "Notwithstanding our urgent remonstrances against indiscriminate emigration from West Russia," the Board of Delegates wrote on April 27 in a circular addressed to various New York congregations and charitable societies, "hundreds of Israelites are here, despatched by the Koenigsberg Committee, and utterly penniless." It was a shock; there was no choice, however, but to rally to the occasion. "We cannot see them starve," the circular went on:

> Something must be done for them. The Charity Committee of the Hebrew Benevolent Society have already sent twenty-two West to their friends, and the following gentlemen have consented to take the matter in charge and to distribute, in the most effective way, the means placed at their disposal for the benefit of the immigrants: [a list of names follows]. . . . Please take up a collection among your members at once, as we need a large amount to give temporary relief to those here and soon to arrive, to send them West or South, or enable them to earn a livelihood.

But other measures also were required; another five hundred refugees were already on the way, and the Königsberg Committee had chartered nine ships to send over still more. Their reception, care, and placement was clearly to be a full-time job for a while, and the Board of Delegates had, along with the Hebrew Benevolent Society, accordingly created a separate organization for the task. Called the Hebrew Emigration Aid Society of the United States, it promptly sent out a public appeal for jobs for the

> mechanics among the refugees who would be most happy to find work—coppersmiths, tailors, carpenters, bakers, etc.—women capable of entering domestic service and lads and young men willing to be apprenticed. They are to observe the Sabbath and will be very thankful for employment.

Something entirely new had happened; quite spontaneously, the institutions of New York Jewry had organized themselves to deal with a mass immigrant influx.

The modest effort soon played itself out. On June 8, the New York leaders wrote to the Alliance in Paris that they would not handle shipments of more than a hundred able-bodied persons at a time. The Königsberg Committee was made to comply, and became so scrupulous that it sent only three hundred refugees in the ensuing year; the rest, with the charitable aid of wealthy Russian Jews, were repatriated after all. In 1873, the Hebrew Emigration Aid Society, its funds and functions both rapidly diminishing, was dissolved. In 1878, Wise succeeded in absorbing the New York Board of Delegates into his national Union of American Hebrew Congregations, thereby curtailing but by no means arresting its activities. The episode had passed.

But new forces had been set loose. Jewish immigration from Eastern Europe—mainly from poverty-stricken Galicia—increased during the seventies, albeit modestly; and the vision of an American refuge grew steadily. Simultaneously, generous-hearted American leaders of all faiths were looking with growing concern to the Jewish plight in that part of the world. In the spring of 1880, the Board of Delegates wrote a letter about the Jews of Russia to William M. Evarts, the Secretary of State under President Rutherford B. Hayes, which provoked a thorough and sympathetic investigation of the problem. This made its way to the floor of the House of Representatives that May 21, when Congressman Samuel S. Cox of New York delivered a speech in behalf of the oppressed Jews of Russia and read a letter written by a group of them to their American coreligionists. "We beseech you to come to our rescue," it said,

> to take us out of our bondage, out of our misery; to give us a chance in your great and glorious land of liberty, whose broad and track-less acres offer an asylum and a place for weary hearts and courageous souls willing to toil and by the sweat of the brow earn their daily bread. Come, brothers of Israel in America, come to our help. Give us the means to migrate to your shores.

And their American brethren, ten years earlier, had even rehearsed for the task.

·6·

ISRAEL UNPREPARED

The Alliance Israélite Universelle's call for relief funds in May 1881 had obtained a prompt response in New York. That very month, a coalition of Jewish groups, led by the editors of the weekly *Jewish Messenger*— the family that had founded the Board of Delegates of American Israelites in 1859—and a new philanthropic organization called the United Hebrew Charities of New York, established a Russian Relief Committee, and proceeded to raise funds to aid the victims.

Nothing was said at first about emigration, but the idea was already in the air. Having expressed the requisite "trepidation" at the prospect in its issue of May 20, the *Jewish Messenger* staff and its associates then sat down to a serious contemplation of the inevitable, and presented their conclusions the following Friday in an editorial entitled "Aid for Immigrants." It advocated the establishment by the United Hebrew Charities of an emigration bureau with a representative at Castle Garden, the New York immigrant clearing house. This was deemed "necessary in view of the danger that, unprotected and undirected, many immigrants will naturally fall into bad associations and disgrace and injure the Jewish community."

After the Vienna conference of European Jewish organizations in June, the *Jewish Messenger* endorsed the policy enunciated there of sending at least some of the Brody refugees to the United States. An editorial of July 8 offered an agenda for the receiving of immigrants by organized American Jewry. It consisted of these recommendations: (1) to keep in close touch with the European organizations to make sure that only the young and able-bodied be sent first, the elderly and dependent to come only after the earlier arrivals had established themselves; (2) to organize the reception of the immigrants in New York and other ports, seeing to "their distribution West and South to places where

41

employment is ready for mechanics and laborers"; (3) to establish "systematic employment registers in certain centers like Chicago, St. Louis and Galveston"; and (4) to raise funds "for the reception, transportation and temporary support" of the refugees, "including provision for the beginning of agricultural establishments."

New York had once again seized the initiative in the matter of Jewish refugees and once again come under the spell of the idea of masses of young Jewish farmers and "mechanics" in the making, ready to move on out of the congested streets of the city into the American heartlands. Perhaps recent experience had even given some encouragement for such an expectation. Only a few weeks earlier, the Jewish Emigration Society of Great Britain—one of the organizations that helped Jews from the Continent along on their route to America—had reported with satisfaction

> that the emigration to America is not by any means confined to the poorer classes of Jews. From Germany and Russia large numbers of our co-religionists with fairly well to do means are this year preparing to leave Europe. Many of them intend to make California their future residence, and there devote their energies to the culture of grapes for the production of wine. Texas and Oregon are likewise stated to have been selected by middle class Jews for their future business operations.

The report concluded that, as a result of this trend, "the poorer class" of Jews, when they emigrate, "are likely to find employment with their richer kinsfolk in the Western Hemisphere."

On August 14, the Alliance and Dr. Schafier decided to make their move and send five hundred of the Brody refugees to the United States. "We are assured by the Paris Committee," said the Union of American Hebrew Congregations in an appeal for aid issued four days later, "that the Hebrews selected for emigration to America will be mainly 'young men having a trade or profession and able to work.'" New York believed itself fully prepared. "The Paris Committee of the 'Alliance,'" announced the *Jewish Messenger* on August 19,

> inform us that arrangements are being made for the departure of Hebrew emigrants from Odessa [sic].
> It now becomes the duty of American Israelites to indicate the extent of their interest in their brethren, exiled because of their race and their fidelity to Judaism.
> Committees will be founded in many cities of the Union to raise funds for transportation and temporary support of the emigrants, and to [help them] receive employment, industrial and agricultural.

The article went on to state that "Mr. Jacob Schiff, with characteristic forethought, has sent . . . $500, which is the beginning of the American Fund in aid of the Russian emigrants." Schiff, a wealthy German-born partner in the New York banking firm of Kuhn, Loeb and Company, was beginning to emerge, at the age of thirty-four, as one of the foremost figures in American-Jewish philanthropy.

The first refugees arrived on September 9, and there must have been a widespread sigh of relief at the sight of them: Dr. Schafier, not yet overwhelmed, had been able to conform well enough to the stated policy in this first selection. "If Russia wearies of such residents," the *Jewish Messenger* wrote, "America welcomes them." There were even young people among them who were ready to try out the newspaper's proposal for securing "tracts of land in the Southern and Western States, where a choice will be given to those who are practical farmers to acquire and build up homesteads."

In the meantime, there was more preliminary work to be done. The Russian Relief Committee had been taking care of the new arrivals, but a more encompassing organization was needed. On September 18, a meeting at the Young Men's Hebrew Association of New York established a Russian Emigrant Relief Committee, with headquarters at 58 Saint Mark's Place. "The New York Committee are at work," the *Jewish Messenger* proudly proclaimed on September 23,

> the Board of Delegates cooperate, and they are receiving advice from distant towns, showing that interest is awakened.
>
> At the meeting on Sunday [the 18th], three of the exiles were present, and conveyed a most favorable impression. . . . Their stories of the sufferings at Kieff during the terrible . . . riots was painfully vivid.
>
> Houston and New Orleans are the first Southern cities to welcome the exiles. Surely, the great West will respond promptly.

And at last, in its issue of October 14, Rabbi Wise's *American Israelite* in Cincinnati gave notice of its acquiescence. "The Hebrew Congregations of Cincinnati," it said, "are taking action in raising money for the Russian Emigrant Relief fund." Then it continued: "Seventeen hundred of these unfortunate brethren are now on their way in most destitute condition, and immediate steps must be taken to raise funds and clothing and devise measures for their support." During the very next week, Cincinnati received its own share of the new arrivals.

But the crisis inevitably came. The refugees who arrived after that first happy debarkation in early September soon ceased to be the results of judicious selection; the inundation had begun in Brody, and a greater variety of ages and types were now reaching New York than their hosts could calmly bear. They complained to the Alliance in Paris, and on October 2 its president, S. H. Goldschmidt, sent a defensive reply. "You can judge by the appearance of those who have already arrived in New York," he insisted, "that the emigrants are not badly chosen." As for the demand that they all be mechanics or agriculturists, he dismissed this with his own version of how things really work in the Land of Opportunity. "I know," he declared,

> that the best way of getting on in America is for working men to work for daily wages at anything that comes their way, saving a part of their wages, so that, after some years, having learned the language and acquired experience in different ways, they find themselves in possession of some capital and can set up for themselves. This is the thing to do for the young men we are now sending over.

This, however, was not the central issue in Goldschmidt's letter. The Americans had accused the Alliance of taking care of its Russian-Jewish problem by creating a desire for emigration that was not really there, and the Frenchmen had to make their reply. "You must not believe," Goldschmidt urged, "that the *Alliance* has called forth this desire for emigration. It existed and was spreading." The reason, he said, was mainly that "envy and jealousy, which lie at the bottom of persecution in Germany and elsewhere in Europe, are not likely to exist for many years to come against the Jews in America." And to this moral challenge he added:

> We foresee that emigration from Russia, where there are two-and-a-half to three million Jews, will go on for years, and rather increase than diminish, and the situation of American Jewry may be deeply influenced, for better or for worse, according to the manner in which they behave in this emergency.

It was provocation added to prophecy; and too much for the members of the beleaguered New York Committee. "Send no more emigrants," they at last wired Paris. "Committee must return incapables."

This cable was followed by a long letter, written on October 31 by Manuel A. Kursheedt, secretary of the Russian Emigrant Relief Committee, in reply to Goldschmidt's remarks. "We are compelled to state," Kursheedt wrote, "that we cannot agree with you that emigration to America is the great panacea for the woes of the Russian Jews. The number of persons whose condition can be bettered in this way is comparatively small."

Kursheedt then went on to reiterate the Committee's reprimand.

"It was understood," he said, "that you were to send us only the strong and able-bodied, willing to work and possessing a knowledge of some handicraft," and that any other types "coming over here in any number would only lead to prompt action being taken to secure their return to Europe." Therefore,

> you will doubtless share our disappointment and vexation when you learn that fully one-third of those who have arrived thus far possess none of the requisite qualifications, and that their unfitness must have been apparent to your agents, if they exercised any discrimination whatever, and that not over one-third are really desirable emigrants.

What, then, had been sent over? "Many of the arrivals," Kursheedt explained, "are not as represented on the descriptive lists, very few are farmers in the American sense; for a farmer here needs a much more varied knowledge than a farmer in South Russia." Instead, most of the emigrants "that we have seen are clerks or tradesmen; they know no handicraft and wish to peddle. We are overrun with peddlers already, who have become a source of much annoyance to us." Adding that many of the arrivals of this type were "too old to learn any trade, and not a few of them are burdened with large families," Kursheedt went on to describe the results of an effort to reform them:

> Some of the emigrants whom we placed in this city at trades, requiring only light manual labor, remained at work only a day or two, declaring that the work was too hard and too confining to them. You can easily understand how men who have been accustomed to travel around the country selling goods, are unable to stand the close confinement required of an ordinary factory employee.

To bring the point home, Kursheedt injected a reference to "emigrants of other faiths coming here," who

> are either skilled mechanics, or else able-bodied laborers, who can and are willing to live on almost any kind of food, and, working on railroads, canals and the like, must endure considerable exposure and fatigue. To send our people to labor in that way would be cruel and futile.

The New Yorker's great fear was over the emerging Jewish social problem in New York, which was due to the fact that the "great bulk" of these emigrants "settle in this city and crowd the filthy tenements in a certain section on the East Side." Kursheedt, for the benefit of his

European colleagues, described what this meant. A tenement, he explained,

> is a house built on a plot of ground usually 25 feet wide by 100 feet deep, part of which is occupied by an open yard and outhouses; upon the small space left a tenement is built five or six stories (étages) in height, with about twelve small rooms on each floor; and two to three rooms are rented to each family. There are frequently twenty-four families in one house; occasionally two or three families occupy the same room or rooms for sleeping, cooking, sitting, working and every possible purpose.

This leads to "demoralization and disease," and a high death rate. "Many of the men are tailors," Kursheedt continued,

> and these—when they have work—sit up half the night in their ill-ventilated rooms, trying to earn a living. Their food is of the poorest: consequently in a few years they break down; their complaints are usually of a pulmonary character, and they live a lingering existence for a few months or perhaps years, and then die, leaving on our hands a widow already worn down with trouble, and a number of little children. In 1871 we only had one Jewish Orphan Asylum in the city which accommodated about two hundred inmates; now we have three such institutions with seven hundred inmates, and they are all overcrowded, and are compelled to refuse many worthy cases for want of room.

This, Kursheedt stressed, was the situation under the "natural influx of Jewish emigrants" of about three to five thousand a year. What, then, would happen if there were "any large increase in the number, especially if the character of the majority of those already sent by the Alliance would render the burden upon us absolutely intolerable"?

The secretary then went on to describe the work that the Americans had been doing—the formation of local relief committees in Philadelphia, New Orleans, Houston, Milwaukee, Louisville, Albany, Rochester, Quincy, and other cities; the participation of major relief organizations in Chicago, Saint Louis, and elsewhere; the efforts to place the immigrants in various parts of the country and on the land—making a special point about the difficulties involved. "The adults who have already arrived here," he stressed,

> have cost the local committee in this city over twenty dollars a piece on the average, and an additional outlay has been entailed upon the committees at the points to which we send them; and this expense—we would emphasize—must be continued until they can earn their bread.

Then there was the cost of sending them outside New York:

> Most of these cities would refuse to join in the movement if we
> sent them the emigrants in the condition they present on landing.
> Their clothing is usually filthy and dilapidated; many have only can-
> vas suits; we have to take most of them to a boarding house where
> they can bathe and refresh themselves, and be furnished with nec-
> essary apparel. All this is expensive as you can readily see. The
> cost of transportation has been as high as twenty dollars in many
> cases, and if there should be, as is daily expected, a cessation of the
> competition between the railroad lines, the rates are likely to be
> higher.

Kursheedt then went on to discuss some of the difficulties involved in
founding agricultural colonies—although the fact was that, at that moment, none had yet been tried with the Russian Jews.

The letter concluded with a series of strictures. "Of course all the
parties whom you send," it said,

> must be able-bodied and, before leaving, provided with clean, sub-
> stantial clothing adequate for our rigorous climate, the cost of cloth-
> ing being much lower in Europe than here. Not over fifty persons
> should be sent in any one week, and not over one hundred and fifty
> per month at present. Strictly accurate descriptive lists should be
> mailed us at least one week in advance of each shipment.... Do
> not send any married men who leave their wives at home, as the
> latter class frequently soon get homesick and cause us trouble;
> above all let us have mechanics or actual farmers or laborers, and
> of course, only those entitled to our special assistance on account
> of being exiles from their Russian homes.

The last specification reflected a problem that was often cropping up:
that of Austrian Jews—and sometimes gentiles—who occasionally insin-
uated themselves among the refugees for an assisted ride to the New
World. This was among several "blunders" often committed by Alliance
agents that the letter now described, culminating in this story:

> One [refugee], Baer Jucht, called at the office of this Society a
> few days since and saw the writer and stated that he ... had just
> arrived here, and that Dr. Schafier had sent him from Brody to this
> country with the promise he would be cared for. He further said
> he was neither a mechanic nor farmer and had so informed the
> Doctor, but that nevertheless the latter, on behalf of the *Alliance*,
> gave him an order for his passage and a few florins besides and
> promised he should be cared for on his arrival here. His name is
> not on the lists you have sent us, but he was carefully cross-exam-

ined and impressed the writer with the truthfulness of his statement.

This example of imputed misrepresentation of the American situation by Schafier and his Brody colleagues provided Kursheedt with a last opportunity to return to the basic philosophical issue of this exchange of letters—the true extent of the desire to emigrate on the part of the Russian Jews. "This desire has been doubtless fed," he now felt able to say, "by the glowing accounts of America given them by persons interested in inducing them to emigrate; if they really knew the condition of affairs here, few would desire to make the change."

These reservations, complaints, and warnings having been aired, the emigration could now continue.

·7·

THE GENTLEMEN OF BRODY

It had soon become clear that Schafier could not carry on the enormous task in Brody without high-level assistance, so at the beginning of October the Alliance had sent its most eminent fieldworker, Charles Netter. Born in Alsace in 1826, Netter had enjoyed a successful and adventurous career as a businessman—living, among other places, in Moscow and London—before settling down in Paris at the age of twenty-five and thenceforth devoting himself to philanthropy. One of the founders of the Alliance, he had established for that organization the Mikveh Israel agricultural school in Palestine and served as its first director from 1870 to 1873. Eager to see the creation of a Jewish farming class, he had been disappointed at the failure of the school thus far to achieve the required transformation among its forelocked young charges, recruited from the religious quarters of Jerusalem, Hebron, Safed, and Tiberias. An attempt made by some of them in 1878 to start a farming village called Petach Tikvah (Gate of Hope) near the school was faltering at this very moment, and Netter had reason to be skeptical about any further such efforts. He was not much in favor of Palestine colonization; as for the dream of making Jewish farmers in the New World, he could only have viewed it with considerable reservations.

Like Schafier, Netter arrived in Brody expecting to spend only a few days there. His quick adjustment to the reality of it is demonstrated by a letter he wrote on October 13 to the Alliance leadership in Paris. "I've been here just a week," it began,

and I think I am fully abreast of the facts of the situation now. We are dealing with an emigration of people of all ages and all classes; although we are working sixteen to eighteen hours a day, I am

49

afraid we are making no particular progress. For every sixty persons we process in a day, a hundred newcomers arrive.

Netter went on to describe how he had organized the operation into three sections: a registration office under Hermann Magnus (a volunteer recently arrived from the Leipzig Relief Committee), an examinations office under Netter himself, and an office under Schafier that made transportation arrangements. "The first office," he said,

> will receive only the men and will fill out for each one a card providing details of accompanying family, which will serve for entry into the second office. The second office will receive the whole families, and examine them regarding the details of their situation, in order to determine whether they should be repatriated or sent on. Once this is determined, the card-bearing man goes to the third office, where he will receive either a subsidy for the return trip to Russia, or the red card that indicates his journey will continue.

But even that poignant situation was more difficult than it seemed at first glance. "It is not sufficient," Netter added, "to send men either to the right or to the left; one must also deal separately with the young, and with the children—for which purpose a fourth office is being opened." And this led to a crucial and impassioned observation:

> We shall never let ourselves be obstructed in the task of making fine adults of these children, who are more handsome and intelligent than people have been inclined to think of those who come out of Russia. People would be quite surprised and become disabused of what they had always thought—in Germany as well—if they could only see who is here seeking our help. The men wear neither caftans nor forelocks; they are handsome, tall, neat, and intelligent. . . . The women are almost elegant. . . . Perhaps as many as half the boys are students of gymnasiums—many of whom had been discharged on the pretext that there were no more places available. After being reproached for not wanting to assimilate, they now find that they have assimilated too much.

This brought Netter to the gist of the problem in Brody: the enormous size and unmanageable variety of the refugee masses, which defied any easy containment in terms of types or numbers such as the Americans had been demanding. "At the beginning," he said,

> we had decided to send over only young men, then, on second thought, to favor the fathers of families. But I believe you cannot adhere strictly to one rule or another, but must take on people as

they come—that you must simply inquire into their personal worthiness and do the best you can, since we cannot do everything.

Which led to another passionate outburst:

It is an enormous calamity that can be dealt with only by an enormous effort. Millions in money would be required to lift up the millions [of Russian Jews] out of slavery before they start seeking the alternative of flight. Is there any better place for our wealthy to spend their millions than here? In doing our duty here, we would show the world Jewish philanthropy in action; that would indeed be a most educational lesson. We must not bury our heads. The upheaval has only just begun. *I fear we shall be inundated. I would like to bring all doubters here for only twenty-four hours—then our cause would be won!*

The last part of the letter was devoted to a description of the exhausting workday. "Officially," Netter wrote,

we begin our work at eight in the morning and officially finish at sunset; but in fact it is otherwise. At six in the morning I can already hear the murmuring of the crowd that has gathered before the door and in the courtyard. I get up and hastily write a few letters, which I find no time to finish and which I defer to the next morning—so that the following day the same thing happens. I step out into the corridor and go to the office of my assistant, which is already overflowing with petitioners. The men are bad enough, but worst of all are the women—the mothers, holding children on their laps!

Then the work actually begins. "Every petitioner," Netter continued,

finds his own situation to be the most urgent, everyone wants to be the first, and much of the time needed for doing business is lost in talk. Recently, a crowd that had gathered in front of my office in the morning was so large and demanding that it took me almost an hour just to get inside. Yesterday evening, quite late, I finally was able to dare going out into the street to get a little air; when I got back, I found the corridor of the hotel overflowing with people, and I had to begin working anew.

This led to a concluding wish:

I do not want to—or rather, I cannot—lengthen the workday any more, for the strain is too great already; but I hope we will have gone through our list of refugees in another twenty days.

It took only one more day for Netter to realize that this wish was a vain one and, indeed, to succumb to a passing mood of despair. "I am besieged," he wrote to the Alliance on October 14, almost before the ink on the previous day's letter was dry, "and dare not even show myself in the street any more; so that I have no choice but to be in my office all day." This led him to a stark conclusion, somewhat at variance with the spirit of the day before:

> The emigration must be held up at all cost, until we have brought some peace and quiet to this overwhelmingly crowded place. . . . The emigration must be held up in clear and no uncertain terms, and, considering the situation in Brody, must even be turned back—otherwise we shall have here all the beggars in the Russian Empire, and what then? How shall we separate the good from the bad? The latter are already pressing to the front of the crowd and the former no longer come to us: this is what is happening.

Furthermore, hygienic conditions were being threatened:

> I shudder at the thought of an epidemic, which could easily break out among these masses of unfortunates! When the cold weather comes, the problems will be awful. *And the influx mounts daily!* It must be stopped as soon as possible, or we are heading for a catastrophe.

Netter immediately sent out a proclamation to Jewish leaders in Russia that no new emigrants would be received in Brody; but though this appeared in the newspapers, it had little effect. The word was out that Jews who got to Brody were being sent on to America, and the outflow increased.

For the moment, then, Netter's only choice was to enlarge his staff, and on October 17, letters asking for volunteers were sent out to Paris and Vienna. From the latter city, Moritz Friedländer soon arrived in Brody's autumn mud, followed not long after by three other associates—two of them burly men with military experience, to deal with the importunate refugee mobs. Wary of the hectic conditions at the Hotel Rainer, where Schafier and Netter were lodging and had initially set up shop, Friedländer and his Vienna colleagues prudently took rooms at the Hôtel de l'Europe, in another part of town.

But Netter had in the meantime found supplementary quarters for the operation, a bit more spacious and conveniently removed from the hotel where he slept. Friedländer was to remember well reporting to the new location, and his first encounter with Netter and Schafier—bearded, solemn, and middle-aged, like himself—who now shared the same large office. "When I entered," he writes,

I found Netter surrounded by a dense throng of pushing and shoving petitioners, while Schafier stood next to him, a guardian angel of the unfortunate, and an interpreter not only of their feelings but of their speech. . . . Netter's look seemed to me to betray an unshakable determination, Schafier's an ineffable resignation.

Schafier, recalling the old expression "failed in Brody,"

> stood before me with folded arms, looked at me with his sympathetic, almost—as it seemed to me—pitying eyes, and said: "So you, too, have come to Brody, to 'fail' here, like us?"

The three men soon established their new working routine. "During these days," according to Friedländer,

> Netter and Schafier worked in the supplementary office, which was tucked away in a tiny two-room house in a remote part of town. The second room was where we did our work, while the first was crammed to the rafters with petitioners. The large space around the outside of the house was also always filled with several hundred refugees, clamoring to be let in. The three volunteer helpers from Vienna would station themselves for a while each morning in front of the door and wage a fearful struggle to hold the fort.

The scenes inside were equally dramatic. "In walks a family," Friedländer records,

> that had seen better days not long before, as one can tell by their clothes, now quite worn out, and by the fine bearing of the children. The father holds a one-year-old in his arms, the mother a child slightly older. Four other children entwine themselves around their parents' legs. It is a closeknit family. The mother has entered sobbing loudly, but her sobs have now—at her husband's soothing and a strong, stern glance from Netter—been suppressed into a whimper that shakes one to the marrow. The man puts his papers on the table with a quivering hand.

Then the questioning begins, during which this family seems, in Friedländer's eyes, to become a summary illustration of the "pitiable history of the Russian Jews":

> The mother cries quietly without letup, the two-year-old girl on her arm chewing on a crust of bread. Then, seeing that the child has finished, she thrusts another piece of bread into her mouth to stop her from crying. The other children, frightened, still entwine themselves around the legs of their parents.

Netter has finished questioning the father, and now proceeds to inspect the other members of the family. "As soon as Netter's eyes fall upon the children," Friedländer continues,

> he loses his stern and piercing look and becomes infinitely tender and mild. Taking from his desktop a piece of pastry in a wrapping, ready for the purpose, he divides the sweet among the children, kissing and fondling them as he does so. The parents begin to look hopeful, and the mother laughs through her tears.

Then, after a brief exchange with them in French—an acknowledgment that this was indeed a family of some culture—Netter pronounces the fateful words:

"You have been accepted!"

Immediately the scene becomes animated. "The parents are beside themselves with joy," Friedländer writes, "and the children jump and shout all over the room, without knowing exactly why. Soon the parents are also dancing in their happiness." Friedländer could recall other such occasions, when the joy was so great that people for a moment forgot their own names. And more than once he heard the cry, directed at Netter:

"You are the Messiah! Our true Messiah!"

If Netter was the Messiah of this upheaval, then certainly America was its Promised Land. Such was the import of a "Declaration" drawn up in Brody on October 18 by a group of refugees from Yelizavetgrad and sent, in Yiddish, to the Alliance headquarters in Paris. It said:

> We, the undersigned, Jews from the town of Yelizavetgrad, downtrodden, tormented, and robbed, recognizing the utter sacredness and necessity of the mission that the Alliance Israélite Universelle has taken upon itself, namely:—
>
> 1. Removing all Jews from the Slavic countries in general and from Russia in particular, because among those populations (from which, for the most part, they have remained aloof, especially from the primitive, crude, wild, and rampantly thieving elements among them) their lives and wherewithal not only are not guaranteed, but are actually in danger;
>
> 2. Transferring them to the United States of North America, a country civilized beyond all others, which gives greater guarantees than any other of freedom of personality and conscience and of the inviolability of property, and which acknowledges all civil and political rights to every inhabitant;
>
> —recognizing all this, we pledge solemnly that we will direct all our thoughts, all our attention, means, and strength, to whatever ways

we, according to our ability, can help in the great and sacred task to which the Alliance has now devoted itself. We swear to aid in the work that must be done to better the lot of all Jews, that may serve to unite them, raise them up, and enable them to flourish— we swear to serve the cause of emigration. Not a single Jew must remain in that accursed land, possessed by wild, thieving, blood-thirsty beasts! We will count ourselves fortunate if we are permitted to help, however few Jews we personally can cause to be moved.

This was a passionate commitment indeed; but how ready was America—or, in particular, America's Jews—to meet it?

It is not clear whether Manuel A. Kursheedt's long letter of October 31 had reached the Alliance in Paris by November 16, when its Central Committee held a crucial meeting. What certainly had arrived was the telegram saying, "Send no more emigrants." Consequently, according to the minutes, "several members expressed the opinion that the emigration to America must now be halted, since the Board of New York has indicated in several of its letters its wish to receive emigrants no longer, and the difficulties it has encountered in placing them." But because not everyone shared it, this expression of opinion produced only an ambiguous result. The minutes go on to say that "the Central Committee, while inclining toward this step, did not vote on it definitively." Nevertheless, the telegram then sent to Brody had a definitive tone. "Stop all transports to America," it said. "New York Committee protests. Encourage only repatriation."

There was a stunned reaction in Brody. With the cold weather coming on—it was in fact snowing the day the telegram arrived—Netter, Schafier, and their colleagues had sped up the pace of the transports to two a week, and had been working more furiously than ever. At that very moment, six hundred emigrants were packed and ready to go, and five hundred more were about to be processed; hundreds of others, huddled in wretched quarters all over town, waited their turn. Netter wired Paris that immediate and complete cessation was not possible. Then he and his associates grimly prepared to begin the task of repatriation the following day.

"When we woke the next morning," Friedländer writes,

there was an air of sadness everywhere. The snow lay thick on the ground and a sharp, icy wind blew whistling through the air. As Netter woke up and went to the window, where he saw the crowds gathered in front of the hotel, their teeth chattering, and gazing up at his window, he broke into sobs.

Getting a grip on themselves, the delegates set to their various tasks, calculating, in Friedländer's words: "If we can just 'repatriate' a hundred people a day, then we would most likely have cleared the place out in eight days—provided that the six hundred who have already been accepted are sent on to America." The work they had to do was accompanied by heart-rending scenes. "The shut doors creaked under the weight of their besiegers," Friedländer recalled, "until the panes shattered, so that we could hear the chilling moan, the cry to be let in, which, together with the pleadings of those who stood before us, formed an anguishing concert."

Nor were these petitioners at all ready to accept the claim that the cause of emigration had now "failed in Brody." They waited for a new directive, and even those who had none of the qualifications demanded by the Americans did not give up hope. At one point, Schafier completely lost patience with an old man who did not stop showing up at the door.

"Even if we resume the transports to America," he blurted out, "you don't have a chance of being accepted! You have no trade and you aren't young enough. How will you begin in a new country when you don't even know the language?"

"Oh, if only it happens!" the old man said. "If only it happens—then you'll see. I have a written testimony from our rabbi that I'll be speaking good English in three weeks!"

The suspense had gone on for three days when suddenly a cable came from Paris: "Telegram 'Stop all transports' is apocryphal. We want to slow down, but not to stop." The dissenters in Paris had reasserted themselves.

Netter and his colleagues went back to work, determined at least to get onto the trains all the emigrants who had been in Brody at the time the order to cease had arrived. This was accomplished in a few more days—but the influx into Brody did not stop.

·8·

FROM BRODY TO NEW YORK, I:
THE EUROPEAN JOURNEY

During a typical Brody week in October 1881, two days in every seven were especially busy—the days when the week's transport of emigrants was made ready, then sent on its way. In mid-November, it became four days—two sets of two—as the effort was speeded up. On the first day of each set there was relative quiet in the two rooms of the bureau as the steamship tickets bought by the Alliance were prepared, usually with the assistance of a shipping-company official from Hamburg or Antwerp, and the emigrants were inspected for their state of readiness to move on. "Once the work in the office is done," according to Friedländer,

> the emigrants with tickets assemble that afternoon in their best array, to submit to a final inspection.... Then the staff goes to Netter's office, to compile an exact list of names for the next day's transport, to prepare the emigrants' pocket money for the journey—in packets bearing the name of each recipient—and to get all the remaining details in order.

The reason for the pocket money was made particularly clear by a general circular issued in Yiddish on November 14 over Netter's signature. "Everyone who has been selected for transport to America," it began,

> must provide himself with a shoulder bag containing three loaves of bread and a flask of drinking water. The flask can be refilled with fresh water at the various stations where there are long waits. It is further recommended to bring along some brandy, cheese, and other desirable foodstuffs, since no food or drink will be provided during the entire overland journey.

The point is then driven home to those who may have thought they would be taken in hand every step of the way. "The providing of room and board for passengers journeying to America under the auspices of the Alliance Israélite Universelle," the notice says, "only begins aboard ship." Then some recommendations are given for finding food and shelter for the time between getting off the train and boarding the ship:

> In Hamburg, find a place to stay for two and a half days, in a transients' residence, where you can get room and board at 1.5 marks a day—that is, altogether, 3 marks 75 pfennigs for persons over ten years of age, and 1 mark 88 pfennigs for children under ten—to be paid by the traveler *out of his own pocket.*

Then there was also the matter of the inadequate accommodations aboard ship. "Since only empty bunks have been provided on the ship," the circular continues,

> the passengers should buy pillows and mattresses in Hamburg, as well as eating and drinking utensils, and washing materials, which should cost about 7 marks altogether. Furthermore, you may need a woolen hat aboard ship—which ought to be obtained here in Brody if you also want to protect yourself from the cold on the way to Hamburg.

But this freedom to provide for oneself was not matched by a freedom to make one's own decisions, for

> with every transport from Brody to Hamburg an escort goes along. He holds all your railway tickets, and all who go with him must grant him *full authority to act* without any discussion of the matter, whether it has to do with money or provisions.
>
> Anyone who cannot or will not comply with these regulations *forfeits his right to his steamship ticket.*
>
> In New York the passengers should not expect to be supported by the Committee there.

With these understandings, the emigrants were ready to begin their journey.

"The next day," Friedländer writes, "even in the first gray light of dawn, one can already see whole troops of emigrants with their baggage making their way to the railway station. The train does not depart until about twelve noon, but they are already streaming toward it at six in the morning." They began boarding at around ten, by which time the waiting room had become filled with onlookers of various religions and nationalities. Then came

> the frenetic outbursts of rejoicing, when the departing emigrants shouted their hurrahs for His Majesty the Emperor of Austria, for the Alliance of Paris and of Vienna, and for all the delegates, while speeches were made in Russian, arousing a veritable storm of enthusiasm among the passengers.

Asher Ginzberg, a young Russian intellectual soon to become known to the Hebrew-reading world under the pen name Ahad Ha-am (One of the People), was passing through Brody on a train to Vienna on one of these occasions. "I could see Netter," he was to recall,

> that worthy man, standing in the station and distributing money to the refugees. His face expressed the kindness and compassion he felt for them. The refugees were gay and in high spirits. One could read in their eyes how hopefully they looked into the future. As the train started to move, they called out: Long live Netter! Long live the *Alliance!*

These certainly were the best moments; although even then, had Ginzberg been able to scrutinize Netter's face more closely, he would doubtless have seen very great fatigue. On November 26, Netter was finally to take his leave of Brody, along with Friedländer, and return home. Schafier stayed on, however, awaiting further help from Paris. The onset of winter was to cause a slowdown in the arrival of refugees and allow a breathing spell, but the work in Brody was by no means at an end.

Meanwhile, what of those who had begun their journey to the New World on those trains? The best surviving accounts come not from that fall but from the following spring, when a renewed stream of Brody refugees was to include the articulate young idealists of Am Olam, eager indeed to realize the agrarian ideal that the American Israelites harbored for them. A member of the Kiev group, Israel Kasovich, was to recall that

> the Am Olam group was given a special train, third-class, that cost us only half the regular price, and over which we were allowed to hoist our own flag. And we made a big one, embroidered with the name Am Olam, a large plow next to it, and underneath, the Talmudic motto "If I am not for myself, who is for me?" written in Ger-

man in golden letters. One beautiful morning we gathered in a certain place, and the procession began. At its head were two students carrying our flag, followed by some older members of the group with our Torah scroll. . . . At the station we heard speeches by some Jewish professors who had come from Lemberg and Vienna.

George Price, not a member of any group, made a quieter departure that spring with his parents. "In the evening we arrived at the station," he recorded in his diary for Tuesday, June 13, 1882:

There was an immense crowd. We waited at the station about six hours, and were finally admitted to the platform. They assigned a compartment to ten passengers and gave each of us a loaf of bread and two eggs. The agent walked from car to car and bade the emigrants farewell.

The first stopover was in the ancient and beautiful Galician city of Lemberg, with its population of more than a hundred thousand, about a third of them Jews. Abraham Cahan, who, though an individual emigrant from the north, had joined an Am Olam group while they were all in Brody, arrived in Lemberg with his comrades a week after the Kiev group had passed through with great fanfare. "A committee of local Jewish notables awaited us there," Cahan writes:

We were regaled with tea and rolls—then, later, with soup and meat. We spent a whole day there, and several of us got a good look at the city. The center of Lemberg, with the green lawns of a lovely park, was a delight to see. To the left of it began the Jewish quarter, and I went in to see it.

The next long stop was Cracow, in the westernmost corner of Galicia. Cahan's group was met there by yet another committee offering tea and rolls. Among the good citizens of Cracow, Cahan records,

was a Polish Christian named Onufrowicz who had taken a warm interest in the Jewish emigrants. His name was already known to us in Russia, because he knew Russian well and had been the Cracow correspondent of the Russian-Jewish weekly *Russkii Yevrey (Russian Jew)*. He had gone to welcome the Kiev Am Olam at the station [the week before], bringing as a gift a richly bound copy of Karl Marx's *Capital* in French translation.

From Cracow the pilgrimage route curved northwestward into Silesia, and made its next major stop in Breslau, Germany. "There a committee also came to greet us," Cahan writes, but it was now of quite a different sort. Its members were German Jews, handsomely dressed in the European manner, and clean-shaven. They gave us an excellent meal.

We had a few hours, so I made a tour of the city, and for the first time I observed the difference between a highly civilized country and a place like Russia. I marveled at how neat, clean, and well appointed everybody and everything were.

The Kiev Am Olam had been through there, too, and perhaps it was they or Cahan's group who had been seen at the Breslau station that spring by the great Danish-Jewish literary critic and historian, Georg Brandes, who wrote:

> Day by day, there arrived more groups of Russian Jews. . . . Among the first were sturdy young men, well suited for pioneering. . . .
>
> When speaking to one of these impoverished but energetic students, . . . three different drives become apparent: More or less consciously, he feels that the collective type of land ownership in the Russian commune is in the natural order of things. He also has been inspired by the relatively developed socialist ideas so widespread in Russia. . . . Ultimately, he is imbued with a profound determination and sense of duty to wipe away the old slur that Jews are capable only of trading, and that they desire only to accumulate money.

The most enthusiastic memories of this crusaders' march come from the Kiev Am Olam leader himself, Nicholas Aleinikoff—he who had publicly repented in a Kiev synagogue after the riot in that city. "The news that an Am Olam student group was on its way to America to found communal colonies had preceded us," he said:

> Along our entire route—in Brody, Lemberg, Cracow, Breslau, Berlin, and elsewhere—committees were founded . . . to help us. . . . In Cracow I was presented with a copy of Karl Marx's *Capital* as a gift for the group. In Lemberg the Orthodox Jews presented us with a Torah scroll and a large flag with the words on it, in Hebrew: "The Flag of the Camp of Israel." Our journey from Brody to Berlin was a chain of ovations for us. In every city they had arranged a grand reception.

After a perfunctory stop in Berlin, a few groups went on to Antwerp to embark, but most of the emigrants made their way to Hamburg. There the atmosphere suddenly changed. Israel Kasovich, having taken part in the glorious procession of the Kiev Am Olam, noted: "In Hamburg, however, we were treated like ordinary emigrants. We were all confined in a large barrack which resembled somewhat a public bath-house in Lithuania." George Price, who had received "bread, milk, cof-fee, cigars, cheese, money, candy and other delicacies," as well as "excellent dinners," all free of charge, in cities along the route, found that in Hamburg "we were left to our fate."

There was a Jewish relief committee in Hamburg, too, but by the spring of 1882 the emigrant situation in this port city had become more than anyone could handle. Since the Alliance was no longer buying steamship tickets, those emigrants who did not belong to groups like Am Olam had to rely on their personal resources to see them on their way. Bernard Weinstein, a sixteen-year-old member of the Odessa Am Olam, which passed through Hamburg that summer, saw "hundreds of poor Jewish immigrants going about faint and waiting for miracles—maybe the Committee would ship them out, or they would suddenly get money from home. Meanwhile, many of them had no place to sleep." It being summer, the committee had obtained permission for them to sleep in the streets. Rabbi Isaac Rülf of Memel issued a warning that any Jew who could do so should stay away from Hamburg, "where he would be exposed to starvation, Heaven forfend, as has already occurred."

At this time, few ships went directly from North European ports to the United States. As a rule, the first leg of the sea voyage was made from Hamburg or Antwerp to Hull or Hartlepool on the eastern coast of England. From there, the emigrants would take trains to Liverpool to embark for transatlantic passage: the volume of shipping to America was at this time vastly greater at Liverpool than at any other Old World port.

The short voyage across the North Sea to Britain seems to have been uneventful for most of the emigrants making it in the spring of 1882, although it had been particularly trying for those being sent by the Alliance in the fall. The Alliance had made its transportation ar-rangements with C. Henry Strauss, an Antwerp shipping agent who worked with it chartering ships for the exodus of Jews from Suwalki and Kovno in 1870. Claiming a specialty in the transporting of Jews—he may have been one himself—he handed out advertising leaflets in Yiddish and made much of his ability to arrange for kosher food aboard ship. But two letters written from Liverpool in late October and early November of 1881 show the emigrants finding his services to be less than satisfactory.

The first was written by a young man on October 25 to his father back in Brody. "Be informed," it said,

that I arrived last night in Liverpool, and tomorrow our ship is leaving for New York. I beg of you to go see Herr Schafier and let him know that Herr Strauss treats us worse than like sheep. We get nothing to eat or drink. All the telegrams about this were false. . . . Herr Schafier asked us to write everything about how it went and how Herr Strauss treated us. Dear father, when your time comes to travel, you must take your own food along, and not leave yourself at the mercy of Herr Strauss. . . .

David Braun of Yelizavetgrad—one of the signers of the "Declaration" on emigration to America sent to the Alliance on October 18—wrote a letter to Schafier himself on November 1:

Our health was good in Antwerp, thank God, but though we left there in good shape things began going badly on the trip to Liverpool. [We were treated terribly.] If someone wanted so much as a little hot water [for washing], he would get hit in the back of the neck. To put it briefly, all the good will that the Alliance had created was completely lost after we left Antwerp. We were called stupid fellows, pigs. . . .

Although England was looked upon primarily—by the emigrants and by the English themselves—as a corridor leading from North Sea ships to British-owned transatlantic ones, it often proved a difficult obstacle to get through. More and more of those who were paying their own passage had to stop there indefinitely. Harris Rubin, a young emigrant from Lithuania, found himself in London in March 1882 and wondered if he would ever get farther. The previous month, a London organization—called the Mansion House, or Russo-Jewish, Committee—had been formed to aid the riot victims, and some of the emigrants with problems were being sent down to its offices from Liverpool. Rubin, who wanted to become a farmer in America but did not belong to a group and needed money to go on, had turned to this Committee for help.

"I reported to the place," he later wrote,

and there found a long hall where there was a long line of gloomy faces. . . . There were benches all around the hall occupied by women and bundles and children of various ages and many howling babies. The hall was filled with a frightful noise and clamor.

Many of these were of the age and type that were not particularly wanted by American-Jewish leaders; but even the young, would-be farmer Rubin had trouble getting through. "Your card indicates," a clerk told him, "that you are married and that you have left your family behind. We can't give you preference over whole families who have been waiting a long time and who have priority over you. And above all, people like you who have left their families behind should not be eligible at all." Rubin thought for a while of settling in London, thereby to join the rapidly growing Jewish immigrant population of the East End—a situation so alarming to many British Jews that they were now taking the lead over the Alliance in pressing the New York Committee to accept more immigrants. Rubin was to make it across, after all; but even among those who did not, in the years to come, "about ninety per cent of the immigrants in London," according to the recollection of one of them, "had it in mind to go to America by saving up enough fare."

Liverpool was a happier point of arrival for those who had come in groups, having rounded up their funds at home and booked passage all the way to America. Alexander Harkavy, a nineteen-year-old scholar, had emigrated that spring of 1882 with a group of young people from Vilna who decided to join forces with the Kiev Am Olam and meet them in Liverpool. Harkavy's group arrived first. Then, as he later wrote,

> four days later the [Kiev] group arrived. Great joy filled our hearts when we learned that our allied group had made it. In high spirits we rushed to greet them. After a meeting between the leaders of our two groups, the creation of a legal union was announced: henceforward, we were like brothers of a single society. The Kiev group with which we had joined had seventy members, men and women. Most were young intellectuals, dreamers just like ourselves . . . That very day, the ship *British Prince* stood at the harbor ready to accept passengers for America. It was destined to take us as well. Just an hour after our union we went down to the ship together. That evening the *British Prince* hoisted anchor, and began to transport us to our ultimate destination: the New World.

To reach it, there only remained the joys and agonies of the Atlantic crossing.

·9·

FROM BRODY TO NEW YORK, II: THE OCEAN

For young Harkavy's combined Kiev and Vilna group, the Atlantic voyage proved to be as euphoric as the embarkation. "The boat *British Prince* was like a city floating on water," he writes,

> so great was the number of its passengers. All its passengers were Russian immigrants; all, save members of our group, were travelling to America as individuals, seeking to improve their position by their own brains and brawn; this one through handiwork, that one through peddling. Members of our group saw themselves as superior to this multitude. "The other passengers are not like us," said we to ourselves, "we are not merely going to America for simple comfort, we are idealists, eager to prove to the world that Jews can work the land!" In our imagination, we already saw ourselves as landowning farmers dwelling on our plots in the western part of the country. So certain were we that our aims in the New World would be achieved that even on the boat we began to debate which kind of community institutions we would build, which books we would introduce into our library, whether or not we would build a synagogue and so forth (with regard to the synagogue, most of the views were negative). We danced and sang overcome with joyous expectations of what America held in store for us. In spite of our seasickness, storms, and tempests which visited us on our journey, we were happy and lighthearted. All the days of our Atlantic voyage were filled with joy.

Such has always been the way of groups of hardy students traveling in pursuit of idealistic adventure; and the rare fact that this was a ship filled entirely with Russian-Jewish emigrants also made for the best possible atmosphere among them. But most accounts of the Atlantic crossing are not so deliriously happy.

For one thing, there was what Abraham Cahan—traveling, as ever, a week after the Kiev Am Olam, on a ship called the *British Queen*—described as "the dreadful, salty, suffocating smell of the cellar called 'steerage,' " filled with "shallow wooden boxes that they called beds." Actually, in this era when steam had almost completely replaced sail on the transatlantic lines, and the rush of passengers ready to make a voyage of ten to fourteen days instead of the month or two it used to take was influencing shipping companies to improve their accommodations, steerage was no longer quite the hellhole it once had been. In the old days, it had been simply a collection of tiers of rude bunks set up in the hold in places where cargo would otherwise have been stored, dank and even more nauseous than what Cahan experienced. By the 1880s, when ships were being built entirely for passengers, steerage was the section—by then usually located toward the bow—in which the most minimally adequate quarters were left over for those who paid the lowest fares.

Never comfortable, these dark dormitories varied greatly in quality all the same. Israel Kasovich, overlooking the euphoria that Harkavy had remembered for the same voyage, was to recall accommodations that were among the worst. "We were all herded together," he writes,

> in a dark, filthy compartment in the steerage. We learned that our vessel had formerly been a cattle ship and had just been converted into a passenger boat. Our compartment was enormously large, and wooden bunks had been put up in two tiers, one on top of the other. Here men, women and children were herded together.

Harris Rubin fared a little better; he was taken with a group down below after boarding,

> and each of us received a stack of straw, a quilt and a dipper for water. The women were taken to one "stateroom," the men to another. On the walls were shelves, one above another, with barely enough room for a person to squeeze in. These were to be our beds.

Bernard Weinstein, whose group sailed directly to America from Hamburg on the German steamship *Wieland*, took his place in steerage along with a group of Polish peasant immigrants. "The women carried large packs filled with bedclothes on their heads," he recalled:

> They were bringing all their possessions to America with them. They jostled and shoved and ran down into the ship. Everyone wanted to grab a good place on board. On the shoulders of each

immigrant hung a little pack filled with tin eating utensils and they clinked. It made one laugh rather than cry. The families were given cots that could accommodate six to eight persons. My friend and I went with the single people and we were given the worst location, in the bow of the ship, where the pitching and rolling was dreadful.

But Weinstein was only sixteen years old. "Who cared?" he adds. "We were going to America!"

The worst problem in steerage—bad anywhere, but especially there—was seasickness. "I tried to fall asleep," Weinstein writes of his first night at sea, "but the ship was rocking like a seesaw, and all the tin utensils kept banging against the wall in a musical rhythm that was simply deafening." Many of his fellow immigrants became "deathly ill." George Price, who also sailed directly from Hamburg to New York, similarly noted: "the clattering of the dishes, the groans and wailing of the men, women and children, the bad effects of nausea," which "could drive anyone insane." Harris Rubin, who had wisely remained on deck until late the first night, was in his bunk just falling asleep when he heard the sound of something dropping from above him. "Help, save me!" came the cry from the upper bunk. "What's the matter?" Rubin asked. "I feel very sick," was the reply, "—a little water, I'm dying." Rubin got off his shelf-bed

with the greatest caution because I didn't want to be hit by the contents of the stomach being steadily disgorged by my upper neighbor. When I got up and walked by the women's quarters, I heard more screaming. Other men were up to help the sick. In a little while our whole stateroom was filled with sick and "nurses." There was a running to the sailors for water and to the doctor for help and medicine. Instead of water and medicine we received a bawling out for having disturbed their sleep.

Rubin may have been among the "nurses" that first night, but he was not to be spared. "For the next couple of days," he writes, "those who first became seasick did recover and then others became sick. I was among these." "Hundreds of people had vomiting fits," writes Kasovich,

throwing up even their mother's milk. . . . The confusion of cries became unbearable, and a hundred persons vomited at one and the same time. I wanted to escape from that inferno, but no sooner had I thrust my head forward from the lower bunk I lay on than someone above me vomited straight upon my head. I wiped the vomit away, dragged myself onto the deck, leaned against the railing and vomited my share into the sea, then lay down half-dead upon the deck.

Cahan was spared this particular affliction, though he had brought along a supply of two dozen lemons just in case. Not that he found no use for them. "One day," he writes,

> I saw on deck a young man going from passenger to passenger, begging for someone to give him a lemon for his wife, who was suffering greatly. I gave him all my twenty-four. Afterward, they never stopped thanking me. The wife kept insisting that I had saved her life.

Lemons were often enough all that one could accommodate. On the *Wieland*, as Weinstein recalled, water would not do, for the water on the ship was bad and too much of it caused a stomach ache. As for food: "During the period of seasickness," Rubin mournfully records, "no one was at all interested in eating." "Panic-stricken," wrote Price of the time of seasickness, "the passengers huddled together on their cots and spent six days practically without food."

But to make matters worse, Rubin adds, even after recovering,

> we had the desire to fill our stomachs but nothing to fill them with. It was not because there was any lack of quantity. The tables were loaded with bread, butter, herring, cake and potatoes in their skins and we were free to take as much as we wished. But the trouble was that we could not put the stuff in our mouths. The butter smelled like old wax, the herring like raw fresh fish. The cake was mouldy. The bread and potatoes without good reason had a nauseating taste.

Price also observed: "The bread and meat were impossible to eat, and no other food was to be gotten. There was not enough sugar to go around. They charged five pfennigs for a lump of sugar and even at that price it was not always available." Often, the very atmosphere in which meals were taken was enough to discourage the appetite. Weinstein's experiences of mealtimes aboard the *Wieland* had a prison-like quality. "We 'below-decks' passengers," he writes,

> lined up with our tin utensils and waited our turn, our "ration." When I stood before the cook for my portion, he poured into my tin bowl some kind of black soup and held out a piece of dry bread. I went back to my "private cabin" to have breakfast. But I couldn't eat the stuff they had given me.

Food was a frequent subject of complaint, especially among those pious emigrants who wished to maintain their lifelong adherence to *kashrut*. "Some of the emigrants who arrived on the *Helvetia*, of the National Line, last week," noted the *Jewish Messenger* of November 25, 1881,

> complained of the food given them on the voyage, asserting that it was not prepared according to the Mosaic dietary laws, as promised by the agents of the line in Europe. This is the second time this complaint has been made.

"As for the so-called kosher meat," says Harris Rubin of his voyage, "hardly anyone touched it, some because of their strict observance of dietary laws and some because it made them sick. That meat was about as kosher as I [these many years later] am 25 years old." Yet when Passover came while they were at sea, Rubin and other Jewish passengers managed to hold a Seder, with wine, matzoh, and other necessary components that had been provided by the London Committee.

Conviviality and companionship were indeed among the most important elements of life on board—the companionship of sacred occasions, of the Sabbath or a holiday, or simply of talk and song. In the case of youthful groups like the Am Olam, one did not have to search at all for such things. Abraham Cahan also was able to strike up a friendship with the steerage steward, who was known to the immigrants simply as "Mister." Cahan made "Mister" his first English teacher: "I used to show him a word in my dictionary or in my *Teach Yourself*, and he would tell me how to pronounce it." Soon Cahan became useful to him. "Whenever he had to say something to an immigrant," Cahan writes,

> he would bring me along, write down the words, and I would look up their meaning in my dictionary. Then I would explain what he wanted to the immigrant. And, conversely, when an immigrant wanted to ask him something, I would look up the words in the Russian-English part of my dictionary and say them to him.

Bernard Weinstein had no such luck with the German crew on the *Wieland*, some of whom called the Jewish immigrants "swine" and "Russian pigs." Distancing himself from them, he found his solace in a Jewish group who assembled to talk every day on deck, their conversation dominated by a few socialists who spoke hopefully of "colonies" and "communes" in America.

Weather permitting, the deck was the most desirable place for steerage passengers to be. "We went up on deck and the sun was shin-

ing," wrote Weinstein of the morning after his first queasy night at sea;
"we became merry." Harris Rubin remarks that "the first week of our
trip was quite pleasant. We spent most of the time on deck looking at
the sea and talking about America." As the day waned, the mood might
change. "In the evenings," says Cahan,

> when the sky was clear, we would gaze at the enchanting colors of
> sunset—gaze and give vent to our rapture. Then, as the magical
> hues extinguished themselves one by one, our hearts would reach
> out with longing. We would then gather together and sing Russian
> folk songs—the plaintive and colorful airs of the villages of Great
> Russia and the Ukraine.

Other passengers—most of those with Cahan, apart from the Jews, were
English, Swedish, or Norwegian—would listen, and some would take
their turn at singing. Then the Norwegians would break into dancing.

Only bad weather could interrupt such idylls; when it came, it
brought a special terror to those who had never known the sea. After
eight tranquil days, Harris Rubin and his fellow passengers experienced
a storm of particular ferocity. "The whole sea was an expanse of moun-
tainous waves and the ship was battered about like a splinter, up one
wave and down another, and the storm continued to worsen." The passengers were warned not to go up on deck. "In our stateroom," Rubin
writes,

> we were not able to stand or sit and if we attempted to lie down in
> our bunks we were shaken out. Trunks, benches and other objects
> slid from one side of the ship to the other. Monday morning when
> some of us wanted to poke our heads out of the door leading to the
> deck it was frightening to see the huge waves black as ink which
> appeared ready to swallow the entire ship. Everything on deck was
> covered with ice. The raincoats worn by the sailors on deck seemed
> to be made of tin because of the freezing. Everyone in our quarters
> was very frightened, especially the Jews. The women were crying.
> The men gathered together and were reciting psalms.

The storm grew worse that night, but it was the beginning of Passover,
and the Jewish emigrants decided to hold the Seder they had been planning. At first they did not think they could do it;

> there were, however, some women who had taken tablecloths from
> their suitcases and spread them over some tables, and on these
> tables portions of matzoh were placed. Some better families had
> brought their own matzoh, wine and Passover whiskey and these

were placed on the tables. But everything placed on the tables had to be securely held by someone.

They proceeded through the Haggadah as best they could, but then:

> When we reached the point . . . of reciting the *Hallel* psalms, there was such an alarm and such loud crying by the women that the non-Jewish passengers, the sailors, and even the captain came running to our quarters. No one, however, interfered with us. As a matter of fact, the captain was quite pleased.

They finished the service, went to bed, and tried to sleep. At about three in the morning, they were awakened by shouts. Leaping from their bunks, they found the man who was making the noise and asked what was the matter.

"You're asking what's the matter," he said. "Don't you realize the storm is worse? Don't you know one of the masts has been broken? How can you sleep in such a situation?"

"What can we do?" they asked.

"Recite psalms!" he said.

The Jewish men thereupon went back and recited psalms, to the annoyance of other passengers whose sleep they disturbed. But when some of these complained to the captain the next morning,

> he upbraided them for interfering with us. "They are praying to God for you as well as themselves," he said, "and instead of being grateful to them you are laughing at them and disturbing them because you're losing a few hours' sleep." To us he expressed the hope and expectation that the storm would abate the next day. The next morning the storm decreased and in the afternoon the weather was pleasant.

There was still one matter to be settled with God, however. During the storm, even the less pious among the Jews had pledged that if they were spared they would not eat any *chometz*—food ritually unfit for the festival—for the whole eight days of Passover. The trouble was, there was not much Passover food left. "So from Monday evening until Friday," Rubin concludes,

> we survived on a few pieces of matzoh which we received twice a day, which we would not have eaten if we had not been so hungry, and some potatoes that had been steamed in their skins. By Friday all the matzoh had been consumed, so Friday evening and Saturday morning breakfast consisted of matzoh crumbs and for the rest of Saturday we had only potatoes. And since the very pious did not

eat the potatoes they in fact fasted that day. But we didn't feel too hungry that day because we were told that we were to arrive in New York. . . . In the afternoon we saw land and we were no longer thinking about eating. On Saturday evening we stopped a short distance from the port and on Sunday, April 4th, on the eve of the last day of Passover, a smaller ship took us to Castle Garden.

The good Lord had brought them to the American Promised Land with not a moment to spare. "We felt relieved," George Price wrote of seeing an American pilot ship that had come to guide them in:

To the west boats and ships passed at regular intervals and a few lighthouses were in sight. It is impossible to describe the joy and excitement; and the exclamations, "Hail Columbia," "Land," were uttered by everyone. We beheld with our own eyes the magnificent shores of America.

PART THREE

Fathers, Mothers, and Exiles

·1881-1887·

·10·

THE HEBREW
EMIGRANT AID SOCIETY

On the shores of America, renewed efforts were being made to cope
with the swelling masses of refugees arriving in spite of all admonitions
and protests. In November 1881, after getting Kursheedt's letter off its
chest, the Russian Emigrant Relief Committee had awoken to the fact
that it lacked the capacity to deal with the emerging situation. This
point had been pressed home by Julius Bien, national president of the
B'nai B'rith, an organization founded in 1843 as a Jewish fraternal order
that was now increasingly devoting itself to philanthropy and the defense of Jewish rights abroad. Throughout the crisis of October, Bien
had persisted in advocating the acceptance of as many of the refugees
as possible.

The result of his agitation had been conveyed in an announcement
in the November 25 issue of the *Jewish Messenger*. "For a few weeks
past," it said,

> the gentlemen composing the Russian Emigration Committee have
> been laboring under the most adverse circumstances. With a task
> of the greatest magnitude, they have, up to the present, been com-
> pelled to work with facilities of an exceedingly meager nature. They
> have come to the conclusion that, in order to carry out their work
> in a proper manner, it is necessary to have a regular organization,
> with a general office in the city, a lodging house, employment bu-
> reau, etc., and which will extend assistance, not to Russians alone,
> but to Hebrews of every nationality arriving on our shores.

A meeting was called for the following Sunday, the 27th, to be held at
11:00 A.M. at one of the Hebrew orphan asylums.

The two hundred who attended spent much of the time listening to a debate between Bien and several men who were still reluctant to undertake the scheme. One of these was Jacob H. Schiff, who thought it to be "smacking of sectarianism." He asked if any other race or nationality had such an agency. "Plenty of them," he was told, and an official of the Hamburg-America line, present at the meeting, described the ones that had been set up in America by German and Irish groups. The example of the German Emigrant Aid Society in particular seems to have made an impression upon this gathering of Hebrew ladies and gentlemen mainly of German birth or descent. But most compelling of all were the reports then given on the desperate condition of so many of the recent arrivals. "Who," asked Bien, "is going to Castle Garden tomorrow morning to look after those five hundred Russian Jews there?" With that, a vote was taken, and the Hebrew Emigrant Aid Society of the United States was brought into being.

Establishing headquarters in a basement at 15 State Street, near Castle Garden, the Society—under its president, J. Stanwood Menken, and its secretary, Manuel A. Kursheedt—immediately devoted itself to the principal tasks stated in its charter. These were:

> 1. To afford aid and advice to emigrants of the Hebrew faith coming to the United States from countries where they have suffered by reason of oppressive laws or a hostile populace.
> 2. To afford aid and advice to emigrants desiring the help of the Society in settling in the United States upon lands of the Society or otherwise; and to check pauperism by discouraging the emigration of persons incapable of labor and by assisting and directing the needy to industrial or agricultural employment or pursuits.

To the latter end, the Society called for the establishment of committees and emigrant aid societies throughout the United States, which were to find appropriate jobs and housing in their localities.

Responses were particularly good in the South, just emerging from Reconstruction and eager for fresh blood to help develop its economy; no leader in that region proved more enthusiastic than the Governor of Louisiana, S. D. McEnery. This was no doubt due to the lively interest in the emigration that was being shown by the New Orleans Jewish community, which had achieved a particular prominence and fullness of integration into the general life of the city. Governor McEnery, thinking of the Homestead Act of 1862, seems to have become inspired in that moment with a vision of Jewish farmers taming the marshy wildernesses of his state. "Louisiana will welcome your people and give them homesteads," he had written to the New York Committee in November,

"160 acres to each family. Our state favors the movement and will act liberally. We have room for hundreds."

The reply was that at least thirty people would be sent right away. "The New Orleans Committee," according to a newspaper account,

> were empowered to rent a suitable home for the emigrants, the expenses to be defrayed by the State, the local Committee providing food, clothing, etc. An agent was appointed to select land, to locate the people and to see to their wants. 132 families are to be sent to New Orleans for the present. They will consist of farmers and mechanics, carpenters being especially in request. . . . Each family arriving will be provided by the general committee with sufficient means to give them one year's support until they have been enabled to raise a crop. Horses, mules, and oxen, as well as all the implements and utensils, will be furnished by the Committee, so that a year hence the immigrants can shift for themselves and become good and taxpaying citizens of Louisiana.

A good part of the Jewish communal life of New Orleans, including the Ladies' Hebrew Aid and Sewing Society, pitched into the task.

It did not take long to perceive, however, that few of the refugees were either qualified or inclined to become American frontier farmers, and that among those who were, group settlement rather than homesteading was the method they preferred. There was, in fact, one group most eager to give it a try that fall, months before the arrival of any of the Am Olam organizations, with which it was not affiliated. It had crystallized in Yelizavetgrad after the riots, under the leadership of Herman Rosenthal, a thirty-eight-year-old printer and scholar who had served with the Red Cross in the Russo-Turkish War of 1877–78, and who persuaded about seventy of his fellow townsmen to follow him in what he regarded as the only remaining solution to the Russian-Jewish problem. He and his comrades had managed to put together $5,700 out of their own pockets; and by the beginning of December the New Orleans Hebrew Emigrant Aid Society was searching for an appropriate piece of land for them.

The best offer came from two Jewish brothers, Isidore and Henry Newman, who owned a large tract in the township of Sicily Island, 350 miles northwest of New Orleans, in Catahoula Parish. It provided for the sale of twenty-eight hundred acres for $19,600 ($7 an acre), payable in yearly installments of $2,000, which did not have to begin until three years later, on January 1, 1885; moreover, no interest would be charged until the start of 1887, after which it would be 6 percent. The Newmans would also pay the taxes until January 1885. One could not have asked for more generous terms. As for the land itself, it was rich and half under cultivation already and, according to a hopeful report issued by

J. Stanwood Menken after a personal visit, "not subject to overflow," even though it was located precariously in a marshy district between the Mississippi and Ouachita rivers. The climate was also good, Menken reported, with temperatures rarely rising above ninety degrees in summer or falling below thirty-two in winter. Menken also felt good about the surrounding population, which, he said, numbered "about 11,000, among whom are Germans, Irish, and Israelites, who seem to be prosperous and contented."

The neighbors appear to have been enthusiastic about the prospect. On December 5, a mass meeting was held in the nearby town of Harrisonburg, "for the purpose of inviting immigration" in general, and the Yelizavetgrad group in particular, to Catahoula Parish, according to a local newspaper. "Whereas," the participants resolved,

> our State has suffered for years because of the lack of immigration, and much of her soil is but poorly and partially tilled; and
>
> Whereas, a number of Russian immigrants, lately driven from their homes by religious intolerance, have, like our forefathers, sought the shores of America for the purpose of enjoying civil and political liberty,

it was resolved to assist the new settlers as much as possible. Ten days later, the New Orleans Hebrew Emigrant Aid Society published an appeal "To the People of Louisiana," which said:

> Having completed our organization under the laws of the State, and concluded the purchase of a large body of the finest land in Catahoula Parish on most favorable terms, we have the pleasure to announce the establishment of the first Russian Colony in America.
>
> As it is universally conceded that, in order to develop the wonderful resources of our beloved State, the prime factor is *immigration*, we are proud of having formed a *nucleus* around which the oppressed citizens of Europe can gather with confidence in our desire to protect and encourage them.
>
> The Governor of Louisiana is a member of this Association, and has given not only his sanction to the enterprise, but every assurance of protection and assistance.
>
> It is with confidence that we then appeal to our fellow citizens of all sects and nationalities to contribute all they can spare for the relief and comfort of the new colony.

The contributions poured in. "$5,000 were collected," according to the *Jewish Chronicle*, deeply concerned from its London vantage point,

> in addition to contributions of provisions and agricultural implements. One firm gave twelve ploughs and eighteen sets of har-

nesses, while another promised to present all doors and window sashes required for the houses to be erected. Other donations, such as furniture, seeds, and implements, were likewise promised. Great care was made in the selection of implements, livestock, etc. Assistance has been freely offered on all sides.

With this help, temporary quarters were built, and by the beginning of 1882, the 151 settlers—fifty-one men, thirty-four women, and sixty-six children under fifteen—were in Sicily Island embarking upon their new adventure.

Now there were international matters to attend to. "Mr. Moritz Ellinger," announced the *Jewish Chronicle* of January 27, 1882, "lately coroner for New York City, a well known American Israelite, has arrived in London . . . as delegate of the Hebrew Emigrants' Aid Society of America." The Bavarian-born Ellinger, a prominent member of the B'nai B'rith and editor of its journal, the *Menorah Monthly*, had been sent by the Society to try to coordinate its efforts with those of the European refugee organizations. There had been difficulties to resolve; but beyond those, now that there was talk of holding another international conference on the refugees, Ellinger had come armed with a sweeping proposal.

It was presented in the form of a letter of instructions from the Hebrew Emigrant Aid Society to Ellinger, which he made public upon his arrival in London. "Dear Sir," it said:

> By a resolution of the Executive Committee, confirmed by the directors, you have been requested to visit Europe as the delegate of the Society and to present to the Central Committee of the Alliance Israélite Universelle at Paris, the Anglo-Russian Jewish Relief Committee of London, and the Hebrew Congregations of Berlin, Vienna and other cities, the suggestions of the New York Committee relative to the reception, distribution and settlement of the Hebrew refugees from the cities and villages of South Russia.

Since the authors of the letter well knew that their suggestions were not always taken seriously, they now prefaced them with a plea for sympathy and understanding. "When the news of the persecution of our brethren . . . reached this country," they went on,

> it could hardly be believed by us that in this century such a wholesale infliction of misery on peaceable people and their defenseless families was at all possible. It was considered an exaggeration to think that an emigration of this class would become necessary. Our friends in Europe have been constrained nevertheless to look to

this country as a place of undoubted refuge, security and peace for the exiles. We have been eager to second the movement and could have done so alone, as in previous cases, had the number of destitute emigrants remained within ordinary limits.

This had proved not to be the case, and the result was a heavy burden upon American Jews, among whom, the letter insisted, "there are but an inconsiderable number of very wealthy persons." Rather, "in the exceptional state of affairs now before us it is utterly out of our power to afford adequate and efficient aid."

How much money did they want, then? To be answered in a moment; but first, a few more words about the task at hand:

> The refugees now among us, if considered representative of the emigration to follow, can be divided into trading, artisan, and in some degree, agricultural classes. For the mechanics there is little difficulty. Our anxiety is exerted in behalf of the others. We cannot advise their resort to peddling or small trading, they cannot live as idlers in the American cities; they must labor.

The solution had to be the one found by other immigrant groups, such as the Mennonites from Russia: agricultural settlement. "The settlement of emigrants in large sections of land," the letter continued,

> can be made from the northern part of New York to the Mexican frontier—embracing all varieties of climate and capacity. The location is a detail which must be left to future consideration as the emergencies arise, but in this respect we shall give the best counsel. Such colonies will provide for all the artisans and mechanics who offer [themselves], and the colonists will eventually, from their labor, pay for the land.

In the meantime, however, considerable layouts had to be made for "the transportation to the interior, the outfit, the horse and cattle, the agricultural implements, the seed, and ample provision of food until a crop is made."

Clearly a large figure was coming. "Assuming," the writers calculated, "that 10,000 immigrants are to be provided for in the course of the following year, and that the expense as to each is averaged at the lowest estimate, it requires $1,000,000 to cover the cost." This was of course to be refunded, "but the time when is contingent."

The anticipated moment of stunned silence on the part of their readers was now filled by the letter-writers with a detailed exposition of their program, including administrative and financial arrangements for the various colonies, and the estimated cost per person settled in them. Stress was laid upon the expectation that the European-Jewish aid committees working in Brody and other refugee centers—the Alliance Israélite Universelle and the Israelitische Allianz were to resume their efforts in the spring—would be "systematic" in their selections of emigrants to send across. "The shipments," urged the writers,

> must be regulated according to the ability of the American Committee to receive and distribute emigrants. Only those having a trade or able and willing to settle on the lands of the Society, or to work as laborers on railways and otherwise, should be selected for emigration. The aged and helpless should remain in Europe at least until those on whom they are dependent have been successfully established in their new homes. Absolute paupers must on no account be chosen for emigration. Before sending emigrants to America the difficulties of settlement in the new country must be clearly set forth and only the willing must be transported, and then must abide by the decisions of the American Committee as to provision for their settlement.

A final stricture was underlined:

> that America can receive but a portion of those selected for emigration. Other countries, for instance, Bosnia, Spain, Algeria and Syria [i.e., Palestine], should be adopted as asylums for many, who in such congenial climes can establish themselves with equal readiness.

The last part of the letter returned to its role as provider of instructions to Ellinger. "You are accordingly commissioned and authorized," it concluded, "to represent this Society at such meetings and conferences as shall be held in Europe with a view to facilitate, direct, and successfully accomplish the emigration of Russian Hebrews." At these meetings he was to "submit the foregoing as generally reflecting the conclusions of this Society," and to urge the Europeans to conform to its desires. "*Immediate* action is indispensable," the letter stressed, "as preparations for selecting the immigrants to arrive in the spring must be made during the winter or another season will be lost." The letter was signed by Menken, Kursheedt, and two other officers.

This program was nothing more than a spelling-out of what everyone involved in the rescue, on both the European and the American sides, professed to want. As for the number of refugees it estimated for 1882, the figure of ten thousand was well within reasonable bounds.*

---

*The total Jewish immigration to the United States in 1882 was to be 13,202, although this figure includes Jews who were not Russian refugees.

Nor was the estimated cost per refugee of $100 anything more than modest; so that $1 million was a total justly arrived at. But as a fund-raising goal it was absurd. Perhaps a third or a half that amount could possibly have been raised in the immediate future, but no more. Yet even $300,000 to $500,000—£60,000 to £100,000—was, it must have occurred to the wealthy British readers of the proposal, a huge sum to entrust to people they did not even know. Could the Americans really handle their end of the crisis and that much money all at the same time? This question became especially urgent as the Jewish crisis in Russia deepened and the prospect of a yet larger refugee wave in the spring became real.

·11·

THE DEEPENING CRISIS IN RUSSIA

"The principal source of this movement [of anti-Jewish rioting], which is so incompatible with the temperament of the Russian people," Count Ignatiev had written in August 1881,

> lies in circumstances which are of an exclusively economic nature. For the last twenty years the Jews have gradually managed to capture not only commerce and industry but they have also succeeded in acquiring, by means of purchase and lease, a large amount of landed property. Owing to their clannishness and solidarity, they have, with few exceptions, directed their efforts not towards the increase of the productive forces but towards the exploitation of the original inhabitants, primarily of the poorest classes of the population, with the result that they have called forth a protest from this population, manifesting itself in deplorable forms—in violence.

With these words—which willfully ignored the poverty in which the great majority of the Jews of the Empire were still living—an official policy was being proclaimed, almost before the Jewish blood had dried on the streets, that sought to shift the blame for the disorders from the assailants to the victims.

"Having taken energetic measures," the Minister continued,

> to suppress the previous disorders and mob rule and to shield the Jews against violence, the Government recognizes that it is justified in adopting, without delay, no less energetic measures to remove the present abnormal relations that exist between the original inhabitants and the Jews, and to shield the Russian population against this harmful Jewish activity, which, according to local information, was responsible for the disturbances.

83

Energetic measures had already been taken against the Jewish populations of Kiev, Saint Petersburg, and Moscow, where many lived in violation of the rules of Jewish residency and others could be construed as doing so; often enough, the expulsions took place quite summarily, in the middle of the night. But there remained much to be done. In September, the *Jewish Chronicle* wrote, the government

> charged the Governors of the provinces where Jews reside to assemble commissions of the notables for the purpose of discussing the measures which should be taken relative to the Jews. Their decisions are to be reported to the Minister of the Interior within the period of two months.

An official review of the Jewish question in the land was very much in order, were it only justly conceived. But such efforts already had a dismal record in Russia, and the present one promised from the outset to be no exception. "This order is directed against the Jews in the most unfavorable sense," the *Chronicle* continued:

> In the first place, there is no idea of inviting the Jews to join the commissions, although General Ignatieff had verbally informed the representatives of the Jews in St. Petersburg that such was his desire and intention. Again it appears that all the Commissions will be called upon to do will be to seek for remedies against the evils emanating from the Jews, though, here again, General Ignatieff stated that they would endeavor without prejudice to devise measures for satisfying the Jewish as well as the Christian population.

Indeed, Ignatiev's instructions to the commissions had explicitly asked them to determine "which aspects of the economic activity of the Jews in general have exerted an injurious influence upon the life of the original population, and what measures, both legislative and administrative, should be adopted" to deal with their findings. As for the composition of the commissions, only one of the sixteen had more than two Jewish delegates among many Christians, even though they supposedly represented the provinces—the fifteen of the Pale of Settlement, plus Kharkov—in which Jews were mostly the majority and never less than a substantial plurality.

Yet, despite all this stacking of the deck, the recommendations of the commissions in November turned out to be far less unfavorable to Jews than had been expected. Of the twelve commissions whose reports subsequently became known, five called for the abolition of the Pale and only one for its continuance; the other six gave no opinion on the subject. Jewish commercial activity in the villages—a continuing source of irritation, despite all the expulsions and restrictions of the preceding eight decades—was condemned by a majority of the twelve in only one field: the selling of liquor. Other advances that Jews had made into a rural economy shaken up by the emancipation of the serfs twenty years before—most notably in the purchase of land—were severely criticized only by a small minority of the commissions.

These results were not at all satisfactory to Ignatiev, who now appointed a High Commission to receive the various provincial reports and make its own deliberations. Members of the local commissions were appointed to it, but, as the Saint Petersburg correspondent of the *Jewish Chronicle* wrote,

> the Minister of the Interior has only invited to the High Commission those members of the local commissions which made themselves conspicuous by their hostility to the Jews and by their inimical designs with regard to our coreligionists.

This included the commissioners from Kherson province whose report had recommended that it

> be forbidden to Jews to sell spirituous liquors, to purchase crown lands, to send their children to the gymnasiums, to fill the post of Justice of the Peace, to act as advocates, to employ Christian servants, and to fully live in this country unless they have a settled occupation.

Events in the country at large gave additional incentive to the deliberations of the High Commission soon after it had convened in November. Later that month, the French actress Sarah Bernhardt arrived in Russia to tour in her celebrated role as *La Dame aux camélias*, after having announced that she would donate part of her fees to the cause of Jewish emigration. This reminder of her own partly Jewish origins was too much for some of the anti-Semitic elements in Odessa. Her performance there went peacefully, but when she drove back to her hotel, according to the London *Daily Telegraph*,

> stones were thrown at her carriage by the populace. The following day an anti-Semitic riot occurred, the pretext being that "Sarah the Jewess plundered the people," and that the Jews speculated on the seats for the theater. Windows were smashed and the Jewish houses threatened with plunder and destruction.

There were other such scenes in southern Russia before Bernhardt left the country.

But the worst was only now to come. During the riots of April and May, there had been frequent rumors of an outburst in Warsaw, but nothing had happened. Nor could anything like that have occurred, as far as many contemporaries—in and outside of Warsaw, Jew and gentile alike—were concerned; Warsaw—and, indeed, all of ethnic Poland—were considered to be something apart from the rest of the Russian Empire in their history of Jewish-Christian relations. The five hundred years or so during which the Jews of the region had lived under Polish sovereignty were now often looked upon as something of an idyll, compromised only by foreign incursions: the Khmelnitsky and *haidamak* Cossacks of the seventeenth and eighteenth centuries had made Poles their victims equally along with Jews. And since the partitions of the late eighteenth century, Jews had taken part prominently—perhaps too much so for their own good—in every Polish uprising against Russian rule. The relationship between Jew and Pole had been celebrated by the greatest of all Polish poets, Adam Mickiewicz, who died near Constantinople in 1855 in the arms of his friend Armand Lévy while trying to organize a Jewish legion to fight with the Turks against Russia; a certain nostalgia for that relationship was always to survive among Poles of quality.

But Polish society, too, was responding to the upheavals of the nineteenth century; new classes were on the rise, and Warsaw—with its more than a hundred thousand Jews, forming a third of the city's population—was becoming as worldly and raucous a place as Odessa. This was demonstrated at last on Christmas day of 1881.

Suddenly, during Mass at the Church of the Holy Cross, attended by thousands of worshippers, the cry of "fire" resounded. There was a panic and a rush for the doors, with the result that about thirty people were trampled to death. When the alarm was discovered to have been false, the rumor immediately arose that "Jewish pickpockets" were responsible for it. "Whilst the excitement of the congregants was at its height," according to a contemporary report, "voices were heard inside as well as outside the church, exclaiming that the Jews, having created the panic, should be sacrificed for their crime." A mob was formed, which rushed into Jewish neighborhoods to begin a work of devastation of a sort that had become grimly familiar far away in the south of Russia; the wrecking, looting, and beating were to last three more days.

Other aspects of the scene were familiar, too: "the same culpable supineness which was displayed by the authorities during the riots in Russia proper, characterized General Abelinsky, the Governor of Warsaw, and his subordinates." There was even the clear presence of outside agitators, for "it has been conclusively proved that the persons who hounded on the mob . . . were scarcely able to speak the Polish language, and that their utterances betrayed an unmistakeable Russian accent." That the event had been prearranged was proved by the subsequent discovery that the same false alarm—and the same conclusion as to its origins—had spread in at least one and perhaps three other Warsaw churches that same day. And the last of the familiar elements was the dreadful outcome: "Entire rows of houses have been demolished, and whole streets have been devastated. Six thousand Jewish families have been reduced to beggary, and their losses exceed two million rubles."

In the light of events such as these—which were followed that April by another wave of anti-Jewish riots in southern Russia—Count Ignatiev's High Commissioners saw fit to conclude that Alexander II's "period of toleration" had been unsuccessful, and that Russia should begin to "turn to its ancient tradition . . . according to which Jews must be regarded as aliens." To initiate this process, they recommended to the government a set of "temporary" measures, which became law on May 12. That day, the Reuters news agency cabled a report from Saint Petersburg, saying:

> The *Official Messenger* today publishes the four clauses of the regulations in regard to the Jews, agreed upon by the Committee of Ministers and approved by the Emperor on the [3rd] inst. They provide:
>
> 1. That Jews are henceforth prohibited from settling outside towns and villages, except where Jewish settlements may already exist.
> 2. That all contracts of purchase or tenancy [recently] concluded with Jews are provisionally suspended.
> 3. That Jews are prohibited from transacting business on Sundays and holidays when the business establishments of Christians are closed.
> 4. That clauses 1 and 3 shall only be applied in Governments where Jews are permanently settled [i.e., the Pale of Settlement].

This assault on the economic foundations of the lives of tens of thousands of the Tsar's Jewish subjects was accompanied by a promise to deal severely with the perpetrators of riots. The rest of the Reuters dispatch said:

> The *Official Messenger* today states that by command of the Emperor it is publicly made known that the Government is firmly resolved to punish inexorably all outrages against the persons and property of the Jews, seeing that the latter are under the protection of the laws, which are equally binding upon all His Majesty's subjects. The governors and other authorities are, therefore, commanded on their personal responsibility to take timely measures for the prevention, or as the case may be, immediate suppression

of outrages against Jews. Any remissness in this respect will entail dismissal from office.

To prove the point, Count Ignatiev himself was dismissed at the end of the month, apparently on account of his own remissness in dealing with the new wave of riots in April. But this was hardly likely to placate the Jews of Russia, who were not at all convinced that the rioters were being punished "inexorably" by the courts, or satisfied that the "May Laws," as they were henceforth to be known, were merely temporary; indeed, along with so many of the other burdens of tsarism, they were to remain in force until the Revolution of 1917.

More than ever, emigration was the tempting alternative to Saint Petersburg's intolerable solutions to the Jewish question. "If the Eastern frontier is closed to the Jews," one judge had called out, after his verdict criticizing the Jewish victims had aroused an objection that the Pale was at fault, "the Western frontier is open to them. Why don't they take advantage of it?" In fact, the ease with which the Jewish refugees were crossing the frontier—the majority of them armed with passports, at that—was a constant source of amazement to the officials at Brody and other such locations. And the reason for this was not hard to find. "The Western frontier," Count Ignatiev had told an interviewer in January, "is open for the Jews. The Jews have already taken ample advantage of this right, and their emigration has in no way been hampered." Speaking later that month to Wickham Hoffman, the American chargé d'affaires in Saint Petersburg, Ignatiev claimed that the provincial commissions had unanimously recommended the expulsion of the Jews from Russia. "We have, then," he said to Hoffman, exaggerating the figures, "on the one hand, 5,000,000 Jews, Russian subjects, clamoring to be freed from all special restraints, and we have on the other, 85,000,000 Russian subjects clamoring to have the 5,000,000 expelled from the Empire. What is to be done in such a case?"

In the eyes of the Jewish wealthy and privileged of Russia, this apparent zeal on high levels to solve the problem by letting their people go was precisely what was worrisome. The Poliakovs and the Günzburgs, pioneers in Russian banking and railway-building, lived lives in Saint Petersburg and on their country estates that were more like those of the Rothschilds in the West than anything remotely experienced by the vast majority of their Jewish compatriots. The late Evzel Günzburg, founder of the dynasty—who had received the title of "baron" from the grand Duke of Hesse-Darmstadt for handling his financial affairs—lived, according to his great-granddaughter Sophie, in a house in Saint Petersburg "with ninety-two suites, some elegant, others more simple. It had only two stories but occupied a large area and had many interior courtyards." His grandson David, Sophie's father, lived two months a year in a country home in Podolia. "The estate was large," according to Sophie,

> including our house, a huge garden, the caretaker's house and garden, the stable, barn, chicken yard, laundry, houses for the coachmen and their families, the laundress, and so forth—about fifty persons in all.

Near the house was the family's sugar factory, and about eighteen miles away was a typical small town of the Pale of Settlement called Khashchevata. "Two or three times a year," Sophie writes,

> our parents would visit this town, sometimes taking us along. . . . The crowd would swarm about the carriage so that it could not move ahead. My parents would descend. Then the "attack" would begin. They kissed my mother's hands, her shoulders, the hem of her gown. . . . About fifty people clothed in rags would follow her everywhere.

The Jews of the town would beg for help, and the Günzburgs "recorded each case, distributed candy to the children and money—a good deal of money—and even promised to attend to every request."

Yet, with a few exceptions like the good Barons Günzburg, the rich Jews of Russia were not known for generosity toward their less fortunate coreligionists. "Our wealthy Jews hold their purse-strings tightly and jealously," wrote an angry Russian-Jewish student in his diary early in 1882; "only very rarely do they indulge in magnanimity." An American-Jewish newspaper had written in the wake of the riots of April and May 1881:

> Nobody will accuse us of lack of sympathy for our brethren in the Russian Empire. But when we hear of "rich Jewish merchants" apprehensive for their villas near Moscow, or their granaries at Odessa, we desire to know why those Hebrews do not sacrifice something for their brethren who suffer from poverty and popular abuse? There are several notable exceptions, like Baron Guinzburg; but the great bulk of the more fortunate Hebrews in the Russian as in the Roumanian cities, are to be condemned for their lukewarmness. Were they half as considerate for their unhappy coreligionists as are the Hebrews of Western Europe and America the wrongs of a generation would at least have approached a remedy.

This lukewarmness was a triumph of tsarist policy, which for generations had sought to widen the gulf between the Jewish masses and the rich, allowing the latter to live in splendor outside the Pale, far from the sight of extensive Jewish poverty, and to exclude themselves from the humbling experience of military service.

But now many of the rich Jews of Russia had become concerned over the emigration of their poorer coreligionists, for any mass flight of Jews was compromising to the secure status in Russian society that they considered themselves to have attained. "I hear," wrote the Saint Petersburg correspondent of the *Jewish Chronicle* in the issue of March 24, 1882,

> that some opulent Jews in St. Petersburg have had the *naïveté* or shamefacedness to assure General Ignatieff that the Jews in general had no idea of emigrating, and with this assurance they coupled the hope that his Excellency would restrain intending emigrants from leaving the country. It is not enough that these monied men should regard with indifference the sad conditions of their poorer brethren, but they actually have the audacity to attempt to close against them the only door of deliverance now open to the bulk of the sorely tried Jewish population of Russia.

Baron Horace Günzburg, the son of Evzel and the present leader of the family, was as worried as other wealthy Russian Jews about the emigration, but he had consistently sought a more humane way of dealing with it. From the start of the crisis the previous spring, he had been prominent in the giving of funds, not only for the relief of the victims, but for the resettlement of as many of them as possible in farming colonies in the south of Russia. In April 1882, with the acquiescence of Count Ignatiev, he called a meeting of Jewish notables in Saint Petersburg. For three days they deliberated, and concluded by placing at the forefront of their resolutions one "to reject completely the thought of organizing emigration, as being subversive of the dignity of the Russian body politic and of the historic rights of the Jews to their present fatherland." Only after this resounding statement of loyalty was it placed upon the list of resolutions "to point to the necessity of abolishing the present discriminating legislation concerning the Jews," to make quite clear to the government "the passive attitude of the authorities" during the riots, and to petition the government for financial aid for the victims. The last was never to be forthcoming. As for the rest, the answer was given a few weeks later, when the May Laws were promulgated.

For many thousands, in spite of the Jewish notables—and perhaps to some extent on account of them as well—the door of emigration remained the only reasonable way out of a life that had become untenable.

·12·

COPING WITH THE FLOOD

Charles Netter had quit Brody for good in November, but now that spring was on the way, Schafier, Friedländer, and Magnus were back there to resume work at their end of the emigration, which had been temporarily halted during the cold months. According to a dispatch sent from that town on March 1, 1882,

> at least 600 families, numbering about 2,400 souls, have been waiting their turn here for several months to be despatched to the United States, in the meantime, however, suffering great distress. Although these people receive relief partly from the *Alliance* and partly from help sent to them from England, the amount which falls to the share of each individual is so small that it barely suffices to purchase the dry bread which is the staple food of the refugees.

But any hope that the resumption of movement would alleviate this situation was in vain; the renewal of rioting in Russia, along with the spreading knowledge there that a network of committees was now functioning to send Jewish refugees to America, was about to give rise to a spring flood of fleeing humanity.

The outflow swelled through March and April, reaching such a height in May that about fourteen hundred refugees arrived in Brody during a single week. "A despatch from Brody, published in Vienna on the 12th inst.," reported the *Jewish Chronicle* on May 19,

> states that 900 refugees from Russia arrived there on the previous day by railway. Five hundred others, who had crossed the frontier clandestinely, also reached that town [on foot]. Two Jewish deserters [from the army] were stated to have been shot by the Cossacks on the frontier. A camp was formed at Brody for the fugitives.

By this time, there were about twelve thousand refugees in Brody, several thousand of whom were gathered in the "camp," a textile factory. George Price, there at this time, described the scene in his diary:

> Approaching the entrance to the textile factory, I see thousands of people running back and forth. When I entered the courtyard I beheld a mass of hungry and thirsty tattered humans. Hawkers of soft drinks run back and forth trying to sell their wares, but they find no customers because no one has money.

Price also beheld a strange sight. At one end of the courtyard was a building with about thirty windows, where all the factory's machinery was located, and in which none of the emigrants were housed. "The exterior of the building," Price noticed,

> seems to be plastered with people. . . . From a distance, it looks as if the walls are covered with ants moving one on top of another. Upon closer observation one is chilled at the sight. Here a Jew clad in rags and perspiring, who seems to have been here many hours, has managed . . . to get midway through the crowd. He tries to figure out a way to get to one of the windows as quickly as possible. He does a somersault hoping to hurdle over the heads of several people and thus advance his position. This causes chaos. He is beaten, his clothes are rent and finally, still alive, he nears the window, only to be pushed back by a strong, armed man who has tried to clear a space. He falls and drags others with him. Immediately the space is occupied by others. . . . The mob pays no attention and goes on fighting and mauling each other to get closer to the windows.

What was happening at the windows? "The situation is as follows: Inside the building a member of the committee walks pompously from window to window and distributes red cards at random. He gives a card to one man at one window and to several at another."

Brody had by now become a chaos, in which several competing rescue committees, having entered the fray alongside the Alliance Israélite Universelle, were moving refugees without screening them. The alternative of repatriation had been abandoned in the wake of the renewed rioting, since, as Schafier put it, this "would have been to expose them to certain death." But even indiscriminate shipments needed organization, and the rate at which people could be moved out no longer came near that at which they arrived. People simply had to wait and put themselves at the mercy of the situation. "Distressing appeals are being received from the fugitives," wrote a correspondent from Brody that May, "who complain of the insufficiency of the relief funds to defray the expenses of their passage to America, most of the money being employed for their sustenance [in Brody]."

Yet even sustenance was becoming a losing battle. "The sanitary conditions of the place are becoming worse," wrote the same correspondent later in the month. "Yesterday, in the crowded quarter, three children fell sick of measles and one of smallpox." The lack of bread even provoked a rebellion. "Last night," read a Reuters telegram sent from Brody on May 30, "there was a tumultuous gathering here of the Jewish emigrants from Russia, who noisily demanded bread and means to continue their journey. The authorities were compelled to employ force in order to restore tranquillity." George Price saw the outcome the next morning in the factory courtyard:

> They summoned twenty soldiers with bayonets and placed them near each window. The emigrants then came to the windows one by one and received cards. . . . But though there was order near each window itself, further back the same old chaos prevailed. The only difference was that a few days ago the emigrants held on to the bars and were beaten by their own fellows, but today they stood near the soldiers, and at the slightest move were struck by guns and bayonets and lost consciousness.

The same day, delegates from the Israelitische Allianz of Vienna arrived to investigate, "and after examining into the conditions of the emigrants," according to the Brody correspondent, "convinced themselves that no bread had been distributed to the Jews in the most thickly populated quarter up to 7 o'clock yesterday evening, when the children were almost starving." Count Potocki, the Governor of Galicia, also appeared in Brody to investigate the situation.

In times of international crisis such as this, England had never failed to heed the call of responsibility; but on this occasion her response had been delayed somewhat by the delicacies of domestic politics. In April 1880, William E. Gladstone had returned to the office of prime minister at last, after six years in opposition to the government of Benjamin Disraeli. One of the basic matters of contention between them in the field of foreign policy had been their respective attitudes toward Russia, especially during the crisis that had culminated in the Russo-Turkish War of 1877–78, when Disraeli's fondness for Turkey had led him to the brink of war at its side, and Gladstone's loathing of the Ottoman menace had caused him to see Russia as a bastion of Christian civilization in the Near East. Disraeli was now dead, and Gladstone's world was beginning to change; but English Liberals, however dismayed they were at all that was now happening in Russia, were still little inclined to offend

their Prime Minister. Still, Russia was going beyond all decency, and
even Gladstone was soon to acknowledge the fact.

By the end of December 1881, a Russo-Jewish Committee had been
formed to meet the crisis, but it did rather little until it organized a
large meeting at London's Mansion House on February 1, 1882. Presided over by Lord Mayor Whitaker and other Christian as well as
Jewish notables—including Cardinal Manning and various members of
the Rothschild family—this gathering "to express public opinion on the
outrages inflicted upon the Jews in various parts of Russia and Russian
Poland" obtained considerable publicity for its cause, as well as the
endorsement of Prime Minister Gladstone. A permanent committee was
established, contributions were solicited, and in scarcely more than two
weeks the Mansion House Russian Jews' Relief Fund could claim an
endowment of £42,550.

Apart from sending protests to the Russian government, the main
work to be done was that of helping the bottlenecked emigration get
back into full motion, starting in England itself. "A communication was
received from the President of the Jewish Board of Guardians, Mr. Lionel L. Cohen," read an item about Anglo-Jewry's central charitable organization in the *Jewish Chronicle* of February 17,

> stating that a number of the refugees from Russia and Russian
> Poland had arrived in this country during the last few months. The
> majority of them were able-bodied men, some single, and some with
> families, and the great majority were emigrants en route to Ameri-
> ca, whose journey hither has been defrayed by communities of the
> Jewish persuasion abroad, but who lacked the means to proceed
> further, and therefore applied to the Board for that purpose. A few
> individual cases remained in this country, but they were all entirely
> destitute. With a view of preventing an influx of helpless poor from
> the Continent, the ordinary rules of the Board restricted the relief
> granted to persons resident at least six months in this country, but
> that provision had necessarily been relaxed in the present emer-
> gency in favor of the Russian refugees. The Board now applied that
> . . . they might be permitted to draw on the Mansion House Fund
> for this purpose.

They were immediately granted £500; but this lasted only a week. "A
large number of Jewish refugees from Russia," reported the *Chronicle*
on February 24,

> have within the past fortnight reached London and are still arriving
> here every day. They are being energetically dealt with by the staff
> of the Jewish Board of Guardians, the principal portion of the work
> falling upon the zealous Secretary, Mr. M. Stephany. We announce

last week that the Committee of the Mansion House Fund have made a grant to the Board of £500 towards the relief of the refugees. This sum has been exhausted. Another grant of £500 was made on Wednesday, and further grants are anticipated to adequately deal with the increasing number of refugees arriving here.

The machinery of passage was soon in full motion, and refugees now went through London as well as Liverpool, many of those from the capital being embarked at Gravesend. "The vessel left Gravesend at one o'clock on Tuesday morning," ran a typical account,

> Mr. Stephany being on board to the last moment. The refugees were loud in their expressions of gratitude for the attention which had been paid to them. They were, as a body, of fine physique and intelligent appearance. All seemed, with scarcely an exception, of a far superior class to the usual poor Jews that reach London from Poland.

But this picture was to darken as the spring rush began out of Brody—and now out of other refuges as well, such as Königsberg, as the uprooted of Warsaw began to appear. "A letter was read from the Jewish Board of Guardians," said an item of March 3, "stating that the number of Jewish refugees in London had so greatly increased during the past few days that they had to authorize a special administration to deal promptly with the cases that arose." The situation soon became grimly clear. "The influx of Jewish refugees from Russia continues in an unabated stream," reported the *Chronicle* of March 24:

> They arrive in London at the rate of nearly a hundred a week. As we have mentioned, a special department of the Jewish Board of Guardians has been created to deal with these cases. The Rev. [Rabbi] M. Keizer has charge of this department, and he is assisted by the members of a special Conjoint Committee, consisting of representatives of the Committee of the Mansion House Relief Fund and the Board of Guardians. . . . The members of the Committee attend in rotation at the offices of the Board, and every case receives very careful consideration and is only dealt with after minute investigation.

What investigation had revealed was this:

> Those who came to London at first were chiefly from a few centers such as Elizabethgrad, Kieff and Odessa. But during the past fortnight refugees have arrived from all parts of Russia and Poland. The task of relieving them becomes increasingly difficult. . . . Those only who are strictly "refugees" from violence and

oppression being assisted by the Conjoint Committee, the remainder are relieved by the Board of Guardians in the usual way. In
fact, it is a serious feature of the present movement that a very
large accession to the mass of foreign poor in London will result.
In Germany, few appear to be relieved in any other way than by
merely being assisted to London.

The Mansion House Fund decided to address itself to the problem
at its source and, to this end, turned to one of its members, Laurence
Oliphant, a fifty-two-year-old journalist, novelist, and travel writer, who
had in recent years achieved note by publishing a viable program for
Jewish colonization in Palestine. A Christian himself—indeed, a sectar-
ian mystic—Oliphant had traveled in Russia and long been interested in
the Jewish problem there. Accordingly, in a late-February meeting of
the Mansion House Fund,

> a special sub-committee was appointed to deal with the Jewish refu-
> gees now in Galicia by . . . sending Mr. Laurence Oliphant, with or
> without a second commissioner, to Galicia, to classify the refugees
> according to their several callings, and after such classification to
> select for colonization those who, being farmers, mechanics, opera-
> tives or laborers, would be serviceable in agricultural settlements;
> next, to select those who, belonging to other trades, would not be
> serviceable in an agricultural settlement, but might find employ-
> ment in Europe or in the British colonies; and finally, to deal with
> the residuum in such mode as might be found desirable.

Ten thousand pounds was voted for the purpose, and Oliphant—eventually to be joined by two other members of the subcommittee—was
soon off to Brody, making stops for discussions in Berlin and in Vienna
on the way.

There remained the American side of the problem. None of the British
leaders of the emigration had ever taken seriously Ellinger's request
for $1 million, although they certainly endorsed in principle the program
he had brought over with him. In any case, the crucial decision regarding his proposal was to be made at an international conference scheduled for late April in Berlin. Until then, the Mansion House Fund had
only to proceed according to its own imperial lights. Refugees were
already being canvassed for those who would be willing to try to settle
as farmers in South Africa or western Canada, and a few such volunteers were sent off that spring.

But the United States of America was where the vast majority of
them wanted to go, and the British remained convinced, despite all pro-

tests from the Americans, that there really was room there for them all. The only obstacle to getting them there, as the Mansion House people saw it, was the American Jews themselves. For example, on March 20, the Hebrew Emigrant Aid Society had sent a telegram from New York to the conjoint committee saying: "Only young unmarried refugees should emigrate hither. Send neither families nor farmers. Cable receipt hereof." What on earth could this mean?

A letter of explanation from Manuel A. Kursheedt arrived about three weeks later. "Our reasons," it said,

> for urging upon you not to send us families are: first, the families sent heretofore consist, as a rule, of a man and wife and several children under twelve years of age. It is almost impossible for even a mechanic to support a family here until he becomes acquainted with our language, and the manner in which the work at his trade is performed in this country; and in the meantime, he is a burden upon our charities, and is likely to become a pauper. The only trade which may be said to be carried on here the same as in Russia is that of tailoring, but owing to the large influx of tailors during the last few years, the prices paid for ordinary work are barely sufficient for the support of a single man, much less for a man burdened with a family.

As for the second of the unlikely prohibitions in the telegram:

> We beg you not to send farmers, because we find by experience that very few of the so-called farmers are fit for farm work in this country. Unfortunately, reports have been spread industriously in Russia to the effect that every emigrant coming over here would receive land already under cultivation, and the result has been that many persons who never planted a seed in their lives have, on their arrival here, styled themselves farmers in the hope, thereby, to make sure of acquiring land. We have now on our hands many more farmers than the money at our command will enable us to colonize. Besides, the season for planting is rapidly advancing, and agriculturists arriving here after the first of May could do very little in the way of farming until next spring, and, in the meantime, we would have to support them.

Kursheedt then explained how, on the other hand, it would be easy to take on single men and women between eighteen and twenty-five who were not farmers, by placing the men in factories and the women as domestics. In tones certain to raise the hackles of his readers, he said, "There is no doubt that a large portion of the emigrants are merely the dregs of the [London Jewish] populace," and urged:

We must beg you to exercise the utmost caution in sending persons to inland points in this country. One case of mistake I deem it my duty to mention. A family consisting of a man, wife, and four children, and two grown nephews arrived . . . with tickets to Atalanta, Illinois. Never having heard of that place, and being unable to imagine why they should be sent thither, I enquired of the man, "Why are you going there?" He handed me a paper with the address of his brother, by which I found that he wished to go to Atlanta, Georgia, a city situated in an entirely different direction, the distance between the two points being over five hundred miles.

Kursheedt concluded by saying that he and his colleagues were "anxiously awaiting intelligence from our delegate, Mr. Ellinger," as to the result of the forthcoming Berlin conference.

Lionel L. Alexander, secretary of the conjoint committee, replied. "It is difficult to see what more can be done," he protested,

even by the light of the facts communicated in your letter. The European committees have done their best to mitigate the distress in Russia and also to prevent the emigrants arriving destitute on your shores, but as you observe yourself, even if they were to withhold the aid altogether, it would have but a very insignificant effect in arresting what is the natural flow of emigration.

We will continue as far as we possibly can to discriminate the character of the emigrants we send you and we must most emphatically demur to the remark that the dregs of the population were sent who were here before the outrages in Russia. It is true some have been a few months here trying in vain to obtain their livelihood, but the papers of every refugee are carefully scanned, the most searching enquiries are made into every case, and it can only be in few and isolated instances that any persons have eluded the scrutiny of the Committee. Of course mistakes may occur like the geographical error you indicate respecting Atlanta, but it would be impossible to devote more scrupulous care to the task than is done by the gentlemen who attend daily to receive the applications of the refugees. Indeed, our anxiety has been to spare as much as possible the Mansion House Fund and strictly to limit every disbursement to the requirements of those whose claim to the title of refugee is absolutely incontestable.

But these civil tones concealed a fury that had already revealed itself at the most recent meeting of the Mansion House Fund, when the conjoint committee presented a memorandum that began:

The Committee being without sufficient information as to the nature and extent of the organization of the Hebrew Emigrants'

Aid Society of New York, and the telegrams from that Society, contained in Mr. Ellinger's [portfolio], not being of a reassuring character, are not prepared at present to forward to that society any further funds.

The Committee are of the opinion that if the Land Scheme, which has hitherto been tried by the Society on the miniature scale of a settlement [in Louisiana] of twenty-five families only, be of practical value, the 300,000 Jews in America will, if they have confidence in the scheme, readily find the money for the purchase of the land, especially as their contributions to the Relief Fund have hitherto not been in proportion to their number and wealth.

Instead, the plan now presented was "to forward no more emigrants to New York, except in special cases, such as when an emigrant has relatives already established there and ready to receive him," but, rather, to "give all future emigrants 'through' tickets to American towns other than New York or certain towns in Canada, distributing emigrants in due proportion, so that no town be unduly burdened." Money for personal expenses—$25 for each head of family, $15 for the wife, and $10 for each child—would be disbursed among the refugees in the form of bank drafts redeemable only at the predetermined destinations. "The Committee are of opinion," the memorandum concluded,

> that the mode of distributing the Common Fund here indicated will be found preferable to that of placing the fund into the hands of a public body in America: (1) because there probably does not exist any such body as would command the full confidence of all the local committees in Europe; (2) because the creation of such a body ad hoc would involve loss of time; (3) because distribution by such a body would involve a center of action, at which all emigrants would have to attend on arrival in America, and such convergence would be at variance with the principle of dispersion, which by decentralizing, is intended to minimize the strain on any one place; (4) because under the method proposed there would be one investigation only, and this investigation would result in fixing at one and the same time the destination of the refugee and the sum needed for his settlement.

This certainly was a comeuppance, although surely nothing the Americans had done or neglected to do warranted the proposed invasion of their countryside without their intervention. The Mansion House Fund prepared to embark upon this program; but then the matter was brought up at the Berlin International Jewish Conference, which convened on April 23, and which was attended by Moritz Ellinger representing the American position. The upshot was a compromise resolution, whereby the Conference authorized the Mansion House Fund to "direct the dispersion of refugees in transatlantic places; and regarding their settlement in the United States, to establish with New York the principles under which they shall be settled in America." But the Hebrew Emigrant Aid Society did not get its $1 million; rather, its financial affairs were left to itself and to London's good will. The Mansion House Fund was thus really left in control of the transatlantic phase of the emigration.

But the situation could not last; by the second week in May, the Mansion House Fund, now bearing the entire cost of emigration from Brody to somewhere on the American continent, was spending £5,500 a week on the operation. By that time, George S. Yates, a Mansion House representative from Liverpool, had arrived in New York to see if the differences could not be ironed out after all. And, indeed, a few days after his arrival, Yates

> publicly stated that he was favorably impressed with the work of the Hebrew Emigrant Aid Society, and the methods employed by its committee for the distribution of the emigrants. Since he had been in New York he had changed his mind as to the methods to be employed by the English Committee in sending over emigrants to inland points in this country, and he had become convinced that all refugees should be sent in the first instance to the Society in New York, in whose hands should be placed all monies intended as grants for those emigrants.

Before the end of May, Yates had wired the Mansion House Fund:

> Aid Society enjoys confidence and cooperation of leading Jews. Am personally favorably impressed. Influential Committee formed. Organization rapidly developing on sound basis. New York should control dispersion of emigrants. Delegates from principal cities meet there next month to arrange concerted action throughout States. Send to New York 200 selected emigrants. Remit funds to Society.

Thus another George from England had—perhaps with a sigh of relief—granted Americans their independence once again. In this case, it was freedom to have the now almost completely uncontrollable flood of emigrants fall directly upon their heads.

·13·

THE WELCOME

"Suddenly a small barge arrives," wrote Bernard Weinstein,

> with half a dozen men in brass-buttoned uniform. All steerage passengers were ordered out of the hold and onto the deck and were lined up in rows. Every passenger was inspected, and we were vaccinated. Soon barges came with boats in tow, and took us steerage passengers to Castle Garden.

Then still the immigrant reception center of New York—and the main one for the United States—Castle Garden stood at the southernmost tip of Manhattan Island, adjacent to Battery Park. It was, in the words of a contemporary guidebook, "a singular-looking circular structure of stone," topped by a cupola, "to which have been added several outbuildings of wood, all enclosed on the land side by a high wooden fence." Originally a Dutch fort—it had been on an island, connected to the mainland by a short causeway over a channel that was later filled in—this amphitheatric structure had been roofed over and become New York's main opera house and civic center a few years after the War of 1812. Celebrated foreign visitors had often stopped there, the virtual entranceway to the city and to America beyond—the Marquis de Lafayette, on his return visit in 1824 to the Republic he had helped create; Louis Kossuth, the fighter for Hungarian independence, in 1851. It had become a symbol of American liberty by 1855, when it was designated New York's immigrant clearing house.

"As soon as the barges are loaded," the guidebook explains,

they are cast off, and are towed to Castle Garden, while the steamer proceeds to her pier in the North* River. When the barge is made fast to the landing at Castle Garden, the baggage is taken into a hall of the building, where it is claimed by its owners, and examined by the Custom-House inspectors.

Once past inspection, the baggage was put into a room for temporary storage. "The surgeon of the establishment," says the guidebook,

then examines the emigrants to see that no paupers, or criminals, or persons affected with contagious or infectious diseases are among them. After the inspection is over, the emigrants are passed into the rotunda, or principal hall of the building.

This great central hall, lined on one side by a series of enclosures containing postal and telegraph offices, railroad-ticket and currency-exchange counters, and a buffet, was otherwise partly encircled by the tiers that remained from its days as a theater. In the rotunda, the immigrants lined up, filing

one by one, by the registration desk, where their names, age, nationality, destination, the vessel's name and date of arrival, are carefully registered, as a means of identifying the person should it be necessary to do so at any time in the future.

In the best of times, this was a situation likely to be unpleasant, but in 1882, it was sometimes terrifying. Owing only in part to the spurt of Jewish refugees, this year was seeing the largest immigrant influx in American history to date: the official total for 1882 was to be 788,992. The facility at Castle Garden—which had been completely under New York State jurisdiction until the U.S. Supreme Court ruled this to be unconstitutional in 1876, but which had not yet been fully transferred to federal authority—was not equipped to handle its part of such a load, and this shortcoming was displayed to the immigrant at every turn, beginning with the brusque treatment meted out by the inadequately trained state officials.

"If we thought," wrote an infuriated George Price, "that they would greet us in New York as they did in the European cities, we were greatly mistaken. The transfer from the boat to Castle Garden was nothing more than going from the frying-pan into the flame." To him the building was "a Gehenna, through which all Jewish arrivals must pass to be cleansed before they are considered worthy of breathing freely the air of the land of the almighty dollar."

*Subsequently Hudson.

What above all shocked people arriving that spring and summer was the scene in the great enclosure that had been built around the landward side of the building to accommodate the recent overflow. "The Castle Garden Plaza," observed a startled Alexander Harkavy, "was filled from one end to the other with immigrants." Price, hearing "the shrieks of children and the curses of women confined" there, viewed the scene with suspicion. "In the spacious courtyard of this institution," he wrote, "which is surrounded by high walls so that no one can enter or leave except through the gate, at which are stationed half a dozen guards, those immigrants who have not as yet been admitted have to find a place for themselves."

Actually, admission was not the problem in most cases; the court-yards and outbuildings had simply filled up with new arrivals—mainly Jewish refugees—who did not know where to go next. "Those of the new-comers who have friends awaiting them," the guidebook says,

> are allowed to depart with them, after the latter have satisfied the authorities as to their real characters; others who wish to remain in the rotunda are allowed to do so for a stated time; those who wish to go to a boarding-house are recommended to houses licensed by, and under the supervision of, the Commissioners; and others still, who wish to proceed at once to their destinations in other parts of the country, can purchase their railway tickets and have their baggage checked at the offices in the building.

But few of the Jewish refugees had friends or relatives awaiting them, or had any particular destinations; nor were they eager to expend their meager resources on boardinghouses until they found more permanent arrangements. It was indeed customary to let immigrants sleep a few nights on the stone tiers in the rotunda until they got themselves located. Most of them had, after all, brought bedding along; Abraham Cahan spent a night that way, though he found that "the stench was terrible, as if a thousand cats were living there." But there was no longer room for everyone to sleep inside, and whole families—doubtless preferring the summer skies to the stench of the rotunda anyway—had camped out, not only in the courtyard, but even beyond the gate that Price had thought to be so forbiddingly guarded. "On the adjoining streets," wrote Harkavy, "—State Street, Greenwich Street, and even at the top of Broadway—women sat on the ground, babies in hand, for want of a home." For the newest arrivals it was disheartening to "step out of the barges into the great courtyard of Castle Garden," as Bernard Weinstein did,

> and see hundreds of people: men, women, children, our Russian Jews. We see that they are living there in Castle Garden without

a roof over their heads. They sit on the ground, a few on the grass. We go around asking people—these "new Americans"—how it's going here in America, and they start to cry. They want to go home again.

"The great steamships heading back to Europe," wrote Cahan as if to emphasize the point, "sail by a short distance away."

At this height of the Jewish influx, the Committee of the Hebrew Emigrant Aid Society fared no better than the Castle Garden authorities. They were now at two locations: the main office at 15 State Street—just a few steps across from Battery Park and under the elevated railway—which served as an employment and housing bureau; and a shelter facility, with a restaurant, at 27 Greenwich Street. Both had more work than they could handle. As Bernard Weinstein remembered it, the Committee's representatives at Castle Garden "used to give out tickets to the immigrants a few times a day, with which you could go to a more or less Jewish-type delicatessen on Greenwich Street (a few blocks from Castle Garden) and get several sandwiches of stale bread and moldy sausage." Impressions of the employment bureau were even worse. When George Price got to it, the crowd

> was so immense that it would have been easier for a camel to pass through the eye of a needle than for the mass of [Jewish immigrants] to get to the door of the Committee. The door was guarded by two tall policemen. . . . Woe to the member of the Committee who dared to enter or leave. The mass crowded around him and from the questions, threats and attacks, his life could have been in danger.

Israel Kasovich encountered a similar scene there:

> At the door stood a policeman, who behaved anything but gently. Near him stood a Russian Jew employed by the Committee, and he bellowed even worse than the policeman. It was impossible to get inside. If someone needed help, he had first to procure a ticket, and then stand in line and wait his turn.

Even when one got in, the worst moments often came in the direct confrontations between the immigrants and their American Hebrew benefactors. Abraham Cahan found little gratification when he got into the Society's employment office:

> An American Jew conversed with me in German, which he butchered in his way and I in mine. We didn't understand each

other very well, and ended up in mutual dissatisfaction. I left with the feeling that he was a heartless bourgeois—and he probably thought of me as a "wild Russian," as they used to call us immigrants behind our backs, and sometimes to our faces.

The "wild Russians" soon had a name for these bourgeois American Jews of German extraction: "Yahudim," a mocking variant on the Hebrew word for Jews (*Yehudim*) that conveys an image of starchiness to the point of absurdity. The whole situation had the shape of an impending class struggle; indeed, the "Yahudim," still thinking of themselves as patient benefactors, were often to be the employers of Jewish immigrant labor—and the bosses against whom strikes were led. Weinstein was convinced that the Society's employment bureau even occasionally sent immigrants to shops on strike to work as scabs.

To make matters worse, the bureau was not even giving satisfaction in what it had professed was its most cherished aim—agricultural settlement. To be sure, very few of the arrivals had really wanted to be farmers, but now the Am Olam groups were arriving, filled with bucolic visions they and the American Israelites had once shared for them, and doubtless having some inkling of the Sicily Island project— the only one of its type to have been initiated so far. They were doomed to disappointment. When the Kiev Am Olam group arrived at Castle Garden on May 31, its leader, Nicholas Aleinikoff, went right to 15 State Street to find out what plans had been made to settle his group on the land. "The officers of the Society received our leader politely," Alexander Harkavy writes,

> but informed him that in the existing circumstances they could not do a thing for our group. . . . After a short while our leader returned to our camp and told us everything that the Society's officers had said. Our spirits sank. "No more hope of working the land! Our dreams ha‧ come to nought! Alas that we have reached such a state!"

For Israel Kasovich, it was more than he could bear. "I had come to America to become a tiller of the soil," he wrote, "and now I was to become a peddler!" He was to return to Russia four months later.

In this atmosphere, the Society's efforts to improve matters by expanding its facilities that summer—doubtless with a sudden influx of sterling from London—did not fare too well. Two large shelters were established—one on Green Street in Greenpoint, Brooklyn, and the other on Ward's Island—but neither was liked by those who had to use them. "While it was true," Harris Rubin conceded of the Greenpoint shelter,

that this immigrant house provided warm cooked meals at tables
and real beds for sleeping, in some respects it was less desirable
than Castle Garden. The beds were dirty and filled with little crea-
tures. . . . The discipline was militaristic and the man in charge was
an angry old German Jew. . . . If one of us wanted to go somewhere
or even write a letter, it was necessary to get permission from that
despot.

The disappointed Kiev Am Olam also stayed at Greenpoint, and Harkavy agreed with Rubin: "The superintendent was a pious old German
Jew whose devotion to every rule was absolute. Since we couldn't follow
every detail of every rule there were always arguments between us."

According to Rubin, the daily routine consisted of being "selected,
dressed in white uniforms, and given the job of washing dishes, cleaning
beds and so on." George Price thought the place to be "in reality . . . a
sort of workhouse."

Harris Rubin summed up the essence of the situation in Greenpoint
by fondly remembering a day he and some other immigrants had spent,
while still at Castle Garden, visiting a group of Orthodox Jews at their
synagogue in New York. "In a sense," he reflected,

it was natural that there be a difference. In the synagogue the Jews
were plain folk like us who had felt the Russian whip and the bitter
taste of being immigrants, and they empathized with us. On the
other hand, in this immigrant house we were dealing with a committee of an organization run by German Jews who did not have
too much love for Russian Jews but provided help out of a cold
sense of philanthropy, and therefore the system and discipline which
resulted were suited to uncivilized recipients which they considered
us to be.

Clashes were inevitable. The high-spirited Kiev Am Olam group
would arouse the superintendent's anger "in very strange ways," according to Harkavy: "for example, at night when he was in bed one
would begin to yell, another to dance, another to screech like a chicken,
another to sing like a cantor, another to sermonize like a preacher, another to spin rhymes like a jester and so forth." But the trouble could
occasionally rise above the level of mere pranks.

The situation was at its worst on Ward's Island, just east of Manhattan, in the fork made by the convergence of the Harlem and East
rivers. Temporary barracks had been built there on the grounds of a
former lunatic asylum, alongside the old immigrant hospital; the money
for this shelter had been donated by Jacob H. Schiff, and it came in time
to be known as the Schiff Refuge. In March 1882, it had not yet been
finished, but it was already open and, for the time being, a matter of

pride. "Three weeks ago," wrote a reporter for the *American Israelite* in its issue of April 7,

> upon a dull, gray Sunday afternoon, I made a visit to Ward's Island, New York, where the Jewish fugitives from Russia were domiciled in a temporary asylum [on land] provided by the United States Government. All the refugees had assembled in a large hall in the lower part of the building to celebrate the festival of Purim, and at least a hundred voices united in singing the strange, melancholy melodies of the Russian folk songs. Even those of the immigrants who had found employment in the city returned to the island to pass the holiday with their wives and children or with their companions in exile.

Eager to point out that these were not at all the shriveled and bearded Talmudists that had been feared, the reporter continued:

> Curious foreign types surrounded me on every side; tall, muscular Russians, with vigorously defined faces, high Mongolian cheekbones, broad brows, and in many cases fair northern hair and complexion, but always with the Oriental element, flashing dark, keen and unmistakeable from the eyes.

Thus, he concluded, "New York has boldly proclaimed her sympathy with the victims of Russian barbarity."

But by the end of summer, the inadequacy of the Schiff Refuge had become clear, and the tensions there between staff and inmates were reaching a danger point. George Price, arriving when some seven hundred refugees were housed there, was in time to witness the consequences. Referring to the director, a man named Blank, as "the Father," Price described him as

> an American Jew who looked down upon the earthly beings, as the immigrants were called and not in a friendly tone. His assistant, the Hungarian Jew [Zadok], was a brazen scoundrel and treated the immigrants like cattle. The other Russian Jews [Aaronson, the commissary of the stores, and about half a dozen subordinates], who through flattery managed to secure soft jobs, imitated them in behavior. The food fed to the immigrants was poor and spoiled.

Here were a typical day's meals:

> At seven in the morning the bell summoned everyone into the mess hall. There each was given a slice of soft half-baked bread and a large cup of a black, muddy beverage which the officials graced with the name of coffee. At 1.00 P.M., they served lunch consisting

of bread of the same quality, a sort of liquid in which very often, instead of grains of cereal, there floated worms, and finally a slice of smelly meat. On [Saturdays] and holidays they added a plate of some sort of fruit dish, which they called *tzimmes*, of a somewhat suspicious quality. At night they again served a slice of bread with the muddy liquid—coffee.

It was on account of the *tzimmes*, according to Price, that a major outburst occurred on Saturday, October 14—"a revolution in minia-ture," as he called it, an "immigrant uprising." Tension had reached a new height the day before, when a woman begging for some medicine had been slapped by Zadok; some other women had protested, and the Hungarian had responded, according to Price, by threatening them with a revolver. The next morning,

at coffee time, there reigned an ill-boding quietude. The men drank their liquid in silence and with an indignant expression. . . . The women, who at such meals were usually noisy, whispered among themselves, silently clenching their fists under their aprons and behind the servers' backs. Even the children seemed to have be-come participants in the conspiracy and they did not shatter the air with their customary unbearable shrieking, crying and wailing.

After breakfast, a delegation went to see "the Father" to complain about his assistant, but they were rudely brushed off. By dinnertime, it needed only "a spark to touch off their stormy passions." That spark was the *tzimmes* served for dessert.

As it was handed out, a young immigrant whom Price calls "A" and who had quarreled with the waiters, was passed by. "The young man protested," Price relates,

and began to shout and curse the waiters. To the scene of argument and shouting came running the hateful Zadok and he, of course, sided with the waiters. The argument resulted in a heated quarrel. Because of Zadok's threats, "A" grabbed a bowl with the *tzimmes* and hurled it into Zadok's face. Other waiters ran to the scene and wanted to have him and those who came to his aid arrested. The rest of the immigrants gathered about and a fight ensued. Zadok and his agents, quite dishevelled, were thrown out into the yard.

At this point, "the Father" sent for the police, who arrived in half an hour. They tried to arrest "A" and his cohorts, but

in front of the policemen there stood a large crowd of children, women and men, and this human wall seemed unapproachable. But when the policemen, with raised clubs, began to swing them to the right and to the left without regard for the children and the women, the crowd retreated. Within a short while, however, stones came flying at the police.

In a few moments the

> entire Jewish sector of the island turned into pandemonium. Shouts, wailing, cursing and moaning, children's crying, the whistling of the police, the groans of the wounded—all blended into a horrible uproar. The Jews fought desperately, but the armed policemen and the Committee's staff succeeded in arresting half a dozen Jews together with "A". Half-dead and beaten, they were thrown into an ambulance and transported to the prison hospital.

This aroused others to greater fury, and they stormed the residence of "the Father," who would have been "torn . . . to pieces had he not fled through the window, jumped into the bay and swum to the opposite shore where he was rescued by the police."

Peace finally was restored, and the next day, delegates came from the Hebrew Emigrant Aid Society to investigate the causes of the trouble. Apart from the food, the chief complaint was "the Father" and his staff. The delegates agreed to replace them, and a few days later, the directorship was given to a Russian Jew long settled in the United States. Other reforms were made, and since the investigators concluded that the disturbances had been caused by "a few ignorant immigrants and those unable to find employment," greater efforts at job placement were made. The owner of a Long Island fruit-canning factory provided work for several hundred of the men, women and children—"at half the standard wages," according to Price—and they were transported there daily. They even held a strike and got a raise in pay. Another group was sent to the Greenpoint shelter, where they held a hunger strike, and were eventually placed in factory jobs.

"A number of young people, among whom also was I," Price concludes, "were sent to a farm, where we first learned to know the American type of work and the language." But this hardly was the return to the soil of anyone's dreams.

·14·

INTERLUDE:
THE ZEAL OF A CONVERT

"The imperative necessity of reforming the organization and methods of the Hebrew Aid Society on Ward's Island," began a letter in the New York *American Hebrew* of Friday, October 20, 1882, "is brought into painful prominence by the scandalous affair of Saturday."

The writer was Emma Lazarus, a thirty-three-year-old poet and essayist who had once been a disciple of Ralph Waldo Emerson and had found her main inspirations in the literature and art of England, Germany, and Italy. The daughter of a wealthy Sephardic sugar manufacturer of New York, Emma had known Jewish piety and observance since childhood and had written an elegy, "In the Jewish Synagogue at Newport," when she was eighteen. But as a writer and a poet she had found her religious faith primarily as a universalist until recently.

The change may have begun in 1881. The most eminent Sephardic Jew of the century, Benjamin Disraeli, had died that spring; a few days later, the anti-Jewish riots had broken out in Russia. But the effects of these events were not to show upon her until a year later. In the April 1882 issue of *The Century*, a magazine to which she was a frequent contributor, Emma published an article on Disraeli to commemorate the anniversary of his death. In it, she touched with some pride upon the Sephardic aspects of his character, judging him to be, despite his boyhood conversion to Christianity, a representative type of Jewish personality of the epoch. To emphasize her point, however, she let slip a few remarks that she may subsequently have regretted. "He knew himself to be the descendant," she wrote of Disraeli's Sephardic heritage, as against what some considered the Ashkenazic one to be, "not of pariahs and pawnbrokers, but of princes, prophets, statesmen, poets and philosophers." This was all very well for a Disraeli or a Lazarus; but

what was it saying about the wretched refuse of Russian Jewry streaming into New York harbor at that very moment?

The point might have gone unnoticed, except that Richard Watson
Gilder, editor of *The Century*, had taken advantage of an opportunity
few editors could have resisted. He had received a manuscript on the
anti-Jewish riots of 1881 by Madame Zinaida Ragozin, the aristocratic
Russian gentile who had witnessed the rioting in Yelizavetgrad. She
had something of an international reputation as an Orientalist and eth-
nologist, and in her article, Madame Ragozin followed her vivid description of the riots with a long analysis of the Jewish situation in Russia.
It was rather forgiving of the rioters and critical of the people—"pariahs
and pawnbrokers" would correctly sum up part of her characterization
of them—who were the victims. It was well written and bound to be
controversial, and Gilder, stating in print that he intended to run a
Jewish response to it, published it in the same April issue that contained
the Emma Lazarus essay on Disraeli. Did he already have it in mind to
ask her to be the respondent? In any case, he knew how to provoke her.
"Here's something you'll be surprised at," he told her as he handed her
the April *Century*.

Surprised, indeed; for the reply she wrote—which was published in
the next issue—shows her aroused to a fury rarely to be found in her
writings until that moment. "In the April number of *The Century*," she
wrote with overflowing scorn,

> Mme. Ragozin set forth the "Russian side" of the question, which
> appears to her sufficient explanation of a state of affairs character-
> ized by the London "Times" as "a scene of horrors that have hith-
> erto only been perpetrated in mediaeval days during times of war."
> Murder, rape, arson, one hundred thousand families reduced to
> homeless beggary, and the destruction of eighty million dollars'
> worth of property—such, in fewest words, are the acts for which an
> excuse is sought.

Madame Ragozin had based her analysis partly upon the writings of the
late Jacob Brafmann—"a Jewish apostate in the pay of the Russian Government," as Lazarus vividly describes him—who had published a book
in 1869 depicting Jewish community traditions and Talmudic law as an
obnoxious state within a state. "For the subtle meaning of the Talmud,
we need not go to a bribed renegade," Lazarus retorts, and refers her
readers instead to "the writings of Emmanuel Deutsch, the Jewish
scholar, said to be the original of George Eliot's 'Mordecai' [in *Daniel
Deronda*], and ... of the orthodox Christian clergyman, Dr. Franz
Delitzsch, one of the greatest living Orientalists," both of whom had

published recent works emphasizing the Talmud's humanistic aspects. After all, she asks,

> If a Moslem were to print an expurgated copy of the Bible, citing all the barbarous passages and omitting all the humane and noble features, what would Islam think of the cornerstone of Christianity? Yet this is precisely what the Jew-haters have done with the Talmud.

She concedes that "no one will deny" the argument that "the Jews are as a rule shrewd, astute, and sharp at a bargain." Moreover,

> that a rapacious envy of their gains is at the bottom of all the religious and political outbreaks against them, I am as firmly convinced as is Mme. Ragozin herself. But none the less is it a fact that this envy, ashamed to appear under its proper name, seeks to disguise itself under the mask of any and every other sentiment—patriotism, self-preservation, religious zeal, righteous indignation in a thousand forms.

And here her own indignation rises to a height. "But is it not as puerile as it is monstrous," she writes,

> to assert that the Christians, who outnumber the Jews by millions, who have the whole power of the law and the throne to back them, not to speak of the prejudice of the whole civilized world in their favor, can find no other weapons than tyranny, violence, and murder to preserve them against the Jew, who has nothing but his wits?

In this polemic, Emma Lazarus had discovered a new voice, to be heard henceforth in her poetry as well as her prose. "O deem not dead that martial fire," she wrote just a few weeks later of the spirit of ancient Israel,

> Say not the mystic flame is spent!
> With Moses' law and David's lyre,
> Your ancient strength remains unbent.
> Let but an Ezra rise anew,
> To lift the *Banner of the Jew!*

That she had undergone a virtual conversion from American Israelite to Jew became evident that fall, when she published a collection of her poems in one volume along with *The Dance to Death*, her verse tragedy of medieval German-Jewish life. The title she gave the book was *Songs of a Semite;* her dedication page for the drama reads: "This play is dedicated, in profound veneration and respect, to the memory of George Eliot, the illustrious writer, who did most among the artists of our day towards elevating and ennobling the spirit of Jewish nationality." Lazarus was far from being the only Jew of that day to have felt a quickening of national spirit upon reading *Daniel Deronda.* And had George Eliot also awakened an Ezra in her?

For with this quickening had come another conversion as well: the shy spinster, hitherto at times a virtual recluse, now became something of a social activist and a preacher. This was the personality that was presenting itself—immediately upon publication of *Songs of a Semite* — in the letters column of *The American Hebrew* in the wake of the unhappy mutiny on Ward's Island. "Such a riot," she chided,

> is the inevitable consequence of a prolonged encouragement of idleness and pauperism, uncontrolled by the necessary forces of intelligent authority. Given between six and seven hundred men, and women and children (of whom twenty-two young girls are the only ones for whom a show of employment is provided), subsisting month after month upon public and private charity and placed under the direction of a single officer who is expected with the aid of the inefficient assistant to personally arrange and overlook every detail of the establishment—and the unavoidable result of utter demoralization and mutiny becomes simply a question of time.

A larger and more efficient administration, better hygienic conditions, stricter rules of organization—these are among the reforms she suggests; but the nineteenth-century moralist welling up in her is also after bigger game.

"It has been well said," her letter continues,

> that philanthropy is no longer a moral luxury to be safely indulged in according to the chance inspiration of the benevolent. It is recognized by modern thinkers as a difficult science only to be properly applied by carefully trained minds and skillful hands. Those who have studied the question thoroughly by the light of modern biology and sociology, assert that there are but two gifts which can with justice and safety be freely dispensed among the poor, viz: *Education and Work.*

The two elements overlap. First, of education:

> It must be remembered that not only the children but the full-grown inmates of this peculiar institution require instruction in the language, manners and customs of America. The refugees have now

been occupied over a month, and not a single practical step has been taken to provide tuition. The swarms of children that infest the place literally run wild in every stage of dirt and raggedness. If the asylum is to be only temporary, it is all the more essential that no delay should occur in the establishment of some organized system of instruction. . . . Moreover, work could thus be furnished for several of the more deserving and educated among the Russians themselves, by employing them as teachers.

Which brings the argument to the main point: work. "The only way," the letter goes on,

to prevent these refugees from sinking into a condition of hopeless pauperism, is to exact from every individual some equivalent, however small, for the benefit he receives. A character strong enough to resist the baneful effect produced by the habitual acceptance of alms, is so rare as to be practically non-existent. And yet to this fatal influence all these emigrants are persistently subjected. The only experiment that has been made in the direction of work, is the opening of a sewing school. The accommodations and appliances thus far allotted have been so inadequate that less than two dozen girls have been enabled to profit by it. But the diligence manifested by these, and the strong desire testified to by the majority of the women to join the class, prove that the wretched idleness of the emigrants is by no means a voluntary one.

And then this new-frocked preacher of the age of Social Darwinism makes her philosophical summing-up:

Employment and Education—Education and Employment—we cannot often enough repeat these words which should be the motto of the institution. Mr. Spencer and Mr. Darwin, not to cite less authoritative names, have pointed out the thoroughly maleficent effects of an ignorant philanthropy, and the portentous evils of that short-sighted charity which neglects to take into account the laws of nature and of natural selection. In justice to future generations, in justice to ourselves, in justice to the objects of our sympathy, we must not only dispense those gifts which strengthen the character and the mind, but we must study how best to avoid the risk of enfeebling the race by pauperization, and the artificial preservation of the vicious and the idle. "Charity is a work of science, not of mere sentiment."

Practicing what she preached, Emma did volunteer work at Ward's Island; and two weeks after printing this letter, *The American Hebrew* began a series of didactic pieces by her called "An Epistle to the Hebrews." "Not for the sake of those who have mainly begotten in us the faults inseparable from long subjection to oppression and contempt," she explained in the first installment,

> but for our own sakes, for the sake of the coming generation, I shall endeavor to impress upon my readers the urgent necessity for reform along the whole line of Jewish thought and Jewish life, and for a deepening and quickening of the sources of Jewish enthusiasm.

Emma Lazarus had found her mission.

·15·

RETURNERS TO THE SOIL, I: PALESTINE

In honor of the Jewish New Year that September, Emma Lazarus had written a poem that contained this stanza:

> In two divided streams the exiles part,
>   One rolling homeward to its ancient source,
> One rushing sunward with fresh will, new heart.
>   By each the truth is spread, the law unfurled,
> Each separate soul contains the nation's force,
>   And both embrace the world.

And, in fact, after the initial rush to the West, the emigration movement had also begun sending a stream, much smaller but equally inexorable, to the "ancient source" in Palestine.

Throughout the centuries, even in the worst of times, Palestine had never been completely devoid of Jews, and there almost always had been Jewish emigration there, however small. The first three-quarters of the nineteenth century had seen a particularly large influx, and by the end of 1881 there were about twenty-five thousand Jews in Palestine (in a total population of about three hundred thousand), fifteen thousand of them in Jerusalem, where they made up half the population. The vast majority were pious immigrants from Eastern Europe who had gone to the four holy cities of Jerusalem, Hebron, Safed, and Tiberias to pray at the source; scarcely productive, they relied for sustenance mainly upon the *halukkah*, a system of reverent contributions from the Jewish communities of the Diaspora. There were also Jewish merchants, artisans, and laborers, many of them descended from the ancient Jewish communities of the Middle East and speaking Arabic as their mother tongue. But there were virtually no Jewish farmers, de-

116

spite occasional attempts to found agricultural colonies—most recently by members of the Alliance Israélite Universelle's Mikveh Israel school near Jaffa.

The idea of a Jewish return to the soil of Palestine was not completely new in 1882, but it had warmed up to a special intensity only in the few preceding years, in large part because of the promotional efforts of a succession of highly interested English Christians. In 1840, Lord Palmerston, then the British Foreign Secretary, had pondered the Jewish return to Palestine as a practical and desirable development in international relations; beginning in 1865, the surveys and excavations conducted by the London-based Palestine Exploration Fund had aroused other high-minded English men and women to the idea. Foremost among these had been George Eliot, whose 1876 novel, *Daniel Deronda,* inspired Jews throughout the world with its vision of a Jewish National revival in Palestine. But equally important on the practical level was Laurence Oliphant, who had submitted his proposal for the Jewish colonization of Palestine to Prime Minister Disraeli in 1878, then gone there himself to scout out locations, publishing his findings the following year. When Oliphant went to work for the Mansion House Fund in February 1882, he made it quite clear that he was interested in getting some of the emigrants to go to Palestine. He was not to be disappointed.

Like the stream of emigration to America, the one to Palestine arose in the first instance as a spontaneous flow. Odessa in particular was, after all, a Black Sea port, vastly nearer to Constantinople than to New York; and Constantinople was the main stop on the way to Palestine, itself a part of the Empire of which that ancient city was the capital. By the end of January 1882, according to a report in the *Jewish Chronicle,* it was "the intention of 500 Jewish families in the district of Odessa to quit the country and settle in Jaffa in Palestine." Few participants in this initial surge seem to have been prospective farmers. "From divers places," wrote the *Chronicle*'s Jerusalem correspondent on January 27,

> envoys have arrived here, charged to secure eligible [commercial and industrial] sites for their brethren who are to follow next spring. A Russian gentleman . . . has assured me that many Jewish capitalists of his country were firmly resolved to settle at Jaffa in order to erect factories there.

Not that all those who were heading for Palestine in this moment were capitalists, either. On the contrary, some observers were worried at the possibility of "an influx of Jewish paupers." America was, after all, a "land of opportunity," and those who did not get to farms or factories there could still become peddlers; but in Palestine, a large number of unemployed did not stand a chance.

Then came those who were convinced, like the Am Olam with regard to America, that the only viable and significant way into life in Palestine was through the establishment of farming communities. This idea sprang from student circles similar to those that had given rise to the Am Olam movement just before it—in some cases, even from the same people. Chaim Khissin, a seventeen-year-old Moscow gymnasium student, wrote in his diary in March 1882 that

> the problem "Whither emigrate?" faces us with a choice between Palestine and America. Considering the laws of Turkey and of the United States, the level of wages and the measure of public security, it is not hard to choose. So I am going to America, only to America.

Yet scarcely more than a month had passed before Khissin was persuaded to join a group of young people determined to go and farm in Palestine that very spring. At this time, another member of the group, Israel Belkind, met Abraham Cahan fleeing Russia on account of his political activities and planning to take refuge in Switzerland. Belkind tried to persuade him to come along to Palestine instead but, failing that, suggested that he at least join an Am Olam group going to America; Cahan, when he got to Brody, did precisely that. In that moment, the gap between a Palestinian and an American choice was not wide for some young idealists; although it is clear that the main energies for the former were coming from those who were better versed in Hebrew and the Haskalah, the foremost publicists of which were now, like Peretz Smolenskin, urgently advocating Palestine. "Many of our unhappy brethren have emigrated to America," ran a characteristic statement issued in February by a Palestine-oriented group in Yelizavetgrad, "but we are against that, because the Jewish element which reigns in the United States loses in time the Jewish national spirit. Acting upon this ground, we prefer to go to the Holy Land and try our fortune on the ruins of our former greatness."

This preference for Palestine swelled in Rumania even earlier than in Russia. A newly revived nation that had achieved independence from Turkey largely under Russian tutelage, Rumania, with its half-million Jews, had tended to learn Russia's lessons in its treatment of that population as well. In particular, the Jews of Moldavia, in the north of Rumania, who were socially and culturally a virtual extension of southern-Russian Jewry, had felt keenly the moral impact of the riots, and were responding to it in their own way. Laurence Oliphant, in Paris on

his way to Brody at the beginning of March, received news there from
Galatz in Moldavia that greatly impressed him. "There is an immense
movement going on in Roumania," he reported to a colleague back in
London, "and subscriptions amongst Jews alone there for Palestine colonization purposes, it is hoped, will amount to fifty thousand francs a
month."

The current in Rumania quickly swelled and overflowed into Russia. In its issue of March 17, the *Jewish Chronicle* observed

> that the many societies for the colonization of Palestine which exist
> in Roumania have now taken practical steps towards beginning a
> well-equipped emigration of settlers with capital from Roumania to
> Palestine. A movement to the like effect is on foot in Russia. Our
> correspondent on the Russian border believes that more than a
> thousand Jewish families are prepared to embark in agriculture and
> manufactures in Palestine.

The movement reached a new height during Passover. By the first week
in May, Oliphant could write from Jassy in Rumania:

> On the 3rd I attended a meeting of delegates from twenty-eight
> Palestine colonization committees. There are forty-nine in the coun-
> try altogether. It was very interesting and encouraging. My cor-
> respondence from all parts of Russia tells me that the movement is
> universal.

His vision seemed about to be realized. "It is true that I have somewhat
delayed my journey to the East," he had written some two weeks earlier to the editor of a Hebrew journal,

> but the fault is not my own, since I was induced to make it my first
> business to visit Brody in order to bring help to the starving fugi-
> tives in that town, and to assist them in their desire of settling in
> America. This mission I have undertaken, not because I personally
> wish to send these poor people to America, but because I know that
> they are dying of hunger, and because funds have been raised for
> the purpose of sending them. . . . I enter into these particulars so
> that you may not think that . . . I have changed my mind with
> regard to an emigration to Palestine.

Indeed, by the time he was in Jassy, Oliphant had resigned his position
with the Mansion House Fund, and a few days later he was on his way
to Constantinople to try to negotiate with the Turkish government for
an organized Jewish emigration to Palestine.

Meanwhile, other central protagonists in the unfolding drama of

Palestine colonization were appearing on the scene. In its May 5 issue, the *Jewish Chronicle* carried a letter from the Holy Land by one S. D. Levontin, announcing that he had formed "a committee whose task it is to establish the colonization of our brethren in the Holy Land on a rational basis," which was now searching for suitable locations and making a worldwide plea for financial aid. Born to a Hasidic family in White Russia in 1856, Levontin had received a secular education and, before emigrating, had worked in Kremenchug near Poltava as a bank clerk. A Palestine emigration group formed in his home city had sent him in February on the mission he was now announcing. Levontin had found an important ally in Haim Amzalak, a Sephardic Jew living in Palestine who, having been born in Gibraltar, was a British subject and was serving as British vice consul in Jaffa. Since there were Ottoman restrictions on the purchase of land by Russian or Rumanian Jews, Amzalak was to be the group's titleholder in any transaction. At the end of May, Levontin and his associates announced the drawing-up of a charter for a colony to be called Rishon le-Zion (Hebrew for "First in Zion"), still in search of a location.

Levontin was interested in colonizing the poorer Jewish emigrants, who, he wrote, "are arriving here almost daily in large numbers." Jaffa, he went on, "threatens, I fear, to become another Brody." But another type was now preparing to take on the task he had in mind. "We have organized a group of intelligent young people," wrote Chaim Khissin that same month, "who intend to emigrate to the Holy Land and to devote themselves to farming there." During Passover, two student organizations, one in Khissin's Moscow and one in Kharkov, had come into being, discovered each other, and merged, taking the name BILU.* "These are the main facts about our organization," Khissin went on:

> we are called Bilu, have a membership of 525 people belonging to several groups, all of which are under the leadership of the Kharkov group which is known as the "Central Bureau." This bureau will conduct all the affairs of the pioneers until the entire membership has been brought to Jaffa.

Advance parties from the Central Bureau were sent to Constantinople to try to negotiate a land purchase, and to Jaffa to rent and prepare temporary quarters. The first to arrive in Jaffa was Israel Belkind, who had recently persuaded Abraham Cahan to go to America.

Then a major obstacle hurled itself in the way of all these plans. For more than a year, a nationalist revolt in Egypt had been eroding the

---

*Acronym for *Beit Ya'akov, lekhu v'nelkha* (O House of Jacob, come ye, and let us walk), Isaiah 2:5.

already weak authority of the Khedive in Cairo, a local ruler ostensibly subject to the Sultan but in fact a puppet of Great Britain and France. The situation was reaching a point of crisis that May, and the Sultan now looked with a troubled eye upon any potentially threatening new developments in the region, especially in Palestine. "When, therefore," explained the *Jewish Chronicle*'s Constantinople correspondent on May 21,

> the news reached here that the Russian and Roumanian Jewish populations proposed concentrating their immigration to [the Sultan's] dominions upon that province alone, and that many had already arrived there, he foresaw possible interference on the part of the Christian Powers whose religious quarrels over the holy places led to the Crimean War; he vaguely feared the creation of a new Jewish nationality with the inevitable Protectorate on the part of a European power which might lead to absorption or independence, and he was reminded by the Sheikh ul Islam of certain uncomfortable passages contained in the Koran, and of other prophecies familiar to Moslems, foreshadowing the final doom of Islam when the Jews were restored to the land of their fathers.

Whereupon the Sultan made a crucial decision and

> caused instructions to be sent to his consular agents in Russia and Roumania informing them that, while he was perfectly ready to permit the Jews to emigrate to his dominions, provided they became Ottoman subjects, he would not allow them to settle in Palestine.

The consuls were to require a signed statement of every prospective Russian or Rumanian Jewish emigrant to the Sultan's territories, promising they would apply for Ottoman nationality and not settle in Palestine.

Khissin and his Bilu comrades were in the midst of preparations to depart when,

> like a thunderbolt, the news came that a notice was pinned on the door of the Turkish consulate at Odessa, saying that the Sultan forbade Jews to enter Palestine. This was confirmed in the press. Cables were sent to influential people to put things straight. Oliphant answered: "I am going to Constantinople at once. I cannot tell you the whole story in a telegram."

The reply to all such inquiries was ambiguous. "The Bilu central office in Odessa wrote to us on May 25," Khissin's diary continues,

> that the Sultan was not against Jews going to the Land of Israel; the notice in Odessa merely signified official Turkish fears lest poor Jews pour into Constantinople and swell the proletariat, which the Turkish Government would not like at all, but once it was persuaded that Jewish entry into Palestine would be carefully organized, it rescinded the order.

It was true that, according to a contemporary news report, some two hundred Russian-Jewish families who had reached Constantinople were "now starving in the streets"; but the view circulating among the Bilu comrades that this was the reason for the Ottoman immigration restrictions remained to be tested. Khissin and his immediate group armed themselves with a document that would ostensibly enable them to land at Jaffa, on the basis of an assurance that they were part of an association that was solvent and mutually supporting. For the rest, the time-honored Ottoman custom of *baksheesh* was to be substantially relied upon.

"The tumult is quieting down," Khissin was at last able to write at the end of July,

> the engine hisses and roars, the boat is getting ready to leave. After the last quick embraces, the passengers hurry to their places; the police leave; the third deafening whistle blows; the sailors move about briskly, pulling in the gangplanks, and gradually the ship begins to move away from the harbor. . . . The S.S. *Russia* is carrying me away from Russia . . . under full steam.

Departing from Odessa onto the Black Sea, Khissin and his five companions—ranging in age from seventeen to thirty, and including one girl—faced a much shorter stretch of open sea than their compatriots who were going to America. But three days was time enough for the ship

> to play tricks and consequently almost everyone suffered badly from seasickness. I had been determined to stay on my feet. I wanted to experience the feeling of facing the storm and outfacing it! But as we approached Constantinople I, too, succumbed; it still seems to me that the ground is shaking under my feet!

Then, on the night of August 1, they dropped anchor at the entrance to the Bosporus, and the next morning they entered Constantinople harbor. "While we were still some distance away," Khissin writes,

we had become aware of a flotilla of small landing craft and before
we had a chance to stop, it had completely surrounded us. The
boatmen, as nimble as monkeys, climbed right up the ship's side.
In a moment the deck was thick with them, and they were pester-
ing the passengers with offers of service.

But Khissin and his friends knew that a member of the Central Bureau
was to meet them before they accepted any such offers. "Then a young
man," he continues,

> came over to ask whether we were "the students from Kharkov."
> After he had shown us his credentials from the Bureau, he took
> complete charge. He called over one of the Turkish porters, who
> gathered up our belongings and we were off, but an inspector went
> through all the other landing craft checking every passenger for
> sealed packages. When he came over to our landing craft, one of us
> produced some papers for the sake of appearances, but our escort
> gave him a meaningful wink and the inspector took off. When we
> landed, the customs officials who had come to meet us went away,
> likewise, after a little whispering between them and our agent.

Khissin spent a week in Constantinople, and did not greatly enjoy
the experience. "The city is densely populated," he noted,

> and land is scarce and dear; they have solved the problem by put-
> ting up tall apartment buildings, which are very dirty. Each house
> floor belongs to a different owner. The streets are narrow and paved
> with cobblestones. Some kind of local superstition prevents the peo-
> ple from driving off the great number of fat, lazy, dirty dogs who
> lie about on the street. The passers-by walk around them. They live
> completely at their ease, feeding on the garbage which the apart-
> ment dwellers throw down into the street!

On the other hand, Smyrna—at which Khissin and his companions put
in on the steamer *Lazarev* two days after their departure from Constantinople—proved a delight to their eyes. "Smyrna lies in the lowest
part of the bay," he writes:

> Mountains, terraced with vineyards, rise behind the city. A beau-
> tiful, wide street paved with small granite brick runs along the
> seashore, and a one-horse *konki* travels down its length. . . . We
> were stunned by the beauty of the buildings along the waterfront.

Never very far from shore, the *Lazarev* nevertheless encountered
a heavy storm off Mersina, near the northeasternmost corner of the

Mediterranean. "Everyone was ordered away from the stern," according to Khissin;

> the hatch was battened down ; sails were unfurled, and the captain, standing on his bridge, gave orders to weigh anchor. They were raising the anchor when the ship suddenly lurched, leaped, and sprang into the air twice! I shall never forget those horrible leaps! Everything fell: suitcases, bundles, all kinds of objects began to roll across the deck; then there was a great crash and a violent uproar. Terrified passengers fell upon their knees with cries of "God have mercy!" and the Jews recited the "Shema Yisroel."

Then the storm passed safely, and the rest of the journey consisted of a quiet succession of calls down the Levantine coast—at Alexandretta, at Tripoli, and at Beirut—where Khissin and his friends had pleasant encounters with the local Jewish communities and made their first thorough acquaintance with the Sephardic pronunciation of Hebrew, which they would find prevailing in Palestine.

At last, at five o'clock in the morning of August 21,

> we approached Jaffa. Like all coastal cities it is very pretty from the sea. It looks like an immense, flat-topped pyramid composed of buildings that rise in layers. At the water's edge there is only a stone wharf built to accommodate small boats. There are no piers for large boats; they must drop anchor out in the bay. Before we arrived the sailors told us that the sea is almost always very choppy close to shore. The small craft coming out to take off passengers sometimes rise to the level of the ship and sometimes seem to fall away beneath it. When this happens, the boatmen simply toss the passengers down into the boat where their companions catch them.

The sea was calm that day, so that Khissin and his comrades did not have to suffer this particular indignity; but their boat ride to shore proved unhappy all the same. When they got there, it was discovered that their papers were not acceptable after all, and they were not permitted to land. Both Belkind and Levontin eventually arrived to intercede for them, but for the moment at least, the young pioneers had no choice but to return to the *Lazarev* and wait while strings were frantically pulled for them ashore.

"Is the colonization of Palestine by Jews from Russia and Roumania desirable?" Charles Netter had asked in a letter written to the *Jewish Chronicle* from Paris on March 15, then proceeded to explain why he did not think so. He began by listing the attempts made by Westerners in recent years to found agricultural colonies in Palestine—by some Americans outside Jaffa in 1867, by Germans near Jaffa and Haifa in 1870, by Orthodox Hungarian Jews from his own Mikveh Israel school at Petach Tikvah in 1878—and noting that they all had either failed or been forced to rely upon charitable support. Then he enumerated what he considered to be the reasons for these failures: the inferior quality of the land available from Arab owners, who held on to the best tracts; the difficulty for Europeans of working in the hot Middle Eastern sun; the ability of Arab farmers, with their lower standard of living, to undersell Europeans; poor conditions of public security; and a vindictive Ottoman system of taxation. To these he added some problems applying particularly to Jews—the ancient religious prescriptions regarding soil cultivation in Palestine, the fact that few Jews were experienced as farmers, and the hitherto lacking organization of effort to return to the soil. Netter, who also expressed fears regarding the implications of Jewish nationalism in the new Palestine movement, argued firmly for America as the better alternative.

The rebuttals came quickly. One of them, a week after Netter's letter was published, used his own successes against him: wasn't the Mikveh Israel school, the writer asked, a working farm and therefore an example to the contrary? But even more forceful than counterargument was the pull of events. Netter's own Alliance Israélite Universelle, though still officially frowning upon Palestine as an alternative to the United States, had in fact been sending small numbers there: in January, Schafier himself had arrived in Jaffa from Brody, bringing in tow a group of twenty-eight orphan boys to enroll in Mikveh Israel. All that spring and summer, news was being published about groups of young Russian and Rumanian Jews eager to go to Palestine and become farmers—and some were getting through in spite of the Sultan's restrictions. The Bilu finally had landed, thanks to Belkind's maneuverings and *baksheesh*, and the leaders of the well-organized Rumanian movement were using tactics of their own, which included an attempt to argue for their rights as former Ottoman subjects and the ardent interventions in their behalf that were being made by Oliphant in Constantinople. Moreover, by the end of August, Levontin's Rishon le-Zion group had purchased about eight hundred acres just southeast of Jaffa, settling upon it nine of its own subscribers, as well as six families who had arrived from Russia unaffiliated and destitute, and who were to be allowed to pay for their plots on easy terms over a five-year period.

All this, combined with the fact that Khissin and eighteen of his Bilu comrades had now settled at the Mikveh Israel school and were learning to be farmers, finally made the situation in Palestine irresistible to Netter's curiosity; at the beginning of September, he went there to have a look for himself. "At about nine o'clock" one morning that month, Khissin recorded,

> someone shouted, "Netter!" and everyone, in unison, leaned hard on the shovel. . . . Netter appeared, escorted by the entire administration of the school. . . . He came over to us, greeted us, questioned [us] about our life, where we lived, about the work—and all this with great concern. Before he left us, he said, "Keep up your work, gentlemen, and don't lose courage. I wish that I, too, had the good fortune to be able to devote my energies to farming on this Holy Land of our ancestors, but I am already past the age for such things," and he continued on his way.

Netter clearly was impressed by this group of elite, secularly educated young Russians, and he put them to work laying the foundations of a house for themselves on the Mikveh Israel property. As for the school's Petach Tikvah plot, northeast of Jaffa, he settled upon it a number of destitute Russian-Jewish families who had been barely surviving in Jerusalem. He probably intended to go on training the Bilu group at the school for a while and eventually settle them as nuclei in Petach Tikvah and other colonies. But he never had a chance to demonstrate what his plans were.

"About ten days ago," Khissin wrote in his diary on October 4,

> we heard that Netter wasn't well. Two days later we were told to stop working on the foundations for the house and not a stone has been laid since. We have now been told that Netter suffered from a chronic liver ailment and that during this whole period of illness he refused to see a doctor. He died on Monday, October 2, at 6 p.m.

"It is believed," said the *Jewish Chronicle*, "that whilst at Brody he imbibed the seeds of the disease which has brought his valuable life to an untimely end. . . . He may be said to have literally died in harness."

Yet, in this final chapter of his life, Netter had seen the momentum of a new kind of Palestine colonization increase, and he had helped it to do so. It is clear that, even before he left Paris, he and the Alliance leadership had decided they would use their influence to get outside help for the colonists; his instructions for this journey included the provision that he "concern himself with the settling of those immigrants who were working at the agricultural school in Jaffa." Meanwhile, as he had made his way to Jaffa, the director of the Mikveh Israel school, Samuel Hirsch, had departed from there for Paris, evidently to discuss the same question. And arriving in Paris at about the same time was an emissary from the Rishon le-Zion colony, Joseph Feinberg, sent to

Europe to try to obtain financial support for the enterprise. When he got there, he found a letter of introduction to the French Chief Rabbi, Zadoc Kahn, awaiting him; it had been written for him by Netter. Soon Feinberg got in to see the thirty-seven-year-old Baron Edmond de Rothschild, leader of the Paris branch of that family, who had actively concerned himself with the plight of the refugees in Brody. The Baron had by this time already had an important conversation with Rabbi Samuel Mohilever of Radom, who had been active at Brody and also carried a letter of introduction from Netter. Rabbi Mohilever was an ardent advocate of the Jewish return to Zion. The upshot of these encounters was that the Baron made a substantial contribution to Rishon le-Zion and began taking a highly auspicious interest in Palestine colonization in general.

Hirsch and Feinberg returned triumphantly to Palestine, and by the end of November the Bilu group—now reduced, by the attrition of despair and departure, to only nine in number—were transferred to the freshly viable Rishon le-Zion. In the meantime, two Rumanian colonies had been established in the north—Samaria, near the coast just south of Haifa, and Rosh Pinna (Cornerstone), in the Galilee, northeast of Safed. Both settlements were located outside the Sanjak of Jerusalem, which alone the Turkish government regarded as Palestine, and were therefore not subject to the prohibition against Jewish immigration. At least, this was a point that had been argued successfully by Laurence Oliphant, whose influence in Constantinople as a British spokesman no doubt had greatly increased that summer and fall, when Her Majesty's forces bombarded unruly Alexandria, crushed the insurgent Egyptian nationalists at Tel el-Kebir, and occupied Cairo. Oliphant was a virtual proconsul of Empire among the Jewish colonists of Palestine when he personally took up residence in Haifa at the end of November, determined to watch over the fate of his charges.

Palestine now had four Jewish settlements; despite Charles Netter's death, they were in good paternal custody.

·16·

RETURNERS TO THE SOIL, II: THE UNITED STATES

The zeal for agricultural colonization in the United States continued, even after the first experiment ended in disaster: in May 1882, immediately after the spring planting, the Sicily Island colony had been destroyed by a Mississippi flood. All its members survived, but only one of them, its president, Herman Rosenthal, was determined to try again. Still believing that the Jews of his adopted country ought to "establish a class of a half-million farmers and workers living by the sweat of their brows," he organized a new group of twelve families, and with funds provided mainly by the Alliance Israélite Universelle, had started a new colony—gratefully named Crémieux—in South Dakota by the beginning of August.

Nor was the Hebrew Emigrant Aid Society daunted by the Sicily Island flood; it presided over the founding of two new colonies that spring. One, at Cotopaxi, Colorado, was established under the Homestead Act: seventeen Russian-Jewish families, farming 160 acres each, were there by the end of the year. The other was at Vineland, in southern New Jersey, a town founded twenty-one years earlier as an experiment in creating a model farm community. In 1882, New Jersey's commissioner of immigration, Augustus Seeman, was an owner of a Vineland Realty Company; entitled to office space at Castle Garden, he was able to proclaim from there the virtues of his Cumberland County promised land not only to interested immigrants, but to the representatives of the Hebrew Emigrant Aid Society, who bought twelve hundred acres of it. During May and June, four hundred immigrants—including 160 children—were sent down to the new Vineland colony, called Alliance by its sponsors, and housed in temporary barracks, called "Castle Garden" by the occupants. Individual family farming on a cooperative basis was the eventual goal, but for the time being, everything was done communally under one supervisor, a Protestant American from Hartford named A. C. Sternberger.

Meanwhile, the Hebrew Emigrant Aid Society had sent a representative, Julius Goldman, to the West to examine the feasibility of colonization there. Traveling for five weeks, Goldman examined possible locations, mainly in the Dakotas, and looked over the Irish immigrant colonies that had recently been established in Minnesota by the Catholic Church. He pronounced the latter successful, but by the time he wrote his report after returning to New York at the end of May, he had—perhaps at the sight of the huge influx that had come through Castle Garden in his absence—begun to take a dim view of the Jewish colonization program. "It has been generally observed," he wrote,

> that of the refugees who have thus far landed in America a great majority have expressed the desire to become farmers; but there can hardly be a doubt in the mind of anyone who has spoken to these people that only a limited number are sincere in this desire, and a still less number have a distinct idea of what farming in this country—and more especially in the Northwest—really means.

He concluded that he was "fully convinced that our society is not able to undertake the work of colonization on a large scale, and that a special organization is demanded," though he admitted "that our society cannot entirely and absolutely shake off the task."

In the end, this proved to be another sign that the Hebrew Emigrant Aid Society had begun to sink under the load being dumped upon it through the gates of Castle Garden. Its expenses for June mounted to almost $36,000; by mid-July, they were reaching $2,000 a day—far more than even the most generous contributions could continue to support. Manuel Kursheedt resigned, and the *Jewish Messenger*, hitherto the Society's ardent supporter, began to recommend that it disband and turn over its duties to the United Hebrew Charities. This view was heartily seconded by the *Jewish Chronicle* in London, which, never assuaged by the favorable assurances of George S. Yates, thought that the Society should be allowed to "die the natural death which seem[s] impending."

Ironically, this fate was then rendered the more inexorable by a sudden stemming of the tide of emigration. After his dismissal in May, Ignatiev had been replaced as Minister of the Interior by Count Dmitry Tolstoy, a man of similarly reactionary and anti-Semitic views, who nevertheless could not tolerate the disorder that had spread through the realm under his predecessor. Vowing to prevent any further anti-Jewish rioting, he significantly abolished the suspect Holy Brotherhood that fall. Russian Jews seemed suddenly less inclined to leave the country—although, whatever their bent, Tolstoy made it more difficult for them to do so, imposing stern restrictions upon emigration and having the border thoroughly patrolled. The Austrian police responded in kind by closing the border more tightly. Moreover, in August, as it became clear that Jews in Russia were now safer, an international Jewish conference at Vienna decided to resume the policy of repatriating most of the Brody refugees, sending only small groups elsewhere, and these only to West European countries, mainly France, Belgium, and the Netherlands. The result was that, by mid-November, fewer than four hundred refugees remained in Brody.

Nothing was left for the Hebrew Emigrant Aid Society but to die its natural death. The first organ to expire was the Greenpoint shelter, which closed its doors on September 13; this was followed by the closing of the main office at 15 State Street on September 22. Then the Greenwich Street restaurant and shelter went on November 3. Only the Ward's Island facility was to last until, completely vacated, it closed the following spring. On November 10, the files of the Hebrew Emigrant Aid Society were turned over to the United Hebrew Charities, which had created an Emigrant Aid Committee for the purpose.

The new committee was run by a man who had already made himself into an immigrant reception institution in his own right. Born in Piotrków in Russian Poland in 1823, the son of a well-to-do and scholarly merchant, Michael Heilprin had spent his young manhood in Hungary, where he worked as a bookseller and served the revolutionary government of 1848 as a press secretary. After settling in the United States in 1858, he had written a widely read polemic against slavery in the New York *Tribune*, then become an editor of Appleton's *New American Cyclopedia*. Deeply moved by the riots in Russia, he had become active with the Hebrew Emigrant Aid Society, "worked for the immigrants literally day and night," according to Abraham Cahan, "and spent on them a large part of his meager savings." Cahan, along with other immigrants, felt a warmth toward Heilprin that they did not feel for his German-Jewish colleagues.

A strong believer in Jewish agricultural settlement, Heilprin had become the director that spring of a new organization called the Montefiore Agricultural Aid Society. Once the Alliance colony had been founded, he made Vineland his special preserve, and saw to the establishment of two more colonies in that area by the end of the year, with the help of funds from Jacob Schiff, Jesse Seligman, and other prominent Jewish philanthropists.

Then, in January 1883, Heilprin scored the greatest triumph to date in the American Jewish colonization movement. In spite of everything, some members of the Odessa Am Olam group had managed to stay together, and Heilprin, with the aid of $5,000 contributed by Schiff and others, bought 780 acres for them in Oregon, on the Pacific Coast. By the end of the month, twenty-one men and five women between the ages of twenty and thirty were established at the site, which they called New Odessa. "Our long wanderings over the vast land of America have come to an end," one of them wrote, "and a new life begins for us, which enables us to turn in earnest to our spiritual, moral, and physical development." There was work to do right away, since adequate quarters had to be built, and there was income to be earned by cutting and selling lumber—for some six hundred acres of the land was forest. "As soon as we assembled," the writer continues,

> we threw ourselves heart and soul into our work, which, in spite of the meager food we received and the generally unfavorable circumstances of our life, was crowned with a measure of success. . . . Our food consisted of bread, potatoes, peas, beans, and a little milk. We suffered greatly from the cold, for we were short of quilts. . . . Nevertheless, we industriously wielded ax, hammer, and saw, and by the end of the month we managed to furnish 125 cords of wood [for railroad ties].

That spring and summer, several new members joined the colony, including a non-Jewish family of four. Its father, William Frey, was a Russian nobleman of German extraction—he had been born with the name Vladimir Heins—who had emigrated to the United States in 1875 to found a Christian communist colony in Kansas. That experiment had failed, and Frey had then lived for several years on the Lower East Side of New York, where, after imbibing a version all his own of the Positivism of the French philosopher Auguste Comte, he had become a popular lecturer and proselytizer. Frey's arrival in the colony meant he would inevitably try to make it over according to his own vision, even though several members did not share it.

By the beginning of August, thirty-six men and seven women—including four married couples—with four children were living in three wooden buildings of two to five rooms each. "This is our daily schedule," according to a letter of August 2:

> We work from six o'clock in the morning until half past eight, [when] . . . we have breakfast. Work is resumed at ten and continued to four in the afternoon. Between four and five o'clock is dinner, followed by a rest period and intellectual activity. Monday, Tuesday, Thursday, and Friday [evenings] are devoted to the study of mathematics, English, and to Frey's lectures on the philosophy of Positivism. On Wednesday, current events are discussed, and on Saturday, the problems of the commune. On Sunday, we rise at six

and a lively discussion begins on the subject of equal rights for women. . . . After breakfast, one member goes to survey the farm, another reads a newspaper or a book, the rest sing, shout, and dance. At four o'clock, dinner is served. Two men wash the dishes, the choir sings, the organ plays. . . . At seven in the evening begins a session of mutual criticism; then the work for the week is assigned.

But, for all this communal culture and rejoicing at the organ in the religion of Positivism, the central fact of life at New Odessa was hard, grinding toil—and a monotony and oppressiveness that soon became worse than that. For, quite naturally under the circumstances, "a lot of trouble arose over sexual matters," according to Abraham Cahan, who was soon to hear the group's story. "There were various instances of jealousy," he explains: most of the members were "single young men. There were too few girls. The result was several love entanglements, some out in the open, others not." The situation was aggravated by the general lack of privacy. "When anyone wanted to be alone, even for a short time," Cahan continues,

> this was not easily accomplished. The single men all slept together in a barn. Each married couple had a separate room, but they were unable to have complete privacy there. Let them try to spend a few hours together in their room apart from the others; suddenly one of the members walks in with a book and sits at their table to read. He is asked nicely to find another place. But he protests in the name of communism. The room belongs just as much to him as to them, he says, and their request that he leave it is a violation of communist ideals.

Frey's religion of Positivism also caused a division between its adherents and its opponents. It advocated vegetarianism, which hardly was popular among the nonadherents. Moreover, not everyone enjoyed Frey's singing and organ-playing. Paul Kaplan, the group's nominal leader, would stand apart during these sessions with a sardonic smile on his face, thereby "spoiling the happy mood of the other members."

In November 1887, after more than half the members—including Frey and his family—had already given up, Kaplan and the few that had remained left New Odessa and returned to New York. By this time, Crémieux and a nearby Am Olam colony in South Dakota had also failed. Nor had a few scattered attempts made in Texas and elsewhere succeeded. Only the colonies in southern New Jersey had survived and were expanding.

The Palestine colonies, which were proliferating as well as expanding, had been doing far better, thanks mainly to the continuing attention and support of Baron Edmond de Rothschild. But the American Jewish colonization, if it had not found its Baron, had at least found its bard. These somewhat Whitmanesque lines had appeared in the March 1887 issue of *The Century:*

1. Vast oceanic movements, the flux and reflux of immeasurable tides oversweep our continent.
2. From the far Caucasian steppes, from the squalid Ghettos of Europe,
3. From Odessa and Bucharest, from Kief and Ekaterinoslav,
4. Hark to the cry of the exiles of Babylon, the voice of Rachel mourning for her children, of Israel lamenting for Zion.
5. And lo, like a turbid stream, the long-pent flood bursts the dykes of oppression and rushes hitherward.
6. Unto her ample breast, the generous mother of nations welcomes them.
7. The herdsman of Canaan and the seed of Jerusalem's royal shepherd renew their youth amid the pastoral plains of Texas and the golden valleys of the Sierras.

They were among the last lines Emma Lazarus would write.

·17·

MOTHER OF EXILES

It was in 1883 that Emma Lazarus had made her principal bid for immortality, by identifying her poetry with a world-famous symbol of the immigrants whose cause she had espoused. Indeed, she had been among the first to perceive what that monument symbolized.

Working their way through scale models of increasing size, and with a steel frame designed by Gustave Eiffel—who was soon to build a monumental structure of his own—Frédéric Auguste Bartholdi and his assistants at the Paris foundry of Gaget-Gauthier had painstakingly bolted copper plate to copper plate to complete, by the fall of 1883, a figure of "Liberty Enlightening the World" that stood 151 feet above the Rue de Chazelles, a little more than half a mile to the northeast of the Arc de Triomphe. This was the triumph of a French vision that reached back a hundred years to the Enlightenment and encompassed the revolutionary and Napoleonic ideals that ensued. It now was to be the bequest of that tradition to the American democracy; in the words of its first sponsor, Edouard René de Laboulaye, a distinguished legal scholar and admirer of the American Constitution: "This Liberty will not be the [French Revolutionary] one wearing a red bonnet on her head, a pike in her hand, who walks on corpses. It will be the American Liberty, who does not hold an incendiary torch but a beacon which enlightens."

The fires of this ideal had cooled somewhat on the American side, however. According to the agreement whereby the statue was to stand in New York harbor as a gift from France, it was up to the Americans to supply the pedestal, but this was still in doubt when Bartholdi finished his work. An American Committee for the Statue of Liberty had been organized in 1876, but there was a good deal of opposition to the whole idea in the press, especially in New York; and in March 1883,

Congress—which had granted the use of Bedloe's Island as a site—rejected a request for $100,000 toward the erection of the pedestal. The Committee considered abandoning the project, and Philadelphia—soon followed by other cities—offered itself as an alternative home for the statue. Funds had been collected, but not nearly enough.

Then the spirit of the project began to undergo a change of character. This change was above all represented by the entry upon the scene of a new and powerful champion in the statue's cause—Joseph Pulitzer, himself a gift from Europe to the United States. In 1883, he had just arrived in New York, the successful publisher of the Saint Louis *Post-Dispatch*. Taking over the New York *World*, he launched an appeal for support of the statue that year and got little response. But things were to be very different the second time around.

On July 4, 1884, the completed statue in Paris was formally presented to the American Minister there; the following month, the cornerstone for the pedestal—a design by the New England architect Richard Morris Hunt—was laid at Bedloe's Island, after which further construction was stopped for lack of funds. By the beginning of 1885, the Paris statue had been dismantled, and its component copper plates were in crates awaiting shipment to New York. This was the point at which Pulitzer stepped in again.

In two years, the *World*'s circulation had risen from a few thousand to well over a hundred thousand daily and more than two hundred thousand on Sundays. Its readership consisted mainly of ordinary working people, and a substantial portion of them were immigrants, like Pulitzer himself. It was to their democratic instincts that the *World* appealed in a dramatic editorial on the Statue of Liberty that appeared on March 13. "The $250,000 that the making of the statue cost," the editorial said,

> was paid in by the masses of the French people—by the workingmen, the tradesmen, the shop girls, the artisans—by all, irrespective of class or condition. Let us respond in like manner. Let us not wait for the millionaires to give this money. It is not a gift from the millionaires of France to the millionaires of America, but a gift of the whole people of France to the whole people of America.

The *World*, the editorial promised, would collect its readers' contributions and publish the name of every donor, no matter how small the amount given.

The spirit of what ensued was appropriately summed up by the letter of one donor, a recent Jewish immigrant living in New Jersey. "I am a young man of foreign birth," it said, "and have seen enough of monarchical governments to appreciate the blessings of this republic. Inclosed [sic] please find $2.00 for the Bartholdi Fund." Day after day the lists of names appeared, and increasingly the statue came to be a cause for immigrants above all. On August 11, the *World* could announce that it had raised $102,000—$2,000 more than the goal it had proclaimed in March.

Work was resumed on the pedestal, which was completed by April 1886. The assembling of the statue then began, and for six months all who arrived in New York harbor—travelers and immigrants alike—watched the emerging figure of the lady who, more and more, seemed to have been conceived for the specific purpose of welcoming them to American shores. On October 28, 1886, in a grand ceremony attended by President Grover Cleveland among other distinguished Americans, and by Bartholdi among other distinguished Frenchmen, the statue was unveiled to the cheering of crowds on Bedloe's Island and the sounds of horns and whistles from the many boats parading through the harbor.

These lines by John Greenleaf Whittier were read at the ceremony:

> O France, the beautiful! to thee
>   Once more a debt of love we owe:
> In peace beneath thy fleur-de-lis,
>   We hail a later Rochambeau!
> Shine far, shine free, a guiding light
>   To Reason's ways and Virtue's aim,
> A lightning flash the wretch to smite
>   Who shields his license with thy name!

This was an appropriate view of "Liberty Enlightening the World," of the French vision that had originally conceived and made her. But in the passage from early vision to final realization, the Statue of Liberty had really become something else—something that Joseph Pulitzer had adumbrated and that Emma Lazarus, who was traveling in Europe at the time of the dedication ceremony, had fully perceived three years before. In the fall of 1883, when Pulitzer was also becoming enlisted in the statue's cause, Lazarus had been asked by the American Committee for the Statue of Liberty to write a poem for its fund-raising campaign. Composed on November 2, her sonnet, "The New Colossus," was read a month later during a meeting at the National Academy of Design in New York.

Remembering the Colossus that guarded the harbor of Rhodes in ancient times—and that probably had been among the sources of Bartholdi's idea—Lazarus saw the true nature of the contrast between it and the one she was celebrating when she wrote:

> Not like the brazen giant of Greek fame,
> With conquering limbs astride from land to land;

Here at our sea-washed, sunset gates shall stand
A mighty woman with a torch, whose flame
Is the imprisoned lightning, and her name
Mother of Exiles. From her beacon hand
Glows world-wide welcome; her mild eyes command
The air-bridged harbor that twin cities frame.
"Keep, ancient lands, your storied pomp!" cries she
With silent lips. "Give me your tired, your poor,
Your huddled masses yearning to breathe free,
The wretched refuse of your teeming shore,
Send these, the homeless, tempest-tost to me,
I lift my lamp beside the golden door!"

Identifying herself with this image of a maternal, welcoming America—guardian of a Schiff Refuge for all peoples and religions—Emma Lazarus was able in this moment to see in her own hand not just Ezra's "banner of the Jew" but a beacon held aloft for all exiles. In the statue's vision, Lazarus's Hebraic ideal had become a universalist one, that of a prophet for a new age of migration.

She died of cancer in 1887, at only thirty-eight years of age, before she could see her vision of the statue and the world's become fully one and the same. It was not until 1903 that her poem would be inscribed on a plaque and affixed inside the pedestal of the statue for whom it speaks, and with whom it will be identified for all time.

PART FOUR

The Swelling Stream

·1887-1902·

·18·

RUSSIA, 1887-1891:
EXCLUSION AND EXPULSION

The stream of Jewish emigration had subsided in 1883, but only temporarily. A historic force had been set in motion, and though the worldwide system of care and placement that prevailed in 1882 had to some extent broken down, and American immigration rules had been tightened, new factors had emerged to aid and encourage the flow. Small but substantial communities of Yiddish-speaking Jews were now established in New York and London, as well as in other cities of the United States and Canada. For Jews back home, these places were less and less strange, and often enough an immigrant could find a *landsman*—a person from his home town—or even a relative ready to take him in when he arrived. More and more often did men with families emigrate in advance by themselves, to settle into jobs and residences before sending for their wives and children. And in certain cities, whole Jewish economies had come into being—most notably, the burgeoning garment industry of New York—to provide the most available jobs for new arrivals, along with a growing Yiddish culture that gave the immigrant a comforting milieu and a means of orientation to the wider New World.

And as the new worlds became more inviting, the old one in Eastern Europe became correspondingly less tolerable. To be sure, though the waves of anti-Jewish rioting had repeated themselves in the two or three years following 1881, they had diminished in fury, and by early 1885, many could regard them as a thing of the past. For a moment, in fact, it looked as if the government of Alexander III might reform its ways in Jewish matters. Early in 1883, it had appointed a High Commission for the Revision of Current Laws Concerning the Jews—called the Pahlen Commission, after its chairman—which proved to be notably fair in its deliberations. But the presence of the Commission, which was to remain at work for five years, was not sufficient to prevent a new turn in anti-Jewish policies that became quite clear in 1887.

Among the refugees there had always been numbers of young men of military age, who were avoiding conscription by their flight and were dealt with severely when caught. "Why do they so gladly evade military service?" the Tsar had asked Baron Günzburg in 1881; the notion that Jews were especially prone to this was ever to be prominent in the Russian anti-Semitic outlook. Statistics show that the percentage of Russian Jews in uniform was always about the same as their proportion to the population as a whole; on the other hand, emigrant Jewish folklore abounds with tales of toes shot off on purpose and midnight escapes across the border, all in the name of avoiding the dreaded *priziv*. Jews certainly had more grounds for resenting military service than most other Russian subjects. From 1827 until 1856, they—or, at any rate, the poorer and less fortunate among them—had suffered under the cantonist system of Nicholas I, whereby the normal twenty-five years of military service were supplemented in the case of Jewish recruits by six additional years prior to the conscription age of eighteen. In actual practice, this meant that Jewish boys as young as eight or nine were being forced into a brutish army that in no way sympathized with their religious preferences. Since then, the general conditions of military service had been reformed—the term of service, for example, had been vastly reduced—and were not substantially worse for Jews than for Christians. But Jews still could not become officers and faced considerable prejudice in the ranks—and besides, what was it all for when one only returned home afterward to become again a second-class citizen?

Whatever the facts of the case, however, the government in 1887 issued a ruling that applied only to Jews: the entire family of any recruit who failed to report was held responsible for his behavior, and had to pay a fine of 300 rubles.

Then an even worse affliction came that year with the official establishment of the *numerus clausus*, or quota, on all levels of Russian education. This was in some ways the most radical reversal in tsarist policy regarding Jews to have occurred in generations. The main thrust of that policy—for all its contradictions, most notably the enormous mistake known as the Pale of Settlement—had hitherto been assimilatory: Jews as such were disliked and suffered accordingly, but Russified Jews fared better, and converts to Christianity best of all. Even the horrors of the cantonist system had been meant for the sake of assimilation, and the entire educational structure had always been completely open in principle to Jews who wanted to take that route. Education had been an effective assimilator—although, far too often in the eyes of the ruling classes, Russification had meant radicalization for Jewish students.

The frequent radicalization was surely among the reasons for the decision to impose a quota upon Jewish students; but it could not have been the only one. In the general atmosphere of European anti-Semitism in the 1880s, Jews simply were perceived by their enemies—even in Russia, despite widespread and persisting Jewish poverty there—as getting too far too quickly. And education was always one of the areas in which Jewish gifts readily displayed themselves. The *numerus clausus* had already been introduced informally in 1885 and 1886, by means of instructions from the Ministry of Education to the various provincial administrators allowing them to impose quotas as they saw fit. The law of July 1887 formalized this and established quotas for the entire realm. Within the Pale of Settlement, the proportion of Jews in all secondary schools and institutions of higher learning was limited to 10 percent. Outside the Pale, it was to be 5 percent in most places and 3 percent in Moscow and Saint Petersburg.

In these circumstances, the Jewish struggle for a good secular education had to be engaged in arenas other than the scholastic one alone. Bribery was often required. It was not even out of the question for a Jewish family to pay the tuition fee of one or more Christian students in a particular school in order to get a ratio whereby their child could be admitted under the quota.

The classic depiction of this situation is found in Sholom Aleichem's story "Gy-Ma-Na-Si-A," which depicts the struggles of a Jewish father to get his son into a type of school whose name he can't even quite pronounce. Failing after the best efforts—which include not merely the bribing of school officials, but the earning of top entrance marks by the son—to get his boy into the local gymnasium, the father proceeds to look elsewhere, anywhere. "We traveled from one end of the country to the other," he confides. "Wherever there is a city, wherever there is a *Gymnasia*, there we went. We registered him, he took his examinations, he passed with top grades—and he *didn't* get in. Why not? Because of the quota. Always the quota." Finally however, the parents discover

in Poland somewhere, a certain *Gymnasia*, a *komertcheska*, they called it, a business school, where for every Christian they were willing to take in one Jew—a quota of fifty per cent, that is. But here was the catch. Every Jew who wanted to have his son admitted had to bring along with him a Christian boy, and if he passed the examination, this Christian, that is, and if all his fees and expenses were paid, then there was a chance! In other words, you had not one headache, but two.

Though a Christian boy is found, a shoemaker's son, this hardly means the end of troubles. The Christian boy fails the exam the first time

around and has to be coached; his father objects to a school with so
many Jews in it and has to be persuaded; the Jewish mother insists on
moving to the town where her son is going to school; the Jewish father
fails in the business he has been forced to neglect for so long—and, in
the end, the gymnasium boy becomes a revolutionary, taking part in a
strike against the school. Sholom Aleichem thus deftly sums up the
struggles of an entire era.

For many among the student generation, the answer was to give
up on Russia altogether. When Chaim Weizmann reached university
age in 1892, even though he had succeeded in getting a gymnasium
education in Pinsk, he had little doubt of the choice he was then to
make. "All my inclinations," he writes in his memoirs, "pointed to the
West, whither thousands of Russian Jewish students had moved by now,
in a sort of educational stampede." For him and others like him, education in the West meant Germany, Austria, Switzerland, or France.
Few yet thought of the United States as a haven for intellectual fulfill-
ment—and for the strictly religious, it was still a place to be avoided.
Nevertheless, more and more parents of small children were looking to
it as a better horizon for their children's educational and even spiritual
future. Whatever the combination of factors—and though not all Russian-Jewish emigrants were going there, just as not all Jewish immigrants there were from Russia—the years in which the *numerus clausus*
was first tentatively introduced and then fully imposed show a sudden
leap in Jewish immigration into the United States, starting with a new
high of 16,862 in 1885 and ascending to 33,044 and 28,881 in 1887 and
1888 respectively. A small and relatively elite emigration also continued
to Palestine.

By the beginning of the 1890s, Jews were leaving Russia at the
rate of about fifty thousand a year; but their natural increase was then
about a hundred thousand a year, so that they were still populating
Russia faster than they were leaving it. The fact remained that emigration was an arduous and frightening upheaval, and that Russia still was
home, the overall quality of life there even improving for many Jews in
spite of all the setbacks and disasters.

But the better-off and the better-educated were in for a new series
of shocks. In 1888, the Pahlen Commission was dissolved, and none of
its relatively liberal recommendations were accepted. Then, the following year, the relatively fair-minded Count Tolstoy died, and was replaced at the Ministry of the Interior by I. N. Durnovo, with Vyacheslav
von Plehve as his assistant—two reactionaries of notably anti-Semitic
views. These were preludes to the disaster of 1891.

By that year, Moscow had a Jewish population of about thirty thousand, some of them illegal according to the rules of Jewish residency,
but the great majority living there as of rights that had become estab-

lished under Alexander II. Not only were Jews of the wealthiest category permitted, but also artisans, students, and military veterans. In
the course of some two decades, this policy had vindicated itself in the
lively contribution Jews had made to the economic life of the ancient
capital—a fact well appreciated by Governor-General Dolgurokov, who
had been appointed to the Moscow post by Alexander II. Then suddenly, in February 1891, Dolgurokov was replaced by the brother of
Alexander III, the Grand Duke Sergey, and troubled rumors began. It
was thought that the Tsar, influenced by the Slavophilism of some of
his advisers, was planning to remove the throne from the would-be European capital that Peter the Great had built on the Baltic and bring it
back to Moscow. It soon became apparent that the Tsar and his brother
felt it necessary to precede this act with certain rites of purification.

It was on March 28, the first day of Passover—that annual season
of Jewish tribulations in Russia—that the following edict was published
in the city:

> Jewish mechanics, distillers, brewers, and, in general, master
> workmen and artisans shall be forbidden to remove from the Jewish
> Pale of Settlement as well as to come over from other places of the
> Empire to the City and Government of Moscow.

An era of salutary permissiveness clearly was being brought to an end;
but otherwise the announcement was ambiguous. Did it mean that Jews
in the stated categories already settled in Moscow could feel secure?
There was hope that it did—until the next day, at any rate. On March
29, a supplement to the edict appeared:

> A recommendation should be made to the Minister of the In-
> terior, after consultation with the Governor-General of Moscow, to
> see to it that measures be taken to the effect that the above-men-
> tioned Jews should gradually depart from the City and Government
> of Moscow into the places established for the permanent residence
> of the Jews.

Yet some ambiguity remained: didn't "above-mentioned Jews" refer to
those who had not yet come to settle?

It did not. That very night a cordon of police, firemen, and Cossacks
led by General Yurkovsky surrounded the Jewish settlement in the Zar-
yadye quarter of the city. This was where about half the Jews of Moscow lived—including virtually all the "illegals" and most of the
population of Jewish poor that had grown in spite of everything. In
principle, the object of the raid was to weed out the "illegals" for immediate expulsion; but that was not the way it was in fact handled.

"Under Yourkoffsky's personal supervision," according to Harold Frederic, a *New York Times* correspondent,

> the whole quarter was ransacked, apartments forced open, doors smashed, every bedroom without exception searched, and every living soul, men, women, and children, routed out for examination as to their passports. . . .
> As a result, over 700 men, women and children were dragged at dead of night through the streets to the . . . police stations. They were not even given time to dress themselves, and they were kept in this noisome and overcrowded confinement for thirty-six hours, almost all without food, and some without water as well. Of these unhappy people, . . . some were afterward marched away by *étape*, that is, chained together with criminals and forced along the roads by Cossacks.

The latter were summarily shipped to the Pale.

The more prosperous of the city's Jewish artisans—those who, though originally registered under that category, had gone on to found flourishing businesses—were given from three months to a year to leave, the difference often depending on their ability to bribe the authorities. Their lot was exemplified by that of "H.P."—one of scores of Muscovite Jews interviewed that year by two Americans, J. B. Weber and Walter Kempster, who had been sent by the U.S. government to investigate the causes of immigration from Eastern Europe. A fur manufacturer, "H.P." had been in Moscow fourteen years, was one of the pioneers of his industry in Russia, and had fifty employees, all of them Christians. But, despite his wealth and wide reputation, he was registered as an artisan—a Jewish one—and therefore had to leave.

"I could stay here and continue my business if I was willing to be baptized," he told his American interviewers,

> but this would be to violate my conscience and my honor. Without conscience or honor, I could not succeed in anything. I don't believe that God constrains men to any particular form of worship. I respect all religions, and believe that the differences are necessary to the advancement of civilization; but every man has the moral right to remain loyal to his own convictions.

As for the rights he sought, they were not much to ask for in the ears of two Americans. "I neither demand nor require the rights of the nobility," he assured them:

> what I would like are simply the rights of those drunken peasants you see sleeping on the street. When I try to complain, I am told:

You are a Jew. If I break the law, then punish me; but don't punish me if I haven't done anything wrong. . . . I have earned a reputation for uprightness; I have been able to raise as much as 200,000 rubles in loans for my factory. I have a right to be proud of these proofs of confidence in me. But now my capital and stock are done for because I am a Jew. I have ruined no one; on the contrary, I have helped many poor people, because I have never forgotten that I was poor myself when I came to Moscow.

Some of those in this situation were to seek new homes in the Pale and in Russian Poland, but others were determined to go on to Britain and the United States. By the end of the following year, only some ten thousand Jews—a third of the 1890 population—were left in Moscow.

"As Moscow is the heart, the core of the real Russia," wrote Harold Frederic, "so her treatment of Jews during the terrible year 1891 most truly typifies the persecution throughout the empire." To bring this point home, Frederic offered a translation of a letter written to the Tsar on May 15, 1891, by Israel Deyel, a Jewish corporal in the army reserves, who had been living in Moscow. "Most Serene, Mighty, and Exalted Sire and Emperor, Alexander Alexandrovitch, Autocrat of all the Russias, Most Gracious Father," it begins:

> We, most faithful subjects, reserved Jewish soldiers and under-officers, venture to lay at the feet of your Imperial Majesty our most humble petition not to extend to us the Law of 28th March of this year, touching the transportation of Jewish artisans from Moscow and the Government of Moscow, and not to subject us, soldiers, both artisans and nonartisans, to removal from these places.
>
> May it please your Imperial Majesty to have your most gracious attention drawn to the fact that the above-mentioned Law, subjecting thousands of poor Jews to utter ruin, must press with special harshness and injustice upon us soldiers, who have borne your Majesty's Imperial service, and who, at the first call of their country, must advance again to serve Throne and Fatherland.

Corporal Deyel, for all his humility of tone, does not now hesitate to press the point. "A non-Jewish soldier," he continues,

> when going forth to fight and die for his Fatherland, may find strength in the trust that the dear ones he leaves behind will be watched over by the community, and receive the paternal care of the Government, and the generous favor of the monarch. But a Jewish soldier has to face death for his Fatherland with the bitter consciousness that it has separated him as an outcast from all the other children, humiliated him, and by its laws has deprived him of

the means to decently exist himself, and to provide for the family he leaves behind.

He concludes with the "humble prayer" that

our Fatherland render us justice, and your Imperial Majesty show his exalted grace, to the end that all reserved and retired Jewish soldiers and under-officers, whether they be artisans or not, may graciously be granted the right to live unreservedly through the empire.

Corporal Deyel was sent to jail for his impertinence.

·19·

IN THE NEW CURRENT

"The measures now being enforced against the Jews which are equivalent to their wholesale expulsion," said an article in the August 1891 issue of the American journal *The Forum*,

> do not appear to me to be altogether a misfortune to the Russian Jew. I think that the worst thing that could happen to these unfortunate people would be to continue for an indefinite period the wretched existence which they have led up to the present time, crowded together in narrow streets, merely vegetating without hope and without a future, reduced to a condition incompatible with the dignity of human beings. The only means to raise their condition is to remove them from the soil to which they are rooted and to transport them to other countries, where they will enjoy the same rights as the people among whom they live and where they will cease to be pariahs, and become citizens. What is going on in Russia today may be the prelude to their beneficent transformation.

This lordly opinion was not being idly expressed; the writer was Baron Maurice de Hirsch of Paris, who had continued to involve himself in the cause of the Russian-Jewish emigrants since his first donation to it of 1 million francs in 1881, and who was now about to create a project for them of far more gigantic cost.

Moritz von Hirsch had been born in Munich in 1831 to a Jewish banking family that had been wealthy for three generations. His grandfather Jacob Hirsch had been court banker to the Bavarian crown and awarded a baronial title for his service. Hirsch's mother had come from another banking family, the Wertheimers. After young Moritz settled in Brussels—where he Gallicized his first name—and went to work for the banking house of Bischoffsheim and Goldschmidt, he married Clara

149

Bischoffsheim. In the ensuing years, he went on to amass a fortune all his own, gradually shifting his main activities to railroad-building and taking a prominent part in the great extension of track then going on in southeastern Europe and Turkey under the aegis of the Austro-Hungarian and Ottoman empires. He moved to Paris, then—after his only child, Lucien, died in 1888 at the age of thirty-one—devoted more and more of his time and resources to philanthropy. It was in 1888 that he had offered 50 million francs ($10 million) for the establishment in Russia of agricultural settlements, workshops, and arts-and-crafts schools for Jews; but when the Russian government demanded complete control of the money, he had withdrawn the offer.

In the wake of that unrealized project, Hirsch had begun to interest himself in Jewish agricultural settlement in the New World. But, assuming that there was relatively little land left in the United States for such purposes, he set his eyes upon Argentina. In 1887, Julio Roca, the President of that still largely unsettled and fertile country, had sent agents to the Pale of Settlement to encourage Jews to colonize the Entre Ríos province as farmers, on what they were told would be easy terms. A favorable response had come from about 130 Jewish families in Kamenets-Podolsk, who were then transported from Odessa by the Alliance Israélite Universelle. Once they arrived, however, they found themselves completely without the wherewithal to establish themselves on the land, and were reduced to beggary. This was the condition in which they were discovered in 1889 by Professor Wilhelm Loewenthal of the University of Lausanne, a sanitary engineer who had been sent by Baron de Hirsch to examine possible sites for colonization. Loewenthal gave them money and told the Baron about them when he returned to Europe in March 1891.

Hirsch not only sent them financial aid, but decided to treat them as the nucleus of the project that now took full shape in his mind in the wake of the renewed persecutions in Russia. In the fall of 1891, he established a stock company in London called the Jewish Colonization Association, with a capitalization of 50 million francs, the amount he had offered for the thwarted project in Russia three years before. Through this company he proposed to transplant twenty-five thousand Russian Jews to Argentina in 1892, and then increase the number progressively, so that, at the end of twenty-five years, a population of 3.25 million would have been resettled there. The Russian government, once again eager to be rid of the Jewish poor, was so gratified at the proposal that it even considered offering a small bonus for each person thus resettled.

The Jewish Colonization Association acquired well over a million acres in Entre Ríos, and settled the Kamenets-Podolsk families and other new arrivals in three settlements—Moisésville named for the leader of the original Exodus, and Mauricio and Clara, named for the leader of this one and his wife. But with the United States an increasingly viable prospect for Jewish emigrants, few of them were attracted to the Argentine wilderness. In 1892, not twenty-five thousand but more like twenty-five hundred Russian Jews went to Argentina under Hirsch's auspices, and about half of them stayed in Buenos Aires. The numbers were to grow smaller. Indeed, at the very brink of his project, even the Baron had been persuaded to hedge his bets and divert some of his resources to the United States. At the beginning of 1891, a group of American-Jewish philanthropists—including Jacob Schiff and several former officers of the Hebrew Emigrant Aid Society—had asked him to endorse the work that had been begun by Michael Heilprin, who had died in 1888. The result was that, in February 1891, the Baron de Hirsch Fund, with an endowment of $2.4 million, had been established in New York. Later that year, the enduring agricultural settlements in southern New Jersey were joined by the new Hirsch colony of Woodbine.

There was little evading the United States fever of the day. " 'America' was in everybody's mouth," wrote the memoirist Mary Antin of the scene in her native Polotzk in 1891:

> Business men talked of it over their accounts; the market women made up their quarrels that they might discuss it from stall to stall; people who had relatives in the famous land went around reading their letters for the enlightenment of less fortunate folks; the one letter-carrier informed the public how many letters arrived from America, and who were the recipients; children played at emigrating; old folks shook their sage heads over the evening fire, and prophesied no good for those who braved the terrors of the sea and the foreign goal beyond it. . . .

She tells of how, at the end of that year's Passover seder, the traditional cry of "Next year in Jerusalem" was replaced or supplemented in many homes by "Next year—in America." Her own father left that year for the famous land, to get started before sending for his wife and children. He was one of 111,284 Jewish immigrants to reach the United States in 1891—a new enormous leap provoked by the expulsion from Moscow. The impact of that expulsion had been felt with particular intensity in the northwestern provinces of the Pale, into which the Moscow refugees poured in large numbers. Polotzk got hundreds of them, says Mary Antin, "bringing their trouble where trouble was never absent, mingling their tears with tears that never dried."

For this and other reasons, the emigration fever moved from south to north at the beginning of the nineties, and it was now the turn of the "Litvaks"—the Jews of the six northwestern provinces of Lithuania and

White Russia—to provide the principal energies of movement across the Atlantic. For the most part, they were in humbler circumstances and less assimilated to Russian culture than their coreligionists to the southeast, where the Palestinian idea had originated and was now taking greater hold. "The Palestine movement," wrote a Kiev correspondent in the July 24, 1891, issue of *The American Hebrew*, "has its most fervent adherents in the southern provinces—in those of Poltava, Ekaterinoslav, Kiev, Kherson and Odessa—while the American exodus comes from Lithuania and the Polish provinces." But the Palestine exodus was still only a trickle; the Antins of Vitebsk province were joining a flooding stream.

In the spring of 1894, when she was thirteen, Mary Antin set out with her mother and three sisters to be reunited with their father in Boston. They traveled through Vilna, headed for Eydtkühnen, just across the border in East Prussia. "Mechanically," wrote Harold Frederic of a scene he observed at this border in 1892, the emigrants

> obey the train officials who at the Russian terminus order them out of the cars. The men drag out the big hempen bags and boxes which they have had with them, and cluster about the baggage vans to watch for the appearance of their other chattels. The women and children huddle together on the platform, looking with furtive fright upon the strange new scene. At last all are passed through the station building and emerge at the other side upon another platform, where an empty train is drawn up. On these carriages are painted German words; the trainmen wear a novel uniform and have their trousers outside their boot-legs.

Then, according to Frederic, a "curious thing" happens:

> There are Russian soldiers, with a non-commissioned officer, stationed at every carriage door. Each male Jew must now show his passport bearing the police stamp of permission to leave the empire, and explicitly stating the size and personnel of his family. He has had to spend money, and sometimes weeks of time, to secure the permission. If now there is any informality about it, or if the examining sergeant or gendarme chooses to suspect one, the Jew is roughly put to one side, perhaps to be detained at the local prison, perhaps to be sent back to the hole whence he is fleeing.

Clearly, the border passage at Eydtkühnen in 1892, dominated as it was by the Prussian rigor, was more difficult than the one at Brody had been ten years before, where Russian indifference had reigned in alliance with the Austrian *Schlamperei*. In the case of the Antin women two years later, it was harder still, for there had been a cholera epidemic in 1893, and there was much precaution as a result. In their case, it was German gendarmes who entered the train on the Russian side of the border. A German physician put them through

> a searching examination as to our health, destination, and financial resources. As a result of the inquisition we were informed that we would not be allowed to cross the frontier unless we exchanged our third-class steamer tickets for second-class, which would require two hundred rubles more than we possessed. Our passport was taken from us, and we were to be turned back on our journey.

The German officials may have been adding corruption to rigor: at this time, permission to pass through Germany was being granted to emigrants on condition that they held steamship tickets for a German line, but there was no general requirement as to class. The German doctor may have decided that a family of five women should have a stateroom of their own for reasons of hygiene or propriety, or he may simply have had connections with the Hamburg-America line.

The women were reduced to despair. In Germany there were emigration committees to help in situations like this—there was one right across the border in Eydtkühnen—but what could they do in a forlorn Russian frontier village? Some of the German officers took pity on them and suggested they go see a certain Herr Schidorsky, a prominent Jewish resident of the nearby town of Kibart. As it turned out, Schidorsky could help them: his brother was chairman of the Eydtkühnen committee. In three days of using family connections, during which the Antins stayed at his house, he obtained permission for them to cross.

In principle, from the moment they crossed into Germany, the Russian-Jewish emigrants of that time were in the charge of its charitable Jewish organizations. The Alliance Israélite Universelle and the Mansion House Fund having faded from the picture with the passing of the crisis of 1882, Germany—from which many more ships were now sailing the whole way across the Atlantic—had in fact become the European crux of the emigration movement. As far back as the Berlin Jewish conference of April 1882, a Central Committee had been established in the German capital to supervise a network of emigration committees throughout the country. In May 1891, this Committee was reorganized, and took upon itself and its affiliates the task not only of facilitating the emigrants' journey from frontier town to port, but of examining them as to their fitness to pass American immigration rules. For this reason, the affiliates had come to be known as *Sichtungskomitees* (examination committees). To many emigrants, they proved to be only slightly less upsetting than the German frontier authorities.

As it happened, the Antins were spared the rigors of the Eydtkühnen *Sichtungskomitee* when they crossed—though this was to be only a temporary respite. Meanwhile, the scene at the Eydtkühnen station was chaos. "There was a terrible confusion in the baggage-room where we were directed to go," Mary writes:

> Boxes, baskets, bags, valises, and great, shapeless things belonging to no particular class were thrown about by porters and other men, who sorted them and put tickets on all but those containing provisions, while others were opened and examined in haste. At last our turn came, and our things, along with those of all other American-bound travellers, were taken away to be steamed and smoked and other such processes gone through.

"One of the unfortunate consequences of this eagerness on the frontier ... to at all hazards keep the exodus moving," Frederic wrote,

> is that very little inquiry is made there as to the fitness of the people for emigration. They are sent on to Berlin and Hamburg, where the local committees must bear the responsibility of detaining and sending back the worthless ones, and of deciding what the others are good for and where they are to go.

This is the unpleasant discovery the Antins were to make.

After a day and a night in a packed train sitting on their luggage, the Antins arrived at Berlin—though not quite in it. For Mary, it was just a whirl of fleeting images of shops, crowds, and passing trains seen from her own train's windows, since the emigrants, in Frederic's words, "are not allowed to enter Berlin, but are conveyed around the outskirts of the capital by the Ringbahn to Ruhleben, and thence, after an hour's inspection and rest, are sent westward." Mary writes of this:

> In a great lonely field, opposite a solitary wooden house within a large yard, our train pulled up at last, and a conductor commanded the passengers to make haste and get out. He need not have told us to hurry; we were glad enough to be free again after such a long imprisonment in the uncomfortable car. All rushed to the door. We breathed more freely in the open field, but the conductor did not wait for us to enjoy our freedom. He hurried us into the one large room which made up the house, and then into the yard. Here a great many men and women, dressed in white, received us, the women attending to the women and girls of the passengers, and the men to the others.

"At Ruhleben," according to Frederic's more sanguine account, some members of the committee are present whenever one of these Jewish refugee trains arrives. Every immigrant is given a cup of sweetened tea and a roll of *kosher* bread upon coming out of the carriage—the children getting milk instead of tea. On their departure—generally an hour or so later—each is given a bowl of peasoup and more bread. A physician is also constantly in attendance.

But Mary Antin could only recall a scene of

bewildering confusion, parents losing their children, and little ones crying; baggage being thrown together in one corner of the yard, heedless of contents, which suffered in consequence; those white-clad Germans shouting commands always accompanied with "Quick! Quick!"; the confused passengers obeying all orders like meek children, only questioning now and then what was going to be done with them.

"Pathetic stories were told me in Berlin," Harold Frederic concedes, after his interviews with the *Sichtungskomitee,*

of the terror and ignorance of the earlier refugees, who came shortly after the fierce Passover persecutions [of 1891]. The committee had arranged with the railroad authorities for the use of a disused tunnel in which to feed and examine the exiles during the halt at Ruhleben. The panic-stricken wretches could with difficulty be brought to comprehend that at last they were among friends. They were afraid to eat the food set before them for fear it was not *kosher;* they fought against giving up their tickets, to be exchanged for others; especially they were terrified at being compelled to enter the tunnel, which seemed to them like another Russian prison. Some were found who, at the sight of this, suspected that they had been brought to Siberia instead of Germany. One woman, rather than go into the tunnel, snatched up her two babes, and, screaming as she ran, leaped upon the track before an advancing train, and was reached at great risk by a veritable hair's breadth.

To Mary, though spared the anxieties of the tunnel, it was no wonder

if in some mind stories arose of people being captured by robbers, murderers and the like. Here we had been taken to a lonely place where only that house was to be seen; our things were taken away, our friends separated from us; a man came to inspect us, as if to ascertain our full value; strange looking people driving us about like dumb animals, helpless and unresisting; children we could not see, crying in a way that suggested terrible things; ourselves driven into a little room where a great kettle was boiling on a little stove; our bodies rubbed with a slippery substance that might be

any bad thing; a shower of warm water let down on us without
warning; again driven to another little room where we sit, wrapped
in woollen blankets till large, coarse bags are brought in, their contents turned out and we see only a cloud of steam, and hear the
women's orders to dress ourselves, quick, quick, or else we'll miss—
something we cannot hear. We are forced to pick out our clothes
from among all the others, with the steam blinding us; we choke,
cough, entreat the women to give us time; they persist, "Quick
quick, or you'll miss the train!"

Then they are off to Hamburg.

"About eight o'clock we reached Hamburg," Mary continues. Of
the Hamburg Committee, Frederic writes: "One of the most significant
features of their work is the cordial assistance it has from the police
and Stadt authorities. The two cooperate as if they were parts of a
single body." The Antins were again confronted by

a gendarme to ask questions, look over the tickets and give directions. But all the time he kept a distance from those passengers
who came from Russia, all for fear of the cholera. We had noticed
before how people were afraid to come near us, but since that mem-
orable bath at Berlin, and all the steaming and smoking of our
things, it seemed unnecessary.

"After their reception at the station," Frederic continues, "the
tickets given them at the frontier are examined, or new ones given
them, and records made of all the names, and other particulars. They
are then allotted to certain lodging-houses, with which contracts have
been made." Mary was both fascinated and frightened by the journey
to her lodgings: fascinated at seeing a large Western city at last—with
its "splendid houses, stone and brick, and showy shops," and, most
amazing of all, an electric trolley car—but frightened at the way they
had been packed onto a high open wagon, looking "like a flock of giant
fowls roosting, only wide awake. . . . Something made me think of a
description I had read of criminals being carried on long journeys in
uncomfortable things—like this?" Even more depressing was the end of
the ride, "in front of a brick building, the only one on a large, broad
street, where only the trees, and, in the distance, the passing trains can
be seen. Nothing else."

"Small *Sichtungskomitees* sit nightly," Harold Frederic had written of the Hamburg lodginghouses, "and pass upon every individual
case of the thousands presented. Such help as is necessary is extended."
Mary and her family, after being ushered into the brick building and
down a corridor, had a less than helpful experience in the

small office where a man sat before a desk covered with papers. These he pushed aside when we entered, and called us in one by one, except, of course, children. As usual, many questions were asked, the new ones being about our tickets. Then each person, children included, had to pay three marks—one for the wagon that brought us over and two for food and lodgings, till our various ships should take us away.

Mary's mother was expected to pay 15 marks, but by now she had no more than 12 in her possession:

The man in the office wouldn't believe it, and we were given over in charge of a woman in a dark gray dress and long white apron, with a red cross on her right arm. She led us away and thoroughly searched us all, as well as our baggage. . . . When the woman reported the result of the search as being fruitless, the man was satisfied, and we were ordered with the rest through many more examinations and ceremonies before we should be established under the quarantine, for that it was.

After a doctor's examination, they were sent to "Number Five," one of several low buildings in a long yard. On the inside, it

looked something like a hospital, only less clean and comfortable; more like the soldiers' barracks I had seen. I saw a very large room, around whose walls were ranged rows of high iron double bedsteads, with coarse sacks stuffed with something like matting, and not over-clean blankets for the only bedding, except where people used their own. There were three windows almost touching the roof, with nails covering all the framework. From the ceiling hung two round gas lamps, and almost under them stood a little wooden table and a settee. The floor was of stone.

Mary and her family "had no idea how long this unattractive place might be our home." It was to be their home for two weeks.

As for food, Frederic had written that "a generous midday meal is furnished at the Jewish soup kitchen." He had seen

a half dozen members of the committee here each day, superintending the affair. When the thick pea-broth had been handed about, two of these committeemen stepped forward with bowls and tasted it. Then, as by a signal, the hungry people hastened to eat. They had been waiting for this proof that the soup was prepared in *kosher* fashion. . . . The bread was all in small rolls, each of which had pasted on the crust a little paper *kosher* label.

Frederic also saw each refugee being given "one-third of a pound of meat, with potatoes and greens." Looking into an adjoining storeroom, he saw "barrels of peas, of flour and of sugar. I noted with curiosity that these were all of the most expensive variety."

The Antins, along with everyone else in Number Five, rushed out "in less than a minute" when the call came for dinner, which was being served in the yard. "In the middle of the yard," Mary recalled,

> stood a number of long tables covered in white oilcloth. On either side of each table stood benches on which all the Jewish passengers were now seated, looking impatiently at the door with the sign "Jewish kitchen" over it. Pretty soon a man appeared in the doorway, tall, spare, with a thin, pointed beard, and an air of importance on his face. It was ... the overseer, who carried a large tin pail filled with black bread cut into pieces of half a pound each. He gave a piece to every person, the youngest child and the biggest man alike, and then went into the kitchen and filled his pail with soup and meat, giving everybody a great bowl full of soup and a small piece of meat. All attacked their rations as soon as they received them and greatly relished the coarse bread and dark, hot water they called soup. We couldn't eat those things and only wondered how any one could have such an appetite for such a dinner.

They learned why that evening and the next morning, when both supper and breakfast consisted only of "two little rolls and a large cup of partly sweetened tea."

For two weeks, the main recurring event "was the arrival of some ship to take some of the waiting passengers." For steerage passengers, this was on a first-come, first-served basis. "When the gates were opened and the lucky ones said goodbye, those left behind felt hopeless of ever seeing the gates open for them." At last the Antins' turn came, one day late in April, during Passover, when they boarded the German steamship *Polynesia*.

In steerage, Mary and her family experienced seven days of seasickness; but then they were up and about, spending as much time as possible on deck, where the atmosphere was friendly and cheerful, and "the sailors and girls had a good many dances." There was some rough sea, but on the seventeenth day out, everyone gathered in excited anticipation. It was a glorious day in May; then: "Oh joyful sight! We saw the tops of two trees!" There was a general shout. Soon steamers and boats were passing by in all directions, and men stood up in them, waving their hats. "Oh, what a beautiful scene!" Mary wrote of the shore north of Boston. "No corner of the earth is half so fair as the lovely picture before us. It came to view suddenly—a green field, a real field with grass on it, and large houses, and the dearest hens and little chickens in all the world, and trees, and birds, and people at work." Soon they saw the wharves of Boston. "One of us," Mary records,

> espied the figure and face we had longed to see for three long years. In a moment five passengers on the "Polynesia" were crying, "Papa," and gesticulating, and laughing, and hugging one another, and going wild together. All the rest were roused by our excitement, and came to see our father.

·20·

REBUILDING THE GATE

But there was a final agony to be endured before one's feet could actually touch the ground. "What followed was slow torture," Mary Antin writes after recording the first happy sight of her father waiting on shore. "Why so many ceremonies at the landing?" The "ceremonies" were the rituals of the American immigration authorities. Actually, Mary's ship had been met by a little steamer while still at sea, and from it had boarded several men who proceeded to give a medical examination, checking to see that all passengers had been vaccinated—as Mary, her mother, and her sisters had been during the voyage. Now, at Boston itself, came the turn of the customs officials. "Each person was asked a hundred or so stupid questions, and all their answers were written down by a very slow man. The baggage had to be examined, the tickets, and a hundred other things done before anyone was allowed to step ashore." Mary could only reflect on the irony of having to wait like this, after all they had been through, only a few yards away from the man down on the dock for whom they had done it all, "unable to even speak to him easily." But then:

> Oh, it's our turn at last! We are questioned, examined, and dismissed! A rush over the planks on one side, over the ground on the other, six wild beings cling to each other, bound by a common bond of tender joy, and the long parting is at an END.

Frustrating as it was at Boston, however, the situation was worse in New York. It was, to be sure, the most dramatic. "The last day of our journey comes vividly to my mind," wrote Emma Goldman, a Jewish native of Lithuania, of her arrival in New York in 1886 at the age of seventeen:

160

Everybody was on deck. [My sister] Helena and I stood pressed to each other, enraptured by the sight of the harbor and the Statue of Liberty suddenly emerging from the mist. Ah, there she was, the symbol of hope, of freedom, of opportunity! She held her torch high to light the way to the free country, the asylum for the oppressed of all lands. We, too, Helena and I, would find a place in the generous heart of America. Our spirits were high, our eyes filled with tears.

But if the gateway had been gloriously embellished by Bartholdi's female colossus, the harshness of landing there was as bad as ever. "Gruff voices broke in on our reverie," Emma Goldman recalled:

We were surrounded by gesticulating people—angry men, hysterical women, screaming children. Guards roughly pushed us hither and thither, shouted orders to get ready, to be transferred to Castle Garden. . . .

She found the scene at Castle Garden "appalling, the atmosphere charged with antagonism and harshness. Nowhere could one see a sympathetic official face; there was no provision for the comfort of new arrivals, the pregnant women and young children."

The gravity of conditions at Castle Garden and the reasons for it had not been lost upon the Federal authorities. In the decade preceding 1890, 5,246,613 immigrants had entered the United States—almost double the number that had entered from 1871 to 1880, and about two-thirds the number that had entered during the entire period from 1820 to 1880. Congress, responding to the Supreme Court ruling of 1876 that immigration could not be controlled by the separate states, had finally made a decisive move in 1882, placing immigration entirely in federal hands and tightening the rules for entry. Nativist reaction to the influx began rapidly rising in 1882; in fact, its worst manifestation that year was the Chinese Exclusion Act, which barred further entry of the people who had for years been providing the major work force in the Western states. A separate immigration act in the same year showed some of the same spirit by forbidding entry not only to all convicts, lunatics, and idiots, but also to persons "likely to become a public charge"—a rather elastic category that was to be an excuse for increasing severity for decades to come.

Another important modification of the immigration rules had come in 1885, when the Foran Act—in response to lobbying by the increasingly organized labor movement of the United States—banned the importation of "contract labor." From then on, no unskilled worker (the rule did not apply to professionals) could enter the country if a specific job, other than one offered by relatives, was awaiting him. But the implications of the act's language went further: by making it unlawful "to assist or encourage the importation or migration of aliens" under such conditions, the act made it possible for the authorities to rule against all "assisted immigration." Money or tickets could no longer be provided to immigrants by anyone but themselves or their relatives. Gone was the old charitable international system of the emigration of 1881 and 1882. There was still work for the network of European committees to do, in the way of advising, screening, and providing accommodations through the stages of the emigrants' journey; moreover, they could still subsidize people who were going to other countries. But they could not openly provide cash to their America-bound charges, lest the beneficiaries be sent summarily back across the ocean.

The process of centralization was completed in 1891, when Congress passed a law establishing a Bureau of Immigration under the aegis of the Treasury Department. The law tightened regulations further. Steamship companies were now held responsible for any ineligible immigrants they brought and were required to carry back free of charge anyone who was rejected. And Congress addressed itself to the Castle Garden problem. A congressional committee had examined conditions there the previous year and found them most unsatisfactory. Immediate replacement was recommended, and Castle Garden was shut down; pending the establishment of a new site, the Barge Office, a short distance away at the Battery, served as the immigrant clearing house.

The location of Castle Garden on the New York mainland, where exploiters could wait for immigrants as they stepped out the gate, impelled a search for a new site among the islands of the harbor. One was found near the Jersey shore, just to the northeast of Bedloe's Island, virtually in the shadow of the Statue of Liberty: it was a three-acre sandbank that the Indians had called Gull Island. Purchased by the Governor of New Amsterdam in 1634, it then became a favorite site for oystering and was known as Oyster Island to the Dutch. After going through a succession of private owners, it ended up in the possession of the heirs of one Samuel Ellis, who sold it in 1808 to New York State, which in turn sold it to the federal government to be the site of a fort. Called Fort Gibson, the federal military installation had seen little action, and it was abandoned by the army in the 1860s; but the navy, which had established a powder magazine there in 1835, continued to use it for that purpose down to 1890.

Congress appropriated $150,000 for construction of the new immigration station on Ellis Island; by the time it opened on January 1, 1892, the cost of building it had mounted to $500,000. Nor was this yet the massive brick-and-limestone complex known to later generations. The first buildings of the Ellis Island immigration center, constructed on an iron framework, were of buff-painted Georgia pine with roofs of slate.

The two-story main building was about four hundred feet long and 150 feet wide, with four-story peaked towers at each of its corners and two smaller towers straddling the harbor entranceway: it was described in its day as a "ramshackle pavilion," looking a bit like a drab and massive seaside-resort hotel. Nearby were smaller wooden buildings, including a hospital, a dormitory for detainees, a bathhouse, and a power plant. Some of these structures had been converted from the old facilities of Fort Gibson and the naval powder magazine. There also were residences for officials who lived on the Island.

As at Castle Garden—which was soon turned into the New York Aquarium—the Ellis Island routine began with the boarding of all incoming passenger ships in the harbor by inspectors from the Immigration Bureau. "As the vessels proceed to their docks," said a *New York Times* article of January 1897,

> the passenger lists are examined by the inspectors. Cabin passengers' tickets and declarations are scrutinized as well as steerage passengers' and if any cabin passenger is thought to be a person who comes within the restrictive clauses of the law he is compelled to go to Ellis Island and await investigation [along with all the steerage passengers]. When the vessel has reached her dock the immigrants and their baggage are taken by barge to Ellis Island and there they are all inspected and their baggage is examined.

"The main building on the island," the article continues, "has a great room on the ground floor, into which the immigrants are sent." An article appearing in *Harper's Weekly* before the opening of the facility described how the immigrants, numbered and tagged, were to

> ascend to the second story for medical inspection and interrogation. Some [will] be detained for further physical examination; the others will continue on and into the great second-story room, to be separated into ten lines and to march through that number of aisles between the desks of the so-called "pedigree clerks," who will cross-examine them as the law requires.

"If any immigrant fails to pass an inspector," the *Times* article adds,

> he or she is at once sent before the Board of Special Inquiry for further examination; if the board finds that the immigrant should not be allowed to land, he or she is put in the detention pen to await a re-examination for his or her return to the place from which he or she came.

The immigration officials, according to the *Times*, were

particularly solicitous about women and children, and hedge them around with the safeguards of the law and of the church to which they belong. If a woman or a child is not met by friends or relatives, she is detained until someone whom she names can be communicated with and until it is determined to be safe for her to land.

Women with children coming to join their husbands could be met by the latter right there in the main building. Jake or Yekl, for example, the fictitious immigrant antihero of Abraham Cahan's 1896 novel, *Yekl: A Tale of the New York Ghetto,* found himself standing one morning "with an unfolded telegram in his hand . . . in front of one of the desks at the Immigration Bureau of Ellis Island." The moment he entered the big shed,

> he had caught a distant glimpse of Gitl and Yossele through the railing separating the detained immigrants from their visitors. . . . Presently the officer behind the desk took the telegram from him, and in another little while Gitl, hugging Yossele with one arm and a bulging parcel with the other, emerged from a side door.

In this case, the shock of reunion after a three-year interval was not a happy one; but that—along with all such cases—was another story.

"Every immigrant is permitted to land in this city as soon as possible after he has disembarked from his ship," the *Times* article assures its readers. "Beyond the aisles and desks of the questioning inspectors," says the *Harper's Weekly* article, the immigrants

> will find two great pens of enclosures. . . . Into one will go those whose destination is New York City or its suburbs; into the other will be put the greater number who are about to begin another journey to distant States and Territories.
>
> On this second floor, conveniently arranged, are spaces for the railroad ticket sellers, the clerks of the information bureau, for the telegraph and brokers' counters, and the lunch stand.

At last, for those just hungry to land, the *Times* concludes: "All come ashore at the barge office at the Battery."

·21·

JEWISH NEW WORLDS
IN THE 1890s

What was the immigrants' next step when they got off the boat at the Barge Office pier? For most of them, it was another boat ride, either to Weehawken or to Forty-second Street, where they could resume their journeys inland on the Pennsylvania or New York Central Railroad. But for those remaining in New York—as a majority of the Jews were doing—this last stage of their exodus could be made by wheel or even on foot.

Many of them were met by relatives or friends, waiting on the street alongside the Barge Office. Others, like Abraham Cahan, or the fictitious hero of his novel about an immigrant, *The Rise of David Levinsky*, stepped forth alone into Lower Manhattan. Levinsky writes that the "cries of joy, tears, embraces, kisses" among those meeting at the Battery "intensified my sense of loneliness and dread of the New World"; but he did not have to walk far to begin feeling less lonely. One only went a few blocks north, to the General Post Office, just south of City Hall, then turned eastward, following Park Row and then East Broadway, to begin experiencing what Cahan described this way in his autobiography:

> My first visit to the Jewish quarter was late one afternoon. I went along East Broadway. On some of the stoops sat Jews. A few of them were old men, with white beards and with skullcaps on their heads. I felt as if I was home again.

Historically, there had never been a specifically Jewish quarter of New York City. Sephardic Jews had lived all over town, and the wealthiest German Jews were building their mansions on upper Fifth Avenue and its environs. Middle-class German Jews had lived in German neigh-

borhoods, mainly east of the Bowery and south of Fourteenth Street,
the "Lower East Side" in the broadest sense. It was partly owing to
this presence in the area that Grand Street east of Broadway had become the city's main department-store artery and Canal Street its pri-
mary source of wholesale textiles and clothing—both these new forms
of enterprise having developed primarily under the initiatives of German Jews. And it was above all the lure of the garment trades in this
area that had begun causing large numbers of East European Jews to
settle into it.

"When I first arrived," Cahan writes,

> the center of the Jewish quarter was between East Broadway and
> Grand Street and between Suffolk and Allen. There was also an-
> other center, a smaller one, several minutes away from East Broad-
> way, at the corner of Bayard and Mott streets (on the other side of
> the Bowery).

The latter center, which was soon to be the heart of New York's China-
town, had been the first place where Russian Jews clustered in the city;
but in the 1880s, it was rapidly superseded by the center at which East
Broadway and Canal and Essex streets converged. As for the previous
inhabitants of this sector, its large Irish settlement was moving eastward, toward the East River, and its Germans were reassembling above
Houston Street in the area soon to be known as Dutchtown. During the
1890s, virtually the entire area east of the Bowery, between Houston
Street on the north and East Broadway on the south, to within a few
blocks of the river, became Jewish; only along the river itself, to the
south and to the east, did there remain an area that was primarily Irish.

During that same decade, the Lower East Side—or, in particular,
its "ghetto"—took on a character that made its way into American folklore. For observers like Jacob Riis, with his social-reformer's eye, it
was a place of filth, squalor, overcrowding, and intolerable conditions.
For others, like Hutchins Hapgood and Lincoln Steffens, it was the home
of a culture more vital than any they saw elsewhere in American life.
It was in fact both, its cultural vitality—represented by the two popular
institutions evolving there, the Yiddish theater and press—expressed
in forms that both served the people and were the vehicles of their
hopes. In a culture that had been uprooted and was in upheaval, these
secular institutions were for the time being no less important than the
synagogue. Religion was still somewhat in abeyance among the immigrants, more and more of whom were willing to work on Saturdays to
make ends meet. There were few rabbis of East European orthodoxy
to guide them. Rather, in the 1890s, the principal shepherds of their
souls were old secularist radicals like Abraham Cahan, Bernard Wein-

stein, and Nicholas Aleinikoff, who had now become their journalists, labor leaders, and social-reforming lawyers. Cahan in particular was on his way to achieving a moral influence over the Jewish immigrant as great as that of any rabbi in the old country, first as editor of the *Arbeiter Zeitung (Workingman's Journal)*, then as editor and cofounder, in 1897, of *The Jewish Daily Forward*.

Not that the charitable involvement—and therefore the influence—of the old German-Jewish leaders had disappeared. The United Hebrew Charities remained the preeminent institution of its type in New York, and its Immigration Bureau was still the main one watching over the problems of Jews arriving at Ellis Island. The continuing benefactions of a Jacob Schiff were expressed in such establishments as the Educational Alliance—an adult education center for the immigrants, at the corner of East Broadway and Jefferson Street—and the Henry Street Settlement, the crowning development of the settlement-house movement that had made its way from London's East End to New York's Lower East Side during the 1880s and 1890s.

If the Lower East Side was becoming both the cultural capital and the largest single repository of Jewish immigrants in the United States, it was nevertheless not without its equivalents in other American cities. Similar neighborhoods had sprung up in Baltimore, Philadelphia, and Boston, all of them prominent ports of entry, and above all in Chicago, to which some two thousand refugees had been sent during the crisis of 1882. A magnet for the new immigration from Eastern and Southern Europe in general, that muscular capital of the Midwest quickly became the seat of the second-largest Jewish population in the country: from ten thousand in 1880, its numbers rose to about sixty thousand in the next two decades. Its West Side ghetto, centering upon the convergence of Maxwell and Halsted streets, became very nearly as celebrated—or infamous—as the one in New York. A resident recalled:

> Chicago, especially the West Side, then was a place of filth, infested with the worst elements any city could produce. Crime was rampant. . . . Jews were treated on the streets in the most abhorrent and shameful manner, stones being thrown at them and their beards being pulled by street thugs.

Yet, for all the poverty and squalor, the place was teeming with vitality. "There was hardly a streetcar where there were not to be found some Jewish peddlers with their packs riding to or from business." Another observer remarked: "In all but the severest weather, the streets swarm with children day and night. On bright days, groups of adults join the multitude, especially on Saturday and Sunday, or on the Jewish holidays." By the end of the 1890s, Chicago Jewry was even to have two Yiddish newspapers of its own.

Canada was also receiving its share of the Jewish influx into North America. As in the United States, the earliest Jewish population there had been primarily Sephardic, then had become increasingly German, but on a much smaller scale. In 1871, when the general population of the newly constituted Confederation was 3,689,257, its Jews numbered 1,333; in 1881, on the eve of the Russian-Jewish influx, they had reached 2,393. The next two decades saw about twelve thousand new Jewish arrivals, the vast majority of them from Eastern Europe.

By the end of the century, then, substantial Jewish communities had come into being not only in Montreal—always to be the largest in Canada—but also in Toronto and in far Winnipeg, to which the Mansion House Fund had sent refugees in the spring of 1882. The Canadian Pacific Railway, still under construction, provided many jobs—even in Montreal, where Jews worked for it as locksmiths, tinsmiths, and carpenters; although there, as in most large North American cities, the needle trades tended to draw Jews in the largest numbers. A Baron de Hirsch Institute was opened in Montreal in 1891 with a donation from the Baron himself, to help the Jewish needy and settle as many of them as possible on the land as farmers.

In Australia and South Africa—once again with a starting fillip from the Mansion House Fund—a significant though small Jewish immigration had begun, though it was to grow large only after 1900. In the last two decades of the century, when the preponderant rush was to the English-speaking world, the only other major refuge apart from North America for Jews was the old mother country herself, founder of that tradition of liberalism and tolerance that the Jewish uprooted were now embracing with such passion. Though not without its own peculiar traditions of anti-Semitism, England had by now proved itself to be the foremost friend of the Jewish people among the great nations of the Old World. The fact that it had expelled its original Jewish community wholesale in 1290 seems only to have made this outcome more likely: the English people had thereby avoided the worst qualities of the medieval Christian-Jewish relationship, and been able to lay the groundwork for their own quintessential middle class without the Jewish competition that had so often irritated Central and East Europeans. As a result, Britain proved able to accommodate a steady and moderate influx of Jews starting in the late seventeenth century, and by the middle of the nineteenth, the oldest Anglo-Jewish families—Sephardic and German, as in North America—had done quite well on the whole, some of them moving into the uppermost circles of that island's society.

For all the attractiveness of Britain, however, its Jewish population in 1880 had not numbered more than fifty thousand. Approximately twice that number were to arrive in the next twenty years, virtually all from Eastern Europe. The result was a transformation in the general character of British Jewry and of the East End of London: by the end of the nineties, London, with a total Jewish population of about 150,000, was the third city in the world in the size of its Jewish immigrant population, exceeded in this respect only by New York and Chicago. Petticoat Lane was described in 1892 by its son and chronicler Israel Zangwill as

> the great market-place, and every insalubrious street and alley abutting on it was covered with the overflowings of its commerce and its mud. Wentworth Street and Goulston Street were the chief branches, and in festival times the latter was a pandemonium of caged poultry, clucking and quacking and cackling and screaming. Fowls and geese and ducks were bought alive, and taken to have their throats cut for a fee by the official slaughterer. At Purim a gaiety, as of the Roman carnival, enlivened the swampy Wentworth Street, and brought a smile into the unwashed face of the pavement. . . . The famous Sunday fair was an event of metropolitan importance, and thither came buyers of every sect. . . . A Babel of sound, audible for several streets around, denoted Market Day in Petticoat Lane, and the pavements were blocked by serried crowds going both ways at once.

Here, too, was a special vitality amid the poverty, and some autonomous institutions. The Yiddish culture of the East End was in some ways the predecessor of its New York equivalent. It was to London that the great Yiddish actor Jacob P. Adler had first brought his troupe after being expelled from Russia in 1883; and it was in London that the first successful Yiddish socialist newspaper in the world, the *Arbeiter Freind (Workingman's Friend)*, had appeared, under the editorship of Philip Krantz. But by the end of the eighties, both Adler and Krantz were in New York. Other prominent Yiddish writers and intellectuals followed a similar route, starting as socialist exiles in London, then following the main route of Jewish migration to the New World. There also were, as in New York, charitable institutions founded on the East End by the wealthy members of the old Anglo-Jewry—such as the Poor Jews' Temporary Shelter at 82 Leman Street, which housed the needy up to two weeks at a time.

But, though London was the overwhelming refuge of Jewish immigrants in Britain, it was not the only one. Between 1880 and 1900, the Jewish population of Manchester grew from five thousand to twenty-five thousand, the second-largest in the country; a similar growth occurred in Leeds, then the third British city in Jewish population. Ireland, Wales, and Scotland also felt the impact. Glasgow, which had nearly six thousand Jews by 1900, even developed a Jewish dialect of its own: "Aye, mon," went the classic sentence, "ich hob' getrebblt mit de five o'clock train."

Although a constant trickle of Jews entered Paris and a small Yiddish-speaking community evolved there, the only major Jewish refuges of this epoch that were not part of the English-speaking world were Palestine and Argentina. These were also the two countries to which the most grandiose visions of Jewish colonization attached.

In Argentina, the main impetus for Jewish immigration continued to be provided by the Jewish Colonization Association, even though the actual agricultural settlement formed a relatively small part of the picture. By 1900, there were 17,795 Jews in Argentina, of whom more than 90 percent had arrived from Eastern Europe during the preceding decade; though the vast majority had arrived under the auspices of the Association, nearly half were living in Buenos Aires. That city was soon to become a prominent center of Yiddish culture; but during the 1890s its Jewish community was just beginning to discover its New World identity. In 1889, the only Jewish religious leader in all of Argentina had been the English-born Henry Joseph, a fifty-one-year-old Buenos Aires merchant who, for reasons that remain completely obscure, had been ordained "Grand Rabbi" of Argentina by the Jewish General Consistory of France. Joseph had little Jewish education, was married to a Catholic, and saw at least one of his children married in the Church—facts that caused the new immigrants to take a dim view of his qualifications to lead them spiritually, even though he was entirely sympathetic to their cause. "We call Joseph an impostor," wrote one Argentine Jewish journalist. After more of this, Joseph finally resigned in 1894, protesting that "the abuse is too much," and was succeeded in the post by a Russian Jew. Three years later, Buenos Aires Jewry built a large synagogue.

As for the roughly nine thousand Jews who were farming in the Argentine wilderness by 1900, a unique way of life had developed among them. Relations with the storied gauchos, though often tense, had achieved a certain gruff cordiality. One man, describing his mother's life in the early days of the Clara colony, told of how "the *gauchos* around there would often come to her house and sample her baked bread . . . and would often bring our family all sorts of things, good leather saddles, *maté*, and once even helped round up some cows that had drifted away." When it came to emulating the native skills, it could not be said

that the Jews were quite the horsemen as the native *gauchos*, but you know, my parents came from Minsk, where they had a bakery and did not go about riding horses at all till they came to Argentina, and my parents said that the *gauchos* were impressed with us at Clara. We learned quickly.

There even came into being a tradition of stories about a mythical figure named Shmilekl the Gaucho, who was an expert gunman and a political anarchist, and who met his end in a gunfight on the main street of a frontier town.

For all the aura of romance, however, fewer and fewer Jews would settle in the Argentine colonies, and many would leave them. The vision of large-scale Jewish settlement there persisted for a time among some: in the spring of 1895, Theodor Herzl, a young Jewish journalist assigned to Paris and dismayed by the treason trial of Captain Dreyfus, went to see Baron de Hirsch to discuss an idea to send Jews to Argentina as a full-fledged Jewish national enterprise. The Baron refused, and only after that did Herzl—establishing contact with the Hibbat Zion (Love of Zion) movement that had come into being since 1882 in Russia, Rumania, and other countries, dedicated to furthering Jewish colonization in Palestine—focus his aspirations specifically upon the Land of Israel.

The colonization movement in Palestine had by then become, to a very large extent, the personal charity of Baron Edmond de Rothschild. This also meant that he was very much in charge. "The Baron's wish, expressed some time ago," wrote Chaim Khissin on October 18, 1886, "that Rishon le-Zion should be turned over entirely to vineyards is rapidly materializing. About 300,000 vines and a great variety of fruit trees have been planted and have taken root very well, growing unusually fast and strong." But the Baron's wish was the father to greater dependency. "Once the people of Rishon le-Zion had decided that their future depended on the vineyards," Khissin continued,

> they put every effort into cultivating as many vines as they could. One person alone, however, could accomplish little, and it became necessary to hire [Arab] laborers. The [Hibbat Zion] administration gave them only the vines and a napoleon, or a napoleon and a half, per family. As a result, the settlers began to spend almost all of their assistance money on wages for hired hands, while they themselves went hungry and couldn't pay the grocer for such food as they bought.

The upshot, according to Khissin, was that "the Baron has been generous enough to pay their debts." Some of the settlers deplored this situation, among them Khissin, who even returned to Russia for a time, eventually to resettle in Palestine as a physician.

Another man who deplored this system of baronial *halukkah* was

Theodor Herzl, who visited Rishon le-Zion in October 1898. "For a poor village," he wrote in his diary,

> this is a fairly prosperous place. But if one has imagined it as more than a poor settlement, one is disappointed. Thick dust on the roads, a bit of greenery.
>
> The [Rothschild] administrator received us with a frightened air, obviously dared to be neither amiable nor unamiable. Fear of Monsieur le Baron hovers over everything. The poor colonists have swapped one fear for another. We were shown through the wine-cellars with elaborate ceremony. But I have never doubted that with money one can set up industrial establishments no matter where. With the millions which have been poured into the sand here and stolen and squandered, far different results could have been achieved.

Herzl by this time was no longer merely determined to achieve different results; he had set about doing so. His activities in behalf of his Jewish national idea had led to the calling of a world Zionist Congress in Basel in August 1897; a second one had since been held. The result was soon to manifest itself in a transformation in the character and sense of purpose of Palestine colonization, despite the continuing difficulties placed in its way by the Ottoman regime. "Were I to sum up the Basel Congress in a word," Herzl had written in his diary in September 1897, ". . . it would be this: At Basel I founded the Jewish State. . . . Perhaps in five years, and certainly in fifty, everyone will know it." Five years was his dream, but fifty was prophecy.

·22·

RUMANIA, RUMANIA

In May 1899, the attention of people who had concerned themselves with Jewish sufferings in Russia suddenly turned to another country. In Rumania, a long history of Jewish disabilities had culminated in a riot in the Moldavian town of Jassy, where the Jewish community of nearly forty thousand made up over half the total population.

An offspring of the Dacia of Greek and Roman antiquity, the Rumanian nationality had recovered its identity in the Middle Ages in the form of two short-lived principalities: Wallachia to the south, founded around 1290, and Moldavia in the north, founded in the following century. The two principalities had fallen under Turkish suzerainty, but their population remained primarily Greek Orthodox and came to be regarded as a special concern of the Russian Empire when it expanded to world power in the eighteenth century.

In the Treaty of Kuchuk Kainarji in 1774, which ended Catherine the Great's first war against the Turks, Russia was given rights of intervention in Moldavia and Wallachia in behalf of their Christian population. From then on, Russian influence steadily grew: in the Treaty of Bucharest in 1812, the province of Bessarabia was detached from Moldavia and incorporated into the Russian Empire; from 1828 to 1834, the principalities were occupied by the Russians. An ensuing period of French cultural influence—Rumanian is, after all, a Romance language—culminated in a French proposal, at the end of the Crimean War, that the two principalities be united. This arrangement was confirmed by international agreement; in 1862, the newly unified country took the name Rumania, electing—though still under Turkish suzerainty—the Hohenzollern Prince Charles (Carol in Rumanian) as its ruler four years later. Hegemony in Rumania remaining basically an issue between Russia and Turkey, the war that broke out between them in 1877 was fought

173

primarily over that end on Rumanian soil. It was officially ended at the Congress of Berlin in 1878, when Rumania was given her independence by the convening powers on condition, among other things, that she accord full civil rights to her Jewish population—a condition that was promptly ignored.

As in Russia, anti-Semitism on the official level seems almost to have been innate to Rumania's national existence. In 1579, Peter the Lame, Prince of Moldavia, had sought to banish the Jews from his principality on the grounds that their competition was ruining the Christian merchants. In 1640, the Church codes of Moldavia and Wallachia tried to ban all relations between Christians and Jews. The Russian influence in the nineteenth century inspired attempts to banish Jewish merchants and distillers from the villages, to prevent Jews from leasing land and establishing industrial enterprises, and in general to keep them from obtaining full rights of citizenship. Jassy was a major center of anti-Jewish activity: it was there that Greek soldiers, passing through on their own war of independence against the Turks, slaughtered Jews by the hundreds in 1821, and it was the University of Jassy that later became the chief gathering place of Rumanian intellectual anti-Semitism.

In 1870, the U.S. government had demonstrated its alarm at the Jewish situation in Rumania by sending as its consul to Bucharest an American Sephardic Jew, Benjamin Franklin Peixotto, who, it was hoped, would exercise some "moral influence." Instead, severe anti-Jewish riots broke out in 1872 in the cities of Ismail and Cahut. Peixotto conveyed the reprimand of his government, but to no avail, and America sought recourse by appealing to Saint Petersburg. The Russian government denied that anything wrong had occurred. "There is little conception in America," wrote the American Minister to Vienna, John A. Kasson, in 1878 regarding the Jews, "of the tenacity of the prejudice against that race in Roumania, and of the contempt and occasional violence and wrong to which this prejudice leads, as well as to the legal deprivation of the ordinary privileges of good citizenship." Kasson attended the Berlin Congress that year and hoped the problem had been resolved there.

As for the Jews of Rumania themselves, their history was twofold: partly Russo-Polish and partly Turkish. In no other country on the Continent was there so dramatic a meeting between the Sephardic and the Ashkenazic strains. Because the Ottoman Empire had been a major refuge for Jews expelled from Spain and Portugal at the end of the fifteenth century, the Sephardic component of Rumanian Jewry, which predominated in Wallachia, was the more ancient and established: some Sephardim had even served as diplomats at the court in Bucharest. It was Moldavia, in the north, that had become a full and contiguous part of Yiddish-speaking Jewry, beginning in the sixteenth century with a trickle of merchants on the Russo-Turkish trade routes, and culminating in the seventeenth in a large influx of refugees from the Khmelnitsky slaughters. Even by the beginning of the nineteenth century, few Jews of Moldavia spoke Rumanian, while most of those of Wallachia did; and a sense of social and cultural superiority on the part of the Sephardim of the south was as much cherished by some Rumanian Christians as by the Sephardim themselves. A good deal of the Rumanian anti-Semitic policy was dedicated to establishing an invidious distinction between "native" and "foreign" Jews.

Yet the Jewish life in the north seems to have had enough of a whiff of the air coming up from southern Rumania to have evolved, among Yiddish-speaking Eastern Europe, a distinct character of its own. The Yiddish theater was born there in 1876, and though it was largely the work of sojourners—of singers and cabaret-type entertainers from Galicia and Lithuania, and of a Russian *maskil* (exponent of the Haskalah), Abraham Goldfaden—the combination had found its proper milieu in the cafés and wine cellars of Jassy. There was something here of the gypsy-land Rumania of folklore, about which the Yiddish minstrel was to sing:

> Rumania, Rumania, Rumania—
> Geven amol a land a zisse, a sheyne . . .

("Once there was a land, sweet and lovely . . ."), praising its foods, its mamalige, its pastrami, its karnatzl, while raising a glass of wine and bursting into a dance. Characteristic Rumanians of these pioneering days of Yiddish theater were such uncharacteristic East European Jews as: Sigmund Mogulesco (born Selig Mogilevsky), actor, who had begun his career as a performer by singing both in the synagogues and in the churches of Bucharest; Moshe Horowitz, playwright, who had taught geography at the University of Bucharest and probably made a temporary conversion to Christianity; and Rosa Friedman, actress, who had once worked as a dancer in a Constantinople café.

A completely different sort of personality, yet also a typifying Rumanian Jew of this generation, was Rabbi Moses Gaster. Born in Bucharest in 1856 of a Rumanian-Jewish mother and a diplomat father who was a Sephardic Jew from the Netherlands, Gaster was a true distillation of his native land: a Sephardi who spoke Yiddish as well as Rumanian, an ordained rabbi who taught Rumanian history and literature at Bucharest University, and a lifelong adherent of Zionism who remained an eminent scholar of Rumanian folklore even after being expelled from the country in 1885 on account of his prominence in agitating for Jewish rights. Settling in London, Gaster was eventually to become the Chief

Sephardic Rabbi of Great Britain, as well as Theodor Herzl's most enthusiastic supporter there.

The strong nationalist streak in the Rumanian-Jewish character had already manifested itself in 1882, when a passion to colonize Palestine in the wake of the anti-Jewish riots in Russia erupted in Rumania even before it did so in Russia itself. This streak emerged once again in the wake of the anti-Jewish riot at Jassy in 1899, and with characteristic Rumanian panache; only this time the principal target for emigration was the United States.

By the spring and summer of 1900, groups of young Jewish men and women, mostly artisans, had decided to emigrate in groups, and to dramatize their gesture by marching through the Rumanian countryside. They called themselves Fusgeyers (Yiddish for "Goers-on-foot"). "They wear long sandals," reported the Vienna Zionist weekly *Die Welt*, "carry packs on their backs and canteens of water on their shoulders. They go along with walking sticks in their hands, and some groups bring along tents and lanterns." Many of them wore distinctive uniforms and caps, in the manner of scout groups, and gave themselves such names as The Wandering Jews, The Rumanian Exodus, The Bucharest Foot-Wanderers, and One Heart, as well as the more prosaic Students, Workers, and Clerks of Galatz. One group entirely made up of young women—of Fusgeyerkes—called itself Bas-Ami (Hebrew for "Daughter of my People").

Going by circuitous routes from one town to another before reaching the Austro-Hungarian border, the Fusgeyer bands were usually met by enthusiastic demonstrations in Jewish communities—and often among Christians as well—accompanied by donations of bread and produce. Some of the groups gave performances, in that way raising money as well as presenting their cause. One of their songs went:

> "Mama, where has Papa gone?"—
> "Off in search of bread and money!
> Now sleep, my child, just sleep!"

> "But it's dark and cold inside the house
> And so long a wait till morning."

> "Off to far America,
> To other countries, too,
> In search of work, of work . . ."

> The child grows still and thinks his childish thoughts,
> Then later asks again:
> "He's gone away but he'll come back tomorrow?—

No, Mama? But why away so far?
Here, Mama, here in our own house
Is where we have no bread!"

The Fusgeyers also distributed brochures in Rumanian. "We were and are women workers," began one item in the Bas-Ami leaflet. "We have worked all our lives, from earliest childhood. . . . Through drudgery and toil we earned our bit of bread. And now—a shudder goes through us at the thought of having to beg for your pity and mercy."

One of the first of these groups was called The Barlad Wayfarers, after the Moldavian town in which it was founded in April 1900. "At that time," remembered Jacob Finkelstein, who belonged to it, "there existed in Barlad, where I lived, a young Jewish amateur theatrical group. I belonged to it myself. We used to organize theatricals from time to time. From the proceeds we used to buy wood for the poor or help them out in other ways." But now they decided to serve their own needs. "Listen," their chairman said one day, "I have a plan for getting to America without money. We'll go on foot. We'll go from town to town giving performances until we come to a seaport. Even when we run low on money, there'll be rich Jewish communities willing to help us out."

And so the expedition was organized. Passports were obtained with *baksheesh*. Tents were purchased, as well as a horse and wagon, for carrying supplies and transporting the group's two women, who were to ride on ahead and arrange for accommodations at each town chosen for an overnight stay. A young man who had been a cornetist in the Rumanian army was to be the group's field captain. And a route was decided upon: from Barlad in eastern Moldavia southwestward along the foothills of the Carpathians into Wallachia, then northwestward at Ploesti (about thirty miles north of Bucharest) and straight across the border pass to the Hungarian town of Bracsov—an ambling route that totaled nearly two hundred miles.

On the appointed morning, there was a large gathering in town of onlookers and participants, friendly Christians as well as Jews, and merchants, grocers, and bakers, who loaded up the young adventurers with free food and supplies. Speeches were made, with expressions of remorse that these young people had to resort to flight. Then,

the speeches finished, our captain gave a signal on his cornet, and the march began. The order was thus: he went first, then after him two men with flags—one of them the Rumanian colors and the other the Jewish national blue and white. On we marched, simple soldiers four abreast, and at the end of our columns the wagon with baggage.

The pomp lasted to the outskirts of town, where the marchers were besieged by parents, sisters, and brothers. "With heavy hearts we were finally able to tear ourselves out of the arms of our dear ones, and we began the long march that was to stir all of Rumania."

That night they reached the outskirts of Tecuci, which had a large Jewish population, and camped in a field. They sent their two representatives in the morning:

> It was not long before they came back informing us that we were being awaited with great impatience, and that a committee headed by the president of the Jewish community had organized a great welcome ceremony for us. They had hired the Municipal Theater for a performance, and the tickets were sold out.

Christians as well as Jews came out to see the Fusgeyers as they marched into town. "The nearer we got, the thicker became the crowd, and by the time we entered, the crush around us was so great we could barely get through." They were escorted to the Hebrew School, where speeches were made and they were served lunch "by the richest women in town. After the meal, the town's rich men brought us to our quarters." Two evenings later, on Saturday, the scheduled performance was given at the Municipal Theater. "The audience could not stop marveling at how a group of nonprofessional artists could perform so well. We put on a play called *Madly in Love*, and earned almost 800 francs for it." On Sunday they took their leave, their wagon loaded with free food, learning with satisfaction that a new Fusgeyer group had been organized at Tecuci under their example.

Proceeding from one town to the next, they passed through a village where the local great landlord stopped them and asked why they were emigrating. "Our captain explained that we were good artisans and couldn't get work." The nobleman replied sadly:

> "Listen, my friends, if I'd had the chance I would have done what I could to dissuade you. My Rumanian brethren don't understand that they are driving the best elements out of the country. The best artisans—who also are loyal patriots—are leaving. This brings us no honor. But I have no right to reproach you. It is your right to live just the way I and other Rumanians do."

Eventually, the wayfarers arrived in Ploesti. It was already

> a large, wealthy city, with a rich Jewish community. We sent our two representatives ahead to say we had arrived . . . and after a few hours they returned with some spokesmen for the Jewish community, including a rabbi. That was something new for us. We were

brought into a girls' school for lunch, which turned out to be strictly kosher, because the rabbi ate with us.

They were brought to their quarters, where they stayed for a week, since it was Shavuoth (Pentecost):

> The president of the Jewish community gave us special treatment. And we gave a theatrical presentation that brought us material success as well as esteem. We took in over 1,000 francs. Then we were given a splendid farewell ceremony: two representatives of the Jewish community gave speeches, as well as several prominent Christians. We sang heartily as we took our leave.

The Jewish-community president said they might have difficulties at the border, and urged them to contact him if they did, since his brother was the Chief Rabbi of Budapest and would be able to help.

Whatever problems existed at the border were partly due to the Israelitische Allianz of Vienna, which did not want to deal with this disorganized migration. In early July, the Allianz was even to ask the Budapest Jewish leadership to intercede with their government and request that it close the border to the Fusgeyers. The Budapest Jews replied on July 13. "To the distinguished directors of the Israelitische Allianz, Vienna," their letter went:

> In regard to your important letter of July 10, we have the honor to express our opinion that it is simply out of the question for *us*, as a Jewish institution, to advocate to our government that it take measures against our Rumanian brethren to limit their freedom of movement. That would indeed be an unfortunate move, upon which the enemies of the Jewish people would look with satisfaction. We beg of you to understand our position and be assured that we are taking upon ourselves every burden required to help our coreligionists on their journey. We have written in the same sense to the Jewish communities along the border.

The Barlad wayfarers were stopped at Predeal, the last railway station on the Rumanian side. "People *ride* through here," said the border official, "they don't go on foot." They immediately telephoned the Jewish-community president in Ploesti, then sold their horse and wagon to get money for food. After three or four days, a man came from Budapest and obtained permission for them to cross.

The young Rumanians were put on a train to Budapest, then took a boat from there up the Danube to Vienna. The Israelitische Allianz, receiving them in Vienna in spite of everything, moved them right on, providing fourth-class train tickets to Frankfurt. Going thus from committee to committee, the wanderers made their way to Rotterdam, and from there, by ship, to London—where they suddenly encountered new difficulties. Presenting themselves at the Poor Jews' Temporary Shelter, they were told that its services were only for residents of the country, not for emigrants passing through. To get help, they tried to contact the most eminent Rumanian Jew in London, Rabbi Moses Gaster, but he was away on holiday. Finally, Herman Landau, director of the shelter and one of the first Polish Jews to have risen to wealth and eminence in England, admitted them, but not without calling them a bunch of "vagabonds, Rumanian *schnorrers*" in good Yiddish. Eventually, Landau arranged for their passage from Liverpool to Quebec in what turned out to be a particularly vile-smelling steerage.

The group spent about three weeks in Canada, most of them working as laborers in the construction of a bridge over the Saint Lawrence. When they had earned enough not to appear as potential public charges—and with their "assisted immigration" behind them—they entered the United States as passengers on a train that took them to New London, Connecticut. From there, they boarded a boat to New York. On the trip, they sang Fusgeyer songs, to the delight of the other passengers.

When they reached their destination, "we were allowed to disembark without any formalities," Finkelstein concludes his narrative. "We got off, we were in New York, and we were free."

·23·

THE HEBREW IMMIGRANT
AID SOCIETY

One night in June 1897, the huge wooden facility on Ellis Island caught fire and burned to the ground. Work began on a fireproof structure of brick, limestone, and cement to replace it, while its functions were once again carried out in the Barge Office. Three and a half years later, Ellis Island was reopened.

"The Bureau of Immigration will be transferred from its present quarters to the new station on Ellis Island the 15th of this month," reported *The New York Times* on December 3, 1900. "The transition from the cramped and badly arranged quarters which the bureau has occupied since the fire that destroyed the old station on the island in 1897 will be marked." The new station had been designed by the New York firm of Boring and Tilton, whose plans were accepted by a panel of the American Institute of Architects. "The wisdom of their choice of plans," the *Times* continues,

> can best be understood by studying a description of the station. The main building, situated in the center of the island, is 385 feet in length and 165 feet in width. The body of the building is 62 feet high, while the four towers at each corner are 100 feet from the ground to the top of the domes. The style is a conglomeration of several styles of architecture, the predominating style being that of the French Renaissance. The material used in the construction is brick with light stone trimmings, harmonized so as to make the general effect as attractive in appearance as possible. The spires of the towers are copper covered, and in the top of each is an observatory from which a splendid view of the harbor and city may be had.

But, as the writer justly observes, it was the "interior arrangements" that were the most important. "When the immigrant is landed

181

from the barges," the article continues, "he will pass through an imposing private entrance, made as nearly as possible free from the observation of the curious, besides protecting him during bad weather." Right inside was a large ground-floor room in which the heavy baggage was temporarily stored. The immigrants then struggled with their hand luggage up a long flight of stairs; at the top stood a group of medical inspectors, watching to see how well they managed the ascent.

One passed from the stairway into the Great Hall. More than two hundred feet long and one hundred feet wide, with a vaulted ceiling fifty-six feet high, and surrounded by great arched windows and an observation gallery, this huge room was filled with rows of latticed, iron-pipe railings, forming a maze of open passageways along which the new arrivals lined up to await their turns at the various stations. At each station, according to the *Times* article, the immigrant was

> inspected by the medical authorities and . . . the officials of the other branches of the service who pass upon his eligibility to land. Every inch of space on this floor is utilized. The railings forming the network of the aisles in which the immigrants are placed in alphabetical order, according to nationality, give the great amphitheater the appearance of an immense spider web.

To observers in the gallery, the tired, poor, and huddled masses in the maze below could look like sheep being led through pens.

The vast majority of the arrivals at Ellis Island made it to shore, but the process was unpleasant, whatever the outcome. The first shocks came with the succession of medical inspectors the immigrants began to encounter as soon as they passed from the stairway into the Great Hall. One's certificate of the vaccination usually obtained aboard ship had to be displayed prominently; very often it was pinned to one's clothing. Then the immigrant had to pass scrutiny as not belonging to any of the categories of medical undesirables, which included:

> all idiots, imbeciles, feeble-minded persons, epileptics, insane persons; persons of constitutional psychopathic inferiority, persons with chronic alcoholism . . . ; persons afflicted with tuberculosis in any form or with a loathsome or contagious disease; persons not comprehended within any of the foregoing excluded classes who are found to be and are certified by the examining surgeon as being mentally or physically defective, such physical defect being of a nature which may affect the ability of such alien to earn a living.

Many of these categories were easy for the inspectors to spot at a glance, but others required a closer look, especially problems of the eyes. At this time, trachoma, a severe and contagious form of conjunctivitis that can cause blindness, was widespread among the European emigrating classes, and—though it was curable—the United States authorities regarded its presence in an arriving immigrant as grounds for immediate deportation. There was, consequently, a separate station for eye inspection, and the quick though necessarily uncomfortable maneuver performed there by the examiner—he had to evert, or roll back, each eyelid over an instrument that many of the examinees were sure was a button hook—was to become a virtual medieval horror in immigrant folklore, all the more so because the possibility of rejection at this point was frighteningly real.

At the various stages, each person in whom a possible defect was spotted was marked accordingly with chalk on the shoulder of his or her clothing—an "L" for lameness, for example, or an "Ft" for foot problems, an "H" for heart, a "C" for conjunctivitis, and a "CT" for trachoma. Persons so marked were sent to separate rooms for closer examinations, often while the rest of the family waited in breathless fear. Sometimes the problem was such as could be cured by a few days of medical care, and, on a newly dredged part of the ever-growing island, there was a hospital for just this purpose. There were also dormitories for the families of the hospitalized, as well as for persons detained for any of a variety of other reasons.

Once the obstacles of the medical examinations had been passed, there remained the final and often most vexing one, at the desks of the immigration officers. A basic list of twenty-nine questions had to be answered satisfactorily; this had first been submitted to the immigrant in the form of a manifest at the port of embarkation. Here is a summary of a typical questionnaire as filled out by a Jewish immigrant of this period:

(1) Full name: *Litschky, Samuel;* (2) age: *32;* (3) sex: *male;* (4) whether single or married: *single;* (5) calling or occupation: *watchmaker;* (6) whether able to read or write: *yes;* (7) nationality (the country of which a citizen or subject): *Polish;* (8) race: *Hebrew;* (9) last permanent residence: *Warsaw, Poland;* (10) name and complete address of nearest relative or friend in country from which immigrant comes: *Moisse Chisznak, 67 Neminov, Warsaw, cousin;* (11) seaport of landing in the United States: *New York;* (12) final destination, if any, beyond port of landing: *Bridgeport, Connecticut;* (13) whether having a ticket through to such final destination: *yes;* (14) whether alien has paid his own passage, or has been paid by any other person or by any corporation, society, municipality or government, and if so, by whom: *by brother Jozef;* (15) whether in possession of thirty dollars: *$35;* (16) whether going to join a relative or friend and, if so, what relative or friend, his name and the com-

plete address: *Jozef Litschky, 287 Fairfield Avenue, Bridgeport, Connecticut;* (17) whether ever before in the United States and, if so, when and where: *no;* (18) whether ever in prison or almshouse or an institution or hospital for the care and treatment of the insane or supported by charity: *no;* (19) whether a polygamist: *no;* (20) whether an anarchist: *no;* (21) whether coming by reason of any offer, solicitation, promise or agreement, expressed or implied, to perform labor in the United States: *no, though brother knows where he can find work in a jewelry store;* (22) general condition of health, mental and physical: *good;* (23) whether deformed or crippled: *neither;* (24) height: *five feet, five inches;* (25) weight: *158 pounds;* (26) complexion: *dark;* (27) color of hair and eyes: *brown, black;* (28) marks of identification: *scar, left shoulder, from a fall;* (29) place of birth: *Warsaw, Poland.*

These questions presented a maze of difficulties for the immigrants. How, in particular, did one answer the delicate question number 21? To say one had a job waiting was possible grounds for deportation as "contract labor"; but Litschky, like many others, could not resist mentioning there was *some* job prospect, in order to show he was not likely to become a public charge. This was a point on which Litschky was bound to be cross-examined by the Ellis Island inspectors: how formal was that arrangement with the jewelry store? As for number 15—the amount asked for steadily rose through the years, but there was in fact nothing in the law stating how much money the immigrant had to have with him; and if he had, like Litschky, a ticket to his destination and was being met there, even less cash would have been sufficient to satisfy the authorities that he was not likely to become a public charge.

But it was quite clear that if an official wanted to be tough, the immigrant had to be shrewd or lucky to get through, and was at a great disadvantage if he knew nothing about U.S. immigration laws. He needed someone to advise him.

Ever since the work of the Hebrew Emigrant Aid Society had been taken over by the United Hebrew Charities in 1883, the latter had maintained a representative, first at Castle Garden, then at the Barge Office, and finally at Ellis Island, to meet arriving Jewish immigrants and help them with their problems. In fact, it had been the same man the whole time, Abram White. Honorable and industrious by all accounts, White was nevertheless becoming less and less satisfactory in the eyes of Russian-Jewish observers. For one thing, the only foreign language he spoke was German, which made communication with the Yiddish-speaking immigrants only minimally workable, and did not warm them to him at all. Since a large part of his job consisted of helping immigrants find their relatives and desired destinations—in Atlanta instead of Atalanta, for example, or on Houston Street instead of in Houston, Texas—the linguistic difficulty could be a formidable obstacle. Furthermore, many thought that White did not do enough to oppose the negative decisions of immigration officials; one account says that in his entire career he appealed deportation orders against Jewish immigrants only twice.

White's detached approach seemed to reflect the outlook of the United Hebrew Charities toward the immigrants, which had an air of "uptown" condescension. Its report of 1888 had said:

> Few of the European Jews who have arrived here within the past few years may be styled exiles for religion's sake; and the sympathy that was generously extended without question or reservation to the saddened victims of oppression prior to 1884, cannot be expected to be offered to people who rush to America merely to better their financial and social conditions, Jews and Christians alike.

This attitude of tried patience could still be found in subsequent reports, such as the one for 1894, which said in part: "These people are dazzled by the brilliance of the city, and believe that there is room for everyone in the Metropolis." Such an outlook was becoming an increasing source of irritation to Russian Jews, even when accompanied by charitable acts; and as some of the latter prospered, they naturally sought to create charitable institutions of their own.

In New York, the first important step of this sort with regard to helping immigrants was taken under the leadership of Kasriel Sarasohn, editor of the Yiddish New York *Tageblatt (Daily News)*. Sarasohn had called a meeting, which was held on November 18, 1889, in Pythagorean Hall, at 177 East Broadway, and created a Hebrew Sheltering House Association—an updated version of the traditional Jewish Hachnosses-Orchim ("Welcome to Guests," the Hebrew commandment of hospitality to wayfarers).

Establishing itself first on Essex and then at 210 Madison Street, the Association provided temporary quarters for new immigrants and had a recreation hall. In 1890, more than three thousand immigrants passed through the shelter, staying an average of six days each. In an 1894 issue of one of Sarasohn's newspapers, a contrast was offered between this Association and the United Hebrew Charities. "The *Hachnosses-Orchim*," the article said, "was organized by poor Russian Jews. When an immigrant arrived, they would let him stay in the home for a few days before telling him to go out and look for work." At the United Hebrew Charities, on the other hand, he "would find an imposing building that swelled his expectations. But when, after calling again and again and again, he would not even get a chance to say he was hungry, he would become frantic." The article cautioned:

> We do not want to criticize our German brethren. We have our faults too. . . . [But] it is up to us, the Russian Jews, to help our poor countrymen and keep them from being insulted by our proud brethren to whom a Russian Jew is a schnorrer, a tramp, a good-for-nothing. . . . In the philanthropic institutions of our aristocratic German Jews you see magnificent offices, with lavish desks, but along with this, morose and angry faces. A poor man is questioned like a criminal. He trembles like a leaf, as if he were standing before a Russian official.

Yet the Hachnosses-Orchim was not entirely exclusive of "uptown" generosity, however condescending; Jacob Schiff and others of his circle were among its financial supporters. If a need was now being felt for more charitable initiatives toward the immigrants by people who had been Russian-Jewish immigrants themselves, no one was proclaiming this more strongly than some of the German-Jewish leaders. At the October 1901 annual meeting of the United Hebrew Charities, its president, Henry Rice, deplored the recent closing of a branch on the Lower East Side with these words:

> This [branch of the] organization was composed of our down-town coreligionists of Russian birth, and we had hailed with gladness the formation of this association, as an attempt upon the part of the more fortunate of the Jewish immigrants to assist their suffering brethren. Alas! that our fond hope should so soon have been blasted. The reason given for the discontinuance of the Auxiliary Society is "lack of funds." I cannot help but think and to express my opinion frankly, that it is rather due to a lack of sympathy upon the part of those able to render aid in our work. I do not hesitate to arraign the down-town people severely. . . . They are giving some of us tangible ground for saying: "Why should we German and American Jews devote our time and money to help the Russian Jews when those Russian Jews who are well able to do so refuse to aid?" And if our down-town friends should protest against my words of reprehension and blame, I shall answer them, that I shall be only too glad to retract provided they show by their actions, and not merely by empty words, that they are willing to do their duty.

President Rice made the point more imperatively at the 1902 annual meeting when he said: "It is time that our East Side coreligionists awoke to the knowledge of their delinquency and aided the work of the society, if not to the extent of their duty, at least to the extent of their ability."

In fact, a group of Lower East Side Jews were awakening at that very moment to the problems on Ellis Island. At the beginning of the year, the young, reform-minded President, Theodore Roosevelt, learning of corruption in the administration there, had appointed William Williams, a Wall Street lawyer of similar outlook, as Commissioner of Immigration. Williams had dealt promptly with such abuses as the selling of false citizenship papers and a variety of kickback arrangements between Island officials and concessionaires. But these were the days when reformers of a certain type were expressing their zeal through an organization called the Immigration Restriction League, and Williams had responded to their influence, tightening the exercise of restrictions upon entry. By December 1902, the New York *Evening Post* could observe:

> In carrying out the plans of the immigration authorities at this port to restrict undesirable immigration, an even more rigid inspection than has prevailed hitherto has been instituted at Ellis Island. As a result, there are more detained immigrants at the island in proportion to the number being landed from steamships than ever before. The several boards of special inquiry sitting daily have as many cases as they can attend to.

The Board of Special Inquiry, "that terror of the immigrant," as *The New York Times* called it, was now making abundant use of the adjoining "dormitory for the unfortunates labeled 'excluded.'" This part of the Island's ritual was being watched with great care from the observation gallery by opponents of severe restriction, and by the newspapers of the various immigrant groups. "Is it surprising," wrote an eminent historian and defender of restrictionist policies,

> that the casual and tenderhearted visitor who leans over the balcony railing or strolls through the passages, blissfully ignorant of the laws and of the meaning of the whole procedure, should think that he detects instances of brutality and hard-heartedness? To him, the immigrants are a crowd of poor but ambitious foreigners, who have left all for the sake of sharing in the glories of American life, and are now being ruthlessly and inconsiderately turned back at the very door by a lot of cruel and indifferent officials. He writes a letter to his home paper, telling of the "Brutality at Ellis Island."

Such letters and comments were indeed filling the foreign-language newspapers of New York, with the Yiddish ones especially likely to see intimations of anti-Semitism in the phenomenon.

The crucial response to this situation evolved out of a decision made that August 30 at a meeting of a Lower East Side *landsmanshaft*, or mutual-aid society of immigrants from the same town or region in the old country. This *landsmanshaft* was the Voliner Zhitomirer Aid Society—former residents, that is, of the town of Zhitomir in the Russian province of Volhynia—which, since it lacked quarters of its own, was holding its meeting in a downtown lodge of one of the old German-Jewish fraternal societies, the Independent Order Brith Abraham. In charge of the meeting were three prospering members named Max Meyerson, Abel Cooper, and Harris Linetzky. The incident that concerned them was the recent burial in the Randall's Island Potter's Field of a Jewish immigrant without friends or relatives who had died in the Ellis Island hospital. Until the beginning of 1901, the United Hebrew Charities had seen to the burial of Jewish paupers, but they had relinquished that responsibility for lack of funds. The men of the Zhitomir *landsmanshaft*, shocked at the Potter's Field story, wanted to organize a society to see to the burial of such persons in Jewish cemeteries.

"In order to arrange that," according to a participant,

> they sent a committee to the immigration station [at Ellis Island]. When the committee arrived there, they found the *living* immigrants in great need of help. They saw the condition—especially the mental condition—of the immigrants. They saw that the immigrants did not understand the Jewish representative at Ellis Island, who spoke German to them. They especially saw the tragic situation of those immigrants who were detained for deportation.

The committee returned from the island with a new sense of what its task should be. In a short time, the group was collecting funds for a new organization, soon to be called the Hebrew Immigrant Aid Society.

This clearly was a challenge to the monopoly over Jewish immigration problems hitherto held by the United Hebrew Charities. It was a challenge not warmly received by, for one, that resolutely "uptown" organ, *The American Hebrew*, which announced on January 16, 1903:

> The Hebrew Emigration [sic] Aid Society has appointed J. D. Eisen its representative at Ellis Island. For some time the East Side people have been greatly agitated about what they term abuses of immigrants. They have created considerable disturbance in the Yiddish press and have made charges against the immigration bureau which, from what can be gathered, are inaccurate and often wilful misrepresentations of fact. The United Hebrew Charities has placed Mr. Abram White at Ellis Island to do all in his power to help incoming immigrants of our faith. Mr. White's labors have been capable in every respect. But the Hebrew Emigration Aid Society desires to have its own representative, and so has appointed Mr. Eisen.

The Hebrew Immigrant Aid Society, then, was another of the growing manifestations—along with the Jewish labor movement, the Yiddish press, and the Isaac Elchanan Yeshiva, founded in 1896 to train Orthodox rabbis on American soil—that "downtown" was suddenly quite ready to start tending to its own affairs, even when this meant occasionally snubbing the charitable hand extended from "uptown." Yet the fact that these lines of rivalry were never as clear-cut as many of their protagonists were inclined to think, was shown in this case by the obviously enthusiastic support given to its immigrant-aid offspring by the Independent Order Brith Abraham, which was at this time engaged in a rivalry with the older B'nai B'rith to become a defense organization of national significance. "A petition signed by several grandmasters of Jewish orders," continues *The American Hebrew* article of January 16, "has been forwarded to Washington calling attention to abuses in the administration of the bureau at New York." This drew a quick response from the B'nai B'rith national president, Leo N. Levi, who addressed a meeting a few days later at his organization's "Roumania and Justice Lodge" on Forsythe Street and, according to *The American Hebrew* of January 23,

> spoke against the attempts of certain Jewish fraternal organizations to discredit the Bureau of Immigration and the present national administration. He said that there was no organization that could justly claim to be the representative of all phases of Jewish life better than the B'nai B'rith, which had undertaken the work of helping the Roumanian Jews.

Levi was doubtless remembering with nostalgia the work of Benjamin Franklin Peixotto, B'nai B'rith's most distinguished emissary to the world at large, a generation before. But though the paternalism of such giants of American Jewry was not yet a thing of the past—Jacob H. Schiff, for one, had a good many years of major philanthropic achievement and community influence still ahead of him—it was becoming less and less possible for them to act effectively without taking into consideration the will of the new Russian-Jewish masses in America. This was sometimes even acceptable to them; but they remained wary, too.

PART FIVE

The Era of Pogroms

· 1903-1909 ·

·24·

CITIES OF SLAUGHTER, I: KISHINEV

At the beginning of 1903, the Jewish population of the Russian Empire was about five million, and its outlook was not without a certain hopefulness. Alexander III had died in 1894, and the new Tsar, Nicholas II, had not yet shown to the wide world his innate weakness, susceptibility to obscurantism, suspicion of political change, and personal hostility to Jews more profound than that of any of his predecessors. No major anti-Jewish incidents had yet occurred in his reign; indeed, there had been no significant riots in almost twenty years. The Jewish middle classes found ways to advance their lot and educate their children in spite of everything, the tradition-minded poor went on struggling to maintain lives of humble piety, while a newly emerging Jewish proletariat—along with a young generation of radical intellectuals—were finding creeds and modes of action that they believed would eventually bring liberation not only to themselves but to all mankind.

The Russian radicalism of the 1880s, for its Jewish and its gentile adherents alike, had still been marked almost entirely by the native Narodnik tradition, peasant-oriented and largely immune to the influence of West European socialism. But in the ensuing years, economic and intellectual change had deeply affected it; rapid industrial progress was creating a small but substantial Russian proletariat, and Marxian socialism—which had founded itself upon the working class and not the peasantry—had come in from the West and taken firm hold upon the revolutionary intelligentsia. These developments made the radical movement in Russia even more congenial to Jewish participation than it had ever been. For one thing, Marxism—founded by a Jew, albeit a renegade who deprecated the people from which he had sprung—had already shown, in Western Europe, a greater capacity to appeal to Jewish intellectuals than any of the socialist theories that had preceded it,

perhaps on account of its instinctual messianism and complete sociolog-
ical grasp of the urban realities in which the newly emancipated Jewries
found themselves. For another, a portion of the Jews of the Russian
Empire, particularly in the provinces of Lithuania and Poland in the
northwest, had begun to form itself, quite spontaneously, into an organized industrial working class.

The movement had begun in the quintessentially "Litvak" cities of
Vilna, Bialystok, and Minsk, where some of the most powerful and ancient intellectual traditions of Jewish Eastern Europe now mingled with
the conditions of industrialization. There, in factories that produced textiles, brushes, and cigarettes, among other things, a Jewish proletariat
had emerged by the beginning of the 1890s that was in a way a Marxist
vision come true—for even before the ideology came along to confirm
them in their outlook, they were marked by a class consciousness, a
bent for intellectual self-improvement, and a sense of goals larger than
their own interests, all of which had come out of their particular ethnicity. For a moment, this group had even formed one of the spearheads
of Russian Marxism. In 1897, the year of the first Zionist congress and
as if in response to it, some of this group's leaders had gathered in Vilna
and organized a Jewish Workers' Federation (a "Bund" in Yiddish) of
Russia and Poland—soon to be known to Jews on both sides of the Atlantic simply as "the Bund." This was the first party of Marxist persuasion in the Russian Empire; it was only in the following year, partly
through the initiatives of the Bund, that the Russian Social Democratic
Party—soon to be the party of Lenin, Trotsky, and Stalin—was brought
into being at Minsk.

Preaching Marxism in the Yiddish language, the Bund could for the
moment regard itself as the Jewish antithesis of Zionism, which it looked
upon as a bourgeois and reactionary nationalism. What it did not yet
perceive was that, among the new Social Democrats, its own ethnocentrism could be suspected of the same tendency. The Bundists were
to discover this to their surprise in 1903, when the Social Democratic
Party was to reject them.

That was to be the year of a shocking realization for Russian Jews
in general, as they discovered they still were aliens in a larger world
that, in places, seemed almost to have taken them in. For 1903 saw a
sudden revival of anti-Jewish rioting—and in a form that made the riots
of the 1880s seem to belong to a bygone age of civility.

The scene was again southern Russia, and again a city notable for its
relative modernity and the degree to which its Jewish population had
become assimilated. Kishinev, like Odessa a hundred miles to the southeast across the Dniester, had also once been in Turkish hands. First
occupied by the Russians in 1812, it still had a mainly Asiatic and Balkan

character when the poet Alexander Pushkin lived there some ten years later. In its narrow streets and passageways, one would encounter, according to a contemporary of Pushkin's, "Moldavians in tall, round hats . . . others in hats not so high; all wore a kind of kaftan similar to a priest's cassock, but multi-colored. Under the kaftan they wore a second, narrower kaftan, then a skirt, then trousers." There were Greeks, Serbs, Albanians, and some Jews at that time, but Moldavians were the largest element—for Kishinev was the capital of Bessarabia, part of the historic Dacia. Hardly more than fifty miles east of Jassy across the border, Kishinev was culturally and economically a wayward part of Rumania.

Situated in a fertile wine-growing region, this former dusty village had grown into a handsome and prosperous southern city by the beginning of the twentieth century. "Its leading boulevard, Alexander Street," wrote the Irish national leader Michael Davitt in 1903,

> would do credit to any American city. It is more than twice the width of Broadway, New York, is planted on both sides with acacia trees, and can boast of imposing public buildings, substantial shops, banks, and jeweler's stores.

The town hall, Davitt continued,

> built, like most of the prominent structures of the city, with a whitish stone, is situated near the middle of the leading thoroughfare and wears a stately and striking appearance. The streets are all wide and run, as in American cities, at right angles to each other in uniform arrangement. They are nearly all planted, a feature which adds greatly to the beauty of the city, in combining the light green foliage of the acacia trees with the bright, clean look of the houses and public buildings.

At the Royal Gardens and People's Park at the center of town there were military-band concerts in the evenings, which attracted "large crowds of well-dressed citizens, officers of the garrison, youth, and particularly ladies." All in all, Davitt concluded, Kishinev,

> in its chief business and fashionable districts, has the look of a comfortable, fairly wealthy, up-to-date bourgeois center, and a well-governed municipal community; a most unlikely place, in the eyes of a visitor, to offer itself as a theater for one of the most abominable tragedies in modern times.

Like that part of Europe on both the Russian and the Rumanian side, Kishinev had seen a rapid growth in its Jewish population through the nineteenth century. From just a few hundred at the end of Turkish rule, it had grown to number 50,237 in the census of 1897, or 46 percent of the whole. By 1903, when the total population of Kishinev was about 130,000, it included some fifty thousand Jews and an equal number of Moldavians, who together outnumbered the roughly eight thousand Russians there. The rest were Bulgarians, Serbs, Greeks, Macedonians, and a small number of Germans, who were among the city's most prominent citizens: the mayor that year, and for a twenty-five-year period, was a man named Karl Schmidt. It was Schmidt who told Michael Davitt that Kishinev, which had been "on a level with an average Turkish town" only thirty years before, owed its "rapid rise and prosperity, and its present flourishing trade solely to the Jews. They built up its commerce, organized its banks, developed its general business, and made it the handsome, thriving city it is today." Moreover, Jewish brokers had spread prosperity over the adjacent countryside, by turning the Moldavian wine-growing into a flourishing business.

Yet it was the Moldavians, above all the peoples in the town and the region, who continued to harbor a virtually medieval hatred toward the Jews in their midst. The Moldavians are "not an intelligent race," Davitt candidly opines, "and are even more superstitious, if possible, than the average Russian Mujik." Certainly many of them were showing themselves susceptible to a revived medieval superstition that had swept through Hungary in the eighties and was now having a vogue in Rumania: the ritual murder charge—the notion that at Passover some Jews seek at all costs to obtain, for murky religious purposes, the blood of a Christian child. Around the beginning of 1903, a newspaper in Barlad—from which Jacob Finkelstein's group of Fusgeyers had gladly departed three years before—printed an article that said:

> The recent ritual murders committed by Jews in Austria, Bohemia, Hungary, Germany and Russia must still be fresh in everyone's mind. And how many children have disappeared in our own country! How many mutilated bodies have been found, while the criminals have remained undiscovered! Who are these criminals— these bloodthirsty murderers of our prattling babes? They are the fanatical Jews that infest our land. These monsters are the slayers of our Christian children. They are the criminals—the Jews who have invaded our country like locusts.

The Barlad journalist did not even leave it to readers to draw their own conclusion. "The time for peaceful and legal restrictions is passing away," he said. "Let all good Rumanians raise their heavy sticks and kill these parasites of their country."

There was by now a direct transmitter of such sentiments to the Moldavian kin over the border. Pavolaki Krushevan, a Moldavian born in Kishinev in 1860, had taken over a moribund Russian-language newspaper of that city in 1894 and transformed it into a successful daily called *Bessarabetz (The Bessarabian)*. At first liberal in tendency, it soon turned to an anti-Semitic policy. This brought it not only greater popular success—it attained the relatively high circulation of twenty thousand—but also the approval of the Russian Governor, who saw to it that no other paper was published in the entire province. Addressing itself, in Davitt's words, "to the police, soldiers, workingmen, Seminarists (Kishinev possesses half-a-dozen Royal and Educational Colleges, gymnasiums, and high schools), and to all the lower employees of the Governor's, Post Office, Telegraph, and other public departments," Krushevan's *Bessarabetz* was soon regularly carrying such headlines as: "Death to the Jews!," "Crusade Against the Hated Race!," and "Down with the Disseminators of Socialism!"

By early 1903, Krushevan, having fallen into financial difficulties at home, had temporarily repaired to Saint Petersburg, where he began publishing another anti-Semitic newspaper, *Znamya (The Banner)*; but he seems to have gone on directing *Bessarabetz* from there. It was rumored that when the anti-Jewish violence finally broke out in Kishinev, he made his way back there in disguise. But he had so successfully established an atmosphere of hatred that his presence was hardly needed. Nothing more was required than the proper events, or pseudo-events; *Bessarabetz* would provide the suitable misinterpretation to ignite his well-made fuse.

As Passover ominously approached, the first sign of brewing trouble appeared in the town of Dubossary on the Dniester, scarcely more than twenty miles northeast of Kishinev. In its issue of March 20, 1903, the London *Daily Mail* carried a report of "a shocking ritual murder" committed there. "A village boy," it said,

> who was sent to a Jewish tobacconist to make a purchase, mysteriously disappeared. The next day he was found with eighteen wounds, dead, in the garden of the tobacconist. The villagers, having joined forces, armed themselves with crude weapons and are besieging the town. They threaten to lynch not only the tobacconist, but all the Jews who fall into their hands.

The Jews of Dubossary, however, organized themselves in self-defense, and no incidents occurred. The mood of violence then subsided long enough for some facts to emerge. The London *Jewish Chronicle*—which reprimanded the *Daily Mail* for uncritically using the term "ritual murder" in its account—was able to offer a clarification on April 17.

"There in a fruit garden close to the river," its correspondent wrote of Dubossary,

> was found the corpse of a nineteen-year-old Christian named Ru-balenko. He was the sole heir to a considerable fortune, on which his numerous poor relatives had cast envious eyes. The post mortem examination ordered by the police having shown that the young man had been murdered by a pitchfork, the body was buried. Four-teen days later the government procurator received an anonymous complaint that the corpse had been interred without a medical ex-amination. The boy was exhumed, and further examination proved that the complaint was groundless and had probably been made with the object of diverting attention from the actual murderer. In order to put the authorities on the wrong scent or to make the crime the occasion for anti-Jewish disturbances, various reports were circulated among the people, the sole aim of which was to stamp the case as one of ritual murder.

Eventually it was to be proved that the murder had been commit-ted by a rapacious uncle; but all this factuality was beside the point for Krushevan's cohorts. "The anti-Semitic papers, such as the *Bessara-betz,*" continues the *Jewish Chronicle* correspondent,

> lost no time in working up a case implicating the Jews, and every day they published fresh reports which were calculated to influence the people against them. These papers outvied each other in their intentions. First we were told that Rubalenko was not nineteen but twelve, and next day his age was reduced to ten; then it was stated that, accompanied by a friend, the unfortunate young man had en-tered the shop of a Jew to make a purchase, but had not left it, his companion being sent away with reassuring expressions. One news-paper having asserted that the body had been stabbed in eighteen places, another capped this statement by giving the number of stabs as thirty-seven, while yet a third announced that there were no stabs at all on the body, but that all the blood had been drawn from it by means of scarcely visible needle pricks in the veins of the hands and feet, and that the eyes, ears, mouth and other apertures had been sewn up.

All this was having considerable impact in Kishinev—the more so after the death of a Christian girl who had poisoned herself and gone to a Jewish hospital there for treatment. Soon printed handbills of a type grimly reminiscent of 1881, asserting that the Tsar had given permis-sion to inflict a "bloody punishment" upon the Jews, were being distrib-uted throughout the city. The local authorities made no effort to suppress them.

The authorities were in fact behaving even worse than had ever been the case in 1881. In the atmosphere of mounting tension, a group of Kishinev's Jewish leaders, according to Michael Davitt,

> visited the Governor and warned him that Krushevan's incitations could lead to murder, unless restrained. General Von Raaben assured the deputation that all necessary precautions would be taken, but no attempt was made by him to stop the appeals of the *Bessarabetz* to the popular anti-Semitic hatred.

The deputation also went to the chief of police, who said it would "serve the Jews right if they were driven from the city for encouraging the propaganda of socialism." Feelings of this particular sort had been running even higher than usual since the murder the previous spring of the Governor of Vilna by a young Bundist named Hirsh Lekert. In this moment, the Jewish Bund could be seen as representing the very soul of radicalism in Russia, a perception that was readily passed on by some to the Jews in general. More than ever, highly placed persons in Saint Petersburg also saw things this way. But if, in 1881, those in official positions holding such views had merely connived at anti-Jewish vigilantism, their successors were now willing to take a more active part in it. Such is the conclusion that must be drawn from the fact, subsequently uncovered, that a high police official from Saint Petersburg arrived secretly in Kishinev and then departed, shortly before the riots broke out.

It was also a few days before Easter Sunday—the threatened day of vengeance against the Jews—that a "band of strangers" arrived in the city, according to Michael Davitt, "comprising thirty Albanians and some Macedonians, believed to be brigands, brought especially for an attack on the Jews." The fateful day—April 6 in Russia, April 19 in the West—dawned with ominous quiet. "Easter came," wrote the Kishinev correspondent of a Saint Petersburg newspaper,

> all the shops were closed, and a festive stillness reigned everywhere. The people, deprived for unexplained reasons of the public refreshments [usually] provided for them, streamed towards one of the squares where private individuals had erected drink stalls and buffets. In the crowd were to be seen a few Jews who had come thither to witness the amusements.

At noon the church bells rang; for some, this was a signal.

"Suddenly at noon," the correspondent continues,

> the surging multitude broke loose. Some Jews emerged from the crowd and hurried to their own locality, followed by a band of

Christian roughs, who threw stones at them and shouted: "Down with the Jews!" This cry acted like an electric current on the people, who without this incitement were already ill-disposed towards the Jews. Immediately the mob dispersed in various directions, and especially towards Alexander Street, in the vicinity of the new market. Exclamations of "Hurrah! hurrah!" broke from the throats of thousands of half-drunken individuals. The noise of the smashing of windows and of the cracking of doors mingled with the screams of the maltreated Jews and the cries of terror of their wives and children—a terrific cacophony that caused consternation among the population in the center of the town.

According to Davitt, the outburst was organized by a group whose leaders were young seminarists disguised as laborers. Leading the Albanian and Macedonian brigands who had come to town a few days earlier, along with fresh enthusiasts, they formed

thirty bands, averaging fifty each, with a Seminarist on a bicycle directing the attack. Some of the bands were composed of the lower employees of the various departments of the municipality—the telegraph, post office, [etc.]—but artisans and laborers, and Moldavians from the suburbs, formed the greater body of the rioters, with the Albanian strangers.

"In half an hour," wrote the Saint Petersburg journalist,

the mob took possession of the approaches to the railway station, where frightful scenes were witnessed that beggar description. Every Jew who was encountered was beaten until he lost consciousness; one Jew was dragged under a tramcar and smashed to death. The miserable dwellings of the poor were rifled of their contents, which were removed into the street and piled into a heap. Immense clouds of feathers rose in the air.

The main work of the mob that day was the looting and demolition of Jewish shops as well as houses. One of the first establishments attacked was Feldstein's saloon on Armenia Street. It was only some forty paces from a police barracks, but the soldiers and police patrolled the street without interfering, according to Davitt,

during the five hours occupied by the mob in demolishing the saloon and destroying fifteen thousand roubles' worth of wines. A safe containing a large sum of money was also broken open and robbed. While that section of the mob was thus employed, the leader of the gang found in the kitchen of the family residence the meat for the family's dinner. He put it on a stick, mounted to the roof of the saloon, which is of one storey, and, addressing the mob, the police and the military in the street, declared, "Here are the remains of a Christian child found in the house of the wealthy Jew, Feldstein."

The Feldsteins had found shelter in the home of one of their employees. Some of their wealthy coreligionists had fled to the countryside, but the vast majority of the Jews of Kishinev, and virtually all of the poor among them, were hiding in cellars, lofts, or sheds. In the evening of that first day, the looting began to give way to murder and rape. Yet by ten at night, when a strange silence descended over the city, the worst seemed over. This, however, proved only to be a prelude to unprecedented horrors.

The next morning, the mob reappeared and headed straight for the Jewish quarter. "At No. 13 Asia Street in the Bender Rugatka quarter," Davitt wrote, "some of the worst outrages were perpetrated. Twelve families, all Jewish artisans, lived in the yard. A mob of Moldavians, some Russian workingmen, and a few Albanians, attacked the occupants." Eight of the men had escaped somewhere—exemplifying an aspect of Jewish behavior at Kishinev that was to cause indignation among Jews throughout the world—while four remained behind to defend themselves and the sixteen women and children who had taken refuge with them in a loft under the roof. "One Mottel Greenspoon, a glazier," Davitt writes, "was stunned by a blow from a bludgeon, and the Albanians mutilated him while still alive." The other three men were also killed, and feathers were dumped on them. "As an act of desecration of the dead, two drunken women, one Moldavian and one Bulgarian, trampled on the body of Greenspoon as it lay mutilated in the yard." The mob then forced its way into the loft, where "all the women and girls were violated." A two-year-old was strangled and its tongue cut out.

"The scene of the most diabolical crimes," Davitt continues,

was the Skulanska Rugatka suburb, eighty per cent of the population of which are Moldavians, the Jews forming the remainder. This is the residence of the poorer class of the workers of both races. The mob broke into the yard on the evening of the second day, Monday, April 20. Twenty-five persons, mostly women and children, hid themselves in a carpenter's shed owned by one Grillspoon. The houses in the yard were demolished, and the mob was going away when the cry of a child in the shed indicated the place of concealment of the women. The shed was instantly attacked by Moldavians, led by a father and a son, who were neighbors of the Jews. Grillspoon, the owner of the shed, was killed, together with four other artisans, who were defending the place, and one woman, the wife of the owner, was murdered after violation.

The mob also found a thirteen-year-old girl, who was raped by at least a dozen men. Then they killed her, and "fought for her body like famished wolves after life was extinct. When found the next morning by her relatives, the body was seen to be literally torn in two."

Sadistic barbarities reminiscent of the Middle Ages had emerged with the fury of the mob. Meyer Weissman, who was blind in one eye, "had a very small store in one of the poorest Jewish quarters of the city," Davitt writes:

> The mob attacked and demolished his little grocery on Easter Sunday. He offered them all the money in his possession to spare his life. It was a sum of sixty roubles. The leader took the money, then said: "Now, we want your eye; you will never again look upon a Christian child." He implored them to kill him instead of making him blind for life. They gouged out his eye with a sharpened stick, and left him.

Davitt, who listened to Weissman's story from his bedside in the Jewish hospital of Kishinev, found lying in a bed nearby one Joseph Shainovitch,

> whose head had been battered with bludgeons, and the victim left for dead. He told me that it was the same gang who killed his mother-in-law, by driving nails through her eyes into the brain.

This was too much for Davitt. "This story I refused to believe," he writes; then adds: "But from no less than six different sources, one of them being a Christian doctor, I learned that the facts were as stated by Joseph."

Hard for a good man of the nineteenth century like Davitt to believe; but it was the twentieth that had just begun.

Abraham Cahan

Nicholas Aleinikoff

Alexander Harkavy

Chaim Khissin

Some emigrants, 1881–1882

Steerage passengers on deck,
SS *Pennland*, 1893.
(*Photograph by Joseph Byron*)

Immigrants on Atlantic
liner, about 1906.
(*Photograph by
Edwin Levick*)

Steerage passengers on deck,
about 1910.

Laurence Oliphant

S. D. Levontin

Charles Netter

Michael Heilprin

Jacob H. Schiff (twenty years later)

Some of those who helped, 1881–1882

Baron Maurice de Hirsch

Early Jewish settlers in Mauricio, Argentina

Children orphaned in the Kishinev pogrom, about to
go to the United States.

Emigrants about to leave Bremen for Galveston aboard the
SS *Breslau*, July 1912.

The Galveston Plan

Israel Zangwill

דזשייקאב שיף : — ‏(אין זיין ספיטש איבער אימיגרייישאן) נעה אין די וועסט, בלייב ניט אין נױארק. שטעל ניט אין געפאהר דעם כלל ישראל׳ !

וו. ר. הירסט : — ‏(אין אוונינג דזשורנאל) מר. שיף, איהר האט א טעות. אין צפאהל איז מאכם. צוואעס און צושפרייים איבער׳ן גאנצען לאנד איי
סלײנע גרופען, קענען די אידען זיך ניט ערווארבען קיין מאכט און קיין איינפלוס. זאל ער בלײבען אין ניו יארק.

עמיגראנט : — איך זאל שױן אזוי מעהר פֿון צ א ר ניט וויסען, ווי איך וױים ניט וועמען צו פֿאלגען.

A 1906 cartoon in the Yiddish satirical journal *Der Groyser
Kundes* ("The Big Prankster"), that shows Jacob H. Schiff and
William Randolph Hearst arguing over where the Jewish
immigrant should settle. The confused immigrant
reflects that he had more clarity from the Tsar than he
is getting from these two gentlemen.

Kitchen, Hamburg Emigrant Barracks, 1905.
(*Courtesy of the Leo Baeck Institute, New York*)

Ellis Island Passover Seder, 1913.

HIAS office, East Broadway, 1916.

John L. Bernstein, President
of HIAS, 1917–1926.

HIAS office. (*Photograph by Alter Kacyzne*)

Waiting for visas outside the American Consulate.

Warsaw, 1920

·25·

IN THE WAKE OF KISHINEV

"Arise and go now to the city of slaughter," the Hebrew poet Chaim Nachman Bialik wrote after being sent to Kishinev on a fact-finding mission,

> and go into the courtyards,
> And with your eyes you will see and with your hands you
> will feel on the fences,
> And on the trees, and on the stones, and on the plaster
> of the walls,
> The splattered blood and the dried brains of the victims.

The world had been aroused to indignation at the news of Kishinev, where the Jewish death toll had reached forty-nine and hundreds had been raped and injured. "I understood the horror," said the great writer Leo Tolstoy in a public statement,

> and felt intense pity for the innocent victims of mob savagery, mingled with perplexity at the bestiality of the so-called Christians, and aversion and disgust for the so-called educated people who instigated the mob and sympathized with its deeds. Above all, I was horrified at the real culprit, namely the government, with its foolish, fanatical priesthood and gang of foolish officials. The Kishinev crime was a consequence of preaching lies and violence, which the government carries on with such stubborn energy.

But Bialik—the great poet of the Jewish nationalist revival—had nothing to say in his elegy on the subject of government culpability.

213

Rather, what appalled him most, after the slaughter itself, was the behavior summed up this way by Michael Davitt:

> Apart from the desperate and hopeless efforts of the forty mur-
> dered men to save wives and daughters, and a solitary attempt at
> organized resistance . . . the 10,000 or 12,000 Jewish men of Kishi-
> nev offered little or no resistance to the 1500 or 2000 Moldavian and
> Russian assailants of their women, homes and property. Ninety per
> cent of them hid themselves, or fled to safer parts in and out of the
> city for refuge.

Bialik put it this way:

> See all this, but also see: in the darkness of that corner,
> Under where that matzoh lies, behind that cask,
> Hid husbands, bridegrooms, brothers, peering through cracks
> At sacred bodies flailing under the weight of monsters. . . .

A new determination arose among Russian Jews, especially the
young, not to let such scenes be repeated. When a riot broke out that
summer at the town of Gomel in White Russia, a Jewish self-defense
group stood up against it with a courage that became celebrated.

Kishinev and Gomel brought a new surge in emigration, and a new
sense of urgency among those concerned with Jewish refugees. On June
29, 1903, an international conference was convened in Berlin under the
auspices of a formidable young organization, the Hilfsverein der
Deutschen Juden (German-Jewish Aid Society).

Created two years earlier, the Hilfsverein had not been intended
primarily for emigration work. Like that of the Alliance Israélite Universelle, its professed purpose was to provide relief to Jewish communities in the less developed parts of the world. Also like the Alliance, it
made its Jewish work serve as an extension of the mother country's
interests. If the Alliance's activities among the Jewish communities
of North Africa had made it a bulwark of French influence there, the
Hilfsverein sought to do the same in areas into which German influence
was extending—above all, at that moment, in the Ottoman Empire. In
Palestine, Hilfsverein cultural work had already embarked upon a course
so energetic that the Jewish educational system there was to become
largely Germanized in the next ten years.

Such a powerful presence could not keep itself entirely out of emigration problems, particularly since Germany was still the country tra-
versed by the great majority of the Russian-Jewish emigrants on their
way to transatlantic ports. Indeed, one of its principal aims in this field

was to reduce the number passing through—although this was a problem of some delicacy, because German shipping lines did not find Jewish business unwelcome. What the German authorities found intolerable were Jewish emigrants entering the country with tickets for non-German lines, or without tickets at all, and there were times when they refused entry to such persons. The Hilfsverein relayed such refusals to the Jewish newspapers of the world, often suggesting new routes, such as one that went directly from the Russian port of Libau in Latvia, or another from Trieste.

The Berlin conference of June 1903, then, while giving solid support to a Kishinev Relief Committee organized to aid victims on the spot, came up with a unanimous decision "to oppose" emigration from Russia "in every possible way, harsh though such a step might appear. It was pointed out that there were no funds for the purpose, and that emigration at this juncture would result in a terrible catastrophe."

The American and British representatives at the conference were entirely acquiescent in this resolve. Native reactions against immigration were reaching a point of crisis in both their countries. In the United States, a 1903 immigration law added categories to the list of undesirables, notably anarchists and prostitutes. President William McKinley had been assassinated two years earlier by Leon Czolgosz, a self-proclaimed "anarchist" of Hungarian extraction—albeit a native American—and the fear of foreign radicals was on the rise. As for prostitutes, the phenomenon called "white slavery"—the importation of women by procurers for professional purposes—was never large, but it was sufficiently present for outraged puritanism to be added to the moods of mounting immigration restrictionism. It was to become extremely difficult, if not impossible, for a young woman immigrant to be admitted if she did not have immediate relatives either accompanying her or awaiting her at the port of entry.

In the United States, neither anarchism nor white slavery was considered to be the fault of Jewish immigrants exclusively, but the tendency in Britain was to see it that way. Since Britain was not the immense receptacle of immigrants of all kinds that North America was, the term "alien" had become a euphemism for the only substantial group arriving there, the Jews. Agitation against unrestricted alien influx had been led since 1901 by a group of Conservative Members of Parliament who combined a solicitousness toward the working-class vote—aliens had been competing for jobs in this era of growing unemployment—with a peculiar brand of gentlemanly anti-Semitism. The group's leader, Major William Evans Gordon—who sat for the increasingly Jewish district of Stepney, and whose endeavors had led to the appointment of a Royal Commission on Alien Immigration in March 1902—was a friend of the young Chaim Weizmann's, and seems to have been entirely respectful of the abilities of Jews and concerned about them as victims of Russian persecution. He just did not want any more of them crowding into the East End of London. This was also more or less the attitude of the Prime Minister, Arthur James Balfour, who had friends among the Anglo-Jewish elite and was to prove to have enormous reserves of admiration for the Jewish people as a historical phenomenon, but who was fearful of the social effect in England of "an immense body of persons who, however patriotic, able, and industrious ... remained a people apart, and not merely held a religion differing from the vast majority of their fellow-countrymen but only intermarried among themselves."

Such a combination of attitudes produced a most unusual result. Even before the Aliens Commission published its findings in August 1903, recommending restrictive immigrant legislation, the Balfour government made an offer to Theodor Herzl—who had appeared before the Commission as a witness—of territory for Jewish settlement in East Africa. Coming in the immediate wake of Kishinev, the offer caused an upheaval in the Zionist movement, first of joy at this show of recognition by a great power, then of dissension by those who saw it as a potentially harmful diversion from the aim of reconstituting a home for the Jewish people in Palestine. Herzl died a year later hoping an accommodation could be made, but the mounting opposition to the idea among Zionists, along with British second thoughts, led to its complete rejection by the Zionists in 1905.

An Aliens Bill was passed in 1905. It imposed a milder set of restrictions than had evolved in the United States since 1882. Meanwhile, many responsible Englishmen remained attached to the idea of Jewish settlement somewhere in the world under their flag. Rabbi Moses Gaster had scathingly referred to the East Africa offer as "blood money" paid in advance for the Aliens Bill, which everyone knew was aimed at Jewish immigration above all. The issue was to arise again with historic results in years to come; in the meantime, Jewish settlement in British territories throughout the world was on the rise. Canada welcomed more than two thousand Jewish immigrants in 1903 and nearly twice that number in 1904. South Africa, in which Jewish immigrants had played a substantial role in the recently ended war against the Boers, was becoming a major refuge, particularly for Jews from Lithuania. By 1904, the number of Jewish arrivals there was averaging about two thousand a year, and a census that year showed their numbers in the country to have reached more than thirty-eight thousand. Even distant Australia was beginning to experience a Russian-Jewish immigration, though its numbers were still only in the hundreds.

As for Palestine—ever an area of special British concern—its Jewish population of about forty thousand was now being augmented by a new wave of immigration, or *aliyah*,* stirred up by the riots at Kishinev and Gomel. A small group of young men and women from Gomel who arrived there as settlers in January 1904 had since come to be considered the beginning of a new type of Palestine colonization. Members of that town's celebrated self-defense group, they were of the new Labor Zionist persuasion, which had come into being partly as a response to the Bund's accusations against Zionism as a bourgeois ideology. These young Labor Zionists were determined to become workers in Palestine and remain such, unlike the early Hibbat Zion settlers, who were by now mostly employers of Arab labor on their Rothschild-supported farms. This new phase of Palestine settlement, in which an authentic collective-farm movement was to be begun, is now known as the Second Aliyah.

But the foremost objective of Jewish emigrants was still the United States. In spite of tightening restrictions, the annual number of Jewish arrivals there increased from 57,688 in 1902 to 76,203 in 1903, and was to reach 106,236 in 1904—the highest numbers since the previous peak years of 1891 and 1892. And the rate of detentions at Ellis Island increased correspondingly—so much so that, in September 1903, President Theodore Roosevelt would visit there in response to complaints. "The President inspected every part of the work," according to a report, "and held an impromptu examination into the case of a Jewish woman, detained since July with her four children." The problem was that the husband who had come to claim her was out of work and suffering ill health, but the President saw to it that she was admitted. Another Jewish immigrant was admitted when the President discovered that, though he was being detained for having insufficient funds, he was in possession of more cash than Jacob Riis—who was in the presidential entourage—had had when entering the country over thirty years before.

When the President was not around, such work was primarily handled by the Ellis Island representatives of the various immigrant organizations. The Jewish ones included not only, as always, Abram White of the United Hebrew Charities, but now also a delegate from the National Council of Jewish Women—which had been founded in 1903 to deal with the problems of unaccompanied female immigrants—and one from the Hebrew Immigrant Aid Society. Now looking benignly upon the latter, *The American Hebrew* commented on July 1, 1904:

> The Hebrew Immigrant Aid Society is one of those organizations of which little is heard. Founded by East Siders, its work at

*Hebrew for "ascent," *aliyah* is the term for Jewish emigration to Palestine.

Ellis Island is in reality national, not local. The other day, a man who had relatives in Philadelphia but who arrived at this port was sentenced to be deported. Through the efforts of the Society, the man was ultimately permitted to land on our shores. This is but one of the numerous instances in which the organization has interested itself in those unfortunate wanderers. Its officer at Ellis Island knows well the character of the immigrants, speaks their language and understands their position, having been an immigrant himself.

This was quite true; the Society's officer at Ellis Island was now that same Alexander Harkavy who had sailed to the United States with the Kiev Am Olam in 1882. Since then he had worked as an agricultural laborer in Pawling, New York, then as a bookstore clerk on the Lower East Side, had spent a year in Paris from 1885 to 1886, and been a teacher and an editor of various journals, mainly in Yiddish. Interested in linguistics—an older relative of his in Russia, Abraham Harkavy, had been a distinguished Slavic philologist—he had composed several handbooks of the Russian, Hebrew, and Yiddish languages and was working on a major Yiddish-English dictionary.

The relationship Harkavy had developed with the immigrants at Ellis Island is well illustrated by an article that appeared in the April 15, 1904, issue of *The American Hebrew.* "One of the pleasantest, and at the same time most touching Seder services that have ever been held in this country," it ran,

was that given at Ellis Island, at which ninety immigrants celebrated the Passover. Through the generosity of [some of the immigration officials], who also defrayed the expenses of the Seder, the tables, utensils, table linen, and in fact everything to be used for the service, were entirely new. The prayers were read by one of their own number.

After the services, an immigrant who knew he had to be deported, on account of ill health, addressed the assemblage, thanking God that his brethren could find comfort in the thought that they could respect their religious observances undisturbed, and notwithstanding he was not allowed to remain in this free country, he still had none but good words for it, and had no fault to find with those who could not conscientiously allow him to remain.

The government officials made arrangements to have the boats leave at a later hour than usual for the benefit of those living in the city who remained until the celebration was over. The Hebrew Immigrant Aid Society supplied matzos, cider, tea and Hagadahs.

Messrs. A. White, A. S. Schomer [a well-known philanthropist] and A. Harkavy had charge of the arrangements.

·26·

CITIES OF SLAUGHTER, II:
1905

Russia's imperial ambitions in the Far East had led to friction with Japan, and to war between them in February 1904. Once again, along with those Russian subjects who enjoyed equality of rights, Jews were expected to don uniforms and lay down their lives for a country that had never really let them in. Even Port Arthur, where Jews joined in to withstand the long Japanese siege, had been banned to them as a residence shortly before the outbreak. "This is not the time to irritate old wounds," the Russian-Jewish newspaper *Voskhod (Dawn)* advised its readers as the war began:

> Let us endeavor, as far as it is in our power, to forget also the recent expulsion from Port Arthur, the riots of Kishinev and Gomel, and many, many other things. . . . The Jews will go forth into battle as plain soldiers, without any hope of attaining an officer's rank, or shoulder-straps, or distinctions—the blood of our sons will flow as freely as that of the Russians.

This proved to be true. On November 29, 1904, an order was issued to the 27th East Siberian Regiment of Sharpshooters that began:

> Corporal of the 7th Company, Joseph Trumpeldor, addressing a petition to the Captain of the Company, writes: "I have been left with one arm, but that one is the right arm. Therefore, wishing to share in the fighting with my comrades as heretofore, I beg to request your Honor to plead for me that I may be furnished with a sword and a revolver."

The order states that this request should be inscribed "in gold," not only on account of its obvious gallantry, but "all the more because

219

Trumpeldor is a Jew." There was a problem, however: a pistol and sword were the equipment of an officer, not of an ordinary man of the ranks. Trumpeldor could not conveniently fire a rifle, but to give him the weapons he required meant promoting him—about which, with his record, there would have been no hesitation had he not been a Jew. All this considered, the order concludes,

> I promote Trumpeldor to the rank of Junior Sergeant-Major for his fighting merits and for his dauntless bravery in battle shown by him many a time in the field. Trumpeldor's good education . . . gives me ground to believe that, in the capacity of a commanding soldier in the ranks, he will be no less useful than when he was only a private soldier, and that, on the other hand, he will not make his subordinates feel that he is a man of a different religion; on the contrary, as a commander he will deserve their personal regard as well as their official respect. How can one fail to respect a man, especially if that man is of a different religion, who offers his life to his country when he is no longer obliged to do so?

The twenty-four-year-old Trumpeldor, son of an army veteran, went back to Port Arthur and was taken prisoner when it fell on January 1, 1905.

"The fall of Port Arthur marks the beginning of the end," said the London *Jewish Chronicle* on January 6, noting the "racial" significance of the event. "It is an event of historic importance, which sets a different stamp on the old European conception of the decadent East, and shakes the diplomacy of the West to its very foundations." But how, the *Chronicle* asks, has this shaking of Russia's racial arrogance affected the lot of its Jews? "The war," it goes on,

> has been as baneful to Jewish interests as all hostilities between the nations usually are. It has driven vast numbers of our coreligionists—according to one account, as many as 50,000—into the battle line. It has left the families of the Jewish soldiers . . . in the Ghetto slums. It has sent Jewish doctors in shamefully disproportionate numbers to the East, while their non-Jewish competitors were left to appropriate their practices at home.

Noting that Jewish heroism at Port Arthur "has won the applause even of the *Novoye Vremya*," the prominent Saint Petersburg newspaper whose hostility toward Jews was rarely concealed, and has even "extorted the admiration of the Tsar," the *Chronicle* nevertheless feared that "little recollection will remain of these things once the smoke of battle has cleared away. That was the experience of the Russo-Turkish campaign, and will probably be repeated. Whatever other virtues war may evoke, racial gratitude is not one of them."

Certainly gratitude toward the Jews was never the predominant feeling among Russians when revolution was in the air, as it was now. On Sunday, January 9, 1905, the strain of modern warfare produced a historic eruption in Saint Petersburg. As the priest Father Gapon led a peaceful procession of workers through the streets, carrying a petition to the Tsar demanding better working conditions, more land for the peasantry, and a constitution granting representative institutions, nervous soldiers began firing upon them. It was the beginning of a countrywide wave of strikes and demonstrations.

What might this mean for the Jews of Russia? The *Jewish Chronicle*, which already had noted that the war "has provoked riots which have brought the Jews of thirty-five Russian towns to absolute ruin," broached the question by interviewing David Soskice, the Jewish editor of a London-based organ of Russian exiles. Soskice was sanguine that, far from representing a danger for the Russian Jews, the revolutionary movement was their best guarantee of ultimate equality. "Twenty years ago," he said, "no one would have thought of asking equality for Jews. Now, all the workers and students, and the Liberal parties in general always demand it." This was on account of Jewish participation in the movement. "The 'Bund,'" he pointed out, "is the strongest, the best organized, and the most influential of all the Reform organizations, and a great percentage of the revolutionary leaders are Jews." He was not ready to grant that this fact could itself be a source of trouble. "Then," the interviewer pressed, "you do not agree with those who fear that the outbreak of general revolt will be the signal for the commission of atrocities against the Jews?" "If such a thing were attempted," Soskice replied,

> the Jewish members of the revolutionary forces will be strong enough to stop it. If it had not been for these organizations there would have been repetitions of the Kishinev massacre all over the country. During the general strike in Odessa in July, 1903, the Jewish and Christian workers fraternized. "There are no Jews and no Christians in this matter," they cried, "there are only workers." So there were no anti-Jewish disturbances, although the local administration tried its best to get up a riot. No! I repeat that the revolution will bring about the equality of the Jews. Zionism is a dream. This is the real salvation.

The *Chronicle*, along with other observers, remained less sure. "The anti-Semites, headed by [the chief of police, General D. V.] Trepoff, the Dictator of St. Petersburg," it said on February 10, are reported to be daily spreading the report that the revolt was the work of the Jews, who were in alliance with the Japanese and the English. . . . Easter, the usual season of alarms, is not very far off now; and we hope that the utmost vigilance will be exercised over the movements of the Russian anti-Semites, whether official or non-official.

By this time, the distinction between official and nonofficial had become obscure where reactionary anti-Semitic organizations were concerned. A number of these had suddenly materialized, including one called the Union of the Russian People, which counted landowners and priests among its leadership but filled its ranks with hordes of toughs and hooligans who soon came to be known widely as the "Black Hundreds." Working with the connivance and frequent cooperation of the police, these groups were preparing for Easter by disseminating such slogans as "Slay the students and the Zhids!" and distributing proclamations like this:

> The shouts "Down with autocracy!" are the shouts of those blood-suckers who call themselves Zhids, Armenians and Poles. . . . Be on your guard against the Zhids. All the misfortunes in our lives are due to the Zhids. Soon, very soon, the great time will come when there will be no more Zhids in Russia. Down with the traitors! Down with the Constitution!

"As the Russian celebration [of Easter] draws near," declared the *Jewish Chronicle*, "the reports of preparations for a widespread massacre grow more and more definite. Many Jews are hurriedly leaving their place of residence. The flight has already set in at Kishinev and Lodz." But alongside the example of Kishinev stood that of Gomel. "In yet other cases," the article continued,

> the Russian Jews are wisely looking to their own defense. Organizations for mutual protection are being founded. The Odessa Jews have not hesitated to announce publicly that they are organized and armed, and that they are resolved to defend themselves. At Kishinev, we are told that the Jewish population are creating a special town militia for the maintenance of order.

Easter Sunday passed quietly; the disasters came the following day, some in unexpected places. "The disturbances here on Monday," said a May 4 report from the Crimean town of Melitopol,

> began with brawls in the street. A crowd armed with sticks fell upon the Jews, but also damaged and plundered the property of

Christians. A row of shops was set on fire. On the arrival of troops order was restored.

Cries of "Kill the Jews" had been heard, and at the end, thirteen of them lay dead. There was a massacre of Jews that same day at Simferopol, also in the Crimea. But the worst disaster of that Easter Monday was in the old troubled heart of the Ukraine, after all. "A bloody encounter took place yesterday in the town of Zhitomir," said a news report of Tuesday, May 2,

> the Christians in the place having made an onslaught upon the Jews. Numbers were killed on both sides. A late despatch last night stated that the fighting still continued then, the Jews defending their homes with great bravery.

A Reuters report from Saint Petersburg amplified this:

> Details regarding the disorders at Zhitomir are now coming to hand. There appears to have been some free fighting between Christians and Jews, both sides being armed. Up to yesterday twelve persons had been killed and fifty injured. Notwithstanding the repressive measures adopted by the authorities, worse is feared today.

Openly led by Black Hundreds, the Zhitomir rioting went on for three days, with plunder, mutilation, and the murder of fifteen Jews.

As the rioting spread, a new word made its way into the languages of horrified Western observers. As far back as 1882, some German journals had taken to using the Russian word *pogrom* to describe the anti-Jewish rioting. The German version then made its way to London on the pages of *The Times* and the *Jewish Chronicle*, who, on the same day—March 17, 1882—both published translations of an appeal by Rabbi Isaac Rülf of Memel, which said in part: "and seeing that the *Pogromen* against the Jews must at once be put an end to. . . ." The *Jewish Chronicle* had parenthetically translated the word as "outbreaks," whereas *The Times* had gone a step further and offered "riots against the Jews" as the meaning for this context. The best explication of the word, which suddenly became widespread in English during and after the riots of 1905, was to be given by the Westminster *Gazette* in June 1906:

> The Russian word "pogrom" (pronounced with stress on the final syllable) is generally translated "desolation, devastation." The word is related to the Russian words *grom*, thunder, the thunderclash, and to *gromit*, to thunder, to batter down as with a thunderbolt, to destroy without pity.

It was henceforth to refer to the kind of pitiless destruction of Jews and their property that had by now become a Russian trademark.

Yet the pogroms of that spring, bad as they were, turned out not to be the worst ones the revolutionary year 1905 had to offer. The opportunity for a new and unprecedentedly destructive wave came on October 17, when the Tsar, responding to months of revolutionary disturbances, finally issued a manifesto promising constitutional reforms and a Duma, or national representative assembly. For a moment, there was joy throughout the land, shared by Jews and Christians alike. "The whole country was jubilant," recalled Arnold Margolin, then a young Jewish lawyer of Kiev. "Never in my life have I witnessed such an outburst of exuberant joy. In the throngs on the streets of Kiev I saw men and women of all ages weeping with overwhelming happiness." But by the end of the day, Jews in Kiev were being shot at.

Odessa provides an example of what now began to happen. The good news reached there on Tuesday, October 18, according to an account in the *Jewish Chronicle*. "It produced a great outburst of jubilation, with red flags in evidence everywhere." But something ominous was in the air:

> Jews were said to have joined the demonstration. According to one account, they pulled down the Tsar's emblems from the Town Hall, and cried, "Down with the Emperor!" This, it is said, so irritated the Russians that they attacked the Jewish inhabitants of the town and wrecked their shops. A big melee ensued in Dalmatzkaia Street between the Jews and students, and the police, soldiers and Cossacks. There was much firing, and about 150 persons were reported killed and wounded.

The *Chronicle* went on to point out that

> there was another side to the story. . . . "The police and Cossacks," said Reuter's Agency, "are showing indignation at the Tsar's manifesto, and appear to be openly provoking disorders in order to have the opportunity of quelling them, and thus to take revenge for the recent public rejoicing. In other words, the carnival of blood was organized and carried out by the partisans of the old *régime*, and was quite independent of any specifically Jewish provocation.

A calculated pattern soon became evident, described in this summary by the Russian-Jewish historian and eyewitness S. M. Dubnow:

> In connection with the manifesto of October 17, the progressive elements would arrange a street procession, frequently adorned by

the red flags of the left parties and accompanied by appropriate acclamations and speeches expressive of the new liberty. Simultaneously, the participants in the "patriotic demonstration"—consisting mostly of the scum of society, of detectives and police officers in plain clothes—would emerge from their nooks and crannies, carrying the portrait of the Tsar under the shadow of the national flag, singing the national hymn and shouting, "Hurrah, beat the Zhids! The Zhids are eager for liberty. They go against our Tsar to put a Zhid in his place." These "patriotic" demonstrators would be accompanied by police and Cossack patrols (or soldiers), ostensibly to preserve order, but in reality to enable the hooligans to attack and maltreat the Jews and prevent their victims from defending themselves. As soon as the Jews assembled for self-defense, they would be drawn off by the police and troops. Thereupon, the "patriotic" demonstrators and the accomplices, joining them on the way, would break up into small bands and disperse all over the city, invading Jewish houses and stores, ruin, plunder, beat and sometimes slaughter entire families.

In Odessa the carnage lasted four days, leaving more than five hundred dead—some four hundred of them Jews—and hundreds wounded. Other cities struck that fall were Kishinev, Kiev, Romny, Kremenchug, Chernigov, Nikolayev, Yekaterinoslav, Kamenetz-Podolsk, and, as if to complete the grim circle, Yelizavetgrad.

·27·

WANDERING SCHOLARS, I:
SHOLOM ALEICHEM

"Life returned to normality," recalled the youngest daughter of the Yiddish writer Sholom Aleichem who was then living in Kiev,

> although it was never to be the same again. When we went back to school, to the same classes, the same schoolmates, we Jewish girls kept to ourselves, not mixing with the others as we used to do, even avoiding our best friends if they were gentiles. There was curiosity in the eyes of the "others," as if they wanted to ask us questions, but we looked away from their glances. We did not blame them. Their fathers had taken no part in the pogrom. Yet they had done nothing to stop it.

"My, my, how much water has flown under the bridge!" Sholom Aleichem's Tevya the Dairyman says. "We have lived through a Kishinev and a Constitution, through pogroms and disasters of every kind." Even Tevya, normally on good terms with the gentiles of his village, had been through some of it. Coming home one evening, he finds the "whole village" waiting in his yard, "from the mayor, Ivan Poperilo, down to Trochin the Shepherd, and all of them looking stiff and strange in their holiday clothes." Greeting them warmly, but with trepidation in his heart, he asks what has brought them, and the mayor says, "We came here, Tevel, because we want to beat you up." "*Mazel-tov*," replies Tevya, forcing himself to remain calm, "why did you get around to it at this late date? In other places they've almost forgotten all about it." The mayor explains: "It's like this, Tevel, all this time we've been trying to decide whether to beat you up or not. Everywhere else your people are being massacred, then why should we let you go? So the Village Council decided to punish you too. But we haven't decided what

226

to do to you. We don't know whether to break a few of your window-panes and rip your featherbeds, or to set fire to your house and barn and entire homestead."

Tevya pleads with them in the name, not of *"your* God or *my* God," but "of the God who rules over all of us," and this has some effect. "It's like this, Tevel," the mayor says, "we have nothing against you your-self. It's true that you are a Jew, but you are not a bad person. But one thing has nothing to do with the other. You have to be punished. The Village Council has decided. We at least have to smash a few of your windowpanes. We don't dare not to. Suppose an official passed through the village and saw that your house hadn't been touched. We would surely have to suffer for it." So they smashed his windows, and let it go at that.

It was enough for Sholom Aleichem, among many others. At the end of his novel of Kiev in 1905, *In the Storm*, he shows a railway station after the pogrom, crowded with Jews,

> with valises, sacks, packages, and pillows, pillows, pillows! Their faces were terrified, their eyes darting about in every direction. They trembled when they heard a shout or even a whistle. . . . From the way they were talking one could surmise that these were emi-grants, because one could hear the words, "escort," "Hamburg," "ship ticket," "America." The word "America" was heard more often than any other. The word "America" had for them a special magnetism, a kind of magical meaning. It stood for an ideal of which many, many had long dreamed. They imagined America to be a kind of heaven, a sort of Paradise. "We hope, God Almighty, they will let us in and not, God forbid, send us back."

By the end of 1905, Jewish immigration into the United States was to reach the new height of 129,910 for the year, and continue rising. That December, Sholom Aleichem left Russia with his family, intending to resettle in the magical land. His daughter, Marie Waife-Goldberg, writes of him:

> For my father, the material advantages of America were of secondary importance. He saw in his own emigration to the Golden Land a symbolic act. He was going along with his own people; the folk writer, as he liked to call himself, would journey with his own folk; he would be with them, with his pen and his heart, as he had been with them all these years in [his fictional towns of] Kasrilevka and Yehupetz.

"Hey, we're going to America!" says Sholom Aleichem's Mottel the cantor's son, and like a true emigrant he even has second thoughts:

Where is America?—I don't know. I only know it's far, terribly far. You've got to ride and ride to it such a long time, until you get there. And when you get there, there's a "Kestle-Gartle." There, in "Kestle-Gartle," they strip you naked and look in your eyes. If your eyes are healthy, that's good. If they aren't, then—sorry, back you go!

There are grounds for hesitation: Mottel's older brother, Elihu, thinks that if their widowed mother doesn't stop weeping, she'll surely make her eyes too bad to pass the immigration authorities; also, they will be leaving their dead father behind in the cemetery; and Pessie, the neighbor, keeps telling of the hard time her relatives in America are having "making a living" (*machen a leben*, a piece of Americanized Yiddish that had made its way back to the old country). But in the end, Mottel's family decides to go, and they are in the wagon with the wheels turning, and that is all that matters: "We're going," Mottel cries, "we're going, we're going to America!"

"Do you know where we've gotten to?" Mottel soon asks. "All the way to Brody! I think we're getting close to America."
"Brody, in Austrian Galicia," writes Marie Waife-Goldberg,

was only a short distance from Radziwill, the town in Western Ukraine which was our last stop in Russia. But between the two places lay centuries of progress. Brody seemed to us a different world. The stores were clean, modern, their windows displaying a profusion and variety of beautiful objects, small comforts, household goods, knickknacks, at moderate prices. But over and above the standard of living we noticed the atmosphere of ease and relaxation, the sense of freedom; no one seemed to be afraid, whether of the government, the police, or their neighbors.

But equally surprising was

the extreme poverty of the poor Jews. The social and economic contrast between rich and poor, modern and old-fashioned, was greater in the Jewish community in Galicia than in Jewish Russia. There were Jews in modern dress, beardless or with side whiskers like those of the Kaiser, sitting in the cafes reading the highbrow German newspapers of Vienna and Budapest; in contrast, there were Jews with long, thick *payes* (earlocks) wearing Hasidic garb— large circular stiff hats, long jackets that reached to their knees (even on the youngsters), with white socks and black slippers—but all this incredibly worn and ragged. My father, who had seen much Jewish poverty in the Russian *shtetl*, was shocked by the threadbare tattered clothes of most of the Jews on the streets of Brody.

"A nice city, this Brody!" says Mottel all the same:

It's not at all like the city, the streets, the people back home. Even
the Jews are not like the Jews back home. That is, the Jews are
the same as ours, only more so. Their *payes* are a lot longer. Their
gabardines almost reach the ground. They wear funny hats, belts,
shoes, socks, and their wives wear wigs.

But the most amusing thing about the Jews of Brody was the way they
spoke. "They spoke Yiddish," says Marie Waife-Goldberg, "but with an
accent of their own, a sort of cockney Yiddish, and in a singsong. . . . It
pleased my father to talk with them in their own accent and rhythm."
"But their language," Mottel exclaims,

oy, that language! They call it "German." It's not at all like what
we speak. That is, the words are the same, only opened out. For
instance: *vuss* is *vass*, *duss* is *dass*, *shlufen* is *shlafen*, *broyt* is
brayt, *fleysh* is *flaysh*. . . . And the way they talk! When they talk,
they sing.

While Mottel goes about Brody, blinking wide eyes at the wonders
of the world, his mother frets about their baggage, which they had
entrusted to an old woman when sneaking across the border, and which
has not yet shown up. "The bedclothes!" she cries. "The pillows! How
can we get to America without bedclothes, without pillows?" The baggage and bedding never do turn up, and, to make matters worse, the
Brody hotel at which they have been staying severely overcharges them.
But they move on to the next station in their journey.
    "We packed up and went to Lemberg," writes Marie Waife-Gold-
berg,

where the devotion of my father's admirers came to our rescue. In
this modern city, with its considerable Jewish intelligentsia, there
was even a local Yiddish newspaper. . . . Even before the notice of
our arrival appeared in the newspapers, our presence in the city
became known and a stream of admirers came to our suite in the
hotel.

Mottel and his family made a much humbler entry, but it was no less of
an event for them. "Lemberg, you see," says Mottel,

is nothing at all like Brody. . . . Clean, spacious, beautiful—a sight
for sore eyes! Sure, there are streets in Lemberg where, if you
walk on them in the summer, you have to wear high galoshes and
hold your nose, just like in Brody. But in the middle of town there's

a park where anybody can go for a walk, even the goats. It's a free
country. On Sabbath, Hasidim with their big fur hats go around
freely and openly, and no one says a word.

The important thing for Mottel's family was the local emigration committee of the Israelitische Allianz. "At last," Mottel rejoices,

> we found the committee! A tall house with a red roof. First you
> have to w... outside a little. That is, not a little, but quite a lot.
> Then they open the doors. You have to go upstairs. There you find
> a lot of people. Mostly our Russians—emigrants, they're called. Al-
> most all of them are hungry, and lots of them have little suckling
> babes. Those who don't have suckling babes are hungry, too. They
> are told to come tomorrow. Tomorrow they are told again to come
> tomorrow.

Mottel learns that many of them are fleeing pogroms, all of them are
going to America, "and none of them has the money. A lot of them have
been sent back." Finally, in walks a kindly doctor, who gives away his
breakfast to some of the emigrants, listens to their stories, and is told
by Mottel's mother of the loss of her family's bedclothes and baggage.
He is perplexed. "And tickets you have?" he asks. "Money you have?"
Mottel's mother says yes, and the doctor says:

> There you are, then, thank God! I'm jealous. Let me ask you
> for something—don't think I'm joking, I'm being serious. Take my
> breakfast, take my emigrants, take my committee, and give me
> your railway and steamship tickets and I'll go to America right
> now. What can I do here all alone, heaven help me, among so many
> poor wretches?

The travelers go on to Cracow.
   There now takes place an inevitable parting of the ways between
Mottel's family and their creator. Sholom Aleichem, after all, was a
famous Yiddish writer, not a poor cantor's orphan. After doing a reading and lecture tour in Galicia, he placed most of his children in school
in Geneva, while he, his wife, and their smallest child went on, first to
England and then to America, to pave the way. But his keen eye remained watchful of the travails of the humbler Russian-Jewish emigrants.
   "If you want to go to America," Mottel observes at this point,

> you should go only with emigrants. When you travel with emi-
> grants, you have it good. You come to a city, you have to find an
> inn. You've got to have a place ready before you arrive, and a

committee does that. A committee sees to it that everything's ready for you.

' Such proved to be the case for Mottel and his family in Cracow, but first

> we were driven into some kind of place—or cell, or stable. We stayed there till morning. Then someone came from the committee and took down all our names. . . . Then they took all of us to a big hotel. A big room with lots of beds and I don't know how many emigrants. "It looks like one of our poorhouses," said my mother.

The emigrants at the "hotel" told one another stories, not all of them encouraging. There was one about steamship tickets told by a man named Topolinsky. In his town, he said,

> there is a company that claims to be selling steamship tickets to America direct from Libau. They got hold of a young man, coaxed sixty-odd rubles out of him, and gave him a card with a red eagle on it. The young man gets to Libau, wants to board the ship, takes out the card with the red eagle on it, and presents it. Nothing doing! It wasn't a steamship ticket, it was somebody's good-luck charm!

Mottel also hears many stories about the cities that lie ahead on the emigration route: Hamburg, Vienna, Paris, London, Liverpool. "As for Hamburg," Mottel records, "everyone says it should burn up right now. Hamburg, they say, is Sodom. There they force emigrants into a bath,* and treat you worse than prisoners. Nowhere are there such villains as in Hamburg." Mottel's family takes the Vienna route instead.

In Vienna, overwhelmed by the size and splendor of the greatest city they had ever seen, the travelers at last find their way to the Israelitische Allianz—or simply "Allianz," as the emigrants call it:

> Who is this "Allianz"? I can't really tell you. I only hear people talking about "Allianz! Allianz! Allianz!" All the emigrants are mad at "Allianz"! They say that "Allianz" does absolutely nothing. "Allianz," they say, has no pity on anyone. "Allianz" hates Jews.

Mottel expects "Allianz" to have a beard and a red nose. But

> "Allianz" doesn't open the door so quickly. You can ring till your heart breaks—he has time. You think we're the only ones? There

---

*In Yiddish, to put someone "in a bath" is to confuse or deceive him; in this case, Mottel is also referring to a literal bath.

are others besides us. They also want to see "Allianz." They look at us as we ring. "Ring a little more; maybe they'll open up for you, maybe you're luckier?" That's what they say, the emigrants, and they laugh.

Finally the doors open, and a man holds back the emigrants as they push in. When his family's turn comes, Mottel is startled to enter and see a group of men without head coverings or beards sitting at a table and smoking cigars. Asking which one is "Allianz," Mottel's mother tells her tale of the bedding lost at the border. They speak to her in German and she doesn't understand a word. The family moves on to Antwerp.

The committee in Antwerp was Ezra, created in 1905 at the sudden increase in the use of that port by emigrants who, avoiding Germany, were traveling there by way of Vienna and Basel. *Ezra* means "help" in Hebrew and is a feminine word (the Biblical Ezra bore a masculine Aramaic name of the same derivation), so Mottel takes this Antwerp counterpart of "Allianz" to be a lady—and much gentler, too:

> "Ezra" is not like "Allianz." "Allianz" throws people around like balls of dough, and "Ezra" doesn't push you around at all. You can come to her whenever you like and talk your heart out. Everything you say gets put down in a book. A young lady named Fräulein Zeitchik sits there and writes. A very nice young lady.

Ezra, like the Hamburg committee, was screening undesirables according to American immigration rules, and was performing the eye examination. At its offices Mottel meets a girl of about ten named Goldie, who has had to stay in Antwerp while her family went on to America because she has trachoma. She is having treatment, and hopes to become well and join them. But now disaster strikes Mottel's family: Mother, as everyone feared, has trachoma. What are they to do? For a moment, they think of going to Canada. Then they decide to go to London and see if they can get by its committee.

"It's a lot of fun at the London committee," says Mottel,

> just like in all the other committees. In the courtyard emigrants are scattered around like garbage, and inside the building men are sitting and smoking cigars and saying to one another, "All right!" The difference is that the German committeemen have their mustaches curled up and speak German, while the London committeemen have shaved their faces completely and say, "All right!" What fun they are.

Mottel and his family find they do not like the East End.

Miraculously, they are able to move on. They sail in steerage on the S. S. *Prince Albert*, eating potatoes the whole way because there is no kosher kitchen on board, getting seasick, observing Yom Kippur, and spending most of their time on deck. Finally, they are in New York harbor. "So there we are," says Mottel triumphantly,

> we've arrived already. Arrived in America. But what now? The passengers from first and second class have been let off on a ladder of some kind with maybe a hundred steps. So what's to become of *us?* We're in America, too.

"That is," Mottel soon concludes,

> people say we're in America. We really haven't seen America yet, because right now we're still in "Kestle-Gartle." That is, it once was called that. Now it's not called "Kestle-Gartle" any more, but "Eli's Island."

Fearing the worst at Ellis Island, they at first, surprisingly,

> were led into a huge brightly lit room and were given food and drink and everything was free, no money needed. Dear, good people! But what now? . . . One by one we were led through long passageways with occasional little openings at the sides. Everywhere we turned, yet another pest with buttons on his uniform looked us over, musing, peering, and tapping.

Then fearful things did happen:

> Before doing anything else, with a little white paper they turned our eyelids inside out, to examine our eyes. Then the rest of our parts. And every one of them puts on you a mark with a piece of chalk and makes a motion with his hand which way you should go, right or left . . . Only then did we look around for one another. Until then we were so rattled we couldn't find one another. And we were as frightened as calves being led to the slaughterhouse.

But, once again miraculously, Mother's eyes are passed.

Mottel and his family have one final matter to take care of. A young man named Mendel, who had become separated from his parents when leaving Russia, and whom they had befriended aboard ship, was being held in detention. What could they do for him? "As luck would have it," Mottel records, "we have reached a society on Ellis Island that calls itself Hachnosses-Orchim." Mottel means the Hebrew Immigrant Aid Society, which was soon to merge with the Hebrew Sheltering House Association, or Hachnosses-Orchim. "This society," Mottel continues, "has its own man on Ellis Island. A very good, kind man. We were sent to this man." They tell him Mendel's story, and the good man—probably Alexander Harkavy—gets to work on the problem. "He goes off somewhere, comes back, then goes off again." Soon he appears with Mendel and proceeds to give him "a whole sermon."

"Remember, my lad," he says, "that we are responsible for you and you must behave. For the next two years you are under our supervision. We'll be watching you. If you don't behave properly, you'll be sent right back where you came from!"

As for Sholom Aleichem himself, he arrived in New York with his wife and youngest child on October 20, 1906. Traveling cabin class, he did not have to go through Ellis Island, and the committee that awaited him was one organized by Jewish notables to meet the famous Yiddish writer. During the ensuing festivities he met Mark Twain, to whom he was introduced as the "Jewish Mark Twain." Whereupon the American author replied to the interpreter, "Please tell him that I am the American Sholom Aleichem." If this is so, can Mottel be called the immigrant Huckleberry Finn?

·28·

GALVESTON

The pogroms of 1903 and 1905 had an impact upon the institutional life of American Jewry. As late as the 1890s, American Jewish leaders had relied largely upon European initiatives to fund the mass emigration and provoke their governments into making official protests against the persecutions in Russia and Rumania. But it suddenly became the turn of the Americans to take the lead in these matters.

It was in late 1905 that funds for overseas relief were raised to any substantial degree for the first time among American Jews. An *ad hoc* National Committee for the Relief of Sufferers by Russian Massacres raised $1.25 million within a month. Its leaders—among whom were Jacob Schiff and other eminences of German-Jewish descent—perceived that a more permanent organization had to be founded. A meeting in New York of Jewish notables from all parts of the country in February 1906 resulted in the creation of the American Jewish Committee, which was soon to become the equivalent of such organizations as the Alliance Israélite Universelle and the Anglo-Jewish Association.

This, and an effort that was to begin a little over two years later to organize a New York "Kehillah"—a single body to bring under one umbrella all the institutional activities of the city's Jews—represented the full ascendancy of the old German-Jewish notables of the United States. It also represented the perhaps inevitable triumph of New York over Cincinnati in national Jewish leadership—Rabbi Isaac Mayer Wise had died in 1900—and the preponderance of philanthropy over religion as the central identifying factor in American-Jewish life. And at the forefront of these philanthropic trends was the personality who so typified them that many observers were inclined to characterize them under his name as "the Schiff era."

Born in Frankfurt in 1847, Jacob H. Schiff had arrived in the United

235

States for the first time when he was twenty, and then, after a return to Germany three years later, settled permanently in New York in 1873, at the age of twenty-six. Making his career and fortune as the guiding spirit of the investment banking firm of Kuhn, Loeb and Company, this short but commanding man with the well-tailored figure and neat Van Dyke beard continued to maintain personal, financial and sentimental connections with his native Germany as well as with other parts of Western Europe. He also was passionately American and just as passionately Jewish. As such, he harbored a loathing for anti-Semitic Russia that had become legendary: it was well known that, in 1904, he had floated an enormous loan to the Japanese government that helped it to victory over Russia. And, as such, he was not just opposed to immigration restrictionism, but actively sought whatever means possible to make the new Jewish arrivals into completely viable Americans.

Foremost among the problems that had always concerned Schiff was the ever-growing Jewish congestion in certain neighborhoods of New York and other American cities. By 1906, the Lower East Side of Manhattan had become one of the most densely populated areas in the world. The Chicago ghetto was not far behind, and other cities serving as main ports of entry, particularly Boston, Philadelphia, and Baltimore, seemed to be heading in the same direction. New Jewish arrivals were naturally attracted to the familiar atmosphere that had developed in these communities, in which one could have no trouble adhering to a more or less traditional way of life and even get through without having to learn much English. This, combined with the fact that these, except Chicago, were the places where one got off the boat, made them irresistible to the vast majority of newcomers. But could they go on absorbing the influx?

For Schiff, this became the overriding question. Efforts at agricultural colonization, while not failing completely—the settlements in southern New Jersey were surviving—had produced relatively meager results. Jews coming to the New World to seek their fortunes were, on the whole, no more eager to become farmers than most people in that era. On the other hand, with American industry and commerce expanding rapidly, there were many jobs and business opportunities available in the country's vast hinterlands. Here the Jewish immigrant masses could easily be absorbed, if only they were willing to go. A substantial portion of the earlier German-Jewish immigration had done this, and many had made their fortunes retailing on the frontier.

A first attempt to deal directly with this problem had been made in 1901, when a national conference of Jewish charitable organizations created the Industrial Removal Office. Making its headquarters in the

United Hebrew Charities building at Second Avenue and East Twenty-second Street, the Industrial Removal Office acted primarily as an information-gathering center regarding employment opportunities in other parts of the country. By the end of 1905, some forty thousand Jewish immigrants had been transferred to the West and Southwest largely through its efforts. But it was felt that a more decisive action was needed.

Schiff was the man to take it. As far back as December 1904, he had written to his friend Paul Nathan, president of the Hilfsverein der Deutschen Juden, that the European emigration committees should consider directing their charges to such ports as "New Orleans, Charleston, Savannah, and Galveston; also Montreal." Among those concerned with the problem, thought had been given in particular to ports on the Gulf of Mexico, which led directly to the new lands of opportunity in the Southwest and beyond. Early in 1906, F. P. Sargent, the United States Commissioner of Immigration, suggested to Schiff that the problem of congestion in the East might be solved by some systematic plan to send immigrant ships directly to Gulf ports. Schiff was quite interested in the idea, and that spring, while visiting London, he mentioned it to the writer Israel Zangwill.

This was only a few months after the Seventh Zionist Congress had definitively rejected the East African territorial offer made by the British government in 1903. Herzl was now dead, and Zangwill, convinced of his own claim to preeminence in world Jewish leadership, had resigned from the Zionist Organization with a group of associates and formed a Jewish Territorial Organization (ITO) instead. The ITO stood on the principle that a territory for autonomous Jewish settlement could yet be found somewhere other than the apparently unobtainable Palestine. In the early throes of grandiose schemes that were to extend all over the world, from Africa to Australia to South America, Zangwill was at first hearing so seized with Schiff's idea of a mass Jewish immigration to the American Southwest that he suggested the establishment of an autonomous Jewish territory there (Arizona and New Mexico were not yet states). Schiff politely informed him that this would be repugnant to American ideals, but tried to persuade him that the ITO could be greatly helpful in carrying out his program, which was not unrelated to its own. Zangwill, reluctant to set aside his vision, was interested in what Schiff had to say all the same.

Back in New York that summer, Schiff wrote to Zangwill that

in this existing emergency the Jewish Territorial Organization, if for the time being it will occupy itself with something which is immediately practicable and sidetrack its cherished project of find-

ing a separate land of refuge where the Jew can live under autonomous conditions, can be of very great service to the momentous
and pressing cause which we all have so very much at heart.

He then spelled out his latest thoughts on the subject:

What I have in mind is that the Jewish Territorial Organization
should take up a project through which it shall become possible to
direct the flow of emigration from Russia to the Gulf ports of the
United States—notably New Orleans—from where immigrants can
readily be distributed over the interior of the country, I am quite
certain, in very large numbers. From New Orleans, for instance,
railroad lines diverge to the Pacific Coast, to the North and Northwest, as well as to the South and Southwest, which provide easy
and cheap transportation to these sections.

Such were the words of a man who had been instrumental in the building of many of these railroad lines and who was known for being inti-
mately familiar with the conditions surrounding virtually every mile of
track. The final lines of his letter reverberate with the passion of a man
of power, eager to achieve control of a situation that others had allowed
to get out of hand:

A proper and thoroughly organized movement of the Russian
emigration, such as I have outlined above, has never been attempted. It has been left more or less—rather more—to the agents
of the steamship companies to direct emigration, and the consequences show themselves, and are increasing to a menacing extent,
in the congestion at New York, Philadelphia, Baltimore, and Boston.

Zangwill remained reluctant, while Schiff continued to bombard him
with suggestions. "I had a conference yesterday," he wrote to the noted
author on October 25,

with Messrs. Cyrus Sulzberger, Oscar Straus, and Professor [Mor-
ris] Loeb upon the project about which we have been recently corresponding, and we have reached the conclusion that the [Industrial]
Removal Office at New York, with the experience and connections
it has already secured, would be well in position to undertake the
carrying out of my project, as far as the labor on this side is concerned.

"With this in view," he goes on, reflecting the discussion they had been
having about location,

it is proposed that the Removal Office create an organization at New Orleans or Galveston, or both, to receive arriving immigrants and at once forward them to their destination, which latter is to be previously arranged for through the New York organization of the Removal Office. To accomplish this properly, it is thought that the Removal Office should have sixty days' previous notice of the initial embarkation of emigrants for New Orleans or Galveston, and that the first shipment should not exceed 500 persons.

This was where the European side came in. "It would be left to the ITO," Schiff continues,

> allied in this, as I hope, with Dr. Paul Nathan's Hilfsverein, to father the movement in Russia, to gather the proposed emigrants, to arrange steamship routes, etc., and for any expense attached to this the funds would have to be found in Europe.

Not that this meant any niggardliness on the part of Schiff, who tells Zangwill that his own contribution to the project at this stage will be $500,000. "This project," he concludes significantly, "is now to a great extent in your own and your friends' hands, and I shall look forward with deep interest to see what can be done with it."

Zangwill went on resisting for a while. In Vienna at around this time, he gave a talk on emigration that did at first sound like an endorsement of Schiff's idea of distribution. "On a misty summer day," he said, "New York is like a hell and I could never conceive how these poor Jews can bear the heat in their small, narrow rooms." But then he went on to say:

> Nevertheless, I have the feeling that were I a Russian immigrant I would give the following reply to the suggestion of moving away: No, I would say, here my soul at least finds satisfaction. Let your millionaries move to other cities, they possess so many resources. I possess only my Jewish atmosphere.

This seems almost to have been intended as an affront to Schiff. But Schiff is not likely to have known about the speech. What he surely knew about was a series of indiscretions Zangwill was to pronounce to Alexander Harkavy of the Hebrew Immigrant Aid Society on January 7, 1907, calling America "the euthanasia of the Jew and Judaism" and concluding, "If I had my way not a single Russian Jew should enter America."

Harkavy's interview with Zangwill was to be published in the New York *Herald* at almost the very moment when the Industrial Removal Office was establishing in Galveston—which alone had been chosen for

Schiff's project—a facility called the Jewish Immigrant Information Bureau. This was being done with the cooperation of the ITO after all, which would be supervising the shipment of the first groups of immigrants to Galveston later that year. The embarrassing episode of the interview must have given Schiff pause about the volatile and histrionic Zangwill's reliability, even as they were beginning their partnership. What it also certainly did was cause Schiff to look with a jaundiced eye upon the personality and activities of Alexander Harkavy.

·29·

WANDERING SCHOLARS, II:
ALEXANDER HARKAVY

When news of Jacob Schiff's plan to divert Jewish immigrants to Gulf of Mexico ports reached the Lower East Side in the fall of 1906, there was inevitably some opposition to it. The Jewish immigrant community there had by then achieved a vigorous identity, and many of its leaders were growing resistant to the charitable ministrations and dictates of the "Yahudim" uptown—especially from one with such authoritarian inclinations as Jacob Schiff. Socialism of the Bund variety was strong among these leaders, and they tended to see in the philanthropies of a capitalist like Schiff a compromise to their aspirations for a Yiddish-speaking proletariat. The Galveston plan was bound to seem an attempt to impede the growth of the Lower East Side Jewish community, which was gaining in votes and political strength, and was seeking to send a socialist representative to Congress. The plan was opposed vigorously that fall by William Randolph Hearst, editor of the *Journal*, who wooed the Jewish voters of the Lower East Side during his ultimately unsuccessful bid for the New York governorship.

Alexander Harkavy—who was now conducting the affairs of the Hebrew Immigrant Aid Society as a virtual one-man operation, even though he was officially only its Ellis Island representative and not its president—shared fully in this attitude. And he also had reasons of his own for disliking the Galveston plan and Schiff's intervention in immigrant affairs in general. Galveston, after all, would mean a large-scale diversion of Jewish immigrants away from Ellis Island, and a consequent diminution in Harkavy's role, to Schiff's advantage. It may well have occurred to Harkavy that if Abraham Cahan had transformed *The Jewish Daily Forward* into a major seat of power and influence almost overnight, then a position in control of the immigration process itself could achieve similar stature. But it had to be real control, and this

241

meant challenging Schiff's authority at the European sources to which it had now reached out.

An essential element of the Galveston plan was the agreement being arrived at with the German shipping companies—among which Schiff had considerable influence—to carry Jewish immigrants directly to the Gulf of Mexico without stopping at the Northern U.S. ports. Harkavy, on the other hand, believed that it might now become possible to bypass Germany almost completely in the Jewish emigration routes from Eastern Europe. Since the Revolution of 1905 and the convening of a Duma the following May, Russia had become a country in which reformers on both sides of the Atlantic could place some hopes. Harkavy had hopes not only that the Jewish situation in Russia might now improve, but also that the Russian government might become more cooperative in facilitating the emigration of those who wanted to leave. Among his justifications for such hopes was the fact that a newly organized Russian Volunteer Fleet had carried as many as twenty thousand Jewish emigrants from Libau to harbors in Western Europe and even the United States since the beginning of the year. Moreover, the Dutch, Belgian, and French ports had been sending increasing numbers across the Atlantic; these were emigrants who had reached the ports either by ship from Libau, or overland through Austria and Switzerland—once again, bypassing Germany. That fall, Harkavy decided to go to Europe himself to see what he could do for the trends in the emigration process that he favored.

Making a point of sailing on a ship of the Russian Volunteer Fleet, Harkavy left New York on the S.S. *Petersburg* on November 13, 1906. During the twelve-day voyage to Rotterdam, he discussed with the ship's captain, J. G. Skolsky, how regulations and conditions could be improved for the benefit of the emigrants. Skolsky, who thought he could find ways of embarking emigrants who had not yet obtained passports, assured Harkavy that the Russian Volunteer Fleet would listen to any suggestions the Hebrew Immigrant Aid Society wanted to make. He even promised to obtain permission for Harkavy to enter Russia on his present tour—a promise that was not to materialize. Harkavy also examined the kosher kitchen on the ship and tasted its food.

At Rotterdam, a major alternative to the German ports, Harkavy visited all the large emigration facilities, eager to find them in the best possible condition. So marked was his concern that the director of the Holland-America line, whom he went to see the first day, feared at first that he might be a U.S. government official. The director at last agreed to take him to see the "hotel" in which the line housed steerage passengers waiting to embark. It had bedrooms, bathrooms, a dining room, and a café, and was much like shipboard: the bunks, for example, were arranged one over the other as in steerage. Harkavy asked stern questions about the handling of baggage, the loss of which was the most frequent complaint he heard from immigrants. He also asked how carefully the line was handling the inspection of emigrants as to physical fitness—for those rejected at Ellis Island had to return to Europe at the shipping company's expense. He was assured that great care was taken in this matter, and that the unfit were, as he jotted in his diary, "returned to the countries whence they came." He received the same assurance the next day from officials of the Rotterdam Montefiore Society, an old Jewish relief organization now engaged in emigration work.

Later the second day, Harkavy visited the Hotel Canada, a favorite lodging for emigrants using the British lines and the Russian Volunteer Fleet, and therefore of particular interest to him. After interviewing some of the emigrants there, he wrote down emphatically that, in general, they

> must avoid Germany, which does not pass persons intending to go by lines other than German. They must in consequence make a long route. They have to go by way of Austria to Basel, Switzerland; from there to Antwerp and then to Rotterdam. To enable them to make such a route reductions are allowed in transportation. Only "prepaids" come to Rotterdam. Nonprepaids desiring to avoid Germany go from Basel to Havre and thence to Liverpool. It is claimed by those who are in a position to know that this route is making Germany relax her severity to emigrants entering her borders.

It was indeed stories of German severities—above all, of the "bath" at Hamburg that Mary Antin had experienced and Mottel and his family preferred to avoid—that were causing more and more of the emigrants to seek routes through other countries.

After a stopover in Amsterdam, Harkavy moved on to Antwerp, where he went to look at Mottel's beloved Ezra committee. Its president told him that the committee had been formed two years before on account of a case of "ill treatment of a woman passenger" by a steamship agent, who apparently sold her a ticket below cost and then tried to reclaim the difference by luring her into white slavery. At the Belgian Red Star line office, where Harkavy again asked about the physical inspection of emigrants, he was told that "extreme care" was taken, but that "rejected emigrants have no confidence [in the company's decision] and make all sorts of efforts to be permitted to embark." It may be recalled that Mottel's mother, found in Antwerp to have trachoma, had moved quickly on to London. In any case, Antwerp as a port of embarkation for emigrants proved to have problems in Harkavy's eyes:

conditions in the emigrant hotels were poor, and there were no kosher facilities aboard the ships of the Belgian Red Star line.

Harkavy seems to have been particularly interested in the possibility of a route through France and its ports, and in the prospects of obtaining an alliance with the Jewish Colonization Association in Paris of the kind Schiff had been seeking with Zangwill's Jewish Territorial Organization. Baron de Hirsch having died in 1896, the JCA was now administered by Rothschild family interests and was to some extent involved in Palestine colonization; but the main thrust of its activities was still toward Argentina and the New World. Harkavy went straight to its offices when he arrived in Paris on December 13. Its secretary, E. Schwarzfeld, told Harkavy that the JCA could obtain reductions of 25 percent on steamship tickets to the United States, and of 30 to 40 percent on railway fares, even on the American side. But the problem was that this clearly would be "assisted emigration," and therefore contrary to U.S. law. Schwarzfeld suggested that the emigrants might get around this problem by forming mutual loan societies, to which the JCA would extend its benefits and protection.

On Saturday, December 15, while still in Paris, Harkavy briefly put on another of the professional hats he had worn throughout his life and careers—that of journalist. He evidently had made arrangements with New York newspapers to send them occasional articles from Europe, and he was clearly determined to use these as opportunities to publicize his own position on, and role in, Jewish emigration. That day, he interviewed the social philosopher Max Nordau, one of the most celebrated nonfiction writers of the period, whose reputation had been further enhanced by his close association with Theodor Herzl in the founding of the Zionist movement. Harkavy evidently hoped to elicit from Nordau sentiments on American Jewish immigration that would support his own.

"America saves the man, not the Jew," cautioned the Zionist leader in response to Harkavy's questions; but he added, "Under present conditions, however, it is fortunate that the country is open to our people." Harkavy then asked him pointedly what he thought about the problem of congestion in New York and other cities, and he replied:

> Jews in America should live in groups in order to be able to preserve their character and ideals. Their dispersion would cause the disappearance of Jewish traits. Influenced by foreign surroundings, Jews lose their identity. To preserve their character in foreign environments, Jews must organize.

Harkavy could not have put it better himself; but Nordau, a cosmopolitan citizen of Western Europe as well as a Jewish nationalist, then had a qualification to add:

However, Jews in America should not go to extremes. They should not congregate in too great numbers. Jewish immigrants in that country should Americanize themselves, and in such a manner that their ideals should remain beside their Americanism.

The argument had been given back to Jacob Schiff, who doubtless read this interview when it appeared in *The American Hebrew* of December 21.

Harkavy now went to see what was happening in Germany. The notorious severities of the German route were in fact being mollified, especially in Bremen, which was becoming Hamburg's chief rival as a North Sea and transatlantic port. Visiting Bremen first, Harkavy went to the offices of its shipping line, the North German Lloyd, which was carrying 250 Jewish passengers a week to the United States. The company was building its own emigrant halls, and was in the meantime sending the steerage passengers to hotels, including one with a kosher kitchen called the Hotel Stadt Warschau (City of Warsaw). Harkavy went to see it, and found its proprietor, F. Missler, an agent of the North German Lloyd, to be a "champion of the emigrant." Missler had much to say about the differences between Bremen and Hamburg in this matter. "Criticizes treatment of emigrants at Hamburg," Harkavy wrote. "Discussion on treatment of emigrants at controlling stations. Says abolition of the 'Bath' is now under consideration and assures it will be accomplished. Claims to be one of those who are agitating against that system." Missler also was for letting emigrants awaiting passage move about town as they pleased, instead of being penned up like prisoners. "Emigrants' liberty," he proudly asserted, "will not be impaired in Bremen as long as I live." At dinnertime, Harkavy saw "hundreds of Jews at the tables" of the dining room, which they called the *Volksküche*—People's Kitchen.

In Hamburg, Max Ohrt, the bureau chief of the Hamburg-America line, told Harkavy that the whole matter of the "bath" was "under consideration and it is hoped that the system will be abolished." Riding out to the suburb of Veddel, where the company had its well-known *Auswanderer-Hallen* (emigrant barracks) on the south shore of the Elbe, Harkavy had a chance to see German efficiency working at its best for the emigration system. He saw

an emigrant city. Buildings for all purposes: examination rooms, baths, kitchens, dining rooms, sitting rooms, bedrooms, baggage alcoves, disinfecting rooms, toilets, etc. Music stand and churches for all denominations. Protestant church, Catholic church, and synagogue.

The place also provided a display of German severity; for it was divided into two sections, a *Reine Abteilung* and an *Unreine Abteilung*, for "clean" and "unclean" passengers, the latter being those who had not yet undergone the medical examination. Room and board were 1.60 marks a day for adults, half that for children, and there were separate bedrooms for families. There was a kosher dining facility for Jews, where a typical dinner consisted of bouillon, vegetables, and half a pound of meat. Emigrants who had passed their medical examinations were free to go about the city. One official said the company had thus handled forty-five thousand emigrants in 1906.

In Berlin, Harkavy visited the headquarters of the Hilfsverein der Deutschen Juden and interviewed its president, Jacob Schiff's friend and associate Dr. Paul Nathan. When asked by Harkavy if he had a message for American Jews, Nathan replied carefully:

> Jews in America should be good citizens, but they need not on that account give up their ideals. Personal convictions are private affairs. Economically it is undesirable that they should live in great numbers together. Jewish ideals may well be preserved in small communities.

Harkavy should not have expected anything different. He asked Nathan whether he was "a Zionist or an assimilator," and the latter replied, "I am neither one nor the other," repeating the point for emphasis. This endorsement of Schiff's position was not published by Harkavy.

With the new year, Harkavy was in London to examine the last station in the European part of the emigrants' journey. He visited those bulwarks of social responsibility, the Jewish Board of Guardians, the Anglo-Jewish Association, and the Poor Jews' Temporary Shelter. The Board of Guardians spokesman told him that the organization took in persons rejected at American ports for trachoma or other diseases, tried to cure them, and, if successful, sent them back to the United States. At the Anglo-Jewish Association, Harkavy spoke to its secretary, M. Duparc, who was also the editor of the *Jewish Chronicle*. Insisting that the Association had nothing to do with emigration, Duparc nevertheless had something to say about an emigration matter of particular concern to Harkavy and to Schiff—that of Jewish congestion in American cities. "It is natural—said he—that Jewish emigrants should go to New York, but it is not desirable that they should live in great numbers together. Jewish congestion, he thinks, will create animosities, envy, etc." Harkavy could not resist pointing out that "Jews living together in great numbers form a political power," but the respectable Duparc replied that "that in itself is injurious."

On Sunday, January 6, 1907, Harkavy stopped in at the Poor Jews' Temporary Shelter, which now not only offered up to fourteen days' lodging at 1 shilling a day—no charge for the destitute—but was also willing to take in emigrants. It was now partly an emigration society, sending agents to Gravesend to meet new arrivals, and aiding transportation to Canada at reductions of 35 percent and more on steamship tickets. Harkavy found its conditions and equipment "simply admirable."

The next day Harkavy again put on his journalist's hat, and rode out to Israel Zangwill's country home at Haslemere for the most important interview of his journey. Off the record, he discussed the Galveston idea with Zangwill, and may have found that the author still had mixed feelings on the subject. But he could not have realized how far the writer's irrepressible impulse to *épater le bourgeois juif* would go. When he asked Zangwill for his opinion on emigration to America, the latter replied for publication:

> America is the euthanasia of the Jew and Judaism. The stronger force always absorbs the weaker. The Jewish force has been the stronger in the past only when persecuted. In the social anti-Semitism of America lies the Jews' only hope.
>
> The Jewish masses who are now pouring into America are the most civilized element in the whole immigration. Not only do they represent an ancient, highly moralized civilization, but their acquaintance with Hebrew and Yiddish literature puts them on a far higher scale of literateness than the bulk of the immigration.
>
> The Russian Jews in particular have so great a capacity for idealism that it is almost their destruction in the world of practice. Witness, for example, their rejection immediately after the Kishineff massacres of England's offer in East Africa because it was not Palestine.
>
> Such an idealistic element is just what latter day America needs. Their language, Yiddish, has produced several masterpieces of literature, as anyone may convince himself by reading the work of [I. L.] Peretz, "Stories and Pictures," recently published in an excellent English translation by the Jewish Publication Society of America.
>
> It is a great pity that the highly complex culture of the Russian Jew must be swallowed up in Americanism and produce no distinctive fruits. If I had my way not a single Russian Jew should enter America.

This potpourri of thoughts and provocations was published in the New York *Herald* a few days later, and provoked an irate editorial in the January 18 *American Hebrew* under the title "The Euthanasia of the Race." Jacob Schiff's response is not on record.

After a brief sojourn in Liverpool, where he looked over the emigrant facilities of the Cunard and White Star lines, Harkavy sailed from there on January 12 on the S.S. *Campania.* Inexhaustibly, he checked out the steerage conditions aboard. "About three hundred Jewish passengers," he recorded. "Asked whether they were satisfied with the food, they answered affirmatively. They make, however, some complaints of ill-treatment on part of attendants." There was a kosher kitchen, which he visited, as well as the general kitchen for steerage, which, on account of the vats of boiling potatoes, was "full of steam, like a Turkish bath. Steerage in general," he concluded, "makes unfavorable impression."

Harkavy arrived in New York on Saturday, January 19, brimming over with ideas for making the world a better place for emigrants.

· 30 ·

MR. SCHIFF STEPS IN

Upon his return, Alexander Harkavy spoke to a large and appreciative audience at the Educational Alliance about his experiences and observations in Europe. Later in the year, he began publishing a semiannual news sheet, half English and half Yiddish, called *Der Yiddisher Emigrant*. Distributed through the various emigration societies in Europe, including a new information bureau in Saint Petersburg, the paper provided the emigrant with exact information about such matters as American entry requirements, how to arrange for transportation, how to handle baggage, the facilities available en route, and so forth. There was no editor's name on its masthead, but every line bespoke the presence of the affable, dark-mustached intellectual who had created it. The little Hebrew Immigrant Aid Society, which had an annual income from contributions of about $7,000 and was operating at a deficit, could scarcely afford this added expense, but the immigrant businessmen who headed it must have been on the whole rather proud of the gifted Harkavy and his works.

To be sure, he sometimes created problems that might not have arisen under someone of a less flamboyant and literary temperament. One particularly disturbing incident was the outcome of an impulsive gesture he had made at Ellis Island almost two years before. One day late in 1905, a group of fifty-five Russian peasants had arrived as immigrants with virtually no money in their possession, and had been detained for deportation. Harkavy, who spoke good Russian, had promptly taken up their cause. According to an account written years later by one of his colleagues, he had interceded directly with Commissioner William Williams, arguing that these men were able bodied and not likely to become public charges, that they were farmers by training; that they surely would obtain work. But the Commissioner would not yield. Finally the Commissioner said, "Mr. Harkavy, if you are so sure that these men are not going to become public charges, why not have the Hebrew Immigrant Aid Society give a guarantee for them?"

This certainly was more than Harkavy had bargained for. Few of his colleagues were likely to look upon any group of Russian Christian peasants otherwise than as potential makers of pogroms. But, on the other hand, this was 1905, a year of revolution and hoped-for reconciliations. He accepted the challenge and "generously signed a guarantee for these Russian peasants. In the afternoon of that day," continues the account of the colleague, John L. Bernstein,

he brought them to our office. When we saw him bring fifty-five men, we told him, "Mr. Harkavy, you know our conditions. You know we cannot make ends meet. You know that we cannot even care adequately for the Jewish immigrants. We cannot send them to the [Hebrew] Sheltering House; there is no room for them. What are we going to do with them?" And Mr. Harkavy naively said, "What did you want me to do? Did you want me to permit them to be deported?"

Bernstein does not indicate what, if any, was the reply to that question. "So we did the best we could," Bernstein continues:

We lodged them in some hotels on the Bowery, paid fifteen cents a night for them. After a little while they obtained work and they became self-supporting—except one of them who met with an accident and entered a public hospital in Philadelphia. Six or eight months later, we received a bill from the hospital for about $110, which we paid.

And that, apparently, was that, until 1907.
"About two years later," Bernstein's account goes on,

Mr. Harkavy received a letter from the Russian Embassy in Washington asking him to call. He did. He was told that the peasants for whom the Hebrew Immigrant Aid Society gave a guarantee wrote to their home town complaining that every nationality had a representative at the Immigration Station except the Russians, and that they would have been deported were it not for the favor extended to them by a Jewish organization. Their complaint reached the Duma, the Parliament of Russia. The Duma appropriated 20,000 roubles a year for the purpose of maintaining a Russian Repre-

sentative at the Immigration Station and a house for sheltering the
Russian immigrants. The Duma inserted a provision that inasmuch
as the Hebrew Immigrant Aid Society aided Russian subjects of
the Jewish faith, six thousand roubles of that appropriation should
be contributed annually by the Russian Government towards the
work of [that organization].

Harkavy was no doubt pleased at this result of his personal initiative. But his sentiments were not those of all his colleagues. "We called
a meeting," Bernstein writes,

> to consider the offer of the Russian Government. It commenced at
> five o'clock in the afternoon and continued until two o'clock in the
> morning. All this time was occupied in discussing whether to accept
> or reject the six thousand roubles. Some of our directors were in
> favor of accepting the money. Others felt that we ought *not* to put
> ourselves under obligation to the Czarist Government, and that
> governments do not give money without exercising some sort of
> control. We did not like to have a representative of the Russian
> Government look at the list of our immigrants—many of whom had
> left Russia illegally. Moreover, we thought that the Jewish public
> in the United States would resent our accepting a subsidy from the
> Czarist Russian Government. A motion to reject the proposal was
> finally *carried.*

This was probably the first significant rejection that Harkavy had experienced in the organization; it was not to be the last.

In the American-Jewish institutional world, the young Hebrew Immigrant Aid Society was something of a maverick. The organization still
considered to be chiefly responsible for the problems of immigration was
the United Hebrew Charities, under whose umbrella the Industrial Removal Office and the Jewish Immigrants' Information Bureau at Galveston carried on their work. Even the chronic complaints about the
effectiveness of the Charities' representation at Ellis Island had been
put to rest in the spring of 1906, when Abram White died and was
replaced in the job by a Jew of East European origin, a lawyer named
I. Irving Lipsitch. From then on, the names Lipsitch and Harkavy regularly appeared together in newspaper accounts of the Jewish situation
at Ellis Island—both of them, for example, running the annual Seder
there, as well as the New Year's and Day of Atonement services. But
it is not likely that all went smoothly between them. How was it decided
which case went to which man? They must have been in constant rivalry.

There can be no doubt, however, which man had the approval of

Jacob Schiff. The United Hebrew Charities had long been one of his principal philanthropies, and Alexander Harkavy was an irritating man. Moreover, adding to feelings of irritation at this time was the situation at Galveston. A major financial panic occurred in 1907, and immigration took a sudden dip as a result. A disappointingly small number of Jewish immigrants were arriving at Galveston, a name scarcely as attractive to them as New York, even in the best of times. Meanwhile, Harkavy and the Hebrew Immigrant Aid Society went on quietly ignoring the Galveston plan altogether.

When it came to indigenous Lower East Side organizations that cared for immigrants, Schiff had a long-standing preference for the Hebrew Sheltering House Association, another of his charities since its inception in 1889. Like other "uptown" philanthropists, Schiff recognized that it was important to nurture a class of charitable workers and leaders of East European origin. Among these, he could not have found any more suitable to his own ideals than the founders of the Sheltering House, Kasriel Sarasohn, who died in 1903, and his son Eliezer, who was carrying on all his father's works. Pillars of "downtown" respectability, they published a newspaper, the *Tageblatt (Daily News)*, that was pious in religion, conservative in politics, and an archrival to the Yiddish socialist press. In fact, a fierce contest for influence and circulation was going on at that very moment between the *Tageblatt* and Abraham Cahan's *Jewish Daily Forward;* by the end of 1907, the *Forward*, even though it had briefly been forced to declare bankruptcy on account of the financial crisis, was clearly pulling ahead. So also was the Jewish labor movement, which was spreading as a major vehicle of self-improvement on the Lower East Side.

Undaunted by these more unruly manifestations of ghetto autonomy, Schiff continued to put his money on people like the Sarasohns; early in 1907, he had decided to make a major benefaction to them. For some years, the Sheltering House had been diverting a growing part of its facilities to caring for the Hebrew aged, its role in immigration thereby diminishing. But the newly appointed Immigration Commissioner at Ellis Island, Robert Watchorn—who was regarded much more favorably by Jewish leaders than Williams had been—now suggested that the Sheltering House could take in as many as a hundred detained Jewish immigrants at a time if only it would turn over the care of the aged entirely to other institutions. Schiff liked the idea and therefore made an offer: if the Sheltering House would "cease to care for the aged and give shelter only to the immigrants," he would take over the $40,000 mortgage on the building at 229–231 East Broadway that the Association had recently bought. Furthermore, he was ready to provide another $5,000 or $6,000 for building improvements. "Among the improvements intended for the building," according to the *American*

Hebrew of April 19, 1907, "are the installing of electric lights, marble hallways and shower baths."

This could hardly be refused; by the summer, the work was completed. And right across the street, staring at this magnificently renovated edifice from its newly occupied quarters on two floors of the modest building at 234 East Broadway, was the Hebrew Immigrant Aid Society.

There had been cases of collaboration between the two organizations. The Hebrew Sheltering House did not have a representative at Ellis Island, and the Aid Society did not have a shelter: each had something to offer the other. To be sure, the Sheltering House would now have been likely to turn to Lipsitch rather than to Harkavy to do its work at Ellis Island. But, apart from certain obstacles—the largest of them being Harkavy himself—it was bound to strike some people in both organizations from now on that a merger between them would make perfectly good sense.

This idea came up palpably in February 1908. The time was ripe for it. The United Hebrew Charities, affected by the financial panic of 1907, had been forced to close its doors for a while in December. Meanwhile, the Hebrew Immigrant Aid Society was itching to expand. "At the information bureau of the Society," ran an *American Hebrew* article of January 31, 1908, "18,000 people received advice . . . and a man is in constant attendance there to help the immigrants find their baggage." Furthermore, "a new manager has been secured, Mr. Samuel Mason, who has already become invaluable." Yet the facilities were quite limited. "The work among detained immigrants proves to be a costly enterprise," the article points out, "for the detained are aided absolutely free of charge, and the messages and telegrams that they have to send to friends or relatives are numerous and oftentimes at great distances." A few months later, the same paper was to stress that the Society's most "pressing need is for a large building on the East Side in which to carry on the multifarious activities connected with immigration." And there was one right across the street.

It was a matter of establishing the right points of contact, and the person who could do this turned out to be Morris D. Waldman, a forty-eight-year-old native of Hungary and veteran of American-Jewish charitable work. Waldman had been the first director of the Jewish Immigrants' Information Bureau in Galveston, but in January he had been called back to New York to serve as manager of the financially troubled United Hebrew Charities. Shortly after that, Waldman relates in his memoirs—with a few of the defects of recollection that must come when writing forty years after the fact—

I received a call from two gentlemen, one an elderly man whose name I do not recall [Max Meyerson] and a young man named Samuel Mason. They were the president and executive director, respectively, of a recently [sic] organized "Hebrew Immigrant Aid Society." It was a tiny society of recent immigrants from, as I recall, the Ukrainian section of the Russian Pale who wished to be helpful to their fellow immigrants from East Europe.

Waldman writes that the two visitors "repectfully begged for permission to place one of their own representatives at Ellis Island"; since they already had Harkavy there, however, this formulation cannot be quite correct. What is more likely is that, since the United Hebrew Charities was just then in abeyance, the two men were suggesting that there continue to be only one Jewish representative at Ellis Island, with their own man wearing the hat for Waldman's organization as well.

It happened that, at this very moment, the United Hebrew Charities, as part of a general trimming of its sails, was eager to get out of immigration work, which it had never regarded as properly an activity of its own. Waldman does not mention this explicitly, although he does say that

from the very beginning of my association with the "Charities" in 1900 I engendered the feeling that the U.H. Charities, a "relief" organization, out of consideration for wise public relations . . . should not operate the Ellis Island Bureau because in the public mind it tended to stamp all Jewish immigrants as dependents because they were the objects of "charitable" ministrations on arrival.

Waldman was therefore quite ready to consider the proposal that Mason and Meyerson had made to him, and to go beyond it.

"About this time," Waldman continues,

Jacob H. Schiff asked me to call on him—as he was in the habit of doing not infrequently to seek information or counsel as to whether and to what extent he should contribute to institutions who continuously kept begging for financial support. This time he wanted my advice with regard to an appeal that had been urgently made of him to destroy a mortgage he held in the sum of $45,000 (if my memory serves me accurately as to the amount) on the building owned and occupied at 229 East Broadway by the Hebrew Sheltering House as a free lodging house and public kitchen for Jewish vagrants and other destitutes. The governing Board of this institution were all lower East Side residents, most of them not long in the country but who had modestly prospered. The majority of the members of the Board, as I recall, also came from the Ukrainian

section of Russia like those of the younger Hebrew Immigrant Aid
Society.

Waldman did not know that a few men were actually on both boards,
but his administrator's mind was arriving at a conclusion.

"As Mr. Schiff was presenting his situation to me," Waldman continues,

> the idea occurred to me that here was an opportunity to do a con-
> structive community welfare job. I told Mr. Schiff of the request
> made of me by the officers of the Hebrew Immigrant Aid Society
> and of my favorable reaction to it for the two reasons already men-
> tioned. I added a third which I believe also made an impression on
> that farsighted little gentleman.

And he proceeded, according to his account, to outline a prophetic vision
of the American-Jewish future:

> I ventured the prediction that in the light of the heavy immi-
> gration from East and Southeast Europe and the phenomenally
> rapid adjustment to their new environment of these intelligent,
> hardworking and thrifty newcomers, a quarter century hence the
> "German" Jews in America would relegate themselves to the back-
> ground in Jewish community affairs, indeed, that many of them
> would become biologically absorbed—"assimilated" was the word
> used then—in the general Christian community. By that time the
> newcomers would prosper substantially in commerce and the
> professions and not only develop communal institutions of their own
> but would gradually infiltrate into the "ritzy" managing boards of
> the old and venerable institutions established before their arrival
> and even become the dominating elements in the older institutions.
> I carried on that train of thought to the conclusion that I would
> regard it as advisable for us to encourage them to assume respon-
> sibility as time went on, thus preparing them for the bigger tasks
> they would eventually take over.

These reflections were bound to make a strong impression upon
Schiff, some of whose foremost charities, such as the Educational Alliance and the Henry Street Settlement, were already being absorbed
and transformed by the very people they had been founded to help.
Meanwhile, what of the particular organizations under discussion, about
which Schiff certainly had some ideas of his own? Waldman went on to
say significantly that the way the East European Jews currently "were
managing the little institutions they had already established was quite
primitive in comparison with the advanced practices of the older institutions." Then, getting to the point,

I told him that I believed that, well intentioned as the governors of the Hebrew Sheltering House were to offer free lodging and meals to Jewish vagrants without inquiring into their personal affairs or attempting to do something that might put them on their own feet and make them self-supporting and self-respecting, they were doing more harm than good; that such charity of the heart but not of the mind tended to pauperize them.

Schiff, who had already been telling the Sheltering House people such things himself,

listened with obviously earnest attention to all I said. Then, in reply to his query "What do you advise me?" I made the specific suggestion that the Hebrew Immigrant Aid Society and the Hebrew Sheltering House should effect a merger—a compatible marriage, I predicted, in view of the close *landsmannschaft* relation between the people on the two boards.

Such a sanguine view of their compatibility could only have come from an outsider. "Further I suggested," Waldman goes on,

that the request of each organization be granted, opportunity to the one to operate at Ellis Island, to the other the gift of Mr. Schiff's mortgage provided they would accept two conditions. One condition was to be that the Hebrew Sheltering House cease operating as a free lodging house for vagrants and use its facilities exclusively for the temporary shelter of immigrants pending their reunion with relatives and friends in other parts of the country. The other condition was that the operations of the Hebrew Immigrant Aid Society at Ellis Island were to be confined to service at Ellis Island for the time being under the supervision of a Committee on Immigration.

Here a whole new concept entered the picture, one that Schiff was bound to like. "The latter committee," Waldman's account goes on,

was to consist of representatives of the following organizations actively interested in the problems of immigration, the United Hebrew Charities, the Baron de Hirsch Fund, the Industrial Removal Office, the Clara de Hirsch Home for Working Girls, the [consolidated] Hebrew Immigrant Aid Society and Shelter House, and the New York section of the National Council of Jewish Women. . . . Further, that this overall committee should have the exclusive authority to deal on behalf of the constituent agencies with immigration legislation and the government authorities.

Here indeed was a program for replacing "primitive" with "advanced practices" in immigration work. "Mr. Schiff said he liked my idea and authorized me to go ahead, promising to make a gift of his mortgage loan to the H.S.H. if they complied with my proposed program." If Mr. Schiff also gave a thought in that moment to the personnel at Ellis Island, he must have realized that another virtue of this scheme was that it could serve to put the unruly Alexander Harkavy under better control.

·31·

THE HEBREW SHELTERING AND IMMIGRANT AID SOCIETY

The idea presented by Morris Waldman to Jacob Schiff of a merger between the Hebrew Immigrant Aid Society and the Hebrew Sheltering House Association certainly appealed to the latter organization. *The American Hebrew* of February 21, 1908, reported:

> At a meeting of the directors of the Hebrew Sheltering House, 229 East Broadway, on February 16, it was decided to appoint a committee to confer with the directors of the Hebrew Immigrant Aid Society as to merging the two societies. As some of the directors of the Sheltering House are also directors of the Aid Society, it is thought such a merger may be brought about.

The American Hebrew thought so, too: its headline over the article said, "Hebrew Aid Societies May Unite."

But the Hebrew Immigrant Aid Society as a whole evidently did not think so—not yet, at any rate, despite the firm support for the proposal that Samuel Mason and some other directors undoubtedly gave. The opposition was surely led by Alexander Harkavy, along with others desirous of keeping their indigenous little organization free of "uptown" control. These forces hung in the balance for the rest of the year. In the meantime, the little society went on as usual, *Der Yiddisher Emigrant* continuing to come out, and work being done of the sort summarized in this typical month's report:

> 714 immigrants guided to their destination—326 went south of 14th Street; 136 north of 14th; 127 to Brooklyn; 3 to Jersey City; 8 to Long Island City; 114 to 39 various cities . . .
> 321 were women and children; 82 taken around before relatives

258

were located; 72 advertised for in local Jewish papers; 91 telegrams, 93 letters to relatives and friends . . . 101 pieces of clothing distributed; 3,000 copies of periodicals distributed at Ellis Island . . .

Eight friendless immigrants were provided with employment. . . .

In 19 cases, lost baggage was regained. . . .

For 3 deserted wives their husbands were located, and for two of them a reconciliation was effected.

Two marriages of immigrants who traveled as companions with the intention of marrying later were performed before they were admitted to the country.

The Society's sense of a distinct identity was made clear in an *American Hebrew* article of June 5, which said that it "is not, properly speaking, a charitable society. The coming alien does not want charity, though he wants very badly advice and cooperation."

By the end of the year, however, a desperate appeal for funds had to be made from this proud stance. "We want your help," said the Society's notice in the *American Hebrew* of December 25, 1908,

and we come to ask you for it. Let our appeal be as honest as our strivings are simple. We are free from high-flown aims and subtle motives, that would need much explaining. We are not a party; we carry on no propaganda that we need seek justification in the eyes of such as would oppose us. We are in opposition to no one man, to no one set of men. We are at variance with nobody's views.

Clearly, some replying is going on here—perhaps to accusations not only that the Society is too much opposed to Mr. Schiff and his friends, but also that it is too much a prey to Lower East Side radicalism. Perhaps someone, thinking of the previous year's offer from the Duma, even claimed it was too susceptible to Russian influence, for the appeal ends: "The Immigrant Societies of other nationalities are subsidized by their respective governments; but we are Jews; we have nobody to back us up. We help one another. Please help us." Just below this notice, *The American Hebrew* amiably reprinted an excerpt from *The Reform Advocate* that said: "The Hebrew Immigrant Aid Society of East Broadway is doing wonders, considering how it is neglected and wholly overlooked by the wealthy."

The Society was undergoing a crisis, and at the beginning of 1909, after the annual meeting on January 2, this produced a polarization of its membership. If there was, on the one hand, a group more convinced than ever that the proposed merger was the only solution, there now was another, led by Harkavy, that was considering a complete break with the Society and the creation of a new organization. On Sunday,

January 10, *The Jewish Daily Forward* carried an announcement for an
"American-Jewish Society for the Regulation of Immigration," among
whose signatories were Harkavy and such radical and intellectual em-
inences of the Lower East Side as the labor Zionist Nachman Syrkin,
the Yiddishist nationalist Chaim Zhitlowsky, the economist and former
Duma candidate Isaac Hourwich, and the writers David Pinsky and
Leon Kobrin. There is a political tinge to the thing, and such signs of
Harkavy's imprint as a call for

> the creation of a modern, scientific system of information, which
> will provide some enlightenment to the masses while still in their
> home countries about the prevailing conditions in the various trades,
> the possibilities of one city or another for becoming new centers of
> Jewish immigration, and new Jewish agricultural settlements.

"This great task," the announcement pointedly concluded, "has not been
attempted by anyone until now."

The Jewish Daily Forward, that great organ of Lower East Side
socialism, was the natural place for this announcement, although some
of its signatories doubtless knew that its editor, Abraham Cahan, was
already taking the paper in a direction somewhat at variance with the
spirit of the proposed new society. A practical man and now a successful
one, Cahan was no longer very patient with airy schemes devised in
Hester Street cafés, and was capable of seeing virtues in the established
institutions of American-Jewish life no matter what their provenance.
Two days after the announcement, he ran an editorial on "The New
Emigrant Society" that stated his position very carefully. "In Sunday's
Forward," it said,

> the declaration was published of the new immigrant society, which
> has been founded here for the purpose of defending the interests
> of Jewish immigrants en route to America and upon their arrival
> here. Among the signers of the declaration were many names known
> from the radical movement—a guarantee that the new organization
> has a truly dedicated set of collaborators.

These last words were faint praise from an editor who was no longer
the good friend he had once been of some of these collaborators.

"This is a veritable link," the editorial continues,

> in a chain of organizations starting in Russia and going through the
> various lands in which our wanderers have settled. If the work it
> is undertaking is carried out successfully, then the now forlorn and
> helpless immigrant will find in the new body a guide and defender.
> The various injustices that befall him from the moment he

leaves home will now have an organized power to reckon with. The shipping companies will perhaps be forced to respect the new society more than they have respected the complaints of each isolated immigrant.

We at the *Forward*, for example, receive complaints from Jewish immigrants from time to time about the treatment they get aboard the ships, about the food, about anti-Semitic slurs. We try to investigate these complaints, but the steamship companies of course deny them, and in general it is not easy to ferret out the conditions in one place or another, to see if it is possible to redress the grievances. But the new society expects to have the means for making such investigations with the support of various countries, and for bringing about rectifications. Things like this will be its task.

We wish this new organization success.

Having given this friendly pat, the editorial now takes a glance at the organizations that already happen to exist. "The Hebrew Immigrant Aid Society," it continues,

is already a success. It does enormous good for our immigrants in its own humble way, and this shows that it is possible to do good for the immigrants when the undertaking is properly organized and is in the proper hands.

Is this a warning about practicality to the intellectuals forming the new organization? After all, from the practical point of view, even the "uptown" institutions could have value; for example:

The [Industrial] Removal Office is not our own institution—it is run on the money of the Baron de Hirsch Fund. But so far as we can gather from many sources, it is one of the most useful of institutions aiding the immigrants, helping hundreds of them to move on from New York to other American cities. The new organization will probably have close relations with this institution and with the Hebrew Immigrant Aid Society.

Or ought to have, at any rate, these words imply.

Cahan's caution may have been shared by Alexander Harkavy, who, despite his role in the proposed new organization, apparently had not left the Hebrew Immigrant Aid Society just yet. He clearly was the spirit behind another explosive display made by the Society's more vehemently anti-uptown elements, and directed against its would-be partner across the street. "The annual meeting of the Hebrew Sheltering House Association," reported *The American Hebrew* on January 15,

was held last Sunday afternoon [January 10] in the rooms at 229
East Broadway. There were about two hundred persons present to
listen to the annual report, but the matter which drew the greatest
attention was an answer made by the director of the home to a
private circular which had been issued by the Hebrew Immigrant
Aid Society, attacking the work of the home. The two organizations
do very similar work. Mr. Jacob H. Schiff, who has been one of the
most liberal supporters of the Sheltering House, denounced the attack made in the circular.

The contents of the circular were not divulged, but the article makes it
clear that it was sent anonymously to the Board of Directors of the
Sheltering House, who had no doubt at all that it was written by the
"managers" of the Hebrew Immigrant Aid Society.

What could the circular have said? Surely there were invidious remarks about the obviously "charitable" nature of the Sheltering House,
in particular about its persistence in still partially housing the destitute—something for which even Schiff had criticized it. And, in general,
there must have been much said against the aura of an organization
supported by the uptown rich that, in the eyes of some critics, did not
represent the Jewish popular will. Perhaps the circular even squarely
addressed itself against the "one man" with whom it was chiefly at
variance. At any rate, that man got the point, and took its remarks
sternly to heart.

"Such an attack as has been mentioned should be treated with the
utmost contempt," Schiff told the January 10 gathering:

> I have been in this city forty years. In all that time I have never
> known until now of one society engaged in a work of a nature anal-
> ogous to another making an attack upon that other association. It
> should be treated with silent contempt. I do not like to withdraw
> my support from any organization which is engaged in the work of
> charity. It is no use concealing the name of the association to which
> I refer. It is the Hebrew Immigrant Aid Society. This society does
> work which is of a most worthy nature and does accomplish great
> good, but when managers stoop so low as to send anonymous cir-
> culars attacking another association which is engaged in kindred
> work, such men should not be supported as long as they are in
> charge of such an organization.

This was the death knell of the Hebrew Immigrant Aid Society, at least
as it had hitherto been constituted. The idea of a merger between it and
the Sheltering House was almost a year old, and Schiff was in no mood
to wait any longer. He went on to promise that he would hold the mortgage on the Sheltering House without interest for ten years, and then

would eliminate it "if the directors had satisfied him that the work had been carried out for which they had organized." What better way could this be accomplished than through the merging of forces that Waldman had proposed a year ago?

All that was required was the departure of the troublemaking elements in the Hebrew Immigrant Aid Society. This did not happen immediately. On March 20, the *Forward* carried an unsigned appeal for that beleaguered organization, describing its activities—including *Der Yiddisher Emigrant*—and quoting letters praising it. "But the Hebrew Immigrant Aid Society," the article stressed,

> is not a rich or an aristocratic society. It is a people's institution. The Jewish masses created it and they maintain it. It has no philanthropists or great benefactors, and that is why the Society turns to the ordinary people and to their organization for help.

Such sentiments were having their last gasp.

"Sheltering House and Immigrant Aid Unite," proclaimed the headline in the April 2 *American Hebrew*, describing an event that had in fact occurred more than two weeks earlier, even before the appeal in the *Forward*. "A committee," said *The American Hebrew*,

> consisting of Max Meyerson, John L. Bernstein, Arthur Concors, Abel Cooper and Max Sincoff, representing the Board of Directors of the Hebrew Immigrant Aid Society, met in conference with a similar committee representing the Hebrew Sheltering House on Tuesday, March 16, to discuss the advisability of amalgamating both institutions.

These men were among the founders of the Society that had started out so quietly in 1902. "We have learned," they stated officially,

> that the Hebrew Sheltering House Association, which is sheltering chiefly immigrants, has ample room for conducting the work now carried on by the Hebrew Immigrant Aid Society: that the latter organization can save the cost of rent, besides . . . facilitating the work in behalf of immigrants, if it were to amalgamate with the former organization.

They furthermore had learned, they wrote, "that if amalgamation were to be effected, the combined body would be left alone to do all the work for the Jewish immigrants on Ellis Island, except the work on behalf of unaccompanied girls, which is now being carried on by the Council of Jewish Women." This, along with their proposed title for the new organization—the Hebrew Immigrant Aid Society and Hebrew Sheltering

House Association—suggests a hope that they would not be entirely swallowed up by Mr. Schiff's people.

The name adopted at the unification meeting a few days later was the Hebrew Sheltering and Immigrant Aid Society. This, while more succinct than the other, implies a tilting in the direction of the Schiff forces, as does the fact that the president chosen was Judge Leon Sanders, who had held that position with the Sheltering House Association. Furthermore, the representative at Ellis Island was to be I. Irving Lipsitch, who had been representing the United Hebrew Charities there for the past three years. Alexander Harkavy's name disappears from the roster completely. Mr. Schiff, elected an honorary vice president, had his way in this matter as in so many others.

PART SIX

Shadows of War and Revolution

· 1905-1917 ·

·32·

THE FAILURE OF
RUSSIAN LIBERALISM

Even as the new aid society came into being, Jewish immigration to the United States went into a decline: from an all-time high of 153,748 in 1906, the figure descended to 57,551 in 1909. In the New World, there still were economic problems left over from the panic of 1907, and Russia was once again in an era of hopefulness.

The Duma promised by the October 1905 Manifesto had convened in May 1906. It was not quite a democratic institution: voting for it was indirect and based on a property qualification. Furthermore, the left-wing socialist parties, who had boycotted the elections, were not represented in it. Still, it was dominated by a liberal optimism whose champions were among the noblest political spirits in Russia. Of the nearly five hundred delegates, some 150 were members of the Cadet Party (the abbreviation, in Russian, of "Constitutional Democrat"), which consisted mainly of university graduates and professionals who aspired to remake the Russian political system in the image of Western Europe and North America. A true embodiment of Cadet ideals was the thirty-five-year-old lawyer and former Minister of Justice, Vladimir Nabokov, father of the future novelist of the same name. "In 1895," the novelist has written, his father

> had even made Junior Gentleman of the Chamber. From 1896 to 1904 he lectured on criminal law at the Imperial School of Jurisprudence (*Pravovdenie*) in St. Petersburg. Gentlemen of the Chamber were supposed to ask permission of the "Court Minister" before performing a public act. This permission my father did not ask, naturally, when publishing in the review *Pravo* his celebrated article "The Blood Bath of Kishinev" in which he condemned the part played by the police in promoting the Kishinev pogrom of 1903. By imperial decree he was deprived of his court title in January 1905,

267

after which he severed all connection with the Tsar's government and resolutely plunged into antidespotic politics, while continuing his juristic labors.

The Jewish question remained among the central ones for Nabokov and other liberals of the first Duma, in which twelve Jewish delegates sat, eight of them Cadets, three others aligned with the Trudoviki or Labor parties, and one independent. Indeed, it was over the Jewish question that the 1906 Duma had its first—and last—major crisis. In June, a few weeks after it had convened, a pogrom broke out in Bialystok. "This was," according to Shmarya Levin, one of the Jewish delegates, "an orgy of beastliness after the fashion of Kishinev: bellies ripped open, heads with nails driven into them, children with their brains dashed out, and the rest. Eighty Jews were killed and hundreds wounded. A tremor went through the Duma."

An investigating commission was appointed, but even before its report came out, the Duma was fully prepared to blame the government. On the floor of the assembly, Nabokov reiterated his old charge that the central authorities were often the instigators of pogroms. Prince S. D. Urusov, the one liberal member of the Tsar's Cabinet, stood up and asked: "How was it possible for a government to exist at all if at the head of it stood men with the education of corporals and the psychology of lynchers?" When he was done, some of the deputies turned to face the other Cabinet ministers and shouted *"Pogromshchiki* (Pogromists)!" Urusov resigned from the Cabinet, and the Duma passed a resolution denouncing the government for its responsibility at Bialystok. When the investigating commission produced its report confirming this, the Duma called for the Cabinet's resignation. This was simply to invoke the principle of ministerial responsibility, which usually applied to parliamentary regimes. But did it apply to this one? Was this a parliamentary regime?

The answer came quickly enough. "The deputies," writes Shmarya Levin, "knew that they now stood at the parting of the ways. Two days later, when they turned up at the chamber, they found the doors locked and guarded. Outside was posted the manifesto of the Tsar dissolving the Duma." That night, about half the deputies reassembled in the Finnish town of Vyborg and adopted a resolution calling upon the Russian people not to pay taxes or perform military service until the Duma was reconvened. But the government had already given its reply: elections were scheduled for a second Duma, from which all signers of the Vyborg manifesto were to be banned. In September, another major pogrom—this one led by Russian troops in uniform—took place in Sedletz. Russia battered its Jews and its democratic hopes with the same blows.

. . .

"What can we do with them?" a high official, interviewed by Michael Davitt late in 1903, had asked rhetorically of the Jews:

> They are the racial antithesis of our nation. A fusion with us is impossible, owing to religious and other disturbing causes. They will always be a potential source of sectarian and economic disorder in the country. We cannot admit them to equal rights of citizenship for these reasons and, let me add, because their intellectual superiority would enable them in a few years' time to gain possession of most of the posts of our civil administration. They are a growing danger of a most serious nature to our Empire in two of its most vulnerable points—their discontent is a menace to us along the Austrian and German frontiers, while they are the active propagandists of the Socialism of Western Europe within our borders. The only solution of the problem of the Russian Jew is his departure from Russia.

With remarks of this sort, Russia had already been demonstrating that it was the home of the world's most advanced manifestations of the anti-Semitic sensibility in that moment. But the foremost such demonstration came with the appearance there, between 1903 and 1905, of the pernicious forgery known as *The Protocols of the Elders of Zion*.

First published in August and September of 1903 by Pavolaki Krushevan in his Saint Petersburg newspaper *Znamya*, the *Protocols* purported to be the record of a meeting of Jewish leaders from all over the world. The Zionist congresses were an obvious source of inspiration, though not till some years later did editions of the *Protocols* claim to be minutes of secret sessions held at the First Zionist Congress in 1897. For now, the Russian anti-Semitic imagination was content with the depiction of a gathering at an unspecified time and place of unnamed Jews of great wealth, power, and intellect, to discuss how they would rule the world, and how far they had already come in achieving that end.

How, according to the *Protocols*, was this being accomplished? There were no Jews at the heads of governments or armies, but Jewish wealth and intellect had already become the principal forces behind these, according to the anonymous speaker or speakers, by financing them, by advising statesmen and shaping public opinion through domination of the press, by weakening the moral resolve of nations through the spread of atheism and religious skepticism, by undermining the old social and political structures through the advocacy of free speech, political democracy, and, most recently, socialism and revolution. Jewish power was depicted as invisible, and hence all the more dangerous. "Throughout all Europe," the elder proclaims, and by means of relations with Europe, in other continents also, we must create ferments, discords and hostility. Therein we gain a double advantage. In the first place we keep in check all countries, for they well know that we have the power whenever we like to create disorders or to restore order. . . . In the second place, by our intrigues we shall tangle up all the threads which we have stretched into the cabinets of all States by means of politics, by economic treaties, or loan obligations. In order to succeed in this we must use great cunning and penetration during negotiations and agreements, but, as regards what is called the "official language," we shall keep to the opposite tactics and assume the mask of honesty and compliancy. In this way the peoples and governments of the *goyim*, whom we have taught to look only at the outside of whatever we present to their notice, will still continue to accept us as the benefactors and saviors of the human race.

Out of this disorder, the *Protocols* make clear, will eventually arise a King of the Jews who will openly rule the world.

Had anyone noticed that, while Jews were among the pillars of capitalism, they were among the champions of socialism as well? Or that, all over Europe, Jews had risen in recent generations to considerable eminence in journalism and publishing? Or that, wherever and whenever the old prohibitions upon them had been removed, their intellect and skills had enabled them to move into often influential positions? The explanation for all these disparate phenomena was now at hand for those predisposed to believe it. "Our year 1905 has gone as though managed by the Elders," wrote Tsar Nicholas II in the margin of his copy of the *Protocols*.

Where had these roughly thirty thousand absurd but dangerously influential words come from? Their authorship remains a mystery, but much has come to be known about their origins in other respects. Sergey Nilus, the Russian religious mystic whose presentation of the *Protocols* as the appendix to the 1905 edition of his *The Great in the Small: Antichrist Considered As an Imminent Political Possibility* did the most to popularize them—this was the edition the Tsar had read—wrote that they were smuggled to him from "the secret archives of the Central Chancellery of Zion, which is at present situated in France." He claimed that they had first been written in French—and this is most likely true. For scholarly investigation has since unearthed the source from which the *Protocols* were to a large extent plagiarized: a political satire called *Dialogue aux enfers entre Machiavel et Montesquieu (Dialogue in Hell Between Machiavelli and Montesquieu)*, written in 1864 by a disillusioned republican lawyer named Maurice Joly. In this work, Machiavelli, clearly acting as the mouthpiece for an unnamed Napoleon III, describes to the shocked liberal Montesquieu the methods whereby the republican enthusiasms of the 1848 revolution in France can be—and have been—manipulated into popular acceptance of a tyranny.

There is nothing about Jews in Joly's *Dialogue*. Nevertheless, the author of the *Protocols*, slavishly following its general outline, lifted entire passages from it almost verbatim, changing its import by simple formulas of substitution—turning "the people" into "the *goyim*," using phrases of oligarchy in place of those of autocracy, and replacing the past and present with the future tense. As for the scenario of Jewish elders meeting to plan a worldwide conspiracy, this, too, turns out to have been taken from a nineteenth-century source—an imaginatively sinister chapter in an 1868 novel called *Biarritz* by the German anti-Semitic writer Hermann Goedsche, which depicts a secret midnight gathering of the leaders of the twelve tribes of Israel in the Jewish cemetery of Prague. All this was to be duly exposed to the public in years to come, though even proof of forgery would not be sufficient detraction for those whose imagination had been captured by what they regarded as a fundamental truth. "Did not the ass of Balaam utter prophecy?" Sergey Nilus himself once replied to an interviewer who had raised the question of the *Protocols'* authenticity. "Cannot God transform the bones of a dog into sacred miracles? If He can do these things, He can also make the announcement of truth come from the mouth of a liar."

This wisdom was not to be good enough for Tsar Nicholas II, however, despite his innermost inclinations. Aroused by his initial enthusiasm for the *Protocols* into ordering an investigation of their origins, Nicholas soon learned that the work had been instigated, for reasons of court intrigue, by a high official of the Russian secret police stationed in Paris. The official was thereupon dismissed, and the Tsar wrote on his copy of the report of the affair: "Drop the *Protocols*. One cannot defend a pure cause by dirty methods." The *Protocols* were to enjoy a major revival in the wake of the revolutionary year 1917; in the meantime, Russian anti-Semitism had to turn to other weapons.

In the spring of 1911, the body of a thirteen-year-old schoolboy, Andrey Yushchinsky, was found in a cave in the working-class district of Lukyanovka in Kiev. It was covered with nearly fifty wounds that had been made with a stabbing instrument. This was just a few days before the start of Passover. At the boy's funeral, a mimeographed leaflet was distributed. "Orthodox Christians!" it said:

> The Zhids have tortured Andryusha Yushchinsky to death! Every year, before their Passover, they torture to death several dozens of Christian children in order to get their blood to mix with their *matzos*. They do this in commemoration of our Saviour, whom

they tortured to death on the cross. The official doctors found that before the Zhids tortured Yushchinsky they stripped him naked and tied him up, stabbing him in the principal veins so as to get as much blood as possible. They pierced him in fifty places. Russians! If your children are dear to you, beat up the Zhids! Beat them up until there is not a single Zhid left in Russia. Have pity on your children! Avenge the unhappy martyr! It is time! It is time!

The Christians of Kiev did not respond to this call for a pogrom. Rather, it was the police who responded to the clamors of ritual murder in this leaflet and in the anti-Semitic press, by arresting a Jew some four months later and accusing him of that ancient "crime."

Hardly a model "elder of Zion," Mendel Beiliss was a simple workingman in his late thirties, the father of five children. For fifteen years he had been a dispatcher at the Zaitsev brickworks, the Jewish-owned factory complex where young Andrey, playing hooky from school, had last been seen alive, and where investigators concluded the boy's abduction had taken place. The supposed ritual murderer was not even religious: he regularly worked twelve hours on Saturdays—including, to his advantage at the trial, the Saturday on which the Yushchinsky boy had been killed. And though he spoke Russian poorly—Yiddish was his everyday language—he had served honorably in the army three years and lived on good terms with his Christian neighbors.

It took the Kiev authorities, guided by the reactionary Minister of Justice in Saint Petersburg, I. G. Shcheglovitov, more than two years to prepare their case against the hapless Beiliss, who moldered in a prison cell the whole time. People of good will in Russia and throughout the world watched in disgust, seeing the whole affair a symbolic dramatization of tsarism in decay—a condition also displayed during this period by the collapse of yet a third Duma, which had been elected in 1907 on the basis of a narrow property qualification, and the election of an even more conservative fourth Duma in 1912. To make matters worse, the reform Prime Minister Peter Stolypin had been assassinated by a revolutionary in the fall of 1911.

When the trial finally was held in the fall of 1913, Beiliss's defense lawyers—led by a Jewish attorney, Oscar Gruzenberg, who served without pay—found they were simply delivering the coup de grâce to a case that had begun falling apart on its own. Soon, clearly revealed behind the unsubstantiated evidence against Beiliss was a den of underworld operators, which made its headquarters at the home of one Vera Cheberyak, the mother of the murdered boy's playmate—who had himself died of dysentery before the trial began. Open-minded observers were soon convinced that the Cheberyak gang, against which no official case was ever to be brought, was responsible for the murder of young Andrey, who had found out too many things about them.

Whose decision it had been to simulate a ritual murder never emerged in court. But the most shocking aspect of the trial was the relentlessness with which the prosecution, backed by the imperial Ministry of Justice, sought to prove that a *ritual* murder had been committed. "One can point, with absolute confidence," the elder Vladimir Nabokov wrote of the trial, which he covered for a liberal daily, "to a series of obvious, unchallengeable legal violations condoned with only one purpose—to instill into the jury the belief in the existence of ritual murder among Jews."

The final verdict was delivered by a jury "of practically illiterate peasants and commoners," in Nabokov's words. Two questions had been posed by the court. The first was:

> Has it been proved that on March 12, 1911 . . . in one of the buildings of the Jewish surgical hospital . . . Andrey Yushchinsky was gagged, and wounds inflicted on him . . . and that when he had lost five glasses of blood, wounds were inflicted . . . and that these wounds, totalling forty-seven, caused Yushchinsky agonizing pain and led to almost total loss of blood and to his death?

In other words, had a ritual murder been committed? To this, the jury's reply was: "Yes, it has been proved." The second question was about Beiliss, and it went:

> If the event described in the first question has been proved, is the accused . . . guilty of having entered into collusion with others, who have not been discovered in the investigations, in a premeditated plan prompted by religious fanaticism, to murder the boy Andrey Yushchinsky, who happened to be there, and drag him off to one of the buildings of the brickworks?

To this the jury replied, "No, not guilty."

Beiliss was vindicated; but was Russia?

· 33 ·

IMMIGRATION ON THE EVE

"Charged with the duty of caring for Jewish immigrants to the United States of America," said Judge Leon Sanders in November 1913,

> and knowing that if Mendel Beiliss and his family should decide to make this country their permanent home they would be considered in the light of ordinary immigrants and as such subject to the immigration laws, the Board of Directors of the Hebrew Sheltering and Immigrant Aid Society at its last meeting felt called upon to make certain action.
>
> The rumored offer of theatrical managers to Beiliss, that he should go on the stage, and the sensational reports, as a result of these attempts to capitalize Mendel Beiliss and the Ritual Murder Charge for unworthy purposes, urged the members of the Board to take action which would obviate the likelihood of such offers being considered. No invitation was extended to Beiliss to settle in this country, but the steps taken were solely for the purpose of preventing a degradation of Jews and Judaism, in the event of his coming.

Beiliss was to leave Russia for Palestine the following year, and eventually to settle in the United States; in the meantime, the four-year-old amalgamated Hebrew Sheltering and Immigrant Aid Society was firmly demonstrating a sense of its larger responsibilities.

By this time, the Society—which was becoming widely known under the rubric "HIAS," the initials of the old component Hebrew Immigrant Aid Society—had grown into a national organization with branches in Boston, Philadelphia, and Baltimore, an office in Washington, and a full staff at Ellis Island. It ran an Oriental Bureau, at which Spanish was spoken, to deal with the growing number of Sephardic immigrants from

274

the troubled Ottoman Empire. It published a monthly *Jewish Immigration Bulletin* and could boast that, in 1911, it had persuaded the Ellis Island authorities to install a kosher kitchen. It had even done its share, in April 1912, in giving aid to those survivors of the *Titanic* disaster who were brought to New York.

"The Hachnosses-Orchim, 229 East Broadway, New York," stated John Foster Carr's *Guide to the United States for the Jewish Immigrant*, published in Yiddish by the Connecticut Daughters of the American Revolution,

> gives the immigrant all necessary information and help. The Home of this Society is open day and night. There the Jew can obtain all the help needed to get a friend or a relative off a ship, or find him if he has already set out in this country. Jewish immigrants can go to this Society for information, for addresses, for advice as to how to buy railroad tickets or find baggage. This way, it's hard for anyone to cheat them.

The *Guide* describes the Society's Home on East Broadway, where

> the Jewish immigrant can get all the help possible to find his relatives and friends, or to find work. There are comfortable accommodations for men, women, and children. There is an interpreter for Oriental Jews just as there is for Russian Jews. Pen, ink, and paper are provided free of charge; also newspapers. Immigrants can use this Society as an address to which letters from back home can be sent. There are always good beds free for guests. A doctor and a nurse are always on duty. Guests are provided with tasty kosher food from the kitchen. There is a synagogue where services are held three times a day. All religious requirements are provided for. Prayer is always free. Jews can turn to the Hachnosses-Orchim for information and advice from all parts of the country.

As Judge Sanders was to describe it in one of the annual reports:

> The work of the Society may be said to fall into two broad divisions. The first includes all those activities which center around the entry, reception, and immediate care of the immigrant on landing. The second is concerned with our aid to him in the earlier stages of his stay in this country.

But of the two, the work at Ellis Island was still the most important.

The HIAS staff at Ellis Island, presided over by I. Irving Lipsitch and located in an office just off the Great Hall, was by now doing its work with considerable sophistication. Its main task was to make sure that the Boards of Special Inquiry were excluding as few Jewish immigrants as was legitimately possible from entry into the country. In 1913, thanks largely to its work, only eleven out of more than a hundred thousand Jewish immigrants were deported from the Island on grounds of coming for "immoral purposes," and only five because they were deemed to be contract labor.

A problem that had suddenly become prominent was that of exclusion on grounds of "convictions of crime"; there were seventeen such cases in 1913 as against five the previous year. Some of these judgments had been patently unfair in the eyes of the HIAS representatives. "It is our duty," reported the Ellis Island Committee for 1913,

> to call your attention to the fact that many of the cases held up on this charge were held up by an inspector who employs questionable methods to get the alien to testify against his own interests. This inspector, knowing of the unavoidable usage which compels many immigrants to come here on passports belonging to other persons* (for Russia does not readily allow its subjects to escape from its clutches), puts leading questions to the immigrant, making him believe that the person in whose name the passport has been taken out has been convicted of crime, and that notice of said conviction is on file at Ellis Island. The unfortunate immigrant, thus grilled, and believing he must adhere to the facts stated in his passport, is often led to make damaging admissions, some of them not true, leading to his exclusion.

The report then gives an example:

> An immigrant arrived at Ellis Island under the name of Lebi Zinowoi and came before the abovementioned inspector for examination as to his right to land. The inspector, who had before him the manifest sheet—a very formidable looking document—and many other official papers, asked him his name, which he gave as Lebi Zinowoi, which name he had assumed when he obtained the passport which enabled him to leave Russia, a deserter from the army. The inspector then addressed himself to the immigrant as follows: "You are 22 years old? You came from Odessa? You are a clerk? You paid your own passage? You have $20?" All of these questions the immigrant answered in the affirmative.

Then the inspector's approach took an ominous turn. "We have information here," he said,

> "to the effect that you have been in prison in Russia, but it does not appear quite clearly if you were two or three times in prison.

---

*This was especially the case with young men evading military service.

The writing is somewhat blurred. Tell me how many times you were arrested, and you will be discharged to your cousin who is waiting for you." The immigrant denied that he had ever been arrested but the inspector persisted. "There is no use denying it—you know the United States does not send back prisoners to Russia. I merely want to correct our records."

The technique then began taking effect:

> At this juncture, the immigrant, . . . believing that the inspector really had knowledge . . . that the man whose passport he was using had been in prison in Russia, believing also the statement of the inspector that the Government of the United States does not surrender prisoners to Russia, . . . [decided to say] that he had been twice in prison. The result of this was that he was held for Special Inquiry. This kept him in the detention room without an opportunity to see any representative of this Society or any relative for two days, at the expiration of which time he was taken before the Board of Special Inquiry and put under oath. When he was then questioned regarding his record in Russia he stoutly denied having at any time been in prison, but the Board preferred to accept the statement of the inspector and he was ordered deported.

This was the point at which HIAS could intervene at last:

> This gave our representative, Mr. Lipsitch, an opportunity to interview the immigrant, and he soon discovered the exact state of facts—that the man's name was Zama Kotin, but that he had assumed a false name to agree with the name of the man whose passport he was using, that he was a deserter from the Russian army, that he had never had any trouble with the Russian police authorities, and that he had actually been forced to make damaging statements by the inspector who had examined him. Mr. Lipsitch promptly took an appeal from the excluding decision of the Board of Special Inquiry, and obtained a rehearing before the same Board, at which time the immigrant told all the facts, including his real name and the reason for his having assumed that of another.

The hearing again resulted in a decision to deport him, but Lipsitch was not going to let this one go. "We had determined," the report continues,

> not to permit the deportation of this immigrant without due inquiry in Russia to ascertain if he had told the truth, and Mr. Lipsitch was sent to Washington to see Secretary [William B.] Wilson of the Department of Labor [of which the Immigration Bureau was a subsidiary]. He succeeded in having an investigation made through the State Department, which resulted in establishing the fact that there

was nothing against the immigrant which could prevent him from entering the United States.

The report concludes: "He was released on June 5th, 1913, about nine months after his arrival, and is now a self-supporting, respectable, and law-abiding resident of the United States."

But the greatest number of deportations by far were still those being inflicted under the category of "likely to become a public charge." Of the 903 exclusions of Jewish immigrants for this reason in 1913, 692 had been on medical grounds and eighty-seven for the possession of little or no money. This latter group of cases was particularly vexing to the HIAS officers. "We do not take issue with the authorities," the report for 1913 stated,

> for excluding aliens with unfavorable medical certificates against them, and who may become public charges because of physical disability. But to exclude persons against whom there is no adverse medical report, simply because they have little or no ready money with them, is not dealing fairly with these immigrants. It must be remembered that to come to this country from Eastern Europe requires a large outlay of cash; that these emigrants, passing through foreign countries, the prey of sharks and runners and agents of all sorts, are often despoiled of their funds before arriving at Ellis Island, although their calculation may have been that the money they had when they started should have sufficed to permit them to land. These men spent all they had to get here. To be barred out, in sight of the Statue of Liberty, merely because he had been reduced to his last penny on the way makes the immigrant feel a just resentment against this country. . . . Why should there be an arbitrary rule that an able-bodied alien, lacking only $20 or $25, must be debarred, although the same alien has paid his passage from home, has paid a head-tax of $4 to the government, and in every other respect is capable of becoming a desirable citizen?

Rulings of this sort were part of numerous manifestations that the mood of immigration restrictionism was reaching a new height in the United States. In the first decade of the twentieth century, 8,795,386 immigrants had arrived—more than twice the number for the decade before. And the decade that had begun in 1911 seemed about to exceed even that total: in 1913, 1,198,892 immigrants had arrived, the most that had ever come during a single year. In the eyes of many native Americans, the figures alone were enough to cause alarm, but they were not the whole story. In the course of this "new immigration," as it was now being called, a shift in its main Old World sources had gradually occurred. The "old immigration," broadly speaking, had come primarily from the British Isles (mainly Ireland starting in the 1840s) and north-western Europe (mainly Norway, Sweden, and Germany in the mid-nineteenth century, but hardly at all from France). Now, however, most of the new arrivals were from Southern and Eastern Europe, mainly Italy (the south and Sicily), Austria-Hungary, Greece and the Balkans, and the Russian Empire (more Poland and the Jewish Pale than ethnic Russia itself).

The result was a growing presence of ethnic types that old Americans were not used to, relatively exotic in dress, customs, and religion, and on the whole less educated (with some exceptions, notably the Jews) than preceding waves of immigrants. Moreover, unlike the often idealized model of the "old" immigrants, settling as farmers on the land—which really had in general been truer of the Scandinavian than of the German immigrants, and scarcely true of the Irish at all—the new immigrants of the age of industrialization were clustering in cities and in factory and mining towns, creating ethnic enclaves in which one could not even hear English spoken. The irritation some Americans felt at all this was aggravated by the spread of "racial" theories in an era when such ideas had become popular both in Europe and in America. Those who harbored notions of "Nordic" superiority saw the new immigrants as coming from a variety of inferior stocks that were threatening the very biological stuff of which America was made.

In a country that had known outbursts of know-nothingism and nativism, it was hardly surprising that a concerted opposition to the "new immigration" should have arisen. In 1894, a group of Boston gentlemen had organized the Immigration Restriction League, which soon achieved national prominence. Two years later, Senator Henry Cabot Lodge, representing the viewpoint of the League, had introduced a bill calling for a literacy test to be taken by all immigrants before being admitted to the United States. It was passed by Congress, but President Grover Cleveland vetoed it, calling it a "radical departure from our national policy relating to immigration," which had hitherto been one of providing a haven for the oppressed. Literacy bills had again been introduced in 1898, 1902, and 1906, but they had all been defeated in Congress.

The literacy approach was not to be dropped; meanwhile, however, an immigration act of 1907 had tightened restrictions in other ways—by excluding imbeciles, criminals of moral turpitude, and victims of tuberculosis, and by raising the head tax, first imposed in 1882 in the amount of 50¢, to $4. The act also created a Senate commission to investigate the whole immigration question, under the chairmanship of Senator William P. Dillingham of Vermont, a spokesman for the Immigration Restriction League and the sponsor of the 1907 bill. The Dillingham Commission deliberated for four years, publishing a forty-one volume report in 1911 that essentially endorsed the view that the "new immi-

gration" was on the whole inferior to the "old." The Commission's majority recommended a literacy test, the exclusion of unskilled laborers,
an increase both in the head tax and in the amount of money an immigrant was required to have in his possession, and a quota for each entering "race." With the exception of the last—which was to have its day
in an even more xenophobic future—these recommendations were incorporated into a bill sponsored by Dillingham and Representative John L.
Burnett of Alabama.

Throughout the history of immigration restriction, Jews had been
in the forefront of the fight against it. Along with Armenians and a few
smaller groups, Jews were almost alone among the "new" immigrants
in seeing America as a refuge from persecution and not just a horizon
for social and economic betterment, so that any narrowing of its gateway was for them a particular grievance. Moreover, Jews on the whole,
being among the best educated of the "new" immigrant groups, saw
more of their first-generation arrivals become prominent as American
intellectuals and social activists. The Anglo-Jewish and Yiddish presses
were outspokenly against all attempts at immigration restriction—including the literacy test, on which the Jews as a group would have done
better than most, but which they nevertheless saw as a violation of
American libertarian principles.

In 1905, the National Liberal Immigration League had been created
under the leadership of Edward Lauterbach, once an officer in the old
Hebrew Emigrant Aid Society of 1882 and subsequently on the advisory
board of the reorganized HIAS of 1909, and Nissim Behar, a Sephardic
immigrant who had been born in Jerusalem and educated in Paris under
the auspices of the Alliance Israélite Universelle, for which he had then
worked several years in Palestine as an educator. The League—which
had sponsored a pioneering study in 1906, *The Immigrant Jew in America,* edited by Edmund I. James, the president of the University of
Illinois—led the agitation against the Burnett-Dillingham bill and organized a petition sent to President William Howard Taft with several
hundred thousand signatures on it.

The major intellectual effort against the Burnett-Dillingham bill was
also the work of a Jew—Isaac Hourwich, sometime Duma candidate and
"downtown" radical, who had a Columbia University Ph.D. in econom-
ics. The Dillingham Commission report had asserted that immigration
policy should be based primarily upon economic or business considerations, and had sought to demonstrate ill effects of the influx in these
terms, dwelling in particular on the lowering of wages and production
standards. Two professors, Jeremiah W. Jenks and W. Jett Lauck, had
then published a book, *The Immigration Problem,* attempting to verify
the Dillingham conclusions. This had led Hourwich to take up the cudg-
els; his book *Immigration and Labor,* published at the end of 1912,

offered systematic proof that the "new immigration" was in fact fulfilling the need for a labor force in a rapidly expanding industrial economy. This had taken more courage than met the eye. Hourwich was still a socialist and a friend of the labor movement, but this movement—spearheaded by the American Federation of Labor under the presidency of Samuel Gompers, himself an immigrant—ardently advocated immigration restriction, arguing that the new arrivals competed for jobs and worked for lower wages.

All these efforts had an influence upon President Taft, who, in one of the final acts of his administration, vetoed the Burnett-Dillingham bill on February 14, 1913, sending the pen with which he had done so to Nissim Behar. As the bill returned to Congress, Judge Leon Sanders, the president of HIAS, and Jacob Massel, its secretary, addressed a telegram to a number of senators and congressmen urging them "not to permit the spirit of narrow nationalism to override the just veto of the Chief of the Nation." This was written into the *Congressional Record* for February 17, and two days later the House sustained the President's veto.

The antirestrictionists had once again saved the day, but time was clearly running out on them. Before a new round in the contest could begin, however, one of history's major disasters intervened.

· 34 ·

WAR AND THE JEWS
OF EASTERN EUROPE, I:
1914-1915

Germany declared war on Russia on August 1, 1914, four days after
Austria's declaration against Serbia; it was not until two days later that
war officially began between Germany and France. At its inception, this
was a conflict between the Central Powers and Russia over hegemony
in East Central Europe. And in the heartlands of the conflict lived the
largest concentration of Jews in history.

"When the war broke out," according to an American Jewish Committee report of 1916,

> one-half of the Jewish population of the world was trapped in a
> corner of Eastern Europe that is absolutely shut off from all neutral
> lands and from the sea. Russian Poland, where over two million
> Jews lived, is in a salient. South of it is Galicia, the frontier province
> of Austria. Here lived another million Jews. Behind Russian Poland
> are the fifteen Russian provinces which, together with Poland, con-
> stitute the Pale of Jewish Settlement. Here lived another four mil-
> lion Jews.

This meant not only that the heavily Jewish areas of Eastern Europe
were to become battlefields, but also that the question of Jewish loyalties was going to be a vexing one for all concerned. Russia's oppression
of its Jews had gone on, whereas, apart from the alignments of war,
few Jews anywhere had much reason to dislike Germany and Austria.
And Jews spoke the same language on both sides.

Not that Russia lacked masses of Jewish young men ready to do
their military duty. "We were born and grew up in Russia," proclaimed
the Jewish Russian-language weekly *Novy Voskhod (New Sunrise)* on
July 24, 1914, eight days before the actual outbreak,

here rest the remains of our fathers. . . . The bearers of the ideals of our fathers, the nucleus of world Jewry—the Russian Jews—are at the same time inseparably allied with our mother country where we have been living for centuries and from which there is no power that can separate us, neither persecution nor oppression. In this historic moment, when our fatherland is threatened by foreign invasion, when brute force has armed itself against the great ideals of humanity, the Russian Jews will manfully step forward to the battlefield and do their sacred duty.

And they did: by the end of the year, three hundred thousand Jews were in Russian uniform, forming a proportion of men in service larger than that of Jews in the general population of the country.

Yet this show of loyalty was to little avail. Although rumors spread that the Pale of Settlement was to be abolished, its restrictions continued, even for Jewish soldiers and their families—and for them sometimes with greater severity. In the case of reservists who had been living outside the Pale as a reward for previous military service, the families they left behind when called to the colors were often made to resettle within it. Wounded Jewish soldiers were often returned to the Pale for treatment, even in violation of the imperatives of medical care or safety. According to a 1915 report by the Cadet Party on the Jewish situation in wartime Russia, the authorities tried to send a Private Godewski, "one of whose legs had been amputated, and who found himself at Rostov on the Don for recuperation, . . . to his native village in the Government of Kalisch, where the Germans were already settled." The report adds:

> An apothecary's helper, who likewise had been wounded on the battlefield, was not allowed to remain in Petrograd for his cure, and it was only by virtue of special intercession that he was later allowed to sojourn two months more at Petrograd, with the notice, however, that at the expiration of this period no further extension of his sojourn would be granted.

Even when Jewish soldiers were allowed to remain outside the Pale for hospitalization, their families usually were not permitted out to see them. These restrictions still continued as, after a few months of war, the Pale's boundaries began to crumble in the wake of forced evacuations of Jews from battlefront areas into the interior of Russia.

These evacuations were the outcome of accusations of spying. The Germans had not hesitated to try to exploit anti-tsarist sentiments among Jews in towns they captured. Here is a typical handbill published in Yiddish by the German occupying forces, this one taking on the rumors that the Pale was going to be abolished:

Do not let yourselves be misled by false promises! Did not the
Tsar in 1905 promise equal rights for Jews? How did he fulfill his
promise? Remember the expulsions of Jewish masses from their
long-established settlements! Remember Kishinev, Gomel, Bialystok, Sedletz, and hundreds of other bloody pogroms!

Jews certainly remembered these things, and among the youngest and
most vigorous a few took such steps as to join the Polish legions of Jozef
Pilsudski, which rallied in Austria and fought on its side against Russia.
Doubtless a few also became spies. But it is clear that the vast majority
only gritted their teeth and waited for the war to end with the least
possible harm to themselves and their families. Just to do this was a
special trial for them. "True, all the peoples of the area suffered ravage
and pillage by the war," continues the American Jewish Committee
report of 1916,

> but their sufferings were in no degree comparable to those of the
> Jews. The contending armies found it politic, in a measure, to court
> the good will of the Poles, Ruthenians and other races in this area.
> These sustained only the necessary and unavoidable hardships of
> war. But the Jews were friendless, their religion proscribed. In this
> medieval region all the religious fanaticism of the Russians, the
> chauvinism of the Poles, combined with the blood lusts liberated in
> all men by the war—all these fierce hatreds were sluiced into one
> torrent of passion which overwhelmed the Jews.

But among the bearers of fierce hatreds, the Germans were the mildest.
"In the German newspapers," said a December 1914 proclamation
by the Grand Duke Nicholas, the Russian Commander-in-Chief, "there
have appeared articles, stating that the Germans have found in the Russian Jews faithful allies. . . . In the victory of the Germans, the Jews see
their deliverance from the yoke of the Tsar and from Polish persecution." Surely the Grand Duke knew what he was talking about. As for
his troops—many of whom, coming from regions far from Poland and
the Pale, had hardly known what Jews looked like—they were bound to
think they saw myths confirmed in some of the peculiar aspects of the
Jewish presence that they encountered. A major factor contributing to
"the success of the slander" that Jews were spies, according to the 1915
Cadet report,

> consisted in those special usages of the Jewish inhabitants of Po-
> land which make them appear entirely unlike their own brethren
> in the Russian provinces proper. The Polish Jews have conserved
> their medieval apparel; they speak neither Polish nor Russian, but

Yiddish, a language that was created some centuries ago from German roots with an admixture of Hebrew and Slavonic words.

These were the conditions that

brought about a natural hostility between the Jewish population and the incoming Russian troops, to many of whom this was, perhaps, the first sight of a people of such a character. It was almost inevitable that suspicion should grow up in the ranks of the army against a people speaking a language that closely resembles German, and that the enemy could understand, while the army of their own country, the Russian soldiers, could not.

Suspicion reached a height during the spring of 1915, when the Russian armies were suffering a series of disastrous defeats. In April, some commanders claimed to have discovered a "shocking treachery against our forces by a certain part of the local population, particularly the Jews" at Kushi in the province of Kurland. They reported that Jews of the town had concealed German soldiers in their cellars. An investigation led by two Duma deputies, Alexander Kerensky and N. M. Friedman, proved the report to have been completely false.

A significant factor in the stirring-up of such suspicions was the attitude of many Polish Christians, who were more and more finding in the Jews a focus for their surging nationalist resentments. This attitude had achieved a new fullness of expression just before the war. During the Duma elections of 1912, the Jewish voters of Warsaw—representing half the city's population—had delivered a majority to a socialist candidate. By doing so, they had brought about the defeat there of the National Democratic Party, a new and powerful organ of right-wing, anti-Semitic nationalism. In retaliation, the party's leader, Roman Dmowski, had called for a boycott of goods sold or manufactured by Jews. The effects of this crisis were still being felt when the war broke out. Moreover, since Dmowski's policy—in opposition to that of Pilsudski—had been to collaborate with tsarism, seeking the Russian conquest of Galicia, its seizure from Austria, and its reincorporation into an autonomous Poland, it was easy for his supporters to conceive of the Jews and the Germans as their common enemy.

The grim potentialities of this situation manifested themselves on and near the Galician front in particular. In September 1914, the Austrians had captured the Russo-Polish town of Zamosc, just over the border, but were driven out by the Russians. At once, according to the American Jewish Committee report,

the Poles of the town denounced the Jews to the Russian commander, accusing the Jews of having given aid to the enemy during

the Austrian occupation of the town. Twelve Jews were arrested.
They denied their guilt but were sentenced to death. Five of them
had already been hanged, when, in the midst of the execution, a
Russian priest, carrying an image of the Virgin, appeared and with
his hand on the image took oath that the Jews were innocent and
that the accusation was merely a product of Polish vindictiveness.
He proved that the Poles of the town themselves had supported
the Austrians and that even a telephone connection with Lemberg
could be found. The seven remaining Jews were then set free.

Such incidents proliferated. After the Russian capture of Lemberg
a few days later,

the Poles accused the Jews of firing on Russian troops; as a consequence a great many Jews were arrested, and nearly seventy
were attacked and wounded. But an investigation proved them all
innocent, and . . . the Jews who had been taken as hostages were
released.

When the Russians recovered Kielce and Radom, the Poles plundered
Jewish shops and "denounced the Jews as German sympathizers. Here
also those Jews who were arrested were found to be innocent and released after investigation." At Jusefow, after its recapture, a full-scale
revival of medievalism occurred: "the Jews were accused of poisoning
the wells. Seventy-eight were killed outright, many Jewish women were
violated and all the houses and shops plundered." A visitor to the area
was to speak to a Jewish woman in Soczaczew "whose right cheek was
permanently bruised and scarred by the heavy heel of the local black-
smith as she resisted the dragging off of her husband to be shot" as a
spy for the Germans.

In those parts of Austrian Galicia that Russian troops occupied, the
Jews of course were enemies in fact, however they behaved. And it was
here that the Russian policy of treating all Jews as potential spies was
begun. In the eyes of the Russian authorities, disloyalty was seen to
spill over among the Jews on their own side of the border as language
and customs did. The accusation first became vehement in Lemberg in
January 1915, when the Russian occupiers posted a proclamation all
over the city saying that "the progress of the war has disclosed an open
hostility on the part of the Jewish population of Poland, Galicia and
Bukovina." Only the last two were in Austrian territory; the statement
was therefore to the effect that Polish Jews who were Russian subjects
were also hostile to the Tsar's army.

The excuse had been found for an official beginning of reprisals.
Summary expulsions by local commanders had sporadically occurred

since August 1914, but with the Lemberg proclamation, mass expulsions of Russian Jews from the battle zones into the interior became official policy. "The Supreme Commander-in-Chief," said a circular issued to district leaders at the same time as the proclamation,

> is pleased to order the respective commanders, beginning with that of Bukovina, to expel the Jews immediately after the retreat of the enemy and to take hostages from among the most wealthy or those occupying a communal or other public office. In fulfillment of this command, the Commander-in-Chief has ordered the removal of Jews into the interior of Russia, into districts no nearer than 200 versts [120 miles] from any of the Staffs of Armies, and to prohibit Jews from entering the zone of expulsion.

"Fire! Fire!" cried Chaia Sonia Gussow, awakening her children one bleak spring morning in the Lithuanian village of Pumpian.

There was no fire, explains Don Gussow in his memoir of this time, when the war had caught his mother and her five children waiting to be summoned to the United States by her husband, who had gone there ahead of them in 1913. "However, insofar as Mother was concerned, the entire village was on the verge of total devastation." He explains:

> The year was 1915. World War I had started some months earlier and the Germans were sweeping over Lithuania. Soon the soldiers of the German imperial army with their guns and their trucks loaded with equipment were expected in Pumpian. Since the Russians did not trust the Jews, ... orders had come through to the local officials to drive out the entire Jewish population.... For the Jews, life in Pumpian would end in twenty-four hours. After that any Jew who remained would be shot.

The Gussows were soon on a train heading somewhere eastward.

"At the present moment," according to a report of June 1915,

> there are tens and hundreds of thousands of people adrift in cattle cars, far from their native provinces, deprived of shelter, living on charity. For weeks they were kept in cars on the side tracks. The local populations hiss at them with cries of "spy" and "treacherous Jews."

Many fled to cities within the Pale: the Gussows came to rest in a town near Gomel. Others pushed on into eastern Russia and Siberia.

In the Duma, the Jewish deputy N. M. Friedman read a letter from a Jew who had returned from America to fight and had lost an arm in combat:

> Scarcely had I reached Riga when I met at the station my mother and my relatives, who had just arrived there, and who on that same day were compelled to leave their hearth and home at the order of the military authorities. Tell the gentlemen who sit on the benches of the Right that I do not mourn my lost hand, but that I mourn deeply the lost human dignity. . . .

How long could men like this remain loyal to the Tsar?

·35·

WAR AND THE JEWS
OF EASTERN EUROPE, II:
ISIDORE HERSHFIELD'S MISSION

During 1915, the Central Powers not only recovered all the ground lost against the Russians in the first months of fighting (with the exception of a small part of Galicia) but also extended their front far beyond it to a north-south line eastward of Riga, Vilna, and Pinsk. Most of the Pale of Settlement had fallen under their control, and one may well assume that, among its Jews, there was a widespread sense of relief. The Germans were eager to be correct if not friendly to the Jews there, partly out of determination to show the world—the neutral United States in particular—how much more humane they could be than the Russians in this regard, partly because the many Jews and other liberal spirits in the German ranks responded with sympathy to the indigenous Jewish plight. Jews earlier evacuated by the Russians were allowed to return home wherever possible, and proclamations were issued in Yiddish, among other languages. Emigration to the United States was allowed, to the limited extent that it was feasible, and representatives of American Jewry were occasionally let in to inspect the situation. In 1916, Dr. Judah L. Magnes, along with other representatives of a newly formed American Jewish Joint Distribution Committee, was able to tour German-occupied Eastern Europe and plan the disposal of charitable funds there.

Similarly, the Hebrew Sheltering and Immigrant Aid Society sent a representative, Isidore Hershfield, to Central and Eastern Europe from October 1915 to the following May. HIAS had become concerned about two matters: the stranding of emigrants who had been en route to America when war broke out, and the now frustrated desire for contact between Russian-Jewish immigrants in America and their families back home. One recent case had involved both problems at once. It was that of a Mrs. Greenwood, wife of a New York dental surgeon, who had

gone with her two young children back to Minsk in 1913 to visit her
family. In order, as she imagined, to facilitate her entry, she had managed to obtain a Russian passport for herself under the original form of
her husband's family name, Greengoltz. When war broke out, the Russian Governor of Minsk refused, on account of her passport, to acknowledge her American citizenship and would not let her leave. Her husband
in New York had appealed to HIAS, which contacted the American
consul in Riga.

"Much telegraphic correspondence ensued," said a HIAS report,

> extending over months. Meanwhile, her funds became exhausted
> and her husband sent money for her maintenance. Finally, the con-
> sul informed the State Department that she would be permitted to
> start, if she were provided with means to pay transportation ex-
> penses and a prospective fine of one or two hundred rubles required
> by the Russian government for violating the rules regarding illegal
> residence. Minsk in the meantime had been captured in part by the
> Germans and she left for Moscow, acting upon a suggestion of the
> American consul, to whom she had written when Riga was taken
> by the Germans and communication with its American consul ren-
> dered impossible. Her husband sent her sufficient money to cover
> all her expenses, but it had to be sent to the American Ambassador
> at Petrograd before it reached her.

She was finally able to leave, at the end of September 1915, from the
near-Arctic port of Archangel, on the steamer *Kursk* of the Russian-
American line, and arrived in New York on October 31.

Another problem was that of a girl who had been traveling as part
of a family of a mother and children to join the father in America. When
they reached Antwerp, the girl had been found, like Mottel's Goldie, to
have trachoma. "Shortly after the war broke out," according to the
report,

> the mother and the other children departed for the United States,
> leaving the afflicted child for [what was expected to be] a few weeks
> under medical treatment. When Antwerp was bombarded, the Ezra
> Society, under whose care this child was, was compelled to disband,
> and the parents lost all trace of the child. After tracing the child
> for four months, through Germany, Holland, England and Den-
> mark, the [Hebrew Sheltering and Immigrant Aid] Society suc-
> ceeded in locating her in London, where she had been placed with
> the Poland Street Refuge.

Problems like these, and others, were to be dealt with by Isidore
Hershfield, a forty-six-year-old lawyer, who had been born the grandson

of a rabbi on the Lower East Side of New York. Arriving in neutral Rotterdam on October 21, 1915, Hershfield made contact with the relevant aid societies in Central Europe, especially the Hilfsverein der Deutschen Juden of Berlin and the Israelitische Allianz of Vienna. Through their good offices, he obtained an important concession from the German occupying authorities. Jews in the occupied zones would be permitted to write to their relatives in America—albeit in a highly restricted form. A circular distributed throughout the occupied zones spelled out the form in exacting detail. As translated from the German, it read as follows:

LETTERS TO AMERICA

The direct postal service to America for persons who wish to ask for aid from their American relatives is permitted under the following conditions:

1. All letters must be brief, written in German or Polish, and according to the following form.

To (Name of addressee)
City—Street and Number
We are well, but urgently need financial assistance.
Please help us. We send our best regards.
Name of writer
City—Street and Number

2. In addition to the above information, a death in the family may also be communicated.

3. The letters must be placed in an open envelope, which must bear the following address:

Hebrew S. and I. Aid Society
229 East Broadway
New York City

On every envelope 20 pfennings postage must be affixed.

4. The above named Society in New York undertakes to deliver these letters to the American addressees without charge.

Warsaw, 10th February 1916
General Government, Warsaw

Having accomplished this, Hershfield embarked on a tour of the occupied zones, which turned into an itinerary of devastation and suffering. "In Warsaw," he was to report,

I saw an old man fall in the street and I helped him to a doorstep.
Neighbors revived him with tea. I asked him whether he needed
medical aid and he replied that there was nothing the matter with
him except that he had eaten nothing in two days. In Lublin I saw
in a courtyard a woman who had fainted. When she was revived
she asked for food, which she said she had not had since the preceding day. . . . These conditions of hunger, suffering and disease
exist in all parts of occupied Russia.

He had examples to give, town by town:

> Lodz points to its ruined and silent cotton mills, its unemploy-
> ment, its epidemic of smallpox. Kalisch shows you its main business
> section entirely destroyed by fire, its lace factories burst or dyna-
> mited by the departing Russians. Bialystok points to its dreadful
> epidemic of spotted typhus, and shows you many streets closed to
> traffic, with signs reading, *"Strasse gesperrt. Eintritt verboten.*
> *Fleck Typhus"* ["Street closed. Entry forbidden. Spotted typhus"],
> and bearing a skull and crossbones. Not only are these streets
> closed, but the doors and windows of the houses are nailed up so
> that the occupants cannot leave their homes. The German military
> authorities send a field kitchen into these streets with cooked food
> for the dwellers. Vilna takes you to its poor quarters, where you
> find Jews—men, women and children—living in subterranean cham-
> bers, in sub-cellars, and in rooms opening from sub-cellars into which
> not a ray of light ever enters.

The account pauses over the ancient city of Kovno, once a great
center of Jewish learning. "Kovno," writes Hershfield,

> has been stricken as was ancient Jerusalem at the time of the de-
> struction of the Temple. . . . The city of Kovno had a normal Jewish
> population of about 45,000, and the Gubernia or Province of Kovno
> had in all a population of 190,000 Jews. On the 5th day of May,
> 1915, every Jew—man, woman and child—in the Province of Kovno
> was expelled on twenty-four hours' notice. From this edict of expul-
> sion not one Jew was spared. It included infants, women in child-
> birth, the aged, the sick, the lame, the poor, the wealthy merchant,
> the artisan, the lawyer, and the physician.

This was the particular edict that had struck the Gussow family of Pumpian. "All fled eastward," Hershfield continues,

> because to the West was the German battle front. Passenger trains
> carried many away. Cattle cars, which I have seen labelled "24
> persons or 6 horses" carried a larger number. Freight cars carried
> more. But probably half of these 190,000 wandered away on foot.

Most of these are practically lost in what is now still Russian territory. Those who fled to Vilna and to other places which have since been occupied by the German forces were later permitted to return. The city of Kovno today, however, instead of its normal population of 45,000 Jews, has only about 4,200 Jewish souls. Its business thoroughfares have the silence of a graveyard or a deserted city. Most of the stores are closed and boarded up; the Jewish storekeepers have gone and never returned. I attended Sabbath services in the large Synagogue at Kovno, and I found a congregation of perhaps forty, where ordinarily a thousand worshipped.

As for Warsaw, home of a prewar population of about three hundred thousand Jews, Hershfield perceived that it had

escaped physical destruction, with the exception of its 3 bridges over the Vistula River. These, like all of the bridges, railroad stations, freight houses, round houses and railroad bridges, were dynamited by the Russian army as it fled before the invading Germans. The Warsawites say that a pogrom which would have surpassed in violence and extent any of its predecessors in the history of Russian Jewry had been planned to mark the evacuation of the Russian army. The cossacks were already riding through the streets of the Jewish quarter inciting the Polish populace; the cry of "Zhid" was heard; the Jewish storekeepers had barricaded their stores and the Jewish population had shut themselves within their homes; that night was one of terror for the Jews of Warsaw. The following day was set for the pogrom; but at early dawn, the German army, unexpected for yet two days, entered Warsaw. The Russian forces were compelled hastily to retreat with barely sufficient time to cross the bridges to Praga. They dynamited the bridges behind them and set fire to Praga. The Jews in Warsaw could see the flames in neighboring Praga, and the Jews in Praga thought that the dynamiting of the bridges was part of the dynamiting and destruction of the whole Jewish quarter of Warsaw.

Inevitably, Hershfield pondered the question of the comparative lot of the Jews of the Eastern war zones under the Russians and under the Germans. The German occupation could hardly be described as benign, but to Hershfield, as to virtually every other outside observer, the condition of the Jews under German control was

indescribably better than under Russia. Officially, Germany and Austria make no distinction on religious grounds in their treatment of the inhabitants of the conquered provinces. Such discriminations against the Jews as exist in some places—and they do exist in some places—are due not to any official German or Austrian rule or regulation, but solely to the personal bias or prejudice of the local official or officials in charge. Much of the present oppression, or rather discrimination against the Jews, is not due to any willful desire to oppress or discriminate, but arises from a lack of understanding between the German or Austrian officials and the Jewish residents.

Also allowing for the "turmoil of wartime," Hershfield reaches the conclusion—widespread among American Jews at that moment—that, with regard to the occupied area on the Eastern Front,

> the best possible outcome of the war for the Jews will be its retention by Germany. Equal rights and equality before the law will be assured to them. A system of compulsory elementary education will be planned and enforced, and that will mean that the Poles will lose some of the bigotry and gradually be taught to live on friendlier terms with their Jewish fellow citizens.

As a final point about future possibilities, Hershfield vehemently asserts that

> the most unfortunate thing that can happen to the Jews in occupied Russia will be an absolutely autonomous Poland. The Jews there all agree that an absolutely autonomous Poland will mean such hardships for and oppression of the Jews as will make the rule of Russia by comparison seem a benign form of government.

To this he hastens to add: "It is not for me, however, to make any conjectures as to the political outcome of the war."

·36·

1917

A wave of riots and strikes that began in Petrograd on March 8, 1917, ended a few days later in the collapse of a regime that stood on a structure too weak to hold up under nearly three years of war. Even the small Russo-Japanese War had caused the structure to shake; this time the upheaval was complete, and Tsar Nicholas II abdicated on March 15. A Provisional Government of Cadets and moderate socialists was established from among the Duma leadership, but the real power swiftly fell into the hands of the soviets, the councils of workers' and soldiers' deputies that had sprung up throughout the land and held the railways and telegraphs as well as the instruments of production.

The Provisional Government set out with the liberal optimism of another century, looking forward to a parliamentary regime in the manner of Great Britain or France, planning the election of a constituent assembly to draw up its fundamental laws, and passing a few preliminary ones on the way. At the beginning of April, a decree was issued stating: "All the limitations on the rights of Russian citizens imposed by hitherto existing laws on the basis of religion, creed or nationality are hereby revoked." Foremost among those to whom this was addressed were the Jews, free and equal Russian citizens at last.

Jews throughout the world were as appreciative of this as were their coreligionists in Russia, for until now the war had caused a moral crisis among them and the countries to which they had emigrated in large numbers. People of conscience in Britain and France had been embarrassed at finding themselves in a wartime alliance with the most reactionary power in Europe, and, with their large and articulate Jewish minorities, were especially perturbed by its unregenerate anti-Semitism. Among the more than two million Jews of the United States, their country's neutrality had made possible the expression of widespread sentiments against an Entente that included the Empire of Pale and pogrom.

The British Foreign Office had, in fact, devoted considerable attention to the question of American-Jewish opinion about the war. Britain and France longed for America's entry on their side, and their leaders and administrators believed that Jewish sentiments counted for not a little in the matter. After all, among other Jewish demonstrations of influence in the United States, Louis D. Brandeis had been an adviser to President Wilson and was now on the Supreme Court, and Jacob Schiff had arranged the financing of Japan's victory over Russia. Schiff in particular was a sore point. His loathing of tsarist Russia had been well known, and his sentimental attachment to his German homeland had been not at all diminished by the outbreak of war in August 1914. His opinion had therefore been closely watched in Britain, where ill feeling was aroused by remarks such as this, made by him in April 1915:

> I am afraid England has been contaminated by her alliance with Russia. . . . England has always been our great friend. . . . In England there existed no such thing as anti-Semitism. But now there are, I fear, signs of a change.

Yet Schiff was not so ardently pro-German as some other prominent American Jews were thought to be.

The balance of sentiments against tsarist Russia had been even more pronounced among the East European immigrant masses. "The Jews support Germany because Russia bathes in Jewish blood," the *Tageblatt* had proclaimed on August 2, 1914. "No matter how terrible German militarism may be," said the anarchist *Freie Arbeiter Shtimme (Free Voice of the Workingman)* on November 21, 1914, "the Jews of Russia would profit politically, economically and above all spiritually" from a Russian defeat. As for Abraham Cahan's *Jewish Daily Forward*—by now the preeminent organ of Jewish opinion in America, with a circulation approaching two hundred thousand—its anti-tsarism was abetted by its socialist outlook, which not only favored pacifism but still looked upon Germany as the homeland of social democracy. By the beginning of 1917, its pro-Germanism was considerable.

But the *Forward* was prominent in the expression of gratitude when tsarism was finally overthrown. "That which has long been awaited has finally come," its headlines announced on March 16, 1917, the day the news broke in the West. "A Revolution in Russia, a free Russian people, a free Jewish people in Russia! Is this a dream?" Two days later it sang, "What a day we are living through! What a golden day!" and on the 20th, even before the actual emancipation decree, it proclaimed in a banner headline: "JEWISH TROUBLES ARE AT AN END."

The way now was open for widespread Jewish endorsement of the
United States declaration of war against Germany, which finally came
on April 6. Not that pro-Entente sentiments had been completely non-
existent among American Jews. In December 1915, Professor Horace
M. Kallen of the University of Wisconsin, a prominent Zionist, had been
able to assure some of his British friends after a study of the Yiddish
press that, although its sentiments were

> largely anti-Russian, and . . . this anti-Russian feeling got empha-
> sized in pro-German ways, I was interested and pleased to find that
> the pro-Germanism was not a natural or spontaneous fact, even
> among the writers in those papers which seemed most violently to
> glory in German victories.

Indeed, pro-British sentiments had long been as deeply engrained among
East European Jews as was any admiration for Germany.

The revolution that had occurred in Jewish attitudes quickly made
itself evident. The *Forward*, though its editorial page remained pacifist
a while longer—causing it to be denied use of the mail—opened its other
pages to writers who supported the war effort; by the following year,
even its editorials would concede that "it is no longer a capitalist war.
Neither is it imperialistic or nationalistic. It is a war for humanity." As
for Jacob Schiff, he had announced on May 3, 1917, "I am a German by
birth and I love the German people, but I do not love the German government as it exists today."

The new mood of the Jewish immigrant was well reflected on Sunday, May 6, when a huge American flag was raised in front of the HIAS
building at 229 East Broadway. "Whoever witnessed that spectacle,"
the new HIAS president, John L. Bernstein, was to observe,

> will not forget it for a long time. For blocks around the building
> thousands of Jewish immigrants gathered to express their loyalty
> to the flag that always stood for liberty and justice to Jew and
> gentile, rich and poor, alike. Thousands of voices joined in the Na-
> tional Anthem sung by the immigrant school children with a zeal
> and zest whose meaning could not be mistaken. It plainly said, "I
> owe all I have, my very life, to the Stars and Stripes, and I am
> ready to pay my debt."

But there was a price to pay for this consummation: American-Jewish
groups and individuals could now no longer penetrate to their coreligionists and relatives in Eastern Europe.

In Russia, too, Jews felt a new sense of loyalty to their country and its
future. But what was this future to be? Even apart from the question

of Poland, where visions of independence were inevitably arising, the
Jews of Russia were in political turmoil. Virtually every party and tendency not opposed to the revolution itself could claim some Jewish following. Many Jews were now content to identify themselves politically
as Russians—or Poles or Ukrainians, even as Lithuanians—and some
were zealously assimilationist. No Jews were readier to forget their
ethnic background than those on the far left of the political scale. It was
that quintessential "non-Jewish Jew" of the left, Leon Trotsky, who
had performed the task of ejecting the Bund from the Social Democratic
Party at its second congress in 1903. For him and others like him, one
could not be a Jew and a revolutionary at the same time—even though,
for their enemies, it was precisely the fact they were both that was
significant.

The largest plurality of the political activists who were Jews, however, were affiliated with parties of explicitly Jewish commitment. The
Bund, larger and more powerful than ever, hoped for a new lease on
life in the wake of the March revolution. There was also a nonsocialist
Yiddishist party that advocated Jewish national autonomy on Russian
soil, the Folkspartei, founded by the historian S. M. Dubnow. But by
far the largest Jewish political group—or grouping, since the left-wing
Poalei Zion maintained a separate rubric—were the Russian Zionists.
With a membership of about three hundred thousand in mid-1917, they
were the largest Zionist organization in the world, and the main source
of Palestine settlers. Before the year was out, thirty-nine Yiddish journals and ten Hebrew ones supporting Zionism were to be appearing in
Russia, where none had openly existed before the revolution. On June
7, the Seventh Congress of Russian Zionists—the first to be held openly
on Russian soil—assembled in Petrograd, attended by 552 delegates and
over fifteen hundred Jewish and non-Jewish guests.

"From all corners of our great Russia," declared the Zionist leader
Yechiel Tschlenow, in front of the gathering,

> come to us, together with tears of joy over the emancipation, as-
> surances of unshattered faith in the eternal ideal—the renaissance
> of our native Palestine. Old and young, rich and poor, from the
> front and from the rear, orthodox and freethinkers declare in one
> voice: "Now, even now, freed from the chains of slavery, shall we
> be able zealously and gladly to give ourselves to the service of our
> ideals?"

But it was made quite clear that this resurgence of national feeling was
in no way intended to compromise Jewish loyalty to revolutionary Russia and its war effort. "We beg the Provisional Government to believe,"
Tschlenow said, "that it may fully depend upon our forces and our sup-

port in its heroic efforts directed toward the strengthening of the freedom and greatness of Russia." The spokesman of the Jewish soldier-delegates, pointing out how they had "fulfilled their military duty" even in "a time of outlawry and terrible persecution, under the burden of false accusations," told the audience that now,

> having become free citizens of Russia, and fully privileged members of the army, the Jewish soldiers will continue their efforts in a new spirit of enthusiasm. Believing that the strengthening of the revolution, and the strengthening of the peoples in Russia can be accomplished only through the union of all the peoples and by a strong discipline in the free army, the Jewish soldiers declare triumphantly that they are prepared to follow the call of the revolutionary democracy to defend Russia against her enemies.

This certainly was what Russia's allies wanted to hear. In London, just as concern about American attitudes toward the war had focused to some degree upon American-Jewish opinion, so also was anxiety as to whether revolutionary Russia would stay in the war partly focused on Jewish sentiments there. Considerations such as these were among the factors giving rise to a historic policy statement issued by the British government, which hoped thereby to rally Jewish support throughout the world, issued on November 2, 1917, regarding Jewish national aspirations in Palestine. Presented in a letter to the second Lord Rothschild from the Foreign Secretary, Arthur James Balfour—and hence known to posterity as the Balfour Declaration—the statement read:

> His Majesty's Government view with favour the establishment in Palestine of a national home for the Jewish people, and will use their best endeavours to facilitate the achievement of this object, it being clearly understood that nothing shall be done which may prejudice the civil and religious rights of existing non-Jewish communities in Palestine, or the rights and political status enjoyed by Jews in any other country.

The Balfour Declaration had particular force because, at the moment of its issuance, British armies were making their first inroads from Egypt into Palestine and were about to snatch that country away from four hundred years of Ottoman rule.

This was not the last of the fateful events of 1917; within a week after the Declaration was issued, the Bolsheviks, who had been assuming control of the soviets throughout Russia, seized all the levers of power in Petrograd itself. Lenin wasted no time making it clear what this meant in terms of the Allied war effort; on November 8, the day after the Bolshevik takeover, he called for immediate peace negotiations. Other things were not yet so clear. With regard to Jewish matters, Lenin had written in 1903 that any idea of Jewish nationality was "definitely reactionary." But when the new Bolshevik government issued its Declaration of the Rights of Nationalities on November 15, promising "the removal of every and any national and religious privilege and restriction" and "the free development of national minorities and ethnographic groups living within the confines of Russia," the Jews were specifically included. For a while at least, the euphoria of liberation could continue.

PART SEVEN

Civil Wars
and Devastations

·1918-1920·

·37·

INTERLUDE IN YOKOHAMA

"A miracle then happened," declared the HIAS president, John L. Bernstein, early in 1918, "which promised to put an end to the bulk of the Jewish immigration into the United States. Six million Jews, who for many decades had been deprived of human rights, had overnight become free citizens of a free country. Russia was liberated from the throes of Czardom." What more reason could have remained for great masses of Jews to emigrate?

"Subsequent events, however," Bernstein continued, "converted the miracle into a mirage. Internal strife, civil war, anarchy, have made the lot of the Jew in Russia more precarious than it ever had been." And with these perils, new forms of distress arose.

"The dangerous condition in Russia," Bernstein's report goes on, "compelled the wives and children of Jewish citizens and residents of America to find a new route to this blessed country." These were the women and children left behind by their emigrating husbands and fathers, expecting to be sent for later, and stranded by the outbreak of war. The forced migrations of Jews eastward in 1915, the disruption of revolution and ensuing civil war, and the virtual closing of the Atlantic to all but war-priority shipping had conspired to leave only the long eastern route open to most of them by now. This route, in Bernstein's description,

led through Russia, through Siberia to Harbin, through China to Japan, through Japan to the Japanese port cities of Kobe and Yokohama, across the Pacific Ocean to Seattle, San Francisco and Vancouver, and in many cases across the whole of the American continent to the Atlantic coast, a distance of approximately 15,375 miles.

It was to aid in this passage that HIAS had established branches in Seattle and San Francisco in 1915; but, as always, financing for the journey had to come from the emigrants themselves and their relatives in the United States. "Sufficient money for the transportation of these emigrants," according to Bernstein's report,

> was sent to them by the heads of their families who were residents of the United States, and the women and children started on their long and perilous journey, feeling secure, however, that they had sufficient means to pay for all their needs and for all the necessary transportation. Their security vanished, however, long before they reached the port of embarkation. The depreciation of the Russian money had become so large and its purchasing power so small that their means were exhausted in the midst of their journey.

The result was an unprecedented kind of emergency. "Jewish women and children by the thousands were stranded all through China and Japan without means to proceed further, and without means to supply even their daily wants for food and shelter."

Harbin and Vladivostok were filling up with refugees en route to the ports of Japan, which was in the war on the side of the Entente. In October 1917, there were more than two thousand Russian refugees in Harbin, the vast majority of them Jews. And most of those who got through to Japan were accumulating in Yokohama, where wartime shipping accommodations, even in steerage, were not sufficient to keep moving them out. "Hundreds of hungry, ragged and barefooted women and children," Bernstein reported, "were huddled together in seven small rooms in an old building in the Chinese section of Yokohama."

First to become aroused to do something about the problem was the Jewish community of Yokohama itself, consisting of fourteen families, all Russian or Austrian in origin, which had settled in that thriving international port during the preceding two decades. In 1899, some of them had founded a Jewish Benevolent Association under the leadership of Maurice Russel, an exporter and the Jewish resident of longest standing in all of Japan. This association had made the first efforts to cope with the emerging refugee crisis, but these had not been to everyone's satisfaction. In mid-1917, a younger group of Yokohama Jews—led by Benjamin W. Fleisher, publisher of the country's foremost English-language newspaper, the *Japan Advertiser*—organized an Emigrant Aid Society to deal with the situation.

The president of the Emigrant Aid Society, Benjamin Kirschbaum, described what was happening in a letter he wrote to HIAS in December 1917. "I have lived in Yokohama for almost three years," he said, and have witnessed the passing emigration from the beginning. At first the majority of emigrants were men, but in the last two years the wanderers were mostly women and children. Under the guise of philanthropy, a small group of hotel and restaurant keepers, bankers, etc., fleeced these unfortunates for their own profit, and many hundreds of Yen donated by charitable people for the use of the emigrants wandered into the pockets of these unscrupulous imposters. I was one of those good-hearted, stupid and undiscriminating donors until I learned the true state of affairs.

In Kirschbaum's eyes, the old Jewish Benevolent Association had been at fault for thus letting things get out of hand. He continues:

> Last April, I made up my mind to stop this exploitation. I applied to my friends for financial assistance and, to my great delight, received their hearty cooperation. To Mr. B. W. Fleisher, Editor of the *Japan Advertiser*, I owe my great appreciation. His paper has helped me along in every respect since September 2nd, and also gave me the foundation for the present organization. We need much to make it possible for our emigrants to proceed to America. In exchanging the Russian rouble, the emigrant receives only 12½ sen. The emigration is daily increasing.

It was because of this pressing financial situation that Fleisher himself had written to Jacob Schiff, who responded by promising a gift of $3,000 to establish a temporary shelter for the refugees.

Meanwhile, HIAS had already decided in October to send an emissary to Yokohama to see what could be done. The man chosen was Samuel Mason, HIAS's former founding secretary, who now was editor and publisher of *The Jewish Business Record*. Mason left New York on November 16 and made stops in Seattle, Portland, San Francisco, and Vancouver to consult about ways of improving transportation arrangements with the Pacific steamship companies. Then he sailed to Japan, to arrive in Yokohama on January 1, 1918. He was startled to find that the condition of the refugees was still deplorable, and that the tiny Jewish community of the city had fallen into disarray over the issue.

What had happened was that, before Benjamin Fleisher had obtained the promise of $3,000 from Schiff, other members of the Emigrant Aid Society had approached Morris Ginzburg, a wealthy Russian-Jewish businessman of Yokohama, and obtained a large bequest for establishing a shelter. "The old Royal Hotel at 87 Yamashita-cho," Mason reported,

> had been rented before my arrival by the local Emigrant Aid Society. The funds for the purpose had been provided by Mr. M. Ginz-

burg, though Mr. B. W. Fleisher had secured an option on the premises and was in receipt of $3,000 from our Society transmitted through Mr. Jacob Schiff, for the sole purpose of renting and partially equipping the house as a shelter for war refugees. Mr. Fleisher was not in Japan for a little while, and meanwhile the Emigrant Aid Society had interested Mr. Ginzburg in the work, succeeding in securing a lease for one year on the premises.

With Fleisher away, the Emigrant Aid Society apparently did not know that they had an additional $3,000 to work with.

"Mr. Ginzburg," Mason's report continues,

set aside 12,000 yen [$6,000] upon the understanding that the sum would suffice for one year's maintenance. This was in accordance with an estimate submitted to him by Mr. B. Kirschbaum, the president of the Emigrant Aid Society. The sum was turned over to Mr. Maurice Russel as custodian and administrator. The latter named the house "The Ginzburg Home for Russian Emigrants." This fact gave it the widest publicity in the native and foreign press, and the Home was recognized as an institution.

Mrs. Ginzburg and several other wives organized a "Ladies' Committee of the Ginzburg Home for Russian Emigrants," which collected clothing for the Home's ragged guests. It had been a moment of utter harmony in the Jewish community of Yokohama.

"However," Mason goes on,

it was not long before a clash occurred between the Ginzburg Home, the Emigrant Aid Society, and the Ladies' Committee. Originally, the Royal Hotel had been a well-equipped house. It had everything that a good hotel should have. Electricity, gas, beds and bedding, tables and chairs, dining room, kitchens and store room, well-furnished lounging parlors, a very fine sun room, and even an immensely large skating rink.

For this splendid array of furniture and equipment, the men of the Emigrant Aid Society had been asked to pay an additional 7,000 yen. "But they decided that it was all too good for the purpose. They wanted none of it, and so permitted everything to be sold at auction, including the floor of the skating rink, nearly all of the toilet bowls, all the gas piping, several of the ranges and every one of the electric chandeliers." By the time they were through, the Royal Hotel "had been metamorphosed into a dilapidated building."

The first to suffer from this metamorphosis had been the refugees. "The situation became so aggravated," according to Mason, that at one time serious disorder among the refugees was threatened, one organization throwing the blame for the occurrence upon the other. Japanese police had to be called in to prevent disturbance, and from that time until the night of February 11th, when I officially opened the Home in the name of our Society, a policeman was stationed day and night at the corner.

To make matters worse, there was "an organized gang of swindlers . . . loitering about the Home, with the expectation of finding easy prey among the helpless women and girls." The Yokohama Jews were by now too busy blaming one another for what had happened to concentrate on doing something about it.

"No sooner had I reached Yokohama," Mason continues,

> than I was informed that the "Russian Home" was the filthiest place. The Russian people are so terribly filthy, I was told. Hence the reason for the deplorable state of the "Royal Hotel." No one could pass the place, I was further told, without acknowledging the absolute truth of the statement.

Even before arriving there, Mason "scented the place where the refugees were kept. The odor was exactly as described. I then knew where the house was situated." Mason promptly addressed himself to this problem and to the petty rivalries that had allowed it to occur.

"Suffice it to say," he writes,

> that by January 15th all the three organizations had been dissolved, the lease of the house assigned to our Society and extended to April 1, 1919, and a host of carpenters, plumbers, painters, paper-hangers and electricians installed and working at top speed to make the house fit once more for human habitation.

In addition to improving the physical plant, Mason hired a staff that included a kosher cook, a *shochet* (ritual slaughterer), a *mashgiach* (kosher supervisor), a cantor, a custodian, a night watchman, waiters, maids, a general physician, and an eye specialist, as well as administrative personnel. With the help of the American consul, classes in English and in Americanization were also instituted.

On February 11, 1918, the house was officially reopened as the establishment of the Hebrew Sheltering and Immigrant Aid Society of America. A gala ceremony began at 8:00 P.M. in its main hall. Present, in addition to K. Ando, the mayor of Yokohama, and George H. Scidmore, the American consul, were Mr. and Mrs. Morris Ginzburg, Benjamin Kirschbaum, Maurice Russel, Mrs. Blanche K. Fleisher (her husband still out of the country), Max Sherover (vice president of the late Emigrant Aid Society) and his wife, and several representatives of the Ladies' Society, their quarrels behind them. Also present were

> a delegation of 24 Japanese ladies representing the YWCA; a delegation of 10 ladies representing the Women's Temperance Union; the Chief of Police and his lieutenants, by invitation; and a host of ladies and gentlemen, American citizens and British subjects, visiting Japan, who came at the instance of some of the guests herein mentioned.

Also present were the women refugees currently staying in the Home. The children were in an adjoining room.

"Mr. Mason welcomed the guests," according to an official account, "and outlined briefly the history of emigration from Russia via Japan." After profusely thanking everyone present, as well as the Japanese people in general, he introduced Consul Scidmore, "who was warmly greeted not only by the guests, but by all the inmates, who rose in a body, waved American flags, and warmly cheered the first representative of the American Government that they had ever seen in their lives." Scidmore spoke with admiration of the quality of the emigrants, and said he "was particularly impressed with the fine appearance of the children, all of whom already looked like little Americans, proudly waving the Stars and Stripes."

This evidently was a cue for the children in the other room. "As he concluded his remarks," the official account goes on,

> the doors from the adjoining room swung open, and two little girls in white marched in, bearing an American and a Japanese flag respectively. They halted at the doors as the national hymn of Japan was played, then a company of marching boys with American flags on their right arms entered the room, marched up to the front, lined up facing the platform, and saluted the American flag and the Japanese flag. Then the "Star Spangled Banner" was played, at the conclusion of which the boys saluted the guests and marched out in perfect order.

The next to speak was Mayor Ando, who also said—in Japanese, with an English-language interpreter—that "the appearance of the inmates was a revelation to him, as he thought originally they were all paupers and of an entirely different type of people." Furthermore, he "was pleased at the display of the Japanese national colors and with the respect paid to it by the refugees and the visitors." There were more speeches and presentations. "Several little boys and girls then sang various songs in Hebrew and Russian, and delivered recitations in both languages. The meeting was concluded with the singing of *Hatikvah* by the inmates."

The hopeful atmosphere was maintained some weeks later when a Passover Seder was held at the Home. The menu, for all its misspellings and macaronics, seemed to provide a summary guide to exiles and emigrations throughout Jewish history. It read:

> Gefilte Litvishe and "Morer" Russia
> Potage Egyptiens
> Chremslach a la Wilna
> Afikomen Palestinian
> Compot Americaine

By then, the Home that Mason had created was itself a "Compot Americaine," festooned with American as well as Japanese and Jewish flags, and resounding with so much English of varying degrees of fluency that it was known as the "American House."

·38·

THE LEMBERG POGROM

By the beginning of 1918 the dreary, trench-slogging campaigns of Flanders and Galicia and the desert maneuvers of Egypt and Palestine had become an idealistic crusade, a war to end wars and to liberate the suppressed nationalities of Europe and the Middle East. These were the essential elements of President Woodrow Wilson's Fourteen Points of January 8, which, among other things, called for the autonomous development of the peoples of Austria-Hungary and the Ottoman Empire and an independent Poland with secure access to the sea. In effect, this was to proclaim the end of the Russian Empire in Europe as well as of the Habsburg one—an aim that had not been shared by the provisional government in Petrograd but was now being implicitly accepted by the Bolsheviks.

The Bolsheviks had remained true to their program of withdrawal from the war, and—after an appeal to the Entente to join them in a peace conference, which was ignored—had begun negotiations with the Central Powers in December at Brest-Litovsk. The result—after a separate pact in February between the Central Powers and a Ukrainian government that claimed to be independent—was the treaty of March 3, in which the Bolsheviks signed away all of Poland, Lithuania, the Ukraine, the Baltic provinces, Finland, and Transcaucasia. The Germans and Austrians had meanwhile advanced to a line that extended from the Baltic to Kiev, taking in all the ceded territory and more.

But the war-weary Central Powers soon also succumbed to civil disorder and revolution. The multiracial Habsburg Empire began coming apart in the spring of 1918, when a Congress of Oppressed Austrian Nationalities assembled in Rome. In October, first the Czechs and then the Yugoslavs declared their independence. Austria signed an armistice with the Allies on November 3, and other proclamations of independence quickly followed. By then Germany, too, had fallen victim to internal strife. Under the threat of civil war, Kaiser Wilhelm II abdicated on November 9, and a newly proclaimed German republic concluded an armistice two days later. Eastern Europe was in a virtual state of anarchy: even when the new regimes were able to establish some authority, it was not clear what the frontiers were to which their authority extended without dispute.

For no state was this problem greater than for the newly reborn Republic of Poland, proclaimed on November 3. The old Poland had been a multinational state, so that one could not go far from Warsaw in any direction without running into some conflicting national claim. In the next three years, the Poles, under the command of General Jozef Pilsudski, were to become engaged in six different wars, some of them overlapping.

The first of these was against the Ukrainians, or, specifically, against the "West Ukrainian Republic" that declared itself on October 31, 1918, in the region known to most of the world as Eastern Galicia and called "Eastern Little Poland" by the Poles. At the end of the war there were still more Poles than Ukrainians in the whole of Galicia—about 3.7 million of them as against 3.3 million Ukrainians, or Ruthenians, as this group is more properly called in its Galician segment. The balance was far different in Eastern Galicia, however, where there were only some 1.3 million Poles, as against virtually the entire Ruthenian population of Galicia; but even there the Poles were preponderant in the cities, as they were west of the San River. This was especially true of the capital—called Lemberg by the Austro-Germans, Lwów by the Poles, and Lviv by the Ukrainians—where more than a hundred thousand Poles and only forty thousand Ruthenians lived.

Yet nowhere in Eastern Galicia, not even in Lemberg, were the Poles a clear majority. For, apart from the German population of about 3 percent found in most Galician cities—mainly the administrators of the Habsburg Empire—there was also a large Jewish presence. In Lemberg the Jews had numbered about fifty-seven thousand in 1914; owing to the wartime influx of the refugees, this figure had climbed to seventy thousand by 1918—about one-third of the city's total population.

Where, then—among Poles, Ruthenians, Germans, and themselves—did the Jews stand? It was the old question, compounded by the peculiar complexities of Eastern Galicia. The Jewish presence in Lemberg was almost as ancient as the city itself—certainly as ancient as the Polish occupation in 1340 of this vestige of a Ruthenian principality that had been overrun by Tartars. Casimir the Great, eager to establish a mercantile class, had encouraged Jewish settlement in this crossroads of Europe and the East, as he had in other cities under his rule. Even

after the partitions and the general economic decline of Galicia, the Jews
of Lemberg created one of the great communities of Israel in Eastern
Europe, a major center of Haskalah in the early part of the nineteenth
century and of Zionism by the end of it.

But Jewish Lemberg was not dominated by ethnocentrism alone.
In the middle of the nineteenth century, a strong current of German
assimilationism had arisen there, along with a religious reform movement influenced from Berlin and Vienna. Another turn began in 1867,
when the Habsburg regime designated Galicia as a region of Polish
cultural autonomy, reestablishing in Lemberg the ancient Jan Kasimir
University, along with a new Henry Sienkewicz school for secondary
education. There followed a steady Polonization among some of the more
assimilation-minded Jews of Lemberg, such as the novelist Wilhelm
Feldman, who wrote in Polish and spent the war in Berlin as a representative of Pilsudski's Polish Legion.

But there was no simple cultural route for the Jews of the city to
follow. For one thing, the Habsburg government had recently also allowed Lemberg to become a center for the lately emerging Ukrainian
nationalism, which was less trouble for it than the Polish variety, and
had established a chair in Ukrainian history and literature at the Jan
Kasimir University. And for all this, the pull of German culture had
remained strong among the upper classes of Lemberg Jewry, as did
Yiddish among its vast majority. Moreover, in spite of all the assimilationism, those two variants of Jewish national feeling, Bundism and
Zionism, had remained predominant.

Whatever the Jews of Lemberg were among themselves, however,
their political choice with respect to the world around them had become
reduced, by the end of October 1918, to two stark alternatives: Polish
or Ukrainian? Certainly there were Jews who regarded themselves as
Poles of the Mosaic persuasion. As for Ukrainian, this scarcely had attracted Jews as a national identification; on the other hand, Jewish delegates were participating in the Rada, or Ukrainian National Council,
in Kiev, which had acknowledged the principle of Jewish national autonomy within its jurisdiction. Consequently, there was widespread feeling
among the Jews of Lemberg that Ukrainian control was more desirable
than that of the Poles, who were reluctant to consider Jewish national
claims of any sort.

Other considerations also favored the Ukrainians. They were the
majority in Eastern Galicia as a whole. Moreover, the tottering Habsburg regime, still holding on for dear life at the end of October and
hoping for a revived national federation under its control, had thrown
its support behind them. Lemberg was full of Ukrainian troops.

On the other side of the picture, however, not only did the Poles
far outnumber the Ukrainians in Lemberg itself, but the Polish Legion

had made the city its headquarters throughout the war. More recently, other clandestine Polish military organizations had established themselves there, lacking nothing but arms. Under all these circumstances, the Jewish leaders of Lemberg perceived that their only viable position in the Polish-Ukrainian conflict was neutrality.

The showdown began early in the morning of November 1, when the Austrian Viceroy officially departed and handed over power to the Ukrainian authorities. Ukrainian troops immediately occupied the key buildings of the city—the police station, the post office, the railway and tram stations, the government bureaus, the banks. "What a strange picture Lwów was on this All Saints' Day, 1918!" writes Rosa Bailly, a Polish memoirist of these events:

> The bells were ringing, calling the faithful to worship. Gentlemen in ceremonial dress, ladies in their Sunday clothes, hurried through the streets. People were going to the cemeteries to light candles on the tombs for the Day of the Dead. They had armfuls of chrysanthemums to carry. But in this whitish fog, the trams were at a standstill in the street, singly or in long lines. And soldiers were standing around them making the passengers get out, examining their papers and searching their clothes. At this station no more trains were leaving. . . . The streets were as yet fairly calm. The Jews chatted under the carriage-entrances, the citadel looked empty. . . . Here, there and everywhere posters in Ruthenian would be stuck up on the walls.

Few people could read them. "These cyrillic characters," Bailly writes, "so strange to the people of the west, spell Russia, Asia, with all their complications." What they said was:

TO THE PEOPLE OF LVIV

1. By the will of the Ukrainian people on the Ukrainian territory of the former Austro-Hungarian Monarchy a *Ukrainian State* has been established.
2. The highest authority of the Ukrainian State is the Ukrainian National Council.
3. As of today, the Ukrainian National Council has taken over the government in the capital city of Lviv and in the entire territory of the Ukrainian State.
4. Further orders will be issued by the civil and military organs of the Ukrainian National Council.
5. The population is requested to observe order and to comply with these instructions.
6. Under such conditions the security of public order, of life

and property as well as the provisioning of foodstuffs is completely guaranteed.

Ukrainian National Council

Lviv, November 1, 1918

This was a virtual signal for the beginning of guerrilla warfare in the streets. Passing Ukrainian troops would suddenly find themselves attacked from hidden entranceways, their arms taken from them. By early afternoon, Polish forces had gathered in the newer, southwestern part of the city at the Henry Sienkewicz school, which quickly became the headquarters of their resistance and was attacked three times before the day was over. An informal army consisting of some fifteen hundred men, women, and young boys—including even a few toughs and criminals—was hastily assembled under Captain Czestaw Maczyński, and it soon took over other locations in the predominantly Polish western part of Lemberg.

Meanwhile, there was the question posed by the Jewish quarter in the whole northern part of the city, which stood between the two forces. "What would the Jews decide to do?" Bailly asks:

Some of them were already fighting alongside their Polish comrades against the aggressor, yet an even larger number dreamed of the day when they would be able to live in an independent, Jewish state, and the Ukrainians had declared their sympathy with the Zionist cause. These latter had, therefore, placed all their millenarian hopes in the newcomers. As for the vast majority of them, they preferred to keep out of harm's way.

This assessment was essentially correct. On the morning of November 1, Jewish leaders had assembled in the main synagogue and officially proclaimed their neutrality. Delegates were sent to both the Polish and the Ukrainian authorities to announce this position.

At the same time, for purposes of self-defense—and self-defense alone, it was emphasized—a Jewish Security Committee and a Jewish Militia were established under the direction of several Austrian-army veterans. A proclamation was drawn up in several languages, saying:

TO THE JEWISH POPULATION IN LEMBERG!

The latest events touch strongly upon the entire local Jewish population. In these perturbed times no single Jewish party may defenselessly surrender the life and property of seventy thousand Jews. It is necessary that in the opening hours we find ourselves united and resolved to be able to represent Lemberg Jewry. For this purpose a Jewish Security Committee has been formed today, representing all the Jewish parties of Lemberg. The Security Com-

mittee has taken on the difficult task of seeking ways and means to
maintain peace and order in the Jewish quarter and protect the
property of the Jewish population. This Committee bears responsibility for all these things and calls upon the Jewish population to
heed its commands, to exercise self-discipline, and to maintain the
strictest neutrality, whereby any assumption of a position for one
side or the other is to be avoided and no credence is to be given to
wild rumors. A Jewish Militia has been formed under the command
of the Security Committee. Jewish streets and institutions will be
guarded and defended. It will know of every outburst of panic or
fear; prudence and calm are to be exercised.

The Jewish Militia of some two hundred men—ranging from soldiers in
Austrian uniform to Hasidim in beards and fur hats—soon became "the
most popular organ in Lemberg," according to Joseph Tenenbaum, one
of its leaders.

Yet many Poles thought it was a secretly pro-Ukrainian organ.
Rosa Bailly insisted that it was "supplied with arms by the Ukrainians," though a British investigating commission the following year was
to conclude that it gave them no armed assistance. In any case, the
Polish view tended to be, as Bailly writes, that

the mere existence of this militia was a help to the enemy, as it
transformed the important and sizeable Jewish quarter into a form
of buffer state behind which the Ukrainians were free to concentrate their forces. One more difficulty to add to the problem of
Lwów's defense.

And she cannot refrain from adding testily:

Was it really formed with the aim of keeping order in the Jewish quarter and to preserve its neutrality? This, at least, was what
its leaders claimed, and they sought Capt. Maczyński's blessing,
although they took ten days before they finally went to see him.

This was the understanding they then reached with the Poles:

AGREEMENT
Between the Jewish Militia and the Polish Commander
Reached on November 10, 1918, in Lemberg

I.
The Jewish Militia has the task of maintaining order and security in the parts of the city inhabited by Jews; it may not take
part in the fighting either on the side of the Poles or on that of the
Ukrainians.

II.

The members of the Jewish Militia carry weapons and are identified by a white band on the left arm, which is their insignia, as well as by identity cards issued by the Militia Command.

III.

The Command of the Jewish Militia is to send in a list of its members and must give notice of changes in it every three days.

IV.

The district to be covered by the Jewish Militia is limited to the following streets: [the streets of the Jewish quarter are named].

V.

The Polish Commander will watch over the neutrality of the Jewish Militia.

This was signed by Polish and Jewish representatives and published in the Polish Command's official newspaper, *Pobudka.*

Rosa Bailly writes of this agreement: "Maczyński was quite worried, though, as [Lieutenant Roman] Abraham's reports had on several occasions made it clear that the Jewish militia supported the Ukrainians, who had supplied it with arms." And—Bailly is clearly implying—how can one doubt the testimony on this point of Lieutenant Abraham, a Jew himself, but one loyally fighting with the Polish forces? Certainly, no matter what the Militia did, rumors of Jewish betrayal to the Poles could not be quelled. "New kinds of heroes have come along," a *Pobudka* article sardonically announced on November 8:

On Cracow Place the Jews, not giving a thought to the neutrality so loudly proclaimed for them by their communal leaders, have added Ukrainian stripes to their Zionist ones and are helping their friends harass the Polish population.

This attitude was not changed by the November 10 agreement. On November 17—six days after the European armistice, which passed in Lemberg as though nothing had happened—*Pobudka* carried an item sarcastically entitled "The Neutrals" that said:

In our military circles there are complaints that the Jewish population is shooting at our patrols from their windows, and civilians who go into the quarter tell of things done by the Jews against the Polish population that are absolutely irreconcilable with their proclaimed neutrality. We present an official eyewitness statement, which goes thus:

"I know with complete certainty that in the Jewish lodging-houses in Zolkiewska and Cebulna Streets, whole weapons stores have been set up for the use of the Jewish population. In confirmation of this I can say that, on November 10 at eleven o'clock, I myself witnessed a band of armed Jews rushing out of the temple in the direction of the Schlossberg and beginning to shoot. Turning around, they said: 'That's nicely done.' Furthermore, I myself saw a Jew in Cracow Place firing a revolver at the Christian population. I have also heard about many Christian businesses being robbed and plundered."

As Tenenbaum suggests, reports like this were helping to implant the "pogrom idea" among the Poles of Lemberg. This idea grew more intense during a truce from November 18 through 20, when Polish reinforcements arrived from Posen and Western Galicia, under the command of General B. Roja. By then there had been anti-Jewish riots in the west of Poland, in which legionaries had either participated or done nothing to restore order. It was no secret that the new troops were bringing the pogrom mood with them—indeed, that they, in the words of a British investigator the following year, "were promised three days' free looting of the Jewish quarter." Joseph Tenenbaum occasionally heard the Polish soldiers singing:

> General Roja's coming with his young men,
> The Jews are going to have a wedding!

He also heard of increasing talk to Jews of a "Day of Reckoning."

But first came a day of victory. On November 21, the Poles made a large-scale attack upon the citadel, the last bastion of Ukrainian resistance. The Ukrainians were routed, and the city of Lwów—if not yet the surrounding countryside—was completely in Polish hands. It was a time for celebration.

On November 22, the sun rose on "streets gay with bunting," in the words of Rosa Bailly:

> Polish flags fluttered from every window and the whole town was red and white. . . . The morning brought a bewildering succession of scenes that were as touching as they were comical. People ran to and fro to pass the glad tidings on to their friends and relatives, without even pausing to dress, still in slippers and dressing gowns.

Then the Polish soldiers began marching through the streets:

> Their fathers and mothers, sisters and brothers were dotted amongst the cheering crowd and eager eyes sought each other out. . . . Everywhere there were tears of joy and gratitude, and,

longing to embrace those youngsters who had brought them deliverance, the crowd strained forward, its arms outstretched towards the soldiers. . . . Soon the procession was one seething mass of soldiers and civilians.

At this very moment, however, a celebration of another sort was taking place in the Jewish quarter. "On November 22, in the early hours of the morning," Tenenbaum writes,

> the frightened population of the Jewish quarter heard the whistling and hooting of Polish soldiers coming in, accompanied by shooting and harmonica-playing, as well as by curses and foul names called out to the Jews.

On some of the Jewish streets, plundering had begun as early as 4:00 A.M., but most of the rioters had waited until dawn. By eight o'clock the Jewish Militia had assembled, but this was very late. "The real pursuit of Jews had begun at seven in the morning. It began according to a plan worked out with military precision."
And it went like this:

> Machine guns and armored cars were stationed on the thoroughfares of the Jewish quarter and the streets were raked with fire, so that no one dared step out of his house. The machine guns were placed at the following locations: at Cracow Place near the State Theater, and at the entrances to Boznicza, Cebulna, Teodora Place, Zolkiewska, etc. At the same time, patrols were organized and every larger one was assigned to an area in which it could "work" without restriction or curtailment. A headquarters for the plundering legionaries was set up in the State Theater, where orders were issued and reports received. A large reserve squad—of robbers and murderers—also was posted there. . . . The Jewish quarter was cut off from the rest of the city by a powerful military cordon, through which no unauthorized person could enter or leave.

"And now," writes Tenenbaum, "the witches' sabbath began!"
Patrols of ten, twenty, or thirty men, each led by an officer, went through the streets carrying hand grenades and rifles with fixed bayonets, and banging on doors. Any door not opened immediately was opened with a hand grenade. Then the patrol would split, part of it guarding the street entrance to see that no one left, and part going through the building, "with a flood of foul curses and wild shouts of rage, spraying shots in every direction." All cash and valuables had to be handed over, but then the victims were usually beaten anyway. "You Jews," ran the typical speech, "have shot at us, thrown hot water and

lye on our fighters, sold us poisoned cigarettes, given millions to the Ukrainians—Poles can't tolerate Jews any more, today you have to die." Men, women, and children were murdered. A young woman was to report that

> a body of soldiers came to her house, shot her father, her brother and her brother-in-law, and would have shot her, but she gave them 3,000 crowns and they went away. The soldiers came again at about 12 o'clock in the day and shot her brother, who was still living, though previously wounded, dead. They broke open the safe and stole the silver plate. Another body of soldiers came to the house about 5 o'clock. She had by then taken refuge on the third floor with a Polish woman, who when the soldiers came a third time sent them away.

Shops were plundered, the booty loaded onto army trucks. When the looting was accomplished, the rioters turned to burning. It was later reported that "many buildings were set on fire with petroleum obtained from a store; as the occupants ran out to escape the flames they were shot down in the street in cold blood by Polish soldiers." That night much of the Jewish quarter was in flames.

"It must be borne in mind," writes Rosa Bailly,

> that the Ukrainians were still in the vicinity, namely at Kozielniki and at Dublany only a few miles distant from the town they had just lost but to which it was possible they had not yet renounced all claim. At dusk, the sky on the eastern horizon was aglow: it was the Polish villages of Bilka Szlachecka and Bilka Krolewska that were going up in flames.

She seems not to have noticed the glow in the northern sky, much closer by. The fires in the Jewish quarter continued and were renewed the following day; at ten in the morning, the three-hundred-year-old Vorstädtische Synagogue burst into flames. "The synagogue was burned," according to the British report, "the safe being opened by means of machine-gun fire, and the scrolls of the law were burned and everything of value removed."

One of the British investigators adds: "A large number of the civilian population of Lemberg, wealthy middle-class people, joined in the plunder of the Jewish shops." At the end of three days of rioting, seventy-two Jews lay dead and 443 were wounded. Thirty-eight buildings had been burned to the ground.

"On Thursday, November 28," Joseph Tenenbaum writes,

was the funeral of the pogrom victims, men, women and children, and the defiled holy scrolls. A cortege of twenty thousand mourners accompanied the victims. The Chief Rabbi Dr. Guttman began the funeral services but collapsed, and only fragments of syllables were torn from his stricken voice. The whole community broke out in anguish of frenzy. Tears flowed, hot, bloody, disconsolate tears. Only this gift could they offer the dear ones on their eternal journey. After the laments, there was silence, and then as from nowhere a thousand voices, a thousand cries, a collective oath: NEVER AGAIN SHALL THIS HAPPEN TO US!

·39·

POLAND AFTER LEMBERG:
AN ITINERARY

"The news that reached London in November 1918 concerning pogroms in what had been Russian Poland and Galicia," writes Israel Cohen, a Manchester-born journalist and Zionist activist,

> aroused so much alarm that the British Government issued a warning against further excesses. The newly formed States in Eastern Europe were solemnly admonished that if they indulged in bloodshed at the birth of their independence they could not reckon upon the help of the Western Powers in the task of their reconstruction. But despite this warning, further messages arrived of more serious outrages against the Jews in Galicia.

The Zionist Organization in London, under the leadership of Dr. Chaim Weizmann and triumphant in the wake of the Balfour Declaration and the British occupation of Palestine, decided to send a representative to Poland to investigate. "Owing to the difficulties of travel at the time," Cohen continues,

> and also to the nature of the intended mission, the consent of the British Foreign Office was necessary. Dr. Weizmann interviewed Sir George Clerk, Secretary to the Foreign Secretary, Lord (then Mr. Arthur James) Balfour, on the subject and proposed that I should undertake the mission. Sir George approved of the proposal, and Lord Balfour agreed to provide the requisite facilities.

The thirty-nine-year-old Cohen, who had visited Galicia in 1906, left early in December and, after meeting with Jewish and Polish leaders in Paris, Vienna, and other cities, arrived in Cracow on January 1, 1919. By that time another pogrom, milder than the first, had occurred in

321

Lemberg, and anti-Jewish excesses were going on all over the country. But the Polish leaders to whom Cohen spoke in Warsaw—which was still under the temporary regime of General Pilsudski when he arrived— were determined either to minimize them, to explain them away, or to claim they had not happened. Foreign Minister Leon Wasilewski told him flatly that there had been "no pogroms, and the reports were exaggerated." When Cohen mentioned the matter to Stanislaw Grabski, a leader of the National Democrats, the reply was that "nothing would be gained by inquiry or prosecution, that Jews had fought on [the] side of Ukrainians, had poured boiling gruel on Polish soldiers, had caused 30,000 Poles in Galicia to be hanged and had greatly profited by war." Cohen adds in his diary: "I questioned all these charges."

The British journalist had two brief interviews with the great pianist and symbol of the Polish national ideal, Ignacy Paderewski, just back from the United States, where he had lived throughout the war. During the first one, a "friendly talk in English" in Paderewski's hotel suite, the composer assured him "he would keep his promises given to the Jewish leaders in America, that he would do all in his power to improve the Jewish position in Poland. Protested that he was philo-Semitic and that the stories about his being anti-Semitic were untrue." The second meeting took place five days after Paderewski had become Prime Minister of the new Polish Republic. "He was finishing supper with American Mission: came into ante-chamber (typewriter, beer bottles, etc.). Offered me a cigarette: had animated conversation on Jewish situation." However, Cohen's diary goes on,

> I regretted to note that Paderewski had become less conciliatory than at our previous interview. He said military raid on Jewish quarter Nalewki [in Warsaw] last Saturday and Sunday was necessitated by search for weapons in fighting against Bolshevism. I pointed out that no weapons had been found in Jewish houses, but soldiers had robbed and assaulted Jews. I asked whether Government would issue condemnation of pogroms. He replied there had also been pogroms in Whitechapel and Cardiff (a gross exaggeration), and those in Poland were caused by resentment against Jews for having sided with Germans.

The Prime Minister went on to complain

> of the part played by Jews in the Bolshevist movement, whereupon I observed that Jewish Bolshevists were but a small fraction of Russian and Polish Jews, that Jews had killed Bolshevist leaders, and all Jewish parties [were] opposed to the movement. In reply to question whether Government would give Jews compensation, he asked whether Poland would be compensated for her losses in war,

and concluded by assuring me he would keep his promise to Jewish leaders in America to do utmost for just treatment of Jews.

The next day, January 23, Cohen interviewed Jozef Pilsudski, the Garibaldi of Polish independence, at his headquarters in the Palace Belvedere. Pilsudski, Cohen writes,

> came in with a slow step, coughing. He was in military attire—with black trousers, grey tunic with high collar and white cuffs; and as he bade me be seated, I noted the resolute and furtive look, the drooping moustache, and the close-cropped hair, which picture postcards throughout the country had made familiar. He was obviously suffering from a cold, and had a couple of handkerchiefs peeping from a pocket in addition to the one that he was using for his nose.

Speaking German, Cohen explained that he had "come from England to study the Jewish situation in Poland owing to the unfavorable impression that had been created by the pogroms."

"The pogroms were caused," said Pilsudski, "by the sudden collapse of Austrian rule and the absence of authority, and by the hatred of Jewish dealers—the only class who had profited in the war. It is true," added the general, who had always obtained strong support from the Jews and was considered friendly by them, "that dealers in all parts of the world have profited. But as so many Jews in Galicia were engaged in trade, hatred was easily directed against all Jews."

"Didn't the Polish landlords and peasants also profit by the war?" Cohen asked.

"If they did, it was through dealings with Jews. . . ."

Cohen let the matter drop. "Doesn't the Government intend issuing a condemnation of the pogroms?"

"How can you expect that the Government would say that it disapproves of pogroms? That would suggest," the Polish leader explained illogically, "that the Government consists of pogromists. It is understood that the Government doesn't approve of the pogroms or of violence of any kind against anybody."

"Then what about the shooting in the Jewish quarter Nalewki last Sunday, when several Jews were wounded?"

"I don't think the affair was serious, and have not yet received a full report about it. I must inquire." Then Pilsudski relented a little. "I must say that the Poles are not philo-Semites. That must be admitted. The Jews in Poland form a very large number and are a foreign body whom one would like to get rid of." Having made that admission, he then added: "On the other hand, it must be said that the Poles are by nature not a wild people, and the present violence cannot continue. Secondly, as soon as the independence of Poland was declared, equal rights were granted to all Jews exactly as in all Western democracies. There were no exceptional laws for Jews."

Cohen protested: "But the Jews *are* in an exceptional position, which makes their equal rights quite illusory. For example, in certain districts of the Kielce province Jews are not allowed to vote at the forthcoming election unless they sign a declaration that they regard themselves [as] members of the Polish nationality."

"Yes, I have heard something to that effect, but nothing very definite."

Cohen then brought up the matter of Jews in the Polish railway service, more than a thousand of whom had been dismissed.

"I must make enquiries into the question," Pilsudski replied. "I presume that the Jews were employed by the Germans, and as all people who worked for the Germans are hated they were dismissed."

It was a familiar argument. "But Poles also worked for the Germans," Cohen rejoindered. "Were they dismissed?"

"The Poles worked on the railways before under the Russian regime, so they remained."

"Yes, but there were other Poles, too, who rendered Germany political aid," Cohen maintained, and gave examples.

"Those people had, of course, to disappear from public life as they had so compromised themselves, and they will not be able to resume their activity for some years."

Cohen riposted: "Because a few Jews worked with the Germans, all Jews in Poland are made to suffer; but as for the Poles, only those suffer who were the actual offenders."

"In these confused times and our present disorganized conditions, you can hardly expect strict justice."

Cohen then appealed for justice at least for a few, bringing up the case of four Lemberg Zionist leaders who had been interned by the Polish government three weeks after the November pogrom.

"I can't do anything in this matter at present," Pilsudski said, "as it was a military measure designed to secure the tranquility of the people in Lemberg. If I were to release the hostages it would cause considerable discontent among the Poles."

"Is there any specific charge against the hostages?" Cohen asked.

"None," said the general in all honesty; "if there were, we should make short work of the matter. It is said that they were not neutral in the fight between the Poles and the Ukrainians, but whether they were so or not is difficult to say. Besides," he added, "the hostages have nothing really to complain of. I sent my adjutant to Baranow to see how they were accommodated. They are in a castle and quite safe. I have already issued an order that as soon as the situation at Lemberg is eased, all hostages—both Ukrainians and Jews—are to be released. The situation in Lemberg is, indeed, distressing. . . ."

"It was nearly ten o'clock when the train steamed into Lemberg fully two hours late," writes Cohen in his diary for the morning of January 26. Entirely in Polish hands, Lemberg was still at war with the nearby Ukrainian forces and being bombarded by them.

"No sooner did I get outside the station," Cohen continues,

> than my ears were assailed by the dull boom of a cannon. I expected everybody to fly for shelter, but nobody seemed to mind. There were no cabs or taxis to be seen, nor trams nor even tram lines; for the electric power station had been badly damaged by the Ukrainians, the trams were rendered useless, and the tram lines were buried under mud and snow.

There were sleighs that would carry people's baggage, but Cohen found a Jewish porter without a sleigh who could manage his handbag and attaché case on foot, and the two set out for the Hotel Krakowski.

"The long sloping street that led from the station to the city showed traces on every side of the fierce battle that had raged there in the early half of November." Even though Lemberg had been captured by the Russians and retaken by the Austrians during the war, it had not known bombardment or fighting within its streets until now. The result was that it

> was now nearly as badly bruised and battered as many a town in Flanders. . . . Not a single building, public or private, had escaped injury, for the machine guns had wrought havoc on every side. The walls looked stricken with smallpox, and the windows were everywhere plastered over with paper, for there was no glass to be obtained. . . . My porter told me that he had been in Lemberg from the outbreak of the war, but since the signing of the Armistice it had been worse than ever before.

At one corner, Cohen and the porter saw a group of shivering women taking turns at drawing water from a pump, and, farther on, some disheveled Ukrainian prisoners being led by an equally dejected-looking band of Polish legionaries. Then they entered the Jewish quarter:

> We turned into the Karl Ludwig Street, where a number of young children between the ages of six and twelve were hawking sweets, cigarettes and newspapers. These tattered traders—their faces pinched and blue with cold—were Jewish children, many of

them orphans, over whom had swept a few weeks ago the horrors of a barbarous pogrom, but who stood eagerly discussing business with one another, and keeping a wary eye open for customers. *"Lemberger Tageblatt!"*—*"Papirossen* (cigarettes)!" piped the infant voices irrepressibly, whilst overhead cracked the roar of cannon. They had seen death so near that invisible guns had no terror for them.

It was not until the next day, after a cold night in the Hotel Krakowski, that Cohen was taken by a local Zionist leader

through the streets in which the pogrom had taken place. The traces of the great outrage were still evident in abundance. There were cracked and broken windows, jagged gaps in iron shutters that had been forced open with a bayonet, heaps of debris still lying on the floors of some looted shops, which their owners had not the heart to clear away. Some of the windows were pasted over with paper, others were covered with boards. Many shops were still closed; others were beginning to re-open with small stocks.

Everywhere they turned, Cohen and his companion were met with stories of assault, robbery, rape, and massacre, and the British journalist regretted that his fingers

were so numbed with the cold that they could not record a tithe of what I heard. Yet everything paled into nothingness when I came into the street where blocks of houses had been wilfully burned to the ground by means of petroleum brought on military lorries; all that remained were portions of brick walls and the damning charred patch on the front of each house, showing where the firebrand had been laid. A synagogue, too, had been utterly demolished, with its priceless treasures of scrolls of the Law, and ritual ornaments of gold and silver, handed down by the exiles from medieval Spain, and two other synagogues had been despoiled, and damaged and robbed even of their charity boxes.

Cohen stayed in Lemberg three and a half days,

and with each succeeding day I became more and more penetrated with the sense of depression that held everybody in thrall. The bitter, biting cold, the dirt and darkness, the famine prices, the lack of amusement—the orchestra at the Krakowski formed the sole entertainment in the city—the isolation from the outside world, the general insecurity, the ceaseless bombardment, all contributed to plunge the inhabitants into the abyss of despair. The liberty of small nations, the right of self-determination! What a mockery these words sounded to the innocent sufferers of Lemberg! "If only Wilson would come here for a short time!" they sighed.

One of Cohen's guides had pointed to the pockmarks left by machine-gun bullets on walls all over the city, and told him that people were calling them "Wilson's Points."

· 40 ·

THE UKRAINIAN HOLOCAUST, I:
FROM NATIONAL UPRISING
TO POGROM

As for the Ukrainians, of the many currents of national feeling released by the fall of tsarism and the voice of Woodrow Wilson, theirs was among the most vexing. Did that vast and fertile region in the south, the name of which meant simply "borderland," really house a distinct nationality? The Great Russians of the north had never thought so, and were inclined to look upon "Little Russia" as a southern region of their own in which the peasants spoke a different dialect. Ukrainian speech was rare in its cities, where Great Russian, Polish, Jewish, and other non-Ukrainian groups predominated, and where the indigenous middle and working classes had become largely Russified. As for the Ukrainian rural gentry, they, like their celebrated offspring Nikolai Gogol, had become completely Russian.

But in the nineteenth century's atmosphere of romantic nationalism, a Ukrainian movement had come into being. Its first great representative had been the poet Taras Shevchenko, born in 1814, who had written verse in Ukrainian and prose in Russian. "As a natural result of centuries of oppression of the Ukrainian language and culture," wrote Arnold Margolin, a Jew of Kiev who spoke Ukrainian poorly,

the Russian and Polish intelligentsia far outnumber the Ukrainian, and Russian and Polish literature are far richer. Nevertheless, Ukrainian peasants have always cherished the memory of their ancestors who fought against Tartar, Polish and Russian invaders. Their folklore and folk songs have earned—and deserve—worldwide admiration and recognition.

By the time of the revolution, the foremost intellectual representative of the Ukrainian ideal was Professor Michael Hrushevsky, who had held

328

the chair in Ukrainian history and literature at the Jan Kasimir University in Lemberg.

It was Hrushevsky who, along with a novelist named Mark Vinnichenko and a journalist turned army officer, Colonel Simon Petlura, had proclaimed a "Ukrainian Conference" in March 1917. Organizing what passed for elections in the nine provinces it considered Ukrainian, the Conference then yielded to a central Rada of six hundred members, with Vinnichenko as Prime Minister. Like the Provisional Government in Petrograd, the Rada in Kiev was composed of a wide range of political tendencies that excluded only the far left, with the difference that they all in varying degrees supported some kind of Ukrainian autonomy. In a proclamation, or "Universal," of June 23, 1917, the Rada proclaimed an Autonomous Ukrainian Republic, which would affiliate with the forthcoming All-Russian Constituent Assembly, but would accept its legislative supremacy only as a "matter of form."

The Rada was not sure what kind of federative arrangement with Petrograd it ultimately foresaw. But no such arrangement was to the liking of the Provisional Government—which could not, however, as a liberal institution, oppose separate national aspirations altogether. A tug-of-war ensued between Petrograd and Kiev, resulting, on the one hand, in a reduction of the Ukrainian territorial claims from nine provinces to five, and, on the other, in a second "Universal," which further strengthened Ukrainian autonomous institutions. This quarrel was superseded by the Bolshevik takeover in November.

The Bolsheviks would not recognize the Rada. True, they had spoken up for the rights of nationalities, but in the Ukraine they would not allow this principle to be implemented under any authority but their own. For its part, the Rada responded with a third "Universal," on November 20, claiming the right to exercise unrestricted authority until the convocation of the Constituent Assembly. The result was an outbreak of civil war between two ill-organized armies. Kiev and its environs remained under the control of the Rada for the time being, but on December 26, Kharkov fell to the Bolsheviks, who proclaimed there a "Provisional Ukrainian Soviet Government." By the beginning of January, they had taken Yekaterinoslav, Odessa, and Nikolayev.

But there was still the Great War itself to put out of the way. On January 8, 1918, peace negotiations with the Central Powers were begun at Brest-Litovsk. The Soviets were represented by their Foreign Minister, Leon Trotsky, but, to everyone's surprise, a Ukrainian delegation also appeared, led by three students of Professor Hrushevsky. Trotsky denied the existence of the "Ukrainian Popular Republic" they claimed to represent, but they were soon seated.

On January 18, an All-Russian Constituent Assembly finally met in Petrograd, and the Brest-Litovsk negotiations were recessed. The Bolsheviks had not won a majority, and there were rumors that they would oppose the Assembly with force. "Notwithstanding these bad omens," recalls Arnold Margolin, who went representing the Labor–People's Socialist Party from Kiev,

> a solemnly hopeful spirit pervaded Petrograd on the memorable morning of January 18, 1918. Early in the morning crowds began to fill the streets and to wind their way slowly toward the Tauride Palace where the Constituent Assembly was to meet. Among these processions could be found the flower of the Petrograd intelligentsia, and there were many who had spent years in prison and in exile for fighting Russian autocracy.

The euphoria soon ended. "About eleven o'clock," Margolin continues,

> some of these processions were entering the streets which led directly to the Tauride Palace. I was in one of them, and saw how suddenly, without the slightest warning, bullets began to rain from above upon the front ranks passing through Liteiny Prospect. A similar fate befell others in the side streets. The guarding of the Tauride Palace was entrusted to Kronstadt sailors—at that time the most reliable force of the Bolsheviki—and machine guns had been placed in all the corridors and entrances.

A day of speechmaking was allowed, but on the 19th, troops loyal to the Bolsheviks dispersed the Constituent Assembly.

This was the last straw for the Ukrainians. "The dispersion of the All-Russian Constituent Assembly," Margolin writes,

> signified the frustration of the plan to introduce a democratic form of government and a genuine federative system in Russia. It was clear that all talk by the new masters of Russia about the self-determination of nationalities was but lip-service to their previous promises.

On January 25, the Rada issued a fourth "Universal," declaring the Ukraine to be an independent state.

When negotiations were resumed at Brest-Litovsk on February 1, the Ukrainians were even more eager to come to peace terms than the Soviets were. Kiev was under siege by the Red armies, and some Ukrainian regiments had gone over to their side. In a few days, Kiev was to be taken, and the Rada to retire to Zhitomir while Petlura's depleted forces tried to hold out in northern Podolia. Meanwhile, both Germany and Austria had begun to favor Ukrainian national aspirations, the for-

mer seeing a new ally and major agricultural supplier snatched out of
the Soviet underbelly, the latter dreaming of a possible new component
in an expanded Habsburg Empire. On February 9, the Ukrainian delegates signed a separate peace with the Central Powers. Trotsky thereupon abandoned the conference, declaring that a state of neither war
nor peace existed between the assembled nations.

On February 17, Germany denounced the armistice with Russia,
and, without Austrian participation, its armies began advancing eastward. Their aim was twofold: to establish a cordon in the north until
the Soviets made up their mind about peace terms, and to occupy the
whole of the "independent" Ukraine to protect it from the Red armies.
Unopposed by Soviet troops, the Germans had occupied Kiev by March
1 and reinstated the Rada there. Two days later, they had covered all
of the Ukraine, and occupied the districts of Vitebsk, Mohilev, and Gomel in the north. That same day, Lenin repudiated the stand taken by
Trotsky, who was now Minister of War, and signed the Treaty of Brest-
Litovsk.

Under treaty arrangements, the Ukraine was to supply grain to
the German army. In just a few weeks, however, it became clear that
the grain sources were not meeting their quotas and not all Ukrainian
leaders were eager to cooperate with their German protectors. Vinnichenko and Petlura were among the quietly resistant elements. There
finally was a showdown in April, when the Rada was dispersed and a
Ukrainian puppet head of state was installed by the Germans under the
ancient Cossack title of "hetman."

General Pavel Skoropadsky was actually the descendant of a Ukrainian hetman who served under Peter the Great; otherwise, he was
scarcely a Ukrainian at all, and spoke only Russian. He had a sentimental interest in the region, but was firmly opposed by the Rada. Consequently, according to Arnold Margolin, "after the Ukrainian parties
refused to take part in his government he appointed as Prime Minister
a Ukrainian landowner of Russian orientation who, in turn, chose as his
ministers like-minded Russians and Ukrainians." The Ukraine in general and Kiev in particular quickly became a major refuge for Russians
of the overthrown privileged classes. It also became a center of wartime
prosperity, in which, according to the official German account, "illegal
commerce and speculation flourished." The Germans, for their part, got
their grain quotas, and remained satisfied even against growing under-
currents of opposition.

This opposition reached a head in July, when the German Commander of the Ukraine, Field Marshal Hermann von Eichhorn, was assassinated by a terrorist, and when several socialist parties formed a
"National Union" under Vinnichenko and Petlura, who headed a five-

member Directory. When the collapse of the Central Powers became imminent in October, the Directory prepared to take power, and Petlura retired to Belaya Tserkov to organize an army.

In the weeks following the November 11 armistice, the Ukraine fell into disarray. The Germans, attempting an orderly evacuation, ran into constant interference from Petlura's troops and from angry mobs convinced they were carrying off great quantities of loot. The Soviets moved steadily into the growing vacuum from the north and the east, and were soon back in Yekaterinoslav and Poltava. There now also appeared in refugee-filled Kiev a "South Russian Center" that aimed to restore a united, non-Bolshevik Russia and supported the "White" armies of General Anton Denikin, who, with British help, were fighting their way up from the remote Kuban and were now in command at Rostov. As for Allied troops, apart from those that were aiding the counterrevolution in the east and the northwest, some were in Rumania watching over the situation in the Ukraine; in mid-December, the French were to make a landing at Odessa.

For a time, the Hetman held out in Kiev. Then, on December 11, Petlura met with German leaders at the Kasatin depot and arrived at a crucial agreement: the Germans would be guaranteed an orderly evacuation if Kiev—then still defended by their troops—were surrendered to the Directory. Three days later, Skoropadsky fled to Germany in disguise, and on December 19, the Directory returned to its home city. As the year 1919 dawned, the principal task facing the restored Ukrainian regime was that of war with the invading Red armies. But what happened next also turned out to be the greatest disaster to befall Ukrainian Jewry since the days of that early hetman for whom one of the new Cossack fighting brigades was named—Bogdan Khmelnitsky.

The Ukraine was the main population center of Russian Jewry; its million and a half Jews were more than 60 percent of the Jewish population of Russia without Poland. It was also the old heartland of pogroms, yet this fact had caused surprisingly little bitterness on the part of Jews there, who were inclined to see pogromists originating more in an urban rabble than in the solid Ukrainian peasantry. Of the latter, Arnold Margolin could write:

> The [Ukrainian] farmers usually surpass their Russian and Polish neighbors in being excellent gardeners and husbandmen, and in what one calls in America "pride of one's home." Ukrainian farms are noted for their neat, white-washed houses, set amid flowers and orchards and simply adorned with an evident appreciation of beauty. Serfdom was introduced later in the Ukraine than in either Russia proper or Poland; it lasted for a shorter time, and could not, there-

fore, completely eradicate the old ideals of individual freedom and human worth.

For Margolin, who had been one of Mendel Beiliss's lawyers, the Ukraine presented a democratic vista that was virtually American. "There is no Ukrainian aristocracy," he writes,

> for whatever nobility there may have been has long since become extinct or completely Russified. Ukrainian leaders are an integral part of the nation; they spring from and work hand in hand with the peasants, artisans, factory workers, and shopkeepers. Thus, like the Czechs, the Ukrainians are a genuinely democratic nation, without any remnant of aristocratic or feudal psychology. In this they are akin to Americans.

This appreciative spirit had led Margolin to represent the Ukraine in the ill-fated Constituent Assembly, and to sit in the Rada.

Indeed, there had been fifty Jews in the six-hundred-member Rada that assembled in March 1917, representing a wide range of political opinions, including Bundism and Zionism. Proclaiming itself in favor of "personal-national autonomy" for the country's minorities, the Rada created separate ministries for Russian, Polish, and Jewish affairs. On January 9, 1918, it had issued a decree guaranteeing to each the "independent organization of its national life."

But forces were now also at work tending to stir up old resentments. Bolshevik rule in particular, wherever it was established, brought an unprecedented and, to many, irritating experience: Jewish officials. The people who had been banned from government posts by the tsarist regime were now coming into Ukrainian communities as representatives of a new order, threatening the economic basis of their existence. Not that all Bolshevik officials were Jews by any means, but a few were sufficient to make the peasant, in the words of a contemporary observer, become

> suspicious of the entire Jewish population, regarding all Jews without exception as members of the Soviet regime, which enabled them to exercise power against the Christian population. The idea took firm root in his mind that the Jewish nation was endeavoring to dominate over the Christian peasant.

Even during the period of Skoropadsky's rule, as the compiler of the official German account saw it, "Jews were frequently the transmitters of Bolshevik propaganda."

Such suspicions had been aggravated by the ambivalent position assumed by some of the Ukrainian Jewish parties after the Bolshevik takeover. The Rada was not so firmly supported by the Russified urban working classes and bourgeoisie as by the rural peasantry, particularly its more prosperous elements, but this was precisely the constituency between whom and the Jewish labor parties there never had been much mutual amiability. The Bund had never fully shared the enthusiasm for Ukrainian separatism and, after abstaining in the vote of the third "Universal," had actually voted against the fourth, which proclaimed Ukrainian independence. The other Jewish labor parties—the United Jewish Socialists and the Poalei Zion—had abstained.

"At this time began the first threats of the Ukrainians against the Jews," according to Elias Heifetz, the above-quoted contemporary observer. Among some opponents of the fourth "Universal," the idea of a protest strike had been discussed. This had led one Ukrainian deputy to say to his Jewish colleagues:

> "Yesterday, one of your men in the council of labor delegates advocated the general strike. Do not play a double game. Say openly what you want. Restrain your people from such steps. We feel that we shall soon be unable to curb the anger and the hate of our people."

But if the revolution had on the one hand introduced Ukrainians to the myth-inspiring image of the Jew-Bolshevik, the German occupation had helped perpetuate the old one of the Jewish middleman. "The well-being of the population both Christian and Jewish had increased considerably," Heifetz writes of the occupation:

> It was the time of unlimited speculation in goods and money, of smuggling in and out of Russia and the neutral zone. The peasants, however, could not increase their earnings in the same measure as the others. The products of the land were taken from them by force, at low prices, and carried to Germany.

The official German account says bluntly of this commerce:

> Even the authorized trading, the object of which was the despatch of parcels of food to their homes, brought the [German] soldiers into undesirable contact with the population—especially with Jews who had most of this commerce in their hands.

On the basis, then, Heifetz continues,

> of exaggerated reports of "the wealth of the Jews," there developed among the peasants a feeling of envy and a desire for city

products (manufactured goods, shoes), of which there was nothing in the Ukrainian village, rumor having it that the Jews in the larger centers enjoyed a superfluity of such things.

The overthrow of Skoropadsky had brought a new moment of hopefulness, and, with the revived Jewish Ministry, a Provisional National Council of the Jews of the Ukraine was convened in Kiev in November 1918. In January 1919, Abraham Revutsky, a member of the Poalei Zion and the Minister of Jewish Affairs in the Ukrainian People's Republic, issued a proclamation in Yiddish, which ran in part:

> The stormy surge of popular anger has overthrown the regime of the Hetman and put an end to the reactionary rule of aristocrats and capitalists. The working classes of the Ukraine have power back in their hands. They will use it to shape a new society, to break the chains that enslave toiling mankind.
> Together with the Ukrainian revolution the Jewish revolutionary democracy has come to power. . . . The Ministry of Jewish Affairs lives again. From now on the Jewish people of the Ukraine can realize full rights to their language and culture, and to an autonomous restructuring of every aspect of their lives.

But even as these words were being written, the dire events that would give the lie to them were already unfolding.

Early in January, copies of a startling telegram from the town of Romny were received by Chairman Vinnichenko and by the Jewish National Council. It read:

> On January 2 at the Bakhmatch central station acts have been committed throwing into the shade all the horrors of the Middle Ages and reviving in our time memories of the Inquisition that was thought long ago dead and gone. Echelons of soldiers passing through the station or staying there, aided by the local garrison, made Jews leave the trains in which they were traveling and subjected them to cruel tortures. First they were going to shoot them all, then to shoot every fifth man, and were already proceeding to select the victims. Finally they decided merely to flog them. Every one of the Jews was robbed of all his baggage and money, and then beaten with ramrods on the naked body. . . . This was done by order of the *ataman* of the regiment. Several were beaten senseless; other victims have disappeared, and their fate is unknown.

This was signed by the Council of the Jewish Community of Romny.

There had already been such incidents in late December, but far worse was now coming. Next to fall victim was the Jewish community of Berditchev. "On January 5, 1919," according to a communication sent by D. Lipetz, Berditchev's new Jewish mayor,

> at 7:00 A.M., Mr. Souprenenko, the head of the Criminal Investigation Department, called on me to tell me that the town was menaced by a pogrom. He said that the "Battalion of Death" had arrived in town the night before for the purpose of "punishing" the Jewish population.
>
> Persistent rumors were circulating that the "Battalion of Death," on arriving at Berditchev (on January 4) had committed a regular pogrom at the railway station. It was said that, in consequence of that massacre, a wagon full of dead bodies and two wagons full of wounded Jews had been discovered; the victims were Jewish passengers travelling by trains passing through Berditchev, whom their tormentors had removed from the trains. Inquiries established the truth of the reports, but it was impossible to ascertain then what became of the wounded and the arrested. About midday the "Battalion of Death" entered the town and the massacre began.

Fifty-eight Jews were killed and over two hundred wounded, but this, too, was to be swiftly outdone. What had suddenly emerged were bands of Cossacks, calling themselves "Setcheviks" and "Haidamaks" like their ancestors, who were ostensibly fighting for Ukrainian independence but were taking out their wrath upon Jews. The band of Setcheviks called the Battalion of Death, commanded by one Ataman Palienko, now turned its attention to Zhitomir, the capital of Podolia. A Soviet regime had just proclaimed itself there, but it had neither a strong popular base nor a well-organized military machine. The Setcheviks made contact with its leaders on January 6 and, according to the report of a subsequent Committee of Inquiry, proceeded to woo them by claiming they were "supporters of the Soviets, but were against the 'Jews,' that they were Bolsheviks, but that they were against the Commissars, and that they intended occupying the town only for a few days, in order to loot, and that then they would leave."

January 7 was a day of great anxiety for the Jews of Zhitomir, who had heard rumors of what happened at Berditchev. Between ten and eleven that evening, Palienko's troops began arriving by train, and the Ataman himself appeared a few hours later. The looting began in the morning. "About 8:00 A.M.," according to the Committee of Inquiry, "soldiers in helmets were already breaking the panes of a shop at the corner of Mikhailovsky and Great Berditchev Streets. At the same time the looting of shops in Petrograd Street was in full swing."

At about 9:00 A.M., a truckload of soldiers arrived in Alexander II Place, in the Jewish quarter. They fired upon the crowd, then bombarded houses, and a new phase of the violence began:

In the center of the town, on the Place and in Great Berditchev Street, Kiev Street and Mikhailovsky Street, an almost uninterrupted gun and rifle fire went on. From time to time the deafening noise of a bomb or grenade exploding was heard; these were used to break open the doors and shutters of the bigger shops. From the shops thus opened, goods were carried away by soldiers of all kinds, in helmets, in caps and in red hoods, in various uniforms, or simply in ordinary clothes, but with full fighting equipment. When selecting things in the shops, the soldiers threw a part of the goods from the shops into the street and onto the pavements. Crowds of women, girls, and children eagerly snatched up the loot and carried it away. In looting the shops the soldiers were joined by civilians who, to judge by their clothes, came from the suburbs and lower quarters, by some minor officials and also by men from the neighboring villages. Among the crowd of looters and robbers were seen a few persons who undoubtedly belonged to the intelligentsia: civil servants and students. The pogrom was carried on without hurry and methodically, with an apparent assurance of absolute impunity. One street after another was visited quite systematically; or, in a given street, first of all the shops on one side were looted, and then all the shops on the other side.

The first two days were devoted to robbing and looting, during which there was scattered killing but not yet any wholesale massacres. Then, on the evening of the 9th, Palienko spoke at the Town Hall before the mayor and other municipal leaders:

"Ukraine is surrounded on all sides by enemies. These include the Entente, the Cossacks of the Don and the Kuban, the Poles, the Rumanians, the Russians, the Jews and the Bolsheviks. All Jews are Bolsheviks.... I have been sent to punish Zhitomir. I have already punished Berditchev. Rovno, knowing of my coming, is trembling. Zhitomir I shall clear so thoroughly that it will not contain any more Soviets of Deputies, or any parties whatever. It shall be clean. It is fortunate for the town that I have not met here any resistance, because otherwise I would have razed the town to the ground, and not left one stone on another."

The next morning, a new kind of anti-Jewish violence flared up. At first it was perpetrated in the outlying parts of town, "mainly by the scum of the local population," but then the troops in the center took up the task. Groups of five to seven soldiers, sometimes led by officers, would break into Jewish homes, usually claiming to be looking for Bolsheviks—even when the home was that of someone known to be an opponent of Bolshevism. Then they

assembled the tenants, ordered them to stand up against the wall, not excluding small children, threatened to shoot them, jeered at them, insulted them, and stripped them of all their valuables, including wedding rings, money and clothes, and sometimes shot to death perfectly innocent persons who had given up absolutely all they had to the assassins.

This slaughter took place without interference from the town authorities. One Jewish woman, Genia Psachis, later testified that she took it upon herself to telephone the headquarters of the local military garrison, asking for help. "Are you a Jewess?" she was asked. She replied that she was not a Bolshevik. "But are you a Jewess?" "My misfortune is to be a Jewess," she said at last. With that

the representative of the [military command], who was speaking to Miss Psachis over the telephone, said that there was an order to kill the Jews. These last words made the witness drop the telephone receiver because she saw that it was useless to ask . . . for help.

By the time the violence ended two days later, 105 Jews lay dead. But this was still only the beginning.

·41·

THE UKRAINIAN HOLOCAUST, II:
FROM POGROM
TO ANNIHILATION

The collapse of their visions of a better future in a storm of murderous anarchy had not fully come home to the leaders of Ukrainian Jewry at the beginning of February 1919. Shortly after February 6, when the Bolsheviks had retaken Kiev and the Directory moved to Vinnitsa in Podolia, Abraham Revutsky, Minister of Jewish Affairs, tried to start bringing the pogromists to justice. A group of Jewish notables—consisting of delegations from ravaged Zhitomir and Berditchev, and of members of a new All-Ukrainian Central Jewish Relief Committee—had gathered in the temporary capital to discuss what action to take. Revutsky approached them and suggested they go to the Commandant of the Vinnitsa district, Ataman Kovenko, and demand an investigation of the pogroms—something the Directory had so far not been moved to undertake. But they demurred, I. M. Guiterman of the Relief Committee objecting that Kovenko was as guilty as anyone.

Revutsky did not disagree, but would not let the matter drop. The question had to be answered: how guilty were officials of the Ukrainian regime? One evening, as the Jewish group sat in the dining room of the Savoy Hotel, where the Directory was making its headquarters, Revutsky asked them to accompany him to his room, where he said some key personages were gathered. The facts of what had been happening had to be ascertained. They complied, and in Revutsky's room found five people waiting—one civilian and four military men, two of whom were atamans. Revutsky called the meeting to order and began, according to the official report of this event,

with a somewhat lengthy speech in the Ukrainian language, drawing attention to the heavy tasks awaiting the Ukrainian army, and the demoralizing influence of the pogroms, and concluded by saying

339

that the rumors of Ukrainian troops having taken part in the pogroms were a serious charge against the authorities, and that if such rumors proved true it would mean that he, Revutsky, as one of those authorities also was responsible for the pogroms.

This was politic, but did he really believe the pogroms could be attributed to lawless civilian elements and not to troops under Ukrainian command? Now, at any rate, was the time to see. He had brought leaders of the Battalion of Death to the meeting, Revutsky said, so they could "make clear to the representatives of the towns that had been victims how false all such rumors were."

It was the turn of the soldiers. One got up, an officer from Eastern Galicia, and began by protesting of "his personally good relations with Jews, saying that he had many friends among the intelligentsia at Lvov." He went on to say that

> during the pogrom he was not at Zhitomir, but was sent by Kovenko to ascertain who was responsible for that pogrom. Palienko, according to this officer, was at the railway station and did not have enough troops to stop the pogrom, which started before he came to Zhitomir. The officer asserted that Palienko on the third day of the pogrom stopped it in the center of the town, but in the outskirts it still went on, as there were not enough troops to send to the outskirts also. Palienko, according to this officer, took very stern measures to stop the pogrom, having many pogrom-mongers shot, and the officer showed some photographs of such robbers shot dead. The officer further stated that the pogrom had been made by those units who declared themselves on the side of the Bolsheviks, together with Jews who took a permanent share in the pogroms.

The report does not record the reaction to this last assertion.

Ataman Kovenko then got up. Barely able to control his fury at the accusations that had led to this meeting, he began

> at first indeed with a slight restraint, but later giving complete rein to his passion, till his last words were shouted quite hysterically. Kovenko said that he had known even before that the Battalion of Death, which was the pride of the Ukrainian army, was innocent, and that it was being libelled for perfectly definite purposes. Kovenko emphasized several times that the most active part in the pogrom was taken by the Jews themselves, whom he charged with the desire of undermining the national rebirth of the Ukraine, and that they sympathized with other nationalities.

Kovenko then turned his fury upon Revutsky, whose attitude he especially resented, he said, because the Minister of Jewish Affairs was a member of the same party as the late [Ber] Borochov, who had inspired him, Kovenko, with the national idea, and that he was aware that at the meeting of the Council of Ministers, Revutsky had spoken of him (Kovenko) as the man guilty of the pogrom.

Had Borochov, the founder of the Poalei Zion, really been Kovenko's mentor? If so, that had happened in a world now irretrievably lost.

When Kovenko finished, I. M. Guiterman, along with two delegates from Berditchev, E. Krasny and Madame F. Nierenberg,

> commenced asking some questions of the Galician officer and of Kovenko. Guiterman stated that two days before the beginning of the pogrom at Zhitomir, namely on Monday [January 6], the Committee of the *Folkspartei* (Jewish Popular Party) in Kiev had received a letter from one of its members, Hofman, who was nearly beaten to death at Fastov by some men belonging to the Battalion, which at that time was proceeding to Berditchev and to Zhitomir to "learn the Jews." In this way the letter warning them of the arrival of the Battalion at Zhitomir to make a pogrom reached Kiev, as Guiterman said, actually before the pogrom commenced.

Seeking to depict the Battalion's commander as an outlaw, Guiterman took the accusations a step further, raising the matter of a robbery that had occurred at the Azov-Don Bank at the apparent instigation of Palienko. This aroused the hitherto silent second Ataman, who turned out to be Palienko himself. He "began in confusion to defend himself, saying that as he had no money to feed his men he took money from the safe at the Azov-Don Bank for a few days."

Now Madame Nierenberg spoke up. "In a sharp tone," the report says,

> she gave details of the part played by Palienko and his men during the Berditchev pogrom and she said that Palienko and his men were the organizers of the pogrom. All the time that Mrs. Nierenberg spoke she was interrupted by Palienko, Kovenko, and others. Krasny stated that Solodar, the deputy mayor of Berditchev, had said that Palienko had declared at Berditchev, in an official statement, that he was going to Zhitomir to teach the Jews a lesson.

Then Guiterman returned to the fray,

> and his words this time, according to the evidence given by the witnesses, caused a veritable explosion. Up to this point the meeting had borne the stamp of a conference, though a stormy one, but after this speech confusion reigned supreme. All those present jumped up from their places and, pale with excitement, kept on

shouting as if to drown one another's voices. Guiterman [had] asked Palienko how it was that, if indeed he did not have enough men to stop the pogrom in the town, seventeen men were killed at the station, where he himself and all his staff were present.

This had been too much for Kovenko, who "jumped up, his face all flushed," struck the table with his fist, and shouted:

"Yes, we have killed, we are killing, and we shall kill! This very night, here at Vinnitsa, fifty men shall be hanged. We sent the Battalion to Zhitomir and to Berditchev, and we knew why we were sending it. When the Battalion was leaving Kiev they were in such a hurry that they upset all the cabs on the Kreshchatik, and the Battalion knew why they were hurrying so. It is my Battalion. It is the pride of the Ukrainian army. If Palienko had not been arrested we would not have surrendered Kiev. Now that Palienko has been released he will retake Kiev. I am chief of the gendarmes and I am not ashamed of it."

If it was not quite clear to Kovenko's listeners whether he was talking about killing Bolsheviks or killing Jews, they surely realized by now that for many of the atamans there was no difference. When Revutsky feebly protested that he was only seeking the rehabilitation of the Ukrainian army, Kovenko snarled: "I don't want your rehabilitation!"

But this was merely the voice of utter contempt; it was now about to be outdone. The one officer who had been silent spoke up at last, and the chill of a new and unprecedented kind of terror passed through the room. "The worst impression, almost like a nightmare," the report continues,

was made on the witnesses by the replies of a young officer, apparently 22–23 years of age, with the face of a typical criminal and degenerate who, whenever he spoke—so the witness Guiterman stated—was encouraged by glances from Kovenko. When Kovenko said that at Zhitomir Bolsheviks only were killed, that officer confirmed it by saying that, when Palienko's detachment was approaching Zhitomir, there came out of the trenches two Jews with "beards like this" (illustrating with a movement of his hand), and when he asked them why they were shooting at the Setcheviks, the Jews replied that "they hated the Ukraine." "And so," the officer concluded, "I stabbed them to death."

The young executioner went on to assert

that Jews had participated in the pogrom, saying that he himself had shot, as he thought, three Jews who were carrying off loot. He also said that he had found on two Jews who were taken to the railway station proclamations against the Directory. On Mrs. Nierenberg's asking what was done to those Jews, the reply was, "I cut them to pieces."

The next day, Guiterman asked Revutsky why he had called the conference. "Revutsky replied that he wished to ascertain who were the persons really guilty of the pogrom. When Guiterman asked whether he had succeeded, Revutsky replied, 'The pogroms were organized by Kovenko.' " And, indeed, a few days later, Kovenko, as chairman of the Supreme Committee of Inquiry, canceled any trial or further investigation of Palienko.

It was at this moment that the war against the Jews of the Ukraine took a turn that would make Palienko seem relatively mild.

In mid-February, the pogroms made a sudden leap from established traditions of anti-Jewish violence into the modes of a newly dawning era. The man chiefly responsible for this was the commander of a brigade of Zaporog Cossacks. Ataman Semosenko was about twenty-three years old, of poor physique, and suffering from venereal disease. A veteran of the Tsar's army, he was by all accounts a capable military leader, if high-strung and somewhat impulsive. Early in February, Semosenko had arrived with his own "Petlura" Brigade and the Third Haidamak Regiment in the modestly thriving Podolian town of Proskurov, whose population of fifty thousand was about half Jewish.

These troops had come from the front lines to rest and carry out garrison duties. But suddenly, on the morning of Saturday, February 15, they were faced with a Bolshevik uprising in the town. It was a quiet affair. From their headquarters in a building owned by a man named Trachtenberg and located on Alexander Street, at the edge of the Jewish quarter, the Bolsheviks had moved out swiftly at 6:00 A.M., occupying the postal and telegraph office and arresting the military commandant of the town. Then they had marched to the railway yards, where the Cossacks were sleeping in freight cars. The Cossacks awoke and quickly dispersed them; some of them retreated to the nearby towns of Felshtin and Yarmolintsy. The Cossacks then marched into Proskurov, and Semosenko proclaimed himself its military commandant. According to a Committee of Inquiry report, Semosenko then

celebrated his assumption of office by arranging a grand banquet for the Haidamaks in which he treated them liberally with liquor. After the dinner he made a speech to them in which he set forth the difficult position of the Ukraine, also the great things they had already achieved in the field, and stated that the worst enemies of the Ukrainian people and of the Cossacks were the Jews, who must all be exterminated to save the Ukraine and their own lives. He called on the Cossacks to take an oath that they would massacre the whole Jewish population, but they must also swear that they would not loot the possessions of the Jews, as looting was not worthy of Cossacks. The Cossacks were made to take an oath on the regimental color that they would kill but not loot. When a lieutenant suggested instead of massacring to levy contributions on the Jews, Semosenko threatened to shoot him.

Only one officer stood up, a captain, who said he would not allow his men to kill unarmed civilians; he and his men were dispatched to a post outside the town. Then

the rest of the Cossacks, having formed themselves in battle order, with the band in front and the sanitary train at rear, proceeded to the town and marched through Alexander Street, at the end of which they dispersed into the side streets which were all inhabited by Jews only.

It was the Sabbath, and most of the Jews of Proskurov had not been aware of that morning's Bolshevik attempt. Some had heard shooting, but that was no longer an unusual sound. They had gone to synagogue, returned home to their Sabbath meals, and then, "as was their habit, the majority went to sleep." This was the situation at two o'clock that afternoon, as Semosenko's men marched into the quarter.
"The Cossacks," according to the report,

who scattered in groups of five to fifteen men over the Jewish streets, entered the houses with the greatest sang-froid, unsheathed their sabres and calmly proceeded to massacre the inhabitants without regard to age or sex. They killed alike old men, women, children and even infants in arms. They used not only sabres, but also bayonets.

Firearms were used sparingly, but people who tried to escape into the street were shot at. "When the Jews heard of the massacre that had commenced, they tried to hide in lofts and in cellars, but the Cossacks pulled them down from the lofts and threw hand grenades into the cellars." One young survivor was to recall how

the Cossacks killed his younger brother in the street near his house, then entered the house and cut open his mother's head. Other members of the family tried to hide under beds, but when a small brother of his saw his mother dead, he got out from under the bed and kissed the dead lady. Thereupon the old father also came out from his hiding and was shot dead by a Cossack who fired two shots at him.

Another house was set upon by

> eight men, who began breaking all the window panes. Five men entered the house while three remained outside. Those in the house seized the old man Krotchak by his beard, dragged him to the window of the kitchen and threw him out of the window to the other three, who killed him. Then they killed the old woman and her two daughters.

In another house "a young girl was tortured a long time before they killed her."

The massacre went on until 6:00 P.M., when Commissar Taranovitch, one of the town councilors, finally realized what was happening. "He ran to Semosenko and insisted that he should order the massacre to be stopped. Semosenko paid no attention whatever to his words. Then Taranovitch went to the telegraph office and by direct wire informed the provincial authorities at Kamenetz of what was going on at Proskurov." Taranovitch was put in touch with the area's commanding general, whom he informed of the situation, and who immediately wired Semosenko ordering him to stop the massacre.

"All right," said Semosenko, "it will do for today."

A signal was given to the troops by trumpet. "Thereupon," runs the account, "they fell in at the place previously appointed, and, in orderly ranks, as on a campaign, singing regimental songs, marched to their camp behind the station."

As night fell upon the Jewish quarter, the outcome of the day's horrors presented itself in a sudden and dramatic display: all the lights went on. Proskurov was electrified, but, in conformity to the limitations of that time and place, the central power was switched on only at night. Since most of the town's Jews were religiously observant, they customarily left their lights on when going to sleep Friday night, heeding the proscription against handling electric currents on the Sabbath. As a result, the lights of individual homes, never turned off, went on all at once with the return of power that grim Saturday evening. Scenes of domestic slaughter were framed in window after window. Moreover, "the fact that everybody had been killed in a particular house could be seen," which proved of advantage to those who now began looting.

"Next morning there still continued isolated murders of Jews on the streets as well as in the homes. The Jews remained in hiding and very few ventured abroad." One who did later described how he "put on peasant clothes and went along Alexander Street near some Haida-

maks who were talking to some of the local residents. He heard the
Haidamaks saying that until two o'clock they would go on killing individual Jews and at two they would repeat the massacre of the previous
day." But this was not to be their pleasure, after all. The town councilors, Polish and Ukrainian Christians, called an emergency meeting and
prevailed upon Semosenko to stop the killing. At first he objected, maintaining that "the Jews themselves were to blame for all that had happened, as they were all Bolsheviks to a man, and conspired to kill all
the Haidamaks and other Cossacks." Then he relented: his men, after
all, were not without something to do, for at this moment they were
waging a pogrom in nearby Felshtin. Declaring martial law in Proskurov, Semosenko issued this proclamation:

Proskurov, February 16, 1919
Garrison Service

I call on the population to cease its anarchist demonstrations,
for I am sufficiently strong to fight you. I specially warn the Jews
of that.

Know that you are a people disliked by all nations, yet you
cause such trouble to Christian people. Do you not want to live?

So long as you are not attacked keep quiet. Wretched nation,
bringing trouble on innocent gentiles!

Ataman SEMOSENKO
Commander of the Zaporog Cossacks Brigade

On Monday morning, the survivors of the wretched nation, relieved
for the moment of fear of further slaughter, went to work burying their
dead. Bodies had lain where they had fallen since Saturday, and many
of those in the streets were now "half eaten up by swine." Peasants'
carts were "laden with the corpses and taken to the Jewish cemetery.
The whole day corpses were brought there till the cemetery was full of
them." Individual bodies that could be identified and cared for by surviving relatives were buried in individual graves; but this was not possible for the vast majority of the dead. "Peasants were hired to dig an
enormous pit which was to be used as a common grave for all the victims."

Twelve hundred men, women, children, and infants were buried
that day. And all around, the slaughter continued.

·42·

IN THE EYES OF
THE CIVILIZED WORLD

Among Jews in the Ukrainian government, there was none more loyal than Arnold Margolin, Associate Minister for Foreign Affairs. Persisting in the belief that the pogroms were the work of "criminal elements" and that the Directory should not be held responsible, he nevertheless could not allow the latest violence to go by without protest. In March 1919, he wrote to K. Matsievich, the Ukrainian Minister for Foreign Affairs:

> The heavy, responsible task which rests on all members of the government is now further complicated by the tragic fact that the Jewish pogroms do not cease, and by the realization that the administration has proved powerless to check the terrible violence and murders which took place in Proskurov, Ananiev, etc. I well know that the government does all that is in its power to fight the pogroms. I also know that the helplessness of the government in this struggle weighs heavily upon all its members and deprives them of that spiritual balance and that calmness which are so indispensable for fruitful labors for all the peoples of the Ukraine. My own sufferings as a Jew, however, are further intensified by the consciousness that [the] results of the anarchy from which the other elements of the population suffer in the main only economically prove dangerous and fatal to the very existence of the Jewish people.
>
> In view of the above circumstances I do not feel capable of continuing my labors as Associate Minister of Foreign Affairs and I therefore request to be permitted to relinquish the above named post.

· · ·

This was accepted, but he was then persuaded to take an assignment as a member of the Ukrainian delegation to the Peace Conference in Paris. He was there by mid-April.

"It was recognized very early in the course of the Peace Conference," Prime Minister David Lloyd George was to recall,

> that the question of the protection of the minority population in the Succession States was one of paramount importance. There was common agreement amongst all the parties concerned that assurances for the protection of these minorities must be given as one of the essential conditions of a peace settlement.

To this end, representatives of various minorities were gathering in Paris, as well as of the succession states that would contain them.

Jewish delegations came not only from Poland and the Ukraine, but also from Czechoslovakia, Rumania, and other new or newly expanding countries of Eastern Europe, as well as from Britain, France, and the United States. Arriving from February through April, they soon displayed two basic tendencies. The Jews from Eastern Europe tended to want not merely civil equality, but status as a national minority within their respective countries. But the delegates of the Anglo-Jewish Association of London and the Alliance Israélite Universelle of Paris had an entirely different outlook. Lucien Wolf of the Anglo-Jewish Association, a lifelong fighter for Jewish rights in Eastern Europe, had just lost a battle against the Zionists at home when their conception of Jewish nationality became incorporated into the Balfour Declaration; he was determined not to lose again in Paris. For him, the task was to see to it that the Jews of Poland, Rumania, and other countries in which they had suffered disabilities be guaranteed the full citizenship enjoyed by their coreligionists in such countries as Great Britain and France, and nothing more. The conception of a Jewish national entity in Poland or the Ukraine was to him as unthinkable as it was in his own country or the United States.

"It is to be borne in mind," had countered Louis Marshall, president of the American Jewish Committee, in December,

> that we are dealing with Eastern European conditions, not those which prevail in the United States, or in England, France and Italy, where the populations are practically homogeneous, and where the term "national" has reference to a political, as distinguished from an ethical, unit. . . . We must be careful not to permit ourselves to judge what is most desirable for the people who live in Eastern Europe by the standards which prevail on Fifth Avenue or in the States of Maine or Ohio, where a different horizon from that which

prevails in Poland, Galicia, Ukrainia, or Lithuania bounds one's vision.

These observations were written the day after a meeting in Philadelphia on December 18, 1918, had created an American Jewish Congress, a long-sought alternative to the lordly American Jewish Committee. Based on a following of largely East European origin, the Congress was, unlike the Committee, outspokenly Zionist, and included the words "national rights" in its recommendations to the Peace Conference regarding East European Jewry. Yet, despite all differences, the Congress had elected Marshall as well as Jacob Schiff of the Committee to its roster of officers, and was sending Marshall, along with Judge Julian W. Mack of the Committee, in its delegation to Paris. This had alarmed the editor of the non-Zionist *American Hebrew*, Isaac Landman, who asked Marshall to clarify his position on matters like "national rights"—which is what he was doing in the above-quoted letter.

Time and again Marshall had stressed, and would continue to stress—albeit with diminishing emphasis—that he was not a Zionist, but he and his colleagues were more pragmatic on this issue than their counterparts in the Anglo-Jewish Association. The American Jewish Committee had already produced a carefully worded endorsement of the Balfour Declaration the previous spring, and was about to take the same approach to "national rights." It was above all Marshall and Mack who now took the lead organizing the Jewish groups in Paris—with the continuing exception of the Anglo-Jewish Association and the Alliance Israélite Universelle—under a single umbrella, called the Comité des Délégations Juives auprès de la Conférence de la Paix.

On May 10, 1919, the Comité presented to the Peace Conference a memorandum on minority rights, in the form of a model treaty. Most of it spelled out proposed rights for national minorities in general without specifying any particular group, with two exceptional clauses. The final paragraph of Clause 5 read:

> Within the meaning of the articles of this chapter, the Jewish population of —— shall constitute a national minority with all the rights therein specified.

Apart from this specific mention of Jews, the only other passage clearly referring to them was Clause 8, which read:

> Those who observe any other day than Sunday as their Sabbath shall not be required to perform any acts on their Sabbath or holy days which by the tenets of their faith are regarded as a des-

ecration, nor shall they be prohibited from pursuing their secular affairs on Sunday or other holy days.

The signatories of this memorandum included not only Judge Mack and Louis Marshall, but also some prominent Zionists, notably Nahum Sokolow, one of the architects of the Balfour Declaration.

But though the principle of Jewish nationality did obtain recognition from the Peace Conference in the case of Palestine, it was doomed to disappear under the rubric of "minority rights"—that is, civil equality for minority groups, but not necessarily any national cultural institutions for them—in the case of Eastern Europe. President Wilson, though a warm friend of the American Jewish Congress—which had been created under the initiative of his colleague Justice Louis D. Brandeis—feared the consequences of a national identification for the Jews of Eastern Europe, and found, along with other Allied leaders, that imposing the principle of minority rights upon Poland, Rumania, and others was problem enough. At a plenary session on May 31, the Rumanian delegate spoke out vehemently against "any interference by any foreign governments in the application of her domestic laws."

For all this indignation, it was in particular Rumania's persistent violation of the rights of her Jewish subjects, along with the continuing pogroms in Poland and the Ukraine, that dramatized the need for special provisions for minority rights, even apart from any Jewish national claims. Poland in particular aroused concern on this issue. Its leadership remained intransigent, refusing in the first place to acknowledge that pogroms were occurring, then arguing that the reports of them were greatly exaggerated and resisting all suggestions that any form of international guarantee for Jews and other minorities in Poland—such as Ukrainians, Lithuanians, or Germans—was necessary. On February 28, the *Jewish Chronicle* reported:

A Jewish deputation interrogated General Pilsudski and M. Paderewski on the subject of the recent pogroms. General Pilsudski replied that the feelings entertained towards the Jews were much worse than had been demonstrated by the pogroms at Lemberg and Kielce and that it was impossible to stop this free utterance of opinions in a free state. The General described the attitude of the Jews to Poland as hostile, and said that this description was proved by the fact that the Jews had drawn the attention of the whole world to the pogroms. He added that it was naive of the Jews to believe that other countries would help to improve their situation. In reply to a request by the deputation to state the proofs he had of the alleged hostile attitude of the Jews, he said that there were no such proofs, but that there was a general feeling that such was the case.

As for Paderewski, he told the deputation "that he disapproved of pogroms, but refused to do anything about them."

By the end of May, further pogroms had occurred in the areas in which Polish troops had established their rule, most drastically at Vilna and at Pinsk. "How do you account for the latest pogroms in Poland?" a *Jewish Chronicle* interviewer asked Israel Cohen, who said:

> "None of the malefactors responsible for the pogroms of last winter has been punished. Hence the Poles, both military and civilian, consider they are pursuing a policy approved of by their Government when they organize assaults, outrages and robbing expeditions against the Jews. . . . The Polish Government is to be blamed most emphatically for the latest outburst of pogroms. Last November and December it had the excuse that it was only newly formed, but since then it has done absolutely nothing to prevent a recurrence of the outrages. . . . Even Major Luczynski, who ordered the massacre of Zionists at Pinsk by a machine-gun, has not yet been punished."

In the end, Poland was made to acquiesce on the minorities issue. In the general treaty to be signed with Germany, this clause was inserted:

> Poland accepts and agrees to embody in a Treaty with the Principal Allied and Associated Powers such provisions as may be deemed necessary by the said Powers to protect the interests of the inhabitants of Poland who differ from the majority of the population in race, language or religion. Poland further accepts and agrees to embody in a Treaty with the said Powers such provisions as they may deem necessary to protect freedom of transit and equitable treatment of the commerce of other nations.

Accordingly, the Polish Minorities Treaty was drawn up and was signed by Poland and the Great Powers at Versailles on June 28. Its crucial provision was Article 8, which said:

> Polish nationals who belong to racial, religious or linguistic minorities shall enjoy the same treatment and security in law and in fact as the other Polish nationals. In particular they shall have an equal right to establish, manage and control at their own expense charitable, religious and social institutions, schools and other educational establishments, with the right to use their own language and to exercise their religion freely therein.

Moreover, two articles—10 and 11—specifically applied to Jews. The former provided for Jewish educational autonomy; the latter forbade compelling Jews "to perform any act which constitutes a violation of their Sabbath" except in cases involving military service.

Premier Georges Clemenceau, who had been the Peace Conference's preeminent supporter of the new Polish state, wrote a long covering letter to the draft copy of this treaty when it was sent to Paderewski on June 24. With respect to Articles 10 and 11, he said:

> The information at the disposal of the Principal Allied and Associated Powers as to the existing relations between the Jews and the other Polish citizens has led them to the conclusion that, in view of the historical development of the Jewish question and the great animosity aroused by it, special protection is necessary for the Jews in Poland.

Noting that the clauses referred to had "been limited to the minimum which seems necessary under the circumstances of the present day, viz., the maintenance of Jewish schools and the protection of the Jews in the religious observance of their Sabbath," Clemenceau insisted that they did "not constitute any recognition of the Jews as a separate political community within the Polish State."

So much for the nationality of the Jews in, for example, Eastern Galicia—where the West Ukrainian government was to collapse completely the following month—and similarly vexed areas in the new Poland. Now it was the turn of the Ukrainians to show where they stood on the Jewish question.

The Ukraine had been utterly neglected in relation to the Polish question at the Peace Conference. Its delegation had not even been invited and had no official recognition. It obtained occasional glimmers of encouragement, but Clemenceau's firm resistance to any Ukrainian entity that would encroach upon Polish claims induced a massive general indifference to it. Moreover, with the French in Odessa, the English helping the White armies of Denikin, and the Americans in Siberia with Admiral Alexander Kolchak, all seeking the revival of some traditional Russian sovereignty, the idea of an independent Ukraine carried little appeal among them.

Nor was its cause at all helped by the ongoing chaos in that country and the horrifying reports of pogroms. A few leaders had become aware of this. Even among the atamans, there now was some concern that the depredations would cause the Ukraine to lose all claims in the court of world opinion. On April 13, Ataman Melnik of the Ukrainian General Staff issued an order that read in part:

The Black Hundreds, Bolsheviki, leaders of armed bands, and common robbers are conducting among our Cossacks an active agitation for the plundering and annihilation of the Jewish population, which is alleged to be responsible for all that is happening among us, in Ukraine, as well as in the realm of Moscow. These elements are striving by hook or crook to institute Jewish problems in Ukraine in order, under their cover, to perpetrate their black deeds. The Black Hundreds and the marauders think that the occurrence of pogroms and of other forms of anarchy will hasten the arrival in the Ukraine of the Allies, who will enthrone a new Tsar and who will return them to their old estates; while the Bolsheviki and various plunderers and robbers simply crave to fill their own pockets, and, while plundering Jews, they sink their claws also into others who happen to fall into their hands. . . . The Cossacks' task is to conquer the enemy, whoever he may be, not to fight women, children, old men, against whom you are being incited by our enemies, in order that our people and our sovereignty may be besmirched in the eyes of the world. Henceforth I command you to arrest all persons who will be discovered conducting pogrom agitation among the Cossacks, and to bring them before the Extraordinary Tribunal.

This shifting of blame was now to become a common practice in the Ukraine. It was easy to do, since there were no longer any clear lines of responsibility in the anarchy that prevailed. In the non-Bolshevik areas, much of the situation had fallen under the control of roving independent bands led by the *batki*, or "little fathers," who rarely kept to any loyalty but themselves. A typical *batko* was one Grigoriev, who had begun as a supporter of the Bolsheviks but had renounced that allegiance in May 1919, writing to another Ukrainian commander, still loyal to the Red flag:

Why do you stand up for the hooknosed commissars? Stop being a fool. Let's take Odessa again and rob so that the place will be pulled to pieces. Warm greetings.

Your brother,
Grigoriev

In the ensuing weeks, Grigoriev took his turn as the foremost of the pogromists, leading his men in the murder of some six thousand Jews.

By the end of July, however, demoralized by drink and loot, Grigoriev and his men met their match in the most powerful *batko* of them all, Nestor Makhno. A self-educated peasant and professed anarchist, Makhno had also begun as a fighter with the Soviets, but his break with them had been wrought by the Bolshevik leadership, who found him completely unreliable. From then on, Makhno, who established a realm of his own in the plains between Yekaterinoslav and the Sea of Azov,

fought against both Reds and Whites—and against Grigoriev as well.
Finally, in a conference at the village of Septovo on July 27, Makhno
denounced Grigoriev for supporting the Whites and conducting pogroms; then Grigoriev was shot by one of Makhno's aides. The following
day this proclamation was issued by Makhno:

> The assassination of the Ataman Grigoriev on the 27th of July
> in the village of Septovo, circuit of Alexandria, Government of
> Kherson, by the ideal leader of the insurrectionists, the Batko
> Makhno, must be regarded as a necessary and required historical
> act, for Grigoriev's policy, acts and aims were counter-revolu-
> tionary and had the main purpose of supporting Denikin and other
> counter revolutionists, as is proved by the Jewish pogroms and the
> arming of the thugs. . . .
> We cherish the hope that now no one will be found who will
> sanction the Jewish pogroms, and that the working people will in
> their honesty rise against the counter-revolutionists like Denikin
> and the others, as well as against the Bolsheviks and Communists
> who are establishing a dictatorship by force. . . . Down with Jewish
> pogroms! Long live the revolutionary uprising of the Ukraine! Long
> live the [independent] Ukrainian Socialist Soviet Republic! Long
> live socialism!

Despite all these protestations, Makhno and his men were eventually to
be the murderers of thousand of Jews themselves.

It was not until August that Commander-in-Chief Petlura, claiming
to stand far above the smoke of anti-Jewish slaughter, saw fit to issue
a statement on it. Like many others, he began by laying the blame on
anyone but the Ukrainians. "Our free but not yet entirely liberated
country," he wrote,

> is still defiled by the stench of the dying wild beast—our enemy.
> Not satisfied with the honest blood of our soldiers, it wanted more
> blood, innocent blood, the blood of peaceful inhabitants who have
> not done any wrong. The "dark men," the "black hundreds," and
> the "red hundreds" are all one pack. A set of *agents provocateurs*,
> having like cowards thrown away their arms, have come out of their
> holes and resumed their shameful occupation in a new field.
> Weaving their subtle and shameful thread of provocation, they
> stir up pogroms against the Jewish nation, and manage to involve
> in this terrible business a few of the less steady elements of our
> army also. In this way they are endeavoring to sully our fight for
> freedom in the sight of the world and to ruin our national cause.

Petlura now addressed himself to "the less steady elements" of his
army:

Officers and men! It is time we knew that the Jews, like the majority of our Ukrainian population, have suffered from the Communist-Bolshevist invasion and have become aware where the trouble is. The best Jewish parties, like the "Bund," the "United Party," the "Poalei Zion," the "Volkspartei," have resolutely ranged themselves on the side of the Independent Ukrainian State and are working for it hand-in-hand with us.

It is time we understood that the peaceful Jewish population, their children, their women had, like ourselves, been enslaved and deprived of their national liberty. The population has nowhere else to go, it has been with us since olden times and has been sharing in our joys and our sorrows. The chivalrous host which is bringing fraternity, equality and liberty of all peoples of the Ukraine must not listen to bandits and agitators who are thirsting for human blood. This army must not be the cause of any disaster to the Jews. Those who allow such crimes are traitors and enemies of our country and must be cut off from all human intercourse.

Officers and men! The whole world is witnessing and admiring your gallant deeds of liberation. Do not sully them even accidentally by any unworthy deeds and do not shame our State in the eyes of the whole world. Our many foes within and without are already making capital out of the pogroms; they point scornful fingers at us and jeer at us, saying that we are incapable of forming an independent state, and that we must again fall under the yoke of foreign domination. I, your Ataman-in-Chief, do tell you that it is just at the present time that in the international court the question is being decided as to whether our independent life is to be or not to be. . . . I order you to expel from your midst anybody who incites you to commit pogrom crimes, and to hand them over to be tried in court as traitors against the country. . . .

The Government of the Ukrainian People's Republic, well understanding all the harm which pogroms inflict on the State, has published an appeal to all the inhabitants of our State to oppose all acts of enemies inciting the pogroms against the Jews.

It was getting late to redeem the Ukraine in the eyes of the world, but Arnold Margolin had not given up the struggle. In May he had gone to London, hoping to persuade the Foreign Office that the Ukraine, rather than Denikin's army, deserved its support. While there, he talked to a *Jewish Chronicle* interviewer, insisting that the Rada had shown itself "willing to grant more concessions to Jews than had any other constituent assembly in history." When asked how he reconciled his attitude with the pogroms, he said:

There is this difference between the pogroms which have unhappily taken place in the Ukraine and those which occurred under the Tsarist regime. Whereas the latter were instigated and con-

nived at by the authorities, the Ukrainian Government has stead-
fastly set its face against the pogroms, and it had no part in or
sympathy for them. At the time of the Petlura *coup d'état* at the
end of November 1918, I myself read, in numerous towns and villages in the Ukraine, proclamations issued by the Government
strongly condemning the pogroms. . . . The proclamations declared
that pogroms must tend to discredit the Ukraine in the eyes of the
civilized world, and those who took part in them were no friends of
the country. . . . I must unhappily admit that the last pogroms as
to which I have information—those of February and March last—
were very bad, thousands of Jews being killed. They were instigated by criminals, Black Hundreds, and Bolsheviks who wished to
discredit the Ukrainian Government. . . . The prevalence of pogroms in the Ukraine may be partly attributed to the fact that the
Ukrainians, although constituting a distinct political entity, were
subject for 300 years to Russia, and have acquired, as an evil in-
heritance, what I may call the pogrom habit. It is at least a matter
of satisfaction that there is no anti-Semitic tendency in the Ukrainian Government, which differs in this respect, very notably, from
that prevailing in Poland.

The tragic Margolin was always to maintain—even after settling in the
United States—that Denikin's troops were worse pogromists than Petlura's.

Certainly Denikin provided no respite in the anti-Jewish reign of
terror. "I had not been with Denikin more than a month," writes John
Ernest Hodgson, a British journalist,

before I was forced to the conclusion that the Jew represented a
very big element in the Russian upheaval. The officers and men of
the army laid practically all the blame for the country's troubles on
the Hebrew. They held that the whole cataclysm had been engineered by some great and mysterious secret society of international
Jews who, in the pay and at the orders of Germany, had seized the
psychological moment and snatched the reins of government.

This was when the *Protocols of the Elders of Zion* was being revived
among the White armies, a copy of Nilus's edition having been found
among the Tsarina's possessions after she, her husband, and their children had been executed by the Bolsheviks at Yekaterinburg on July 16,
1918. Hodgson noticed that the idea of a Jewish world conspiracy among
Denikin's officers

was an obsession of such terrible bitterness and insistency as to
lead them into making statements of the most wild and fantastic
character. Many of them had persuaded themselves that Freema-

sonry was, in alliance with the Jews, part and parcel of the Bolshevik machine, and that what they called the diabolical schemes for Russia's downfall had been hatched in the Petrograd and Moscow Masonic lodges. When I told them that I and most of my best friends were Freemasons, and that England owed a great deal to its loyal Jews, they stared at me askance and sadly shook their heads in fear for England's credulity in trusting the chosen race. One even asked me quietly whether I personally was a Jew. When America showed herself decidedly against any kind of interference in Russia, the idea soon gained wide credence that President Woodrow Wilson was a Jew, while Mr. Lloyd George was referred to as a Jew whenever a cable from England appeared to show him as being lukewarm in support of the anti-Bolsheviks.

Hodgson concluded that, as the war went on,

> it became increasingly plain that pogroms were to be expected after a final victory of the anti-Bolsheviks. . . . There were hundreds of well-authenticated cases in which Red Commissars had done relatives of anti-Bolsheviks to death under the most cruel and revolting circumstances. . . . As relatives of the latter who were fighting with Denikin held all Red Commissars to be Jews, crimes of revenge against the Jews will be constant throughout the country for many years to come. The horror of injustice of pogroms never seemed to enter into the minds of my friends—they were under the complete control of a fierce and unreasoning hatred.

The slaughter continued into the summer and fall. Here is a typical scene, occurring in September at Fastov, near Kiev, after the Bolsheviks had tried to capture it, and Denikin's Cossacks returned:

> In the first three days robbery and murder were perpetrated mainly at night. During the nights the whole population could hear shooting and desperate cries now from one direction, now from another. At first murders were not so frequent, but they became more and more so. By about the third day cossacks were already walking about the town, quite openly looking for Jewish houses and when they found one, doing whatever they liked. They were also stopping Jews in the streets. Sometimes they would simply ask, "A *Zhid?*" and put a bullet through his skull. More often they would search the man, strip him naked, and then shoot him. Many of the killers were drunk. . . .
> About the second or third day they began to set fire to Jewish homes. The reason for this was that the *pogromshchiki* wanted to destroy the traces of their worst crimes. In one house on the corner of the Torgovy Square, for instance, were fifteen corpses, including

many young girls who had been killed after being raped. They set
that house alight to cover up those crimes. . . .

Somewhere between fifteen hundred and two thousand Jews were killed
at Fastov, and another four hundred wounded; about two hundred buildings were burned to the ground, so that a thousand families were left
homeless.

The Jewish death toll in the Ukraine for 1919 is not known exactly.
At least thirty thousand were murdered instantly, but a great many
more died subsequently on account of wounds, so that the final figure
may be more than a hundred thousand. Hundreds of Jewish communities lay in ruins. It was the worst holocaust the Jewish people had ever
known.

·43·

WANDERING SCHOLARS, III: CROSSING THE ZBRUCZ

In the first months of 1920, the White armies collapsed; Kolchak abdicated and was shot; Denikin resigned and left his failing command with General Baron Peter Wrangel. The Ukrainian anarchy was steadily being replaced by Soviet power. Only the Poles remained.

On May 6, Polish troops entered Kiev and provoked a massive counterattack. They evacuated on June 12. "We ran all the way to Kiev," a Polish fighter was to say, "and we ran all the way back." Two Soviet armies, one in the north led by M. N. Tukhachevsky, the other dominated by Sergey Budienny's "Red Cavalry" in the south, made a two-pronged assault on the retreating Poles, the former heading for Warsaw, the latter for Lemberg. Isaac Babel, a young journalist assigned to Budienny's forces, was to remember the July day on which the Zbrucz River—the Polish ethnic frontier—was crossed, "our train of supplies stretched out, a noisy rearguard on the highway that went through Brest to Warsaw and had been built by Nicholas I with the bones of the muzhiki."

Babel, a middle-class Jew from Odessa, now could see a Jewry different from what he had known as he followed the cavalry into some of the most ancient and tradition-bound heartlands of his people. In Berestechko, he writes in *Red Cavalry*, his fictionalized account of the campaign, he saw "branches extending across three centuries, . . . still greening in Volhynia with the warm rot of olden times." Rebellious against his own bourgeois background, caught up in the spirit of the revolution, the twenty-six-year-old writer noted, to be sure, that the Jews of Berestechko "bound together with the threads of profit the Russian muzhik and the Polish nobleman, the Czech colonist and the Lodz factory. They were smugglers, the best on the border, and almost always stern in their faith."

But these Jews of religious orthodoxy and petty capitalism also were Jews of darkness and fear. Noting that in back of the typical Jewish house of Berestechko there would always be "a barn of two or sometimes three stories," Babel observed that

Sunlight never gets into them. These barns, dark beyond description, stand in place of our courtyards. In them are secret entrances to cellars and stables. In times of war these catacombs provide shelter from bullets and marauders. Human refuse and cow dung then pile up in them for days. Terror and despondency fill the catacombs with the corrosive stench of tainted sour excrement.

Even now, this town with a Jewish majority "stinks relentlessly, and everyone reeks of rotten herring."

Yet, during this pilgrimage, Babel also discovered the Jewish soul preserved in a purity untainted by the civilization of Odessa or Warsaw. It was embodied in the old shopkeeper Gedali, dreaming of an International of good people—one without all the shooting—and ruminating like a Talmudist over the meaning of present history:

"But the Pole shot, my kind gentleman [Gedali protests], because he was Counter-Revolution. You shoot because you are Revolution. But Revolution—now, this is a Rejoicing. And a Rejoicing does not love to have an orphan in the house. A good person does good deeds. Revolution—now, this is the good deed of good people. But good people do not kill. That means bad people are making Revolution. But Poles also are bad people. Who, then, can tell Gedali where is Revolution and where is Counter-Revolution?"

Still, for all his doubts, this "founder of an unworkable International" is clearly more on the side of the Russian Revolution than on that of the Pole, that "mad dog" who plucks out the Jew's beard and has caused Gedali to go nearly blind.

Was the Revolution—now Bolshevik—the side that Jews mainly were on, then? At this moment, the defense of Warsaw was being prepared. "The Bolsheviks have captured Brest-Litovsk and have crossed the Bug below it," wrote Lord D'Abernon, the British Ambassador to Berlin, in Warsaw as an observer, in his diary for August 3, 1920. "The retreating Polish troops omitted to destroy the bridges and the passage of the river was badly defended." It would be any day now. Meanwhile, D'Abernon had made a tour of the defenses being set up in the largely Jewish suburbs north of the city, along the Ostrow Road. "This road," D'Abernon writes, is the main artery of communication between the capital and the northeastern frontier. I therefore expected that it would be blocked with troops and munition wagons, also with refugees flying before the Bolsheviks. As a matter of fact there was very little traffic on it. . . . In the villages some preparations were being made for defense, but nothing of a very serious character.

Did all this tranquillity have something to do with the fact that the population here was largely Jewish? Does D'Abernon see some hint that these people would not be unhappy to see the Soviet armies come?
But he continues:

> Curiously enough most of the people I saw who were engaged in putting up barbed wire and other forms of protection were Jews. This was surprising, as the Jews are suspected of being an element friendly to the Bolsheviks, but the feeling here between Christians and Jews is so strong, suspicion is so rife, that it is difficult to ascertain the truth about anything.

Sympathetic with the Polish cause and aware of complaints against the Jews, the Englishman D'Abernon could nonetheless see the Jewish side of the story. "As an indication of the feeling between Poles and Jews," he goes on,

> I may recount the following. Two private soldiers who were on the box of my car shook their fists as they passed Jews putting up wire entanglements; not that they objected to the work that they were doing, but merely as a normal expression of spontaneous antipathy.

This antipathy had grown worse than ever under the impact of the Soviet invasion. As far as many Poles were concerned, almost every Bolshevik commissar was a Jew. Even Russian gentile revolutionaries did not seem to them as bad. On August 6, D'Abernon spoke to a member of a Polish delegation just returned from unsuccessful negotiations with the Soviets at Baranowicze. "He describes the Russian officers," D'Abernon recorded,

> as very much of the French Revolution 1793 type, young, enthusiastic, with flaming eyes and long hair, but completely under civilian commissars. Most of the commissars are Jews, but not those who were sent to Baranowicze. The Poles esteemed it an act of courtesy that Christians were sent.

A week later, D'Abernon spoke to some Bolshevik prisoners, "mild, downtrodden peasants without enthusiasm, fanaticism or conviction," who claimed that

Jewish commissars did everything in their division—commandeered food—gave orders—explained objectives. When the soldiers asked about peace, the commissar told them Poland has asked for peace but in conjunction with England—Bolsheviks will have nothing to do with England!

This at the very time when Leon Kamenev—another Jewish Bolshevik—was the Soviet government's representative in London.

This fearsome Jewish image bore the stamp of Trotsky, the man who had refused to make peace at Brest-Litovsk and was now, as Minister of War, leading the Soviet armies on all their fronts, traveling with furious energy from one to another in his private train. "One of the most surprising results of the interviews with the prisoners," D'Abernon observed,

> was the entire lack of enthusiasm or conviction regarding the Soviet Government, although there was evidently a genuine universal respect for Lenin, who is esteemed the working-man's friend, in contrast to the feeling about Trotsky, who is generally detested and feared.

The prisoners were widely of the view that Trotsky was determined to go on waging war under all circumstances. "The bellicose section" of the Soviet regime, they believed,

> have a strong hold, and now contend that the regime can live only by war. So long as there is war, the driving force is exerted by the commissars, backed by the Chinese units which are placed at their disposal, and by the terror which the Cheka and its network of spies and denunciators inspire. . . . The general impression gained from the interviews was that Trotsky had rendered such services and gained so strong a position that Lenin will be unable to get rid of him. . . . The general impression conveyed was that the Jews and the Jewish commissars were universally detested and the latter particularly feared.

Who, then, was this new Jewish-Bolshevik personality? Babel describes one leading a Soviet infantry detachment near Lesknow:

> A stooping youth in glasses was walking up and down along the front line. A sword dragged at his side. He hopped along with a dissatisfied look, as if his boots hurt him. This chosen and beloved ataman of the peasants was a Jew, a near-sighted Jewish youth with the absorbed and emaciated look of a Talmudist. In battle he exhibited a circumspect courage and coolheadedness that seemed like the absent-mindedness of a visionary.

And there were women, too: the Bolshevik revolution had shown no discrimination regarding sex, as it had shown none regarding ethnicity, in the appointing of its cadres. Indeed, a considerable—and often grim—folklore was developing around the mythic figure of the female Jewish commissar. Captain Arthur L. Goodhart, an American Jew serving with a commission in Warsaw investigating the Polish pogroms, had heard statements in the fall of 1919 about Jewish women signing death warrants for the Bolsheviks. "This fantastic story," he wrote,

> about Jewish girls signing death-warrants is one of the most frequent that is told in Poland. In every Bolshevik city captured by the Poles some person claims to know about one of these women.

The confrontation at Warsaw began on August 15 and lasted five days, during which the Poles held firm. Soon the overextended Red armies were retreating; near-defeat was turned by the Poles into a victory that enabled them to roll back their territorial claims all the way to Pinsk. By the end of the year, with the White armies defeated, the border situation between Poland and Russia stabilized, and was to remain so for years to come.

But the impact of the Jewish-Bolshevik myth was only beginning to make itself felt.

"The Poles are afraid," a Ruthenian peasant had told Babel's narrator at Zamosc, another scene of Red Army defeat. "The Poles are slaughtering the Zhids. . . . The Zhid is blamed by everyone, by our people and by yours. Very few of them will be left after the war. How many Zhids are there in the world?"

"Ten million," answered the narrator conservatively.

"Only two hundred thousand will be left," cried the peasant, vague in his figures but exact in the spirit of his terrible prophecy.

PART EIGHT

The End of the Classic Emigration

·1920-1932·

·44·

THE REFUGEES OF 1920

"It is doubtful if in any of the devastated areas of the war there is as much human suffering as exists along that great stretch between Congress Poland and the Bolshevist line."

This was set down in his diary for July 1, 1919, by Colonel W. R. Grove, a representative of the American Relief Administration, organized under the chairmanship of Herbert Hoover to provide food and other supplies in the devastated areas of Europe.

"Meanwhile," wrote the Oxford historian H. N. Brailsford, also doing relief work in the area,

> this borderland population is enduring famine. One may discuss whether there is much absolute scarcity of food in Congress Poland. There is no doubt when one crosses the Bug, and conditions grow worse as one approaches Russia. . . . On the way we met at stations west of the Bug scores of peasants from the eastern side who had made a two days' journey of the utmost hardship to buy flour, which was unprocurable in their own districts.
>
> At Pinsk even the hospital and the Jewish orphan house and alms house were without bread. . . . Typhus is raging everywhere, and is even worse in the villages than in the towns. . . . It will be followed in the summer by dysentery or cholera. The police told me that at Pinsk men and women frequently fainted on the streets. I saw at Pinsk the body of a middle-aged Jew, who had just fallen dead on the street. It was so emaciated that it might have served for a lesson in anatomy. I went into many houses filled with refugees. About half of them were lying ill. . . . The Jewish Cooperative stores were closed, for they had nothing to sell.

In 1919 and 1920, European distress was greatest in the areas
where Jews were most thickly settled. "Brest [-Litovsk] is a city which
was totally destroyed, and the majority of people did not return to their
homes," according to the report of an American-Jewish relief organization working in the area, about a city whose prewar population of
some sixty thousand had been more than 70 percent Jewish. "The small
towns surrounding Brest are still in a worse condition," the report continues discussing the environs, also thickly Jewish, for in them

> the farms are absolutely neglected and the peasants are not at
> home, having been driven to Russia. The food question is a very
> bad problem here at present. For example, I visited a town last
> week named Werhovitch, which is about 110 kilometers from Brest,
> where I found that this town, which before the war contained 100
> families, at present contains only 30 families. They are living in four
> houses and 25 people there are sick with typhus and some with
> malaria.

As for the small towns in the Pinsk district, the field representative
found the situation in them "quite impossible." The town of Telechany
was "entirely destroyed," the people there "living in trenches. The same
situation exists in Lubishay, where people are existing on potato peel-
ings, where sickness is raging terribly."

The organization making these observations was the American
Jewish Joint Distribution Committee, which had come into being in New
York during the first year of the war. It was made up of three component organizations. The first had been the Central Committee for the
Relief of Jews Suffering Through the War, formed under the aegis of
the Union of Orthodox Congregations on October 4, 1914; its president
was Leon Kamaiky, publisher of the *Tageblatt* and an officer in the
Hebrew Sheltering and Immigrant Aid Society. A few days later, the
American Jewish Committee called a conference to deal with the prob-
lem, and an American Jewish Relief Committee was formed. These two
groups—one "downtown," the other "uptown"—federated in November
into a Joint Distribution Committee. The third component emerged in
August 1915: the People's Relief Committee, essentially an organ of the
Lower East Side labor movement. This was never an easy alliance.
When Dr. Judah L. Magnes left in the summer of 1916 to tour the
Eastern war zones, he was not accompanied by representatives of the
two "downtown" committees, who objected to the composition of his
delegation. But there was some harmony in 1919, when the Yiddish
writer Sholem Asch, a member of the People's Committee, traveled in
Lithuania as the representative of the Joint Distribution Committee as
a whole.

The "Joint," as the organization had quickly come to be called in Europe, was working alongside Hoover's American Relief Administration, as a result of personal representations in Washington by its president, Felix M. Warburg. Hoover had at first objected to working with an autonomous private body and had asked that the Joint contribute $1 million to his own effort. Warburg had objected to this, insisting that money contributed by American Jews toward the relief of their coreligionists in Eastern Europe should not be used indiscriminately among populations that included pogromists. A compromise was reached, whereby the Joint would contribute its funds to the whole operation, but would be able to operate autonomously in Eastern Europe alongside Hoover's Administration. In fact, it gave $3.3 million, half of which was advanced on behalf of another concerned American ethnic organization, the National Polish Relief Committee.

The man sent as the Joint's chief representative was Boris D. Bogen, a fifty-year-old social worker who had been born to a privileged Jewish family in Moscow and had learned Yiddish only after his emigration to the United States following the expulsion of 1891. "With the arrival of Dr. Boris D. Bogen in Warsaw, February 9th, 1919," writes Colonel Grove,

> the American Jewish Joint Distribution Committee started its relief operations on a scale quite large for a private organization. While the work was largely among the Jews, a great deal of it was of a non-sectarian nature, and they contributed liberally toward the general relief.

Working from Warsaw, Bogen sent out food and health missions to wherever it was possible to reach during the Polish-Soviet war and the chaos in the Ukraine. Captain Arthur Goodhart, a young American-Jewish officer serving with former Ambassador Henry Morgenthau's commission to investigate the Polish pogroms, observed Bogen's work in the Polish capital. "This morning," he entered in his diary for July 19, 1919,

> we drove to the Jewish quarter to see the milk depots of the American Joint Distribution Committee. We were accompanied by Dr. Boris Bogen, who is at the head of all Jewish relief in Poland. He is one of the few men whom the Poles and the Jews agree in liking. At each one of the depots there was a long line of little children clamoring to get in. Two young men at each place were trying to keep the lines in order, but every now and then the starving children broke away and tried to rush through the doors. They were of all ages—little tots two years old and even tiny babies carried by their elder sisters of ten or twelve. The rooms in which the milk

and biscuits were distributed were kept spotlessly clean and seemed to be managed with the greatest efficiency. Dr. Bogen had given a number of young Jewish girls a course in American social service before he put them to work in the depots.

Bogen also organized other services, chief among them a system for transferring funds directly from American Jews to relatives in Eastern Europe. This was placed under the direction of Isidore Hershfield, who had traveled in the area for HIAS in 1916 and was now part of Bogen's staff in Poland.

Yet, despite the fact that refugees from eastern Poland and the Ukraine were beginning to flock into Warsaw by the thousands, Bogen showed no interest in the question of emigration. Colonel Grove provides an illustrative example. "On the 20th of March [1919]," he writes,

> Dr. Bogen brought into the office a Jewish boy named Abraham Lichowicki, fourteen years old, who lived at Pinsk. He was small for his age. His father went to America and had made arrangements to get his family to the United States just as the war was breaking out. As a result the family could not go. When the Germans entered Pinsk they drove out all the civilian population and sent this boy with his mother, his sister two years older, and three younger children to a point near Warsaw. The mother had recently died but the family returned to Pinsk upon the departure of the Germans in January 1919. They had no funds. The boy sold his mother's fur coat for 200 rubles and that had all been used up but five rubles, so the boy determined to make a break for America. He heard there was an American Mission in Warsaw, whereupon he took three pounds of bread and five rubles and started for Warsaw, leaving two pounds of bread for the family, believing that the American flour would arrive in time to keep the family from starving. He could not buy a ticket for five rubles, which would have been equivalent to about forty cents of US money, so he had to travel by his wits over the 300 miles. He was assisted by passengers who kept him hidden from the conductors, and in some cases was assisted by the conductors themselves by simply ignoring his presence. He said that all the people in Pinsk were opposed to Bolshevism. . . . Dr. Bogen provided financial aid for his return to Pinsk.

Was this the only way such problems were going to be handled? The mere presence of Americans in Warsaw was reawakening the passion to emigrate. "During the afternoon," Captain Goodhart noted one July day, there was a rush of men and women at our headquarters who wanted to go to America. A rumor had somehow started that the Mission was helping people to obtain passports. The crowd in the hall became so great that we had to assign a man to explain again and again that we were only an investigating Commission. Even then most of the people refused to go, as they thought this was only a trick to put them off.

The next morning, Goodhart writes, the crowd at the door

was even greater than that of yesterday evening. But today there were more women than men. One of them told me that her husband had left for America six years ago and she had not heard from him since the war had started. She could no longer support her children here, so her only chance now was to go to New York. "But how will you find him there?" I asked her. "Oh," she answered, "I remember his face perfectly well."

The problem of emigrating husbands separated by the war from their families back home had become a main concern of the Hebrew Sheltering and Immigrant Aid Society. When more or less normal transatlantic shipping resumed in the fall of 1919, the New York headquarters of HIAS found itself inundated with thousands of letters from American Jews asking for help in bringing over relatives who had been left behind. A committee was sent to Washington in October to discuss the matter with William Phillips, an assistant secretary of State—for it was the State Department that had issued stringent rules regarding the admission of immigrants under wartime conditions, and these rules were still in force. Under them, passports were being visaed by American authorities only at the countries of origin. But virtually no visas were being issued in Eastern Europe at that moment, largely out of the fear of typhus and of Bolshevism. The HIAS committee persuaded Phillips to allow the emigration of relatives, provided they were vouched for by their families in the United States. HIAS then appointed a delegation to go to Poland, under the direction of Leon Kamaiky.

What then happened many times over is described in a HIAS report:

Mr. "A" wrote to us from St. Louis, Missouri, that he had heard we were sending a Commission to Europe, for the purpose of reuniting families, and asked if we could facilitate his reunion with his wife and children from whom he had been separated for several years owing to war conditions. This letter reached us in January 1920. We immediately replied, assuring him of our desire and readiness to be of service to him and enclosed a registration blank for him to fill out with the object of giving us all the necessary information concerning himself as well as the relatives intending to come here. He returned the registration blank, filled out to the best of his knowledge and ability.

This registration blank was taken, with thousands more, by our Commission to Europe.

The commission, consisting of Kamaiky, Jacob Massel, and Louis Busker, left New York on February 5, 1920, and arrived in London eight days later. After discussing the refugee situation with Jewish leaders in London, it made stopovers in Rotterdam, Antwerp, Brussels, and Paris, where colonies of Jews fleeing Eastern Europe had gathered, stranded because their papers were not in order. "The passport situation abroad is complicated," Kamaiky wrote in his report:

According to the ruling of the State Department, an emigrant destined to the United States must have his passport visaed by an American Consul in the country to which he owes allegiance. Thus, an emigrant living in Poland must secure this visa from the American Consul in that country. However, owing to the extraordinary conditions which prevailed, a large number of emigrants, among them women and children, could not possibly remain in Poland until the Polish Government issued passports to them. These people went to France, Holland or Belgium, minus passports, and were successful in obtaining them from the Polish Consuls in these countries. The difficulties arose when the emigrants applied to the American Consul for visas. They were told to return to Poland and have their passports visaed by the American Consul there. This was impossible.

To deal with such problems, a HIAS office was established in Paris.

There was, in fact, an even greater problem than this one regarding the visaing of passports. "When an emigrant is already in possession of a bona fide passport from his Government," Kamaiky continues,

and where no reasons that would militate against granting a visa exist, the American Consuls require an affidavit from the relative in America, setting forth the latter's willingness to receive the emigrant and his ability to take care of him. Some emigrants have letters to the effect from their American relatives, but the American Consuls will not recognize them. It becomes necessary to communicate with the State Department in Washington, and as this is done by mail, several months elapse before a final answer is received. This means that the immigrants spend all their available money while waiting. Their plight, in consequence, is pitiable.

On top of all this, the consuls had to refer all visa applications to the Military Intelligence Department, "which keeps these applications for a very long time. They are returned with an approval or otherwise, no reason being assigned in cases of refusals."

With these and other difficulties to iron out, the HIAS delegates arrived in Warsaw at the end of March and made their headquarters in a courtyard at 34 Muranowska Street, in the heart of the Jewish quarter. "As soon as it became known that we were in Warsaw," Kamaiky recalled, "we were besieged by persons anxious to join their relatives in America. The clamor for help and for guidance was insistent and the work would admit of no delay. We began immediately." First there was the matter of passports. "Six to eight weeks," according to Kamaiky,

> would elapse before a passport was issued to emigrants. It was a long and wearisome process. We made representations to the Polish authorities, and at our request a ruling was issued whereby passports are issued in Warsaw to applicants within two or three days after application is made, upon presentation of proof from the applicant's native town that he or she is a law-abiding citizen.

This greatly speeded up the process, clearing the way for attention to be given to the visa problem.

"In order to procure a visa," Kamaiky wrote,

> every applicant must come personally to the American Consulate in Warsaw and fill out an application. Attached must be an affidavit in duplicate from the relative in America stating that such relative is willing to receive the immigrant and is in a position to take care of the new arrival. Where more than one person is concerned, the name, age, and relationship of each person must be given. The applicant must also furnish four photographs, and in the case of women going to their husbands, the marriage certificate (*ketubah*) must be produced.
>
> Three to fourteen days elapse before a visa is granted.

The HIAS delegates went over this situation carefully with the American consul and arrived at some new arrangements. It was decided that the visa applications could be handled at the HIAS office. "With the limited staff at the disposal of the Consulate, it was not possible to fill out more than fifty applications for visas daily. We [now] filled out five hundred applications every day, having 12 clerks on duty for this particular work." There was also the cumbersome matter of the affidavits. "We found out," Kamaiky writes,

> that fully ninety per cent of the affidavits which had been sent from America were lost in the mails, never reaching the addressees. We pointed out that the sole purpose of the affidavit was to show that

the relative in America was desirous of having his family with him and asked why a letter to that effect would not suffice.

The consul granted HIAS the authority to obtain such letters, which he would take as sufficient grounds for the granting of visas.

The commissioners now addressed themselves to the matter of transportation. The traditional routes had been disrupted by war and its aftermath, and Germany was in no condition to deal with a large transmigration. Kamaiky and his associates decided to look to the Baltic port city of Danzig, which had been separated from Germany at the Paris Peace Conference and made a "free state," with use of its port guaranteed to Poland. "After studying the situation there," Kamaiky writes,

> and then consulting the Warsaw and Danzig representatives of the various steamship companies, the conclusion was arrived at that the easiest route for emigrants would be by way of Danzig. The journey by rail to Western Europe is attended by overwhelming troubles and even by danger. It means fully two weeks of misery. And moreover the emigrants arrive in countries the languages of which they do not know. The women and children suffer most.

On the other hand: "From Warsaw to Danzig there is a daily train service, the journey taking only twelve hours. We arranged for special trains for emigrants." As for shipping:

> No steamers ran direct from Danzig to New York, and so we came to an arrangement with the Cunard and White Star Companies to carry emigrants on small steamers to English ports, where they would be transferred to the big liners going to America. The French Line agreed to take emigrants to Havre and there put them on trans-Atlantic steamers.

There remained the question of how the emigrants who went to Danzig would be sheltered and fed until they boarded ships. "We discovered in Troyl, a suburb of Danzig," Kamaiky goes on,

> a camp that had been built by the Germans for war prisoners. Everybody claimed to be the owner of that camp. Finally we came to an understanding with the authorities of Danzig by which we could use the camp for Jewish emigrants. The Danzig authorities were to manage the camp while we were to regulate prices. It was agreed that emigrants should be charged sixteen marks for a night's lodging, which included transporting baggage from railroad station to camp and from camp to steamer. Food, including medicine that

may be necessary, was charged at the rate of twenty-two marks a day per person.

As for food, an abundance of fish was available in Danzig, but no meat, so an arrangement was made to bring kosher meat from Posen twice a week.

Discovering, moreover, that the strains of uprooting and the vagaries of prices and exchange values were causing many emigrants to run out of money, the commissioners adopted Isidore Hershfield's method of arranging the transfer of funds from American relatives. The Warsaw office of HIAS would cable the New York headquarters, asking it to contact the relatives concerned

> and request that the money needed be sent at once. The [HIAS] commission paid dollar for dollar. That is, whatever amount was intended, in American dollars.

In the typical case of Mr. "A," for example, according to a HIAS report,

> our Commission cabled to us that they had located the family, but that they lacked funds. On the same day we wired Mr. "A", informing him of the contents of the cable and advising him to send the necessary sum in accordance with the request. Two days later we were in receipt of a Western Union Telegraph Order for the amount, and this was immediately dispatched to our Commission.

There was to be some criticism of both HIAS and the Joint from American financial circles, who maintained that this was banking without a license. But the two organizations insisted that there was no other way, and HIAS was eventually to obtain a banking charter.

Danzig now presented difficulties. "Soon after the emigrants began to arrive in Danzig," Kamaiky writes,

> a quarantine order on the part of the American government went into effect. Every emigrant passing through Danzig had to undergo a quarantine of twelve days. The American Government doctors rigidly examined the persons going to the United States.

By the time Kamaiky left Danzig in July, "there were no less than 2,100 immigrants in quarantine." Then came the Soviet attack on Warsaw in August. As HIAS President John L. Bernstein later wrote:

> Many immigrants who were at that time in Warsaw were not residents of Warsaw, but were people who came from all corners

of Poland . . . and were waiting for money from their husbands in
this country. But they had to be shipped in a hurry, because the
government had issued an order that everybody should leave . . .
as the Bolsheviki were only three miles away.

The HIAS office, remaining open in Warsaw until the last possible minute, helped thousands to evacuate to Danzig.

The *Jewish Chronicle,* not perceiving that HIAS was a separate
organization from the Joint, otherwise aptly described what had happened:

> The influx of about 10,000 Jewish refugees and emigrants (*en
> route* to America) into Danzig created a formidable problem for the
> local Jewish leaders, who found themselves unable to assist the
> large number of the starving Jews. The American Joint Distribu-
> tion Committee, however, took matters in hand, and opened res-
> taurants, a credit Society, and an information bureau. It also
> brought an American Consular representative to Danzig to facili-
> tate the visa of the passports. It even arranged social and literary
> functions for the emigrants who were awaiting accommodation on
> the ships going to America. In view of the changes in the military
> situation, the American members of the Joint Distribution Com-
> mittee are returning to Warsaw to resume their activities.

Actually, the Joint was worried about the large Jewish emigration to
the United States that HIAS was now facilitating—that September, Ellis Island received a record-breaking 18,691 immigrants in a single week,
a large proportion of them Jews—at a time when immigration restrictionism was having a major new surge.

Meanwhile, what of those uprooted Jews in Poland whose lives had been
affected by all these efforts in their behalf? The family of Chaia Sonia
Gussow, who had spent the latter part of the war in the town of Schlutzk
working as a domestic servant, was now ready to go. In 1919, she set
out from there with her two sons, aged eleven and eight. They went to
Bialystok by horse and wagon, then rode 120 miles to Warsaw by train.
The Polish capital was to be their home for almost a year. "The Warsaw
ghetto of 1919," recalls Don Gussow, one of the sons,

> included thousands upon thousands of refugees or immigrants, like
> us, from Russia, Lithuania, Latvia, and other Eastern European
> countries. With more than a million Jews packed into it, the place
> was unbelievably crowded, with ear-shattering noises and an as-
> sortment of smells. The cat and rat population seemed as large as
> that of the milling human inhabitants.

The lodging they found was a one-room flat in a group "of buildings around one of the series of courtyards which comprised the ghetto area. Each courtyard was a city unto itself."

At first, the Gussows had gone for help to the Joint office, as well as the American consulate, in a fruitless effort to have their passport visaed. But in February 1920, the new HIAS office became their chief recourse. It "was located on the ground floor of an old four-story building, situated in a quiet street several blocks from the main thoroughfare. . . . Mother, tired and excited, tried to explain the purpose of her visit to an attendant as we entered." A clerk took down all the relevant information:

> He asked Mother to give him Father's exact name, where he came from, when he had left for the United States, the city in which he now lived and worked, his age, whether she had other relatives in the United States, when she last heard from Father, did she possibly have his last address, and many other questions.

But it took some time to locate Simche Gussow in New York, during which Chaia Sonia experienced the theft of all her money and belongings. HIAS thereupon lent her money, and she and her children ate in its soup kitchen until she found work as a domestic in the home of a well-to-do Warsaw Jewish family.

Finally, one morning in late spring, the Gussows received news that Simche had been located in New York and had sent them money for their journey. A few days later, they were on an early-morning train. "Late in the afternoon," Don Gussow recalls,

> when the sun began to set, we arrived at Danzig. Shortly after we got off the train and collected our few bundles of belongings, a HIAS representative came over and made an announcement. "American travellers please follow me."
>
> What a wonderful sound these few words had as they came from the mouth of the middle-aged woman. We were now "American travellers." She said it first in Yiddish. Then she repeated it in German, Polish and Russian.
>
> We followed her gladly. Soon we were lined up before a bus and told to get in "carefully and slowly. There is plenty of room for all of you." The HIAS people, fully experienced in their dealings with immigrants, knew and could appreciate their anxieties. Then the woman explained that the bus would be taking us to the embarkation camp, where we would prepare for our trip to America.
>
> It was dark when we resumed our journey, and we could see little on the hour's drive to the camp. Soon we were on the outskirts

of the city, near a body of water. Through the window came smells of coal and tar.

When we reached the camp area, we saw electric lights in the camp, a change from the gas lamps in our Warsaw flat. As we were led off the bus, we were lined up in front of a large, wooden building, and at intervals groups went inside for registration and room assignments.

The Gussows were eventually to find themselves in a large barracks room, with rows of beds, some of them two-tiered bunks, clean if not private, but first they were separated from one another for washing and delousing. The two boys experienced the first showers of their lives, after which they were issued new underwear and clothing.

Another refugee family of that year was that of Moses and Minke Gingold, who with their five sons, aged four to twelve, had set out in the spring from their home in Brest-Litovsk once and for all. When the Jews of that city had been evacuated by the Russians in August 1915, the Gingolds had gone to live in the townlet of Antopol, about a hundred miles to the east, in the home of Minke's mother. There, for four years, Moses had helped his mother-in-law at her stall, selling geese in the local market. Returning in 1919 to the ravaged Brest-Litovsk, now under Polish rule, Moses tried to resume his dry-goods business. But a fight with some anti-Semitic toughs on the steps of his store caused him to decide to emigrate to the United States. Minke had two brothers and a sister there, all now American citizens. It was the sister, Fanny Glosser, her husband a partner with his brothers in a department store in Johnstown, Pennsylvania, who was reached to sign an affidavit for the Gingolds. Sworn by her and her husband before the Americanization Committee of the Board of Commerce in Detroit, where they were then residing, it said in part:

> Fanny Glosser, age 35, and Nathan Glosser, age 37, 298 Kirby Avenue, East, Detroit, Michigan, being duly sworn upon their oath, say that they are the sister and brother-in-law of Minke Gingold, age 37, and the sister-in-law and brother-in-law of Moses Gingold, age 37, and the aunt and uncle of their five sons . . . all residing at Brest, Litowski, Poland and desirous of coming to the United States to join these affiants.

That spring, the Gingolds, too, found themselves first in Warsaw and then in Danzig, where the boys received fresh school-type uniforms after their haircuts, delousing, and showers.

It was on a bright morning in September 1920 that Chaia Sonia Gussow arrived with her two young sons in New York harbor on the

S.S. *Susquehanna,* an American ship that had sailed the whole distance from Danzig. So also did the Gingolds sail the whole distance, on a Belgian Red Star ship, the S.S. *Kronlund,* which arrived in New York on October 17, 1920. They were among the families who were making it to America just in time; in a few months, the doors of immigration were to swing almost completely shut.

·45·

CLOSING THE GATES

In the United States, 1920—the year in which the Treaty of Versailles was rejected by the Senate—had begun with the great "Red Scare," then undergone the most disturbing anti-Semitic episode in the nation's history; from August through October, it had seen the largest Jewish influx ever recorded for an equivalent period; and the year ended with a precipitous drive in Congress toward some drastic form of immigration restriction. These events are significantly connected.

On the night of January 2, 1920, A. Mitchell Palmer, the United States Attorney General, brought his long-time pursuit of radicals to a climax with a network of raids in thirty-three cities. His agents—many of whom had been undercover members of radical organizations—entered cafés, club rooms, pool halls, bowling alleys, and private homes, rounding up more than four thousand suspects. Convinced that most radicals were aliens, Palmer had set special rules for the latter among the captured. Anyone claiming American citizenship, according to his instructions, had to "produce documentary evidence of same." Aliens in particular, upon arrest, were to be "searched thoroughly; if found in groups in meeting rooms, line them up against the wall there and search them." Special detention arrangements were made for alien radicals, who were subject to swift deportation hearings; hundreds were to be deported in the coming months.

Italians were prominent among foreigners suspected of radicalism, but a special onus fell upon Russian Jews, émigrés from the Bolshevik homeland of Trotsky and Lenin (who many thought was a Jew). Americans, haunted by images of radicals like Alexander Berkman and Emma Goldman, found it easy to imagine that there was a good deal of Bolshevik sympathy among Russian-born Jews in the country. That there was some there can be no doubt; the communist Yiddish-language daily

Freiheit (Freedom) was soon to exist in New York as case in point. The fact that a vastly greater number read *The Jewish Daily Forward*, which was from now on to devote much of its energies to an anticommunist crusade, did not help in the eyes of many. For the *Forward*, still nominally socialist, had been radical and pacifist enough during the war; the fact that it had welcomed the Russian Revolution of March 1917 doubtless aroused suspicion among those unaware that, by 1920, it was with equal vehemence repudiating the one that followed in November.

But whatever the political attitudes of Jews, ordinary Christian middle-class Americans knew only that frightening things seemed to be happening in Central and Eastern Europe. REDS ATTEMPT TO STORM WARSAW, began the terrifying headline in *The New York Times* of August 16, 1920,

> BARBED WIRE CHECKS FIRST ASSAULT;
> SOVIET PLAN FOR WORLD RULE TOLD

And the article that followed began:

> Soviet Russia intends to seek an alliance with Germany to make war on France, and, if this is successful, to undertake a conquest of England and, eventually, America, officials of the Bolshevist regime told the Associated Press . . . today.

There unquestionably were Jewish names prominent among the stories of revolution—Rosa Luxemburg in Berlin, Kurt Eisner and Gustav Landauer in Bavaria, Béla Kun in Hungary, to name a few, in addition to those well known in the Russian Revolution itself. Some people inevitably saw significance in this.

One such was Henry Ford. On May 22, 1920, Ford's personal weekly newspaper, a sixteen-page tabloid called the Dearborn *Independent*, suddenly began a series of articles under the general title "The International Jew." The first said:

> There is a super-capitalism which is supported wholly by the fiction that gold is wealth. There is a super-government which is allied to no government, which is free from them all, and yet which has its hand in them all. There is a race, a part of humanity, which has never yet been received as a welcome part, and which has succeeded in raising itself to a power that the proudest gentile race has never claimed—not even Rome in the days of her proudest power.

The kinship between these sentiments and those of the *Protocols of the Elders of Zion*, which had made its way in English translation across the Atlantic, were to be explicitly established in the ensuing series of articles, which would stretch out for more than a year.

Who wrote them? Certainly not Ford himself, who would not have had the time—they were rarely of fewer than three thousand words each and often a good deal longer—and who, when he finally relented under severe criticism in 1927, was to claim he had been deceived and not given a clear idea as to their content. There was more than one possible culprit on his staff, if the articles were produced entirely by the paper's staff and not at least partly by outside contributors; in any case, this was beside the point. Ford had lent his enormous prestige to the most resounding display of political anti-Semitism America had ever experienced, and its impact was serious. In particular, it was bound to have an impact on those who were contemplating the new surge of postwar Jewish immigration with dismay.

"One of the Commissioners of the Hebrew Sheltering and Immigrant Aid Society of America," ran a *New York Times* item on August 17, 1920,

> Leon Kamaiky, publisher of the Jewish Daily News of this city, returned recently from Europe, where he went together with Jacob Massel, to bring about the reunion of thousands of Jewish families who were separated by the war. Mr. Kamaiky has been abroad since last February. . . .
> In an article in the Jewish Daily News describing conditions in Eastern Europe, Mr. Kamaiky declared that "if there were in existence a ship that could hold 3,000,000 human beings, the 3,000,000 Jews of Poland would board it and escape to America."

In the interview that ensued, Kamaiky told the *Times* reporter, among other things: "We made it possible for all Jews of Poland who want to come to America to be able to do so." Did this mean, alarmed readers were bound to say, that HIAS was planning to bring over three million Polish Jews? Just a few weeks later, as record-breaking numbers of Jews began pouring into Ellis Island, the United States Commissioner there said something must be done to stem the tide. Congress, which had finally succeeded in passing a literacy law in 1917 and had more recently tightened the rules against the immigration of political undesirables, in late November 1920 began a drive to stop it completely.

"Would Bar All Aliens for Six Months," said a *Times* headline on December 2. The article ran:

> Complete stoppage of immigration for six months, while Congress is drafting a general law to cover the whole question, is proposed in a bill which Senator King, a Democratic member of the

Immigration Committee, is preparing for introduction soon after Congress meets.

Senator King said that the admission of aliens to this country must be made more difficult, and that it was necessary to prohibit all persons who were inoculated with "red" tendencies from entering the United States.

The House Immigration Committee will meet tomorrow to begin work on bills dealing with immigration. . . .

The House Committee was tougher than its Senate counterpart. Its chairman, Representative Albert Johnson of Washington, introduced a proposal to ban all immigration for two years. This caused the chairman of the Senate Committee, Senator Colt of Rhode Island, to remark critically: "This talk about 15,000,000 immigrants flooding into the United States is hysteria and not based on actual information." As for the minority members of the House Committee, they were scandalized at the way the Johnson proposal had been pushed over their heads. Representative Isaac Siegel, one of two Jewish members of the Committee, both from New York, issued a statement of protest to the press. "Mr. Siegel said," according to *The New York Times* on December 8,

> that it was an insult to the House that a bill of such proportions should be reported without a committee hearing, as was the case in this instance. The minority of the committee, he said, had not had an opportunity to present its report or be heard. . . .
>
> He charged that the bill resulted from Henry Ford propaganda against the Jews.
>
> "The point about the whole proposition is the fear of the large number of Jews coming in," Mr. Siegel said. "Otherwise we would have had a full bill reported. . . . The majority report reads just like Ford propaganda."

Representative Johnson defended his bill in the House debate on December 9. "The fact is," he proclaimed,

> that the new immigration is not of the kind or quality to meet the real needs of the country. We are being made a dumping ground. We are receiving the dependents, the human wreckage of the war, not the strength and virility that once came to hew our forests and till our soil.

With the proposed ban on immigration whittled down to one year, the Johnson Bill was passed in the House on December 13.

Senator Colt, however, doubtful about the drastic nature of the ban, called for hearings on the bill before his own committee. The sessions began on Monday, January 3, 1921. The first witness was Representative Johnson, who presented a memorandum prepared by his own committee and "declared that unless an emergency act was passed, European immigration would flood this country as soon as the war passport system went out of existence."

Among the Jewish witnesses were Louis Marshall of the American Jewish Committee, who called the Johnson Bill "an insult to the great number of American citizens whose parents were of foreign descent"; Morris Rothenberg of the American Jewish Congress; and Judge Leon Sanders and President John L. Bernstein of the Hebrew Sheltering and Immigrant Aid Society. Sanders insisted that "the present inrush was not abnormal, being . . . the checked flow of six war years." Bernstein felt put upon to clarify a misunderstanding. "The very first thing that the [House] Immigration Committee says in this report," he said,

is that it has confirmed a statement by one of our men. "The Committee has confirmed the published statement of a commissioner of the Hebrew Sheltering and Immigrant Aid Society of America, made after his personal investigation in Poland to the effect that if there were in existence a ship that could hold 3,000,000 human beings the 3,000,000 Jews of Poland would board it to escape to America."

Bernstein scoffed, "On this statement the House Immigration Committee builds the so-called emergency," and then proceeded carefully:

Now, all of you who are acquainted with poetry and oratory can well understand that that statement was not made by the gentleman to indicate that there are 3,000,000 people ready to come to America, but merely that the conditions six months ago were such that 3,000,000 people would like to come to America if they could.

I remember a few years ago a statement in a book on America, written by a foreigner, to the effect that every school boy in America has the desire, ambition and hope to become the president of the United States. Now, I think that statement in the main is true, but that it should not give us the right to suppose that in the next generation there will be about 10,000,000 Presidents of the United States.

This fanciful argument could hardly have placated those senators who suspected that the HIAS office in Warsaw was sending over as many emigrants as it could, and Bernstein's next remarks suggest he realized this. "There is another reference in this report," he said, which I believe is directed to this Society, because there is no other Society just like it, and we are operating in Europe to a small extent. It says in this report:

"One immigrant aid society which has offices in Poland is said to be planning to send 250,000 emigrants of one race alone, the Jewish, to the United States within the next three years."

And this is from a report by one of the consuls. Now, gentlemen, . . . our most prosperous year was the year 1919. . . . During the year 1919 we obtained the largest contributions, both in membership and in donations, that we have ever received, . . . and the amount of the contributions was $325,000. . . .

Now, I will leave it to you, gentlemen, how much of that $325,000 will be left us to undertake this great plan that somebody is reading, about the bringing over of 250,000 emigrants here?

Then Senator Hiram Johnson of California bluntly asked if HIAS encouraged or discouraged immigration. Bernstein replied:

Well, to be perfectly frank, we do neither. But here is what we do. A man comes to our office for advice; we give it to him. And remember, we do not come in contact with any person unless he is already an emigrant, because we have no offices throughout Europe. . . . Every person who wants to leave Poland . . . must come to Warsaw to get his visa. . . . And by the time the immigrants come to Warsaw they are on their way. . . .

Then he put it more succinctly:

Our work in Poland is merely police work. We are trying to prevent the emigrants in Poland from being exploited, cheated and swindled, and we are succeeding about as much as the New York police force is. There is cheating and there is swindling and there is exploiting of the immigrants all over Europe.

He ended with some remarks about Immigration Commissioner Wallis, accusing him of having created the present atmosphere of emergency and describing him as insufficiently experienced for his job.

It did not take long for the Senate Committee to conclude that there was no danger of an overwhelming influx of immigrants in the near future and that consequently there were no grounds for a general prohibition. But it did not conclude that there was no danger at all. On the contrary, in its efforts to gauge current American public opinion on the subject, the Committee had moved steadily toward the views of Senator William Dillingham of Vermont. That old champion of restrictionism, who was no longer chairman of the Committee but was still a member of it, had come firmly to the conclusion that the current crisis once again lay in the distinction between "old" and "new" immigration.

"The immigration of the present year," he stressed in a report a few weeks after the end of the Senate Committee hearings,

> has very largely come from southern and eastern Europe and in the opinion of the committee the largest immigration of the imme- diate future will also come from that section of the world. . . . It was the new immigration coming in unprecedented numbers which created our postwar problem and . . . it is the impending return of this movement to its prewar status which in the opinion of the committee constitutes the present emergency. Unlike the older im- migration, which distributed itself to every part of the country, entered every branch of its activity and was, as a rule, quickly and thoroughly assimilated, the new immigration has consisted largely of single men, it has gone directly to the cities and to manufacturing centers, and has remained there. It has moved in racial groups and to a large extent has maintained them, and compared with the older immigration it, as a rule, shows a slighter tendency to become American citizens and the number who have gone to the land have been negligible.

Therefore, Dillingham's report concluded:

> The Committee are of the opinion that in the present emer- gency a restriction should be applied to the type last described and are convinced that such restriction should be accomplished through some measure that will insure definite effectiveness.

The measure had, of course, already been determined by Dil- lingham long before and incorporated into a bill submitted by him on December 12, 1920: a quota system. The new bill was presented in April, 1921, and it prescribed:

> That the number of aliens of any nationality who may be ad- mitted under the immigration laws to the United States in any fiscal year shall be limited to 3 per centum of the number of foreign- born persons of such nationality resident in the United States as determined by the United States census of 1910.

This provision, scheduled to apply until June 30, 1922, meant a radical reduction in the immigration from Italy and Eastern Europe. Passed by the House on April 22 and by the Senate—where the vote was seventy-eight to one—on May 3, the bill was signed by President Harding and went into effect in June. As a result, Jewish immigration—which was still coming mainly from the low-quota countries of Eastern Europe—was to be reduced to a little over fifty thousand for the fiscal year 1921–22, as against nearly 120,000 the previous year. The gates of the Golden Land were swinging shut.

·46·

ORGANIZING EMIGRATION

On Sunday afternoon, June 5, 1921, at a moment agreed upon, President Warren G. Harding pressed a button in the White House that caused bells to ring at a building in New York where nearly five thousand persons were gathered and overflowing into the street for a dedication ceremony. The building was the old Astor Library on Lafayette Street, erected in 1854 with the bequest of a fabulously successful immigrant and long since a favorite retreat of immigrants seeking self-education. Its book collection having been passed on to the New York Public Library at Fifth Avenue and Forty-second Street ten years before, the Astor Library building had been falling into disuse until it was purchased at the beginning of 1920 by the Hebrew Sheltering and Immigrant Aid Society of America. The purchase price of $325,000, along with the $175,000 cost of converting the building into the full-scale shelter HIAS had long dreamed of—with dormitories, a cafeteria, a reading room, a roof garden, as well as living quarters and abundant office space—had been covered by an intensive fund-raising campaign throughout the previous year. "I am informed," President Harding said in his telegram of congratulations, "that the purchase of the new home was made possible through gifts from persons who came to America as immigrants. It seems to me there could be no more emphatic testimony to the usefulness and effectiveness of your society's work for Americanization."

These words came from the man whose signature on the immigration-quota law less than three weeks before threatened to make the facility obsolete even before it opened. Even at the time of the purchase in January 1920, when the many thousands of emigrants in Warsaw had signaled the possibility of the largest Jewish influx ever, Jacob Schiff, opening the fund-raising campaign with a contribution of $10,000, had suggested that the building was "perhaps a bit large." Schiff had since died, as if to symbolize the end of an era. Would there be any more tired, poor, and huddled masses to receive at John Jacob Astor's democratic palace?

The leaders of HIAS had been dedicating themselves to this question for more than a year. In this respect, too, a new era in the history of the emigration was manifesting itself. Until the war, HIAS had been almost entirely an American organization for American purposes, active only at the receiving end of the emigration route. But the problems of war had caused it to begin intervening in Europe and Asia. It was in particular Leon Kamaiky's mission in 1920 that wrought a startling transformation in the overall character of the Society's activities. Arriving in Poland for the ostensibly limited purpose of reuniting broken families, the HIAS representatives quickly turned themselves into a major force in the emigration process.

But the good people of HIAS were amiable benders of rules, not breakers of laws. There were still tens of thousands of Jewish refugees in Eastern Europe—the exodus from the Ukraine was only now reaching its height and overflowing into Rumania—but these were far too many for the new American quotas. The vast majority of them had to be settled elsewhere; and with Russia gone over to communism, and Poland and Rumania zealous to be rid of as many Jews as possible, no responsible persons spoke any longer of repatriation. This meant that an organization as deeply concerned in the entire Jewish emigration process as HIAS had become had to make Europe a principal center of its activities. And HIAS, youthful, rambunctious, was eager to do so; indeed, it was inclined to take over Jewish emigration activities in Europe.

But, in emigration matters as in everything else, Europe had proud and august institutions that did not welcome the incursions of brash Americans. One such institution was the old Jewish Colonization Association, or JCA. Recognizing the need to coordinate Jewish emigration problems throughout Europe, the JCA had called a conference of French and British organizations, which was held in Brussels on June 7 and 8, 1921.

Among those who attended, but not as a delegate, was Adolph Held, then the European representative of HIAS. In his late thirties, Held was a new type of American-Jewish leader. Born in Eastern Europe, he had emigrated to the United States with his family as a child and been educated at the College of the City of New York. He was active in the Lower East Side labor movement, and had served for a number of years as business manager of *The Jewish Daily Forward*. Since the war, he had gone into immigration work and joined the HIAS Board of Directors. Earlier in the year, he had been part of a group sent to

Warsaw to relieve Kamaiky's delegation, and had since established himself at the HIAS office at 16 Rue Lamarck in Paris, hoping to make it a permanent center of European activities.

The transcript of the Brussels conference gives clear indication that some of the other delegates, in particular the hosts from the JCA, were not happy with either Held's presence or his general aspirations. "May not the HIAS," asked Held, hitherto silent, at the end of the first morning's session, "join in with the JCA in studying practical implementations of the questions raised here?" There clearly was some reluctance on this point among the delegates. Louis Oungre of the JCA, the conference chairman, replied by addressing the assemblage in general. "Are you," he asked, "of the opinion that the HIAS should be charged jointly with the JCA to examine the questions placed here before you?" The vote was affirmative, but this proved to be only the prelude to abrasive confrontations.

There seemed to be some suspicion among the delegates, for example, that HIAS was involved in the traffic in illegal visas that had recently surfaced in Eastern Europe. Suddenly, during the first afternoon session, Oungre turned to Held and asked: "We would like to know what measures the HIAS is taking to fight against the traffic in visas." Held replied:

> It is very difficult to combat false visas. The dealers in them are everywhere. And since people very often have difficulty obtaining visas through proper channels, as in Rumania, they have recourse to false visas.

Recognizing that more explanation was being sought from him on the role HIAS was playing among fleeing Jews at the Soviet borders, Held went on to say:

> At HIAS, we organized ourselves just like the traffickers in visas. At the border, we attracted the emigrants, but not by the same methods or with the same results as the traffickers. We take charge of the money they have on their persons, we buy them railway and steamship tickets, and visas, at reduced prices. . . . For those who present themselves to us at the border, we obtain all the necessary papers.

This may not have quelled all suspicions, but Held, now that he had the floor and was talking about various problems of the emigration, took the opportunity here to make a major proposal. "The JCA and the HIAS," he said, must take the lead in organizing all this, and HIAS will, in this respect, work in full accord with the JCA in order to watch over the wherewithal of the emigrants and prevent agents and companies from exploiting them. We must get all the leading organizations to come together on this, all our strength assembled. Our work until now was in America. But we will devote all our resources to one central organization.

This offer on the part of the upstart HIAS to join the lordly JCA as a full partner in a single European emigration organization did not get a friendly response. One of the JCA delegates, referring implicitly to American laws against assisted immigration, replied haughtily: "Since the HIAS is exclusively occupied with those who have money, from the viewpoint of emigration it has, so to speak, done nothing." Grand Rabbi Israel Lévy of France lashed out at HIAS with an even more arbitrary criticism, complaining that Paris was becoming cluttered with homeless refugees because it had opened an office there.

A debate ensued on the nature of the proposed central organization, since everyone agreed that such a body had to be established. "I would like this central body," Held persisted, shifting his emphasis, "to be a cooperative of all the Jewish organizations and that it not be particularly in the charge of one or another of them." Clearly he felt that, at least if the JCA were not put specifically at the head, HIAS would have a chance to achieve equality and even predominance in the central organization. But at this point he found himself opposed by no less an adversary than Lucien Wolf, the distinguished spokesman of the Anglo-Jewish establishment, who also was the British representative of the JCA. At this time, the League of Nations was creating a High Commission for Refugees, and Wolf, as the JCA's delegate to it, was preparing to report to it on this conference. He was, among other things, determined to be able to say that nothing was being done by the Jewish organizations to stimulate "unnecessary migration." And he was not alone among those present in believing that HIAS, in its zealous border activities, had been a prominent offender on this issue.

"I am of the opinion," Wolf said pointedly in reply to Held,

that the JCA, given its importance, its experience, should have charge of this central body. We [of the Anglo-Jewish Association] are ready to cooperate . . . at the forthcoming Geneva conference on refugees for the solution of the Jewish emigration problem, on condition that we find ourselves dealing with a central organization—and I believe that the JCA can take charge of the formation of such a body.

This was formidable, but Held made a final plea, insisting that JCA control

> would be to impinge upon the independence of the other organizations. In principle, this central body ought not to be placed under the direction of one organization rather than some other. The organizations in other countries ought not to count on such a central body, but should rely on their own countries' funds and groups for the task at hand.
>
> I am therefore opposed to placing the central body under the authority of the JCA. There should not be any authority, any direction, to which one has to submit.

Without further comment, Chairman Oungre submitted the following proposition to a vote:

> The Brussels conference has decided that a central organization should be created under the direction of the JCA, with the cooperation of various emigration committees, for studying the emigration from Eastern Europe.

The transcript then reads:

> (This proposal was put to a vote and it was approved unanimously, except for one vote, that of Mr. Held of the HIAS, who requested that his vote against the proposal be recorded in the transcript.)

There was nothing left for HIAS to do but create a European emigration organization of its own. The roots for one had already been planted in August 1920, when a group of Jewish relief organizations had met at Carlsbad, in the new state of Czechoslovakia, and founded a body called the World Jewish Relief Conference, abbreviated Werelief. This group, which made its headquarters in Paris, had lacked the kind of leadership that HIAS was now ready to provide. Why it came from HIAS and not from the JCA is a question that can only be answered by conjecture. For all its power as an organization that had guided emigrants to Argentina, Palestine, and other countries, the JCA had never been able to offer the United States, which was where most of the emigrants still wanted to go. Only HIAS could offer the prospect of an emigration route that might at least lead there eventually, in spite of the drastic new restrictions. Moreover, the JCA, an organization of elite West European Jews, simply did not have the roots in Eastern Europe that HIAS had, with its many members who had been born there and spoke good Yiddish. And HIAS would cooperate with the Zionists, which the JCA would not do. Last but not least, HIAS had lively financial resources.

It was in October that HIAS and Werelief made their move, convening at the Czechoslovakian capital. "The emigration conference," said the October 7, 1921 *Jewish Chronicle,*

> convened under the auspices of the HIAS (American Hebrew Immigration Aid Society) and the Executive of the Carlsbad Relief Conference, was held at Prague. Thirty-five delegates from fourteen countries attended. . . . They represented twenty-five organizations, including the Jewish National Councils of Poland and Lithuania and the Zionist Organization. . . . A member of the Carlsbad Relief Executive, Mr. [Wilhelm] Latzky-Bertoldi, read an authorized statement from the Soviet representative in Berlin that his Government was ready to facilitate the emigration of Jews. . . . The Conference decided to establish in London a Central Jewish Emigration Bank, with a capital of £50,000. . . .

Establishing headquarters in Berlin, the new organization called itself the Vereinigtes Komitee für Jüdische Auswanderung, or United Jewish Emigration Committee. Its headquarters were called the Emigrations-Direktorium (Emigration Directorate), and it was under the shortened form of this name, Emigdirect, that the organization became widely known. But the main point was made on its printed circulars, which said: "European Representative of the Society 'Hias of America.' "

·47·

BRITISH PALESTINE

Under the law of 1921, only about fifty thousand Jews were entering the United States each year. This was extended into 1923; in 1924, Representative Albert Johnson introduced an even more severely restrictive bill, which became law. Based this time on the "national origins" of the American population in 1890—when the "new immigrant" groups were represented in far smaller numbers than in 1910—the law also reduced the quota of each nationality to 2 percent of what its size had been in that year. Under this drastic reduction, only 10,292 Jewish immigrants entered the country in 1924.

The impact of restriction in the United States had already been felt in Canada in the wake of the 1921 law: 8,404 Jewish immigrants arrived there in 1922, three times as many as in the preceding year. Jewish immigration into South Africa, previously in the hundreds each year, suddenly doubled in 1925, arriving at a figure of 1,353. Jewish immigration to Argentina also nearly doubled between 1922 and 1923, reaching in the latter year an all-time high of 13,701. Brazil, too, now emerged as an important refuge, admitting over two thousand Jews in 1924. But all these figures were relatively small, and became smaller when some of the countries—notably Canada and South Africa—began introducing restrictive immigration laws of their own.

Only Palestine seemed to offer a virtually unlimited horizon for Jewish immigration. When the Balfour Declaration was being formulated in the summer of 1917, an early draft had mentioned "freedom of immigration for Jews," and this was a principle Zionist leaders went on taking for granted even after it was not explicitly included. At the Paris Peace Conference, Chaim Weizmann envisioned, before the Council of Ten, an immigration of "70,000 to 80,000 Jews annually." And, indeed, in the years immediately following the war's end, during which the British military administration yielded to the Mandatory granted to Britain by the League of Nations, Jewish immigration was unrestricted. From the spring of 1920 to that of 1921, an unprecedented ten thousand Jews entered the country; the figure seemed about to grow rapidly.

But this sudden influx may have helped precipitate a crisis in April 1920, when a wave of Arab rioting against Jews occurred. During this first outbreak, Joseph Trumpeldor, the Jewish veteran who had lost an arm at Port Arthur and who had since fought with the British in the Middle East, was killed at the remote northern settlement in which he had been living after the war. Then a new outbreak occurred in May 1921, causing the British administration, under High Commissioner Sir Herbert Samuel—a Jew himself—to call a temporary halt to immigration. This was regarded by many Zionists as an ominous sign, even though the ban was lifted two months later.

The granting of visas to Palestine was thenceforth somewhat more selective than it had been in the first postwar years. A major British-government policy statement on Palestine, issued on July 1, 1922, over the signature of the Colonial Secretary, Winston Churchill—and hence generally known as the Churchill White Paper—while declaring that the Jewish community was there "as of right and not on sufferance," stressed the restrictive principle of the "economic capacity" of the country to absorb new arrivals, and this was to be applied with growing severity. It soon became clear that, in the eyes of the British authorities—among whom enthusiasm for the Balfour Declaration rapidly diminished, especially with the passing of the political generation responsible for it—absorptive capacity was at least as much a political as an economic principle. Jewish economic institutions began to flourish, and there is reason to believe—though this cannot be proved statistically, since the British kept no records of Arab arrivals—that an Arab influx of some substance was drawn overland into Palestine by the employment opportunities created in the major areas of Jewish settlement. But on the political level, the fear remained that too much Jewish immigration would arouse the violent anger of the local Arabs.

Yet most of the period from 1919 to 1924 was relatively idyllic. Known to Zionist historians as the Third Aliyah, this was the classic time of large-scale agricultural pioneering. Dominated by the Poalei Zion and other labor Zionist groups, it was typified by large numbers of young people, mostly from Poland, arriving together to found collective settlements (kibbutzim), clear rocky lands, drain swamps, make new areas fertile, and build roads.

Of the many remarkable young people who took part in this movement, there was one girl who, though born in Russia, had grown up in

Milwaukee, Wisconsin, and had emigrated from there. Golda Meyerson (later Meir) settled with her husband in Kibbutz Merhavia in 1921 and, because they were married and Americans, were accepted there only with some reluctance.

"Since I had been accepted as a member of the kibbutz with such reluctance," she was to recall many years later,

> I took pains to prove that they had been wrong about me, and like the other girls, I insisted on doing any job that the men did. There is a big stand of trees near the entrance to the kibbutz today and at the time it provided our main source of income. The Jewish National Fund paid us six pounds per member to plant the trees. The plot was full of rocks and boulders and we had to loosen them with picks to get some soil in which to plant the saplings. I will never forget the first days I worked at that job. When I returned to my room in the evening I couldn't as much as move a finger but I knew that if I didn't show up for supper they would jeer: what did we tell you? That's American girls for you! I would gladly have forgone supper, for the chickpea mush we ate wasn't worth the effort of lifting the fork to my mouth—but I went. . . .

This predominantly ideological wave of arrivals was superseded by a relatively urban influx beginning in 1924, when the virtual closing of the United States to Jewish emigrants made Palestine the major alternative. Immigration then took a sudden leap, from 7,421 in 1923 to 12,856 in 1924 and an incredible 33,801 in 1925. And yet, ironically, this was also the period of greatest peace between Jew and Arab. At the 1925 Zionist Congress in Vienna, Chaim Weizmann was able to say that Palestine was the quietest part of the Middle East.

But this peace did not last. Once again ironically, the next major Arab outbreak occurred after a precipitous decline in Jewish immigration: as a consequence of an economic slump, a total of barely five thousand Jews arrived in the two years 1927 and 1928. Then, in August 1929, an incident at the Western (or "Wailing") Wall in Jerusalem, at which the most religious elements in Judaism and in Islam constantly found themselves in uncomfortable proximity, led to growing Arab retaliations. Groups of young Arabs suddenly appeared and attacked Jews, first in Jerusalem, then in Hebron, Safed, and other towns throughout the country. When the wave had passed, nearly 150 Jews were dead and hundreds were wounded. It was worse than Kishinev.

A British investigating commission under Sir Walter Shaw came to the conclusion that immigration was one of the irritants causing Arabs to riot, and a decree severely restricting it was issued in May 1930. When this was criticized by the League of Nations Mandates Commission, another investigation was conducted for the British government by Sir John Hope Simpson. This resulted in a White Paper, issued in October 1930 by Lord Passfield (the former Sidney Webb), the Colonial Secretary. The Passfield White Paper was highly critical of the Zionist leadership for various of its policies, and called for the tightening of Jewish immigration, but it met with widespread protest and was quietly withdrawn.

Nevertheless, the situation was ominous as Palestine entered the decade of the 1930s. The few euphoric years of seeming Arab-Jewish reconciliation in the country had ended with the collapse of any real hopes in the riots of 1929. What was even worse, the British administrators had come out of that bitter experience convinced that, among the various Zionist policies that they regarded as incitements to Arab violence, relatively free Jewish immigration was the greatest offender. There was bound to be further confrontation on this issue, even as the grounds for Jewish emigration from Europe started to become more urgent than ever before.

·48·

A POLISH MINORITY

"After dinner," Captain Arthur Goodhart of the Morgenthau Commission recorded one evening in Warsaw in July 1919,

> Colonel Bryant and I went to the open-air Dolina Theatre. Dancing was one of the most important features of the performance, as it always is in Poland. There was also, much to our surprise, a short skit ridiculing the American Mission. In this scene a Jew carrying an American flag refused to permit a young girl dressed as Poland to join the League of Nations. The other piece was a highly dramatic episode in which a Polish girl killed a Bolshevik.

Added to this set of postwar conceptions regarding Jews for some Poles was the image of Zionism, about which the pro-Paderewski newspaper *Rzeczpospolita*, for example, carried a significant item two years later, in March 1921. According to a summary in the *Jewish Chronicle*,

> it accused the Zionists of making efforts to convert Poland into a Palestinian colony and of subsidizing the speculators in Poland. It further charged the Jews with provoking attacks on Poland abroad, with the introduction of Bolshevism into the country, and with avoiding military service and fostering other crimes.

This was a moment when such accusations were on the rise everywhere in the Western world, from Warsaw to Dearborn, Michigan. But the Jewish situation in Poland was unique. The approximately three million Jews there (slightly less in the census of 1921, slightly more in that of 1931) formed about 10 percent of the population—the largest percentage anywhere in the world except Palestine. True, there were several other minorities in Poland, one of them even larger than the

398

Jews: five million Ukrainians, or about 15 percent of the population. But around the Jews there clustered special fears, hatreds, and ambiguities, ancient as well as brand new.

Were they a national or a religious minority? There had long been a Jewish element in the country, especially strong in Warsaw, that regarded themselves as "Poles of the Mosaic Persuasion," exactly like their nineteenth-century Reform counterparts in Germany and the United States. This tendency was still very much in evidence at the war's end. "In the afternoon," Goodhart writes one day in July 1919,

> eleven Assimilators called. These are the Jews who believe that Judaism is only a question of religion. In culture and dress they have become entirely Polonized and speak only Polish as a rule. The wealthiest business men and the leading lawyers belong to this group. In the middle of the nineteenth century they were the spokesmen for the Jewish community, but lately they have entirely lost their influence. This is due in part to the fact that many of them have been baptized.

Diametrically opposite to this tendency, yet in principle the same, was the classic Polish Judaism represented by the Chief Rabbi of Warsaw, Abraham Perlmutter, who also called at the headquarters of the Morgenthau mission. "He was a most venerable-looking old man," Goodhart writes,

> with a long white beard which reached almost to his waist. He was dressed in his finest silk kaftan, which his son whispered to me was only worn on the greatest occasions. . . . When he met Mr. Morgenthau he bowed low and then recited a long speech which he had apparently learned by heart.

Neither of these tendencies ought to have been regarded as a problem by the Polish state, for all either of them wanted was to practice its religion without offense and be left in peace. And the assimilationists could do even better, for they were already producing some of the major figures in Polish cultural and professional life. Yet Polish anti-Semitic zeal extended to both groups.

"A soldier made a shameful attack on the aged . . . Rabbi Perlmutter," the *Jewish Chronicle* was to report from Warsaw on August 6, 1920,

> in a railway carriage at Skiernewitz. He began to tear the Rabbi's beard, and threw him on the ground. A number of Jews surrounded the soldier, and rescued the Rabbi from his hands. Our coreligionists attempted to take the assailant to a superior official. . . . The

authorities censured the Jews for . . . detaining the soldier. The latter . . . was allowed to depart unpunished.

Disabilities of a subtler nature were reserved for the assimilated classes. "Later in the morning we called on Professor Szymon Askenazy," Goodhart had recalled in July 1919, correctly describing him as

> the leading historian in Poland. He is the author of the chapters on Poland and Russia in the *Cambridge Modern History*. He was bitterly attacked by the Russians for predicting the collapse of their empire in these articles. He is one of the very few Jewish professors in Poland—it is even doubtful whether he will be continued at the University [of Warsaw].

Askenazy was indeed to lose his chair; but in this moment his Polish patriotic optimism was unquenchable:

> Professor Askenazy said that he thought that Poland had a bright future. . . . He thought that the sudden development of nationalism, both on the part of the Poles and the Jews, was only a temporary result of the war. The Polish nationalists especially had confused nationalism with patriotism. He defined patriotism as the love for one's country, nationalism as the desire to limit that country to one race.

This question of "race" was above all the source of growing irritation between Poles and Jews. For, if Polish nationalism was at a new height, so also was the Jewish nationalism that had emerged in the late nineteenth century out of the conflict between assimilationism and traditional Orthodoxy, and had obtained renewed confirmation in the Balfour Declaration. Goodhart describes how

> a Committee from the Zionist organization called on the Mission. They seemed to be exceptionally able men, and expressed their ideas in clear and forceful language. In dress and manners they were entirely modernized and were separated by centuries from the kaftaned Jews we had seen in the poor quarter. . . . They said they hoped that the Mission would bring about better relations between the Poles and the Jews, but this could only be done if the truth were established. They wanted separate schools for their children and also the right to manage their own charities and other institutions. They believed that Judaism was a question not only of religion, but also of race. They were anxious to preserve their racial culture, which could only be done if the children were taught in Jewish schools.

Refugees about to leave Bremen for South Africa on the SS *Stuttgart*, October 1936.

Passengers disembarking at Antwerp, June 17, 1939,
after having been refused entry at Havana, Cuba.

SS *St. Louis* passengers boarding the train at Antwerp for Brussels.

The SS *St. Louis*

French internment camp at Le Vernet.
(*Photograph by Gabriel D. Hacket*)

HIAS office, Marseille, 1942.

From Le Havre, February 1940.

From Marseille.

Refugee departures from Europe, 1940–1942

From Marseille.

From Lisbon for Cuba, 1942.

The SS *General William M. Black* arriving in New
York harbor on October 30, 1948, with the first shipment
of refugees under the Displaced Persons Act of that year.

Camp Oswego, Fort Ontario, New York, August 1944.
(*Photograph by Hikaru Iwasaki*)

Displaced persons arriving at the entrance to the
HIAS shelter, the former Astor Library building, on
Lafayette Street in New York, 1949.

A group of Rumanian Jews leaving for Australia under
HIAS auspices, 1946.

Polish Jews crossing Czechoslovakia on their way to
Displaced Persons camps in Germany and Austria, 1946.

From Bergen-Belsen.

Through Marseille.

Children arriving in
Haifa harbor.

Refugees going to Israel under HIAS auspices, 1948–1949

Miksa Frankel and his family arriving in the United
States from Hungary, November 1956.

Soviet Jewish family arriving at Kennedy Airport, March 1972.

The Zionists were now, in fact, to become the predominant element in
the Jewish cultural life of Poland among those members of a younger
generation who sought modernity, especially if they eschewed the politics of the far left. It was not hard for them to develop the consciousness
of separate identity that the Zionist program was founded upon. "From
the fifth grade on," recalled one woman who grew up at this time in an
acculturated Polish-Jewish home,

> I went to school with Christian children. I then began to be aware
> that I am a Jew. After religious instruction and before Catholic
> holidays, the stories were revived about ritual murder and about
> Judas. I personally got along well with Catholic girls. Whenever I
> brought them some goodies before Purim or Passover, they readily
> took it, even though the matzah supposedly had "Christian blood"
> in it. It was no use to try to discuss this matter rationally with
> them. When they had no argument left, they would conclude "it is
> nevertheless true that you use Christian blood in the matzah. We
> were told this." Sometimes they would add, "Jew go to Palestine."

One result of such stimuli was that, in the 1931 census, almost 8 percent
of Polish Jewry were to declare that Hebrew was their mother tongue—
an answer true to Zionist principle though entirely contrary to fact.

Much closer to the truth were the nearly 80 percent who gave Yiddish as their mother tongue. In quantitative terms, Yiddish culture was
declining in Poland, and more and more Jews were speaking the majority language in preference to it: there were now several major Jewish
publications in Polish, including a daily newspaper and a popular illustrated weekly. But the growing national feeling had brought Yiddish
culture to a new height of intensity among its adherents. Warsaw, the
home of such writers as Chaim Grade and the brothers Israel Joshua
and Isaac Bashevis Singer, could claim in the 1920s to be the world
capital of Yiddish literature. Yet, as a center of Yiddish learning, it was
rivaled by Vilna—or Wilno, in its form as the city in Poland it had
become—where the Yiddish Scientific Institute, called YIVO from its
Yiddish acronym, was founded in 1925.

The power of Yiddish as the mother tongue of most Polish Jews
had ample political expression. On the middle-class level, there was the
Folkspartei. Goodhart, who interviewed its leaders, writes: "They took
the same position as the Zionists, as far as matters in Poland were
concerned, but said they were not interested in re-establishing a Jewish
homeland in Palestine." This, translated into terms of the class struggle, was above all the position of the ardently Yiddishist Bund. Poland
alone was now the homeland of this movement, for in postrevolutionary
Russia the leaders of the Bund had elected to become absorbed into the

Communist Party. The temptation to do this was strong in Poland, too, and the question of the relationship with the Communist Party there caused frequent splits in the Bundist ranks.

One effect of this tendency was that the Bund stayed clear of "bourgeois" politics. In the important elections of 1922 to the Sejm—the Polish National Assembly—though twenty-two Jewish deputies were returned, most of them Zionists, not a single Bundist was among them. Not that this exclusion of Jewish radicalism conciliated anti-Semitism in the country. That year, the winning candidate for President of the Republic was Gabriel Narutowicz, a moderate of aristocratic background who was known as a close associate of Pilsudski. For the time being, Pilsudski was retired from active politics, but the influence he and his friends still exercised against the reactionary policies of Roman Dmowski's National Democrats was cherished by liberals and by the national minorities, especially the Jews. Indeed, some of the more extreme elements among the National Democrats took to calling Narutowicz the "President of the Jews." And in December, only a few months after his victory, he was assassinated.

At his trial, the assassin, an artist and a fanatical nationalist named Eligiusz Niewadomski, explained his position. "Jewry," he said,

> has inculcated into socialism morbid poison and creative impotency.
> The era of Utopian socialism was followed half a century later by so-called scientific socialism which will rightly be called the Jewish era. . . . Jewry soon realized to what uses socialism could be put once it got it in its hands. The Jews gave to socialism their theories, distributors, agitators, material help, advertising. . . . And not in vain. They have imbued that idea with all their radical characteristics and with the elements which have been the cause for social degeneration of the moral value of its nationalism.
> The class struggle was invented by them in order to destroy the Aryan nations and thus avert racial animosities and struggles.

Under the circumstances, there was widespread relief among the Jews of Poland when, in May 1926, Marshal Pilsudski staged a military coup and became the effective dictator of the country. Two years later, the Warsaw correspondent of the *Nation* could write that

> the present regime . . . shows signs of wanting to come to an understanding with the minorities. This is especially true in the case of the Jews. Compared to the persecution of the old Endek [National Democrat] regime, the present condition of the Jews in Poland is greatly improved. The Marshal himself is probably one of the best friends of the Jews in Poland, and his administration . . . cannot be accused of lack of good will toward the Jews.

The first years of Pilsudski's rule corresponded to a period when the anti-Semitism that had raged through the Western world at the war's end like the Spanish flu suddenly, after reaching a height in about 1924, fell everywhere into abeyance. By 1931 in Poland, 56 percent of its doctors, 33.5 percent of its lawyers, and 22 percent of its journalists, publishers, and librarians were Jews. There even was soon to be a Jewish flyweight boxing champion.

Israel Cohen was keenly aware of the changes that had come over Poland when he revisited it in 1932, particularly when he got back to the city that was now called Lwów. "As I entered a taxicab outside the railway station," he wrote,

> . . . I could not help recalling and contrasting the very different circumstances in which I had last visited what was then called the city of Lemberg. . . . There [now] were trains and taxicabs in plenty, and everywhere flags were flying, for on the previous day there had been an international motor race.

Returning to the same hotel in which he had stayed in 1919, then "dirty and dilapidated, with no light at night except that of candles in beer bottles," he now found it "resplendent with electric illuminations, in which the brass buttons on the page boys' jackets twinkled with unusual luster."

On the streets of the Jewish quarter, though he saw Jews who "seemed to be just the same, with the same long black coats and black plush hats, from which depended corkscrew curls," he also saw distant signs of progress. "In a dingy square," for example,

> there was a large number of motorbuses with scores of Jews swarming around them. Before the . . . war the Jews from the outlying townlets—Zolkiev, Tartakow and others—used to come into the city by cart or slow train, now they travelled by the popular motorbus for a small fare in order to buy a basketful of wares, which they took back for sale. All these motorbuses, I learned, belonged to Jews.

There had even come into being something of a provincial Jewish nightlife. "In the evening," Cohen continues,

> I was taken to a Jewish café, which seemed to be the resort of all classes and sections of the community, seated at different tables and distributed in different parts. There were business people at one table, lawyers at another, Zionists at a third (distinguished by a little flag with the Shield of David), chess-players at the next, and speculators further on. In a separate room we came across a party

of card-players, who, owing to the heat, were sitting in their shirt-sleeves, whilst others were poring over newspapers. Another door led to a chamber with subdued and variegated lights dimly disclosing a bar and reflected in the polished surface of the parquetry, on which the hired "hostesses" in jet-black were dancing with the gilded youths, one of whom smilingly greeted me with *Shalom* over the gleaming shoulder of his gilded partner.

Not all was well, however. There were signs of the worldwide Depression everywhere. In the Jewish marketplace, "there seemed to be far more sellers than buyers, and nobody's stock would have been worth more than a few shillings." Cohen took a picture of a shoemaker

who sold me the right to photograph him at work for the price of a bottle of beer; and presently I found myself surrounded by a motley crew of beggars and cripples and dwarfs of both sexes, all wretchedly clad, mostly in rags, and some literally in sackcloth. Nowhere had I seen so many misbegotten specimens of humanity within so small an area.

Another economic problem was the competition from the Ukrainians,

especially in the rural districts. For as the Jews were loyal citizens of Poland, the Ukrainians, in their annoyance, were doing their utmost to drive them to the wall. They had established an extensive and successful cooperative organization, particularly for the export of dairy produce; and the young Ukrainians (many of them educated in Prague) who were unable to find an outlet in Government service, were devoting their abilities to commerce.

Above all, there were the unrelenting phenomena of anti-Semitism, the chief reason for what was described to Cohen as

the bleak, blank prospect that faced the Jews of Galicia. Active anti-Semitism was confined to the students, but the Government pursued a subtle and systematic policy which was far more devastating than any attack. It kept Jews out of the civil service, refused to appoint any as teachers in Polish schools, and withheld from them all contracts for military and other supplies, which amounted to vast sums every year.

In general, there was a mood of quiet desperation, broken only now and then by the steadily fading hope of emigration. "As we walked along the busy thoroughfare," Cohen wrote, and I stopped to point my camera at a salesman of shoes, the latter asked me whether the picture was intended for America. "Perhaps," I replied, whereupon he said, "I wish you could pack me in and take me there. That is, indeed, a fortunate country."

It was also almost entirely out of the question, despite all the relatives there who sent money back to Lwów. Palestine was more likely:

> Everywhere there was a passionate desire, on the part of old and young, to emigrate to Palestine, and only recently a party of two hundred had gone out to visit the country and study the possibilities of settlement.

On the other hand, Cohen concluded ominously,

> as the prospects of emigration, whether to Palestine or any other land, were limited, many young Jews were perforce lending an ear to the seductive talk of the Communists. It was a sign of the growing stark despair, which was felt more acutely in the circles of the intellectuals.

But even as despair prodded some Jews to look eastward, the most extreme cause for it was at that moment rising to the west, just across the vexed border with Germany.

PART NINE

The Nazi Menace

·1933-1939·

·49·

GERMANY SUCCUMBS

"From time immemorial," observed the *Jewish Chronicle* in its issue of February 17, 1922,

> Germany has been a hotbed of anti-Semitism second only to the Russia of old; but with this difference. Pogroms were unknown in Germany, where what was called *Salonantisemitismus*, or "Parlor anti-Semitism," was in vogue.
>
> Since then, however, all this has changed, and anti-Semitism is showing its head openly all over the country. The aristocracy [for example] have always been anti-Semitic; under the Republic they are more so than ever. They wish to throw upon the German Jew the responsibility for the downfall of the Empire.

This had been the view of one of Germany's supreme warlords, General Erich Ludendorff, when he wrote the previous year:

> The Supreme Command of the Jewish people worked hand in hand with France and England. Maybe it directed both sides. It regarded the coming of war as a means of realizing its political and economic aims, to obtain for the Jews a State in Palestine, recognition of the Jewish people as a nation, and to secure for it a supreme super-State and super-capitalist position in Europe and America. In order to bring this about, the Jews tried to attain the same position in Germany as they held in the countries which are already in their grip. For this purpose the Jewish people needed Germany's defeat.

These *Protocols*-infused remarks may have been inspired in part by anger at Walther Rathenau, the distinguished German-Jewish indus-

419

trialist, who had directed the country's Raw Materials Department during the war and had had several brushes with the general. It was Ludendorff who had secretly demanded an armistice in the fall of 1918, and Rathenau had opposed the idea. Earlier in the war, on the other hand, Rathenau had opposed the disastrous policy of unrestricted submarine warfare, which Ludendorff supported and which helped push the United States into the fight against Germany. Ludendorff got his revenge for all this in November 1920 when, for the benefit of a Reichstag committee of inquiry, he publicly misquoted a remark Rathenau had made in 1914 criticizing the German military leadership. The effect was to make it sound as if Rathenau had hoped for a German defeat. "For very many people," according to Rathenau's friend and biographer, Count Harry Kessler,

> especially in young nationalistic circles, Ludendorff's misinterpretation stamped Rathenau as a noxious criminal on whom it would be an act of patriotism to take vengeance. From then on he was a marked man.

It was three young nationalists who, on the morning of June 24, 1922, demonstrated their patriotism by murdering Walther Rathenau, by then Foreign Minister of the German Republic, as he rode in his open car from his home in suburban Grunewald to his office in the center of Berlin. All of them were from good families. Two of the assassins were killed while evading arrest; the third, twenty-one-year-old Ernst Techow, explained their views at his trial for murder. Techow claimed that "Rathenau had very close and intimate relations with Bolshevik Russia, so that he had even married off his sister with the Communist Radek." Karl Radek, Lenin's personal emissary to Germany, was actually an acceptable figure in German diplomatic circles at that moment, even though he was a communist and by origin a Galician Jew; in any case, Rathenau's sister was married not to him but to a German banker. But this was only the beginning for young Techow, who told the court

> that Rathenau had himself confessed, and boasted, that he was one of the three hundred Elders of Zion, whose purpose and aim was to bring the whole world under Jewish influence, as the example of Bolshevist Russia already showed, where at first all factories, etc., were made public property, then at the suggestion and command of the Jew Lenin, Jewish capital was brought in from abroad, to bring the factories into operation again, and so in this way the whole of Russian national property was now in Jewish hands.

What Rathenau had actually said, writing in the *Neue Freie Presse* of Vienna in December 1909, was: "Three hundred men, all acquainted with each other, control the economic destiny of the Continent." He had certainly counted himself among the three hundred, but they were far from all being Jews. The essential fact was that young Techow, as the judge elicited, had been reading the *Protocols of the Elders of Zion*.

"Behind the murderers and their accomplices," summed up the judge, a true voice of the Republic in danger,

> the chief culprit, irresponsible, fanatical antisemitism, lifts its face, distorted with hatred—antisemitism, which reviles the Jew as such, irrespective of the individual, with all those means of calumny of which that vulgar libel, the *Protocols of the Elders of Zion*, is an example; and in this way sows in confused and immature minds the urge to murder. May the sacrificial death of Rathenau . . . serve to purify the infected air of Germany, now sinking in mortal sickness in this moral barbarism, towards its cure.

Techow was sentenced to hard labor, but the sickness was spreading.

Writing in the comfort of the Landsberg fortress, to which he had been sentenced after the failure of his November 9, 1923, *Putsch* in Munich— an effort participated in by Ludendorff—Adolf Hitler expounded an anti-Semitism that fused two traditions: German racism and the conspiracy theories of the *Protocols of the Elders of Zion*. This combination produced a particularly volatile and dangerous chemistry.

Racist anti-Semitism had been the characteristic German form of contempt for Jews during many generations. In 1831, Dr. Edward Meyer of Hamburg wrote characteristically of the name Jew that it

> designates not only the religion but a whole nationality. . . . We do not hate the faith of the Jews as they would like us to believe, but rather the many ugly peculiarities of these Asiatics which cannot be laid aside so easily through Baptism: the often recurring shame-lessness and arrogance among them, the indecency and frivolity, their noisy demeanour and their often mean basic disposition.

Some of this is echoed by a writer in 1897, who tells of wandering through the Tiergartenstrasse—a middle-class, predominantly Jewish neighborhood of western Berlin—on a Sunday morning:

> Strange sight! There in the midst of German life is an alien and isolated race of men. Loud and self-conscious in their dress, hot-blooded and restless in their manner. An Asiatic horde on the sandy plains of Prussia. . . . Forming among themselves a close corporation, rigorously shut off from the rest of the world. Thus they live

half-willingly in their invisible ghetto, not a living limb of the people, but an alien organism in its body.

These observations are especially significant because they were made by Walther Rathenau, who was not alone among German Jews to feel a deadly ambivalence regarding his origins. Elsewhere, he wrote of "the tragedy of the Aryan race":

> A blond and marvellous people arises in the north. In overflowing fertility it sends wave upon wave into the southern world. Each migration becomes a conquest, each conquest a source of character and civilization. But with the increasing population of the world the waves of the dark people flow ever nearer, the circle of mankind grows narrower. At last a triumph for the south: an oriental religion takes possession of the northern lands. . . .

This is not at all incompatible with a passage in *Mein Kampf*, in which Hitler speculates on the nomad origins of civilization:

> Probably the Aryan was . . . first a nomad, settling in the course of time, but for that very reason he was never a Jew. . . . In [the nomad] the basic idealistic view is present, even if in infinite dilution, hence in his whole being he may seem strange to the Aryan peoples, but not unattractive. In the Jew, however, this attitude is not at all present; for that reason he was never a nomad, but only and always a *parasite* in the body of other peoples.

Mein Kampf abounds with such expressions of the conventional German racist anti-Semitism—including some conveying an almost clinical pathology, such as: "With satanic joy in his face, the black-haired Jewish youth lurks in wait for the unsuspecting girl whom he defiles with his blood, thus stealing her from her people." But the strain of Jew-hatred that appears throughout the book with the deepest and most ominous conviction, for all that, is the one descending from the *Protocols of the Elders of Zion*, about which Hitler writes that the charges of forgery coming from the Jewish-owned *Frankfurter Zeitung* are "the best proof that they are authentic," and that it really is

> completely indifferent from what Jewish brain these disclosures originate; the important thing is that with positively terrifying certainty they reveal the nature and activity of the Jewish people and expose their inner contexts as well as their ultimate final aims.

It was in the light of these "disclosures" that Hitler clearly found the meaning he wanted in the café disputations and newspaper scrutinizings of his youth. "I gradually became aware," he writes of his early days in Vienna,

> that the Social Democratic press was directed predominantly by Jews. . . . I took all the Social Democratic pamphlets I could lay hands on and sought the names of their authors: Jews. I noted the names of the leaders; by far the greatest part were likewise members of the "chosen people." . . . One thing had grown clear to me: the party with whose petty representatives I had been carrying on the most violent struggle for months was, as to leadership, almost exclusively in the hands of a foreign people; for, to my deep and joyful satisfaction, I had at last come to the conclusion that the Jew was no German.

The lesson for more recent years was clear to Hitler, who writes:

> The most frightful example of this kind is offered by Russia, where [the Jew] killed or starved about thirty million people with positively fanatical savagery, in part amid inhuman tortures, in order to give a gang of Jewish journalists and stock exchange bandits domination over a great people.

This is among the main reasons that Hitler concludes the first volume of *Mein Kampf* with a program calling for "A Germanic State of the German Nation." What this was meant to be in practice was not at all clear.

After obtaining the chancellorship of Germany on January 30, 1933, Hitler moved swiftly against the communists and the Social Democrats, and in the wake of the Reichstag fire of February 27, for which the communists were blamed, was soon able to banish these two offspring of Karl Marx from German political life. As for the enemy that Nazism considered to be behind both, the Jews, dealing with them proved a more complex matter. The first weeks after the Nazi accession—and particularly the days after the confirmatory elections of March 5—saw waves of anti-Jewish incidents throughout the country: beatings, daubings, and scattered local boycotts. All this bespoke a Russian type of chaos, and aroused the fury of the press in the onlooking Western democracies. "On the nights of March 9th and 10th," wrote the correspondent of the Chicago *Tribune*,

> bands of Nazis throughout Germany carried out wholesale raids to intimidate the opposition, particularly the Jews. . . . Men and women were insulted, slapped [and] punched in the face, hit over the heads with blackjacks, dragged out of their homes in night clothes and

otherwise molested. . . . Innocent Jews . . . "are taken off to jail and
put to work in a concentration camp where you may stay a year
without any charge being brought against you." Never have I seen
law-abiding citizens living in such unholy fear.

It was not in the interest of the new regime to look as if it could
not control its own vindictive hordes. Moreover, the air of miscellaneous
violence gave the impression everywhere—and to German Jews especially—that anti-Semitism had merely been a demagogic ploy in the Nazi
struggle for power and would now exhaust itself. The answer to all this
was provided by the Nazi leadership on March 28, when it circulated an
order among the party's functionaries throughout the country that said:

> In every local section and organizational arm of the National
> Socialist German Workers' Party, action committees are to be
> formed immediately to plan and execute a boycott of Jewish busi-
> nesses, Jewish merchandise, Jewish doctors, and Jewish law-
> yers. . . . The boycott is not to be casual or miscellaneous; it must
> strike with the force of a single blow. Instructions from the SS and
> SA will be posted at the moment the boycott begins, warning the
> public against entering Jewish business establishments. . . . Its be-
> ginnings will be made known by the posting of placards, announce-
> ments in the press, the distribution of flyers, and so on. The boycott
> is set to strike suddenly on Saturday, April 1, at exactly ten o'clock
> in the morning.

The order was meant as a clear demonstration of the regime's intention
to begin excluding Jews from full participation in German life, even
though this particular boycott was to last only one day. It was also
meant to show that the German people would rally behind such a policy.
"Do not touch even a hair of any Jew's head!" the order warned:

> In that way, international world Jewry will know: the government
> of the national revolution does not hang in empty air, but is the
> representative of the German people in the act of self-creation.
> Whoever attacks it attacks Germany! Whoever slanders it slanders
> the nation! Whoever goes to battle against it is calling sixty-five
> million Germans to battle! We are through with Marxist agitation
> in Germany. . . . National Socialists! Saturday, when ten o'clock
> strikes, Jewry will find out whom it has called to battle.

A vivid description of what happened typically on that fateful morning is provided in *The Oppermanns*, Lion Feuchtwanger's novel of a
Berlin Jewish family during those months of the Nazi takeover. One of
the protagonists, Dr. Edgar Oppermann, sets out as usual for his clinic,

against the warnings of his wife and daughter. "For the Nazis," writes Feuchtwanger, a Jew who experienced that day,

> had directed that on this Saturday, in addition to all other propaganda against the five hundred thousand Jews in the country, a boycott was to be carried out. The Nazis explained that they were forced to give the lie to the statement, endorsed by thousands of documents, that they had employed sinister violence against the Jews. They were giving it the lie by inflicting economic annihilation on the Jews! Many Jews remained at home that day, many others had already left the country. It might be foolish, but Edgar Oppermann could not do otherwise: he went to his clinic.

As he walked through the streets,

> The city looked as though it were a public holiday. People were jostling one another in the streets in order to watch the boycott in operation. He passed innumerable placards: "Jew." "Don't buy from Jews." "Death to Judah." The Nazi mercenaries stood about overbearingly, their legs encased in high boots, and bawled in unison, their silly young mouths wide open:
> "Until the last of the Jews is dead
> There'll be no work and there'll be no bread."

At the clinic, Oppermann performs an operation on a young Christian, Peter Deicke, whose case had been considered hopeless until it was referred to him. Minutes after its successful conclusion, the Brownshirts arrive, drive Edgar and the other Jewish doctors out into the street, and go to the bleary patient's bedside:

> "You swine!" they said to Peter Deicke and on his bandage stamped the words: "I have been shameless enough to allow myself to be treated by a Jew." Then they shouted: "Heil Hitler!" and tramped down the stairs.

Edgar's brother Martin Oppermann, director of the family furniture business, drives to the store and parks nearby to observe:

> They had stationed more than a dozen mercenaries in front of his not particularly large shop, and a man with two stars was in command. All the show-windows were thickly plastered with notices: "Don't buy from Jews," and "Death to Judah." ... "The Jews bring you bad luck," Martin heard the young mercenaries shouting in chorus. He noticed that there was a large sign in the end window inscribed: "May the hands of this Jew rot off."

There were eighteen such placards, and the Brownshirts added insult
to injury by charging the store 2 marks apiece for them. "That day,"
the narrative concludes,

> placards of this sort were pasted on the premises of altogether
> 87,204 Jewish shopkeepers, doctors, and lawyers. A Jewish lawyer
> in Kiel, who offered resistance after an argument arising from the
> mercenaries' demand for payment for pasting up the placards, was
> lynched in a police-cell. Forty-seven Jews committed suicide that
> Saturday.

The day had provided a grim demonstration of what the regime
could do against Jewish businessmen and professionals; within a week,
as if to fulfill its promise, a "Law for the Restoration of the Professional
Civil Service" was passed, which ruled that "officials of non-Aryan origin are to be retired." This applied to all Jewish magistrates and a great
many lawyers, who were swiftly and ruthlessly deprived of their posts.
But businessmen and some other types of professionals—notably physicians—turned out to be a more difficult problem to handle: ideology
and race-hatred were one thing, but running a country was something
else. "In the main," writes the historian Konrad Heiden, who lived
through these events,

> the regime distinguished for a long time between useful and non-
> useful Jews. Jewish lawyers and civil servants were mercilessly
> removed, but Jewish doctors received much better treatment; de-
> spite all the fury against the "Jewish mind," indispensable Jewish
> economic journalists long retained their positions on the business
> press; Jewish technicians kept their places in industry for an aston-
> ishingly long time; after the first boycott mood had cleared, Jewish
> businessmen were graciously assured that they had nothing further
> to fear, and some were prevented by the authorities from emigrat-
> ing or liquidating their businesses—for suddenly they had ceased
> to be Jews and become employers, and employment was what mat-
> tered most to the regime.

In fact, according to Mark Wischnitzer, a historian and social worker
who was at this time with the Hilfsverein der Deutschen Juden in Berlin,

> a special department was set up by the Reich Ministry of Econom-
> ics to deal with complaints of Jewish firms against boycott actions
> or outrages committed by Nazi party members. The Württemburg
> minister of economics forbade discriminatory acts against non-Ar-
> yan workers, artisans and businessmen, on November 24, 1933. The
> Reich minister of the interior [Wilhelm Frick] declared, on January

17, 1934, that anti-Aryan legislation did not apply to the field of private business.

Rather, it was in the cultural fields—those major areas of Jewish subversion and conquest, according to the *Protocols*—that the young regime engaged in its first large-scale purges of Jews. These had begun with the civil-service law of April 7, 1933, then continued from June through October with a succession of laws and regulations excluding Jews from general teaching and from those various communications and entertainment media—journalism, radio, theater, film, and the concert hall—in which they had flourished. The great conductor Wilhelm Furt-wängler, who, as an Aryan, had nothing personally to worry about, wrote a letter objecting to all this to Joseph Goebbels, Minister of Pro-paganda and chairman of the Reich Chamber of Culture, arguing that "in the last analysis I recognize but one dividing line: that between good and bad art." Goebbels had replied: "Art in the absolute sense, as known under liberal democracy, must not be." Indeed, the books that were publicly burned at this time included works by non-Jewish as well as Jewish authors. The refugee exodus of that first year, which included about fifty-three thousand Jews, was essentially the departure of the Weimar culture.

·50·

JEWISH REFUGEES, 1933-1937

Suddenly it was Germany. After more than half a century of an emigration from Eastern Europe, in which a mainly bourgeois and firmly planted German Jewry had presided over the westward passage of the wanderers, they had unexpectedly turned into the victims and refugees themselves. "The center of gravity," observed the HIAS report for 1933,

> had now shifted almost overnight to Western Europe and the problem became more complicated. We are dealing with an element not accustomed to wandering, and the relatives here [in the United States] as well as their people abroad are bewildered and at a loss to know what to do.

In fact, this suddenly uprooted mass of mainly artists, intellectuals, and professionals, most of them middle-aged or older, did not in this first moment of flight readily think of themselves as emigrants. The sudden madness in Germany would surely end soon, and then they would go back. Meanwhile, they did not run far: their chief places of asylum were Belgium, Holland, Switzerland, Austria, even Yugoslavia and Hungary—but above all France, generous to the exiled and the stateless, where a highly visible German-refugee colony formed in Paris. By the end of 1933, they were watching a production of the new work by two of their own, Kurt Weill and Bertolt Brecht, *The Seven Deadly Sins of the Petit Bourgeois*, as if they were still in Berlin.

The initial lack of interest in permanent emigration was indicated by the fact that, in 1933, only 1,445 immigrants entered the United States from Germany, even though its annual quota was 25,967 under the 1924 law. To be sure, part of the problem was the State Department policy on immigrant visas, which, as had now become permanently established, were issued only in the countries of origin. In 1930, responding to the problems of the Depression and unemployment, President Herbert Hoover had ordered American consuls to limit the number of immigrant visas they granted by making severe application of the "likely to become a public charge" principle. By 1933, this had become standard procedure, and restrictionists in Congress took it for granted that even the low quotas established by law would be far from filled in practice. HIAS sent a letter to the new President, Franklin Delano Roosevelt, asking that the 1930 Executive Order be rescinded, but the only reply was an evasive one from the Visa Division of the State Department; this was a delicate matter Roosevelt was not yet ready to take on. But it is not likely that a more liberal policy would have caused the 1933 German quota to be filled; indeed, some sixteen thousand refugees were to return to Germany in 1934.

Zionist feeling aroused by the Nazi takeover, especially among the young, produced a better emigration to Palestine: about sixty-five hundred German Jews went there in 1933. Palestine, in fact, became the one country with regard to which a German-Jewish emigration policy was organized from the outset. By an agreement arrived at in August 1933 between German-Jewish organizations and the Reichsbank, Jewish emigrants from Germany to Palestine could transfer $5,000 of their personal assets at a highly unfavorable rate—better, however, than the nothing with which many refugees had to leave—which they received mostly in German exports at their destination. An office to handle these transactions—called Ha'avarah, or Transfer, in Hebrew—was opened in Tel Aviv. The Ha'avarah agreement soon became a model for other such hoped-for arrangements as the numbers of penniless refugees from Germany mounted.

Concerned observers soon recognized that, in spite of the ambiguities of the situation, a serious German-refugee crisis was in the making, and that improved international facilities were required for the handling of it. In Europe, the HIAS-controlled Emigdirect bureau had finally been approached in 1927 by the Jewish Colonization Association, recognizing that the duplication of such efforts no longer made sense, and a combined HIAS-JCA-Emigdirect organization, called HICEM, had been established. But a higher intervention was now required. In the 1920s there had been a League of Nations High Commissioner for Refugees, the Norwegian explorer and scientist Fridtjof Nansen, but he had died in 1930 and his office, though still in existence, was moribund. In October 1933, the League of Nations Council in Geneva convened to deal with the problem, which was politically delicate. Germany was a new member of the League, and there was considerable reluctance to offend her. "We have no wish," said the Dutch Foreign Minister to the Council,

> to examine why these people have left the country; but we are faced with the fact that thousands of German subjects have crossed the frontiers of the neighboring countries and refuse to return to their homes for reasons which we are not called upon to judge. For us therefore, it is a purely technical problem, and its solution must be found by common agreement.

Pursuing political discretion, the Council established a High Commission for German Refugees, but stationed it in Lausanne rather than Geneva, and made it an administrative council made up of the representatives of fifteen governments. Germany, not at all convinced that these arrangements constituted noninterference in her internal affairs, resigned from the League after all.

As a further gesture to neutrality, the Council appointed as High Commissioner an American, James G. MacDonald, a lawyer and scholar who had been chairman of the American Foreign Policy Association. "MacDonald was physically impressive and morally courageous," in the words of Norman Bentwich, the British lawyer and Zionist leader who worked as his associate:

> He was single-minded in his work, direct in his approach to a problem, had a ready gift of speech, and was prepared to talk in undiplomatic language. He continually crossed the Atlantic, to deal first with the American philanthropic bodies and then with the organizations and governments in Europe.

MacDonald, a Christian, was highly sympathetic to Zionism, and looked to Palestine as the principal refuge for Jews fleeing Germany. During his tenure, Jewish immigration into Palestine reached new heights, attaining an unprecedented figure of 42,359 in 1934, and then 61,854 in 1935. The majority of these were from Poland, but a growing number were from Germany, particularly with the growth of the Youth Aliyah, founded under the leadership of Henrietta Szold in 1933, which sent groups of young people from Germany to collective settlements. It is estimated that some forty-three thousand German Jews went to Palestine from 1933 to the end of 1935.

Until the summer of 1935, all this took place in an atmosphere in which it was hopefully assumed that the Nazi regime had reached the limits of its harassments, and that the vast majority of German Jews—still about five hundred thousand after approximately one hundred thousand had left—would stay put. This was the outlook of the newly created Central Council of Jews in Germany, under Rabbi Leo Baeck, which now and then urged the League of Nations and the world at large not to be too severe in its political treatment of Germany. It was widely assumed at this time that the Jews of Germany were hostages to the good will of the international community, and that the German government treated them in accordance with how it was treated by the world.

There were even some who believed that the Nuremberg Laws of September 1935 were a response to an incident in New York harbor, wherein some Americans had pushed their way onto a German ship and torn down the swastika it was flying. The laws were the first major official move against the Jews in nearly two years. One of them defined citizenship in the Third Reich:

> A citizen of the Reich is only a subject of the state who is of German or related blood, who demonstrates by his behavior that he is determined and suited to serve faithfully the German *Volk* and Reich.

This effectively excluded from citizenship all persons with three or four Jewish grandparents, no matter what religion they professed, as well as many persons with only two. A second law forbade marriage and sexual intercourse between Jews and Aryans, as well as the employment of non-Jewish women under forty-five in Jewish households. A third law made the swastika the official flag of Germany, which the Jews were forbidden to raise over their homes and establishments.

Some thought that the Nuremberg Laws did not necessarily represent a worsening of the situation for German Jews, since they merely defined what were already facts of life and in a sense clarified the hitherto ambiguous status of "non-Aryans"; at any rate, there was no substantial increase in emigration in their aftermath. They were too much for James G. MacDonald, however, who now concluded that the cart was being put before the horse: the problem was not simply the refugees, but the situation creating them. At the end of December 1935, he sent a letter of resignation to the Secretary General of the League of Nations.

"In the period of over two years since the establishment of the office," he wrote,

> conditions in Germany which create refugees have developed so catastrophically that a reconsideration by the League of Nations of the entire situation is essential. The legislative and administrative Party actions against "non-Aryans" were steadily intensified, and culminated in the autumn of 1935, when a series of new laws and

decrees initiated a fresh wave of repression and persecution of a character which was not envisaged in 1933.

Calling for renewed efforts in behalf of refugees, MacDonald adds:

> But in the new circumstances it would not be enough to continue the activities on behalf of those who flee from the Reich. Efforts must be made to remove or mitigate the causes which create German refugees. This could not have been any part of the work of the High Commissioner's office; nor, presumably, could it be a function of the body to which the League may decide to entrust future administrative activities on behalf of the refugees. It is a political function, which properly belongs to the League itself.

The League, he said, must exercise its moral authority and make "a determined appeal to the German Government in the name of humanity and of the principles of the public law of Europe." And he warned: "In the present economic conditions of the world, the European States, and even those overseas, have only a limited power of absorption of refugees. The problem must be tackled at its source if disaster is to be avoided."

The League appointed Sir Neill Malcolm of Great Britain as MacDonald's successor, but for the moment the principal responsibility for the refugee question shifted elsewhere. Jewish organizations in Western Europe, Great Britain, and the United States created a Council for German Jewry to carry on the main work. Its leadership included Zionists, as well as non-Zionists who recognized that, in the circumstances, Palestine had to be looked upon as the major refuge. When MacDonald spoke before the Zionist Congress in the summer of 1935, he had said: "The daily grace in the High Commissioner's Office was 'Thank God for Palestine.' "

Then the lot of German Jewry seemed to improve slightly, or at any rate to become stabilized. "While Jewish organizations abroad are busy with plans for transferring from Germany as many Jews as possible," the *Jewish Chronicle* reported on January 17, 1936,

> it was disclosed in Berlin that opinion in German Government circles is divided as to whether it is entirely wise to prevent a large exodus of Jews. Extremists in the Cabinet are of the opinion that it is worth while to get rid of the Jews at any price. More moderate elements, however, are now beginning to fear that their country is facing an economic collapse and believe that no matter how much Germany wishes to see a decline in her Jewish population, a system of selective emigration must be instituted and the elements useful

to the economic interests of the country must not be permitted to leave the Reich.

The leader of these "moderate elements" was the Minister for Economic Affairs, Dr. Hjalmar Schacht, who had brilliantly engineered the recovery of the German mark in 1924 after the preceding runaway inflation. His present confrontation with the elements who had "Aryanized" German culture in 1933 and were now undertaking the "Aryanization" of the country's commercial and financial life was dramatized in an article, entitled "Schacht vs. Goebbels," that appeared in the *Jewish Chronicle* the following month. It ran:

> Jakob Mendelssohn, a Jewish art dealer at Nuremberg, has been notified by the Reich Chamber of Arts that he has to liquidate his business on the ground that he lacks the qualification required for a responsible share in furthering German culture. It will be remembered that six months ago similar notices were issued to almost all the Munich art dealers. They were withdrawn, however, as Dr. Schacht, the Reich Minister of Economics, insisted that these dealers were under the jurisdiction of the Chamber of Commerce and not under the Chamber of Art.

Schacht certainly was foremost among those responsible for a widespread cleaning-up of anti-Jewish manifestations when Germany played host to the 1936 Olympic Games, at Garmisch-Partenkirchen in Bavaria in February, and in August in the vast Reichsportfeld built outside Berlin for the occasion. "The signs *'Juden unerwünscht'* ('Jews not welcome')," William L. Shirer recalls, "were quietly hauled down from the shops, hotels, beer gardens and places of public entertainment, the persecution of the Jews and of the . . . Christian churches temporarily halted, and the country put on its best behavior." Copies of Julius Streicher's scurrilous anti-Semitic rag *Der Stürmer* were removed from their usually prominent display positions on newsstands, and the new Germany showed the face of a happy land covered with groups of marching, singing, camping youth. Most who went to the Olympics had a wonderful experience and were ready to tell this to a world eager for peace and reconciliation. With Italy playing the role of Fascist villain in ravaged Ethiopia, German troops could even occupy the Rhineland—German territory, after all—in March 1936, violating the Treaty of Versailles, without too much protest from the family of nations.

As for the Jewish question, if there was a preeminent villain in the eyes of the world in 1936, it was Poland. Norman Bentwich, devoting himself at this time to dealing "constructively with the larger Jewish problem

of Europe," considered it to be "most acute in Poland." Marshal Pilsudski had died in May 1935, and the relatively friendly attitude toward
Poland's Jews that he seemed to represent had quickly given way to a
pronounced hostility. Even the moderate Peasant Party was quick to
show a certain influence emanating from Nazi Germany, declaring that
although "all citizens in Poland irrespective of creed and nationality
must enjoy equal rights," the Jews, on the other hand,

> cannot be assimilated and are a consciously alien nation within Po-
> land. As a middle class they occupy a far more important position
> in Poland than in other countries, so that the Poles have no middle
> class of their own. It is, therefore, most vital for the Polish state
> that these middle-class functions shall more and more pass into the
> hands of the Poles. . . . While we profess the principle of equal rights
> for the Jews in Poland, we shall nevertheless aim to solve the Jew-
> ish problem through the emigration of Jews to Palestine and other
> places.

The Peasant Party was determined not to realize this goal "through
fruitless acts of violence, which only brutalize the nation," but the parties of the right did not have such scruples. The National Democrats,
who revived their call for a boycott, also stimulated pogroms. On March
9, 1936, a full-scale pogrom occurred in Przytyk, resulting in the death
of three Jews; many more were to follow.

This was part of a campaign to get masses of Jews to leave the
country. "The Jews," said the anti-Semitic *Dziennik Narodowy (People's Daily)* of Warsaw in August 1936,

> would rather change Poland into a Jewish State than go. They will
> never go of their own free will. They must be forced out by all
> means. A sharp and drastic anti-Jewish campaign is needed all over
> the country, both economic and political.

The government, while expressing itself in more moderate terms, was
essentially in agreement with this view. "Forty per cent of all Jews in
Poland," said a Polish Foreign Office communiqué that summer,

> derive their living from trade. A very great proportion of them are
> in the professions. The present crisis dealt a grave blow to all these
> economically unsound classes of Jews, of whom a million have no
> basis of existence at all. Poland has no capital. She must seek the
> solution of her population problem, at least partially, in emigration.
> This aim, important for the problem of overpopulation as a whole,
> is of equal importance for the Jewish problem in Poland.

The communiqué went on to offer a startling proposal. "Palestine cannot absorb the necessary numbers," it said:

> Jewish emigration must therefore seek new territories overseas. The way to new territories must be found and shown to the Jews by all those countries which are interested in furthering Jewish emigration.

At the League of Nations session that fall, the Polish delegation made clear what was meant by this, proposing that a Jewish colony be founded on the French-held island of Madagascar. This island of about 228,000 square miles in the Indian Ocean off the east coast of Africa then had a population of about 3 million natives and thirty-six thousand European colonists. In 1931, some German writers had proposed it for Jewish colonization, perhaps influenced by the East African territorial offer the British government had made to the Zionists in 1903. Heinrich Himmler, leader of the SS, was said to have suggested the idea to Hitler in 1934. It had evidently already been discussed by Polish and French diplomats as well, and in May 1937, Premier Léon Blum—himself a Jew—consented to the dispatch of a Polish mission to Madagascar to study its possibilities for Jewish colonization. The French Colonial Office then even suggested the plan to representatives of the American Jewish Joint Distribution Committee, who would not consider it.

At any rate, the Polish government had been correct in considering the prospects for Palestine to be fading. In April 1936, a series of Arab demonstrations had quickly spread from Palestine to adjacent areas and assumed the aspect of a general rebellion. When the British government sent a six-man commission there under Lord Peel to investigate, a severe restriction was placed on Jewish immigration. In July 1937, the Peel Commission recommended the partitioning of Palestine into a Jewish and an Arab state, along with continuing Mandatory control of Jerusalem and the route to it; but a British government too weary to implement these recommendations preferred to follow the easier path of immigration restriction. In 1937, only 10,536 Jewish immigrants entered Palestine. This last major refuge for European Jewry was closing down just as the Jewish situation in Germany was about to take a turn for the worse.

·51·

FROM THE *ANSCHLUSS* TO EVIAN, MARCH-JULY 1938

After weeks of threats and intimidations, German troops occupied Austria on Saturday morning, March 12, 1938, without firing a shot. Visiting his home town of Linz later that day, Hitler said: "If Providence once called me forth from this town to be the leader of the Reich, it must in doing so have charged me with a mission, and that mission could only be to restore my dear homeland to the German Reich." That homeland's separate name and existence were swiftly obliterated, and its provinces incorporated into the greater Germany.

The Jewish question was also swiftly dealt with. "For the first few weeks," writes William L. Shirer, who was in Vienna at the time,

> the behavior of the Vienna Nazis was worse than anything I had seen in Germany. . . . Day after day large numbers of Jewish men and women could be seen scrubbing Schuschnigg signs off the sidewalk and cleaning the gutters. While they worked on their hands and knees with jeering storm troopers standing over them, crowds gathered to taunt them. Hundreds of Jews, men and women, were picked off the streets and put to work cleaning public latrines and the toilets of the barracks where the S.A. and the S.S. were quartered.

Thousands of Jews were jailed on various pretexts and their property was confiscated. "The plight of the Jews in Austria," wrote the Vienna correspondent of *The New York Times*, G. R. Gedye,

> is much worse than that of the Jews in Germany at the worst period there. In Austria, overnight, Vienna's 200,000 Jews were made free game for mobs, despoiled of their property, deprived of police pro-

436

tection, ejected from employment, and barred from sources of relief.

It was as if all the energy of anti-Semitism that had been accumulating in Germany for the past five years had been unleashed with sudden force upon Austria, almost all of whose Jews were concentrated in Vienna. Moreover, a man with a bureaucratic apparatus had also suddenly come into being to guide that force—SS Untersturmführer Adolf Eichmann, director of the Department of Jewish Affairs in the Headquarters division of the Reich Security Office. To prepare for this position, he had studied Hebrew and Yiddish and had traveled in Palestine, even letting it be believed that he had been born in one of the German colonies there. Arriving in Vienna less than a week after the *Anschluss*, he quickly established a Central Office for Jewish Emigration in the former Rothschild mansion on Prinz Eugen Street. For, after seeing the wanton brutality and chaos in Vienna, he had decided to introduce order into the handling of the Jewish question. As many Jews as possible had to leave.

"It all went like an assembly line," Eichmann was to say. Jews were called into the Central Office and, one by one, were stripped of their property, livelihood, and rights, then issued a passport with the letter "J" stamped on it, valid for two weeks; at the end of that time, if the bearer had not obtained a visa, he or she was subject to imprisonment in a concentration camp. "It was terrible, terrible," according to the testimony of Dr. Franz Eliezer Meyer, who was part of a Jewish delegation brought down from Berlin to see what was in store for them:

> Like a factory . . . A man was just passed on like an inanimate object. . . . In Berlin it was not like that at the time. We could still argue, at least, with the authorities. At that time we still thought we could tell him "No," and we said that this was unthinkable in Berlin.

The effect this had upon the representatives of foreign governments in Vienna is described by Israel Cohen, who had been sent by the Zionist Organization in London to investigate:

> Thousands of Jews were besieging the Embassies and Consulates of different Governments in frantic efforts to obtain visas. Their state of despair was evidenced by the fact that they began queuing up at midnight, members of a family relieving one another, so as to make sure of being admitted into the coveted presence the following day. At the British Consulate I found the courtyard, the staircase, and the waiting-room crammed with anxious-looking men

and women; and I was told that over 6,000 had already applied for permits for Palestine and the British Dominions.

A new emergency of worldwide import had arisen. "The Jews of the world," reflected the *Jewish Chronicle* on March 18,

> thus find themselves confronted by an additional problem. What is to be done with their gravely beset Austrian coreligionists—and for their other brethren who may be engulfed in the ever-widening torrent of Nazi power and influence? They can open their purses once again. They can appeal with increased confidence to the nations now roused to the German menace. They can ask, with greater force, for the provision of havens for the fugitives.

Of the nations roused to the German menace, the United States was the first to respond to the new problem with an initiative. On March 24, the State Department issued this communication to the press:

> The government has become so impressed with the urgency of the problem of political refugees that it has inquired of a number of governments in Europe and in this hemisphere whether they would be willing to cooperate in setting up a special committee for the purpose of facilitating the emigration from Austria, and presumably from Germany, of political refugees.

At a press conference at his Warm Springs retreat the next day, President Roosevelt announced that he was sending out invitations to twenty-nine nations to take part in a conference for the purpose stated. He also said that he would ask the State Department to combine the German and Austrian immigration quotas and see to it that the resulting total of 27,370 a year be met in full.

Roosevelt was in effect rescinding the Hoover Executive Order of 1930, and this was not without some political risk. In Congress and in the public at large, though there was growing sympathy for the plight of the victims of Nazism, there was no change of heart at all on the subject of immigration: the Depression was still on. A poll published by *Fortune* magazine three months later showed 67.4 percent of the respondents agreeing that "with conditions as they are we should try to keep [refugees] out." Only 18.2 percent in effect agreed with Roosevelt's position that "we should allow them to come but not raise our immigration quotas." A mere 4.9 percent favored raising the quotas. The rest were undecided. In the House, Representative Thomas A. Jenkins of Ohio argued that the President was proposing to "violate the immigration policies under which the Nation is supposed to have been operating for the last 7 or 8 years. . . . For years the policy has been to stay within 10 percent of quotas."

Under the circumstances, then, and despite considerable sympathy for the refugees on the part of a number of people close to the President, there could be no thought of trying to raise the immigration quotas. That could only have been done by act of Congress, and it was feared that any such attempt would result in a backlash and the lowering of quotas. For this reason above all, the State Department communication of March 24 had carried a second paragraph saying that "it should be understood that no country would be expected or asked to receive a greater number of immigrants than is permitted by its existing legislation."

This proviso was convenient for other governments as well, but what about the British Mandatory in Palestine? Immigration to Palestine was controlled by administrative policy, not by legislation. Could the British government be persuaded to liberalize the policy that had become so severe since the outbreak of the Arab rebellion in 1936? The prospects were not good.

It soon became clear that the British were not going to allow Palestine to become a matter of serious consideration at President Roosevelt's proposed conference, which was scheduled to begin July 6 at the French resort of Evian-les-Bains. This was first signaled by the appointment, as chairman of the British delegation, of Lord Winterton, "a notorious opponent of Zionism and a friend of the Arabs," in the opinion of Arthur Ruppin, the head of the Jewish Agency group that attended the conference as observers and consultants. Then the point was made explicit in Evian just before the opening of the conference, when members of the British delegation met with the chairman of the American delegation, Myron Taylor. A former chairman of United States Steel and now an ardent public servant, Taylor said that he and his colleagues wanted to hear Dr. Chaim Weizmann present his case for Palestine immigration during the conference. Sir Michael Palairet, the deputy head of the British delegation, replied that his government "would naturally prefer that this meeting should not take place." And it did not. "Our American cousins," the *Jewish Chronicle* correspondent commented on this matter,

> have an idea, generally exaggerated if not wholly groundless, that their representatives are but children in the hands of our Machiavellian diplomacy. Nevertheless, the obliging silence which Mr. Myron Taylor and his colleagues, whether on their own initiative, or on instruction from Washington, have only too patently felt con-

strained to observe about this particular issue is the kind of thing
that is used to support that transatlantic prejudice.

Not that the British delegation was able to maintain complete silence on the issue. In his opening remarks to the conference, after pointing out that the United Kingdom itself—highly industrialized, thickly
populated, and still suffering grave unemployment—could not take immigrants, Lord Winterton went on to say:

> His Majesty's Government is also studying attentively the pos-
> sibilities that may present themselves for admitting refugees in its
> overseas colonies and territories. The question is not simple. The
> economic and social factors that apply in the United Kingdom also
> prevail in them, yet are more complicated by considerations of cli-
> mate, race, and politics. Many of the overseas territories are al-
> ready overpopulated, others are entirely or in some special way
> inappropriate for the settlement of Europeans, while in yet others
> the local and political conditions hinder or prevent any significant
> immigration. These factors impose strict limitations on the possi-
> bilities for offering asylum to European refugees, but His Majesty's
> Government does not despair that some of its colonial territories
> might play a role in their turn, even if it be a relatively secondary
> role in the contribution to the solution of the problem.

This tepid offering and veiled reference to Palestine finally, under
some pressure, yielded to a more explicit statement on the last day of
the conference, when Winterton said:

> The committee is perhaps expecting me to present some ob-
> servations as the representative of the Power which holds the Man-
> date for Palestine. It has been asserted in some circles that the
> problem as a whole, at least as it concerns the Jewish refugees,
> could be solved if only the doors of Palestine were opened wide to
> Jewish immigrants, without restrictions of any sort. I must state,
> as clearly as possible, that I consider any proposition of this sort to
> be entirely untenable. First of all, Palestine is not a large country,
> and besides, there are special considerations, which come out of the
> terms of the Mandate as well as the local situation, which cannot
> be ignored.

Stressing that the Mandatory's obligation was to facilitate Jewish immigration "under appropriate conditions," Winterton pointed out that
about three hundred thousand Jews had entered Palestine since 1920,
and about forty thousand German Jews in recent years. He reminded
his listeners that the present vexed state of affairs there had led to
"proposals tending to introduce a radical transformation in the political

structure of the country." While these proposals were being investigated,

> it has appeared to be indispensable, not, to be sure, to interrupt Jewish immigration—this has never been envisaged—but to subject it to certain restrictions of a purely temporary and exceptional character, having for their goal to maintain, within reasonable limits, the population within its present numerical proportions, while awaiting a final decision.

Until that time, however,

> our opinion is that the question of Palestine constitutes a separate case, and that it cannot usefully be entered into consideration at this stage with regard to the general problems being examined at the present conference.

Winterton then went on, with no apparent sense of the irony, to suggest that his government might be able to offer some land in Kenya.

During the conference, Australia showed no more generosity than Britain had, even though there had been some hopes regarding its vast expanses and a good deal of talk about organized settlement in the Kimberleys district in the far west. T. W. White, the Australian delegate, pointed out that, though his was indeed a land of immigration, this "migration has been principally British." Alluding to a small Jewish immigration that had been going on—the annual figures were in the hundreds—he said that Australia could do no more,

> for it is understandable that, in a young country, the human influx that one prefers would be that which comes from the source where the majority of its citizens originated, and it would not be possible to grant unjustifiable privileges to a non-British category of subjects without injustice for the others. It is also no doubt understandable that, since we have no actual race problem, we are not desirous of introducing one among us by encouraging any sort of plan of foreign migration in considerable proportions.

The representatives of the Latin American countries expressed reluctance to accept immigrants of the type that most of the German and Austrian Jews were, saying they wanted agricultural settlers. The delegate from Colombia turned the discussion in another direction entirely by raising the moral question in what they were proposing to do. Can a state, he asked,

without shaking the very foundations of our civilization—of all civilization—arbitrarily strip away the nationality of a whole class of
its citizens, thereby making them stateless, whom no country is
obliged to receive on its territory. Can a state, acting in this way,
cast out onto the other states the citizens it wants to get rid of, and
can it unload upon others the consequences of a disastrous internal
policy?

Myron Taylor had put it in a more bluntly American way, speaking
against the mass "dumping" of unfortunate peoples. The question was:
should the legitimate nations of the world in effect cooperate with Nazi
Germany by accepting populations that the latter wished to dump upon
them? Human decency dictated only one course, but it had moral complications—and potential dangers as a precedent, which were signaled
at the conference by the presence of delegates from Poland, Hungary,
and Rumania, who had not been invited but had come as observers. "It
was always a moot point," mused the *Jewish Chronicle*'s correspondent
with regard to those three countries,

> whether a serious mistake was not made in omitting to invite the
> attendance of powers who have also raised the question of "sur
> plus" racial and religious minorities. Because Nazi Germany has
> treated the minorities in question more outrageously, she is, appar
> ently, to receive special consideration. A premium is thus placed on
> persecution.

These were frightening words, but surely no less frightening to the
conference participants was the prospect of having the nearly five million Jews of Poland, Hungary, and Rumania "dumped" upon the world.
How many could imagine that, in just a few years, the alternative was
to be annihilation?

"The published outcome of the conference at Evian," recalled Norman
Bentwich, who had appeared before it as representative of the Council
for German Jewry, "seemed flat, like the mineral water of the place.
The exclusion of Palestine from the survey of countries of settlement
was stultifying." But he also acknowledged that

> something was gained. The American example of re-opening immi
> gration to the limit of the German quota, which amounted to nearly
> 30,000 a year, was followed by a few other states. Notably the Com
> monwealth of Australia, which hitherto had been niggardly in the
> admission of alien refugees, and at the Conference adopted a cau
> tious tone, announced a few months later her willingness to admit
> 5,000 a year.

Even the Jewish Agency's Arthur Ruppin was optimistic in spite of everything. "The conference was poorly prepared," he acknowledged in his diary during the proceedings,

> and its start was rather chaotic. The Jewish organizations also came without a definite plan, but gradually something seems to be taking shape on both sides: (a) a permanent committee is to be formed to deal with the emigration from Germany; (b) the German government must be asked to permit the emigrants to bring out some money; (c) the United States will offer its full quota for Germany and Austria (27,300).

At the conference's end, he said to the press:

> Evian is the first silver lining in the dark clouds hanging over the Jews since the Nazis came to power. There is no reason for pessimism regarding the Evian results. The intergovernmental body which is to be set up will play a big role in the emigration problem.

Ruppin, who hoped the Intergovernmental Committee on Refugees created by the conference would also consider East European Jewry, thought that, even under the current quotas—and assuming that the Mandatory would soon lift its "temporary and exceptional" restrictions upon immigration—the United States and Palestine together could solve the German-Austrian refugee problem "within six years."

·52·

THE NIGHT OF BROKEN GLASS

The *Anschluss* had opened a new era in the growth of Nazi Germany and its relations with the world at large. For all Hitler's previous violations of the Treaty of Versailles—the rearming of Germany, the occupation of the Saar and Ruhr valleys—he had never made any moves beyond the borders of Germany. But now that he had achieved an extraterritorial conquest, it was widely anticipated that he would not stop at Austria. After all, if he was claiming to redeem alienated German populations, there was Danzig and—now most glaringly—the Sudetenland in westernmost Czechoslovakia, containing some three million Germans and surrounded on three sides by the Greater Reich.

The *Anschluss* had barely been completed before Hitler began making known his desire for a Sudetenland settlement; and the appeasement-minded governments of France and Britain hastened to accommodate him. During the course of Prime Minister Chamberlain's three humiliating voyages to Germany during the summer and early fall of 1938, culminating in the ill-famed conference at Munich on September 29, few observers doubted that the fate not merely of the Sudetenland, but of Czechoslovakia itself, was at stake. "Editorial opinion gathered from newspapers throughout the United States," *The New York Times* had reported on September 21, "reveals the sentiment that Czechoslovakia has been betrayed by France and Britain." Moreover, according to the *Times* survey, the feeling was "that war has only been postponed, not avoided."

Nevertheless, Americans shared in the virtually audible sigh of relief emitted by the British and French when Chamberlain came home from Munich—where the Sudetenland had been carved out and turned over to the Reich—proclaiming "peace in our time." President Roosevelt, champing at the bit of isolationism, had even tried for influence in the crisis by sending an open letter to Hitler on September 27. "The government of the United States," he said carefully, "has no political involvements in Europe and will assume no obligations in the conduct of the present negotiations. Yet in our own right we recognize our responsibilities as part of a world of neighbors." There was little more he could do; for, as the *Times* survey of September 21 also had made clear, American editorial opinion held predominantly "that it is not the business of the US to have any part in the affair."

Yet Roosevelt's growing involvement was significant, for there rarely had been a time before this when the Nazi leadership was not concerned about American public opinion. Indeed, this concern had been prominent among the forces tending to apply restraints upon anti-Jewish excesses; Hitler and his henchmen, no less than many of the friendlier statesmen of Great Britain, regarded Jewish influence as significant upon American opinion in general and upon Roosevelt's outlook in particular. But the time for such scruples was rapidly disappearing. First over Austria, and now over Czechoslovakia, Hitler had made the powers of the world acquiesce in his bullying; he certainly was not going to worry any longer about the disapproval of a president and a public determined to stay out of European hot waters. This new unconcern was bound to affect his treatment of Jews.

For one thing, the practice of "dumping" had been markedly stepped up since the *Anschluss*. The most notorious of such instances had been the expulsions occurring that spring in the Burgenland, in eastern Austria. "With ruthless precision," reported the *Jewish Chronicle*,

> the Nazis have been expelling Jews from a fifty-kilometer zone of Austria's territory. . . . One such case was so frightful as to arouse world indignation last week. Fifty-one Jews expelled from the Burgenland province were marooned by the Nazis on a breakwater in the Danube and were rescued by the inhabitants of the Czech town of Theben, who heard their cries of distress.

This was not the end of their troubles, for the Czechoslovakian government, fearing that all of Burgenland's Jews might be dumped into their country, refused to accept them. Some of the group made their way to Hungary, from which they were promptly deported back into Austria; others reached Yugoslavia, where they were taken in reluctantly and on a temporary basis. On September 2, the *Jewish Chronicle* wrote:

> The persistent "dumping" of German Jews across the frontiers of countries bordering on Germany is causing great concern.
> Hardly a day passes without an average of fifty Jews being

forced to swim rivers, climb mountains, crawl through thickets and across marshes to evade detection in passing the frontiers of Switzerland, Holland, Belgium, Czechoslovakia and Luxembourg. They arrive penniless, stripped of everything, their clothing in rags, to face immediate deportation to the Reich unless the local Jewish communities guarantee their temporary maintenance and emigration.

These refugees now total about 10,000, and their sheltering and feeding cost the American Joint Distribution Committee about [$5,000] daily. Their emigration overseas would cost approximately [$1.5 million].

The worst case of dumping occurred in October and was to have historic consequences. The provocation was provided by the Polish government, which issued an order on October 6, to go into effect at the end of the month, revoking the passports of Polish citizens who had lived abroad more than five years, unless they obtained special visas. The German government had no doubt that this was aimed at the roughly twenty thousand Polish Jews still living in Germany, many of them for twenty years or more. If nothing were done by November 1, Germany would have this many stateless Jews on its hands.

"On October 27, 1938—it was Thursday night at eight o'clock," Zindel Grynszpan, a tailor of Hanover, was to recall,

a policeman came and told us to come to Region II [police headquarters]. He said, "You are going to come back immediately; you shouldn't take anything with you. Take your passports."

When I reached the Region, I saw a large number of people; . . . The police were shouting, "Sign, sign, sign." I had to sign, as everyone did. . . .

They took us to the concert hall on the bank of the Leine. . . . There we stayed until Friday night, about twenty-four hours; then they took us in police trucks, in prisoners' vans, about twenty in each truck, to the railroad station. The streets were filled with people shouting, "The Jews to Palestine!"

After that, they took us by train to Neubenschen on the German-Polish border. . . .

When we reached the border, we were searched to see if anybody had money, and if anybody had more than ten marks, the rest was taken from him. . . .

The SS were giving us, as it were, protective custody, and we walked two kilometers on foot to the Polish border. . . . The SS men whipped us and hit those who fell behind, and blood was flowing on the road. . . .

Then a Polish general and some officers arrived. They examined our papers and saw that we were Polish citizens, and they decided to let us enter the country. They took us to a village [Zban-szyn] of about six thousand people, even though we were twelve thousand. The rain was driving hard, people were fainting. . . . There was no food.

The Joint Distribution Committee immediately took the responsibility for these people, and began a new search for funds.

"Dear Herschel," wrote Zindel Grynszpan's daughter Bertha from Zbanszyn to her seventeen-year-old brother in Paris: "You must have heard about the disaster. . . ." He certainly had, for the newspapers were full of it. An unstable young man, living footloose and by now illegally at the home of relatives in Paris, Herschel Grynszpan was, after his fashion, an ardent Jewish nationalist, who had belonged to a Zionist group and once dreamed of settling in Palestine. Now he had a more dramatic idea. Perhaps something in the Paris atmosphere had made him think of Sholem Schwartzbard, the Ukrainian Jew who had shot and killed Simon Petlura on one of its streets in 1926 and, pleading retribution for the murder of his people, had been acquitted by a French court. There had also been a more recent and more pertinent incident. In February 1936, the Nazi leader in Switzerland, Wilhelm Gustloff, had been shot down in Davos by a twenty-five-year-old Jewish medical student named David Frankfurter. A Swiss court had found Frankfurter guilty and sentenced him to eighteen years in prison, and, despite Nazi threats and hints of reprisals, that had been the end of it. Of course, that had been the year of the Olympics, when Germany was on its best behavior.

Between nine-thirty and ten o'clock in the morning of November 7, Grynszpan arrived at the German embassy in Paris with a newly pur-chased 6.35-caliber loaded pistol in his pocket. Claiming to have a pack-age to deliver, he was ushered by an incautious porter to the office of the highest official present at that hour, Third Secretary Ernst vom Rath, and fired five shots at the symbol of Nazism that sat in front of him. Only two of them hit their target, one causing a relatively harmless shoulder wound, the other inflicting severe internal damage. The twenty-nine-year-old vom Rath was still alive when brought to the hospital, but in serious condition. Grynszpan readily surrendered himself to the po-lice.

Vom Rath died on Wednesday, November 9, which happened to be the fifteenth anniversary of Hitler's abortive *Putsch* of 1923. The Führer himself was at a celebration in the Munich Town Hall when he received the news about vom Rath. He left without giving his speech, but he is said to have paused long enough to say to the gathering, "The SA should be allowed to have a fling." The lines of authority leading to the ensuing events have never become quite clear, but, whoever ordered what, the night of November 9–10, 1938, became an opportunity for many Germans to demonstrate what an efficiently organized, countrywide pogrom could be.

"Despite authoritative warnings against anti-Jewish excesses issued before news of the death of Ernst vom Rath," *The New York Times* reported on November 10,

> violent anti-Jewish demonstrations broke out all over Berlin early this morning.
>
> Raiding squads of young men roamed unhindered through the principal shopping districts, breaking shop windows with metal weapons, looting or tossing merchandise into the streets or into passing vehicles and leaving the unprotected Jewish shops to the mercy of vandals who followed in this trail in an unprecedented show of violence.
>
> While crowds were still touring the streets at 7 a.m., viewing the debris left behind in all the principal shopping districts, Berlin fire-fighting forces were striving to control the burning of the city's largest synagogue, in the Fasanenstrasse, in the fashionable West End.

Synagogue-burning, along with window-smashing, proved to be the central activity in the riots that broke out that night, not just in Berlin but in towns and cities all over Germany and Austria. Here is a sample report, delivered the next day by the leader of the SA brigade in Starkenburg, near Darmstadt:

> At 3:00 A.M. on November 10, 1938, the following order reached me:
>
> "At the command of the group leader, the brigade is immediately to blow up or set fire to a total of fifty Jewish synagogues.
>
> "Adjoining buildings occupied by the Aryan population must not be harmed. The action is to be carried out in civilian clothes. Rioting or plundering is to be prevented. . . ."
>
> The flag-group leaders were immediately contacted by me and given detailed instructions, after which they immediately began the operation.

The Brigadeführer then systematically lists the destructions of synagogues—thirty-six in all, in as many different towns—performed by his five flag-groups, designating whether they were "destroyed by fire," "destroyed by explosion," or merely had suffered the demolition of their interiors.

In addition to the enormous destruction of property, sacred and profane, there were beatings, roundups, humiliations, and arrests, large numbers of Jews being hauled off to the concentration camps at Sachsenhausen, Buchenwald, and Dachau. "Towards noon," recalled a teacher at the Baden-Baden gymnasium,

> the main gates were opened and our group, disarmed and arrayed in orderly ranks by the guards, was marched across town behind a Star of David over which was written, "God, do not abandon us." . . .
>
> The parade reached the synagogue, whose top steps were already lined with people in uniform and in civilian clothing. Passing in front of them, we had to endure their petty insults. . . .
>
> The interior of the synagogue had changed completely. It was swarming with SS troops. There were large numbers of them in the women's gallery, where they were laying electric cables. . . .
>
> Suddenly a thick, arrogant voice commanded, "You will all sing the *Horst Wessel Lied.*" We were forced to sing it twice. Then I was summoned to the dais to read a passage from *Mein Kampf.* I began softly, but the SS trooper behind me grew irritated and struck me on the back of my neck. Those who read afterwards received the same treatment. . . .
>
> We were taken from the synagogue to the Central Hotel. . . . Then the Rabbi, ashen-faced, came into the dining room. "Our synagogue is on fire." Now we understood the electric cables. . . .
>
> A bus was waiting outside the door. . . . We ran to the bus, and whoever did not run fast enough was beaten. At the station a train arrived to collect the Jews from our area. . . . After Karlsruhe, when the train branched off toward Stuttgart, the only word to be heard was the terrible name Dachau.

A summary of the work of that night and morning was provided by SS Security Chief Reinhard Heydrich:

> The scope of the destruction of Jewish business establishments and residences cannot yet be set out in figures. As far as can be determined, the figures are: 815 destroyed business establishments, twenty-nine warehouses set fire to or otherwise destroyed, 171 residential buildings set fire to or otherwise destroyed. . . .
>
> As for synagogues, 191 were set fire to, another seventy-six completely demolished. Also, eleven community centers, cemetery chapels, and the like were set fire to, and another three completely demolished.
>
> Around twenty thousand Jews were taken into custody, as well as seven Aryans and three foreigners. The last were held for their own safety.

The dead numbered thirty-six, with another thirty-six in serious condition. The dead and wounded are Jews. . . .

Since the damage of property—much of it owned by "Aryans" from whom Jewish businesses and residences were rented—was heavy, the government saw fit to fine the Jewish community 1 billion marks to cover the costs. This was to be raised by a 20-percent tax on all assets owned by Jews.

·53·

THE NEW REFUGEE CRISIS

The Nazi regime had once again flouted the world's good will, and had delivered a fillip in the face of appeasement. While the governments of France and Britain pondered how best to respond in the face of public revulsion at home, President Roosevelt, free of any pactual obligations, took the occasion to speak out first in the name of outraged democracy. "The news of the past few days from Germany," he said in a statement issued to the press on November 15,

> has deeply shocked public opinion in the United States. Such news from any part of the world would inevitably produce a similarly profound reaction among American people in every part of the nation.
>
> I myself could scarcely believe that such things could occur in a twentieth-century civilization.
>
> With a view to gaining a first-hand picture of the situation in Germany I asked the Secretary of State to order our Ambassador in Berlin to return at once for report and consultation.

The New York Times was careful to stress that the summoning of Ambassador Hugh S. Wilson was "technically . . . not a recall," but added that "actually it carried just that implication."

Prime Minister Chamberlain, who had hitherto avoided the Jewish question as a potential obstacle to good relations with Germany, now realized that it was an obstacle that had to be removed. "In these circumstances," wrote the *New York Times* London correspondent,

> it is felt that the only alternative is to organize and subsidize vast emigration with the least possible delay or to leave the Jews in Germany where their plight would be a constant irritant to Anglo-

German friendship and an obstacle to the "appeasement" on which
Mr. Chamberlain has set his heart.

Emigration had once again become the central issue.

The burden of the emigration problem was still theoretically in the
hands of the Intergovernmental Committee on Refugees created by the
Evian conference. At the end of the formal Evian meetings on July 15,
the committee had transferred its permanent headquarters to London—
for the British, still wary of this American creation in rivalry to Sir
Neill Malcolm's League of Nations High Commission on German Refugees, would not have suffered its being anywhere else. Its chairman
was George Rublee, a seventy-year-old American lawyer and public
servant, and an old friend of the President's. From the outset, Rublee
regarded it as his task to negotiate an emigration agreement with the
German government.

There were already several distinguished Americans, such as the
columnist Dorothy Thompson and the philanthropist Marshall Field, who
were calling upon the country to adopt a more generous attitude toward
refugees; but even among these, there was a sense of the practical problems to be considered. In her *New York Times* column of August 22,
1938, Anne O'Hare McCormick, arguing that Americans were "a society
of émigrés," and that "democracy cannot survive and admit that minorities can be denied the right to existence," had suggested that the United States ought to "take . . . over" the refugee problem and "distribute
over this continent all the citizens kicked out of Germany on racial
grounds." To be sure, "we have at least 10,000,000 of our own citizens
on relief," but, she argues:

> Suppose [the refugees] did not come empty-handed, as they
> wouldn't, because the German government is desperately anxious
> to trade with us and could be forced to make a deal releasing funds
> for their resettlement. Suppose a great proportion brought special
> skills, training and talent that would enrich the communities in
> which they settled. Suppose, as has actually happened in Belgium,
> the refugees started new businesses and gave more jobs than they
> took.

Since German and Austrian Jews were mostly middle-class, it was
reasonable to ask as a condition for freer admission of them that they
be allowed to take some part of their wealth with them. But this is
precisely what the Nazi regime, in economic straits on account of its
rearmament program among other things, was not letting them do. In
the early years of the regime, it had often been possible for an astute
emigrant to get away with something more than half of his personal
fortune, but the chance to do this had been dwindling over the years,

and in the wake of the Kristallnacht—which came while Rublee was waiting for the German government to accept his offer to negotiate—it had been reduced to virtually nothing. By the end of November, a Jew emigrating from the Reich had to turn in 25 percent of his assets as a "flight tax," and 20 percent toward the fine levied against the Jewish community for damaged property. Another 15 percent had to go to a fund to help other Jews out of Germany, and whatever remained had to be deposited in the Reichsbank, which would reimburse the deposit without interest and at only 8 percent of value when the claimant had settled abroad. A person fortunate enough to have had a net worth equivalent to $100,000 would end up with $3,200. Yet even this was more cash than the German government wanted to spare, and it was now pressuring emigrants to take only goods with them when they left the country.

In its issue of November 20, then, *The New York Times* had to carry this bleak report by its Berlin correspondent, Otto D. Tolischus:

> The Evian refugee conference's projects to facilitate the emigration of German Jews with at least part of their possessions, which would enable them to make a new start in a new land, appeared today to have been definitely wrecked by the new German policy of "liquidating" the Jewish question by the Germans' own methods.
>
> This aspect of the new policy, which began with the anti-Jewish excesses November 10 and is being continued with increasingly more drastic government measures, is evidenced by the fact that the German Government has let it be known that it has no desire to negotiate with George Rublee . . . along the Evian lines. . . .
>
> The government, it is understood, is perfectly willing to negotiate for the emigration of Jews from Germany without their possessions with any authority or any country willing to accept them as penniless refugees, but on no other terms.

Then, on December 12, the situation suddenly changed, thanks to the as-yet undaunted circumspection of those Germans whose main concern was international finance. Their balance of trade was suffering greatly—largely, as they saw it, on account of a worldwide boycott of German goods mainly instigated by American-Jewish organizations. Couldn't the two questions, of emigration and of export, be tied together, then? This was how the set of problems was seen by that old force of "moderation," Dr. Hjalmar Schacht, who, as president of the Reichsbank, was still a major financial power in the land, despite his dismissal from the post of Minister of Finance late in 1937.

"It was officially announced tonight," said a *New York Times* dispatch of December 12 from Berlin,

that Dr. Hjalmar Schacht, president of the Reichsbank, would go
to London for a "private visit to the governor of the Bank of England." ...

[Among his reasons] may be discussion of the Jewish refugee
problem. So far the German Government has refused to negotiate
with the Intergovernmental Committee on Refugees sitting in London, on the ground that it is political and anti-German. But London
quarters interested in the emigration of Jews from Germany are
known here to be anxious to discuss some plan for facilitating such
emigration.

Dr. Schacht may be quite willing to discuss unofficially some
plan whereby Germany would facilitate the emigration of some of
her Jews, in return for which Jewish quarters would undertake to
facilitate German exports. How such a plan would work is not definitely known, but it is assumed that it would parallel the
[Ha'avarah] system employed in the emigration of Jews to Palestine. Under that system Jews receive in Palestine, in return for
delivering their property to the German government, an agreed
sum in sterling obtained from the sale of German goods in Palestine.

The plan Schacht quickly proposed after arriving in London was
based on just such a principle. It was for the creation of two parallel
funds, one to be established by "world Jewry," the other to be set up
in Germany as collateral for it and created out of yet another tax imposed upon the German-Jewish community. Each emigrating German
Jew would be granted 10,000 marks credit, to be collected in foreign
currency from the "world Jewry" fund, which in turn would be paid off
with interest from the German one—but only when the profits from
German exports were considered sufficient to justify such payment.
President Roosevelt, when he heard of the plan, wrote to Myron Taylor
that this was "asking the world to pay a ransom for the release of
hostages in Germany, and barter human misery for increased exports."
There also were angry responses from Jewish leaders, many of whom
objected to being put into the position of answering to the Nazi conception of an organized "international financial Jewry." The World Jewish
Congress, meeting in Paris in January 1939, "adopted a resolution declaring Jews would not accept a solution of the German refugee problem
that rewarded the Nazi regime with economic advantages in return for
its policy of expropriation and expulsion."

It was a moral dilemma, but for Rublee it represented an opening
at last, and he had no alternative but to try to improve the terms of the
offer. By January 10, he was in Berlin beginning conversations with
Schacht; by January 19, he had even obtained concessions. But suddenly
it was too late. Hitler helped the good-willed of the world out of their

moral dilemma on January 20 by removing Schacht from his post as president of the Reichsbank. Was it all over, then? Two days later, Helmut Wohlthat, an economist in the Foreign Ministry, was appointed to take over the negotiations with Rublee. The sorely tried American had to start all over again.

Meanwhile, London had been seeking its own form of solution to the newly urgent refugee problem. "The British Cabinet," wrote the *New York Times* correspondent on November 16,

> is understood to have given tentative approval today to a plan for opening thinly settled parts of the British colonial empire as a sanctuary for some of the oppressed Jews and other "non-Aryans" in Germany.
> The plan, which calls for financial help from United States citizens, now has been submitted to Washington as a matter of utmost urgency.

British Guiana was discussed in the Cabinet, and when Mr. Chamberlain aired the plan in the House of Commons on the 17th, he also spoke of Tanganyika. The following week, he outlined a scheme for leasing ten thousand square miles in British Guiana to settle Jewish emigrants. There was little consideration just yet as to how several hundred thousand Europeans, largely urban, middle-class, and middle-aged, could be set down to survive and develop in the midst of a wilderness. Chamberlain granted that the project would cost about £20 million, or $100 million—which was, of course, to be raised largely in the United States— and that "it may be years before the new refugee colonies can begin to flourish."

Such colonial fantasies were prompted by the same concern that had led Lord Winterton to talk of Kenya at the Evian conference—that of avoiding any discussion of Palestine in the refugee context. The problem there was now coming to a head, for, after more than a year's delay and hedging over the Peel Commission's partition proposal, the more recently dispatched Woodhead (called by some wags the "re-Peel") Commission had come in with a recommendation against it. Now a conference of Arab and Zionist leaders was being scheduled to convene in London the following February, to try to make a final determination over the future of Palestine. "It is generally recognized," Chamberlain had said of Palestine during his speech proposing Guiana,

> that that small country could not in any case provide a solution of the Jewish refugee problem, but Palestine has been making its own contribution. No less than 40 per cent of the Jewish emigrants en-

tering the country during the last 12 months have come from Germany.

But that would only have meant a little over five thousand German Jews, whereas Chaim Weizmann thought that a hundred thousand refugees could enter Palestine immediately and be absorbed.

Whatever problems their government was having, the British public were responding to the plight of the refugees on their traditional high level of common decency. At the same parliamentary session at which Chamberlain had made his proposal regarding the wilderness of Guiana, Sir Samuel Hoare, the Colonial Secretary, announced that "an exceptionally large number" of refugee children would be taken immediately into British foster homes, under a program financed by both private contributions and government subsidy.

"A ten-coach train," reported *The New York Times* on December 10,

with 630 happy Jewish children, aged 2½ to 16, left the suburban Huttledorf station tonight for the Netherlands, whence 530 of the children will go to England, the others remaining in Holland.

For the latter hundred, the respite was to prove only temporary.

Meanwhile, President Roosevelt was taking further steps, within the limits imposed by law and public opinion, to deal with the refugee problem. On November 18, he had announced at a press conference that he had instructed Secretary of Labor Frances Perkins to extend the visitor's visas held by some twelve to fifteen thousand German refugees in the country "for a period of six months, which the law permits her to do, and for other like periods so long as necessary." The President, at pains to justify this surprise use of a loophole in the law, pointed out, for one thing, "that the visitors he has in mind are not all Jews, by any means." He also made it clear that he did "not intend to ask Congress to alter existing immigration quotas so as to permit more political refugees to come into the country than are now permitted by law." Then he simply pleaded

that the visitors who are now in the country, and who cannot become American citizens while they are here in the status of visitors, must not be forced to return to Germany to face the concentration camps and other forms of punishment that they believe await them.

The President added, according to *The New York Times*'s summary of his remarks, that the situation has become urgent because the German Government intends to cancel the passports of all its nationals who do not return to Germany before next December 30. This will put the responsible officials in the position of permitting aliens to remain in this country on the strength of invalidated passports, but the President indicated that legal technicalities would not be permitted to stand in the way of the humanitarian purpose.

This stretching of legality was to be "presented to Congress in all its details," for the President was confident, he said, "that Congress would not, by new legislation, force the deportation of the unfortunates who have sought temporary asylum here, any more than it sought to force the deportation of White Russians to face certain death at the hands of the Soviet Union."

That bit of moral arm-twisting accomplished, he moved on to the next aspect of the question over which he proposed to stretch legality a bit. "Under existing law and regulations," he told the gathered members of the press, "an applicant for a visitors' visa may not, at the same time, inscribe himself on the quota list at his place of origin." This meant that a person ultimately seeking admission as an immigrant—the only category from which one could apply for citizenship—could not simultaneously apply for an immigrant visa *and* one allowing him at least temporary refuge there or in any other country. "This situation," Roosevelt continued, "has caused considerable hardship in recent months, particularly in Vienna, Warsaw and Prague, where American consulates are swamped with applications for immigration visas. Many of the applicants are unable, through fear of danger, to await their turns in those capitals." Therefore,

> the State Department has worked out machinery to care for them.
> Such applicants are advised to proceed to any other place they desire, except the United States, and await their turn there. When their number comes up, the consulate of the place they have elected is authorized to examine them and to grant the visas as if the applicant were still at his point of original application.

This was quite at variance with the procedure that had, for example, been so strictly applied in Warsaw at the beginning of 1920. "Under this [new] procedure," the *Times* pointed out,

> thousands of applicants are waiting their turn in the Netherlands, Portugal, Switzerland and Cuba, the latter being probably the most popular place of all because of its proximity to their ultimate destination. For such cases, the President does not intend to take any further steps.

With these last words, it was being made clear that Roosevelt had gone as far as he could go for now. As a coda to the article about this press conference, the *Times* appended some congressional opinions regarding the refugee issue. Among those quoted was Chairman Martin Dies of the House Committee on Un-American Activities, Roosevelt's foremost nemesis and ideological opponent. Firmly opposing any liberalization of the immigration laws, Dies furthermore predicted "that if such a proposal were presented to the House it would not receive more than a hundred votes." There was no evidence in the temper of the day to contradict that estimate. Senator William H. King of Utah, of the Senate Committee on Immigration. was quoted, saying that he

> favored liberalization of immigration quotas, but agreed with Representative Dies that there would be great opposition in Congress to such proposals because of the traditional opposition of Congressmen to extensive immigration and because of lack of jobs for people already here.

·54·

THE COURSE OF THE ST. LOUIS

On January 30, 1939, during a two-and-a-quarter-hour speech to the Reichstag, which, the *New York Times* correspondent thought, for the most part "lacked the militant overtone that had characterized his last Reichstag address," Hitler made some remarks about the Jews that were as terrible as any he had ever uttered. "One thing I should like to say on this day," he said,

> which may be memorable for others as well as for Germans. In the course of my life I have very often been a prophet and have usually been ridiculed for it. During the time of my struggle for power, it was in the first instance the Jewish race that only received my prophecies lightly when I said that I would one day take over the leadership of the State and with it that of the whole nation and that I would then, among many other things, settle the Jewish problem.
>
> Their laughter was uproarious, but I think that for some time now they have been laughing on the other side of their face. Today I will once more be a prophet. If the international Jewish financiers in and outside Europe should succeed in plunging the nations once more into a world war, then the result will not be the bolshevization of the earth, and thus the victory of Jewry, but the annihilation of the Jewish race in Europe.

Subsequent history shudders with the import of these words, but in that moment it was still possible to believe that they were an excess of rhetorical bombast. *The Times* of London could settle for regarding them as a "sinister flourish." As for the *Jewish Chronicle*, it rose to unwonted vituperation, but not to a full perception of what the words have since come to signify. "The suggestion," it wrote,

that "international Jewry" caused the Great War is, of course, a
wicked, aged, and threadbare fiction favored by the anti-Jewish
scum for its own vile purposes. . . .

It is, no doubt, true that Jews would suffer acutely in a new
war. But so would others, for obvious reasons. If they suffered to
a greater degree it would be because of the vicious incitements of
Nazis and their like, and the appetites for theft and murder already
tickled in Germany by the recent pogroms.

Perceptions of what Jewish suffering might be under such conditions were based on what had happened during and after the last war—
which was bad enough. Meanwhile, in the first months of 1939, the reality of the Jewish problem in the Reich was something quite different.
The Nazi rulers seemed bent, not on mass annihilation of the Jews under their rule—which was still inconceivable to most human beings—but
on ejecting them wholesale. The problem was outrageous, but it did not
seem insoluble. Between three and four hundred thousand Jews were
still in the Reich, a number that the United States, Palestine, and other
countries of immigration could have absorbed eventually under the conditions still prevailing in January 1939—as long as there was no great
hurry.

But hopes for this and all other peaceful solutions took a severe
new beating in mid-March when, ostensibly in response to appeals from
the pro-Nazi premier of Slovakia, Hitler dismantled what remained of
the Czechoslovakian state and sent in troops to establish a protectorate
of Bohemia and Moravia. This was a complete violation of the Munich
understandings and another slap in the face to the governments of Britain and France. From that point on, even Chamberlain was prepared to
go to war to prevent any further German territorial expansion.

This new development also had an adverse effect upon discussions
of the refugee problem. George Rublee, after briefly offering his resignation in February, had then valiantly returned to his negotiations with
Helmut Wohlthat. But now 350,000 Jews of Czechoslovakia had suddenly been added to the potential refugee pool. Returning to London in
late March, Rublee informed Washington that the British and French
governments, preparing for war, were no longer ready to commit themselves to the negotiations. Under-Secretary of State Sumner Welles
wired back to him that the "basis of the program continued to exist
despite events in Czechoslovakia."

But a sense that the thrust toward a solution of the refugee problem had been severely curtailed was felt by concerned Americans, too.
The disappointment was reflected in the remarks made by James L.
Houghteling, Commissioner of Immigration and Naturalization, to the
annual HIAS convention on March 19. "Denouncing the dictators for

trying to force us into sacrifices which will help their position at our expense," according to *The New York Times*, Houghteling

> deplored the fate of the Jewish people and declared that with the present crisis in Central Europe the hopes for adoption of the Rublee plan to solve the refugee problem had vanished.
>
> Addressing 3,000 delegates at the annual convention of Hias ... the commissioner defended our immigration laws as generous and liberal but said the "temper of our people" and general opinion in Congress are against increased immigration quotas.
>
> "These are distressing days," he declared. "A great power has been let loose in Europe bound by none of the rules of decency and good faith. This has been accomplished by unreasoning wrath against the Jewish people. Our great President has been a most courageous leader in their defense, just as another President Roosevelt was a valiant defender of the Jews against Russia a third of a century ago."

Houghteling's remarks about the "temper of the people" were well borne out the following month, when *Fortune* magazine published the results of a poll showing that *83 percent* of their sampling of American public opinion opposed any enlargement of the quotas. Only 8.3 percent favored it; the rest were undecided.

The hopes for a substantial Palestine refuge also dwindled rapidly in the wake of Hitler's dismantling of Czechoslovakia. It is likely that the attitude of the Chamberlain government on the question had become firmly fixed even before the conference of Arabs and Jews was convened in Saint James's Palace on February 7. In January, a subcommittee of the Committee of Imperial Defence had, after nearly two years of inquiry, submitted a report saying:

> We feel it necessary to point out at the outset ... the strong feeling which exists in all Arab States in connection with British policy in Palestine. ... We assume that, immediately on the outbreak of war, the necessary measures would be taken ... in order to bring about a complete appeasement of Arab opinion in Palestine and in neighboring countries. ... If we fail thus to retain Arab goodwill at the outset of war, no other measures which we can recommend will serve to influence the Arab States in favor of this country.

Any hopes that the implications of these remarks could be modified at the conference were dashed from the start by the Arab delegates' refusal even to be in the same room as their Jewish counterparts. "The dignity of the occasion," Chaim Weizmann said of the opening,

was somewhat marred by the fact that Mr. Chamberlain's address
of welcome had to be given twice, once to the Jews and once to the
Arabs, since the latter would not sit with the former, and even used
different entrances to the palace so as to avoid embarrassing contacts.

Inevitably, the two delegations were able to come to no understanding, so that the British government was left with the task of formulating
its own policy to impose on both sides. The fact that the conference
broke up in the immediate wake of Hitler's occupation of Prague, and
in face of the growing threat of war, confirmed the outcome. It was the
Arabs, with their ambivalence regarding European conflicts, who had
to be appeased, not the Jews, who had no choice but to be on the side
opposed to Hitler. The British policy, known to insiders for weeks before, was published in a White Paper on May 17. The Mandate, it announced, was to continue ten more years, at the end of which time a
binational Arab-Jewish state was to be brought into being. For the next
five years, a total Jewish immigration of seventy-five thousand was to
be allowed; after that, immigration would continue only if the Arab
majority of the country permitted it.

For Winston Churchill, who delivered a thundering oration against
the policy in the ensuing parliamentary debate, its worst violation was
the granting to the Arabs of a veto on Jewish immigration. "Now, there
is the breach," he said; "there is the violation of the pledge; there is
the abandonment of the Balfour Declaration; there is the end of the
vision, of the hope, of the dream." He did not object in principle to the
limitation upon immigration—no responsible British statesman did—although his own proposals in an earlier debate had allowed a much more
generous quota. The great irony was that the Arabs had immediately
rejected even this latest White Paper policy, since they opposed any
Jewish immigration at all; so that Churchill wanted to know what really
was gained by it. "Can we—and this is the question—strengthen ourselves by this repudiation [of the Balfour Declaration]?" he asked:

> The triumphant Arabs have rejected it. . . . The despairing Jews
> will resist it. What will the world think about it? What will our
> friends say? What will be the opinion of the United States of Ameri-
> ca? Shall we not lose more—and this is a question to be considered
> maturely—in the growing support and sympathy of the United
> States than we shall gain in local administrative convenience, if gain
> at all indeed we do?

The question of American responses to their Palestine policies had
never been taken lightly by the British. The Balfour Declaration itself
had been stimulated in part by the British desire to win American sup-

port for the Allied war effort. And if it had long been believed in White-hall that Jewish opinion counted for a good deal in the American political climate, it was above all believed of the administration of President Franklin Delano Roosevelt, with his power base in New York State and the noticeably large Jewish presence among his advisers and constitu-ency. Indeed, as the President most passionately adored by Jewish vot-ers in all of American history, he was even in danger of bearing a political stigma for this among his enemies at home as well as abroad. If the Nazi organs were regularly calling him such things as "a mere tool of American Jewry," some Americans now were resorting to such sinister word-plays as the "Jew Deal" and President "Rosenfeld."

This surely was why Roosevelt had always hedged his compassion-ate actions on the refugee question with certain precautions, stressing, for example, in each new announcement that Christians as well as Jews were being persecuted in Germany and being helped to escape from there. On the day in November when he announced the extension of visitors' visas for German nationals in the United States who held them, the *New York Times* article added: "President Roosevelt pointed out that the visitors he has in mind are not all Jews, by any means. All shades of political thought and many religions are represented, he said." Two days earlier, after his severe statement about the Kristallnacht excesses and his recall of the American Ambassador to Berlin, his press secretary had felt the need to issue a clarification. "President Roose-velt's criticism of the acts of violence in Germany at his press confer-ence yesterday," according to *The New York Times* on November 17, "was intended to apply to persecution by the Nazis of Catholics and others as well as Jews, it was announced at the White House yesterday by Stephen T. Early, secretary to the President."

Palestine was certainly a matter of concern to Roosevelt, even if his position on Zionist aspirations was not clear. There were Zionists as well as non-Zionists among the Jews close to the President—Rabbi Ste-phen S. Wise, his closest adviser on Jewish affairs, took part as a Zionist spokesman in the conference at Saint James's Palace—but in the refu-gee crisis of that moment, Zionism was not even the issue where Pales-tine was concerned: it was simply a major potential Jewish refuge. In October, Roosevelt had allowed Senator Robert F. Wagner of New York to make this statement to the press after a conversation between them at Hyde Park:

> The President told me that he and the United States Govern-ment were for the maintenance of Palestine as a Jewish National Home without limitation. He assured me also that he was watching the situation closely and that everything within the power of the Government would be done to prevent the curtailment of immigra-

tion. With one power after another driving out the Jews, it is imperative that Palestine be kept open to them without restriction, otherwise they would have no place to go. I believe that we are so situated that we can make our protests to the British Government effective. I am still very hopeful, and I cannot persuade myself otherwise than that Palestine will continue to be used as a Jewish National Home.

This remained Roosevelt's firm feeling in the months that followed, but he also was loyal to another conviction in that grave historic moment—that Anglo-American harmony was of overriding importance in the face of the Nazi threat. Whatever his personal views on Palestine, his representatives at Evian had acquiesced in the face of strong British reservations on the subject, and this pattern was to remain. Upon the appearance of the White Paper in May, he responded, as he wrote to Secretary of State Cordell Hull, with "a good deal of dismay," and added that "this is something that we cannot give approval to by the United States." Yet, though American displeasure was duly conveyed to the Foreign Office by Ambassador Joseph P. Kennedy, and there was considerable outcry in Congress and among prominent American Jews— including men close to the President like Rabbi Wise and Justice Brandeis—the public response of the administration was muffled. Chamberlain had taken his chances on this: "If it was necessary," he had told the Cabinet on March 8, "to face an outbreak of anti-British feeling in the United States . . . it was better that this should happen at a time like the present, rather than at a time of acute international crisis."

The gamble had paid off. In a carefully wrought editorial published the day after the issuance of the White Paper, *The New York Times* caught the mood of those who, without any commitments regarding Zionism, were as worried about Britain's ability to withstand the Nazi threat as they were about the fate of the refugees. "The situation of the Jews in a great part of Europe is completely changed" since the time of the Balfour Declaration, it said:

The pressure on Palestine is now so great that immigration has to be strictly regulated to save the homeland itself from overpopulation as well as from an increasingly violent resistance on the part of the Arabs. Arab national consciousness is enormously quickened not only in the Holy Land but throughout the Arab world. The British position is different also. Today not only imperial interests but the very existence of the Empire are involved in friendly relations with the Arabs. The Zionists, moreover, should be the last to desire hostility between Arabs and Britons. In the event of war a colony dependent for most of its vital supplies on sea-borne traffic could be starved out in a fortnight's blockade. And what would happen to the homeland in peace if the neighboring Arab peoples passed under the influence of the Fascist powers?

These are hard facts. Less than half a million pioneers, builders of a new world that depends on peace, international order and respect for spiritual values, are planted on an exposed coast with millions of Arabs in the background, and in the foreground a strategic ocean highway coveted by rival imperialisms. In honor, humanity, and the defense of its own interests, Great Britain must protect these people to the end. On their part, in the long run, they have not much chance but to employ their proved intelligence and energy, and to cooperate in building up a state wherein they can conserve the wonders they have already wrought.

As for the Zionist leadership in Palestine, their view was to be aptly summed up by David Ben Gurion after the outbreak of war in September, when he would say, "We shall fight with Great Britain in this war as if there was no White Paper, and we shall fight the White Paper as if there was no war." In fact, the war against the White Paper had begun even before it was issued, with a program of illegal immigration that dated back to 1937. Three and a half weeks before the White Paper, on Sunday, April 23, the S.S. *Assimi*, a Greek ship carrying 270 refugees who did not have entry permits, was turned away from Haifa harbor.

By May 1939, then, the Jewish refugee problem had once again become quite clearly what in a sense it always had been: a *sauve-qui-peut*. Ships loaded with refugees were streaming out all over the globe to whatever ports would take them—including Shanghai, which, until the Japanese closed it down in November, was the one place in the world that would take them without restriction. The Nazi regime, still bent on mass emigration as the solution to its Jewish problem, was putting on German ships any Jews who could buy their tickets, show credentials for their reception at some port, and leave virtually all their possessions behind them. Under the circumstances, landing certificates of any kind were at a premium, and soon there was a trafficking in those that circulated most freely. Foremost among them that spring were those that admitted refugees to that favorite threshold for entry into the nearby United States, Cuba.

The government of Cuba was under the nominal presidency of Federico Laredo Bru but effectively under the dictatorship of General Fulgencio Batista, and the two occasionally clashed. One of Batista's friends, Manuel Benitez Gonzalez, held the post of Director General of Immigration, and it was he who, on the basis of a ruling made earlier in the year, was free to issue landing permits to "tourists" at $150 each. Gaining a substantial personal profit from this, Benitez was soon selling permits in large job lots to European shipping concerns, who would then sell them to their own customers at a profit. The Hamburg-America line was an important customer, and a Cuban landing certificate was part of the package this company was offering ticket-buying refugees by the beginning of May.

But suddenly President Bru, objecting to the profits Benitez was making in this way, gave out a decree invalidating the permits. Officials of the Hamburg-America line remained skeptical of its force, however, and, with the backing of the Reich government, did not hesitate to send out, on May 13, a ship containing the largest single load of refugees ever to have sailed—930 Jews out of 936 passengers. This was the ill-fated *St. Louis*.

By the time the *St. Louis* reached Havana harbor on Saturday, May 27, one refugee had died on board and been buried at sea. The worst was now to come. Twenty-eight passengers—the six nonrefugees, and twenty-two others who had taken the precaution to get better papers than those being peddled by the Hamburg-America line—were accepted through customs; the rest were told that they would not be allowed on shore.

This was not the first consignment of refugees to be repudiated at Havana on account of the invalidated landing certificates. At that moment, the *Orinoco* was heading back across the Atlantic with two hundred Jewish refugees who would be landed a few days later in Denmark. But there were several factors unique to the *St. Louis* that were now to bring it into the world's headlines. One was the enormous number of detained refugees aboard—907, of whom more than seven hundred held quota numbers enabling them to wait their turn for American visas, and in whatever country they chose, thanks to President Roosevelt's recent ruling. Another was the determination to resist the order on the part of Captain Gustav Schroeder, a man of honor and old-fashioned German virtue. And another—after Captain Schroeder had remained in the harbor demanding that the Cuban government reconsider its position—was the suicide attempt on May 30 of one of the passengers, Max Loewe, who slashed his wrists and jumped overboard, to be fished out and taken to a Havana hospital. This was followed by threats of more suicides, and from then on the *St. Louis*—which *The New York Times* called "the saddest ship afloat today"—was front-page news.

While the conflicting Cuban political forces confronted one another over the issue behind the scenes, the Joint Distribution Committee sent two representatives to Havana. They arrived on May 28, and ten days of negotiations ensued, during which the Joint offered to post a bond guaranteeing that the refugees would not become public charges during their stay in Cuba. As the offer rose from $125,000 to $500,000, the *St. Louis* discreetly sailed out to the twelve-mile limit and gave its anguished passengers a view of Miami. A group of them even wired an appeal to President Roosevelt to let them land there, but they received no reply. What could he have said? The Atlantic Ocean was at that moment teeming with boatloads of refugees—two more, the *Orduna* and the *Flandre*, together carrying more than 250 Jews with bad certificates, were then steaming toward Havana—that would gladly have "dumped" their human cargoes on American shores had Roosevelt only handed them a precedent. In this sense, the glare of worldwide publicity was most unfortunate for the passengers of the *St. Louis*.

At last President Bru—subjected to anti-Semitic pressures at home—refused all compromises; on the evening of June 6, the *St. Louis* headed back across the Atlantic. But not to Germany. Morris Troper, the European director of the Joint, had been preparing for this eventuality, and from his office in Paris had prevailed upon some of the Jewish organizations in Western Europe to get their governments to admit *St. Louis* passengers on a temporary basis. Those of Great Britain, France, Belgium, and the Netherlands had agreed, so that when the *St. Louis* arrived at Antwerp on June 17, a scene of welcome awaited it at last. "The chief Alderman of Antwerp was present," according to the *Jewish Chronicle*,

> and among those who went on board was the Commissioner of Emigration, who, for over thirty years has been protecting the interests of emigrants passing through Belgium, and representatives of the Jewish emigration society, Ezra, and of the refugee committees. A representative of the American Joint, which made the landing of the passengers possible, and delegates of various Jewish and non-Jewish bodies and Ministries, including the Quakers, had already boarded the steamer from a motor launch at Flushing, where the arduous work of selecting the refugees suitable for each country had begun. . . .
>
> Some 180 refugees arrived in Rotterdam, Holland, on Sunday evening, and temporary accommodations were found for them in the quarantine station. . . . According to a statement made by the Ministry of Justice, it is intended to distribute these refugees among the existing camps, and to prepare them for emigration elsewhere.
>
> Two hundred and twenty-three of the St. Louis passengers landed in France on Tuesday morning from the tender Rhakodis. They were permitted to take up residence anywhere in France, except in Paris.
>
> . . . The tender Rhakodis, with the remaining St. Louis passengers, numbering about 250, arrived at Southampton on Wednesday morning.

Many of the passengers who were landed in France, Belgium, and the Netherlands were again to face Nazi persecution.

PART TEN

The War of Annihilation

·1939-1945·

· 55 ·

THE FALL OF POLAND

In the late spring and summer of 1939, Hitler proclaimed his next desired revision of the Treaty of Versailles, this time with regard to Danzig and the "Polish Corridor." Since the demand for the Sudetenland had turned into the conquest of Czechoslovakia, the Western democracies did not doubt that these new segments of Germania Irridenta were to be mere steppingstones to taking all of Poland. The governments of Neville Chamberlain and Edouard Daladier, repenting of appeasement, were now ready to oppose Hitler's demands even at the price of war; they hoped Soviet Russia would take a similar stance. Instead, on August 23, a nonaggression pact was concluded between the governments of Hitler and Stalin, the latter having viewed Munich as proof of willingness on the part of the Western powers to abandon his country to the German wolves. A secret clause divided Poland into German and Russian spheres of influence.

Hitler invaded Poland in the early morning of September 1, and two days later Britain and France declared war on Germany. On the 6th, French troops entered the Saar basin, but any notions that the Eastern Front might hold out came to an end in a matter of days, as Poland succumbed to the German Blitzkrieg. On the 16th, with Warsaw alone still holding out and being bombed to ruins, Russian troops quickly invaded to establish their claims in eastern Poland. By the end of September, the Polish state having been annihilated between them—this was often referred to as the "Fourth Partition"—Germany, with the Soviet Union seconding the idea, turned to the West to demand peace terms. After all, what war was left for Britain and France to fight?

What was left was a war to wipe out Nazi brutality and its efforts to extend itself over more and more of the Continent. A major voice reemerging in British affairs was that of Winston Churchill, long the most outspoken enemy of Nazi Germany in Parliament, and now once again, as in 1914, First Lord of the Admiralty. In an October 1 radio broadcast, Churchill called for the repudiation of any peace offers from Hitler and, describing Russia as "a riddle wrapped in a mystery inside an enigma," declared that, when the time came, Stalin would not let Hitler overrun the rest of Eastern Europe. France and Britain held their ground.

Meanwhile, news of Nazi brutality in Poland was reaching the West. It was directed not only against Poles, whom Nazis regarded as an inferior race, but against Polish Jews, whom they regarded as inferior even to German Jews. About two million Polish Jews now found themselves under German rule, the other million and a quarter being in the Russian-ruled areas. "First intimations," according to a *New York Times* dispatch from Berlin dated September 12,

> that a "solution of the Jewish problem" in Poland is on the German-Polish agenda is revealed in a "special report" of the official German News Bureau.
>
> In view of the world refugee problem and the individual suffering created in the last six years by Germany's determination to rid her borders of Jews, the implications of the "solution of the Jewish problem in Poland," were it carried out on the German model, are ominous. . . .
>
> As a possible solution of this question, a "purge" is indicated by the Official News Bureau, which continues:
>
> "Removal of the Polish Jewish population from the European domain would furthermore, in the long view, definitely bring a solution of the Jewish question in Europe nearer. For this is just the Jewry which, through its high birth rate and in spite of all existing differences between the two groups, has continually established the large numbers of Western Jewry, whose birth rate is small."
>
> How, however, the "removal" of Jews from Poland without their extermination can halt the alleged "strengthening" of Western Jewry is not explained.

It would seem that the Nazi leadership had not yet worked out their final answer to that question. On September 21, Reinhard Heydrich, chief of the SS Security Division, issued instructions on the handling of the Jews of Poland to the *Einsatzgruppen,* or special task forces, which were taking over from the army the work of policing the country. The instructions called for the gathering of Jews as much as possible from small towns and into large cities, and for the creation of Jewish Councils in those cities, among other things to aid in the work of "evacuation" when the time came. "You must distinguish between the final aim," Heydrich cautioned, "whose attainment will take considerable time, and the steps necessary for reaching it, which can be applied within a short time." The "final aim" was not yet clearly defined, and though it may have included the ultimate possibility of extermination, its more immediate sense still included the notions of emigration and resettlement that had typified the prewar policy. Indeed, what emerged in this moment was some conception of a Jewish preserve, a Pale of Settlement in Poland, which was designated for the vicinity of Lublin. Into this, great masses of Jews were to be dumped, especially from those areas— the old Germany, Austria, western Czechoslovakia, and certain parts of northern and western Poland—that were being claimed for settlement of only ethnic Germans.

"In his Reichstag speech of last week," reported the *Jewish Chronicle* of October 13,

> Hitler announced as one of his "peace aims" the regulation of the question of *Lebensraum* according to nationalities, with reference not only to Poland but also to the whole of southeastern Europe, and added that the German Government hoped, in this connection, to try to solve the Jewish problem.
>
> Commentators on the speech suggested that the Nazis plan to set up an all-Jewish State on part of the German half of Poland. German Jews would be transferred to the new State, it was declared.

Two weeks later, the *Chronicle* conveyed reports that

> 2,000 Vienna Jews have left in a special train for a "Jewish reservation" in Poland, near Lublin. . . . Most of the deportees originally came from Poland during or after the war of 1914–18. It is thought that they formed merely the first of considerable numbers of Jews who will be transported to the new "Jewish Pale" which the Nazis propose to establish.

By early November, the picture regarding the Lublin Jewish reservation was as clear as it was ever going to get. "The determination of the Nazis," said the *Jewish Chronicle* of November 10,

> to concentrate the Jews from the German Reich, the Czech Protectorate and possibly the whole of Poland in a special reservation in the Lublin area seems apparent from reports received by the Jewish Telegraphic Agency from many centers.
>
> It is reported that the Nazis plan to have Greater Germany cleared of Jews by November 1940. The ultimate population of the Pale, if all Polish Jews are included, will be between 3,000,000 and 4,000,000. . . . The Nazis also seem to think that they will obtain a

large amount of foreign exchange from Jews abroad to support the
Jews in the Lublin Pale.

This certainly was something for Jews in the West to contemplate.
What was the character of the refugee problem now? In October, President Roosevelt had called a conference at the White House of some
members of the Intergovernmental Committee on Refugees; there, he
spoke of the enormity of the problem to be confronted by the world
once Nazism was defeated. "All we can do is estimate," he told a group
that included Lord Winterton, Myron Taylor, James G. MacDonald, and
representatives of France, the Netherlands, Argentina, and Brazil,

> that when this ghastly war ends there may not be one million but
> ten million or twenty million men, women, and children belonging
> to many races and many regions, living in many countries and pos-
> sibly on several continents, who will enter into the wide picture—
> the problem of the human refugee.

This was hardly something to be contemplated for the moment by the
governments engaged in war. "I realize, of course," Roosevelt said,

> that Great Britain and France, engaged as they are in a major war,
> can be asked by those nations which are neutral to do little more
> than to give a continuance of their sympathetic interest in these
> days which are so difficult for them.

Stressing that the current "short-range program" was what could and
should be handled by the conference, he said:

> We have with us the problem of helping those individuals and
> families who are at this moment in countries of refuge and who for
> the sake of the world and themselves can best be placed in per-
> manent domiciles during the actual course of the war, without con-
> fusing their lot with the lot of those who in increasing numbers will
> suffer as a result of the war itself.

In other words, the President saw no way of helping people who
were at that time under German control. Whatever potential refugee
problem they represented was, he was saying, for the postwar world to
deal with—an enormity that embattled Britain and France could not
even contemplate for the time being. What had to be dealt with now by
all present was the obligation already incurred, toward those refugees
who had come out of German-dominated areas before September 1—
some four hundred thousand since 1933, according to Sir Herbert Emer-

son, who announced at the conference that the Intergovernmental Committee, over which he now presided, had placed about 250,000 in permanent homes. The task was to do the same for the 150,000 who remained.

Most of these were in still-neutral Belgium and the Netherlands, or in France and Great Britain. The refugees in the latter two belligerent countries had been interned with the outbreak of the war—and, in the case of France, sometimes in such camps as Gurs in the Pyrenees and Le Vernet, under conditions that drew protests from humane observers. "The famous French author, André Gide," reported the *Jewish Chronicle* of November 10,

> criticizes the action of the French authorities in interning all German and Austrian refugees, irrespective of whether or not they are loyal to the Allied cause.
>
> In neutral countries and, above all, in Switzerland, astonishment is expressed at the treatment of refugees in France, M. Gide declares in an interview with the Nice paper, *Le Petit Niçois*. England, he says, has shown her wisdom in interning only those refugees who are really suspect.

But in the wake of the White House conference, France proved ready to relent somewhat in her severities, particularly in the face of appeals from such organizations as HICEM, the European offspring of HIAS and the JCA. "The French authorities," announced the November 24 *Jewish Chronicle,*

> have given permission to the Hias-Ica Emigration Association (Hicem) to send representatives to all internment camps where German-born Jewish refugees are being detained. The representatives are to be allowed to register all those who are eligible for emigration to overseas countries, so as to facilitate their release and departure. . . .
>
> It is estimated that about 2,000 such refugees are at present interned in camps in France. The American consulate has resumed issuing visas under the German and Austrian quotas, and the Hicem will, therefore, be able to help refugees possessing such visas to emigrate.

At the same time, the British government relented in a somewhat different way, allowing the possibility to refugees of a foot in the door of permanent residence. "It is officially announced," according to the *Jewish Chronicle,* that all permits to stay in the United Kingdom expiring during the war are being automatically extended until further notice. There is, therefore, no need to apply for an extension.

But the other side of this leniency was made sternly clear. "New permits for refugees still in enemy countries," the article continued,

are in no circumstances being granted. All permits granted before the outbreak of war have become automatically invalid. The Committees may apply on behalf of those persons who are already in neutral countries and have special reasons to come to England, but the prospects of such applications being granted are small.

This was in conformity with the policy enunciated at the White House conference in October.

But such a policy was based on the assumption that the Jews under Nazi rule, however murderously maltreated, were not being slaughtered. Even Jewish organizations were thinking in terms of handling a problem of mass resettlement, whether eventually or right away. At the White House conference in October, a group representing the American Emergency Committee on Palestine Affairs and the United Palestine Appeal presented "a program for the mass settlement in Palestine of up to 2,800,000 refugees from Germany and other lands," according to *The New York Times*.

But was resettlement still the main thrust of German policy? An alarming new note was sounded in an unsigned report on Polish Jewry that appeared in the *Jewish Chronicle* on December 1. It said:

The campaign of extermination of the Jews which the Nazis started with the occupation of Poland is gaining momentum from week to week. . . .

Underlying all, there is the determination to "solve" the Jewish problem in Poland even more drastically than in Nazi Germany.

The immediate plan to segregate all the Jews from Germany, Austria and Czechoslovakia in a Pale seems to have receded somewhat during the last fortnight and is giving way to plans no less mad and brutal.

A report printed two weeks later explained that Hans Frank, director of the General Government of Poland, called a temporary halt to deportations to the Lublin reservation because of the unsanitary conditions prevailing there. "Particulars of the conditions in the Jewish reservation," the report said, the starvation, the misery of the population, and the spread of disease are of such a character that the Nazi officials themselves informed Cracow, the seat of the Governor General, that they were unable to cope with the difficulties which arose from the continuous dumping of thousands of Jews without any provision having been made for their housing and maintenance. They reported that if the dumping was not interrupted, or the conditions immediately improved, typhoid and other epidemics rampant in the area might spread to the rest of Poland.

Perhaps, then, the true tenor of events in Poland was such as to verify the intention proclaimed by *Der Weltkampf,* a Munich periodical that, according to the *Jewish Chronicle* of January 12, 1940,

has published an article telling the German people that their lives are being menaced by the continued existence in Poland of—according to the writer—a block of five million Jews, avowed enemies of Nazism, and declaring that Polish Jewry must be annihilated. "We know the aims of the Jew and we will act accordingly," the article concludes, recalling Hitler's sinister threat that "a new world war will mean the end of Jewry."

Authoritative reports show that the destruction of Polish Jewry is not merely the dream of Nazi blood-lust but something which is daily being translated into fact.

There follows an unattributed personal account:

A message reaching Budapest declares: "Although four months have elapsed since the war ended in Poland, the territory, as far as the Jews are concerned, still represents a huge battlefield. The writer, who travelled about the country, met thousands of Jewish men, women and children wandering the roads aimlessly, hungry and ill-clad in the bitter cold. They had been driven from their homes. . . .

"A conservative calculation puts the news of deaths from starvation, exposure, forced labor, and epidemics, since the so-called end of the Nazi war, as equal to those from the September bombardments. This latter figure is estimated at 60,000; and thus it would appear that altogether 120,000 Polish Jews have lost their lives during the war and the occupation, apart from the multitudes who have been murdered in cold blood.

"Unless a miracle happens," the message concludes, "the whole of Polish Jewry in Nazi territory (estimated at about two and a half million) will be physically exterminated within a short time."

If this were correct, what miracle could be aspired to but the swiftest possible destruction of the tyrant?

·56·

THE COLLAPSE
OF WESTERN EUROPE

In the first months of 1940, the victimized Jews of Europe had fallen into two categories: refugees and captives. The Jews of Poland, apart from an infinitesimal number able to escape, were captives, either of a vindictive Nazi regime or of a Soviet one that made much of its opposition to anti-Semitism and treated Jewish proprietors no worse than gentile ones in despoiling them. Many of the Jews deported into the Lublin zone, already bereft of everything they owned, found the lure of the adjacent Soviet frontier irresistible. "It has been reported," according to *The New York Times* of March 3, 1940, "that the German border patrols are not too careful about preventing them from fleeing across the nearby demarcation line into Soviet Russia and that many have taken advantage of this." The vast majority of Polish Jewry did not have this option, however, as the Lublin plan declined and the alternative of amassing Jews from all over into large-city ghettos proceeded apace. In April, the ghetto of Lodz—a city being incorporated into the Greater Reich and into which ethnic Germans were being settled—was fully defined and cordoned off. The Warsaw ghetto, with some four hundred thousand Jews, was soon to follow.

As for the roughly three hundred thousand Jews still in Germany and Austria, a semblance of civility was maintained through American contacts. Still neutral, even though it had never returned its Ambassador to Berlin, the United States was able, through its own authorities and through private Jewish organizations, to maintain contact with the Jews of Berlin and elsewhere in Nazi-ruled Europe. "The only country," said the *Jewish Chronicle* in May 1940,

with which the Berlin [Jewish] community is still allowed to communicate is the U.S.A., which is continually sending relief to Germany, not only for the German Jews but also for those in the other enslaved countries. There is no doubt that the American Jews are now the sole mainstay of those three million Jews under Nazi rule; without American support, they would be faced with immediate starvation.

In the case of Poland, this was a matter of subsistence, the Joint Distribution Committee having established soup kitchens in Lodz, Warsaw, and other centers. In the case of Germany and Austria, it meant the continuing possibility of rescue, for American consuls were still issuing visas there.

As for the 150,000 refugees already escaped from the Reich at the outbreak of war who had not found permanent homes, many of them were in internment camps in France, Belgium, the Netherlands, Switzerland, and Great Britain. Now that the war was going on, the old reluctance to accommodate penniless arrivals was hardened greatly by the new fear of a "Fifth Column," a notion originating in the Spanish Civil War that was now demonstrating a capacity to become a popular hysteria. It was particularly rife after the fall of Norway in April, when the emergence of the traitor Vidkun Quisling gave notoriety to the idea of subversion at home. "Disquiet about Britain's 'Fifth Column' is growing," announced the London *Daily Mail* on April 19:

> The people ask that doubtful enemy aliens should be immediately interned and all other aliens strictly examined. . . . The traitors of Norway have shown the perils of the enemy within.

To be sure, as many enlightened citizens perceived, refugees from persecution were not likely to be loyal subversives for the countries from which they had fled. Yet not everyone saw it that way, and, furthermore, there was widespread belief that German spies were sometimes getting through disguised as Jewish refugees. So far, the British government had been proceeding with notable fairness on the question, by establishing a system of tribunals to examine the case of every German and Austrian national still in the country after September 1939. The Home Office designated three categories of "enemy aliens"—category A, to be interned; category B, not to be interned but subject to restrictions; and category C, to remain at liberty. Category C was above all for the refugees, who, according to the Home Office instructions, had left their native countries because they were

> subject to oppression by the Nazi regime upon racial, religious or political grounds. . . . They will be hostile to the Nazi regime and ready to assist this country rather than to assist the enemy.

Of about sixty-nine thousand cases reviewed, sixty thousand were placed in category C. But this liberality was not to outlast the crisis to come.

Meanwhile, plans of large-scale colonization of refugees continued to abound. In Britain, a company anticipating a major exodus of Hungarian Jews made plans to buy a thousand-acre tract in British Honduras. Australians continued to debate the question of whether they wanted such a colony in Kimberleys. In the United States, a scheme for colonization in Alaska, favored by President Roosevelt, was formulated in Congress and then blocked there, largely because of opposition from Alaskan political leaders. A project for the Philippines began slowly taking shape, intended to accommodate only ten thousand refugees. But the only one of these plans to get started in earnest was that which had been initiated in the Dominican Republic by Generalissimo Rafael Leonidas Trujillo. The former President and effective dictator of the country had bought a twenty-six-thousand-acre tract near Sosua from the United Fruit Company for $50,000, originally using it as pasture land. He had recently offered to allow refugees to settle on it and repay him on easy terms through the profits they earned from banana cultivation. With funds from the Joint Distribution Committee, an *ad hoc* organization called the Dominican Refugee Administration, or DORA, was formed. Five hundred German and Austrian families, some of whom had been on agricultural training programs in Germany, were selected as the first colonists.

"The hot sunshine of the deep tropics greeted the Sosua settlers today," wrote Kenneth Campbell of *The New York Times* on May 11,

after the stormy ride over the mountains from Ciudad Trujillo was completed last night.

This morning they spread about the nearer parts of the tract of land excitedly inspecting the varied plant life and admiring the seascape. The first get-together meeting was held on the porch of the main building, at which Dr. Siegfried Klinger and his wife, both Viennese physicians, gave instructions on the proper health routine for the tropics.

The remainder of the day was spent in unpacking. Several days' rest will be necessary to acclimate the new settlers. Their earliest tasks will be that of preparing houses. The type of houses best suited to the Sosua Settlement is a subject for experiment. The settlers who arrived yesterday were quartered in some of the twenty frame houses, with corrugated iron roofs, that are now available. Twenty more houses already on the tract can be fixed up with little effort. These houses are equipped with plumbing and electricity. It is hoped that the new houses to accommodate the coming colonists can be built for as little as $200 each. Samples of native stone are being examined to determine whether it might not be more suitable than wood for permanent residences.

Pointing out that "the exact economic plan under which the settlement is to operate is as yet undetermined," Campbell goes on:

> Each settler will have a house and a parcel of land, probably eight to ten acres. Those receiving land somewhat less fertile than others are receiving more of it. Each settler will probably receive several cows, although for the present livestock is being held cooperatively with the bulk of it likely to be so held in the future.
>
> Each settler is expected to devote certain hours daily to cooperative work and he may use the remaining time for his own enterprises. Probably specific cooperatives will be established for growing bananas, yucca and coffee, each settler joining the cooperative for the work [to which] he is best adapted.
>
> Cooperative work will include road building, which is now badly needed. A negotiable but inferior road links the settlement with the Santiago–Puerto Plata highway, but other roads are little better than trails which become quagmires after heavy rains.

A final important point is stressed:

> The picked settlers making up the 500 families were selected because they intend to remain here. . . . Only those were picked who had little or no chance of migrating to the United States or other countries.
>
> Association officials make it clear that Sosua is in no way a jumping-off place for the United States.

The quiet peopling of Sosua took place on the second day of the most startling event of the war so far: the Germans had invaded Holland and Belgium. Chamberlain resigned in the face of events for which he was not the man required, and Winston Churchill replaced him. The battle of France ensued, Hitler's tanks and planes, along with his highly disciplined troops, pouring in north of the Maginot Line, through the Low Countries and the Ardennes Forest, unleashing a Blitzkrieg unlike any ever seen. Trapped in a pocket formed by the German thrust, the King of Belgium surrendered unilaterally, leaving the French and British troops in that sector to fend for themselves. At the end of May and for the first days of June, three hundred thousand of them staged a miraculous escape across the Channel from the beach at Dunkirk, many transported in small boats, yachts, and fishing craft owned by individual Englishmen who volunteered for the task. Some of these troops were rushed back to the front and the defense of Paris, but it was too late. On June 10, Italy dishonorably entered the war against a crumbling France, invading from the southeast. Paris fell on June 14, and eight days later a new French government under Marshal Philippe Pétain signed a humiliating armistice.

The Britain of Winston Churchill would not give up, nor would a Free French government declared by General Charles de Gaulle in a broadcast from London to the people of France on June 18. But to many Frenchmen, what had occurred was defeat as in 1871, with the loss of Alsace-Lorraine again and the prospect of a German military presence until a permanent peace was signed. British persistence in fighting Hitler simply meant for them a prolongation of the agony they had to undergo in the meantime: that of direct German occupation of some three-fifths of the country, including Paris, the entire north and all of the Atlantic coast down to the Spanish border. The capital of Unoccupied France was established at the resort town of Vichy, under a government headed by Marshal Pétain that claimed to have authority over the whole country, including the Occupied Zone, but which was from the outset a puppet of the German authorities in Paris.

Among its other activities, the Vichy government enacted a series of anti-Semitic laws with a swiftness and a zeal that were perhaps even greater than what the German overlords had required. France, after all, had an anti-Semitic tradition of its own, and an assortment of quasi-Nazi zealots who made themselves at home among the ruling circles in Paris as well as at Vichy. Culminating in the Statut des Juifs of October 3, 1940, these laws defined Jews racially after the German fashion, effectively excluded them from cultural life, journalism, and the civil service, required their registration and the stamping of "Juif" on their identification papers. Moreover—since xenophobia, directed against the huge influx of foreign Jews that had occurred in recent years, was as strong a feeling among some Frenchmen as anti-Semitism—the Vichy government began to take measures against aliens and recently naturalized citizens.

Unoccupied France was now the principal location on the European Continent of Jewish refugees from Nazi Germany. Apart from the large numbers already there when the war broke out—many of them in the detention camps in the Pyrenees and elsewhere in the south—others had since flooded in from Holland, Belgium, and the north of France. In fact, the German authorities in the north had come to regard the Unoccupied Zone as another dumping ground for Jews—much to the chagrin of the Vichy regime, which tried to seal the border between the two zones. In July, the German rulers of Alsace—which had been reincorporated into the Reich—dumped three thousand Alsatian Jews into the Unoccupied Zone. In August, fourteen hundred German-Jewish refugees were sent there from Bordeaux; in October, more than sixty-five hundred Jews from the west of Germany itself were sent in sealed trains to Lyon.

All these actions were part of a vague plan of resettlement that had revived since the conquest of France. As Reinhard Heydrich was to explain to a member of the German Foreign Office the following February, "after the conclusion of peace, [the interned Jews of German-dominated Europe] will be the first transport to leave Fortress Europe in the total evacuation of the Continent that we plan." There now was even a prospective destination for them—Madagascar, that old hope of Polish anti-Semites, was a French colony. In August, SS Lieutenant Theo Dannecker—soon to be in charge of Jewish affairs in Paris—looked into the matter at the French Ministry of Colonies, and gave a report. "Attached," he wrote,

are preliminary studies on the project to transfer about 4,000,000 Jews to Madagascar. . . .

a) First of all, all bureaus in charge of the operation have to make a survey of the Jews under their jurisdiction. They are responsible for such preliminary measures as preparing documents for individual Jews, confiscating and evaluating their property and setting up convoys. The first convoys must include principally farmers, construction specialists, artisans and manual laborers with their families, as well as doctors. These must serve as an advance guard to prepare the way for the masses to come later.

b) Each Jew can take up to 400 pounds of baggage. The farmers, artisans and doctors *must* take along whatever tools and professional instruments they have. Cash and precious objects will be subject to current regulations.

It was a kind of authoritarian nightmare vision of Sosua—or of Zion, for that matter: Adolf Eichmann, who now got to work on the planning of this project, was to claim that he found inspiration for it in the writings of Theodor Herzl, and to describe it as his "great effort to provide a place where Jews could live among their own folk and be glad to get a piece of land beneath their feet."

In the meantime, the Nazis had still not completely sealed off the exits in regions under their control for Jews who could find the legal and financial means to get out. In the East, there was still the Soviet border of occupation for those willing to take their chances with it. And Unoccupied France, which obtained *de facto* recognition from the United States, was now the chief corridor of departure—Italy had been a prominent one until it entered the war—for refugees who could obtain visas to the neutral countries of the Western Hemisphere. From there, they usually would pass through Spain—except when Spain would not let them—to the neutral port of Lisbon.

There an important link in the rescue system awaited them. HICEM, the organ of HIAS and the JCA, was now carrying on its principal work in Lisbon, after a flight from the Nazi onslaught similar to that of the refugees themselves. When France had declared war in September 1939, the headquarters of HICEM were transferred to Brussels in neutral Belgium, although the office in Paris was not closed. With the invasion of Belgium, the Bel-HICEM operation, as it was called, was closed and its personnel escaped to France. When Paris fell on June 14, 1940, the remaining personnel of HICEM, including its American chairman, James G. Bernstein, retreated within hours of the oncoming German troops, establishing themselves first in Bordeaux, and then, on June 26, in Lisbon.

"Apparently nobody wants to know," Hannah Arendt was to write some two years later, "that contemporary history has created a new type of human being—the kind that are put in concentration camps by their foes and in internment camps by their friends."

Arendt was one of the thousands of Jewish intellectuals who had left Germany in the first outpouring of 1933, political as well as racial refugees: in her case, she had had to leave on account of her activities with the Zionist movement. And she was one of the many who had landed in France, to create a brilliant colony of German exiles in Paris. "We were expelled from Germany because we were Jews," Arendt reflected:

> But having hardly crossed the French borderline, we were changed into "boches." . . . During seven years we played the ridiculous role of trying to be Frenchmen—at least, prospective citizens; but at the beginning of the war we were interned as "boches" all the same. In the meantime, however, most of us had indeed become such loyal Frenchmen that we could not even criticize a French governmental order; thus we declared it was all right to be interned. . . . After the Germans invaded the country, the French Government had only to change the name of the firm; having been jailed because we were Germans, we were not freed because we were Jews.

On May 15, upon receiving orders, Arendt and more than two thousand other women had reported at the sports arena, the Vélodrome d'Hiver, and from there had been transported to Gurs. "I was five weeks in Gurs," she was to recall many years later:

> we had been put there by the regular French government during the last weeks of the war as "enemy aliens." A few weeks after

our arrival in the camp—which was a regular concentration camp, originally built for soldiers of the Spanish Republican Army—France was defeated and all communications broke down. In the resulting chaos, we succeeded in getting hold of liberation papers with which we were able to leave the camp.

Such papers were issued to those who could offer assurance of leaving the country soon. Arendt then joined her husband, Heinrich Blücher, and her mother in nearby Montauban to await American visas.

What Arendt was to obtain—through the good offices of her first husband, the novelist Gunther Anders, who was by then living in the United States—was an emergency visitors'. visa. This was another product of President Roosevelt's efforts to find loopholes in the immigration rules in order to rescue victims of Nazi persecution. Having discovered the use of the visitors' visas in the wake of the Kristallnacht in 1938, he invoked it again in January 1940 as a way of rescuing intellectuals and anti-Nazi activists whose lives could be considered in imminent danger from retribution. The idea became especially urgent after the fall of France, and in mid-July, Hamilton Fish Armstrong, the influential editor of *Foreign Affairs*, cabled two appeals to the White House in the name of the many well-known anti-Nazis who were trapped in the Unoccupied Zone. He then sent a list of names, which was relayed to the State Department, and from there sent to the American consuls in Marseille and Lisbon, with instructions to grant these people emergency visitors' visas.

Another *ad hoc* method of rescue had come into being, and the State Department's Visa Division soon found itself besieged by an array of American organizations—many but not all of them Jewish—who were eager to present lists of their own. Among these were the Jewish Labor Committee, the American Federation of Labor, an association of Orthodox rabbis, and also concerned individuals like Rabbi Stephen S. Wise. An Emergency Rescue Committee, concerned specifically with refugee writers, artists, and intellectuals, was formed in New York. The President's Advisory Committee on Political Refugees, which had been created at the time of the Evian conference under the chairmanship of James G. MacDonald, took over the task of coordinating this new emergency visa effort. By means of this program, and with the help of HICEM in Lisbon, the Blüchers were able to sail for the United States early the following year.

·57·

REFUGEES OR SPIES?

The "Fifth Column" fear that had first arisen in Britain with the German occupation of Norway returned in greater strength upon the fall of the Low Countries a few miles across the Channel. Sir Neville Bland, the recent British Minister at the Hague, arrived home convinced that the "Fifth Column Menace," as he called it in the title of a memorandum to the Foreign Office, was in large part responsible for what had happened. Writing of men and women who had been parachuted into Holland ahead of the German troops, and of the danger represented by "the paltriest kitchen-maid," he concluded:

> Every German or Austrian servant, however superficially charming and devoted, is a real and grave menace, and we cannot conclude from the experiences of the last war that "the enemy in our midst" is no more dangerous than it was then. I have not the least doubt that, when the signal is given, as it will scarcely fail to be when Hitler so decides, there will be satellites of the monster *all over the country* who will at once embark on widespread sabotage and attacks on civilians and the military indiscriminately. We cannot afford to take this risk. *All* Germans and Austrians, at least, ought to be interned at once.

On May 30, 1940, Sir Neville conveyed these views in a BBC broadcast.

As fear grew of a German invasion of Britain, such warnings had their effect. As early as May 11, the new Churchill government had declared a "protected" area along the southern and eastern coasts, within which all male Germans and Austrians between sixteen and sixty were rounded up and interned. Later that month, all category-B aliens were arrested. Then, in June, after a roundup of Italian aliens, some

486

thirty thousand refugees in category C were rounded up, the majority of them sent to internment camps on the Isle of Man. These included a number of distinguished writers, scholars, jurists, scientists, and musicians.

But as the battle of Britain began in the air, the presence of so many thousands of "enemy aliens" anywhere in the British Isles was considered a potential danger. Soon they were being sent to the overseas dominions—mainly Canada, whose Prime Minister, Mackenzie King, agreed to take them "because of the danger of having a potential enemy in the midst of the people during the threat of invasion." A stream of shipments of them began flowing across the Atlantic, until, on July 2, the *Arandora Star*, carrying 473 Germans and Austrians and 717 Italians, was torpedoed by a German submarine off the west coast of Ireland; 146 of the Central Europeans and 453 of the Italians were drowned. This caused an angry outburst of public opinion at home that arrested the antirefugee trend.

In the meantime, about nine thousand "enemy aliens" had arrived in Canadian internment camps, just across the border from the United States.

Americans were a whole ocean away from German-occupied Europe, but in an age of aerial warfare, it was a greater proximity to such danger than any they had ever known. Endangered Britain did not seem very far away to people who lived on the East Coast of the United States, especially when Winston Churchill, in one of the most heroic speeches ever made, said on June 4 that if by any chance that island found itself "subjugated and starving, then our Empire beyond the seas, armed and guarded by the British Fleet, would carry on the struggle, until, in God's good time, the New World, with all its power and might, steps forth to the rescue and the liberation of the Old." This was not only an invitation to America to help, but a clear promise that if Britain fell the war would be carried on from Canada.

Under the circumstances, Americans were quite susceptible to the Fifth Column fears sweeping Britain. Joseph C. Bullitt, the U.S. Ambassador to Paris, returned home after the German conquest and said:

> The French had been more hospitable than even we Americans to refugees from Germany. More than one-half the spies captured doing actual military spy work against the French army were refugees from Germany. Do you believe that there are no Nazi and Communist agents of this sort in America?

Americans were already inclined to believe otherwise. In July, *Fortune* magazine published the results of a poll showing 71 percent of the respondents agreeing that Germany had "already started to organize a 'Fifth Column' in this country." In newspapers and magazines there was a virtual hysteria on the subject. The August issue of the *American Magazine* began a series with an article by J. Edgar Hoover entitled "Enemies Within," which was announced as describing:

> Factories sabotaged . . . ships burned . . . machines smashed . . . trains wrecked. . . . In a war of utter ruthlessness the Fifth Column is on the march. . . . Saboteurs are striking at America.

This theme was even taken up by *The New York Times*, which carried an article on August 21 by Colonel William J. Donovan, a Washington intelligence adviser, that began:

> When all allowance has been made for Adolph Hitler's superior armies, his resourcefulness, his daring, and the vital assistance by Germans living within the victim countries, his success can be explained only by another factor. This is nothing less than the presence among the enemies of what, since the Spanish civil war, has been known as the "Fifth Column."

Even Hollywood, that eminent refugee haven, entered into the fray. The first of what was to become a barrage of foreign-agent films was *Confessions of a Nazi Spy*, starring Edward G. Robinson, once a Jewish immigrant from Rumania, as an FBI man; Paul Lukas, a refugee from Axis Europe, as a spy; and produced at the studios of Warner Brothers, sons of a Jewish immigrant family: it seemed an exercise in bending over backward to prove American credentials. First released in the spring of 1939, this depiction of spies entering the United States disguised as refugees had then had a bad reception: there had been protests from the German embassy in Washington, and it had been banned in several countries in Europe and Latin America. But in the summer of 1940, after the fall, with the purported aid of the Fifth Column, of not only France and Belgium, but also of three of the countries that had banned the film—Norway, Denmark, and Holland—it was being rereleased in an updated form that included a series of newsreel vignettes showing the fall of each of the West European countries and suggesting that the Fifth Column was a crucial factor. There were still objections, but, as *The New York Times* wrote, "So expert a spokesman of true German culture as Thomas Mann, however, felt that 'the picture will exercise a splendid influence on the world in general, as it will help people to realize what is going on in the world today.' "

The most significant impact of this "realization" was upon the American government's policy of refugee admission. Restrictionists in

Washington were now determined to restrain the liberal tendencies that Roosevelt had been showing in this matter since 1938. For his own part, the President had to yield somewhat on what was coming to seem a secondary issue, for the restrictionists also represented the forces of isolationism, and his overriding purpose was to become Britain's virtual ally in an undeclared war against Hitler. That fall, as he made a perilous and unprecedented bid for a third term, he took risks enough when he introduced the Lend-Lease policy to aid the British war effort and started the first peacetime conscription in American history. People influenced by voices like that of Representative Martin Dies of Texas had to be granted concessions—indeed, Roosevelt could only have been grateful that, with a war going on that had followed upon a devil's pact between Hitler and Stalin, Nazis in America were as bad in their eyes as communists. "Dies Asks U.S. Ban on [German-American] Bund and Reds," ran a headline over a *New York Times* article of August 27, 1940, which summed up remarks he had made the day before:

> There are 6,000,000 sympathizers with communism, nazism and fascism in the United States, and they are organized and financed into a more dangerous fifth column than any that existed in any of the countries overrun by Hitler, Mr. Dies declared. . . .
> Although this country is in no danger of invasion by foreign armies [he continued], it is in great peril from treason within. . . .
> He charged that both Stalin and Hitler had declared their intention of attacking this country, and he said that nazism had already made tremendous progress in South America.

The implication for admirers of Mr. Dies was that he was fighting a war—the only real one, perhaps—in which the President was negligent.

The man who proved to be in the best position to do something about the possible influx of Fifth Columnists was the Assistant Secretary in the State Department, Breckenridge Long of Missouri. A descendant of the two well-known political families invoked by his name, Long was a Princeton graduate who had first entered public service in the Woodrow Wilson administration. There he came to know his colleague and contemporary Franklin Roosevelt. After several years as a Saint Louis lawyer, Long had been rewarded for his efforts in behalf of Roosevelt's 1932 victory by being appointed Ambassador to Rome. His initial enthusiasm for Mussolini cooled after the Italian invasion of Ethiopia, and he resigned in 1936, an ardent anti-Fascist. In January 1940, he was appointed to the State Department to head a newly created Special War Problems division. The several functions thereby placed in his charge included controlling the issuance of visas.

The first signs of a negative attitude on his part toward refugees, if one takes the evidence of the diary he kept almost daily throughout the war, occurred after the fall of the Low Countries and the invasion of France. His principal task at that moment was to find places on ships that could take American citizens out of the war zones, and he was finding, to his annoyance, that many of them were filling up with refugees. "In the Department," he wrote in his diary for May 17,

> we have been busy trying to evacuate Americans. Our big ships sailing in the Mediterranean are booked up with foreigners, proceeding to the United States in such quantities that they have practically absorbed all available passages so that our own citizens are going to have great difficulty getting aboard. . . . The *Manhattan* sails from New York tomorrow for Genoa, and on her return trip she is sold out to refugees.

To this he added, in a more political vein:

> We are also proceeding with protective measures for our national defense. I had passed by [Sumner] Welles and the Secretary [of State, Cordell Hull] a proposed bill for the Congress for the registration of all aliens now in the country and all aliens in the future arriving and requiring them to report and authorizing their deportation if illegally entered or illegally overstaying. . . . And we will tighten up on our visas from abroad and require additional information with authority to grant visas centered in Washington instead of designated to our Consuls. There are many thousands of aliens, some of them known to be active German agents, and many of them illegally in this country. We have to be very careful in keeping within the provisions of the Constitution, but it is a necessary requirement that we have authority to handle any "4th army" or "5th army" there may be in the United States.

In the next few days, Long and his colleagues worked on security questions. "Still engaged in preparation of papers," he wrote on June 4,

> consultations with Justice and Labor [Departments] and arranging final draft executive orders and telegrams to restrict the granting of visas and to stop up the holes of unauthorized immigrants into the United States.

By June 17, the day France asked for an armistice, the lesson of that country had become clear to Long, and he confided to his diary:

> The problem of refugees is getting to be enormous. France was filled with political refugees from Belgium, Holland, Poland, Ger-

many and a lot from Italy. . . . The English propose to take a number of refugees to Canada. Without passport requirements, which we are now working on, they could simply walk right into the United States.

By June 26, he had a firm policy for at least slowing down the influx. "We can," he wrote in a department memorandum that day,

> delay and effectively stop for a temporary period of indefinite length the number of immigrants into the United States. We could do this by simply advising our consuls to put every obstacle in the way and to require additional evidence and to resort to various administrative devices which would postpone and postpone the granting of the visas. However, this could only be temporary.

This policy was gradually to take hold; for the moment, Long's influence in the State Department was not yet great enough to withstand opposing tendencies there on the refugee issue, probably represented mainly by Sumner Welles. On June 20, when Long was gaining a certain unpopularity by opposing a movement—led by Mrs. Eleanor Roosevelt—to bring over British children into American foster homes during the Blitz, *The New York Times* carried this item:

> The American Consulate in Lisbon was authorized by the State Department today to supervise the immigration quotas of several European countries to facilitate the migration of certain war refugees to this country. The consulate will supervise these for the Belgian, Luxembourg and Netherlands quotas and for part of the British, French, Italian and Swiss quotas.
>
> It will mean that refugees who have made their way to Lisbon can obtain immigration papers there instead of having to communicate with the American Consulates in their native countries.

Moreover, it was only a few weeks after this that the emergency visa program went into full motion.

These clear victories of the prorefugee forces were followed in September by a most humiliating defeat for Long. The *Quanza*, a Portuguese vessel out of Lisbon, had arrived at New York on August 19 and deposited there about two hundred American evacuees as well as a few visa-holding refugees. Remaining on board were over a hundred more refugees holding landing permits for the *Quanza*'s next port of call, Vera Cruz, Mexico. These had been dearly purchased, and, like those of the *St. Louis* a little over a year before, they proved unacceptable upon arrival at the port for which they were designated. The *Quanza* then moved on to Nicaragua, where the refugees were again refused. "Unable to land there," Long continues in his diary,

> they proceeded ostensibly for Portugal and then conveniently discovered that they would have to put in to Norfolk for coal. As soon as it became known that they were to arrive at Norfolk I was flooded with pressure groups and telegrams and telephones and personal visits to permit the landing of persons off of the boat.

Long resisted all such pleas, arguing that, though there now was a category of emergency visitor's visas, the plight of the *Quanza* refugees was not an emergency.

But this largely unpublicized episode was one in which Rooseveltian intervention could play a role, unlike that of the *St. Louis*. It was Mrs. Roosevelt, by this time a major advocate in the cause of refugee children, who telephoned Long to express her concern about "the children and a few other categories" aboard. She had talked to the President about the matter, and asked Long to call him the following day. Long did so, and concluded that "it was apparent that he did not want to talk to me on the subject, and I inferred—and it now seems correctly—that he would leave the matter entirely in my hands." Considering what occurred in the sequel, the President's attitude could only have meant he knew there was nothing more to worry about.

In the course of recoaling at Norfolk, the *Quanza* managed to be delayed more than twenty-four hours, and therefore had to make a formal entry into the port. "Apparently," Long writes, "there was every effort to delay the vessel from sailing and a concerted effort by persons on shore cooperating in the interests of persons aboard." One such person on shore by now was Patrick Malin, a representative of the Presidents' Advisory Committee on Political Refugees. "I . . . agreed with the Department of Justice," Long writes of the situation he had thus been maneuvered into,

> to treat the passengers on the ship on the same basis that we treated persons in Europe, which was: first, we would recognize the recommendations of the Presidents' Advisory Committee on Political Refugees [as to] who were in imminent danger and who were of the leading intellectuals of the liberal movement in Europe; second, recognize the Marshall Field Committee for the saving of British children by taking their recommendations for children aboard, provided they complied with the requirements; and third, to let off the boat for purposes of transit across or through the United States any persons whose travel documents were corroborated to us as authentic.

On the evening of September 14, Malin telephoned Long and told him

> that they had found three children and two mothers, making five; that they had found thirty-five persons who had valid travel documents entitled to travel across the United States—which was greatly to my surprise and far in excess of the number I anticipated and I am sure now was due to a very generous interpretation of the validity of the documents in question; and that he had construed everybody else on the boat to be a political refugee and that they could come ashore.

Long did not take the outcome gracefully:

> I remonstrated violently; said that I thought it was a violation of the law; that it was not in accord with my understanding with them; that it was not a proper interpretation of my agreement; that I would not be a party to it; and that if they did that I would have to take the matter up some other way.

He was not to be so deftly outmaneuvered again.

·58·

THE BARRIERS STRENGTHEN

The month of November 1940 saw significant setbacks in Palestine and in the United States to hopes for escape to those countries from Nazi persecution.

A disaster in Haifa harbor on November 25 brought back to the world's attention the problem of the 1939 White Paper, and of the large illegal immigration that had ensued. "Refugee Ship Off Palestine Is Sunk by Blast," *The New York Times* headline announced, and the article said:

> While the steamship *Patria*, with nearly 1,800 Jewish refugees aboard, was lying alongside the main breakwater in Haifa Harbor this morning, an explosion caused her to keel over and then slowly settle to the harbor bottom. It is feared there were some fatalities.
>
> The refugees aboard the ship—men, women and children—were awaiting transfer to another British colony in accordance with the Palestine Administration's recent decision. Rescue work was undertaken immediately by British troops and the police.
>
> The cause of the blast that sank the vessel has not been determined.

The *Patria* was a British ship onto which the passengers of three smaller vessels—illegal immigrants who had come down the Danube and through the Black Sea straits—were being loaded to be taken to an internment camp on the British-held island of Mauritius in the Indian Ocean. Not until years later did it become known that the explosion was the work of Palestinian-Jewish underground fighters who had sought to hinder the ship's departure but underestimated the charge they laid. Ultimately, the death toll reached over 250. In a gesture of mercy by the British government, the survivors were placed in camps in Palestine.

A radical response to the Palestine quotas, Aliyah Bet, as the illegal immigration was called, had been begun as early as 1937 and taken on its particular character and intensity in Vienna shortly after the *Anschluss*. Negotiations had opened there between young leaders of the radically nationalist Zionist Revisionists and Eichmann's henchmen, all of whom were in agreement about getting as many Jews as possible out of Germany and Austria. The embarrassment this caused to Britain was perfectly satisfactory to the Nazis and of no concern to the young Jewish organizers of the operation—although Chaim Weizmann and other Jewish Agency leaders, eager to maintain good relations with the Mandatory power, were to be officially disapproving of it. The American Jewish Joint Distribution Committee, while not openly supporting the Aliyah Bet, connived at the indirect use of its funds for this purpose.

The process was not too difficult, since Rumania was friendly to Germany and eager to get rid of some of her own Jews. Shipments of illegal refugees could be sent without much interference down the Danube to Rumanian Black Sea ports, from which they would embark for Palestine on ships, often Greek, whose captains were well paid for their efforts. Papers of some kind were needed for passage through Hungary and Yugoslavia, and especially through the Black Sea straits—nonbelligerent Turkey was eager not to clash with British interests—but these, too, could be arranged with the help of the German authorities. The most difficult part of the operation was the actual landing in Palestine. This was almost always done at night, on remote parts of the coast, by means of small boats taking passengers from the ships to the beaches. In one unusual instance, the Greek ship *Parita* had simply run aground on the Tel Aviv shore in July 1939, many of its passengers scurrying to safety past the British police.

There were frequent protests against the White Paper policy from concerned sections of the British public, especially when incidents occurred with illegal immigrants. Winston Churchill, who, though friendly to Zionism throughout his career, found that he could not tamper with the White Paper policy under the strains of war, showed an eagerness to make humane gestures from time to time. It was owing to his order that the *Patria* survivors had been allowed to stay in Palestine, even though the area commander, General Archibald Wavell, had been opposed to doing this. But the attitudes of the Foreign and Colonial offices remained firmly as they had been defined in a memorandum of January 1940:

Illegal immigration into Palestine is not primarily a refugee movement. There are, of course, genuine refugees among the immi-

grants. . . . The problem is thus an organized invasion of Palestine
for political motives, which exploits the fact of the refugee problem
and unscrupulously uses the humanitarian appeal to the latter to
justify itself.

In this view, what was going on was an effort sponsored by the Gestapo
to undermine the British Mandatory authority.

After allowing the *Patria* survivors to stay in Palestine, the British
government then lashed back by suspending the further issuance of
immigration certificates until March 1941. "Summing up the immigration situation since April 1939," said the *Jewish Chronicle* of January
3, 1941,

> a Government statement shows that legal immigration for the pe-
> riod reached 12,270 and "illegal" immigration 16,565. With a fur-
> ther reduction for the "illegal" immigrants, including the survivors
> of the *Patria* disaster, a balance remains of between 36,000 and
> 37,000, to which number Jewish immigrants may be admitted dur-
> ing the next three-and-a-half years, in accordance with the terms of
> the White Paper, which allowed for the admission of 75,000 Jews
> over a period of five years.

Meanwhile, another attempt had been made by Aliyah Bet in the
immediate wake of the *Patria* incident, and it, too, had ended in disaster. In December, the *Salvador*, an unseaworthy Uruguayan freighter,
was wrecked in a storm in the Sea of Marmara carrying 326 illegal
immigrants; 204 were drowned. "According to German sources," reported the *Jewish Chronicle* on January 3,

> the British Consulate in Istanbul has refused to issue Palestinian
> visas to the 122 Jews who were saved when the Uruguayan
> freighter *Salvador* was shipwrecked in the Sea of Marmara while
> on its way to Palestine. . . . The Turkish authorities are said to be
> continuing their efforts to obtain visas for the refugees.

There was not to be another such attempt for a year.

Breckenridge Long was in the meantime recovering rapidly from his
setback in the *Quanza* episode. The decisive role in that had been played
by the Justice Department, under whose jurisdiction the Immigration
Bureau had just been placed. From then on, Long was at war with
certain of its members, "who, for sentiment or for sympathy, are inclined to be soft-hearted" on the refugee issue. Foremost among these
was the Solicitor General, Francis Biddle—the Attorney General himself, Robert Jackson, seems to have remained aloof in the controversy.

Moreover, pitted on the side of Biddle and his men was Harold L. Ickes, the outspokenly liberal Secretary of the Interior, who had become highly sympathetic to the refugee cause. On the other hand, Long was now finding such formidable allies as Martin Dies and the increasingly vehement anti-Roosevelt columnist Westbrook Pegler. Roosevelt's relatively narrow victory over Wendell Willkie in November—a landslide in the Electoral College, but only 55 percent of the popular vote—only worsened the hostility of men like these.

It was Ickes and his assaulting troops who forced the next battle over the refugee issue. Two of the administration's more "soft-hearted" lawyers, Nathan Margold of the Interior Department and David Hart of Justice, had come up with a scheme involving the Virgin Islands. Searching for a place that could be designated a temporary refuge, not subject to immigration quotas or visa requirements, they believed they had found an opening in a clause of the President's April 1938 Executive Order on refugees, allowing the Governor of the Virgin Islands—an American territory not subject to metropolitan restrictions—to admit visitors without visas in emergency cases. The Interior Department, whose jurisdiction this was, presented the idea to the Islands' Governor, Lawrence W. Cramer, who enthusiastically supported it—the refugees would be supported by funds from American-Jewish organizations— and won approval for it in the legislature.

On November 12, Cramer issued a proclamation announcing the policy, and that was when Breckenridge Long got wind of it. "Yesterday," Long wrote in his diary on November 13,

> it developed that the Governor of the Virgin Islands, Cramer by name, under the guidance of the Solicitor in the Department of the Interior and a Mr. Hart in the Department of Justice, had issued a proclamation admitting refugees in the Virgin Islands on their appearance at the port of entry. After a short period of residence in the Virgin Islands and an affidavit that they are bona fide residents they may proceed without visas or other formalities to the United States. There is no consular investigation of the individuals prior to their arrival in the Virgin Islands.

Whether or not Long was correct about the refugees being allowed to "proceed without visas or other formalities to the United States," he doubtless felt such an eventuality was in the offing, and he was determined to prevent it at the source. He was sure this was

> part of a problem which Mr. Hart has indulged in in connection with the President's Advisory Committee. Biddle, the Solicitor General, has been associated with him, but I think he has not quite understood the purposes and objectives.

Long tried calling the President immediately, but was told that he was in his swimming pool and could not be disturbed. Then he turned to Secretary Hull, who "authorized" him to talk to the President. By the time Long reached him at nine that evening, Roosevelt may have had some inkling of what was up. "When I explained the matter to him," Long writes, "he was a little perturbed and asked me to talk to Ickes immediately and to call him back." Long then called Ickes

and found that he knew of the order and had authorized it and that he was an advocate of the whole scheme. He said that he would send his Solicitor [Nathan Margold] around to talk to me in the morning. I told him that our consular activities served as a sieve through which we could strain the applicants. His reply was that the holes in the sieve were too small and that they ought to be bigger and perhaps now we could negotiate and get them bigger. The inference was very plain that he was trying to take into the United States persons whom he thought the Department of State would not admit. He was rather obdurate and a little sarcastic.

Clearly Ickes had hoped to present a *fait accompli* and had been caught in the act. The President was on the spot when Long called him back to report the conversation, and had no choice but to agree to give an order suspending the proclamation until the issues were clarified.

The project was not yet dead, but now it was in the open and vulnerable. At the same time, Long had become a clearer target for liberals. On Monday, November 25, Joseph Alsop and Robert Kintner, in their "Capital Parade" column in the Washington *Post*, revealed that a jurisdictional conflict was going on between the State and Justice departments and that Long was at the center of it. Though they were not clear as to its content, they were critical of Long's refugee policies. "This morning," Long wrote,

the *Post* carried a story very critical about me. . . . The origin of it goes back to the same as the other criticisms which have appeared heretofore but by different columnists. They find their sources in the opposition of various groups to the policy which I have personified officially for the exclusion from the United States of undesirable persons and a very careful scrutiny of all who are permitted to come in. The pressure that has been brought to bear on me the last two months has been astonishing. The opposition is now using me as the fulcrum to pry open the door. I astonished Ickes irreparably by opposing his Virgin Islands scheme, and he is aligned with certain persons in the Department of Justice and in other branches of the government in an effort to unseat me officially.

Long had weapons now, however; the Attorney General, he wrote later,

> has under him a number of persons who have peculiar ideas and radical tendencies and sympathies toward forces which are inadmissible and unacceptable to my mind. And it is these persons and some others whom I do not know or know of whom Dies has investigated and about whom he has files which I understand are highly explosive and which he may release to the detriment of the administration and particularly to the Department of Justice if he and Jackson get into a fight.

"Delays War Haven on Virgin Islands," announced a *New York Times* headline on December 13, and the text summed up a statement by the State Department that the project "has been halted, temporarily at least." The article then quotes Ickes's remarks at a press conference:

> "This department has been in favor of it for some time," he said. "Naturally the Virgin Islands could not take care of many refugees, but even a few lives saved from firing squads and concentration camps are worth while in these days. . . .
> "I think it is regrettable to create the impression that the right of asylum for political refugees, of which this country used to be so proud, has been allowed to die of inanition. . . .
> "Fear has been expressed that some subversive people might come to the Virgin Islands and from there to the mainland," the Secretary continued, "but I don't see how, unless they are long-distance swimmers."

The last word on the subject for the year was delivered in rejoinder to Ickes by a tongue that, if not sharper than his, lashed more violently. "Like the experiment of prohibition," Westbrook Pegler wrote in his syndicated column of December 18,

> Mr. Ickes' proposal may be noble in purpose but, again like prohibition, it is charged with disastrous possibilities, as the people of France could warn us out of their experience.
> Most of these refugees are anti-Fascist, although there will surely be among them some Nazi and Fascist agents. But it stands to reason that a greater proportion of them will be communists who fled over the border into France after the Spanish Civil War and other Communists who, earlier in the general European revolution now in full eruption, escaped from Italy and Germany.

It could hardly be denied that some people with old if not current communist associations were among the refugees from the south of France. "On this subject," Pegler continued, it should be observed that there is in progress in New York and Hollywood a campaign to import a lot of Europeans who are described as intellectuals and writers, and that some of these are the beneficiaries of a great ballyhoo which disarms suspicion.

Americans are told that so-and-so is a great German or French or Spanish liberal and the author of some significant work, and they believe it without trying to ascertain whether the person in question is a Communist or without reading his book.

But at a recent dinner on behalf of this movement in Hollywood the committee in charge included most of the anti-American, native communist film writers and fellow travelers, and the character of this sponsorship naturally creates suspicion. Communists are not interested in relieving distress. They are concerned only in importing reinforcements.

Pegler ended by returning to Ickes with a word of warning:

Mr. Ickes needs watching. He has great powers and is tricky, abusive and high-handed, and here he seems to be shoving into matters which are the business of the Departments of State and Justice and involve the safety of the whole country.

There was France!

The Roosevelt administration, in the midst of constantly imperiled efforts to involve the country more deeply in the war against Hitler, could not tolerate too many flanking attacks of this sort. Breckenridge Long himself had concluded that the attacks upon him seemed "to be joined up with the small element in this country which wants to push us into this war. Those persons are largely concentrated along the Atlantic seaboard and principally around New York." He soon had his way with the Virgin Islands, persuading the navy to declare them a security zone and hence ineligible for foreign settlement. He also was able to whittle down the number of emergency visas granted in the coming months to only half of those once declared eligible.

·59·

THE DESCENT INTO
UNTRAMMELED SLAUGHTER

"It is estimated," said the *Jewish Chronicle* just after the dreadful re-birth of the Eastern Front on June 22, 1941,

> that about 8,000,000 Jews—about half the world's total—live in the battle area between the Baltic States and the Black Sea. When, early in 1939, Professor Burgdörfer, Director of the Reich Statistical Office, quoted this figure at a meeting of the Reich Institute for the History of the New Germany, he described the area . . . as the world's "Number 1 Semitic belt."

With the German invasion of Russia, grim memories of the years 1914–20 inevitably returned—along with some of the actors. "Hetman Skoropadsky, the Ukrainian quisling leader," as the *Chronicle* described him,

> who during the last world war was also appointed by the ex-Kaiser to ruler of the Ukraine, has published in the Russian organ in Berlin, *Russkoe Slovo*, an appeal to all Ukrainians to help Hitler in his war against the Jews and the Communists.
>
> Many Tsarist Russian anti-Semitic leaders who have lived since the Revolution in France, Yugoslavia, Bulgaria, Rumania and Czechoslovakia have been brought to Berlin to assist Hitler in his campaign.

According to the report, a "Free Ukrainian" center had been opened in Berlin, which urged the Ukrainian people to attack the "Jewish Bolsheviks" and invoked the old slogan of the Black Hundreds: "Beat down the Jews and save Russia."

To these old formulas had been added a deadly new combination:

Nazi fanaticism and German efficiency. "A ferocious anti-Jewish campaign," the *Chronicle* continues,

> has been launched in broadcasts from Germany, in the Ukrainian, Lithuanian, Russian, Latvian and Estonian languages. The Nazis are selecting as the special object of their spleen the Soviet Commissar Lazar Kaganovitch, who is a Jew. According to the German broadcasts, it is really Kaganovitch and not Stalin who is "the boss," and he is conducting a "Jewish policy."

There was no ambiguity for Jews this time as to which was the right side for them. "The Jews on the Western Soviet front," observed the *Chronicle*, "will resolutely fight against the Nazi invaders, for they know only too well what conquest would mean."

What conquest now meant on the Russian front was slaughter more terrible than any the war had seen thus far. Those Jews—and other "undesirables," such as gypsies and Soviet commissars—who survived the extraordinarily ferocious clash of armies, in which whole towns were quickly destroyed, were often subjected to the scourge of the *Einsatzgruppen*. These special troops affiliated with the SS, which followed the German armies and operated independently of them, were carrying out an assignment originating that spring with Hitler himself—and since known to infamy as the "Führer Order"—to deal summarily and fatally with "enemies" of the Reich—above all, Jews. The notions of resettlement and the outlines of the Lublin reservation were rapidly disappearing as the German eastern horizon suddenly extended without limit. A typical scene was Lwów. "The last Soviet column marched off on the night of the 28th of June 1941," Joseph Tenenbaum was to write of what had already been the unhappy Lemberg of his youth,

> and the first German patrols entered Lemberg on June 29, at eleven in the morning. With them marched terror. In a matter of hours large posters appeared on the walls inciting the population to wreak vengeance on the Jews, "responsible for the war and the killing of several thousand Poles and Ukrainians." The slaughter started immediately. The "new order" was inaugurated with "unrestrained plunder, violence, torture, mass shootings and murders of the civilian population." . . .
>
> The hunt for Jewish men and women went on unabatedly. Several thousand were herded into the prison on Kazimierzowska Street, others to penal institutions at Zamarstynowska and Jachowicza. The captives were unmercifully tortured and many shot. After two days of massacre only six individuals out of several thousand returned home. The others were exterminated.

Galicia, which had been a much-used dumping ground of Jews by Hungary—especially after its seizure of territories from Rumania the year before—was a scene of particular violence. "Massacres of thousands of Jews deported from Hungary to Galicia," *The New York Times* was to report in the fall,

> and the machine-gunning of more thousands of Galician Jews by German soldiers and Ukrainian bandits are reported in letters reaching Hungary from Galicia and eye-witness accounts of Hungarian officers. . . .
>
> One account by a Hungarian officer told of massacres in the Kamenec-Podolsk region of 2,500 deportees from Hungary, many of whom were originally refugees from other countries, and 8,000 Galician Jews. Other reports place the number of deaths as high as 15,000.

It was the policy of the *Einsatzgruppen* to use the cooperation of local populations whenever it could be enlisted, and none proved more cooperative than the Ukrainians of Western Galicia. "Three days after the first pogrom," Tenenbaum continues about Lwów,

> the Ukrainians renewed their assaults. They had tasted blood and were only too willing to do the bidding of the Nazis, especially since every murderous act was rewarded by pillage. . . . The climactic orgy of indiscriminate murder, however, was yet to come.
>
> On the 25th, 26th, and 27th of July, "action Petlura" was inaugurated. . . . The Germans instigated the Ukrainians to celebrate Petlura's anniversary in July instead of May. The Ukrainian hordes received carte blanche for three days, in which they could do as they pleased, and what pleased them most was the murdering of thousands of Jews.

Actually, the Nazis' foremost surrogate butchers at this time were the Rumanians, who had, along with the Finns and the Hungarians, joined in the war against Soviet Russia, and who quickly displayed themselves as more astute Jew-murderers than the Nazis yet seemed to be. Fighting their way through Bessarabia to Odessa, they rounded up some twenty-five thousand of that city's 150,000 Jews, herded them into the central military barracks, and mowed them down with machine guns.

"The extermination of the Jews," reported the *Jewish Chronicle* in August,

> was recently announced as one of the German war aims in a Russian-language broadcast from Belgrade. "From the beginning of this struggle," the broadcast said, "the German people have declared

war on the Jews." Asserting that victory in the East was certain
after the successes already achieved by the German army, the
broadcaster declared that "everything is moving towards the last
settling of accounts: that is, towards a massacre of the Jews without exception."

Of the Western leaders, it was Winston Churchill in particular who
showed full recognition of the turn Nazism now was taking. On October
25, when he and Roosevelt both issued public condemnations of some
shootings of hostages by the Germans in France, he added:

> The butcheries in France are an example of what Hitler's Nazis
> are doing in many other countries under their yoke.
> The atrocities in Poland, in Yugoslavia, in Norway, in Holland,
> in Belgium, and above all behind the German fronts in Russia, sur-
> pass anything that has been known since the darkest and most bes-
> tial ages of mankind. . . .
> Retribution for these crimes must henceforward take its place
> among the major purposes of the war.

In the United States, the passion for security had reached a new height
even before the German invasion of Russia, which had long been expected. At the end of May, President Roosevelt had declared a state of
"unlimited" national emergency; on June 17, he ordered the closing of
all German consulates in the country, considered to be main centers
of Fifth Column activity. This order was followed the next day by a new
State Department ruling regarding visas, which had been provoked by
the widespread belief that refugees with relatives in Nazi-controlled
Europe were sometimes blackmailed by threats of reprisals into becoming German agents. The instructions given to American consuls abroad
were summarized for the press:

> In view of the increasing number of instances known to the
> Department where persons living in certain countries in Europe
> have been permitted to leave only after entering into an obligation
> to act as agent in the United States for the governments controlling
> the countries from which they desired to depart, the Department
> of State . . . telegraphing instructions to diplomatic and consular
> officers, directed the withholding of visas from aliens having close
> relatives still residing in certain countries and in territories con-
> trolled by these countries.

The instructions had gone on to specify that this ruling applied to all
persons who had "children, parents, spouse, brothers or sisters still

remaining in such territory," though exceptions might be made in "meritorious cases" if they were referred back to the State Department in Washington. "The new Department of State regulations," *The New York Times* observed on June 19, "will cut off the avenue of escape for hundreds of refugees now waiting for permission to enter the United States."

Indeed, disapproval of the new ruling was so widespread that the State Department quickly felt obliged to offer a clarification that in effect modified its position slightly. In an editorial entitled "No Ban on Refugees," *The New York Times* explained the whole situation on June 26. It ran:

> A recent State Department ruling officially explained as "directing the withholding of visas from aliens having close relatives still residing in certain countries and the territories controlled by those countries" seems to have been widely misunderstood. The Department was not so explicit as it might have been.
>
> A supplementary ruling, issued last Tuesday in Washington and taking effect on July 1, clears up the situation. Discretion to grant visas is taken from consuls and transferred to the State Department. If the department is satisfied that the applicant's admission is desirable, that he can secure support, that he is properly sponsored, and that he can obtain the necessary exit permits, transit visas and transportation from the country in which he is residing, he will be admitted. The President's Advisory Committee on Political Refugees, with offices at 122 East Twenty-second Street, New York City, will act as a liaison agency with social service organizations interested in the immigrant. It is thought that this procedure will protect the country against those who might be induced to act as spies because of Nazi threats against close relatives still in the Nazi-controlled areas; that action on visas will be expedited; and that about as many immigrants can be admitted as would be possible under the old system.
>
> In short, the doors are not being closed. They are being more closely watched. We shall continue to receive, to our own great benefit, brave men and women who have refused to live under the Hitler tyranny.

This was still not to the satisfaction of refugee advocates. At the end of July, a group of the most prominent among them—all non-Jews—published a protest that said in part:

> We are aware of the situation which promoted this decision and we are sympathetic with every effort to reduce the toll of treason, spying and sabotage.... But we believe that this proposal is

similar to the policy hastily adopted by the British government a year ago, which proved to be too sweeping in its treatment of aliens, and which had to be mitigated under pressure of enlightened public opinion.

We believe that the denial of the right of American asylum to the victims of political and racial oppression in Europe represents a serious and unnecessary departure from American traditions.

Among the signers were Dorothy Thompson, Marshall Field, Alvin Johnson, Bishop Francis J. McConnell, and William Allen White.

"Personally," wrote Breckenridge Long in his diary,

I am committed to the program to prevent persons coming into the United States who are or who are apt to become the enemies of the United States. I cannot adopt the philosophy that some segment of our constitutional guarantees of liberty attach to an alien outside the United States the moment he applies for a visa to come here, nor can I condone the persons of any race, religion or category who entertain the slightest doubts about the desirability of the United States and its form of Government as compared to their own or some other form and who would serve the interests of another while here, and that mental attitude is going to direct my course in the Department of State as long as I am here.

But for all the growth of his influence, strong opposition continued against him in some government circles. Indeed, it was now stronger than ever at the Justice Department, where Robert Jackson, after being appointed to the Supreme Court, had been replaced as Attorney General by Francis Biddle. "I plainly foresee," Long wrote,

that following that course is going to bring on some more pointed difficulties with the Department of Justice than it has heretofore. I have always been able to straighten them out with Jackson. However, I have had nothing but difficulty with Biddle and his subordinates.

These difficulties, stimulated by adverse public response to the new visa policy, soon came to a head. Even the Secretary of State, who normally did not tread on Long's territory, expressed some concern over this issue. "Hull somewhat uneasy," Long wrote on August 19,

about policy which puts through a careful scrutiny all prospective immigrants who have close relatives in Germany or Russia. There is a recrudescence of criticism from radical elements and organizations interested in getting persons into the United States from the doubtful territory. Welles thought I should see the President and present him with the whole picture.

Sumner Welles was perhaps at this time closer to the President than anyone else in the department, and had been notably sympathetic to the refugee problem in the first crises of 1938 and 1939. Something was brewing, and after Long, at Hull's urging, wrote up a long memorandum on the situation for the President, the latter sent for him "to discuss the immigration problem." Long adds in his diary that this was to be done "before he shall receive the [James G.] MacDonald group." Roosevelt clearly was responding to the proddings of his Advisory Committee on Political Refugees. At their meeting, Long writes, he found the President "keen, well, in high spirits, and thoroughly in accord with our policies and practices." But this was not the first time Roosevelt had made Long believe he was in complete agreement with him when that was not necessarily the case.

This had been the preliminary to a showdown meeting. "At the request of the President," Long writes for September 4,

> attended a conference with him, MacDonald's refugee committee and Attorney General Biddle. They are critical of the Department's policy—consequently of me. Biddle is their advocate. Rabbi Wise and the Archbishop of New Orleans were their principal spokesmen. Various amendments to procedure were proposed.

The discussion soon became heated:

> Wise always assumes such a sanctimonious air and pleads for the "intellectuals and brave spirits, refugees from the tortures of the dictators" or words to that effect. Of course only an infinitesimal fraction of the immigrants are of that category—and some are German agents and others are sympathizers, the last named coming here because it is away from the scene of combat and looks like a safe place. I got a little mad and I fear I betrayed it. . . . Each one of these men hates me. I am to them the embodiment of a nemesis. . . . They would throw me to the wolves in their eagerness to destroy me—and will try in the future as they have in the past to ruin my political status.

But Long's status was secure in the general political climate of the country at that moment. Roosevelt's deepening involvement in the war was becoming precipitous, and the disapproving forces of isolationism—led in Congress by Senator Burton K. Wheeler and Representative John A. Rankin, and on the public platforms of the nation by Colonel Charles Lindbergh—were growing not only shriller but more insistent that Jews

were partly responsible for this trend. That summer, Rankin had made
such an accusation on the floor of the House. Colonel Lindbergh, as
chairman of the isolationist America First Committee, had begun frankly
to place the Jews at the center of the question. "He has told more than
one close friend," according to an August 11 *Life* magazine article about
him,

> that participation in the war against Hitler is sure to cause an in-
> ternal explosion, a bloody revolution in America. . . . He is espe-
> cially concerned with the effect such disasters would have on Jews
> in the U.S. He believes Jews will be blamed for American entry
> into the war and will suffer for it. If that happens, he has said, the
> anti-Jewish outbreaks that will occur here will surpass those in Nazi
> Germany, for Americans are "more violent" than Germans.

On September 11, Lindbergh told a crowd in Des Moines, Iowa, that
"the three most important groups which have been pressing the country
toward war are the British, the Jewish, and the Roosevelt Administration."

Lindbergh had added, on this occasion, that "the greatest danger
to this country" posed by the Jews lay in "their large ownership and
influence in our motion pictures, our press, our radio and our government." Only two days earlier, another leading isolationist, Senator Ger-
ald P. Nye of North Dakota, had argued before a Senate committee

> that a small group of motion picture producers, "all born abroad
> and animated by the persecutions and hatreds of the Old World,"
> have been injecting pro-war propaganda into American films, both
> for financially selfish and "non-American" reasons. . . .

Under the circumstances, it was not easy for Jewish groups to press
for a more liberal approach to the refugee issue, and the contending
forces in the administration moved toward a settlement behind the
scenes that was favorable to Breckenridge Long. On November 5, he
could record in his diary with relief:

> The Attorney General agrees to the last proposal for control
> of entry of aliens! That covers the principle we have insisted upon—
> ultimate control here in this department. . . . Details, in conformity
> with the principle, remain to be formalized. The selection by the
> President of two members of the Board of Review to represent *his*
> point of view—also remains. But the principal object has been at-
> tained.

This left hundreds of cases to be finally decided on by the new method in Lisbon, Casablanca, and Marseille, the main cities of refuge and hoped-for transit across the Atlantic in the fall of 1941. HICEM, which now had offices in all three, could claim that, between June 1940 and the end of December 1941, it had helped a total of twenty-five thousand men, women, and children from these cities to overseas countries of refuge. As for the Jews in those parts of Europe that were directly under Nazi control, their prospects for escape were rapidly disappearing. A wholly new and disastrous chapter was opening in Hitler's war against the Jews, as summed up by this report in the *Jewish Chronicle* of November 14:

> All Jewish emigration from territory controlled by the Reich has been brought to a halt by a new Gestapo measure which forbids the granting of exit visas to Jews regardless of their age. . . .
> The new ban . . . has come as a severe shock to hundreds of Jews who had completed their arrangements for emigration and were hoping shortly to quit Reich territory. Considerable alarm is felt that the Reich's aim in refusing to allow Jews to emigrate is that they may all be concentrated in Poland.

The fear was well grounded.

·60·

RESPONDING TO
THE INCONCEIVABLE

The emergence of Japanese imperial ambition in the Pacific, culminating in the air attacks on Pearl Harbor on December 7, 1941, finally brought all-out American entry into the war. President Roosevelt's declaration against Japan on December 8 was followed three days later by the expected declarations against the United States on the part of Japan's Axis allies, Germany and Italy. The menace in the Far East instilled a unity among Americans that the German one could not. Even Senator Wheeler acknowledged, "The only thing now is to lick the hell out of them," and Colonel Lindbergh sought to be reinstated in the Air Force.

For the next six months, it was the Pacific war that dominated the American headlines, as one loss after another was suffered by Allied forces not yet fully mobilized for war in that area. Indeed, despite the stand that was finally made that summer at Midway Island and then at Guadalcanal, the chief energies of American preparation were quietly being directed at the European sphere: Roosevelt and Churchill had decided, even before December 7, that that was the war to be won first. As American troops began massing in Britain under the command of a hitherto obscure lieutenant general, Dwight D. Eisenhower, the only question of grand strategy being mooted was whether they were to be landed in Western Europe or in North Africa, where the German effort to bail out the foundering Italians was turning into the southern jaw— the northern one being in Russia—of a huge pair of pincers that threatened to close upon the Middle East.

These were the circumstances under which Hitler's war against the Jews became a campaign of annihilation. There is a dreadful irony in the fact that this change was precipitated by the successive entry into the war, in the last half of 1941, of the two powers—Soviet Russia and the United States—without whom Nazi Germany could not have been

510

defeated. Until then, the policy of forced emigration and resettlement of Jews had continued to vie with the as-yet unchanneled impulse of Nazis to wage miscellaneous murder and allow starvation and pestilence to take their toll. But into the atmosphere of savage mutual slaughter that the war with Russia became had been introduced the first program of organized killings. And now, with the United States no longer a "non-belligerent" to be placated hopefully, there was no longer any need to make concessions to American sensitivities.

The feeling among Nazis that the American brake on them was disappearing can be traced at least as far back as the battle of Britain a year earlier. "The Nazis' rage against the pro-British speeches of President Roosevelt," the *Jewish Chronicle* had said in January 1941,

> and his steps to give war aid to Britain have led to a new crusade against the German Jews. Leading Nazis now declare that there is no longer any necessity for Germany to placate public opinion in America by withholding anti-Jewish measures, and that the process of extermination of Jewry in the countries under German control should now be intensified. The Nazis, of course, pretend to hold the American Jews largely responsible for President Roosevelt's policy, and they seem determined to "retaliate" by making their own Jews suffer.

All the more had this become the case with America's official belligerency. In June 1942, the *Chronicle* gave this summary of an article that had just appeared in the SS organ, *Schwarze Korps:*

> The war in Russia and President Roosevelt's policy, which the paper claims is inspired by the Jews, have made it necessary to revise the "magnanimous policy" hitherto followed by National Socialism towards the Jews. Only now, the paper concludes, has it been realized that the Jew is the eternal and implacable enemy of Germany, and, therefore, of the whole of Europe, and that his physical extermination must from now on be the aim of Germany and her allies.

The new program of organizing the destruction of Jews in death camps in Poland seems to have originated in a conference held on January 20, 1942, in a suburban villa near the Wannsee outside Berlin. Here, in guarded language, Heydrich, Eichmann, and other organizers of the war against the Jews discussed a "definitive solution" that involved the mass transportation of the ghettoized populations. At this stage, the plan still called for using some able-bodied Jews for slave labor, but their eventual annihilation was foreseen, along with the immediate killing of the rest. Throughout that winter and spring, camps

dedicated wholly or in large part to annihilation were successively established—first Chelmno, then Belzec, Majdanek, Auschwitz, Sobibor,
and Treblinka. Organized deportations to them of Jews amassed in
freight cars were in full operation by the beginning of April, and the
technique of killing them with poison gas—first carbon monoxide, later
the notorious "Zyklon B"—was in full use. Upon arrival at the camps,
only those Jews who were "selected" for work or experimentation had
a further chance to live; the rest were taken immediately to the gas
chambers—which, in time, were disguised as shower rooms in order to
forestall immediate panic. After asphyxiation, their bodies were cre-
mated. On July 22, the deportations from the Warsaw ghetto to the
death camp at Treblinka began.

Information about what was happening in their home country began reaching the exiled Polish National Council in London, which included two Jews among its membership. Shmuel Zygielbojm, the
Bundist member, received a report from colleagues in Poland, which he
immediately conveyed to the London *Daily Telegraph*. The paper published the story in two sensational installments, on June 25 and 30.
Referring to "the most gruesome details of mass killings even to the
use of poison gas," the articles said that more than a million European
Jews had been killed to date and that the aim of the Nazis was to "wipe
the race from the European continent." On June 29, Ignacy Schwarzbart, the other Jewish member of the Polish National Council, took part
in a press conference at which, according to *The Times* of London, he

gave figures of the massed slaughter and deaths caused by ill-treatment or starvation of Jews in Poland by the Germans. Asked what
could be done now in the matter, he suggested that the Jewish
population of Poland was in danger of annihilation, and only immediate reprisals could deter Hitler from carrying on his criminal
action.

Yet neither man had grasped fully what was happening—that is,
the use of death camps and poison gas for the systematic murder of an
entire people—and Schwarzbart, who grasped it less, greatly confused
the issue by criticizing his colleague's "harmful and irresponsible" pro-
pensity to exaggerate. Insisting that Zygielbojm should have referred
to the Jewish victims as "exterminated" rather than "murdered,"
Schwarzbart clearly had in mind by this his reference to "deaths caused
by ill-treatment or starvation." Germans, in this conception, were behaving so brutally toward Jews as to cause them to die by the tens of
thousands—a horrible phenomenon, indeed, but not precisely race-mur-
der. The uncertainty about the German policy toward Jews in that moment is reflected in a *New York Times* comment of July 4—four days

after that paper had published a summary of the Zygielbojm *Daily Telegraph* reports—which went:

> No figures are available here on Jewish massacres in Nazi-occupied areas except those furnished by refugees and occasional newspaper correspondence from Germany. They permit any conclusion one wants to make, from 100,000 to 1,500,000. As a rule the Germans treat the Jews according to whether they are productive and whether Reich Jews or Jews in Polish and Russian territory.

The uniqueness of this ultimate phase of the Nazis' "final solution" of the Jewish question had not yet impressed itself upon observers in the West. On June 20, it was still possible for a distinguished American rabbi to say in a sermon:

> The dastardly threat of Goebbels that the Nazis will exterminate the Jews if the R.A.F. continues its bombardment of German cities should be clear evidence that the Jews of Germany and occupied countries have been and are merely hostages in the hands of brigands and gangsters.
> Jews have been martyrs before in the annals of mankind, and if the slaying of Jews is necessary to redeem humanity from the blight of nazism those who are the victims will prove again the stuff of which the prophet and the martyr race is fashioned.

The mood of that moment among those who had heard and pondered the news presented by Zygielbojm and Schwarzbart was well expressed on the evening of July 21, at Madison Square Garden in New York, in a "massed demonstration against Hitler atrocities" organized by the American Jewish Congress, the B'nai B'rith, and the Jewish Labor Committee, and held under the chairmanship of Rabbi Stephen S. Wise. This was a heartfelt show of concern at the Jewish plight not only in Europe but in Palestine, which faced the danger presented by Rommel's succession of victories in Libya and western Egypt. Messages were sent to the gathering of twenty thousand by President Roosevelt—whose name was cheered every time it was mentioned—and Prime Minister Churchill. In the course of his message, the President said:

> Citizens, regardless of religious allegiance, will share in the sorrow of our Jewish fellow-citizens over the savagery of the Nazis against their helpless victims. The Nazis will not succeed in exterminating their victims any more than they will succeed in enslaving mankind. The American people not only sympathize with all victims of Nazi crimes but will hold the perpetrators of these crimes to strict accountability in a day of reckoning which will surely come.

Winston Churchill's message endorsed this position by recalling

> that on October 25 last both President Roosevelt and I expressed
> the horror felt by all civilized peoples at Nazi butcheries and our
> resolve to place retribution for these crimes among the major pur-
> poses of this war. The Jews were Hitler's first victims and ever
> since they have been in the forefront of Nazi aggression.

No one challenged the spirit of these remarks, to the effect that the task
at hand—for the sake of the Jews of Europe, as for all else that was
human—was to win the war and bring its criminals to justice. No one
expressed any thoughts of trying to organize some separate action to
avert total annihilation of the Jews under Hitler. The treatment of the
Jews was by far the worst manifestation of Nazi brutality for those
present, but not, as some were eventually to see it, a virtually distinct
war in itself.

Indeed, the remainder of Churchill's message, like most of the
meeting, dealt with the perilous situation of Palestine—here, after all,
was a problem that could be taken on by the normal efforts of war. The
Prime Minister praised the contribution being made by the Jews of
Palestine, ten thousand of whom were in the British armed forces, many
more thousands of whom were in other ways directly involved. This
provoked a discussion at the meeting of the idea of a Jewish Legion,
which had been broached with the British government by Zionist leaders and was still unresolved. Rabbi Wise said:

> We expect that the United Nations, conscious of the peril fac-
> ing Palestine, will enable the Jewish community of Palestine to
> defend itself in order that the Jews of Palestine be not exposed to
> the same fate which has overwhelmed millions of our fellow-Jews
> in Europe.

For the rest, there seemed nothing to do but pray for those millions.
"We join in mourning," said a message from the American Jewish Committee,

> for the destruction of the innocent and helpless victims of Nazi
> terror, and at the same time highly resolve that we shall not permit
> the world to forget these crimes so that the perpetrators may be
> brought to answer for them before the bar of civilization.

The meeting came to its climax with the chanting of the mourner's
Kaddish, led by a group of cantors.

·   ·   ·   ·

A new level of comprehension of the Nazi program of annihilation became possible at the beginning of August, through the medium of the World Jewish Congress headquarters in Geneva. Its director, a thirty-year-old German-Jewish refugee named Gerhart Riegner, had received startling information relayed to him by colleagues from a source they considered unimpeachable, a German industrialist trusted by the Nazis who had leaked information in the past. Riegner brought the information to the American consulate in Geneva, where he was allowed to cable it to Washington, though the opinion there was that the news had the "earmarks of war rumor inspired by fear." This was the message Riegner sent to Washington, and to London as well:

> Received alarming report that in Führer's headquarters plan discussed and under consideration according to which all Jews in countries occupied or controlled Germany numbering 3½-4 millions should after deportation and concentration in East be exterminated at one blow to resolve once and for all the Jewish Question in Europe stop the action reported planned for autumn methods under discussion including prussic acid stop we cannot transmit information with all reservation as exactitude cannot be confirmed stop informant stated to have close connections with highest German authorities and his reports generally speaking reliable.

Along with this message, the American consulate in Geneva relayed Riegner's wish that it be brought to the attention of Rabbi Wise. But in Washington, the State Department's Division of European Affairs, through which the message had to be cleared, decided not to do so. The reasons it gave for this decision were: "the [Geneva] legation's comments, the fantastic nature of the allegation, and the impossibility of our being of any assistance if such action"—stated by the report as only being under consideration—"were taken."

Despite this suppression, the message made its way to Wise after all. In London, Riegner's cable, in accordance with his request, had been passed on reluctantly by the Foreign Office to Samuel Sydney Silverman, an M.P. who was also British chairman of the World Jewish Congress. Silverman sent Wise a telegram on August 29 summarizing Riegner's message—this one managing to pass through the State Department without coming to the attention of the Division of European Affairs. But it did come to the attention of Sumner Welles, who asked Wise to refrain from making the information public until it had been confirmed by the State Department. After all, the source was unknown, and, besides, the only thing really new about the message was the formulation "at one blow," which was as outlandish as it was alarming—and which was to prove untrue. Welles—and apparently the President—

still held hopefully to the view that the mass deportations were for the purpose of slave labor.

In fact, when the news finally emerged with clarity three months later, it was in a form far more detailed and closer to the truth than Riegner's message had been. On November 24, Welles summoned Rabbi Wise to the State Department and, presenting him with new documents relayed from the American legation in Geneva, said: "I regret to tell you, Dr. Wise, that these confirm and justify your deepest fears." He authorized Wise to convey the information to the public, and the rabbi scheduled a press conference for that evening.

But on that same day, the crucial information had already been presented to the world by the Polish National Council, quite clearly at last. Referring to a program said to have been ordered by Himmler, whereby half the Jews of Poland who were still alive were to be exterminated by the end of 1942—a "first step toward complete liquidation"—the Council's report went on to describe the roundups and deportations:

> The most ruthless methods are being applied. The victims are either dragged out of their homes or simply seized in the streets.
>
> The Germans have mobilized a special battalion under the command of S.S. men. . . . The victims when caught are driven to a square where old people and cripples are selected, taken to a cemetery, and shot there.
>
> The remainder are loaded into [freight cars] at a rate of 150 to a [car] that normally holds forty. The floors . . . are covered with a thick layer of lime or chlorine sprinkled with water. The doors are sealed.
>
> Sometimes the train starts immediately on being loaded. Sometimes it remains on a siding for two days or even longer.
>
> The people are packed so tightly that those who die of suffocation remain in the crowd side by side with those still living and with those slowly dying from the fumes of the lime and chloride and from lack of air, water and food.
>
> Wherever the trains arrive, half the people are dead. These survivors are sent to special camps at Treblinka, Belzec and Sobibor. Once there the so-called settlers are mass-murdered.
>
> Only the young and relatively strong people are left alive, for they provide valuable slave labor for the Germans. However, the percentage of these is extremely small, for out of a total of about 250,000 resettled, only about 4,000 have been sent to do auxiliary work on the battlefronts.
>
> Neither children nor babies are spared. Orphans from asylums and day nurseries are evacuated as well. The director of the biggest Jewish orphanage in Warsaw and well known Polish writer, Janusz Korczak, to whom the Germans had given permission to remain [behind] in the ghetto, preferred to follow his charges to death.

Thus under the guise of resettlement in the east, the mass murder of the Jewish population is taking place. . . .

To this Rabbi Wise had nothing to add at his press conference but a grim clarification of the numbers, saying he "had learned through sources confirmed by the State Department that about half the estimated 4,000,000 Jews in Nazi-occupied Europe had been slain in an 'extermination campaign.' "

·61·

A CHOICE WITHOUT PRECEDENT

On December 5, 1942, after the terrible announcement in London by the Polish National Council, *The Times* published a letter from the Archbishop of Canterbury about this "horror beyond what imagination can grasp." Granting that it was "hard to see what can be done," he went on to suggest:

> At least we might offer to receive here any Jews who are able to escape the clutches of the Nazis and make their way to our shores. In comparison with the monstrous evil confronting us the reasons for hesitation usually advanced by officials have an air of irrelevance. Further, it could be announced that any person proved to be directly or indirectly concerned in this outrage would be held responsible when the war is over. But, indeed, the matter seems to be beyond earthly resources. It should be the subject of our constant, united, and most earnest prayer to Almighty God.

The British Chief Rabbi, Joseph H. Hertz, called for a day of fasting and prayer on Sunday, December 13, followed by a week of mourning.

In the meantime, deputations of Anglo-Jewish leaders had been seeking an official response. Considerable alarm had already been aroused in the British press by a statement of Hitler's in September, in which, invoking the threat of annihilating European Jewry that he had made in January 1939, he said:

> At one time, the Jews of Germany laughed about my prophecies. I do not know whether they are still laughing or whether they have already lost all desire to laugh. But right now I can only repeat: they will stop laughing everywhere, and I shall be right also in that prophecy.

518

The feeling had grown that there should be some reply from the Allied governments, and the deputations had been seeing not only British public men but Ambassadors Ivan Maisky of the Soviet Union and John G. Winant of the United States.

Winant cabled Washington on December 7:

> Last week I was asked to petition my government to intervene. Hitler's last speech has intensified this feeling of an impending mass attack and there have been requests to Eden, Maisky and myself that we ask our three governments to take a joint stand protesting against German terrorism and to make it clear that punishment will be meted out to those responsible for Jewish atrocities. Eden looked favorably on this plan as did Maisky, and I would like to give it my support.

In Washington the next day, President Roosevelt received a delegation of Jewish leaders that included Rabbi Wise, Maurice Wertheim of the American Jewish Committee, and Adolph Held representing the Jewish Labor Committee. Roosevelt authorized them to make a statement to the press saying "that he was profoundly shocked to learn that two million Jews had perished as a result of Nazi rule and crimes," and that "the American people will hold the perpetrators of these crimes to strict accountability in a day of reckoning which will surely come." The language was familiar; and Foreign Secretary Anthony Eden and the Soviet and U.S. Ambassadors in London were now preparing a statement that would speak even more strongly for their three countries and their Allies—the whole of what was now called the United Nations.

On the floor of the House of Commons, in response to a question put by Sydney Silverman, Eden presented the statement on December 17. He read:

> The attention of the Governments of Belgium, Czechoslovakia, Greece, Luxembourg, the Netherlands, Norway, Poland, the United States of America, the United Kingdom of Great Britain and Northern Ireland, the Union of Soviet Socialist Republics, and Yugoslavia, and the French National Committee, has been drawn to numerous reports from Europe that the German authorities, not content with denying to persons of Jewish race in all the territories over which their barbarous rule has been extended the most elementary human rights, are now carrying into effect Hitler's oft-repeated intention to exterminate the Jewish people in Europe. In Poland, which has been made the principal Nazi slaughter-house, the ghettos established by the German invaders are being systematically emptied of all Jews, except a few highly skilled workers required for their industries. None of those taken away are ever

heard of again. The able-bodied are slowly worked to death in labor camps. The infirm are left to die of exposure and starvation, or are deliberately massacred in mass executions. The number of victims of these bloody cruelties is reckoned in many hundreds of thousands of entirely innocent men, women and children.

The above-mentioned Governments and the French National Committee condemn in the strongest possible terms the bestial policy of cold-blooded extermination. They declare that such events can only strengthen the resolve of all freedom-loving peoples to overthrow the barbarous Hitlerite tyranny. They reaffirm their solemn resolution to ensure that those responsible for these crimes shall not escape retribution, and to press on with the necessary practical measures to this end.

An unprecedented scene ensued. James de Rothschild stood up and spoke with tears in his eyes. Then, according to one participant, it was "suggested that we stand in silence to pay our respects to those suffering peoples, and the House as a whole rose and stood for a few frozen seconds." David Lloyd George later commented: "I cannot recall a scene like that in all my years in Parliament."

Undoubtedly the Allied leaders, bewildered in the face of this catastrophe beyond all imagination and experience, hoped and even believed they had now done all they could do: promise retribution against the criminals and then get on with the war to defeat them. It had even become possible to foresee an end to that war, for a major turn of the tide had occurred in the preceding weeks. In the first half of November, General Bernard Montgomery had delivered a decisive victory against Rommel's forces at El Alamein in western Egypt, and American troops, with British help, had invaded western North Africa in three major sectors. Meanwhile, the Russians were making a stand at Stalingrad that would finally put an end to the German advance. It was in the flush of these victories that Roosevelt, meeting with Churchill at Casablanca in January 1943, was to introduce the doctrine of "unconditional surrender" and announce it to the press. Churchill, who claimed to have been taken by surprise, would write years later: "There is a school of thought, both in England and America, which argues that the phrase prolonged the war and played into the dictators' hands by driving their peoples and armies to desperation." This bit of rashness on the President's part was perhaps related to the recent news of anti-Jewish slaughter and his vow to seek retribution.

But feelings were now rising in some quarters that prosecution of the war alone was not sufficient to deal with the situation faced by the Jews of Europe. In the House of Commons on December 17, after the moment of silence had been observed, Sydney Silverman pursued the line of questioning that had elicited Eden's reading of the United Nations statement and asked him "whether he is consulting with the United Nations Governments and with his own colleagues as to what constructive measures of relief are immediately practicable." Eden replied, "My honorable friend knows the immense difficulties in the way of what he suggests," then added later, "the House will understand that there are immense geographical and other difficulties in the matter." When asked whether Britain would be ready to accept any refugees who managed to reach her shores or those in her charge, Eden said that "certainly we should like to do all we possibly can," but "there were certain security formalities to be considered." Eden may have had in mind a speech delivered in the House of Lords three weeks earlier by Lord Selborne, the Minister of Economic Warfare, about the "traffic in the sale of exit permits from occupied countries" that he said was still going on. "While His Majesty's Government might, on humanitarian grounds," Selborne had argued,

> have been prepared to overlook isolated instances of payment made to the enemy in the above-mentioned circumstances, it is clear that the matter has reached the dimensions of a regular organized traffic, from which the enemy hopes to derive marked benefit. Indeed, the fact that he has been obliged to resort to this action is a measure both of the difficulties in which he finds himself as a result of the Allied financial blockade and of the advantage that would accrue to him from any serious breach of it.

The "war by refugee" concept—the notion that the Nazis were at times ready to dump large numbers of refugees upon the Allies in order to disrupt their war effort—was dying hard; and who was to say the Nazis would not suddenly reverse their extermination policy and try another mass dumping of populations?

The issue seemed about to be forced in the first weeks of 1943, when the possibility suddenly emerged of a mass rescue of Jews, not from Germany or the territories it occupied, but from its satellites in the war against Russia: Bulgaria and Rumania. Bulgaria, with a Jewish population of about sixty-five thousand, had never been more than a reluctant participant in the anti-Jewish policies thrust upon it by its Nazi ally. In December, the Jewish Agency had suggested to the British Colonial Office—which still had about thirty thousand Palestine certificates to distribute under the White Paper quota—that forty-five hundred children and five hundred accompanying adults could be taken out of Bulgaria and settled in Palestine. Oliver Stanley, the Colonial Secretary, was amenable and, after obtaining Churchill's enthusiastic approval, announced the plan to the House of Commons on February 3.

This was endorsed by a motion, subsequently signed by 212 Members from all parties,

> That, in view of the massacres and starvation of Jews and others in enemy and enemy-occupied countries, this House desires to assure His Majesty's Government of its fullest support for immediate measures, on the largest and most generous scale compatible with the requirements of military operations and security, for providing help and temporary asylum to persons in danger of massacres who are able to leave enemy and enemy-occupied countries.

Another test of this generous attitude was soon in the offing. There had already been signs that Rumania, seeing the prospect of an Allied victory, was prepared to relent in its Jewish policies, in the hope of thereby gaining gentler treatment after the war. In December, the World Jewish Congress had proposed to the government of Marshal Ion Antonescu that terms might be arranged for the removal of seventy thousand Jews from Trans-Dniestria, as the Rumanians called the part of southern Russia they were occupying and into which they had been deporting some of their own Jewish nationals. They would be paid for this in their own currency at the rate of 20,000 lei for each refugee. The news was broken in *The New York Times* on February 13 by its London correspondent, C. L. Sulzberger. "The Rumanian Government," he wrote,

> has communicated to United Nations officials that it is prepared to cooperate in transferring 70,000 Rumanian Jews from Trans-Dniestria to any refuge selected by the Allies, according to neutral sources here.
> The proposal, which was made in specific terms, suggests the refugees would be conveyed in Rumanian ships, which would be permitted to display the insignia of the Vatican to insure safe passage. . . . The Rumanian Government has intimated that shipment to Palestine would be most convenient.

Where else, indeed, could such a large number of Jewish refugees be brought conveniently under wartime conditions from lands bordering on the Black Sea? But this was not a suggestion that the Foreign and Colonial offices were ready to entertain.

On January 20, a long memorandum prepared by the Foreign Office had been delivered to the State Department in Washington, suggesting "the expediency of a private and informal United Nations conference" on the refugee problem. In it, the Foreign Office spelled out "certain complicating factors" in the current situation:

(a) The refugee problem cannot be treated as though it were a wholly Jewish problem which could be handled by Jewish agencies or by machinery only adapted for assisting Jews. There are so many non-Jewish refugees and there is so' much acute suffering among non-Jews ... that Allied criticism would probably result if any marked preference were shown in removing Jews from territories in enemy occupation. There is also the distinct danger of stimulating anti-semitism in areas where an excessive number of foreign Jews are introduced.

(b) There is at present always a danger of raising false hopes among refugees by suggesting or announcing alternative possible destinations in excess of shipping probabilities.

(c) There is a possibility that the Germans or their satellites may change over from the policy of extermination to one of extrusion, and aim as they did before the war at embarrassing other countries by flooding them with alien immigrants.

The problem that the public servants who drafted this memorandum were struggling to cope with was spelled out profoundly, in the Sunday *Observer* of February 7, by Sir William Beveridge, who was at that time making his name in British history by submitting a major report on the social and economic condition of his countrymen. In an article on "The Massacre of the Jews," he wrote, after calling for an improved program of refugee aid and rescue:

When all this has been done, those who have any chance of escape while Germany pursues a policy of extermination are but a tiny fraction of all those now under threat of destruction. With a view to saving lives, not by the hundred, but by the hundred thousand, the suggestion has been made that the United Nations ... should ask Germany, in place of exterminating the Jews, to set them free to leave Germany and lands under German control.

An astonishingly simple suggestion: the request, after all, could only be accepted or refused. If refused, Beveridge went on, "no harm has been done, and, at least, every effort will have been made; the conscience of those who make the request will be clear, and the record of Germany will be blacker still." On the other hand, the request

might receive a favorable reply. Hitler might think he saw an advantage in throwing a large mass of people upon the resources of the Allies to use their food and transport; in place of sending the inhabitants of the ghettoes to slaughter-houses in Poland and Germany, he might send them in train-loads to the borders of neutral countries and leave them there to the responsibility of the United Nations; he might use the Jews in this stage of the war as his armies used the civilian refugees of invaded countries to impede their opponents, as a weapon to stave off defeat.

This was precisely the nightmare scenario of the Foreign Office. "Is that a reason," then, Beveridge asked,

> for not making the request? That is a question which can be answered, with a full sense of responsibility, only by those who are in a position to survey the whole field of war and all its problems of feeding, transport and supply. Only by making such a request can the United Nations hope to save any large numbers of those otherwise doomed.

No statement of the alternatives could have been more clearly made. It was a choice without precedent in history, and a definitive decision in the matter was delivered that March by Anthony Eden during a visit to Washington. Asked by his American counterpart, Cordell Hull, about the possibility of removing the sixty-five thousand Jews of Bulgaria, Eden replied, according to Roosevelt's special assistant Harry Hopkins, who was present,

> that the whole problem of the Jews in Europe is very difficult and that we should move very cautiously about offering to take all Jews out of a country like Bulgaria. If we do that, then the Jews of the world will be wanting us to make similar offers in Poland and Germany. Hitler might well take us up on any such offer and there simply are not enough ships and means of transportation in the world to handle them.

Tens of millions of lives, and more, were at stake in the war effort for which Eden claimed a substantial share of the responsibility, and the Foreign Secretary, weighing four million Jewish lives into the balance, had made his choice. Nor was this a decision, under the immense pressures of the moment, that either the Prime Minister or the President could readily have contested. It was Britain in particular that would have borne the burden of any mass outpouring of refugees.

Nevertheless, among the American public, a clamor was beginning to arise for some kind of separate action in behalf of the Jews of Europe.

·62·

MOUNTING PUBLIC PRESSURE

On February 16, 1943, three days after the publication of C. L. Sulzberger's article regarding seventy thousand Jews of Trans-Dniestria, a large advertisement appeared in *The New York Times*, covering the entire length of a page and six of its eight columns. "For Sale to Humanity," it proclaimed:

70,000 Jews
Guaranteed Human Beings at $50 a Piece

Most of the remaining space was taken up by a letter from the mordant pen of the writer Ben Hecht, and the whole page was signed by a group called the Committee for a Jewish Army of Stateless and Palestinian Jews.

This Committee was the work of a group of young members of the Irgun Z'vai Leumi, the more militant of the two secret Jewish armies of Palestine—the other being the Haganah. This group from the Irgun, which had come to the United States at the beginning of the war to propagandize for its cause, was led by Hillel Kook, scion of a distinguished family that included the former Chief Rabbi of Palestine. To conceal this aspect of his identity, Kook was going under the name Peter Bergson. There was a glamorous ferocity to his ideas of militant Jewish national redemption that, in the midst of news of the Nazi slaughter, had a particular appeal for artists and intellectuals of Jewish origin who had rarely thought about such matters in the past. Ben Hecht became a foremost disciple, and, as one of America's eminent writers, enjoying good connections in New York, Washington, and Hollywood, he proved to be a most valuable partisan of the Irgun cause.

That cause, as now being formulated by Bergson's group, essentially had a twofold aim: (1) the immediate opening of the gates of Palestine to all the Jews who could get there; and (2) the creation of a Jewish army, based in Palestine but ready to fight wherever Jewish interests required it. Both of these really were ideals of Vladimir Jabotinsky, the chief instigator of the Jewish Legion in World War I and spiritual father of the Irgun. And both were still opposed by British policy in World War II—although the idea of a revived version of the Jewish Legion, fighting under the British flag, was not without prospects.

In the February 16 advertisement, however, the principal demand put forward was "that the United Nations immediately appoint an intergovernmental committee to formulate ways and means of stopping this wholesale slaughter of human beings. . . ." The rest of its program was not presented, and as for the seventy thousand of the Jews in Trans-Dniestria, though the advertisement called dramatically for their rescue, it did not make clear how Bergson's committee planned to function in that process. Their sensational way of announcing the 20,000-lei ransom sought by the Rumanian government for each Jew as a sale at $50 a head ("Attention America!!! The great Roumanian bargain is for this month only! . . . Act now!") seemed to imply that each $50 contribution made to the Committee would rescue a Jew. There was a subscription coupon at the bottom of the page, but no clear indication as to what program one's money would be supporting. The American Jewish establishment—led by such men as Rabbi Wise of the American Jewish Congress and Rabbi Abba Hillel Silver of the Zionist Organization of America, both vehemently opposed to the Irgun, as well as by the American Jewish Committee, which was opposed to Zionism altogether—was scandalized by this advertisement, and by Bergson's activities in general.

But the Bergson group was suddenly becoming a formidable presence in a new struggle to arouse American public and government opinion over the slaughter of the Jews of Europe. By the end of February, as Rabbi Wise prepared to lead a mass rally at Madison Square Garden on the evening of March 1, sponsored by the American Jewish Congress, the American Federation of Labor, the Congress of Industrial Organizations, the Church Peace Union, and the Free World Association, the Bergson group was announcing a demonstration to be held in the same arena on March 9.

Wise's rally, which received front-page coverage in *The New York Times*, was attended by a capacity crowd of twenty-one thousand in the arena, while another ten thousand stood in the street to hear the proceedings through loudspeakers. Mayor Fiorello La Guardia and Chaim Weizmann were present to speak in person, and messages were broadcast by Governor Thomas E. Dewey, Senator Robert F. Wagner, and Justice William O. Douglas. Messages were also read from Lord Halifax—the British Ambassador in Washington—and Wendell Willkie, among others; but there was nothing this time from either Prime Minister Churchill or President Roosevelt. "The climax of the meeting," reported the *Times*,

> was reached after Cantor Morris Kapok-Kagan had sung "El Mole Rachamim," Hebrew prayer for the dead, memorializing the Jewish victims of the Nazis. This was preceded by the blowing of the shofar, the ram's horn, by Rabbi Maurice Taub, and as the sounds subsided and Mr. Kapok-Kagan began the prayer the huge audience wailed and wept, while the thousands outside, who heard the proceedings through amplifiers, joined. There followed the reading of the Kaddish, another prayer for the dead, by Rabbi Israel Goldstein, and the reading of the passage from the Psalms by Rabbi Jeb Hoffman, ending with the words, "Save, Lord and let the King hear us when we call."

The "keynote of the meeting," as the *Times* reporter characterized it, was struck by another American Jewish Congress spokesman, Herman Shulman, who called attention to the fact that "months have passed since the United Nations issued their declaration denouncing the unspeakable atrocities of the Nazis against the Jews and threatening retribution," with the promise that "immediate practical steps would be taken to implement it" [sic], and pointed out that nothing had yet been done. In order to promote action, then, the Zionist leader Louis Lipsky presented an eleven-point program, to be submitted to President Roosevelt and the United Nations. It went:

> 1. Through the intermediation of neutral agencies, the German Government and the governments of states it now partly dominates or controls—such as Rumania, Bulgaria and Hungary—should be approached with the view to secure their agreement to the release of their Jewish victims and to consent to their emigration to such havens of refuge as will be provided; and that such neutral states as are in a position to enter into direct discussion with the German Government be urged to make similar representations.
> 2. The United Nations should take steps, without delay, to designate and establish a number of sanctuaries in Allied or neutral states to serve, under agreed conditions, as havens of refuge for those Jews whose release from captivity may be arranged for, or who may find their way to freedom through efforts of their own.
> 3. The procedure that now prevails in the administration of existing immigration laws in the United States, which acts as deterrent and retardation of legal immigration under the established quotas, should be revised and adjusted to the war conditions and

in order that refugees from Nazi-occupied territories may find sanctuaries here within such quotas.

4. Subject to the maintenance of national security, Great Britain should be asked to provide for receiving a reasonable quota of the victims escaping from Nazi-occupied territories and to provide for their accommodation for the duration.

5. The United Nations should urge the republics of Latin America to modify such administrative regulations that now make immigration under the law extremely difficult and to endeavor under existing immigration law to find temporary havens of refuge for an agreed number of refugees.

6. Overriding pre-war political considerations, England should be asked to open the doors of Palestine—the Jewish homeland—for Jewish immigration, and the offer of hospitality made by the Jewish community of Palestine should be accepted.

7. The United Nations should provide financial guarantees to all such neutral states as have provided temporary refuge to Jews from Nazi-occupied territories. The transfer of such refugees to the designated sanctuaries should be undertaken without delay. . . .

8. In view of the fact that planned mass starvation is the design of the Nazi regime in its inhuman warfare, the United Nations are urged to take steps without delay, but with due regard for the economic warfare being waged against the aggressor states, to organize through neutral agencies for the feeding of the unfortunate victims who are doomed to linger under Nazi oppression.

9. It is submitted that the United Nations should undertake to provide the financial guarantees that may be required for the execution of the program of rescue here outlined.

10. The United Nations are urged to establish an appropriate intergovernmental agency to which authority and power shall be given to implement the program of rescue here outlined.

11. It is further urged that steps be taken without delay to implement the declared intention of the United Nations to bring the criminals to justice, to appoint a commission to assemble the evidence on which the trials shall be based and to establish the procedure of such a tribunal.

The State Department, which was to give prompt demonstration that the feelings manifested at the rally had not escaped its attention, must have noticed that there was very little in these demands it would have been free to act upon. The idea of dealing with the enemy in any form, as called for in proposal 1, was even more vehemently opposed by the Foreign Office than it was by the State Department. Numbers 4 and 6 depended upon British acquiescence. Number 8 required dealing with the enemy, whose policy, in any case, had gone beyond the starvation phase to more summary methods of extermination. Latin America was a complex diplomatic issue, particularly because pro-Nazi sentiments and anti-Semitism were a clear and constant danger in several countries. There was, to be sure, the question of the State Department's visa policy raised by number 3—a policy sorely needing reform, yet not really among the central issues in this moment when rescue and not immigration was the immediate imperative. It was not likely, under war conditions, that a normal quota of immigrants could be readily and safely shipped across the Atlantic. Immediate havens of refuge were required.

In any case, the remaining problems seemed to call for international deliberation, and this is what the State Department was prepared to do, in response both to the rally and to the British request of January 20. It had responded to the latter on February 25, and now, on March 3, it published its letter of acceptance. The letter seems to have been intended for the public eye even when written, for it gave the impression that the idea for a conference had originated in Washington rather than London, and listed at considerable length—and with some exaggerations—the things the United States government had done to aid in the refugee crisis since 1933. Then it spelled out its own recommendations for such a conference, the aim of which, it suggested, should be that of reviving the dormant but still-existing Intergovernmental Committee on Refugees. The recommendations were:

A. The refugee problem should not be considered as being confined to persons of any particular race or faith. . . .

B. Wheresoever practicable, intergovernmental collaboration should be sought in these times of transportation difficulty, shipping shortage and submarine menace, to the end that arrangements may be determined for temporary asylum for refugees as near as possible to the areas in which these people find themselves at the present time and from which they may be returned to their homelands with the greatest expediency on termination of hostilities.

C. There should accordingly be considered plans for the maintenance in neutral countries in Europe of those refugees for whose removal provision may not be made. . . .

D. The possibilities for the temporary asylum of the refugees, with a view to their repatriation upon the termination of hostilities in countries other than neutral, and their dependencies, should be explored, together with the question of the availability of shipping to effect their movement from Europe.

Apart from the prudence—which the British shared—of insisting that the refugee problem was not exclusively a Jewish one, these recommendations showed an apparent readiness to ponder whatever parts of the Madison Square Garden proposals could be taken on constructively under the prevailing circumstances.

Then, on the evening of March 9, the Bergson group had its own
Madison Square Garden event—or events, for two sessions of its ninety-
minute presentation were held, one at eight-forty-five and one at eleven-
fifteen, for a total audience of more than forty thousand. No mere
collection of speeches, "We Will Never Die" was a powerful dramatic
pageant created by Ben Hecht and his friends in the arts: Kurt Weill—
a refugee himself—to compose the music, Moss Hart to stage it, Paul
Muni and Edward G. Robinson to recite, along with other well-known
actors and theater artists. "The actors," reported *The New York Times*,

> moved against towering tablets, as of stone, engraved with the Ten
> Commandments. The stage was a grey stone escarpment, with steps
> leading down. Massed choirs sang behind dark blue curtains. The
> scenes were stark, some in sharp candlelight and deep shadow.
>
> Far down on the stage between the towering tablets, the actor,
> Jacob Ben-Ami, intoned a fervent prayer. . . .
>
> Onto the stage shuffled and walked twenty of the rabbinate
> saved from European ghettoes, most of them bearded patriarchs
> clad in black gowns and white prayer shawls. High on the escarp-
> ment, between the Ten Commandments graven on towering stone,
> stood four men clad in spotless white holding aloft the Torah and
> the white light glittered on the spangled velvets that bound them.
>
> The rabbis prayed. . . .
>
> Paul Muni and Edward Robinson, dwarfed by the great stone
> tablets, came through the space between the Ten Commandments.
> Muni moved to the pulpit on the left, Robinson to the right.
>
> Alternately they recited the record that the Jews have written
> into world history, from Abraham and Moses down to our time.
> They recited the names great in the arts, in science, in war. . . .

These ceremonies were accompanied by a chorus of rabbis and cantors
singing Weill's music.

The next day, the Committee for a Jewish Army of Stateless and
Palestinian Jews ran a large advertisement headed "The People Have
Spoken," and thanking the participants in the pageant. A list of supporters of the Committee was presented as if on a permanent letterhead, and included the names of some senators, among them the
chairman of the Senate Defense Committee, Harry S. Truman. Senator
Edwin C. Johnson of Colorado was presented as the national chairman
of the Committee. In a letter featured centrally in the advertisement,
Johnson stated what were now the three demands of the Committee:

> 1. The immediate appointment of an intergovernmental com-
> mission of military experts to determine a realistic and stern policy
> of action to stop the wholesale slaughter of European Jewry.

2. The immediate creation of a Jewish Army of Stateless and Palestinian Jews including Commando Squads which will raid deep into Germany, and Eagle Air Squadrons for retaliatory bombing of Germany.

3. The immediate utilization of existing possibilities of transfer of Jews from Hitler-dominated countries to Palestine or any temporary refuge, as well as the initiation of further possibilities along those lines.

The Bergson committee had thus formed itself into a standing pressure group, dramatic in its methods and demands, and supported by an impressive list of persons, non-Jews and Jews, who were widely known in various sectors of American life. Less glittering was the corresponding group now formed under the leadership of Rabbi Wise, the Joint Emergency Committee on European Jewish Affairs, which was supported by the American Jewish Congress, the American Jewish Committee, the Jewish Labor Committee, the B'nai B'rith, and various religious groups. Wise's organization claimed respectability and Bergson's claimed attention; in any case, their common cause was not well served by being represented to the country by two rival factions.

No further move was made on the Anglo-American refugee conference proposal until Anthony Eden had returned home from his March visit to the United States. Then, on March 23, Viscount Cranborne, the government leader in the House of Lords, read a joint Anglo-American statement that Eden had presented to him. "The question of the plight of oppressed and persecuted persons in Europe," Cranborne read,

> has been taken up between Mr. Hull and Mr. Eden. It has been decided that conversations in connection with this matter should take place in the immediate future. . . .
> The two Governments have previously agreed by an exchange of notes upon the necessity of urgent and immediate action and have arrived at an agenda which they intend to implement in their forthcoming conversations. . . .
> It is expected that the place of the meeting and the names of representatives of the two governments will be announced in the immediate future.

The date and place soon were set: April 19 at Bermuda.

·63·

VEXED BERMUDA

"The Anglo-American conference on the refugee problem which begins in Bermuda today," reflected a *New York Times* editorial on April 19,

> is important both as a symbol of future cooperation among the United Nations and as the first attempt at international collaboration to mitigate the appalling horror of Hitler's war of extermination since the outbreak of that war. In both aspects it appears to be pitifully inadequate.

Noting the conditions for the conference that had been spelled out in the State Department letter of February 25, the editorial called them "good enough as far as they go," but doubted that "they go far enough, or recognize the urgency of the problem."

On the other hand, one of the conference's principal organizers, Breckenridge Long, could ponder his work with some satisfaction. "The 'Bermuda Conference' on Refugees has been born," he wrote in his diary the next day, confusing the two Jewish pressure groups that had emerged in the previous month:

> It has taken a lot of nursing but is now in existence. One Jewish faction under the leadership of Rabbi Stephen Wise has been so assiduous in pushing their particular causes—in letters and telegrams to the President, the Secretary and Welles—in public meetings to arouse emotions—in full-page newspaper ads—in resolutions to be presented to the conference—that they are apt to produce a reaction against their interest. Many public men have signed their broadsides and Johnson of Colorado introduced their resolution into the Senate.

As far as Long was concerned, there was a danger

> that their activities may lend color to the charges of Hitler that we
> are fighting this war on account of and at the instigation and direc-
> tion of our Jewish citizens, for it is only necessary for Nazi propa-
> ganda to republish in the press of neutral countries the resolution
> introduced in the US Senate and broadsides bearing the name of
> high government officials in order to substantiate the charges in
> the eyes of doubting neutrals. In Turkey the impression grows—
> in Spain it is being circulated—and in Palestine's hinterlands and
> in North Africa the Moslem population will be easy believers in
> such charges. It might easily be a definite detriment to our war
> effort.

For all his confusion and hostility, however, Long had noted some
crucial facts. Wise's Emergency Committee, disappointed at the refusal
of the conference to admit any lobbying groups into its presence, had
drawn up a memorandum for it presenting its eleven demands plus one
more, requesting that special passports be issued to stateless refugees.
As for the Bergson group, they had not only begun to present their case
in Congress, but also, on April 13, had run a large advertisement that
in effect derogated the forthcoming conference by not mentioning it, and
that stated what they thought the real aims of the United Nations should
be regarding the Jews of Nazi-ruled Europe. Proclaiming that the "dead
hand of yesterday's politics is still at the throat of the European Jews,"
the text pointed its accusing finger squarely at British policy in Palestine—there were even a few British signers of this advertisement, including Aneurin Bevan, Sir Maurice Bonham Carter, and Henry
Wickham Steed. Moreover, the advertisement vehemently denied that
there was any reason to seek changes in American immigration laws,
or in the reception policies of distant countries like Australia or those
in Latin America. "Even though we welcome *any* possibility to rescue
the European Jews," the text said,

> no considerable number of refugees can be saved immediately by
> changing the immigration laws of the United States or by sending
> them thousands of miles over submarine-infested waters to far-off
> countries. The desperate scarcity of ships, the transportation diffi-
> culties alone, stop that. . . .
>   Such impracticable proposals are put forward either by well-
> intentioned friends who do not know the truths of the situation, or
> by those people who want to confuse the simple issues in order to
> preserve their deadly political positions of yesterday.

The implication here was that British intransigence regarding Palestine was the main reason that the Bermuda Conference was doomed from the start.

The Bermuda Conference held its sessions in strict secrecy, permitting only a handful of journalists on the island at all. "The limits of achievement," glumly wrote Edward T. Sayer, the *New York Times* correspondent at the conference,

> that may be possible as the result of the Anglo-American talks on the international refugee problem—already hinted at by both delegations in press conferences—became more clearly defined at the formal opening of the parley this morning.
> Dr. Harold W. Dodds and Richard K. Law, heads of the American and British groups respectively, sounded as the keynote of the conference the fact that victory was the only real solution.

The limits became yet more clearly defined on the third day of the Conference. "Movement of refugees on a very large scale," Sayer wrote, "is definitely out of the picture." The delegates went on to explain that, though they were "closing the door on any mass project," they were "starting from the basis that every human life that can be saved is something to the good, and we are working on it from that." The focus, apparently, was to be on the individual, not the mass.

As it happened, one of the most enormous of the mass fates of Europe was coming at this very moment to its deadly conclusion. On Friday, April 23, alongside the news report on the fourth session of the Conference, headlined "Refugee Transfer Is Held Unlikely," there was this item, datelined London, April 22:

> Armored cars and trucks have moved into Warsaw, where the ghetto populace is resisting deportation of the city's 35,000 Jews. The battle was still raging when the Polish exile government in London received the latest news last night.
> Those resisting are the most active elements left after the mass murders and deportations of last fall. The Polish underground movement has supplied arms and sent trained commanders for a last stand, which is said to be costing the Germans many lives.

Under such circumstances, the small gestures to which the Bermuda Conference was dedicating its energies were bound to seem very small indeed; in the end, they were even smaller than hoped for. Apart from discussions about the reestablishment of the Intergovernmental Committee and the means of dealing with those neutral countries—

Spain, Portugal, Sweden, Switzerland, and Turkey—to which fugitives from Nazi-held Europe were making their way, the largest issue dealt with was that of sanctuaries. The neutral countries would remain receptive to refugees only if they could be assured that the latter would be removed by the Allies as quickly as possible. But to where?

The discussion centered upon French Morocco, occupied by the Americans, to which it was hoped that several thousand refugees then in Spain could be brought and interned for the duration of the war. But this was a delicate issue. A North African administrative cadre hitherto loyal to Vichy was being conciliated by the American military authorities through General Henri Giraud, whom they had placed in charge. Cautious about the attitudes both of this cadre and of the vast Muslim majority, Giraud was already annoying liberal opinion in both Britain and the United States by not restoring to Algerian Jewry its old rights of full French citizenship, granted by the Crémieux Law of 1870 and revoked by the Vichy regime. The Americans therefore did not consider it possible—no doubt to the ironic gratification of the British, with their similar reserve regarding Palestine—to admit a large Jewish influx suddenly into North Africa at that moment. The idea of camps of internment was suggested by the British, but American military authorities had insisted that their troops in North Africa would not tolerate having Jews penned up in camps. The upshot was that the Americans at Bermuda did no more than agree to look further into the problem.

The Bermuda Conference ended on April 29, amid denunciations by Jewish and concerned Christian leaders in both Britain and the United States. Dr. Frank Kingdon, president of the nonsectarian International Rescue and Relief Committee, called it a "shame" and a "disgrace," and Rabbi Israel Goldstein of New York commented: "The job of the Bermuda conference apparently was not to rescue victims of Nazi terror but to rescue our State Department and the British Foreign Office from possible embarrassment."

Not quite two weeks later, on May 12, Shmuel Zygielbojm, the Bundist representative on the Polish National Council in London, whose wife and children had died in the Warsaw ghetto, committed suicide by taking an overdose of sleeping pills. A few weeks later, a suicide note addressed to his colleagues was issued to the press. "My companions of the Warsaw Ghetto," it said,

> fell in a last heroic battle with their weapons in their hands. I did not have the honor to die with them but I belong to them and to their common grave. Let my death be an energetic cry of protest against the indifference of the world which witnesses the extermination of the Jewish people without taking any steps to prevent it.

A fitting postscript to this season of slaughter, frustration, and despair was provided by the *Jewish Chronicle* on May 28, with an editorial
entitled "Never Again." There had just been an acrimonious debate in
the House of Commons on the results of the Bermuda Conference, during which Anthony Eden had said: "We shall do what we can, but I
would be false to my trust if I raised . . . hopes . . . , because I do not
agree that great things can be achieved. I do not believe it is possible
to rescue more than a few until full victory is won." Quoting these and
other remarks, the *Chronicle* observed:

> In all these circumstances, there is imperative need for plain
> speaking. What we are witnessing today is the virtual abandonment
> of the Jews of the Continent to their fate. . . .
> It comes to this, then, that, whether the Allied Nations are in
> any way to blame or not, the Jews are today helpless in the cross
> of their destiny and powerless to avert by far the greatest tragedy
> even in their blood-saturated annals. . . . In face of it Jews are
> obliged solemnly to declare that the time has come to make the
> repetition of such a calamity impossible. If the world cannot save
> them, then, once and for all, the Jews must be given the inalienable
> human right to save themselves.

Some recitation of the pertinent record ensues:

> Years ago, the present Prime Minister gave the solemn assur-
> ance that thenceforth the Jews would enter Palestine as of right
> and not on sufferance. That pledge was smothered in the mean
> treacheries of the White Paper. . . .
> Then again, when an urgent and insistent clamor went up from
> Jews for the right to fight their own battle as Jews, surely the most
> primitive elementary right in the human charter, it was, again out
> of idle fears, virtually denied them, to the accompaniment of assur-
> ances that others will bring them deliverance at some date that no
> one can even approximately fix.

Then the final plea:

> Jewry can no longer afford the risk of such rebuffs and humil-
> iations. It demands its rehabilitation as a nation, with the power to
> do for itself what the rest of the world cannot do and certainly has
> not done for it. . . . It demands a land in which it can shape its own
> destiny, a land in which it can work out its own policies in advance,

so that its remnants, threatened once again in what must be for long and at best a confused world, will be shepherded in good time into a Jewish haven of refuge, and not become a sacrifice for a world cause and be caught like rats in another mass-murder trap. And that haven can only be the land promised by God and man, the land of Jewish hope. . . .

·64·

THE MOVE TOWARD
RESCUE ACTION

"The refugee question has calmed down," Breckenridge Long noted in his diary for June 23:

> The pressure groups have temporarily withdrawn from the assertion of pressure. Information which we have received indicates very plainly that they now see the correctness of the position which we have maintained from the beginning, which is that we will be glad to help such refugees as find their way out of the clutches of Germany, but that we cannot deal with the enemy on the account of refugees any more than we can deal with them or negotiate with them on any other account.

With that matter apparently disposed of, he was dealing as best he could with the problems taken on by the Bermuda Conference, particularly that of a haven in North Africa. "The British," he wrote,

> have had a little different idea of the program than we have had and they seem to be stressing the point that there must be a refugee camp in North Africa under our control and as a result of our enterprise. We secured the agreement in principle of Giraud acting through [Robert] Murphy and Eisenhower and obtained their consent, but the Joint Chiefs of Staff have not given their consent. The President has taken the position that it would be dangerous to have a large number of Jews sent into North Africa—because of the predominant Moslem sentiment and the inherent antagonism existing between the two bodies.

Pondering such matters suddenly led Long to a significant insight. "The truth of the whole thing," he observed,

538

is that there is no authority in the Government that can make commitments to take refugees in groups and that there are no funds out of which the expenses of refugees could be paid for safe-keeping in other localities.

Indeed, what was required was a separate government agency with the authority and power to deal with the problem as a whole.

Peter Bergson's maverick group had been the first to recognize this; with it as a central point, they now stepped forth once again, but under a new rubric. The Committee for a Jewish Army as such had protested the results of the Bermuda Conference too violently for some of its distinguished supporters: Harry S. Truman, for one, had his name removed from their letterhead. The Committee was not dissolved, but its core members—including Bergson, Ben Hecht, and Eri Jabotinsky, the son of Vladimir—formed a new organization, which gained warm support from Senator William Langer of North Dakota and Representative Will Rogers, Jr., of California. Calling itself the Emergency Committee to Save the Jewish People of Europe, it made its first appearance to the world at large in the form of a well-publicized conference at the Hotel Commodore in New York. Held from July 20 through 25, the conference had as its main format a series of panel discussions presided over by statesmen and prominent writers and intellectuals, including the Nobel Prize–winning Norwegian novelist Sigrid Undset and the brilliant young political columnist Max Lerner.

On August 12, the Emergency Committee ran a large advertisement of the twelve-point program it now was urging upon the governments of the United Nations. It ran:

1. To create an official agency specifically charged with the task of saving the Jewish people of Europe. This agency to be initiated by the United States, and the United Nations to be invited to participate in the agency when organized.

2. To ask guarantees from the Axis satellite countries, through the International Red Cross, Neutral Countries or the Vatican to insure Jews the same treatment given to other nationals.

3. To demand relief from starvation and disease in Axis-held territory by distributing food and medical supplies under the supervision of the International Red Cross, following the precedent established in feeding the starving peoples of Greece.

4. To bring pressure on Axis-held territory through the intermediary of the International Red Cross, Neutral Governments or the Vatican to permit Jews to leave Axis-controlled territories.

5. To urge Neutral Countries—Sweden, Ireland, Portugal, Spain, Switzerland and Turkey—to grant the Jewish people temporary asylum. The United Nations to be called upon to feed and

clothe those refugees and arrange for return to their homeland as soon as safety permits.

6. To urge that foreign exchange controls of the governments of the United Nations be operated in such manner as to make possible financial assistance to Jewish refugees in non-belligerent territory.

7. To convince the governments of the United Nations that they should grant temporary asylum and transit to territory under their control to Jews who cannot be accommodated in non-belligerent countries, with the understanding that these refugees will have no claim to permanent residence.

8. To concentrate particularly on admitting European Jews to Palestine, because of its proximity and the fact that evacuation can be accomplished without diverting shipping space.

9. To ask Neutral Countries to grant transit facilities to all Jewish people passing from Axis-controlled lands to any United Nations territory, regardless of whether the persons involved be refugees, immigrants or repatriates.

10. To use every available means of transportation to rescue the Jewish people.

a) By rail and road into Turkey and from Turkey to Palestine and other Allied territory.

b) By rail and road into Spain, Sweden and Switzerland.

c) Neutral shipping lying idle in United Nations ports can bring 50,000 persons per month to safety. Other idle tonnage of neutral registry can transport many additional thousands.

11. To inform all Axis and satellite governments that they will be held strictly accountable for the death, through murder, torture, deportation, starvation or denial of medical aid, of all Jews in their territories. To warn them further, in line with the announced policy of the United Nations, through the means of radio, leaflets, etc., that just reprisals will be initiated against them immediately for all atrocities and crimes committed against the Jews as well as any other defenseless civilian people.

12. To urge that 100,000 stateless Jews outside of the United States who are not being used for military service, together with the 23,000 in the Jewish Palestinian military force, be employed specifically in such reprisals as well as in the most dangerous military operations against the Axis in general.

These proposals, which were to show considerable vitality in the coming months, revolved around four basic points. First and foremost was the demand for an official rescue agency, which was to be the principal focus of the Committee's action that fall; most of the other points in the program were activities and goals that would be under the aegis of such an agency. Second, the old demand for the opening of Palestine to refugees was reiterated—although, significantly, nothing was made of the issue of Jewish statehood. This was a way of enabling all Jews, including those in non-Zionist organizations like the American Jewish Committee, to join in the demand. To be sure, the proposal for a Jewish army—the third basic point—was in effect the Zionist demand coming in the side door; but it was placed separately at the end, and it was to disappear during the Emergency Committee's ensuing agitation. The fourth basic point, the demand for accountability in number 11, had already been addressed by Roosevelt and Churchill on several occasions, but it was felt that their statements had not been sufficiently concrete; furthermore, no endorsement of the idea had yet come from the third major Allied leader, Premier Stalin. Later that month, this program was formally presented to Roosevelt and Churchill at their conference in Quebec.

If the Bergson group was now showing remarkable coherence, Rabbi Wise's coalition, on the other hand, was having trouble with internal rivalries. For all his endeavors to represent American Jewry as a whole, Wise was, after all, a Zionist, and Zionism was still a divisive issue. But it had been gaining considerable momentum: in May 1942, a conference of worldwide Jewish leaders at the Biltmore Hotel in New York had repudiated the White Paper and called officially for the immediate establishment of a Jewish State and army. Foremost in the establishing of the Biltmore Program had been Wise's colleague Rabbi Abba Hillel Silver of Cleveland, a powerful orator and magnetic personality. Now, at the beginning of September 1943, Wise presided over an American Jewish Conference at the Waldorf Astoria, made up of the tenuous coalition he had established in his Jewish Emergency Committee. The Conference proved quite ready to cooperate on a resolution calling for the abrogation of the White Paper and the opening of Palestine to unlimited Jewish immigration. Then Rabbi Silver stood up and made a speech demanding a Jewish Commonwealth, in defiance of the outlook of some of the major participants in the Conference.

A majority of those present were sufficiently moved by his stand to cause a new resolution to be passed, invoking the Balfour Declaration and then saying:

> The American Jewish Conference . . . calls for the loyalty and faithful fulfillment of the covenant entered into between the nations of the world and the Jewish people.
> We call for the fulfillment of the Balfour Declaration and of the Mandate for Palestine whose intent . . . was to reconstitute Palestine as the Jewish Commonwealth.

The resolution ended with the earlier demands for the abrogation of the White Paper and the opening of Palestine to immigration. But Judge Joseph M. Proskauer, heading the delegation of the American Jewish Committee, issued a "dissent from concurrence" with the resolution, accepting its final points but insisting, with regard to the Jewish Commonwealth demand, "that it is inadvisable to bring to the foreground of public attention at this time political matters that may divide the peoples of the United Nations and create added difficulties."

This was ironic; for, ten days later, at the opening in Columbus, Ohio, of the annual convention of the Zionist Organization of America, President Roosevelt showed himself to be ready once again to give a cautious endorsement to Zionist aims. In a message sent to the convention, after expressing his horror at Nazi cruelties against the Jews, he then expressed his confidence that "the helpful contributions made by American citizens toward the establishment of a national home for the Jewish people in Palestine will be continued." Nothing was said about the immediate future, and this was certainly not an endorsement of the Biltmore Program in all its concreteness. But it was a quiet rebuff to the White Paper, something the President had not shown readiness to deliver in public before this.

The idea of opening the gates of Palestine was given new impetus by an almost miraculous event that now occurred in Scandinavia. In October, when the Nazis suddenly decided to round up the six thousand Jews of Denmark for deportation, the resistance movement in that country succeeded in hiding almost all of them. It soon became clear that they had been smuggled across the water to Sweden.

"It Can Be Done!" proclaimed a large advertisement published on October 21 by Bergson's Emergency Committee to Save the Jewish People of Europe. "Simply by opening its doors," the text said, "Sweden saved the Jewish population of nearby Denmark." This was one neutral country ready to fulfill the moral obligations demanded by the Committee in its program. But still another conclusion was inexorably drawn: "Simply by opening the gates of Palestine thousands of Jews from nearby countries will save themselves." The advertisement called for a mass meeting at Carnegie Hall on the evening of October 31, with a "Salute to Sweden and Denmark" as its stated theme. At the meeting, a petition was circulated calling upon President Roosevelt to establish an intergovernmental rescue agency and to "advise the British Government that it is America's desire that the door to Palestine be opened to refugee Jews of Europe."

Of the four basic demands of the Committee, the one that now seemed about to be fulfilled was the one for a firm United Nations statement regarding retribution. At the end of October and the beginning of

November, the foreign ministers of the United States, Great Britain, the Soviet Union, and China convened in Moscow for the first high-level conference of the Four Powers. Among the documents it produced and made public on November 2 was a "Statement on Atrocities," which was sent to Roosevelt, Churchill, and Stalin and signed by them. Referring to "massacres and cold-blooded mass atrocities" committed by the Nazis, the document—clearly in deference to Stalin's wishes—called particular attention to "monstrous crimes on the territory of the Soviet Union which is being liberated from the Hitlerites." Then, attempting to formulate procedures for the establishment of postwar tribunals, the document proposed that lists of war criminals be compiled in the various "countries in which their abominable deeds were done . . . having regard especially to invaded parts of the Soviet Union, to Poland and Czechoslovakia, to Yugoslavia and Greece, including Crete and other islands; to Norway, Denmark, the Netherlands, Belgium, Luxembourg, France and Italy."

The statement was strong, but, as some critics noticed, in its emphasis on national territories—perhaps once again owing to Stalin's influence—it had omitted any mention of the Jews. In the United States, there was one outstanding critic who could not forgive the omission and who was able to do something about it. The mordant prose of Ben Hecht had been serving Bergson's group well. In September, as part of an advertisement for the Committee for a Jewish Army, he had published a brilliant piece of doggerel chiding the world, faced with "the killing of all the Jews," for being too "busy with other news." On November 5, three days after the publication of the "Statement on Atrocities," the Emergency Committee published an advertisement reproducing the statement and dominated by a kind of prose lyric by Hecht called "My Uncle Abraham Reports."

"I have an Uncle who is a ghost," it begins. Uncle Abraham had been elected by the other two million Jewish victims of Hitler to be their world delegate, and he attended, invisible, all the conferences "on how to make the World a Better Place," where he would sit "on the window sill and take notes." He had of course been to the Moscow Conference, "one of the Finest Conferences he has ever attended," and had listened with excitement to "every word that Eden, Molotov and Hull spoke." After it, he went back to "the Certain Place where the Two Million murdered Jews met," and made his report. "The Conference," he said, "made a promise that the world was going to punish the Germans for murdering all the different peoples of Europe—Czechs, Greeks, Serbs, Russians, French hostages, Polish officers, Cretan peasants. Only we were not mentioned. In this Conference, which named everyone, only the Jew had no name. . . ." A woman ghost from the Dynamite Dumps of Odessa remarked: "If they didn't mention the two million murdered Jews in the Conference, isn't that bad for the four million who are still alive? The Germans will think that when they kill Jews, Stalin, Roosevelt and Churchill pretend nothing is happening." But Uncle Abraham silenced the great outcry that followed and ex-. pressed hope for tomorrow. "My Uncle Abraham," the fable ends, "has gone to the White House in Washington. He is sitting on the window sill two feet away from Mr. Roosevelt."

This piece succeeded in perturbing Roosevelt, and it may have been what moved Cordell Hull to add a mention of the Jews in his report on the Moscow Conference to Congress on November 18. "The Conference," he said at one point,

> also served as an occasion for solemn declarations by the heads of the three governments with regard to the perpetrators of the bestial and abominable crimes committed by the Nazi leaders against the harassed and persecuted inhabitants of occupied territories— against people of all races and religions, among whom Hitler has reserved for the Jews his most brutal wrath.

Congress no longer needed prodding on the issue, however; for the pressures of Bergson's Emergency Committee had caused it to take action more than a week earlier. On November 9, the fifth anniversary of the Kristallnacht, identical resolutions had been introduced in the Senate by Guy M. Gillette of Iowa and in the House by Representatives Will Rogers, Jr., of California and Joseph Clark Baldwin of New York. The common resolution read:

> Resolved, that the House of Representatives (Senate) recommends and urges the creation by the President of a commission of diplomatic, economic and military experts to formulate and effectuate a plan of action to save the surviving Jewish people of Europe from extinction at the hands of Nazi Germany.

Hearings on the resolution were held by the House Foreign Affairs Committee, whose chairman, Representative Sol Bloom of New York, had been a delegate to the Bermuda Conference. Bloom correctly saw the resolution as an attempt to repudiate the work of that Conference, and he turned the hearings into occasions for some bitter debate. The November 19 session, at which members of the Bergson circle were present, became a quarrel over Palestine as well. "The attack on British policy on development of Palestine as a Jewish home," reported *The New York Times*, was pointed up by William B. Ziff, author and publisher, who said that "the true obstacle to solution of the Jewish refugee problem was the complexities of British politics." Emphasizing that he was "pro" and not "anti-British," he declared:

"If the borders of Palestine were thrown open to Jewish immigration, and if the laws which prohibit the purchase of land there by Jews are abrogated, a great part of the problem can be solved."

Dean Alfange, a vice chairman of the Emergency Committee to Save the Jewish People of Europe and titular head of the American Labor Party, said he believed the proposed resolution "would influence Britain to modify her policy in Palestine."

But this was getting into matters that the strategists of the resolution wanted to avoid for now. "Representative Joseph Clark Baldwin of New York, one of the resolution's authors," the article continues,

and Herbert S. Moore, president of Transradio Press, argued that the resolution concerned neither Palestine nor immigration problems, but was an "emergency" step for aiding European Jewry by setting up reservation camps for the temporary care of those escaping the Nazis.

Peter Bergson, also a witness, simply "urged immediate action on the resolution, declaring that 1,000,000 additional Jews would be 'murdered by the Nazis' before an armistice."

Chairman Sol Bloom, seeking to defend himself,

took exception to some witnesses' assertions that it was necessary to create a Presidential commission to explore the refugee problem, declaring that such an organization would be superfluous in view of the existence of an intergovernmental agency revived at the Bermuda conference. He mentioned also his own House Committee.

Mr. Bloom said that two shiploads of 750 refugees each had been transferred from the Far East to Mexico and that "we are taking them out as fast as we can get the ships." He pointed out also that Britain recently extended indefinitely the time previously stipulated [in the 1939 White Paper] for allowing [the remaining quota of] 31,078 Jews to enter Palestine.

Now another opposing force to the proposed resolution entered the picture in the form of Rabbi Stephen S. Wise, ironically playing the role of more militant Zionist than the Bergson group. He appeared before the Bloom Committee on December 2. "Speaking as co-chairman of the American Jewish Conference," reported *The New York Times*,

Rabbi Stephen S. Wise of New York told the House Foreign Affairs
Committee today that the Baldwin-Rogers resolution authorizing
the establishment of a United States commission to save the Jews
of Europe was "inadequate," mainly in its failure to recommend
that Palestine be opened to unrestricted Jewish immigration.

This startled the resolution's supporters:

> Representative Charles A. Eaton of New Jersey, ranking Re-
> publican member of the Committee, questioned the "propriety" at
> this time of serving notice on our ally, Great Britain. Representa-
> tive Will Rogers, Jr., Democrat of California, an author of the res-
> olution, declared:
> "We are fighting a war of alliances and I would doubt the wis-
> dom of injecting this ancient and acrimonious Palestine question
> into a resolution specifically designed for rescue."

The discussions then took another turn when Wise proceeded to
criticize the Bermuda Conference as inadequate. In reply,

> committee members said that the most strategic work of the con-
> ference could not be made public for security reasons. They re-
> vealed that last week in executive session with State Department
> officials the committee was told of the extent of the department's
> activities on behalf of rescuing the Jews of Europe, but that these
> had to remain secret.

A week later, however, doubtless under considerable pressure, the State
Department testimony was released to the press. It had been delivered
by Breckenridge Long, in the form of an apologetic history of State
Department policy regarding refugees and immigrants for the ten years
since Hitler came to power. Long had insisted that "We did every legitimate thing we could do." Without specifically calling for rejection of
the resolution, he made remarks like these:

> There has been an agency of the American Government ac-
> tually attending to these affairs for more than four years. . . . There
> is now an international agency set up at the instigation of and co-
> operating with the United States.
> And I think your committee will desire to consider whether
> any step you might take would be construed as a repudiation of the
> actions of the intergovernmental body which has been associated
> with the American Government in its activities.

The most provocative of Long's remarks, however, was his assertion that in the past ten years the United States had admitted about

580,000 "victims of persecution by the Hitler regime." In his diary a few weeks later, Long was to write:

> I made a statement to the Foreign Affairs Committee of the House which was subsequently printed and in the course of a long four-hour inquisition made several statements which were not accurate—for I spoke without notes, from a memory of four years, without preparation and on one day's notice. It is remarkable I did not make more inaccurate statements. But the radical press, always prone to attack me, and the Jewish press have turned their barrage against me and made life somewhat uncomfortable.

In fact, the problem of memory had been insignificant; the State Department letter of the previous February 25 to the British Foreign Office had claimed the issuance, since the advent of Hitler, of 547,775 visas "to natives . . . of the various countries now dominated by the Axis powers." The actual figure for refugees had been about 175,000.

It was Representative Emanuel Celler of Brooklyn, one of the longest-standing and most outspoken advocates of refugees in the House, who had moved in to catch Long the day his testimony was released. Arguing that Long's 580,000 refugees were "in the main ordinary quota immigrants coming in from all countries and the majority were not Jews," Celler took the opportunity to snipe in public at this old nemesis:

> Mr. Long's statement, the Representative from New York said, "drips with sympathy for the persecuted Jews, but the tears he sheds are crocodile. I would like to ask him how many Jews were admitted during the last three years in comparison with the number seeking entrance to preserve life and dignity. It is not a proud record.
> "Frankly, Breckenridge Long is least sympathetic to refugees in all the State Department. I attribute to him the tragic bottleneck in the granting of visas."

Long complained to his diary: "The Jewish agitation depends on attacking some individual. Otherwise they would have no publicity. So for the time being I am the bull's eye."

The shots had some effect, for Long's influence in the State Department was now declining. Then, in January 1944, as the rescue resolution gathered strength in both Houses of Congress and prepared to face a Senate vote on the 24th, a sudden action by the President rendered it unnecessary.

·65·

THE WAR REFUGEE BOARD

During the preceding year, new sources of initiative regarding the Jewish problem in Europe had been arising within the Treasury Department. The Secretary of the Treasury, Henry Morgenthau, Jr., was the scion of a distinguished American-Jewish family—his father had been United States Ambassador to Turkey during part of World War I—and the only man of Cabinet rank among the Jewish advisers and friends of the President; this certainly was a factor in the department's growing concern over the problem. But the most important initiatives there ultimately came from three young non-Jews: John W. Pehle, Randolph Paul, and Josiah E. Dubois, Jr.

The department's involvement had begun in the spring of 1943 as a result of a suggestion from the World Jewish Congress representative in Geneva, Gerhart Riegner. He had proposed that certain large-scale rescue actions could be carried out in France and Rumania with the help of American funds, including the still-pending proposed rescue of seventy thousand Jews in Trans-Dniestria. American policy forbade any transfer of currency to Axis countries, but, in Riegner's scheme, none would have to occur. The money, which would come from Jewish organizations, would be placed in blocked accounts in Switzerland as a guarantee of postwar payment of debts incurred. Rabbi Stephen S. Wise personally urged this plan upon President Roosevelt, who approved it and informed the Treasury Department to make the necessary arrangements.

State Department approval was also required, however, and there the project suffered a long delay, not only on account of Breckenridge Long—who argued that the money would certainly reach enemy hands—but also because of the continuing resistance of the British Foreign Office in the matter of mass rescue. In a letter finally written to the

548

American embassy in London in mid-December, the Foreign Office explained that it was concerned about

> the difficulties of disposing of any considerable number of Jews should they be rescued from enemy occupied territory.... [We] would be greatly hampered by the difficulties of transportation, particularly shipping, and of finding accommodation in the countries of the Near East for any but a very small number of Jewish refugees. [We] foresee that it is likely to prove almost if not quite impossible to deal with anything like the number of 70,000 refugees whose rescue is envisaged by the Riegner plan. For this reason [we] are reluctant to agree to any approval being expressed even of the preliminary financial arrangements.

This was the point at which concerned persons were bound to realize that none of the old machinery for dealing with the Jewish problem in Europe would suffice. On top of this, Morgenthau and his young associates had been given ample opportunity to discover the obstructionist role that the State Department, and particularly Breckenridge Long, had been playing in the matter. Consequently, at the beginning of January, officers of the Foreign Funds Control Division of the Treasury Department, led by Dubois and Pehle, produced a scathing memorandum to which they gave a title that Ben Hecht might have written: "Report to the Secretary on the Acquiescence of This Government in the Murder of the Jews." It accused members of the State Department not only of failing "to use the Governmental machinery at their disposal to rescue Jews from Hitler," but even of going so far "as to use this Governmental machinery to prevent the rescue of these Jews." It further accused them of covering up their guilt in the matter by concealment, misrepresentation, and the issuing of false and misleading statements about their activities. Changing the inflammatory title to read "Personal Report to the President," Morgenthau, accompanied by Pehle and Dubois, handed it to the President on January 17. They recommended, as did the proposed congressional resolution, that a separate rescue agency be created.

Roosevelt, recently returned from the Three Power conference at Teheran, proved perfectly ready to comply. On January 22, a public announcement was made that, by Executive Order, President Roosevelt had created a War Refugee Board. Stating that it was the policy of the United States government "to take all measures within its power to rescue the victims of enemy oppression who are in imminent danger of death and otherwise to afford such victims all possible relief and assistance consistent with the successful prosecution of the war," the

Executive Order charged the War Refugee Board with the responsibility for carrying it out. The Board's functions, the order continued,

> shall include, without limitation, the development of plans and programs and the inauguration of effective measures for the rescue, transportation and maintenance and relief of the victims of enemy oppression, and the establishment of havens of temporary refuge for such victims. To this end, the board through appropriate channels shall take the necessary steps to enlist the cooperation of foreign governments and obtain their participation in the execution of such plans and programs.

The Board was to consist of the secretaries of State, War, and the Treasury, but was also to have an executive director and a staff all its own. These departments were to cooperate as fully as possible, and the State Department was directed to "appoint special attachés with diplomatic status, on the recommendation of the board, to be stationed abroad in places where it is likely that assistance can be rendered to war refugees." This meant, in effect, that the Board could create an international cadre of its own, with status that only the State Department could confer, though outside its jurisdiction. There would be no ban among this cadre against dealing with enemy governments. John W. Pehle was appointed acting executive director.

What had brought about this sudden leap into action, on the part of the government and of the President? Certainly a major cause was the mounting pressure of public opinion, led by the Bergson committee and its friends in Congress, who had formulated and publicized a useful and viable proposal at last. Politics doubtless were a factor, too; with Roosevelt planning on a fourth term, it was in his interest to head off the congressional rescue resolution, among whose eminent proponents was Senator Robert A. Taft of Ohio, a contender for the Republican nomination. Another important factor was the recent erosion of Breckenridge Long's influence in the State Department, where he had been passed over for the under-secretaryship, after the resignation in September of Sumner Welles, in favor of Edward R. Stettinius.

But surely the most important factor in his sudden readiness to act on the refugee issue was a new willingness on the President's part, in the wake of the Teheran Conference, to defy British reservations in the matter. This was one of the rare independent actions he had taken regarding the war in relation to Britain. And there can be no doubt that it was somewhat embarrassing to the British government. The *Jewish Chronicle* noticed in London

> a certain amount of invidious comparison between the President's vigorous action and the results, so far as could be made known, of

British initiative. . . . Suspicions have been harbored that the British authorities might not be putting forth all the efforts expected of them, and Mr. Eden's reply this week on the subject [in the House of Commons], while reaffirming the Government's anxious sympathy, made no mention of any alteration in the present machinery for dealing with the problem.

Nor was the creation of the War Refugee Board the only action issuing from Washington at this time regarding the Jewish question in Europe that was clearly embarrassing to the British government. Also in January, a resolution on Palestine was introduced in the Senate jointly by Robert A. Taft and Robert F. Wagner—the latter a man whose views rarely strayed far from those of the President, a close personal friend. It proposed that the United States should "use its good offices" to open Palestine to the free entry of Jews and promote colonization there so that it might ultimately become "a free and democratic Jewish commonwealth." That this proposal had the support of the President was to become quite clear in the sequel.

The most formidable challenge to this proposal came from an unexpected source: the War Department. At the beginning of March, Secretary of War Henry L. Stimson prepared to state his case against it before the Senate Foreign Relations Committee, but then—in a decisive move in favor of the War Department position—General George C. Marshall, the United States Chief of Staff, appeared in his stead. Marshall explained to the Committee

the situation in the Moslem world with respect to the resolution, sketched the potentials of trouble if action was taken by the Senate at this time, explained the added military burdens this would place on the Army in a period where every effort was being made to effect huge concentrations elsewhere, and said in effect that he could not take the responsibility for certain consequences.

Marshall, whose integrity was known to be beyond reproach, was one of the most respected men in Washington. The result of his testimony was an immediate announcement by the Senate Foreign Relations Committee that the Palestine resolution had been indefinitely postponed.

But that was not quite the end of it, for there was one man in Washington whose recommendations had even more impact than those of General Marshall—namely, the President, who proved to have something more to say in the matter. On March 9, the two Zionist rabbis Stephen S. Wise and Abba Hillel Silver obtained a presidential audience that lasted about half an hour. When they emerged, they had a state-

ment to make to the press. "The President has authorized us to say,"
they announced,

> that the American Government has never given its approval to the
> White Paper of 1939.
>   The President is happy that doors of Palestine are today open
> to Jewish refugees and that when future decisions are reached full
> justice will be done to those who seek a Jewish national home, for
> which our Government and the American people have always had
> the deepest sympathy and today more than ever in view of the
> tragic plight of hundreds of thousands of homeless Jewish refugees.

The statement had its requisite precautions, but the fact remained
that it was the strongest repudiation of the White Paper the President
had ever publicly delivered. During recent months, the historic relationship between Roosevelt and Churchill had been losing some of its
old intensity. Differences had emerged over the conduct of the war and
the disposition of the peace. The final establishment of personal contact
between Roosevelt and Stalin at Teheran in December, when the President became rather susceptible to the personal influence of "Uncle Joe,"
seems to have been another step in the widening of a gap between
Roosevelt and Churchill. The valiant Britain of 1940 was no longer the
keystone in the fight against Hitler in 1944. Roosevelt was clearly perceiving the relationship as less sacrosanct, and was acting accordingly.
The British could be criticized.

The President, however, was pitting himself not only against British policy in this particular matter, but against his own War Department. The statement on the White Paper was, in the eyes of Senate
supporters of the Palestine resolution, a virtual countermanding of orders by the Commander-in-Chief over the head of his general, and they
took it as license to renew their demands for immediate action. Did
Roosevelt really want things to go this far?

Suddenly, a new and drastic change for the worse occurred in the Jewish situation in Europe. On March 19, Hitler, anxious to shore up his
crumbling Russian front and aware of the wavering resolution of his
East European satellites, sent troops in to occupy Hungary. And in
their immediate wake came Adolf Eichmann and his staff. It was clear
that the eight hundred thousand Jews of Hungary—more than the prewar indigenous population on account of refugees and territorial annex-
ations—were in danger of swift annihilation.

Roosevelt responded on March 24 by issuing the strongest public
statement he had ever made on war guilt and the persecution of the

Jews and taking the unusual step of calling upon the German people to help the victims. "In one of the blackest crimes of all history," he said,

> —begun by the Nazis in the day of peace and multiplied by them a hundred times in time of war—the wholesale systematic murder of the Jews of Europe goes on unabated every hour. As a result of the events of the last few days hundreds of thousands of Jews who, while living under persecution, have at last found a haven from death in Hungary and the Balkans, are now threatened with annihilation as Hitler's forces descend more heavily upon these lands. That these innocent people, who have already survived a decade of Hitler's fury, should perish on the very eve of triumph over the barbarism which their persecution symbolizes, would be a major tragedy.

These last words were a reminder that the long-awaited invasion of Western Europe was now in the offing. Roosevelt then spoke again of the retribution that would follow the Allied victory, "not only to the leaders but also to their functionaries and subordinates in Germany and in the satellite countries." With that he turned to the German people:

> Hitler is committing these crimes against humanity in the name of the German people. I ask every German and every man everywhere under Nazi domination to show the world by his actions that in his heart he does not share these insane criminal desires. Let him hide these pursued victims, help them to get over the borders, and do what he can to save them from the Nazi hangman. I ask him also to keep watch, and to record the evidence that will one day be used to convict the guilty.

Roosevelt added, outside the text of the statement, that it had the support of Prime Minister Churchill and Premier Stalin. He also gave commendation to the work of the War Refugee Board, which was seeing to it that this statement would be dropped by air in leaflets over Germany, and which was now about to devote its best efforts to the situation of the Jews in Hungary.

The new crisis was probably crucial in helping the President realize he could little afford a head-on confrontation with the War Department. In a March 28 press conference, when asked how the Chief of Staff's position on Palestine and his own as expressed through the rabbis on March 9 "stacked up" with each other, Roosevelt took the opportunity to make a carefully covered retreat. The rabbis' authorized statement,

> the President asserted in response to questions at his news conference, conformed to, rather than conflicted with, the position taken

by the military. On the one hand, he said, there was a military
matter, on the other a civilian question for the future to be worked
out in conjunction with the peace. The military aspect, Mr. Roosevelt added, was a temporary bar to further discussion at the present time; a very serious bar, too, he said!

The question of Jewish statehood, then, was being put back on the shelf,
but the immediate issue, after all, concerned refugees and havens.
"Asked whether further immigration would upset the situation in the
Middle East," the press-conference report continues,

> the President said that the immediate problem was what we were
> going to do for those refugees coming out of Europe by two ways,
> through Spain and through the Balkans into Turkey. Not all these
> refugees, he said, were Jews, and he stated that the total was a
> relatively small number.

The supporters of the Palestine resolution in the Senate were to go
on asserting for a while that there was no contradiction between their
own position and the one the President had taken at the press conference. But he had, in fact, deftly sidestepped the whole issue, and in so
doing he had taken some heat off the whole controversy. This restored
some harmony with Britain on the question of Jewish persecution and
how to respond to it. "Foreign Secretary Anthony Eden," according to
a March 30 news dispatch from London,

> appealed today from the House of Commons to European Quisling
> officials to help Jews escape persecution by the Nazis, and implicitly
> promised that they would be rewarded with special Allied consid-
> eration "on the day of reckoning."
> Mr. Eden's unusual statement, which went beyond President
> Roosevelt's recent pleas to the peoples of Germany and occupied
> Europe to aid the Jews and other Nazi victims, declared that the
> British and American governments were discussing further action
> to save refugees.

In the meantime, the War Refugee Board had gone fully to work.

·66·

FINAL EFFORTS

Two decisive triumphs for the Allied cause occurred in the first week of June 1944: not only the long-awaited invasion of France on Tuesday, the 6th, but also, two days earlier, the capture of Rome. The advancement in Italy in particular gave a new coloration to the refugee situation in Europe, for the safe haven that now existed in the south of the country was highly accessible to persons able to escape from Central and southeastern Europe as well as from France. The camps there were being rapidly overtaxed. In the week following the liberation of Rome, a thousand refugees arrived from Yugoslavia alone; they could not be maintained in Italy for long.

The question of Palestine inevitably came to the fore again; in the meantime, the United States, eager to show its own renewed willingness to deal with the refugee problem, took two significant steps. In the first week of June, the Visa Division of the State Department—at the request of the War Refugee Board, and no longer under the control of Breckenridge Long—announced a substantial liberalization of its rules. Still, immigration was not the issue in this moment, which called for quick rescue action. Accordingly, on June 9, President Roosevelt announced that a thousand refugees would be brought immediately from Italy to the United States, "to be placed in an emergency refugee shelter to be established at Fort Ontario near Oswego, New York, where under appropriate security restrictions they will remain for the duration of the war."

These were not to be immigrants or even temporary residents, so "the procedure for the selection of the refugees should be as simple and expeditious as possible, uncomplicated by any of the usual formalities involved in admitting people to the United States under the immigration laws." In fact: "It is contemplated that at the end of the war they

will be returned to their homelands." Some may have suspected that
these people would—as turned out to be the case—have their chance to
become American citizens at the war's end, anyway, but in the meantime, they would technically be internees. On August 4, 984 refugees—
most but not all of them Jewish—from fourteen different countries of
origin, arrived at New York on a ship filled with wounded American
soldiers. When they got off the trains that took them to the camp, a
historic but unused military installation in the northern part of the state,
a message of welcome from Harold L. Ickes was read to them. The
younger members of the group were to become students in the Oswego
schools that fall.

In an editorial of June 16, after Roosevelt's announcement of the
Fort Ontario project, the *Jewish Chronicle* observed that "there will
be nothing but gratitude for the Presidential initiative, so completely
in line with Mr. Roosevelt's previous record in this matter," but raised
the question that the editors saw lying hidden at the core of the situation:

> Why transport the hapless Jews all the way across the Atlantic
> when a country—Palestine—in the very area where they are now
> located can find room for them not only in the proposed insignificant
> numbers but in tens and scores of thousands? Why subject these
> unfortunate people who have been "on the run" from Nazi perse-
> cution for nearly a decade to further wanderings across the Atlan-
> tic? And why employ for their convenience shipping which at this
> moment is of paramount importance to the Allied cause? . . . The
> whole thing does not make sense, and calls for explanation.

Whether Roosevelt had intended it that way or not—and there is good
reason to suspect that it was indeed part of his intention—his Fort Ontario gesture had become yet another of the mounting pressures on the
British government to reconsider its Palestine policy. Yet far more urgent pressures than this one were now forthcoming.

In Rumania, where the threat of Russian conquest had become imminent, the idea of using the Jews of Trans-Dniestria to bargain for
money and mercy from the Allies was still alive. Out of an original
170,000 Jews interned there, some forty-eight thousand were surviving,
subject to slow death from misery, disease, and starvation, but at least
not to deportation and the swift death of the extermination camps. This
store of survivors became the particular concern of the representative
that the War Refugee Board had sent to Turkey, Ira Hirschmann, a
forty-one-year-old department-store executive who had had experience
working with refugees as early as 1938 in Vienna.

Hirschmann was stationed in Ankara, where he worked with the warm assistance of the American Ambassador, Laurence A. Steinhardt. Through Steinhardt, Hirschmann met with the Rumanian Minister to Turkey, Alexander Cretzianu, and urged upon him the cause of keeping the Jews of Trans-Dniestria alive. That spring, as the Rumanian-occupied Trans-Dniestria in southern Russia was about to be overrun by Soviet troops, the Jews there were transferred to Rumania itself; in April, American intervention in Turkey had arranged for a shipment of fifteen hundred Jews to leave for Palestine from the Rumanian port of Constanza. Hirschmann announced this at a press conference upon his return to New York, to the annoyance of the British embassy in Ankara, who described him as "a go-getter, somewhat tenacious of his own ideas and impatient of official methods." But then the Germans refused to grant a safe-conduct, for which they had been indiscreetly approached, and, despite the intervention of the International Red Cross and of the Apostolic Delegate in Istanbul, Monsignor Roncalli (the future Pope John XXIII), the voyage had to be canceled. British authorities, stung by the episode, were inclined to view it as a stunt to favor Roosevelt's prospects in the November elections.

Rumania was out of the war by August and soon to join the fight on the side of the Allies; in the meantime, however, during that spring and summer, a far greater challenge to the British policy on Palestine and refugees was arising in Hungary. The Hungarian chapter of the Nazis' "final solution" of the Jewish question was proving unique in several respects. In the first place, it was being carried out with unprecedented efficiency by Eichmann and his henchmen, now the expert products of an education obtained over the bodies of more than four million victims. Hungary was divided into six zones, in which the roundups and deportations were carried out in successive stages, beginning with those eastern and northeastern parts of the country—including the areas annexed from Rumania and Carpathian Ruthenia at the beginning of the war—in which some of the most ancient and densest centers of small-town East European Jewry were located. Between May 15 and the beginning of July, more than four hundred thousand Jews had been deported from these sectors, mainly to Auschwitz, where over three hundred thousand were sent immediately to the gas chambers. The only significant remaining portion of the Jewish population of Hungary was the two hundred thousand now in Budapest, the last of the six zones, where most of them had been herded into a ghetto.

Another unique aspect of this death campaign in Hungary was that it was being carried out virtually in full view of the world at large. "The Germans' march into Hungary," wrote the *Jewish Chronicle* on March 24, "has given rise to the gravest concern for the fate of the Jews . . . who are now in the country." Noting that although "Jews in Hungary were subject to many harsh disabilities" before the German occupation, including instances of forced labor on the Russian front, the *Chronicle* nevertheless thought that

> their situation was relatively tolerable compared with the conditions under which Jews labor in other Axis and Axis-occupied countries. Comparatively few were interned in concentration camps, and deportations were carried out only in the case of foreign Jews, and then only from the large cities.

But all that had changed as if in a nightmare. "Only a miracle, it seems," the *Chronicle* ruminated on April 7, "can now save Hungary's doomed Jews. Already the dread campaign of terror, so familiar in other countries overrun by the Nazis, is beginning to take shape." And on July 14:

> The deportation of 40,000 Hungarian Jews to the death camps of Poland, where it is known that 100,000 have so far been massacred, has aroused the conscience of the civilized world. . . .

The figures were grossly underestimated, but they were far more than enough: denunciations were delivered by Anthony Eden in Parliament and in all the leading British newspapers.

Yet this had not been the first instance of unhappy involvement in the Hungarian-Jewish extermination on the part of Mr. Eden and the British government. In the preceding weeks, yet another unique aspect of the Hungarian "final solution" had begun to manifest itself. Prior to the fall of France, the Nazi government had often been willing to use its Jewish subjects as hostages for international blackmail, but in the ensuing years, particularly since late 1941, no such inclination had been visible among the German overlords themselves, even though their satellites had occasionally shown it. But now, suddenly, amid the most visible of all the slaughters, the Nazis came up with the most ambitious blackmail attempt they had ever made. On May 19, a Budapest Jew named Joel Brand, who had lived at times in Germany and in the United States before the war, arrived in Istanbul by airplane from Vienna, accompanied by a Gestapo agent. Working for a Budapest Zionist organization called the Aid and Rescue Council, Brand had been assigned to relay to the British embassy an offer that Adolf Eichmann had personally made to him. In exchange for ten thousand trucks and a variety of other items—soap, coffee, tea, chocolate—in similarly large quantities, Eichmann had claimed he would see to the release to the Allies of a million Jews, or roughly the whole surviving Jewish population of Nazi-occupied Europe. The Germans had furthermore specified that the trucks so received would be used only on the Russian front.

British and American authorities were quick to recognize that not the least among the offenses in this proposal was a blatant effort to drive a wedge between the ever-suspicious Soviets and their Western Allies. On the other hand, it was impossible for men of good conscience to dismiss the offer summarily. The question of negotiating with the German Satan over Jewish lives had been largely an academic one before this; now it had to be pondered in all its concreteness. "Everyone with whom I have talked," wrote the Istanbul representative of the Joint Distribution Committee to the State Department,

> recognizes the impossibility of carrying out the proposals as they have been stated, but everyone believes that all should be done to continue exploration until it is definitely determined that no further good can be served by its continuance.

This became most emphatically the position of the Zionist leadership, both in London—where Chaim Weizmann discussed the matter with Anthony Eden—and in Jerusalem. In mid-June, the Jewish Agency Foreign Minister Moshe Shertok (later Sharett) was able to interview Brand in Aleppo, and he returned to Jerusalem convinced that the offer was genuine and had to be investigated. The ambivalence of the British government was conveyed by Eden's remarks to the Cabinet, on June 29, that the plan had

> arrived in circumstances so suspect, and was worded in such a mixture of terrorist threats and blackmail that we should have been justified in rejecting it forthwith. With our well-known solicitude for the Jews and for all who are suffering under the German terror, we have, however, carefully considered what, arising out of this affair, can be done by both [the British and the American] Governments.

By this time, however, the Soviet government had been informed of the affair, and was—without even knowing yet of the German promise to use the desired trucks only on the Eastern Front—vehement in its opposition to making any bargains with the Germans, including this one. This attitude, on top of growing British doubts about Brand—on July 11, Churchill wrote to Eden of the offer, "I would not take it seriously"—caused the entire matter to be set aside. The affair was reported on July 21 by the *Jewish Chronicle*, which demonstrated by its tone that, in this case at least, the behavior of His Majesty's Government on a question of Jewish concern had presented no threat to the delicate balance of the paper's Anglo-Jewish loyalties. "This fantastic and revolting offer," it said, is said to have been accompanied by an undertaking that the war material would not be used on the Western Front.

The report says a prominent Hungarian Jew, in the charge of a Gestapo agent, arrived in Turkey and was instructed to get in touch with intermediaries who brought the proposal to the notice of the British authorities. Authoritative British quarters have since characterized it as a barefaced attempt to blackmail the Allies, whose concern for the fate of Hungarian Jewry has been shown repeatedly.

The British Government immediately consulted Washington and Moscow regarding the proposed scheme, which official British circles regard as a foul and blatant attempt to divide the Allies.

No sooner had this proposal been rejected, however, than there came one from a most authoritative and presumably reliable source: the Hungarian Regent, Admiral Miklós Horthy himself. Responding at last to moral pressure from the Vatican and the International Red Cross, as well as from President Roosevelt and King Gustavus V of Sweden—and recognizing that he would soon have to answer to the victorious Allies—the nominal head of the Hungarian state took the initiative of calling a halt to the deportations on July 7, when the Jews of Budapest were still relatively untouched. He then informed the Allies through Swiss intermediaries that all adult Jewish holders of entry permits to Palestine would be permitted to leave, along with all Jewish children holding visas for any country. The United States government, at the urging of the War Refugee Board, was ready to accept this offer, but the onus was once again upon the British and their Palestine policy. It was the old question.

"According to a report just received from the International Red Cross," Eden wrote in an August 3 memorandum,

the first contingent of a total number of 40,000 Jews are to start leaving Hungary for Palestine in ten days. Palestine cannot accept at the moment anything like so many immigrants.

Moreover, as Colonial Secretary Oliver Stanley told the Cabinet the next day, it "was not clear that the figure of 40,000 might not turn out to be much larger." The authorities on the spot—Sir Harold Mac-Michael, the Palestine High Commissioner, and Lord Moyne, the Minister Resident in Cairo—were firm in stressing how few Jews could be admitted into Palestine at that moment. The upshot was that the British government agreed with the Americans to announce that all Jews leaving Hungary would be accepted, that "temporary havens" of refuge—with no explicit mention of Palestine—would be found for them, while agreeing in private that, as Ambassador Winant wrote to Eden, it was understood between the United States and British Governments that the British capacity to accommodate refugees is limited, so that while the British Government has accepted in principle an indefinite commitment, the British Government rely on the United States Government to assume its fair share of the burden and not to face the British Government with a practical impossibility.

"The State Department made clear," *The New York Times* specified in its report on this joint announcement,

> that the plan did not involve preparation for permanent emigration. It spoke specifically of "temporary havens of safety," using the same term that has been applied to refugee camps set up throughout the Mediterranean area for refugees from Yugoslavia, Greece and France.

Then, as if to "rub it in" to the British, the article went on:

> There was no comment on a question whether the agreement would mean that Great Britain would admit Hungarian Jews to Palestine in the same manner that refugees already have been admitted to a refugee camp at Oswego, New York, but the commitments left this as an open question.

But the several weeks it had taken to arrive at this decision turned out to be too long: in October, the author of the "Horthy offer" was deposed by the Nazis. Eichmann, who had departed from Hungary in July at Horthy's request, returned, and the deportations were resumed.

Another possibility for mitigating the slaughter presented itself at this time, also without successful results. Allied air raids over Eastern Europe from southern Italy had been taking place since December 1943, and were reaching full strength at the time the deportations from Hungary began. First from Jewish leaders in Budapest, then from other sectors in Europe, the plea now arose for Allied bombing of the railway lines leading from Hungary to Auschwitz, and even for a raid on the death camp itself. In June, the War Refugee Board, having received the gist of these proposals, relayed it to the War Department in Washington.

But on this issue, once again, an Anglo-American understanding was in force at the War Department. In January, responding to British fears about what tactical implications the creation of the War Refugee Board might have, the War Department had enunciated its policy:

> It is not contemplated that units of the armed forces will be employed for the purpose of rescuing victims of enemy oppression

unless such rescues are the direct result of military operations conducted with the objective of defeating the armed forces of the enemy.

On the basis of this policy, all proposals from the War Refugee Board
and elsewhere to bomb Auschwitz and the railway lines leading to it
were consistently rejected by the War Department. It is almost certain,
moreover, that none of these proposals ever reached President Roosevelt.

A new hope for rescue, however, had emerged for the remaining Jews
of Budapest. The government of Sweden, along with some prominent
citizens of the country, had become increasingly involved in the effort
to save Jews in Nazi-controlled Europe. One such concerned Swede was
Ivar C. Olsen, who was now the representative of the War Refugee
Board in Stockholm. In June, acting upon a suggestion that had come
to him from the World Jewish Congress, with the endorsement and
financial support of the War Refugee Board and the American Jewish
Committee, Olsen obtained permission to send a Swedish diplomatic
representative to Budapest, bearing the title of third secretary in the
legation but actually charged with the mission of rescuing as many Jews
as possible.

The choice for this task was a thirty-one-year-old architect named
Raoul Wallenberg, offspring of a distinguished family of businessmen
and diplomats, who had studied before the war at the University of
Michigan. Arriving in Budapest early in July, Wallenberg, who was unmarried, was without restraints upon an extraordinary gift of courage
and personal magnetism that he quickly made evident. Discovering that
the Swedish Minister there, Carl Ivan Danielsson, had managed to issue
several hundred Swedish passports to Jews who could show some visible tie with the country, Wallenberg went much further and designed
a "protective passport," which he began to issue freely by the hundreds
and then by the thousands.

At first these were to serve under the "Horthy offer," but when
the Regent was overthrown, Wallenberg, who had already begun to
organize health, food, and relief services for the Budapest ghetto, turned
to more brazen methods. Renting a network of thirty-two apartment
houses and placing them under Swedish protection, he assembled in
them the five thousand holders of his "protective passports," as well as
some eight thousand more Jews. Constantly on the watch for attempted
deportations, he boldly intervened upon them in person several
times, once even racing after a train in his car and stopping it at the
border.

By the time the Russian armies entered Budapest in February 1945, twenty thousand of the Jews who survived in that city could claim they had done so entirely on account of Wallenberg's protection. But by then he himself was a prisoner—taken by the Soviet authorities on January 17, under circumstances that have remained a mystery, as has his fate at Soviet hands.

PART ELEVEN

A World in Search of Peace

· From 1945 ·

·67·

DISPLACED PERSONS

President Franklin Delano Roosevelt died on April 12, 1945, less than a month before the victory in Europe on which he had expended his life's last energies. He did not live to see the retribution, so often promised by him, that was soon to come to the Nazi war criminals gathered at Nuremberg. Nor did he see the full evidence of the horrors they had wrought that suddenly appeared before the eyes of the world only a few days after his death.

The worst of the death factories—those that were in Poland—had been liberated by the Soviets, but it was the British and American troops entering Germany from the west who announced and filmed the dread spectacle of the camps they came upon. The piles of emaciated and rotting corpses at Bergen-Belsen were recorded in newsreels; and at Buchenwald—to which many inmates had been driven on forced marches with the retreating German troops—the burghers of nearby Weimar, still professing ignorance of what had gone on there, were given the benefit of a tour by the occupying forces. "German civilians—1,200 of them—" reported a correspondent,

were brought from the neighboring city of Weimar today to see for themselves the horror, brutality and human indecency perpetrated against their "neighbors" at the infamous Buchenwald concentration camp. They saw sights that brought tears to their eyes, and scores of them, including German nurses, just fainted away.

They saw more than 20,000 nondescript persons, many of them barely living, who were all that remained of the normal complement of 80,000.

Richard Crossman, an Oxford don and former editor of the *New Statesman and Nation*, working with British intelligence at this time, visited Dachau shortly after it was liberated. "As we entered the camp," he wrote,

> we turned left to see the crematorium. We passed a long line of bullock carts—with sullen peasants standing by. The carts were laden with corpses taken from the crematorium. . . .
> Just at the crematorium there were half a dozen camp inmates sitting in the shade of a pine tree, nonchalantly watching the corpses being arranged with pitchforks on the carts. Obviously they were immune to any sense of horror at the sight, and even their sense of smell apparently had been deadened. . . .
> We were walking down the space between the work barracks and the hospital barracks when we saw a column of inmates five deep coming toward us. They were advancing or rather tottering along, in the sweltering heat, so slowly that they scarcely seemed to move. They were obviously so ill that many of them could hardly make the distance.

In the immediate wake of the German surrender on May 8, approximately one hundred thousand Jews, many of them in the condition Crossman described, were counted among the seven million "displaced persons" of Europe, uprooted and homeless as a result of the war. The Jews constituted a special case, since the great majority of those who had lived in Germany and Poland simply refused to return to their homes, if they had any left to go to, regarding themselves as permanently alien to the countries of their birth and of their terrible suffering. Indeed, many of the tens of thousands of surviving Polish Jews who tried returning in the ensuing months found they were not welcome. Unruly elements of the Armija Krajowa, or Home Army, which had served the Polish national cause underground during the war, had appointed to themselves the task of freeing the country from the danger of Bolshevism as they understood it, and were killing and intimidating Jews. "About ten miles to the west of us," wrote one Polish-Jewish survivor, of the period in which he had resettled in his home town of Losice,

> lay Mordy, a small town which had a prewar Jewish population of about a thousand. Now there were thirteen survivors. They were all young, and they too had equipped themselves with weapons and were on guard—until March 27, 1945. The raid the A.K. staged that night was prepared with the care of a full military operation. There was even treason involved. No one ever learned the details, but somehow the normally locked entrances to the houses where the

Jews slept were opened from the *inside*, and all thirteen Jews, including three girls, were slaughtered in their beds. . . .

The news reached Losice the morning after the slaughter. . . . All of Losice's survivors gathered in our apartment and almost without words decided to abandon town.

Under the circumstances, the ranks of the Jewish displaced persons in Germany soon began swelling beyond what they had been at the time of liberation. This produced problems, as the facilities for them became overtaxed, especially in the much-sought-after American zone of occupation. The governing military authorities made an effort to distinguish between what they considered genuine displaced persons—those found homeless on German soil at the time of liberation—and the new "infiltrees." There were frequent efforts to turn back the infiltrees, and consequently, occasional incidents of what seemed to be excessively rough handling by American soldiers.

The situation had become virtually scandalous by the summer, when Earl G. Harrison, a former United States Commissioner of Immigration, was sent by President Harry S. Truman to investigate. Back in Washington in August, he presented a report that began:

> Generally speaking, three months after V-E Day and even longer after the liberation of individual groups, many Jewish displaced persons and other possibly non-repatriables are living under guard behind barbed-wire fences, in camps of several descriptions (built by the Germans for slave-laborers and Jews), including some of the most notorious of the concentration camps, amidst crowded, frequently unsanitary and generally grim conditions, in complete idleness, with no opportunity, except surreptitiously, to communicate with the outside world, waiting, hoping for some word of encouragement and action in their behalf.

Many of the problems of physical conditions were soon rectified, however, as a result of Harrison's report. By the end of the year, Richard Crossman, newly elected to Parliament and appointed to an investigating commission, could conclude from his scrutiny that the Jewish displaced persons, assembled in a large number of centers ranging greatly in size, were living in reasonable conditions. "Some of these centers were camps," he wrote,

> but many of them were blocks of houses or even good hotels commandeered by the military authorities for the purpose. When they were surrounded by barbed wire it was at the wish of the inhabitants who felt safer when they were divided from the Germans by a fence.

That remained the crux of the matter: they were homeless, and in most cases—with the notable exception of those who were either returning to or being accepted by France—they refused to think of themselves as at home anywhere on the European Continent. The mood was captured by a *Jewish Chronicle* correspondent who visited the large Jewish transit camp at Bergen-Belsen that had been built alongside the ruins of the infamous concentration camp, where a special kind of gathering was being held. It had begun on Tuesday evening, September 25, with a procession

> from the Jewish transit camps in Belsen Barracks back to the site of the old, infamous, burnt-out Belsen camp. Here Jews of every country gathered together to commemorate martyrs who were foully murdered in the camp, and who now lie in mass graves.
>
> As the sun slowly sank at the end of the mild autumn day, El Mole Rachamim and Kaddish, recited by a 13-year-old orphan, could be heard in the place which, but a short time ago, resounded with the anguished cries of persons being brutally beaten, the sharp crack of rifle fire and the moans of the dying.
>
> The deeply impressive recital of these solemn prayers was a fitting inauguration of the first Congress of Jewish Displaced Persons, to which 50,000 Jews in various transit camps had sent delegates.
>
> The Congress, which opened on Wednesday, was held in the large Assembly Hall of the Belsen Transit Camp. Above the platform were two Jewish flags, linked by yellow stars and a streamer, on which were inscribed the words: "Open the Gates of Palestine."

Although there certainly were many who wanted to go to America, or to join relatives in various other overseas countries, what seemed to be the overwhelming majority of the Jewish displaced persons found their proper sentiments expressed in that slogan. The Jewish Agency had requested that a hundred thousand refugees from Nazi persecution be allowed into Palestine outside the White Paper quota, and Earl Harrison had recommended in his report that this be done. On August 31, President Truman had written to the new British Prime Minister, Clement R. Attlee, urging him to accept this recommendation.

A crisis was developing over the Palestine issue in the Labour government that the British people had overwhelmingly elected at the end of July. The Labour Party leadership seemed to have backed the position taken by Hugh Dalton at their annual conference in May, when he said it was "morally wrong and politically indefensible to impose obstacles to the entry into Palestine now of any Jews who desire to go there." But this was before they had assumed the responsibilities and embarrassments of power. Moreover, the Labour government's Foreign Secretary turned out to be not Dalton but Ernest Bevin, a gruff trade-union leader up from the workingmen's ranks who had wanted to be Chancellor of the Exchequer, and who seems to have been singularly ill-fitted for the post to which he was appointed. To Bevin in particular, the Truman letter of August 31 was only the beginning of what looked like a series of provocations on the Palestine issue, coming from an American government that was perceived as too much influenced by Jewish voters and yet was unwilling to send troops to Palestine to defend British policies there.

After some weeks of deliberation, the British government replied to President Truman that it did not accept "the view that all of the Jews or the bulk of them must necessarily leave Germany, and still less Europe," since that "would be to accept Hitler's thesis." The letter went on to invite the United States to participate in an Anglo-American Committee of Inquiry to investigate the whole problem of Palestine and the Jewish displaced persons, and to make recommendations.

This was accepted, and a committee of six Britons and six Americans was appointed. They were all non-Jews, but two of the Americans were known to have strong Zionist sympathies: Bartley C. Crum, a San Francisco lawyer who had managed Wendell Willkie's presidential campaign, and James G. MacDonald. Bevin, on the other hand, hoped that his choices would support his policy of repatriation. Indeed, five of them more or less remained on his side, but the sixth, Richard Crossman, who had hitherto shown little interest in the Palestine question and was chosen partly for that reason, was to be catapulted by his experience on the Committee of Inquiry into becoming an ardent supporter of Zionism.

In the course of the Committee's travels, which ranged from London to Washington and back to Jerusalem, Crossman was particularly struck by a group of displaced Jews he encountered in the mountain village of Villach, in Austria at the Italian frontier. "There were housed a small group of Polish Jews," he wrote,

perhaps a couple of hundred men, women and children. Their camp was army huts. They had done nothing to improve it. The furniture was a few old boxes; their beds, boards. When we got there in the afternoon, half the inmates were lying in their bunks, not asleep but just whiling the time away doing nothing.

Crossman had already learned that this passivity, idleness, and refusal to improve their physical circumstances came from a refusal to accept any situation short of the ultimate goal of getting to Palestine. The situation at the Italian border was particularly poignant, since Italy and its ports were now the main route of the illegal immigration.

"Talking to the camp leader," Crossman continued,

> I learned their history. These were Jews who had returned to Poland from the gas chambers of Auschwitz. Thence they had walked in twos and threes southward into Czechoslovakia and southward again into Austria. The grapevine—those mysterious rumors by which displaced person get their news—had told them that the way over the Italian passes was still open and that from Italy they could get a boat to Palestine. But by the time they got to Villach in their twos and threes, the British army had closed the frontier and forbidden anyone to approach within five miles. Firmly they had been shepherded by British soldiers into the disused prisoner of war camp at the edge of the town and for seven long months they had lain in the camp looking at the frontier of freedom just five miles away.

By the time the Committee members had finished visiting places like these, even the more resistant among them had been driven

> to one conclusion. There was no possibility of sending these ... people back to their own countries, because they had no countries of their own. . . . Nor was it possible to resettle them in Germany or anywhere else in Europe. . . . Some fifteen out of every one hundred, we reckoned, were anxious to join their relatives in America or in the British Commonwealth. Another fifteen were indifferent where they went so long as it was right away from the Continent which had become for them one vast Crematorium. The remaining seventy out of each one hundred—mostly young people of tough physique since only the tough had survived—wanted Palestine and nothing else.

Inevitably, then, when the Committee presented its report in April 1946, its central recommendation was

> (a) that 100,000 certificates be authorized immediately for the admission into Palestine of Jews who have been the victims of Nazi and Fascist persecution; (b) that these certificates be awarded as far as possible in 1946 and that actual immigration be pushed forward as rapidly as conditions will permit.

For Bevin and Attlee, this outcome was a virtual betrayal and a capitulation to the Americans on the Committee—even though the report suspended judgment on Zionist aspirations and recommended that Palestine continue under the British Mandate for the time being. Indeed, though the recommendation regarding the hundred thousand was warmly welcomed in the United States, by the President and by Jewish leaders, the report's lack of commitment to Jewish statehood evoked a certain ambivalence toward it on the part of Zionists. Meanwhile, the British government, bolstered by Bevin's statement at the Labour Party conference in June that he believed the Americans wanted a hundred thousand Jews to be put into Palestine "because they don't want too many of them in New York," sought other ways of delaying that outcome.

President Truman had tried to demonstrate that the United States was ready to do its share in absorbing refugees, to the extent that the laws and public opinion would allow. These were severe limitations. In a Gallup Poll published in December 1945, 37 percent of the respondents agreed that they wanted fewer European immigrants allowed into the United States than had been allowed before the war, while 32 percent said they would settle for the same number but no more. Only 5 percent wanted an increase, and 14 percent said they wanted no more immigrants from Europe at all. This was the climate within which President Truman announced, on December 22, that he wanted all the quotas for the coming year met in full on the basis of preference for victims of Hitlerite persecution, at the rate of thirty-nine hundred a month. This was to apply only to refugees who were within the American zones of occupation at the time. It was thought that this would bring a full quota into the United States within ten months.

In practice, this Executive Order proved a disappointment. A HIAS report was to sum up the situation this way:

> Of the 39,000 U.S. quota numbers which were estimated as being applicable to displaced persons in the American occupation zones of Germany and Austria, 25,957 were German quota numbers. Few German Jews were found in Germany. Many were slaughtered. Many escaped and were scattered throughout Europe and America.
>
> Two-thirds of the displaced Jews in Germany and Austria are Polish. They number about 120,000—but the Polish quota is only 6,524 a year. So that we have the tragic spectacle of the major number of the displaced Jews being excluded from this country while the large German quota remains unfilled. Although the U.S. State Department is cooperating with HIAS and issuing visas to displaced Jews up to the extent permitted by law, the over-all quota situation is such that the President's directive is thwarted.

The problem clearly was in the existing immigration laws, and those who were concerned decided that the time had come to try to do something about them, despite the general trend of American public opinion. In fact, a political-action group on immigration policy had been created during the last year of the war; its major participants were HIAS, the B'nai B'rith, the American Jewish Congress, and the American Jewish Committee. It now reorganized itself under the name National Committee on Immigration Policy, and appointed Earl G. Harrison its chairman. This Committee was lobbying for new immigration legislation by the fall of 1946—an outcome that also began to be sought by President Truman, once he had perceived that his Executive Order of December 22 was not working as hoped.

These growing initiatives in response to the displaced-persons problem in Europe now brought to the fore the old tensions between Zionists and non-Zionists in the American-Jewish leadership. Zionists, like Rabbis Stephen S. Wise and Abba Hillel Silver, ardent for the admission of the hundred thousand refugees into Palestine, were now also more determined than ever to see a Jewish State come into being. Non-Zionists, on the other hand, while eager to see the hundred thousand get into Palestine, also wanted to bring the same number of Jewish refugees into the United States. If there were some in the latter group who saw Jewish national aspirations as compromising to the simple claim of admitting a hundred thousand refugees into Palestine, there were Zionists, on the other hand, who feared that the agitation for increased Jewish immigration into the United States would compromise their own demands regarding Palestine. Ultimately, both were to get what they wanted, but not without some bitter struggle.

·68·

WASHINGTON AND JERUSALEM

The Jewish refugee situation in Europe reached a new crisis in July 1946, when a revival of the old ritual-murder accusation in the Polish town of Kielce led to a riot that resulted in the death of forty-one Jews. The trickle of "infiltrees" into the Allied occupation zones in Germany and Austria then turned into a flood. By then, the Jewish masses fleeing from Eastern Europe included growing numbers of the roughly 150,000 Polish Jews who had taken refuge in the Soviet Union during the war. Here was a typical scene in late August at the Danube town of Bratislava, in Czechoslovakia on the Austrian border:

> More than 700 persons a day are pouring into the city after a journey of hundreds of miles to escape the terror in their homeland. At times there are as many as 1,000 Jewish refugees from Poland waiting to continue their exodus. The refugees are received at an emergency reception center in Nachod near the Polish frontier, which has been opened for them by the repatriation office of the Czech government in cooperation with the "Joint." There they are given sleeping accommodation, hot meals, fresh clothing, and thorough medical examinations before leaving for Bratislava.
>
> The refugees are crowded into old box cars, freight trains, anything that rolls on railroad tracks. But although the summer days are hot and the cars are musty and old, there are no complaints.
>
> At the station in Bratislava they are met by Czech officials and "Joint" welfare workers and are marched to a reception center—the old Central Hotel. . . . They are given food tickets enabling them to obtain meals at the nearby kosher kitchens maintained by the "Joint."

The prevailing mood among these arrivals, especially the youthful majority, was for Palestine. "Next morning," the account continues,

> as they wait to go, the sound of singing is heard from the courtyard, and there in the center of the yard 100 orphans accompanying the group are singing and dancing a Palestinian hora. . . .
>   Then suddenly a voice shouts, "Time to go." Then slowly they parade through the streets of Bratislava, on their way once again to be taken to the border from where they will walk across the frontier into Austria and on to Vienna. As the train recedes into the distance the tune of Hatikvah can be faintly heard.

This movement—which was not much interfered with in the American zones of occupation but was sternly opposed in the British—was largely under the guidance of an underground Zionist organization called Bricha (Hebrew for "Flight"). It had come into being toward the war's end under the auspices of Aliyah Bet, forming largely around a nucleus of demobilized members of the Palestinian Jewish Brigade that the British had finally created and that had fought in Italy. The principal Bricha route was to Italy and her ports by way of Austria and Yugoslavia—a network primarily of rough mountain trails paved by false papers and the connivance of friendly or bribed authorities. "Even while fighting was still going on in western Yugoslavia and the Germans were still entrenched in northern Italy," one Bricha worker was to recall,

> Jewish war survivors had begun to travel through Yugoslavia; they were headed for the Mediterranean ports of Greece and southern Italy, from where they hoped to go to Palestine. . . .
>   During the months immediately following the war, all the traffic moving along Yugoslavia's highways was subject to strict control—anyone using the highways had to obtain a special travel permit. Before long, however, our staff had managed to obtain printed forms for all the different types of travel permit issued by the Yugoslav government.

For those who sought to cross directly from Austria, the problems were British opposition—the British occupied the southern zone on the Italian border—and an extremely difficult landscape. "As a result of British pressure on the Italian authorities," another Bricha worker recalled,

> Bricha was forced to close the Alpine border stations which it had operated for some time. We therefore had to start traveling over remote Alpine passes where we would not be likely to be found out. . . . During most of the year the mountain trails were blocked

by heavy snow. The few passes which we found were criss-crossed
by mountain streams so that we had to set up temporary "bridges."

Under such strenuous conditions, it was necessary to be able to get
immediate rest and shelter on the Italian side. "Our immediate problem" the Bricha guide continues,

> was to find a building—or several buildings—near the border which
> could accommodate our workers and the transient refugees. Ex-
> ploring the area in question, we found an Italian border police out-
> post. The house was filled with customs officials wearing every
> conceivable type of uniform—customs, *carabinieri*, security and
> what have you. The commander of Bricha in northern Italy decided
> to add a sprinkling of American army uniforms. One night—it was
> after midnight—we turned up at the outpost after quite a risky
> journey. All of us, from the Rumanian refugee whose entire English
> vocabulary consisted of a faltering "Yes," to the emissary who had
> just arrived from Palestine, were wearing American uniforms. We
> were stopped several times by policemen, but when they saw our
> American uniforms they saluted smartly and, in return for some
> American cigarettes, gave us all the information we wanted about
> traveling conditions on the highways. We rented two rooms at an
> inn near the outpost.

To these were added other amiable techniques:

> On those nights when we moved refugees across the border we
> would throw parties, complete with hired bands, for the *carabinieri*
> and the people of the nearby village. . . . While the Italians were
> busy at our party, we would bring in our refugees. A few of our
> workers stayed at the shindig to make sure that the Italians were
> having too good a time to get suspicious.

Things did not always go so smoothly:

> One day in May 1947, a transport of 390 people, traveling in 15
> cars, set out for Italy from Austria. Somehow the British intelli-
> gence people found out about it, and when the group got to the
> Austro-Italian border, it was stopped by British soldiers. . . . Be-
> fore the British realized what was happening, our 15 cars had turned
> tail and were heading straight back into Austria. The refugees hid
> out for eight days and then crossed into Italy at some other point.

Passage through Italy and outward from its southern ports presented few problems, given the connivance of Italian authorities. The
last difficult phase of the journey was the arrival in Palestine itself,

usually at some forlorn part of the coast and in the dead of night. "A faint light blinked in the distance," one refugee was to recall,

> flickered and went out in the darkness, flashed again and disappeared. A deathly stillness all around. . . . The motor of the ship was silenced, and the beating of sixty hearts was stilled. . . .

The sixty refugees were divided into groups of ten; then a leader spoke:

> "A hundred meters separate us from the shore. The boats are being lowered into the water. Each group will go into its boat quietly. . . . Everything ready?"
> "Yes," a quiet reply issues forth from sixty mouths and is swallowed up in the silence.
> Again that awesome quiet. The sound of metal bars clashing against the sides of the ship. An iron ladder is lowered. . . .
> Someone speaks:
> "First group, ready?"
> "Yes"—ten mouths answer.
> "Follow me!"
> Ten shadows step forward. They go up . . . from the depths of the ship to the deck. . . .
> "Haverim, hurry. Here is the ladder. Go down one by one."
> They descend. There is a small wooden boat. Hands hold the oars, strong, muscular hands. One, two, three . . . ten.
> "All of you, are you ready?"
> A red light flickers and dies out. . . . Agile hands cut through the waves of the sea with their oars. Angry waves bang up against the side of the boat with fury. The waters spray over us.
> Tens, hundreds, wade through the waters of the sea and come toward us. . . .
> We step down and wade through the water up to our thighs. Where are we going? Is this the longed-for shore?

In another few moments, the refugees were in trucks and being driven to a Jewish settlement village.

In the world at large, the Palestine question was becoming one of the foremost issues of the day. On July 22, 1946—hardly more than two weeks after the Kielce pogrom—members of the Irgun Z'vai Leumi planted explosives in a wing of the King David Hotel in Jerusalem, producing a blast that killed ninety-one persons, including Jews as well as Britons and Arabs. Tensions mounted as Mandatory policy became more repressive and the detention camps on Cyprus filled up with illegal immigrants who were caught. That fall, the various participants in the conflict took their positions: the British proposed a division of Palestine into Jewish and Arab provinces under a continuing Mandate; Arab League leaders convening in London called for a Palestinian Arab state; and the World Zionist Organization, holding its Congress in December, called for immediate Jewish statehood. Moreover, in October, President Truman had not only reiterated his call for the admission of a hundred thousand refugees into Palestine, but "also expressed his support of the Jewish Agency plan for a viable Jewish State in an adequate area of Palestine."

Subjected to all these pressures, the British government announced on February 14, 1947, that it had decided to submit the Palestine question to the United Nations. The result was the appointment, in May, of a United Nations Special Committee on Palestine (UNSCOP), made up of eleven members from various countries* not involved in the issue, which proceeded in the course of its investigations to go over much the same ground as had the Anglo-American Committee of Inquiry. Submitting its report at the end of August, UNSCOP recommended "that the Mandate should be terminated and Palestine granted independence at the earliest practicable date," and urged the partition of the country into an Arab State, a Jewish State, and the City of Jerusalem governed by an international trusteeship. These were essentially the same recommendations the Peel Commission had made back in 1937. Now they were strengthened by the authority of the world organization, the willingness on the part of both the Zionists and the American President to accept them, and the weakening of a British Empire that had just granted independence to India.

With the British acquiescing in the plan, the Americans and the Zionists accepting it, and the Arabs refusing to consider it, the United Nations, on November 29, 1947, voted on a resolution that included these essential points:

> The Mandate for Palestine shall terminate as soon as possible but in any case not later than 1 August 1948. . . .
>
> Independent Arab and Jewish States and the Special International regime for the city of Jerusalem, set forth in Part III of this plan, shall come into existence in Palestine two months after the evacuation of the armed forces of the mandatory Power has been completed but in any case not later than 1 October 1948.

There had been a question whether the supporters of this resolution could obtain the two-thirds majority needed to pass it, even with Britain and her friends planning to abstain. But a surprise that had been brew-

*Australia, Canada, Czechoslovakia, Guatemala, India, Iran, the Netherlands, Peru, Sweden, Uruguay, and Yugoslavia.

ing for some months was delivered by the Soviet bloc, whose votes made possible the narrow margin—thirty-three in favor, thirteen (including all eleven Arab states) opposed, and ten abstaining—by which the resolution was passed and the Jewish State brought into being. Communist ideology has almost always opposed Zionism, before that moment and since, but Jewish statehood evidently was seen as a price worth paying to get the British out of there. The only problem remaining for the Jewish State and the refugees waiting to go there was the danger of its being overrun by hostile armies in the Arab-Jewish war that was beginning.

In the meantime, those forces in American society who considered it their country's duty to take on a fair share of the displaced persons—Jewish and non-Jewish alike—had begun setting their own plans in motion. In September 1946, *Life* magazine had carried an editorial that said:

> If we are to remain the leading nation of One World, we also have a deep moral obligation not to be too exclusive. No other nation represents so many blood strains or has amalgamated so many viewpoints; that is an asset in our foreign relations which, if we really believe in it, gives us a special claim to leadership and a special duty to "set an example." The constitution of the United States proclaims the universality of human rights and freedoms, a clause the U.S. has often invoked and argued for. How then can we be so complacent about our immigration policy? Above all, in God's name can we go on doing nothing about those DPs?

In December, at the Waldorf Astoria in New York, a meeting organized under the auspices of the American Jewish Committee created a Citizens' Committee on Displaced Persons, an interdenominational group. Since there was thought to be a total of eight hundred thousand displaced persons still in Europe, the Citizens' Committee decided, in order to include one hundred thousand Jews in the program, to demand a nonquota immigration into the United States of four hundred thousand DPs altogether, to enter during a period of four years.

At the beginning of 1947, the Citizens' Committee launched an energetic campaign, which consisted not only of direct approaches to legislators, but also of appeals to the public through speeches, advertisements, leaflets, radio scripts, and even a short film (*Passport to Nowhere*) distributed nationally in commercial cinemas. By the beginning of April, the Committee's efforts had succeeded in causing a Republican congressman from Illinois, William G. Stratton, Jr., to introduce a bill calling for the immigration of four hundred thousand DPs in four years. "Who are these people?" ran a press release sent out by the Committee after the introduction of the Stratton bill:

> They are the "displaced persons." More than 75 per cent of them are victims of one or another of European dictators, no matter under what cause or name the dictatorship flourished—communist or fascist. They are, these 80 per cent, of the Christian faith, a good many of them Polish and Baltic Catholics. Another portion of them, by far the smallest number, only one out of five, is of the Jewish faith. Some of them are political exiles, and since fascism is nominally dead in Europe today, this means that some of them are exiles from countries now controlled by communism.

These remarks highlight some of the problems faced by the Citizens' Committee and some of the weaknesses of their campaign. Among Americans of restrictionist sentiment, the new "cold war" mood was gaining strength. Did America want to import communists? And this question led to others? "Weren't the DPs *Jews*?" many Americans were asking, according to one national magazine. "Didn't they come from Eastern Europe? And didn't that mean that most of them were probably communists?" This was why the Citizens' Committee was making a special point of saying, in effect, that a refugee from communism was not likely to be a communist. But, in the opinion of some observers, in stressing that only 20 percent of the DPs were Jews, the Committee was—whatever its good reasons for doing so—implicitly suggesting a Jewish quota.

As for Congress, it had just undergone a struggle to pass a bill approving American membership in the newly created International Refugee Organization, the U.N. body that was to supersede all predecessors concerned with that question. It had passed the Senate only after the inclusion of an amendment stating that American membership would in no way "have the effect of abrogating, suspending, modifying, adding to, or superseding any of the immigration laws or any other laws of the United States." This represented the atmosphere at the time the Stratton Bill was introduced.

By the beginning of 1948, the two major issues regarding the fate of the uprooted Jews of Europe—the American-proposed DP legislation and the emerging Jewish State—were approaching final resolution. Of the two, the matter of Palestine was the first to reach its conclusion. On the morning of May 14, the British authorities finally withdrew, announcing the official termination of the Mandate for midnight. That same morning, David Ben Gurion read to the Provisional State Council in Tel Aviv a proclamation establishing the State of Israel, which "will

be open to the immigration of Jews from all countries of their dispersion." In Washington later that day, Eliahu Epstein (later Elath), the
new government's representative there, sent a letter to Secretary of
State George C. Marshall, which was based on the six-hour difference
between Washington and Tel Aviv time:

> I have the honor to notify you that the State of Israel has been
> proclaimed as an independent republic within frontiers approved
> by the General Assembly of the United Nations in its Resolution
> of November 29, 1947. . . . The Act of Independence will become
> effective at one minute after six o'clock on the evening of 14 May,
> 1948, Washington time.

President Truman was prompt in his response. Shortly after 6:00 P.M.
—midnight in Tel Aviv—Epstein received this letter from Marshall:

> I have the honor to acknowledge receipt of your letter of May
> 14, 1948, and to inform you that on May 14, 1948, at 6:11 P.M. Wash-
> ington time, the President of the United States issued the following
> statement:
> "This Government has been informed that a Jewish State has
> been proclaimed in Palestine, and recognition has been requested
> by the Provisional Government thereof.
> "The United States recognizes the provisional Government as
> the *de facto* authority of the new State of Israel."

But at the same time, the domestic matter regarding displaced persons was going less smoothly in Washington. Since the beginning of the
year, restrictionist sentiment in Congress had caused the Stratton Bill
to be shunted aside in favor of two new ones, introduced in the Senate
by Alexander Wiley of Wisconsin and Chapman Revercomb of West
Virginia, and in the House by Frank Fellows of Maine. Both, after some
debate and amendments, called for the admission of two hundred thousand DPs in two years; but among the points on which they differed,
the crucial one from the Jewish refugee standpoint regarded the cutoff
date for eligibility under the proposed legislation. The more liberal Fellows Bill proposed April 21, 1947—the day when the American military
authorities in Germany and Austria ceased to allow any further infiltrees into their zones of occupation—as the date beyond which any new
arrivals in those zones would not come under its purview. The Wiley-
Revercomb Bill preferred the December 22, 1945, cutoff that had prevailed under President Truman's old Executive Order of that date. This
earlier date would exclude from eligibility some seventy-eight thousand
Jews who had arrived in the DP camps in those zones between Decem-

ber 22, 1945, and April 21, 1947—and that seems to have been the main intention among those who preferred it.

A joint Senate-House compromise bill was formulated out of the two, with the December 22, 1945, cutoff date remaining. Passed in June 1948, it became known as the "Displaced Persons Act." President Truman signed the bill reluctantly, and made a public statement:

> The bad points of the bill are numerous. Together they form a pattern of discrimination and intolerance wholly inconsistent with the American sense of justice.
>
> The bill discriminates in callous fashion against displaced persons of the Jewish faith. This brutal fact cannot be obscured by the maze of technicalities in the bill or by the protestations of some of its sponsors.
>
> The primary device used to discriminate against Jewish displaced persons is the provision restricting eligibility to those displaced persons who entered Germany, Austria, or Italy on or before December 22, 1945.

In its annual report for 1948, HIAS—which was to have the lion's share in the work of bringing over and settling those Jewish DPs who were eligible under the new legislation—stated flatly:

> The DP Act of 1948 is not humanitarian legislation; it discriminates against prospective immigrants from the DP camps on racial and religious grounds. It cuts off, as ineligible, all political refugees from Soviet-controlled countries who fled into the Western Zones after December 22, 1945. . . . Another provision is that 40% of the visas must be given to persons from the Baltic countries. It also provides that 30% of the visas must be given to persons who were previously engaged in agriculture. A small percentage of Jews were previously so engaged. . . . Happily, we have good reason to believe that the present Congress [in 1949] will soon amend this law so as to make of it a democratic one designed to admit these war victims and not really to exclude them.

But pending such an outcome, HIAS was doing the best it could with the existing situation.

· 69 ·

PASSAGES FROM
POSTWAR EUROPE

"On Saturday, October 30," reported a HIAS publication in November 1948,

> 813 displaced persons disembarked from the Army transport *General William M. Black* at New York, the first of the 205,000 DPs to come to this country under the provisions of the new Displaced Persons Admissions Act of 1948. With the decks of the Army transport lined solid with human beings enjoying their first look at the famed Statue of Liberty, the *General Black* had a distinctive appearance, with pennants flying from stem to stern and United Nations flags draped over the rails.

The passengers in this historic transport from Bremen had been selected in Germany by the Displaced Persons Commission created by the Act. There were 165 Jews among them, eighty-one of whom had been sponsored by HIAS. The remainder had been helped by two other organizations: the Joint Distribution Committee and a new group called the United Service for New Americans.

With the withdrawal of the Jewish Colonization Association from emigration work at the end of 1945 and the consequent dissolution of HICEM, a good part of the latter's functions had been directly taken over by its American parent, HIAS. From its main office in Paris, HIAS had established branches in or near the DP centers all over Germany and Austria. Its representatives went into the camps and took the emigration process of every individual—whether heading for the United States or some other settlement country—in hand from its inception. "Even before contact is made with a relative," explained a 1948 report,

584

HIAS takes preliminary action for the emigration of a D.P. from Germany or Austria. Our offices establish, for the refugee, proof of nationality through birth certificates and affidavits often obtained from his native land, proof of residence in the occupied zones through sworn affidavits of witnesses, clearance of subversive affiliations through examinations by the U.S. Counter-Intelligence Corps, and other complicated requirements. When contact is made with U.S. relatives or friends, HIAS produces an affidavit for the individual, filed by these American citizens, or gives its own corporate affidavit. Later, when the prospective immigrant is called to an assembly area for processing, HIAS is on hand to guide him through the maze of military and consular interviews, physical examinations, and other routine clearances until he is granted a quota number.

A DP who has made his way through this process becomes one of those who

> are sent to the Bremen staging area where HIAS officials who have arranged their transportation meet them, and arrange for their temporary stay at that port. Before sailing for the United States, the HIAS protégés are briefed on their voyage, given cash grants, and introduced to the HIAS escort who will accompany them on their trip.

Those who did not have relatives or other sponsors waiting for them in New York when the ship arrived were able to stay in the HIAS shelter on Lafayette Street, now at a height of activity. "A group of DPs, colorful and various," runs a contemporary description,

> many of the women with infants in their arms, most of the men with makeshift luggage fastened with ropes and straps, little boys and girls holding on to the clothes of their elders, came through the big double doors of the HIAS shelter at 425 Lafayette Street, New York, deposited their baggage on the floor around the central desk, and looked around at their new surroundings with wide, interested eyes. In the somber eyes of the women and the dark, intense eyes of the men, there were the traces of past horror and the remembrance of tragedy which would never leave their souls.

Then a significant scene ensued:

> One of the men disengaged himself from the little boy who was clinging to his hand and approached the desk. He was middle-aged, bearded, and his worn clothes hung on him in ill-fitting folds. The clerk at the desk looked up at him.

"When do we have to register with the police?" asked the DP.

The clerk shook his head. "You're in America now. You don't have to register with the police."

The DP stared at him in disbelief. . . . Ten years of existing through the horrors of pogroms, concentration camps, DP camps, wandering, makes a man's mind skeptical.

"Not register with the police!" he echoed. "You want to get me into trouble?"

The clerk was calm, almost gentle. "I told you," he said. "You're in America now. You don't have to register with the police. You can go anywhere you want to. No police. You're in America now."

The DP's wife was now standing beside him. He turned to her, and there were tears in his eyes. "Dora," he said to her, "I think we're home."

Yet, for all these efforts, the number of Jewish displaced persons in Europe was not substantially reduced in the two years following passage of the Act. The HIAS representative in Europe, Lewis Neikrug, wrote in the middle of 1950:

Despite the fact that many thousands of DPs and refugees have been resettled in the past year, there is little reduction in the number of refugees in Western Europe. This paradoxical statement is explained once it becomes known that there is a continuous infiltration from Eastern countries into Western Europe—an infiltration of such proportions that it practically offsets the mass of migrants who are continually leaving for resettlement elsewhere. The situation is similar to a boat that is leaking and that ships more water than can be bailed out.

What was at least needed was an extension and widening of the current legislation. In June 1950, after a long battle against the restrictionists who were led by Senator Pat McCarran of Nevada from his position as chairman of the Senate Judiciary Committee, an amendment was passed to the Displaced Persons Act extending its application for another year, increasing the numbers eligible under it by more than 150,000, and changing the cutoff date from December 22, 1945, to January 1, 1949. This bill, like its predecessor, still tended by its broadened definition of a displaced person, to favor refugees from communism rather than the old victims of Hitlerism; it was nevertheless a great improvement, and carried such subsidiary advantages as a provision to admit four thousand refugees from the old Central European Jewish haven of Shanghai.

The upshot, by the end of 1951, was to be a total of almost a hundred thousand Jewish refugees having entered the United States from the time of the Truman directive of December 22, 1945. In the same period, Israel took in about 150,000 refugees from Europe, while smaller numbers found homes in the British Commonwealth and Latin America.

The arrival of refugees into the United States had slowed to a trickle by the beginning of 1953. The European DP camps were all but completely empty. The International Refugee Organization had ceased its operations at the end of 1951. Immigration restriction had been reinforced in the United States the previous year by passage of the McCarran-Walter Immigration Act, which essentially reaffirmed the quota system of 1924 and added tougher screening methods for anyone regarded as politically subversive. It had been passed over Truman's veto, and the newly elected President Dwight D. Eisenhower also disapproved of it, saying in his first State of the Union message on February 2, 1953,

> we are one and all immigrants, or sons and daughters of immigrants. Existing legislation contains injustices. It does in fact discriminate. I am informed by members of Congress that it was realized, at the time of its enactment, that future study of the basis of determining quotas would be necessary. I am, therefore, requiring the Congress to review this legislation and to enact a statute that will at one and the same time guard our legitimate national interests and be faithful to our basic ideas of freedom and fairness to all.

Congress did not take heed, although a piece of emergency legislation, proposed by President Eisenhower and introduced in the Senate by Arthur V. Watkins of Utah, was passed into law that August. It provided for entry during a three-year period of 214,000 new arrivals—mainly refugees from communism—to be admitted outside the quotas.

Nevertheless, the arrival of Jewish immigrants was substantially less than in the immediate postwar years, and the organizations that dealt with them were now confronted with a new kind of problem: how to cut back, for reasons of economy, facilities that had become overextended and that often duplicated one another unnecessarily. There had evolved three major organizations in the field of Jewish refugee and rescue work: the venerable HIAS, the immigration department of the Joint Distribution Committee, and the relatively new United Service for New Americans.

Of the three, the Joint Distribution Committee subsidiary was by far the largest and most encompassing. Created during World War I, the Joint had become a virtual sovereignty during World War II, a constant presence in Europe in one form or another, providing sustenance in the Polish ghettos until American entry into the war made that impossible, engaged in every important refugee operation until Germany's defeat. Its postwar efforts had been similarly far-reaching, involving the feeding of two hundred thousand Jewish DPs in 1945 and more than four hundred thousand in 1947, as well as the supplying of vast quantities of clothing, medical aid, and cash. Its work inevitably spilled over into emigration activity, even though it had once eschewed this and left the work to HIAS, which now ranked second in the field.

In the meantime, American-Jewish response to refugees arriving from the beginning of the Hitler era had given rise to a sequence of organizations intended to aid the new arrivals after they descended the gangplank. The sequence had begun in 1934 with a group called the National Coordinating Committee, which evolved during the war into the National Refugee Service. This, in turn—with the collaboration of the National Council of Jewish Women, which had worked alongside HIAS at Ellis Island since the late nineteenth century—was reorganized as the United Service for New Americans. In this form, the organization had grown into an overseas refugee service as well as a domestic one, whose representatives worked in Europe alongside those of the Joint Distribution Committee and HIAS in the postwar years.

Inevitably, there was criticism of all this duplication of effort and talk of combining forces. But such talk was resisted by Samuel A. Telsey, the president of HIAS from 1947 to 1952, who had publicly stated in this connection in March 1949:

> It is stated occasionally, by some, that there should be an avoidance of duplication of services by the voluntary agencies. The hydra-headed monster of complete centralization and of enforced unity of American Jewry through the power of the purse appears in one form or another, such as additional budgeting, disguised under and in the name of economy and [against] duplication of services. Such centralization is dangerous. . . .

Yet even Telsey agreed that "co-operation and co-ordination among HIAS, JDC and USNA was necessary," and therefore was able to announce

> that after a number of conferences . . . an accord among the three agencies was reached with regard to the services to be rendered to the DPs under the DP Act as now or hereafter in force. A merger of services was effected with JDC in Germany, under the terms of which HIAS and JDC set up, in Frankfurt, a co-ordinating committee for U.S. immigration under the DP Act, headed by two officers of equal rank, one a HIAS and the other a JDC appointee. USNA

was the agency selected to give the ... assurances for jobs and housing required by the law.

This was still only a first step. With the great diminution in the flow of refugees after the termination of the Displaced Persons Act at the end of 1951, it became clear that some more radical form of integration was necessary. In the summer of 1952, Samuel Telsey was replaced as president of HIAS by Ben Touster, who was far more amenable to such an idea. The man who finally put the idea into action was a Jewish community organizer named Edwin Rosenberg, who had been the first president of USNA upon its creation in 1946, and in 1952 was chairman of the Executive Committee of the New York United Jewish Appeal. "When in the summer of 1952," he later wrote,

> a new president was elected by HIAS, a man whom I knew and one who had been active in communal affairs, I thought the time propitious for another attempt to effect a consolidation of the Jewish agencies operating in the migration field. ... I had the privilege of meeting first with some of the top leadership of HIAS, then of USNA and JDC. It was soon apparent to all of us that we had to think in terms of one world-wide Jewish migration agency.

This was still not easily achieved, however. The huge Joint Distribution Committee proved entirely willing to turn over the immigration part of its manifold activities to a new organization, but HIAS was reluctant about the possibility of losing its long-standing identity in a merger with the young USNA. Besides, the USNA, which took pride in having developed new methods in immigrant reception and placement, was also hesitant to renounce its identity and name. More than two years of discussions and then negotiations were required to iron out these and other difficulties. The crucial element of the compromise finally arrived at was indeed the name for the new consolidated agency. The HIAS rubric was simply to be inserted between the first two words of USNA's title: the resulting new name was "United Hias Service." This was felicitous, for the name HIAS had become a virtual piece of folklore, and was to go on being the one fondly used for the organization by its friends, clients, and personnel.

On August 3, 1954, at a meeting of the HIAS board of directors, President Ben Touster announced:

> About 22 months ago a committee was formed, under the chairmanship of Mr. Edwin Rosenberg, consisting of representatives of HIAS, USNA, JDC and the National Council of Jewish Women, to explore the possibilities of establishing a single national and international Jewish migration agency. On January 28th of this year

the Negotiations Committee announced that, after more than 16 months of discussion and study, it had agreed upon a set of proposals to consolidate HIAS and USNA to form United Hias Service, Inc., and that the new agency would take over all the migration services of JDC.

Accordingly, a resolution was passed creating the new organization. Ben Touster remained its president, and the celebrated shelter on Lafayette Street was to continue as its center of activity for a few years more.

·70·

THE END OF
JEWISH EASTERN EUROPE

In the mid-1950s, despite the Hitlerite annihilation and some large-scale emigration to the new State of Israel, the ancient centers in East Central Europe, now under communist control, still had substantial Jewish populations. Rumania, even after enabling about 150,000 of them to emigrate to Israel between 1948 and 1951, had some 250,000 Jews. In Poland there were about fifty thousand, in Czechoslovakia fifty thousand, and in Hungary 135,000. The lives of these communities had been subjected culturally and politically to the constantly shifting winds that came from Moscow and from their own governments, relatively tolerant at some times, redolent of fresh weeds of anti-Semitism at others.

It was Czechoslovakia that had given, in 1952, the most vivid demonstration of the predominant form that anti-Semitism was to take in communist Eastern Europe. The kind of national independence within the communist world that Marshal Tito had pioneered in Yugoslavia was dealt with severely in any of its potential manifestations elsewhere, but it was only when Rudolf Slansky, the former secretary general of the Czechoslovakian Communist Party, was put on trial for espionage in Prague along with thirteen other defendants—eleven of whom, as well as Slansky himself, were identified by the court as being "of Jewish origin"—that Titoism, "bourgeois nationalism," and "Zionism" were linked with one another as the common enemy. The hope, provided in the United Nations vote on the partition resolution in November 1947, that Israel and the communist countries could enjoy a moderately friendly coexistence, now rapidly came to an end. Israel was the homeland of the Zionist menace.

To be sure, the more traditional forms of anti-Semitism remained alive in Eastern Europe, albeit in new permutations. This was especially the case in Poland. "Communist newspapers," ran a report from Poznań early in October 1956,

> published today a frank article on the nature and extent of anti-Semitism in Poland.
>
> The article was written by Professor Tadeusz Kotarbinski, Polish educator. . . . Professor Kotarbinski brought into the open what has been the most important aspect of anti-Semitism in Poland today. That is the number of Jews in leading Government and Communist Party positions. . . .
>
> Professor Kotarbinski said "a minority has become almost a majority in key positions and preference for their own people has not been avoided."
>
> He tried to explain why Jews had so many top jobs. It was, he said, because "after having been hunted by the Nazis they became faithful servants of the Socialist regime." But the Polish masses, he added, distorted this to mean "Jewish plot against Poles and Christians."
>
> The reduction of Poland's Jewish population from more than 3,000,000 to about 50,000 and the elimination of competition between Jewish and gentile merchants by the socializing of trade has eliminated two of the prewar bases of anti-Semitism, he wrote.
>
> But the professor added that there still could be heard such expressions as "God sent Hitler to liberate us from the Jews," and schoolchildren say "Mama does not allow me to be friendly with Jews."

Such feelings were part of the atmosphere in which the spirit of Polish national autonomy was reasserting itself at that time, in the "thaw" that had begun with Nikita Khrushchev's speech denouncing Stalin's crimes at the Twentieth Congress of the Communist Party in February. In Poland, ironically—even though anti-Semitism had been among Stalin's offenses—hard-line Stalinism was represented by several prominent Jews. Agitation in Warsaw against excessive control from Moscow had already led to the removal of the two high Polish-Jewish officials, Jakub Berman and Hilary Minc, who were considered loyal Stalinists. The Polish restlessness, which had erupted in a workers' riot in Poznań that June, reached a crisis in late October with a series of street demonstrations in Warsaw. On October 20, Khrushchev himself was in Warsaw to iron out difficulties, and the upshot was the election of Wladislaw Gomulka—a communist leader who had fallen into disfavor among the Stalinists and was therefore all the more popular among Poles—to the position of first secretary of the Polish Communist Party. Gomulka represented, in effect, the restoration of a certain autonomy for Poland without a complete departure into Titoism. A major confrontation with Moscow had been averted.

Not so in the case of Hungary. Following the Polish example, a series of street demonstrations broke out in Budapest on October 23. This resulted in the reelection to the premiership of Imre Nagy, a former premier who had shown nationalist and liberal tendencies and was, like Gomulka, in disfavor among orthodox Stalinists. But the Hungarian confrontation, exacerbated by the arrival of Soviet tanks in the streets, grew more severe. The rioting crowds refused to relent, and Nagy suddenly made a more decisive turn toward Titoism, above all by announcing that he would withdraw Hungary from the Warsaw Pact, the defensive alliance of the Soviet-bloc countries.

Concurrent with the events in Hungary, a presidential election was going on in the United States, and a growing crisis in the Middle East broke with the sudden invasion of the Sinai Peninsula by Israeli troops on October 29, followed by the Anglo-French invasion of Suez a few days later. By the time the smoke had cleared on November 10, Eisenhower had been reelected, the U.N. was calling upon the French, British, and Israeli troops to withdraw, and Imre Nagy was no longer Premier, having been replaced by Janos Kadar after a few days of bloody street battles.

During the fighting, streams of Hungarian refugees had begun making their way to Vienna, their numbers eventually to reach as high as 170,000. In the United States, the Refugee Relief Act of 1953 was still valid until the end of the year. President Eisenhower, fresh from his landslide victory on November 6, two days later ordered

"extraordinary measures" . . . to get 5,000 Hungarian refugees into the United States through the barrier of the Refugee Relief Act. . . .

To complete the job in the limited time allowed, the tough restrictive Refugee Relief Act may have to be bent, if not broken, the White House said. . . .

Pierce J. Gerity, deputy administrator of the act, said that he was prepared to relax the strict security check required for all refugees and to ease assurance requirements.

The problem confronting the administrators is to compress into seven weeks visa-processing work that normally takes months and sometimes a year or longer.

The act expires December 31 of this year, and with it all legal authority for issuing visas to refugees from behind the Iron Curtain.

In another month, the President's Committee for Hungarian Refugee Relief had been established, and the United States Army Reception Center at Camp Kilmer, New Jersey, was readied to house the new

arrivals. By that time, President Eisenhower had increased the number
to be admitted to 21,500; this figure was soon to rise to more than thirty-
two thousand. Meanwhile, Pierce Gerity had gone to Vienna to admin-
ister the program, along with the representatives of ten private agencies, including the American-Hungarian Federation, the Church World
Service, the Tolstoy Foundation, and United Hias Service. HIAS participated as the one organization to deal with the needs of the approximately twenty thousand Jews among the refugees. Some of these were
to go to Israel, some to the United States, some to other countries in
the West.

"On November 4," Miksa Frankel, a Jewish railway conductor then
living in the Hungarian town of Sopron, was to recall,

> I heard that Russian troops were eight kilometers from our city. I
> did not know if this was true, but I did not wait to check. I left my
> job, went home, and told my wife to get ready. We packed only a
> few extra things for the [three] children. I wore my conductor's
> uniform because it was the warmest and only complete suit I had.

The entire family—including Frankel's pregnant wife—walked twelve
kilometers through cold weather to the Austrian border, where the wife
and children were allowed through by the Hungarian police. Frankel
himself, along with some other men, sneaked across at night. "I went
immediately to the nearest village," Frankel's account continues,

> and there I found my wife and children. We slept in a farmer's barn
> that night, and the next morning one of the townspeople told us to
> go to a displaced persons' camp [at Traiskirchen] near Vienna. . . .
> The children were tired and cold and we decided to take the bus.
> We boarded the bus and I held out money to the driver. He refused
> to take it. "You will be my guest," he said. I later found out that
> our Hungarian money was worthless in Austria.
>
> We were in Traiskirchen that afternoon. Though it was
> crowded, we were given clean quarters. We were given food,
> too. . . .
>
> The next day a man came from United Hias Service . . . and
> questioned me about my relatives in the United States. Two days
> later the man came and took us, this time to Vienna.
>
> In the Vienna office of United Hias, we filled out forms and we
> were told that my sister and brothers in America had been notified
> that I was safe. The United Hias people said my relatives could not
> afford to sponsor me, but that the agency would attend to that
> detail. I was asked to go next door and talk to the Joint people.
>
> The Joint (Joint Distribution Committee) found a place for us
> with a Jewish family in Vienna. Two days later, five o'clock in the
> morning, I was awakened by a telephone call. The United Hias man

asked me to report with my family to the American Consulate at 9 o'clock in the morning. I was there two hours early.

Mr. Gerity ... was giving out visas. Since I had been fully processed by United Hias, I was first in line, and I received the first visa. That night I was on a plane for America. ...

When we landed, we were greeted by government officials and then taken to Camp Kilmer. We filled out papers and six hours later we boarded a bus which took us to the United Hias Shelter in New York.

In this way, United Hias helped bring forth nearly forty-five hundred Jewish refugees from Hungary to the United States. It also helped the placement of the remainder in other countries that welcomed portions of the Hungarian refugee outpouring.

During the ten years that ensued—a period of some quiescence in East European affairs—the major shift in Jewish population from Europe was out of Poland and Rumania to Israel. Gomulka, who tolerated a certain degree of Jewish cultural autonomy, had allowed thirty-three thousand Polish Jews to emigrate to Israel between 1956 and 1958. The Rumanian government, in traditional fashion charging the Jewish Agency a certain amount for each emigrant, had allowed a steady outpouring to continue. The Jewish Agency also took charge of the transportation and placement in housing and jobs of each emigrant to Israel. These, along with political factors, were doubtless as important as Zionist feelings in causing Israel to be the main objective of Jewish emigration in those years rather than the United States—even though, in the latter country, the Immigration Act of 1965 finally abolished the old quota system.

A new turn occurred with the Israeli victory of 1967, after which all the communist-bloc countries except Rumania broke diplomatic relations with the Jewish State. The event also caused new political stirrings in Eastern Europe, most notably in Poland, where some officials and army officers—not necessarily Jewish—openly expressed their anti-Sovietism by rejoicing in the triumph of *"our* Jews over *their* Arabs." If Jews had represented too much Moscow in 1956, they now represented the spirit of opposition to it, but either way meant trouble for them.

Eastern Europe was in ferment again in 1968. This time the way was led by Czechoslovakia, where the year had begun with the dismissal of the hard-liner Antonin Novotny from the party first-secretaryship and the appointment of the liberal Alexander Dubcek to replace him. During the ensuing "Prague Spring," Novotny was also to be induced to resign the presidency of the country.

The "Prague Spring" was ultimately to end in the disaster of summer, with the Soviet invasion of Czechoslovakia and the ousting of Dubcek; but in the meantime, it inevitably sent provocative breezes into Poland. The trouble there had begun almost insignificantly, after performances at the University of Warsaw of the classic play *Dziady (Forefathers)* by Adam Mickiewicz had been closed down in January at Soviet urging. The drama, depicting the oppression of Poland under the tsars, had aroused audience enthusiasms that Moscow found uncomfortably significant. There were student demonstrations against the closing, and two participants in them had been expelled. Protests against this action then mounted, first among the student body and then among Polish intellectuals. On March 8, about four thousand students held a demonstration at the university, which had to be dispersed by the Militia. Some ten days of clashes between students and police ensued at Cracow and Poznań as well as Warsaw—expressions of a mood of student unrest that caught fire all over the world that spring, from France to the United States. It was not until March 19 that Gomulka, his authority seriously shaken, stepped forward to make a public statement on the troubles.

By that time, a whole undercurrent had arisen that was expressive once again of the perennially problematic situation of the Jews in Poland, who were now scarcely more than twenty thousand in number. It had first shown itself on March 12. "In rapid retribution for the Warsaw student riots," Jonathan Randal of *The New York Times* wrote that evening,

> the Polish Government dismissed three high government officials tonight. Meanwhile a campaign accusing pro-Zionist Poles and other Jews of having organized the disturbances became more widespread.
>
> The officials were apparently dismissed because their children had been identified in the press as ringleaders of the demonstrations, which protested Communist party controls over cultural affairs. . . .
>
> Among the children of the officials dismissed tonight, Wiktor . . . Topolski was listed as a member of the Babel club of the Jewish cultural society, which the newspaper Kurier Polski today singled out for responsibility for the riots.

The same article in *Kurier Polski* also named some intellectuals it deemed responsible for the disturbances, a large number of whom were Jews. Moreover, it emerged in the next few days that another of the student leaders was the son of Roman Jambrowski, the last of the old Jewish hard-line Stalinists who had otherwise been purged in 1956; now it was his turn to be removed from office. An ironic generational conflict was taking place—but fathers and sons were all "Zionists" now in hostile eyes. The Warsaw party leader Józef Kepa made it clear, moreover, that the party would not "allow Zionists to seek protection for themselves by accusing others of anti-Semitism."

Gomulka, who was forced to walk a difficult path between his hard-line critics and the more liberal tendencies that had once made him popular, now found that path thickly overgrown with the "Zionist" question. Not particularly anti-Semitic himself—his wife was Jewish— he had no choice but to deal with this question in the course of the nationally televised two-hour address he gave on March 19 before a raucous gathering of some three thousand party members in Warsaw's Palace of Culture. "At no time in his address," Randal reported,

> did Mr. Gomulka accuse Zionists or discredited Stalinists of having organized student demonstrations against Communist cultural controls. . . .
> However, Mr. Gomulka did hold liberal intellectuals, many of them Jews, responsible for the "spiritual instigation" of the unrest, which has turned into the most serious crisis he has had to face since he assumed power in 1956.

On the one hand, he warned: "It would be a misunderstanding if we saw in Zionism a danger for socialism in Poland, for its social-political system." On the other hand, he stressed that "Zionism and anti-Semitism are two sides of the same nationalist medal" that communism rejects along with all other nationalisms. Then he made a startling proposal:

> Analyzing the "self-determination of Jews [who are] Polish citizens," he said "we are ready to offer emigration passports" for Israel for Jews like those who during last June's Middle East conflict "proclaimed their wish to go and fight the Arabs."
> He said these people were "by their hearts and minds not linked with Poland, but with Israel," and were "surely Jewish nationalists."

Gomulka went on to make some sympathetic remarks even about "Jewish nationalists" and to give words of praise for the many Jews holding "important and responsible posts in the party and administration" for whom, as he put it, "Poland is the only fatherland." But the effect of these afterthoughts was lost upon those elements in the party and the government who were eager to have a final purge of Jews, now being offered their "emigration passports." In the next three months, some eight thousand Jewish functionaries at all levels in the party, the government, and the country's cultural institutions were dismissed. Soon

various surviving Jewish cultural institutions were closed down, including the Yiddish daily *Folkshtimme,* and the world-renowned State Yiddish Theater of Warsaw, whose director, Ida Kaminska, now joined the
stream of emigrating Polish Jews.

"As an immediate reaction, in the month following the Gomulka
statement," stated the HIAS *Annual Report* for 1968,

> 44 Polish Jews arrived in Vienna, after having been ousted from
> their positions, deprived of their nationality and obliged to pay out
> substantial amounts for documentation, reimbursement of educa-
> tional costs, refurbishing of their apartments, and other fees.
>
> This movement soon took on major proportions. During the
> last quarter 500–600 Jews were leaving monthly. The total arrivals
> in 1968 reached close to 3,000.
>
> By the end of the year some 750 Polish persecutees had been
> resettled by United Hias Service in various countries in the free
> world, notably in the United States. An additional 750 were in var-
> ious stages of processing; getting their documents in order, waiting
> for consular examinations, learning English, and preparing in
> countless ways to face the task of rebuilding their lives and replant-
> ing their roots in a new country. Approximately 1,500 were reset-
> tled in Israel with the assistance of the Jewish Agency.

This was only the beginning; the stream swelled into the next fall,

> from September to November 1969 when the rate of arrivals in
> Vienna and the Scandinavian countries soared to 1,500 per month.
> During the year 5,144 Polish Jews arrived in Vienna. . . . In addi-
> tion, more than 3,000 went directly from Warsaw to Scandinavian
> and other European countries in 1969. . . . In addition, as of Decem-
> ber 31, 1969, 1,384 Polish Jews were undergoing processing by our
> [HIAS] offices in Rome and Vienna for resettlement in the United
> States and other countries.

Within another few months, the remaining Jewish population of
Poland was no more than eight thousand, consisting mostly of elderly
persons unwilling to give up their pensions. The only significant rem-
nant of the old Jewish Eastern Europe were the nearly three million
Jews still in the Soviet Union.

·71·

SOVIET JEWS

In 1965, they were still The Jews of Silence. When Elie Wiesel went there for that year's High Holy Days, "if possible, to penetrate the silence of the more than three million Soviet Jews who have, since the Revolution of 1917, lived apart from their people," the first Jewish voice he heard was one on a dark street asking: "Do you know what is happening to us?"

The Jewish question was one of the ingrained problems of tsarist Russia that the revolution claimed to have solved, but there were conditions attached. Theoretically free to enter any profession and rise as high as talent would allow, accepted into the innermost governing circles, the Soviet Jew was really expected to offer in repayment the same price that tsarism had so incompetently aspired to—assimilation. Jewish culture in its different manifestations was downgraded in varying degrees, and each took its turn in being dealt with quite severely. The Jewish religion—like all religion in the Soviet Union, only more so—was frowned upon, and though it inevitably persisted in provincial strongholds, it was an impediment usually dropped by rising young professionals in Moscow and Leningrad, cities to which Jews flocked in the decades following the revolution. Zionism was not tolerated for long, and was officially nonexistent by 1928. With this proscription there came a gradual eclipse of Hebrew language study, even for religious purposes.

Yiddish culture was a more complicated matter. The vast majority of Russian Jews still spoke Yiddish as their mother tongue at the time of the revolution, and many of them could not yet be reached through any other medium. Furthermore, though the Bund was soon banned, its legacy had instilled the idea of an indigenous Jewish nationality, and it was one that the communist regime, with its complex theory of nationalities, felt bound to accept. If Uzbek was an officially recognized national language, then Yiddish also had to be, and Yiddish culture—through books, newspapers, and, above all, the theater—continued to flourish throughout the 1920s. In 1927, a Jewish Autonomous Province had even been founded, in the remote Siberian region of Birobidzhan on the Manchurian border, where Yiddish could be spoken as an official language—though few Jews settled there and even fewer remained.

During the purges of the late 1930s, Yiddish culture all but disappeared in any of its institutional forms. But then it was revived during the war, apparently to demonstrate to the world that Soviet communism was the opposite of Nazism in its treatment of Jews as in all other respects. To popularize this revival to the Western Allies, and especially to the Jews of the United States, a Jewish Anti-Fascist Committee was created, made up of the foremost Yiddish poets, novelists, and theater artists of the day. They even made an American tour. But by the end of 1949, when anti-Zionism was rising in the communist world and all manifestations of Jewish culture became an enemy in Stalin's eyes, the members of the Jewish Anti-Fascist Committee were in jail. They were soon to be executed.

By the time of Stalin's death in 1953, Soviet Jews were still technically a nationality—their internal passports all accordingly stamped *Yevrey*—but they were virtually without a national culture. Then, after Khrushchev's celebrated denunciation of Stalin in February 1956 and the "thaw" that ensued, there was a gesture at revival, and in 1959, several classic Yiddish authors—from Sholom Aleichem to some lamented members of the Jewish Anti-Fascist Committee—were reprinted in commemorative editions. A Yiddish literary journal, *Sovietish Heymland (Soviet Homeland)*, also was inaugurated that year. Starting as a bimonthly, it eventually became a monthly, but its contents were carefully circumscribed, and there was little in it of a distinctively Jewish feeling.

Such feeling could only be found in fugitive manifestations, as Elie Wiesel first saw, during that 1965 visit, in a Succah somewhere in Leningrad:

> About a hundred *hasidim* had pushed their way in to hear an old Jew, his face glowing and his heart raging with heat, his aristocratic features giving transient bodily form to the angel of hope. Everything he touched took fire. When you shook his hand, you felt strengthened and purified . . . protected.

He also saw the feeling burst before his eyes on the streets of Moscow, when the sun set to begin the festival of the Rejoicing of the Law:

Where did they all come from? Who sent them here? How did they know it was to be tonight, tonight on Arkhipova Street near the Great Synagogue? Who told them that tens of thousands of boys and girls would gather here to sing and dance and rejoice in the joy of the Torah? They who barely know each other and even less of Judaism—how did they know that?

These, in the metaphor of Jewish tradition, were the sparks of Jewish consciousness waiting to be redeemed.

Alla Rusinek, born in Moscow in 1949, had been "the most typical Soviet girl." First a young Pioneer-Leninist, then a member of Komsomol, she was a hard-working student, devoted to communist ideals. "And I loved my country," she wrote, "my Soviet people." To be sure, she happened to have been born a Jew. "I didn't know what it meant but it was written in my identity card: *Yevreika.*" This led quietly to other problems, among her classmates and even in her career as a student—for the revolution had not done away with the instinctual anti-Semitism that discriminates against Jews even when they think just like everyone else. Alla Rusinek began to perceive herself as a stranger and even somehow to be proud of being Jewish. "But where," she wondered, "is a place for me?"

The event that aroused so much of the spirit of dissent in the communist world, among both Jews and gentiles, stirred her as well. "When I heard about Israel in 1967," she writes,

about "an aggressive, capitalist state, an agent of U.S. imperialism in the Middle East," I didn't fail to understand it was my home, my people, defending their young state. I understood that to be Jewish meant to belong to the Jewish nation with its history, culture, religion.

Alla then joined an underground culture of clandestine books and study groups:

I began to study Hebrew. In some old books I learned the first facts about Jewish history: the Maccabees, the Warsaw ghetto. For the first time in my life I went to the synagogue, the only synagogue in Moscow, where I saw thousands of people who looked like me and thought like me. We sang Jewish songs, we danced Israeli dances.

Perhaps she was part of the youthful crowd that celebrated Rosh Hashanah, the Jewish New Year, in September 1968. "A packed congregation of about 2,000 inside Moscow's largest synagogue," reported the *Jewish Chronicle*,

> listened in silence to the shofar while about 1,000 people outside watched a group of youngsters dance the hora and sing Hebrew songs. They were joined by an accordion player. . . .
> Observers have noted with interest that, unusually, Rosh Hashanah this year was treated as a cause for street celebrations by young Moscow Jews.

Then came the Rejoicing of the Law at the end of the New Year cycle, and the scene was a demonstration that what Elie Wiesel had seen three years earlier was now a tradition of overwhelming force. "An estimated 12,000 people in and around the city's Central Synagogue," the *Chronicle* reported,

> most of them young people, cheered lustily, danced the hora and sang Israeli songs.
> Inside the white-domed synagogue itself, the overflow congregation estimated at 2,000 sang "Havah Neranenu" ("Let Us Rejoice") in Hebrew to thunderous hand-clapping.
> During the day, worshippers brought home-made wine with them and drank it in the synagogue's succah, and sang Yiddish and Hebrew songs. Many others brought honey cake and had a "feast" on the pavement.

In a sense, what was occurring was a new and highly dramatic form of the dissident or Democratic Movement that had been slowly gaining strength since the days of the "thaw." Jews and their history had always been prominent in this movement. In September 1961, the non-Jewish poet Yevgeny Yevtushenko had startled the Soviet regime and gained worldwide attention with his poem about the 1941 Nazi massacre of Jews at Babi Yar, calling attention to the special character of Jewish suffering and the persistence of anti-Semitism in Russia. The issue of freedom of expression was raised anew and quite pointedly in May 1968, when a short essay by one Boris Kochubievsky, called "Why I Am a Zionist," was put into circulation. Kochubievsky was arrested in December.

And with that issue of human liberty, another was now brought to the fore. As Andrei Sakharov was to write in the fall of 1971: "The freedom to emigrate . . . is an essential condition of spiritual freedom for all." This, too, was dramatized to the world by Soviet Jews in 1968. On February 15, a group of twenty-six Jewish intellectuals in Vilnius

(Vilna), Lithuania, addressed a letter to the first secretary of the Central Committee of the Lithuanian Communist Party, which reached the American press at the end of the year. It said in part:

> It is known that if the borders were opened up for emigration today, some 80 per cent of the entire Jewish population would leave Soviet Lithuania and go to Israel. They would leave everything behind, despite the unsettled conditions in the Near East, despite the fact that our people here are used to a damp climate, find it difficult to adjust to the climate there, in the main have no knowledge of Hebrew and do not observe religious traditions, and, being mainly employed in services, would not find it easy to become economically integrated into Israeli society.
>
> We face a paradoxical attitude. We are not wanted here, we are forcibly denationalized, oppressed and even publicly insulted in the press—and at the same time we are forcibly detained. As the Lithuanian proverb goes: "He beats and cries with pain at the same time."

Actually, there had long been a trickle of emigration to Israel from the Soviet Union, mainly of elderly Jews who sought to be reunited with their families. In December 1966, at a press conference in Paris, Premier Alexei Kosygin insisted that his government was ready to honor this principle, thus causing perhaps a greater stir than he had anticipated. The following month the *Jewish Chronicle* noted:

> Reports that Soviet Jews were seeking exit visas from passport offices throughout the Soviet Union coincided this week with an assurance by the Soviet Ambassador to Israel that his government favored the reunion of families and that such reunions were already being facilitated.

The reports told of growing numbers of applicants, and Soviet newspapers were soon hastening to publish stories of emigrants to Israel who proved unhappy upon arrival and wanted to return. Such efforts at deterrence became unnecessary, however, after the June 1967 war, when the Soviet Union severed relations with Israel and placed a ban on emigration there.

But the demands to emigrate to Israel that began arising from Soviet Jewry in 1968 soon became a force impossible to resist. Yakov Kazakov, a Moscow Jew in his early twenties who had written a letter in May to the Supreme Soviet renouncing his citizenship—"I do not wish to be a citizen of a country," he wrote, "where Jews are subjected to forced assimilation"—received an exit permit and went to Israel at the beginning of 1969. A prominent reason for his success was that his letter had reached the West and was given extensive coverage in *The Washington Post* in December 1968. The technique of publication in the West was soon used with regularity. A good deal of publicity was accorded a letter addressed on August 6, 1969, to the U.N. Human Rights Commission by eighteen Jewish families of Soviet Georgia, appealing for the right to emigrate to Israel. By the fall of 1970, more than two hundred such appeals had reached the West, from Moscow, Leningrad, Kiev, Minsk, Riga, Vilnius, and Tbilisi. The issue was dramatized to the world in another way as well, as a group of Leningrad Jews who had tried to hijack a plane to Israel were brought to trial. And, meanwhile, Alla Rusinek was one of a growing number of Jews being allowed to depart. She left for Israel in November 1970.

During 1971, it became increasingly clear that a new exodus had begun. In its March issue that year, the *samizdat* or underground Soviet journal *Khronika*, the principal organ of the Democratic Movement, inaugurated a regular section entitled "The Jewish Movement for Emigration to Israel," with reports of protest letters, demonstrations and trials. By then four issues had appeared of *Khronika*'s Jewish-nationalist offspring *Iskhod (Exodus)*, which featured on its first cover the clause from the Universal Declaration of Human Rights that says: "Everyone has the right to leave any country, including his own, and to return to his country." At the World Conference of Jewish Communities on Soviet Jewry held in Brussels at the end of February, General D. Dragunsky, a prominent Soviet "official Jew," told a press conference: "Whoever wants to emigrate to Israel has a juridical right to do so. As soon as peace has returned to the region, the emigration procedure will be speeded up." It was soon speeded up. While visiting Canada in October, Kosygin said: ". . . you know that we are now increasing the number of people who are allowed to emigrate from the Soviet Union. In the past eight months alone 4,450 Jews were allowed to emigrate from the Soviet Union to Israel." Indeed, it was only as he spoke that the real flood was getting under way.

"New Surge of Emigration by Soviet Jews Reported," ran the *New York Times* headline on November 6. Datelined Moscow, the article said:

> Jewish sources report that a new surge of emigration to Israel has been permitted in the last two weeks, raising to some 7,500 the number of Jews who have been allowed to leave the Soviet Union this year.
>
> Moscow's Jewish community is alive with the news that several hundred, including some activists in the emigration protest

movement and a larger proportion of urban professional people than has previously been permitted to leave, have received exit visas.

On Tuesday, Moscow's airport was the scene of an emotional departure for 40 persons flying to Vienna on their way to Israel.

In Vienna, the Jewish Agency office, located at Brahmsplatz no. 3, was busy at the task of receiving the emigrants and arranging their speedy resettlement in Israel. By the end of December, a total of nearly fourteen thousand Soviet Jews had gone this route in 1971.

The applications for exit visas mounted, even though this entailed considerable difficulties for the persons who applied. The first thing a prospective applicant had to do was obtain an affidavit from a relative in Israel. Only then could he or she apply for an exit visa, the cost of which had been raised from 40 to 400 rubles at the end of 1970. To apply, one had to get a character reference from one's place of work—which meant, in effect, advertising one's intention to leave the country, and therefore to become subject to considerable harassment and probable loss of the job. Moreover, when the exit visa was finally received—a process that could drag on for months or even years—automatic loss of Soviet citizenship ensued, and for this a charge of 500 rubles had to be paid. For these reasons, applicants for exit visas were never more than slightly over half the number who actually held affidavits, and often much less. Yet, in 1972, the number of Soviet Jews who left for Israel soared to 31,500, and in 1973 it rose still higher, to 35,300.

The October 1973 war between Egypt and Israel no doubt contributed prominently to a sudden diminution in the exodus in 1974, when—partly owing to an apparent tightening of the government's emigration policy, and partly out of some reluctance on the part of emigrants to go to a newly turbulent Middle East—the figure dropped to about twenty-one thousand; in 1975, it plummeted to 11,700. But now the character of the exodus was changing in other ways as well. There had always been a very small number of the emigrants going to the United States and other Western countries, mainly to rejoin relatives; suddenly, in 1973, this number rose to 4.2 percent of the total. The October War was a factor leading to this rise; another was a ruling issued in August by Attorney General Elliot Richardson greatly facilitating the visa procedures for emigrants with relatives to vouch for them in the United States. In Vienna, the principal first stop of the Soviet emigrants with the Israeli visas they had obtained through the Dutch embassy in Moscow, the offices of HIAS and the Joint Distribution Committee were located in the same building on Brahmsplatz as those of the Jewish Agency. More and more of the émigrés learned that, upon arrival, they could ask to be referred to the American agencies, who were perfectly willing to help them get to the United States or other countries.

This procedure grew in popularity—particularly as the proportions of emigrants released from different regions by the Soviet government began shifting in favor of those from Moscow, Leningrad, and the cosmopolitan cities of Great Russia, and away from the more tradition-bound Jewish communities of Georgia, Lithuania, and White Russia. A diminishing number of them regarded Israel as necessarily preferable to the American Zion, particularly as stories of housing and employment difficulties for Soviet arrivals in Israel began coming back. In 1974, the percentage of "dropouts," as the disapproving Jewish Agency began calling them, rose to 18.8 percent. This was still only the beginning. In 1975, with the overall number of Soviet emigrants at a low point since the beginning of the exodus, more than 37 percent chose to go to America; in 1976, as the emigration figure rose again to more than fourteen thousand, nearly half the arrivals in Vienna applied for American visas. This had been a steady increase proportionately throughout the year, so that by December such applications had become well over half the total.

"More Than Half of Emigrating Soviet Jews Bypass Israel; Reaction by Moscow Is Feared," reported a *New York Times* headline on December 12, 1976. The article said:

> An official Israeli source said today that the percentage of "dropouts," as they are called, reached 54 percent last month. It stands at 47.4 percent so far in 1976.
>
> Israel is worried not only for Zionist reasons—the goal of ingathering as many Jews as possible—but also because it fears that the Soviet Union may use the trend as a pretext for halting emigration. . . .
>
> American Jewish officials share the Israeli concern, but emphasize that they have no reason to bow to the Soviet contention that all Jews leaving the Soviet Union go to Israel. Their primary obligation, as they see it, is to the principle of freedom of movement.
>
> According to an Israeli official deeply involved, Israel subscribes to that principle but would like the American organizations most concerned—United Hias Service and the Joint Distribution Committee—to persuade the Soviet Jews who apply to them for immigration to the United States to go to Israel first, for the sake of the Jews still in the Soviet Union.

This last suggestion was not readily taken, however, since the emigrants who wanted to go to the United States feared that it would be more difficult to do so if they settled in Israel first.

The scene in Vienna that December was described by a Western observer as he followed a group of "dropouts" from their arrival at the railway station through the next phase of their journey into the bewildering Western world. This takes place on the first floor of a large old-fashioned house in tree-lined Brahmsplatz. The square is shabby, a trifle decayed and crammed with parked cars. As soon as one enters the street a sensitive nose can detect the odor of exile. Subdued groups of Jews stare at their unfamiliar surroundings and file up the staircase of Brahmsplatz 3 to be interviewed in turn by representatives of the Jewish Agency, the American Joint Distribution Committee, and HIAS, the Hebrew Immigrant Aid Society. The central lobby is crowded and voluble with chatter, everyone exchanging impressions. Again one is powerfully reminded of Jewish history. There is the smell of Russian cigarettes, pungent sausages, bread and pickles brought for the journey, human perspiration. Children play, cry. Here and there among the Russian speakers one hears a snatch of Yiddish. Several older men are lacking an arm or a leg, casualties of the war. . . .

The first person seen is a representative of the Jewish Agency. It should be explained that wherever the migrant intends to settle he will be travelling with an Israeli document and the Israeli Government has to provide the authorities in Vienna and Rome with a guarantee that Israel accepts full responsibility for him. The Jewish Agency representative tries to find out why the person concerned has decided not to go to Israel and hopes to induce a change of mind. . . .

Those who did not change their minds were put in the charge of HIAS and sent on to facilities in Rome. "Here they stay," according to the HIAS report for 1976,

for a period ranging from six weeks to six months, depending upon the complexity of their case and the availability of visas for the U.S., Canada, Australia and other countries of destination. Because of the growing caseload, the staff of HIAS-Rome was increased from 40 in 1975 to 48 [in 1976].

During their stay in Rome, HIAS provided the emigrants with vocational counseling and courses in English and in American history and culture. To facilitate their sojourn, some basic Italian was provided as well. When at last their turns came to fly to the United States, HIAS agents were waiting at the airports to help them make their entry into a new life and society.

The Soviet emigration figures continued their new ascent. In 1977, nearly seventeen thousand Soviet Jews arrived in Vienna, and in 1978, nearly thirty thousand. In 1979, the outflow reached an astonishing new height of 51,294. With this climb, the proportion of "dropouts" also increased, from a little more than 50 percent in 1977 to nearly 65 percent in 1979. In Israel and at the Jewish Agency offices, there continued to be alarm. "A research study by the [Israeli] ministry concerned with immigration," reported *The New York Times* in August 1979,

> concluded that ... the Hebrew Immigrant Aid Society and the Joint Distribution Committee ... should stop dealing with Soviet emigrants. When [Prime Minister Menachem] Begin was said to have suggested that the agencies confine themselves to those with close relatives in the United States or Canada, the Israeli press commented that an "industry of phoney relatives" would spring up.

And so, as the Soviet-Jewish emigration rose at the end of the 1970s, so also did the temperature of the controversy between the America-oriented and the Israel-oriented.

It had a familiar ring. In 1882, another Muscovite Jew, Chaim Khissin, had asked himself the question "Whither emigrate?" before deciding to go to the Land of Israel instead of the United States. A group of his comrades in Yelizavetgrad had written, it will be recalled:

> Many of our unhappy brethren have emigrated to America, but we are against that, because the Jewish element which reigns in the United States loses in time the Jewish national spirit. Acting upon this ground, we prefer to go to the Holy Land and try our fortune on the ruins of our former greatness.

But at the very same time, another group of Yelizavetgrad Jews had written of "the utter sacredness and necessity of the mission" of transferring their brethren "to the United States of North America, a country civilized beyond all others." Who was right? It would seem that they both were.

The Soviet emigration figures declined sharply as the new decade began, and in 1982 only 2,688 Soviet Jews arrived in Vienna. In the meantime, organizations like the Jewish Agency on one side and HIAS on the other had found other parts of the world in which to do their good works, and even to cooperate in their efforts: for a long time, there had been Jews of the Middle East and North Africa to help from troubled old homes into new lands of settlement; more recently, there was the ancient and imperiled Jewish community of Ethiopia. The hundred-year exodus that had begun in Russia in the 1880s, and of which HIAS and the Jewish Agency also were products, had come full circle. Meanwhile, they had much to do as the next hundred years began.

AFTERWORD

This history of a hundred years of Jewish emigration has fallen, by the nature of the subject, into two main parts: (1) what can be called the classic era, from the upheavals of 1881–82 until the restrictionist American immigration laws of 1921 and 1924; and (2) the period after 1924, which is dominated by the Nazi onslaught of 1933 to 1945 and its aftermath. In some ways, the character of this book differs from one part to the other.

The first part is an attempt to portray straightforwardly, through narrative and illustrative excerpts, the overall character of the classic emigration, and the effort of rescue and assistance that accompanied it throughout. It also describes the worsening pattern of persecution and violence that drove Jews outward from Eastern Europe to lands of refuge in ever-increasing numbers. The story as told here is, I believe, fresh with new details and perspectives, but its essential premises are not likely to be controversial today.

The second part—particularly in its chapters on the Nazi era—is a different matter. In recent years, much controversy—or, rather, a whole literature of accusation—has arisen over the subject of responses in the Allied countries to the Nazi persecution of the Jews.* Could more Jews have been saved than finally were, had there been a more concerned and humane policy regarding their fate among the Allies? Did the Jewish communities of the West properly meet their responsibilities during the crisis? Did the press adequately report details of the catastrophe? These and other questions have increasingly been asked.

And some historians have answered them in ways highly unfavorable to the historic institutions and personalities concerned. Heavy crit-

*For some sample titles, see the notes at the end of this book.

icism has been directed at the governments of the West, and in particular at that of the United States under the administration of President Franklin Delano Roosevelt. David S. Wyman writes in *The Abandonment of the Jews*: "Franklin Roosevelt's indifference to so momentous an historical event as the systematic annihilation of European Jewry emerges as the worst failure of his presidency." Judgments of this nature have cast a dark shadow upon the figure of Roosevelt in the eyes of our contemporaries.

Yet my own researches into that period, reflected in the account on these pages, have brought me to the conclusion that such judgments may be too harsh. Let me not be misunderstood: the years from 1933 to 1945 were marked by widespread indifference and callousness toward Jewish suffering among those who were not its out-and-out perpetrators. But within that atmosphere there were degrees of unconcern and of concern, and it seems to me that Franklin Delano Roosevelt was, in fact, the least indifferent to the Jewish catastrophe of all the heads of government of his time.

It was Roosevelt, for example, who recognized the gravity of the German and Austrian refugee crisis in the spring of 1938 sufficiently to call the international conference on the question held that July at Evian-les-Bains. To be sure, the results of the conference proved inadequate, but few of his contemporaries were inclined to blame him for that, and many—including Jewish spokesmen—continued to praise him for his initiative in the matter. And he continued taking such initiatives. From 1938 to 1940, he kept bending American visa and immigration rules—against formidable opposition in both Congress and the State Department—in such ways as to allow more victims of Hitlerite persecution to find refuge in the United States than otherwise could have.

It is the interval from December 1941, when the United States entered the war as a belligerent, to January 1944, when Roosevelt created the War Refugee Board for the specific purpose of rescuing victims of Nazism, that presents a more difficult problem of comprehension. During this time, we find little effort at direct intervention on Roosevelt's part—or that of his fellow war leaders—in the European-Jewish tragedy. Much has been made by historians of the problem of knowledge: when did the Western democracies learn that the systematic annihilation of European Jewry was taking place, and not just scattered persecutions and murders? The answer is that all responsible and informed persons knew by December 1942. So the question remains: why did it then take more than a year for Roosevelt to take action for the purpose of rescuing the victims to whatever extent possible?

Such a question cannot be answered without reference to the war itself. Certainly at the outset, the leaders of the Allied Powers considered the relentless prosecution of the war to be the only way to deal with the evils of Nazism and to rescue its victims. Roosevelt—along with Winston Churchill, who also was far from indifferent to the Jewish fate—was outspoken on numerous occasions in condemning Nazi crimes against the Jews and demanding retribution at the war's end for those who were responsible. Indeed, his somewhat hasty enunciation of the "unconditional surrender" doctrine in January 1943 may have come out of his zeal for retribution.

The fact remains, however, that after December 1942 the Allied leaders were sometimes confronted with the possibility of taking direct action to rescue Jews. Virtually every one of these possibilities arose in circumstances that demanded weighing it against military considerations. Perhaps the most notable such instance occurred in March 1943, when Anthony Eden, the British Foreign Secretary, refused to consider certain large-scale rescue operations for Jews out of fear that these would hinder the war effort.* Eden's views in matters of this sort were as crucial in Washington as they were in London at the time; it was not until January 1944 that Roosevelt felt some freedom to defy the inclinations of the Foreign Office, as he did when he created the War Refugee Board. This respect for British requirements was also what kept Roosevelt silent until 1944 on the subject of Palestine, where Britain's White Paper policy of 1939 had all but closed off completely the major potential refuge of European Jewry.

No Allied leader would do anything that, in his opinion, threatened even remotely to interfere with the fullest prosecution of the war. This meant heeding one's expert advisers: Winston Churchill, who had vehemently opposed the White Paper from the floor of the House of Commons in May 1939, acquiesced in the position of his Foreign, Colonial, and War offices after becoming Prime Minister and did not try to change the policy. Roosevelt, even after showing readiness to defy the British on Palestine as on other matters early in 1944, found that he could not defy his own War Department, and had to back down on the issue. It was also the War Department that bore the brunt of responsibility in another matter regarding the Jews of Europe for which Roosevelt has too often been reproached: the refusal to bomb Auschwitz or the railway lines leading to it. The War Department rejected all such proposals—none of which seems even to have reached Roosevelt himself—on the basis of a policy opposing the diversion of armed forces for rescue missions. This put it in direct opposition to the War Refugee Board, which, after all, represented the President's desire that rescue be counted an objective of the war.

Any grounds, then, for the claim that Roosevelt was indifferent to the fate of European Jewry turn out to be quite tenuous. There are

*See page 524.

stronger grounds for the claim that there was indifference—and sometimes worse—among people whose advice he had to heed or whose will he could not defy. This was especially true of some of the specimens of biased and narrow-minded officialdom that we are able to glimpse holding crucial positions in the State and War departments, and in their British equivalents. But what about those on the highest levels? Winston Churchill, for example? There is ample reason to believe that his sympathies with the Jewish plight were strong, but that he was even less able to act directly upon them than Roosevelt was. Anthony Eden? He assuredly represents a crucial factor in this problem, and a thorough study of his conscience and behavior with regard to it—to whatever extent that is possible—would be a most significant contribution to the historical discussion. It is beyond my purview. One thing is clear, however: Eden took squarely upon his shoulders—and, I suspect, with full realization of its awfulness—the responsibility for a decision without precedent in history. Any judgment of him should be based on recognition of that fact. In light of it, he does not seem indifferent, either.

In making such a judgment, I think it is a mistake to apply anything like the stark moral criteria we use in judging Nazism itself. In the one case we have a rampant and unmitigated evil, an inexorable bestiality, which could upset mankind long enough to wreak terrible destruction and impose grave moral dilemmas before finally being destroyed itself. In the face of such a fury—and of the heroism that defeated it—a calculus of humane virtues is very hard to apply.

Notes

A PROLOGUE IN ODESSA

Page

3   "And it was on March 1, 1881 . . ."; Pauline Wengeroff, *Memoiren einer Gross-mutter: Bilder aus der Kulturgeschichte der Juden Russlands in 19. Jahr-hundert*, 2 vols. (Berlin, 1908), 2:186. Translated by the author. All dates in this and the following two chapters are according to the Old Style Russian calendar.

4   "Toward the end of the seventies . . .": Israel Kasovich, *Days of Our Years* (New York, 1929), p. 163.

"a silver wreath . . . of a Russian Emperor." *American Israelite*, May 13, 1881.

"It is, we fear . . .": *Jewish Chronicle*, March 18, 1881.

5   "For God's sake, Your Majesty . . .": Konstantin P. Pobedonostsev, *Reflec-tions of a Russian Statesman*, trans. Robert Crozier Long (Ann Arbor, 1965), quoted in Foreword by Murray Polner, p. vii.

"The authorities appear . . .": *The Times* (London), April 21, 1881.

6   "Advices from St. Petersburg . . .": Ibid., April 30, 1881.

"The New York *Herald* . . .": Abraham Cahan, *Bletter fun mein Leben*, 5 vols. (New York, 1926–1931), 1:430. Translated by the author.

Dondukov-Korsakov in Odessa: *The Times* (London), April 29, 1881.

7   "during the Russian Easter . . .": *Jewish Chronicle*, April 29, 1871.

7-8 "It was rumored . . . in the bud." Ibid., June 16, 1871.

8   "Odessa was in the hands . . . occupied by Jews." Ibid., May 10, 1871.

8-9 "On Monday afternoon . . . of their impunity." Ibid., June 16, 1871.

9   "What could not be destroyed . . .": Ibid., May 10, 1871.

"On Tuesday . . . standing below." Ibid., June 16, 1871.

"Four thousand Jewish families . . .": Ibid., June 23, 1871.

"The part the authorities . . .": Ibid., May 10, 1871.

"which states that . . .": Ibid., June 9, 1871.

10   "When Prince Stroganoff . . .": Ibid., June 23, 1871.

2. A SEASON OF DEVASTATIONS

Page
11   "If a statement . . .": *Jewish Chronicle*, June 2, 1871.
12   "Not a single capital . . .": Leon Trotsky, *My Life* (New York, 1970), p. 37.
12-13   "Brother Jews . . .": "Jacob Gordin," in Melech Epstein, *Profiles of Eleven* (Detroit, 1965), pp. 140–41.
13   "The *Zhids* . . .": S. M. Dubnow, *History of the Jews in Russia and Poland*, 3 vols. (Philadelphia, 1916), 2:249.
14   "Inflamed by the drink . . .": *The Times* (London), January 11, 1882.
       "spreading with extraordinary violence . . . without knowing what to do." Dubnow, *History*, 2:250.
       "The authorities were wholly unprepared . . .": Madame Zinaida Ragozin, "Russian Jews and Gentiles—From a Russian Point of View,"*The Century*, April 1882, p. 906.
       "at first as spectators . . .": *The Times* (London), January 11, 1882.
14-15   "was bound to arrive . . . the means at hand." Dubnow, *History*, 2:250.
16   "hated the Jews . . .": General V. D. Novitsky, quoted in Louis Greenberg, *The Jews in Russia*, 2 vols. (New Haven, 1944–1951), 2:21.
16-17   "the air suddenly resounded . . . filled with loot." Dubnow, *History*, 2:252.
17   "When I reached the grain bazaar . . .": Quoted in Ragozin, "Russian Jews and Gentiles," p. 908.
       "The streets . . . . caused a fire." *The Times* (London), May 12, 1881.
       "a rather more malignant character": Ragozin, "Russian Jews and Gentiles," p. 907.
       "Through the uproar . . .": Quoted in ibid., p. 908.
17-18   "an enclosure . . .": Quoted from *Zaria* in the *Jewish Messenger*, June 16, 1881.
18   "The entire behavior of the police . . .": Quoted in Greenberg, *Jews in Russia*, 2:21.

3. DISILLUSIONMENT AND FLIGHT

Page
19   "Bigotry, envy . . .": *Jewish Chronicle*, May 13, 1881.
       "It is officially stated . . .": *The Times* (London), May 19, 1881.
       "There is evidence to show . . .": *Jewish Chronicle*, May 20, 1881.
20   "Ever since the German anti-Semites . . .": *The Times* (London), January 11, 1882.
       "Everyone knows . . .": Quoted in Louis Greenberg, *The Jews in Russia*, 2 vols. (New Haven, 1944–1951), 1:159.
       "to popular reprobation . . .": Quoted in *Jewish Chronicle*, May 6, 1881.
21   "the anti-Jewish movement . . . against the Christians." Ibid.
       "The persecution of the Jews . . .": *The Times* (London), May 19, 1881.
       "that the assertion of the Emperor . . .": Ibid., May 31, 1881.
21-22   "the beginning of a social war . . .": Quoted in *The New York Times*, May 11, 1881.
22   "Good people . . .": Quoted in Lucy S. Dawidowicz, *The Golden Tradition* (New York, 1967), p. 406. I have edited the translation slightly.
       authoritative estimate: Greenberg, *Jews in Russia*, 1:149.
       "The enthusiasm for an idea . . .": *Jewish Chronicle*, March 25, 1881.
23   "We are *Narodniki* . . .": Greenberg, *Jews in Russia*, 1:147.
       "I still remember . . .": In Dawidowicz, *Golden Tradition*, pp. 406–7.

23 "I will never forget . . .": Ibid., p. 414.

"I must admit . . .": Abraham Cahan, *Bletter fun mein Leben*, 5 vols. (New York, 1926–1931), 1:435. Translated by the author.

23-24 "whooping and howling . . . can be observed." Quoted by Axelrod in Dawido-wicz, *Golden Tradition*, pp. 408–9.

24 "that the Jews . . . the Jewish masses." Ibid., p. 408.

"it was only necessary . . .": Quoted in Nora Levin, *While Messiah Tarried: Jewish Socialist Movements, 1871–1917* (New York, 1977), p. 56.

"filled with weeping . . . 'Yes, we are Jews.' " Cahan, *Bletter*, 1:500.

25 "to found in America . . .": Abraham Menes, "Die Am Oylom Bavegung," in E. Tcherikower, ed. *Geshikhte fun der Yiddisher Arbeter-Bavegung in die Far-eynikte Shtatn*, 2 vols. (New York, 1945), 2:208. Translated by the author.

"There is no doubt . . .": In Arthur Hertzberg, ed., *The Zionist Idea* (Phila-delphia, 1964), p. 151.

25-26 "The Jews are removing . . .": Quoted in the *Jewish Chronicle*, May 20, 1881.

26 "Crowds of refugees . . .": Ibid.

"Many refugee Jews . . .": *American Israelite*, May 20, 1881.

"All the available space . . .": *The Times* (London), May 19, 1881.

4. THE BRODY REFUGE

Page

29-30 Galicia: See Norman Davies, *God's Playground: A History of Poland*, 2 vols. (New York, 1982), esp. vol. 2, passim.

30-31 "In many places . . .": Abraham Cahan, *Bletter fun mein Leben*, 5 vols. (New York, 1926–1931), 2:25. Translated by the author.

31 "moth-eaten" old fiacre: Moritz Friedländer, *Fünf Wochen in Brody unter jü-disch-russischen Emigranten* (Vienna, 1882), pp. 14–15. Translated by the au-thor.

"a water carrier . . .": Cahan, *Bletter*, 2:26.

"the synagogue . . . a Russian Jewess." "The Diary of Dr. George M. Price," ed. and trans. Leo Shpall, in *Publications of the American Jewish Historical Society*, vol. 40, no. 2 (December 1950), p. 176.

"God! What Pandemonium! . . . hungry and thirsty." Ibid., pp. 176–77.

32 "Here squats a young mother . . .": Friedländer, *Fünf Wochen*, p. 14.

32-33 The Alliance Israélite Universelle and Brody: Zosa Szajkowski, "How the Mass Migration to America Began," *Jewish Social Studies*, vol. 4, no. 4 (October 1942), pp. 291–310.

34 "They would rather suffer here . . .": Szajkowski, "Mass Migration," p. 303.

"Emigration may continue yet . . .": Elias Tcherikower, "Jewish Immigrants to the United States, 1881-1900," *YIVO Annual*, 1951, p. 159.

"Impossible accept . . .": Szajkowski, "Mass Migration," p. 297.

5. AMERICAN ISRAELITES

Page

35 "It is very philanthropic . . .": *Jewish Messenger*, May 20, 1881.

"It is high time . . .": Quoted in James G. Heller, *Isaac M. Wise: His Life, Work and Thought* (New York, 1965), p. 585.

36 "A free country . . .": Ibid., p. 127.

"a jargon . . .": Ibid., p. 586.

38   "Let our rich Israelites . . .": New York *Herald,* September 26, 1869: quoted in Mark Wischnitzer, *To Dwell in Safety: The Story of Jewish Migration Since 1800* (Philadelphia, 1948), p. 31.
      "no thought of sending over beggars . . .": Quoted and translated from the *Israelitische Wochenschrift* by Rudolf Glanz in "Source Materials on Jewish Immigration," *YIVO Annual,* 1951, p. 155.

38-39 "Notwithstanding our urgent remonstrances . . . earn a livelihood." Morris U. Schappes, ed., *A Documentary History of the Jews in the United States, 1654–1875* (New York, 1971), pp. 538–39.

39   "mechanics among the refugees . . .": Ibid., p. 33.

40   "We beseech you . . .": Ibid., pp. 35–36.

6. ISRAEL UNPREPARED

Page
41   "Aid for Immigrants": *Jewish Messenger,* May 20, 1881.

41-42 Four recommendations: Ibid., July 8, 1881.

42   "that the emigration to America . . .": *Jewish Chronicle,* May 6, 1881.
      "We are assured . . .": *American Israelite,* August 19, 1881.

42-43 "The Paris Committee . . .": *Jewish Messenger,* August 19, 1881.

43   "If Russia wearies . . .": Ibid., September 23, 1881.
      "The New York Committee . . .": Ibid., September 23, 1881.
      "The Hebrew Congregations . . .": *American Israelite,* October 14, 1881.

44   Goldschmidt's letter: Mark Wischnitzer, *To Dwell in Safety: The Story of Jewish Migration Since 1800* (Philadelphia, 1948), p. 43.
      "Send no more emigrants . . .": Zosa Szajkowski, "The Attitudes of American Jews to East European Jewish Immigration (1881–1893)," *Publications of the American Jewish Historical Society,* vol. 40, no. 3 (March 1951), p. 224.

44-48 Kursheedt's letter: Ibid., appendix B, pp. 264–71.

7. THE GENTLEMEN OF BRODY

Page
49-51 Netter's letter of October 13, 1881: Moritz Friedländer, *Fünf Wochen in Brody unter jüdisch-russischen Emigranten* (Vienna, 1882), pp. 9–11. Translated by the author.

52   Netter's letter of October 14, 1881: Ibid., p. 12.

52-54 "When I entered . . . 'Our true Messiah!' " Ibid., pp. 15–28.

54-55 "We, the undersigned . . .": Zosa Szajkowski, "Materialn vegen der Yiddisher Emigratzye keyn America in 1881–1882," *YIVO Bletter,* vol. 19 (March-April 1942), p. 277. Translated by the author.

55   "several members . . .": Zosa Szajkowski, "How the Mass Migration to America Began," *Jewish Social Studies,* vol. 4, no. 4 (October 1942), p. 298. Translated by the author from the French quotation.
      "Stop all transports . . .": Friedländer, *Fünf Wochen,* p. 34.

55-56 "When we woke the next morning . . .": Ibid., pp. 34–35.

56   "Even if we resume the transports . . .": Ibid., p. 36.
      "Telegram 'Stop all transports' . . .": Ibid., p. 39.

8. FROM BRODY TO NEW YORK, I: THE EUROPEAN JOURNEY

Page

57   "Once the work in the office . . .": Moritz Friedländer, *Fünf Wochen in Brody unter jüdisch-russischen Emigranten* (Vienna, 1882), p. 29. Translated by the author.

57-58 Netter's circular: Zosa Szajkowski, "Materialn vegen der Yiddisher Emigratzye keyn America in 1881-1882," *YIVO Bletter*, vol. 19 (March-April, 1942), p. 275. Translated by the author.

58-59 "The next day . . .": Friedländer, *Fünf Wochen*, pp. 29–30.

59   "I could see Netter . . .": Quoted in Mark Wischnitzer, *To Dwell in Safety: The Story of Jewish Migration Since 1800* (Philadelphia, 1948), p. 38.

59-60 "the Am Olam group was given . . .": Abraham Menes, "Die Am Oylom Bavegung," in E. Tcherikower, ed., *Geshikhte fun der Yiddisher Arbeter-Bavegung in die Fareynikte Shtatn*, 2 vols. (New York, 1945), 2:215. Translated by the author.

60   "In the evening . . .": "The Diary of Dr. George M. Price," ed. and trans. Leo Shpall, in *Publications of the American Jewish Historical Society*, vol. 40, no. 2 (December 1950), p. 180.

       "A committee of local Jewish notables . . .": Abraham Cahan, *Bletter fun mein Leben*, 5 vols. (New York, 1926–1931), 2:49. Translated by the author.

       "was a Polish Christian . . .": Ibid., 2:51.

60-61 "There a committee also came . . .": Ibid., 2:51–52.

61   "Day by day . . .": Quoted in Joseph Brandes, *Immigrants to Freedom: Jewish Communities in Rural New Jersey Since 1882* (Philadelphia, 1971), p. 33.

       "The news that an Am Olam . . .": Abraham Menes, "Die Am Oylom Bavegung," 2:220–21.

       "In Hamburg, however . . .": Israel Kasovich, *Days of Our Years* (New York, 1929), p. 140.

61-62 "bread, milk, coffee . . .": "Diary of George Price," p. 180.

62   "hundreds of poor Jewish immigrants . . .": Bernard Weinstein, *Fertzig Yohr in der Yiddisher Arbeter-Bavegung* (New York, 1924), pp. 14–15. Translated by the author.

       Rabbi Isaac Rülf: Elias Tcherikower, "Jewish Immigrants to the United States, 1881-1900," *YIVO Annual*, 1951, p. 161.

       C. Henry Strauss: Szajkowski, "Materialn," p. 276.

62-63 "Be informed . . . stupid fellows, pigs. . . .": Ibid., p. 276.

63   "I reported to the place . . .": Harris Rubin, "Workers on the Land," in Uri D. Herscher, ed., *The East European Jewish Experience in America* (Cincinnati, 1983), p. 20.

64   "about ninety per cent . . .": Quoted in Lloyd P. Gartner, *The Jewish Immigrant in England, 1870–1914* (London, 1960), p. 44.

       "four days later . . .": Alexander Harkavy, "Chapters from My Life," in Herscher, *East European Jewish Experience*, p. 56.

9. FROM BRODY TO NEW YORK, II: THE OCEAN

Page

65   "The boat *British Prince* . . .": Alexander Harkavy, "Chapters from My Life," in Uri D. Herscher, ed., *The East European Jewish Experience in America* (Cincinnati, 1983), pp. 56–57.

66   "the dreadful, salty . . .": Abraham Cahan, *Bletter fun mein Leben*, 5 vols. (New York, 1926–1931), 2:62. Translated by the author.
      "We were all herded . . .": Israel Kasovich, *Days of Our Years* (New York, 1929), p. 170.
      "and each of us . . .": Harris Rubin, "Workers on the Land," in Herscher, *East European Jewish Experience*, p. 22.

66-67 "the women carried . . .": Bernard Weinstein, *Fertzig Yohr in der Yiddisher Arbeter-Bavegung* (New York, 1924), pp. 15–16. Translated by the author.

67   "I tried to fall asleep . . .": Ibid., p. 16.
      "the clattering of the dishes . . .": "The Diary of Dr. George M. Price," ed. and trans. Leo Shpall, in *Publications of the American Jewish Historical Society*, vol. 40, no. 2 (December 1950), p. 180.
      "Help, save me! . . .": Rubin, "Workers on the Land," pp. 23–24.

67-68 "Hundreds of people . . .": Kasovich, *Days*, p. 170.

68   "One day . . .": Cahan, *Bletter*, 2:60.
      "During the period of seasickness . . .": Rubin, "Workers on the Land," p. 24.
      "Panic-stricken . . .": "Diary of George Price," p. 180.
      "we had the desire . . .": Rubin, "Workers on the Land," p. 24.
      "The bread and meat . . .": "Diary of George Price, p. 180.
      "We 'below-decks' passengers . . .": Weinstein, *Fertzig Yohr*, p. 17.

69   "Some of the emigrants . . .": *Jewish Messenger*, November 25, 1881.
      "As for the so-called kosher meat . . .": Rubin, "Workers on the Land," p. 24.
      "Mister . . .": Cahan, *Bletter*, 2:61.
      "swine . . .": Weinstein, *Fertzig Yohr*, pp. 16, 18.

69-70 "We went up on deck . . .": Ibid., p. 16.

70   "the first week . . .": Rubin, "Workers on the Land," p. 24.
      "In the evenings . . .": Cahan, *Bletter*, 2:63.

70-72 The storm at sea: Rubin, "Workers on the Land," pp. 25–28.

72   "We felt relieved . . .": "Diary of George Price," p. 181.

10. THE HEBREW EMIGRANT AID SOCIETY

Page

75   "For a few weeks past . . .": *Jewish Messenger*, November 25, 1881.

75-76 The November 27, 1881, meeting: Gilbert Osofsky, "The Hebrew Emigrant Aid Society of the United States (1881–1883)," *Publications of the American Jewish Historical Society*, vol. 49 (1960), pp. 175–76.

76   "To afford aid and advice . . .": Ibid., p. 186.

76-77 "Louisiana will welcome your people . . .": *Jewish Chronicle*, November 11, 1881.

77   "The New Orleans Committee . . .": Ibid.

77-78 The land offer and Menken's report: Hebrew Emigrant Aid Society of the United States, *Report on the Formation of the First Russian Jewish Colony of the United States at Catahoula Parish, Louisiana*, by J. Stanwood Menken, President (London, 1882), pp. 3–5.

78   December 5, 1881 meeting in Harrisonburg: Ibid., pp. 16–17.
      "To the people of Louisiana . . .": Ibid., p. 4

78-79 "$5,000 were collected . . .": *Jewish Chronicle*, February 3, 1882.

79-81 Moritz Ellinger and his letter: Ibid., January 27, 1882.

11. THE DEEPENING CRISIS IN RUSSIA

Page
83   "The principal source . . . the disturbances." S. M. Dubnow, *History of the Jews in Russia and Poland,* 3 vols. (Philadelphia, 1916), 2:271-72.

84   "charged the Governors . . .": *Jewish Chronicle,* September 23, 1881.
      "which aspects of the economic activity . . .": Dubnow, *History,* 2:272.

84-85 Commission results: Louis Greenberg, *The Jews in Russia,* 2 vols. (New Haven, 1944-1951), 2:28-29.

85   "the Minister of the Interior . . .": *Jewish Chronicle,* November 25, 1881.
      "be forbidden to Jews . . .": Ibid., October 21, 1881.
      "stones were thrown at her . . .": Reprinted in *Jewish Chronicle,* December 2, 1881.

86-87 The Christmas Day 1881 riots in Warsaw: *Jewish Chronicle,* December 30, 1881; January 6, 1882.

87   "period of toleration . . .": Dubnow, *History,* 2:309.

87-88 "The *Official Messenger* today . . .": *Jewish Chronicle,* May 26, 1882.

88   "If the Eastern frontier . . .": Dubnow, *History,* 2:265.
      "The Western frontier . . .": Ibid., 2:285.
      "We have, then . . .": Cyrus Adler and Aaron M. Margalith, *With Firmness in the Right: American Diplomatic Action Affecting Jews, 1840-1945* (New York, 1946), p. 209.

88-89 Sophie Günzburg on her family: Lucy S. Dawidowicz, *The Golden Tradition* (New York, 1967), pp. 248-56.

89   "Our wealthy Jews . . . .": Chaim Chissin, *A Palestine Diary: Memoirs of a Bilu Pioneer, 1882-87* (New York, 1976), p. 263.
      "Nobody will accuse us . . .": *Jewish Messenger,* May 27, 1881.

90   "I hear . . .": *Jewish Chronicle,* March 24, 1882.
      The April 1882 meeting of Jewish notables: Dubnow, *History,* 2:304-7.

12. COPING WITH THE FLOOD

Page
91   "at least 600 families . . .": *Jewish Chronicle,* March 10, 1882.
      "A despatch from Brody . . .": Ibid., May 19, 1882.

92   "Approaching the entrance . . . to several at another." "The Diary of Dr. George M. Price," ed. and trans. Leo Shpall, in *Publications of the American Jewish Historical Society,* vol. 40, no. 2 (December 1950), pp. 178-79.
      "would have been to expose them . . .": *Jewish Chronicle,* March 3. 1882.

92-93 "Distressing appeals . . .": Ibid., May 19, 1882.

93   "The sanitary conditions . . .": Ibid., June 2, 1882.
      "Last night . . .": Ibid.
      "They summoned twenty soldiers . . .": "Diary of George Price," p. 179.
      "and after examining . . .": *Jewish Chronicle,* June 2, 1882.

94   "to express public opinion . . .": Ibid., February 3, 1882.
      "A communication was received . . .": Ibid., February 17, 1882.

94-95 "A large number of Jewish refugees . . .": Ibid., February 24, 1882.

95   "The vessel left Gravesend . . .": Ibid., February 17, 1882.
      "A letter was read . . .": Ibid., March 3, 1882.
      "The influx of Jewish refugees . . .": Ibid., March 24, 1882.

95-96 "Those who came to London at first . . .": Ibid.

96   "a special sub-committee . . .": Ibid., February 24, 1882.
97   "Only young unmarried . . .": Ibid., April 14, 1882.
       "Our reasons . . .": Ibid.
98   "It is difficult to see . . .": Ibid., April 21, 1882.
98-99 "The Committee being without . . . needed for his settlement.": Ibid.
99-100 "direct the dispersion of refugees . . .": Moritz Ellinger, *Report to the Hebrew
       Emigrant Aid Society of the United States* (New York, 1882), p. 19.
100   £5,500 a week: *Jewish Chronicle*, May 19, 1882.
       George S. Yates: Ibid., June 2, 1882.

13. THE WELCOME

Page
101   "Suddenly a small barge . . .": Bernard Weinstein, *Fertzig Yohr in der Yid-
       disher Arbeter-Bavegung* (New York, 1924), p. 18. Translated by the author.
101-02 "a singular-looking . . . of the building." James D. McCabe, Jr., *New York By
       Gaslight* (New York 1882: 1984 reprint), pp. 660-61.
       "one by one . . .": Ibid., p. 661.
102   Immigration figures: The principal sources are Samuel Joseph, *Jewish Immi-
       gration to the United States* (New York, 1914), and Mark Wischnitzer, *To Dwell
       in Safety: The Story of Jewish Migration Since 1800* (Philadelphia, 1948). See
       appendix tables in both books.
       "If we thought . . . almighty dollar." "The Memoir of Dr. George M. Price,"
       trans. Leo Shpall, in *Publications of the American Jewish Historical Society*,
       vol. 47, no. 2 (December 1957), p. 102. This is not to be confused with the
       "Diary of George Price," hitherto cited.
103   "The Castle Garden Plaza . . .": Alexander Harkavy, "Chapters from My Life,"
       in Uri D. Herscher, ed., *The East European Jewish Experience in America*
       (Cincinnati, 1983), p. 57.
       "the shrieks . . . a place for themselves." "Memoir of George Price," pp.
       102-3.
       "Those of the new-comers . . .": McCabe, *New York*, p. 662.
       "the stench was terrible . . .": Abraham Cahan, *Bletter fun mein Leben*, 5 vols.
       (New York, 1926-1931), 2:71-72. Translated by the author.
       "On the adjoining streets . . .": Harkavy, "Chapters," p. 57.
103-04 "step out of the barges . . .": Weinstein, *Fertzig Yohr*, p. 19.
104   "The great steamships . . .": Cahan, *Bletter*, 2:68.
       "used to give out tickets . . .": Weinstein, *Fertzig Yohr*, p. 21.
       "was so immense . . .": "Memoir of George Price," p. 103.
       "At the door stood a policeman . . .": Israel Kasovich, *Days of Our Years* (New
       York, 1929), p. 175.
104-05 "An American Jew . . .": Cahan, *Bletter*, 2:68-69.
105   "The officers of the Society . . .": Harkavy, "Chapters," pp. 57-58.
       "I had come to America . . .": Kasovich, *Days*, p. 177.
105-06 "While it was true . . .": Harris Rubin, "Workers on the Land," in Herscher,
       East European Jewish Experience, p. 31.
106   "The superintendent . . .": Harkavy, "Chapters," p. 58.
       "selected, dressed . . .": Rubin, "Workers on the Land," p. 31.
       "in reality . . .": "Memoir of George Price," p. 109.
       "In a sense . . .": Rubin, "Workers on the Land," p. 31.

106   "in very strange ways . . .": Harkavy, "Chapters," p. 58.

107   "Three weeks ago . . . of Russian barbarity." *American Israelite*, April 7, 1882.

107-09 "an American Jew . . . and the language." "Memoir of George Price," pp. 105–10.

14. INTERLUDE: THE ZEAL OF A CONVERT

Page

110   "The imperative necessity . . .": *The American Hebrew*, October 20, 1882.
       "He knew himself to be . . .": Emma Lazarus, "Lord Beaconsfield," *The Century*, April 1882, pp. 729–44.

111   "Here's something . . .": Heinrich E. Jacob, *The World of Emma Lazarus* (New York, 1949), p. 112.

111-12 Emma Lazarus's reply: "Russian Christianity Versus Modern Judaism," *The Century*, May 1882, pp. 48–56.

112   "O deem not dead . . .": "The Banner of the Jew," in Morris U. Schappes, ed., *Emma Lazarus: Selections from Her Poetry and Prose* (New York, 1967), pp. 35–37.

113   "This play . . .": *Songs of a Semite* (New York, 1882; reprint, Upper Saddle River, N.J., 1970), p. 3.

113-14 Letter on "The Schiff Refuge": *The American Hebrew*, October 20, 1882.

115   "Not for the sake . . .": Ibid., November 3, 1882.

15. RETURNERS TO THE SOIL, I: PALESTINE

Page

116   "In two divided streams . . .": "The New Year: Rosh Hashanah, 5643 (1882)," in Morris U. Schappes, ed., *Emma Lazarus: Selections from Her Poetry and Prose* (New York, 1967), pp. 37–38.

116-17 Palestine in 1882: See Ronald Sanders, *The High Walls of Jerusalem* (New York, 1984), chapter 1.

117   "the intention of 500 . . .": *Jewish Chronicle*, February 3, 1882.
       "From divers places . . .": Ibid., February 10, 1882.
       "an influx of Jewish paupers . . .": Ibid., May 26, 1882. Letter from Colonel Albert E. Goldsmid.

118   "the problem 'Whither Emigrate?' . . ." Chaim Chissin, *A Palestine Diary: Memoirs of a Bilu Pioneer, 1882–87* (New York, 1976), p. 263. I have preferred to use the transliteration "Khissin" of his name in the text.
       Belkind and Cahan: See Ronald Sanders, *The Downtown Jews* (New York, 1987), pp. 38–39.
       "Many of our unhappy brethren . . .": *Jewish Chronicle*, April 21, 1882.

119   "There is an immense movement . . .": Margaret Oliphant, *Memoir of the Life of Laurence Oliphant*, 2 vols. (New York, 1891), 2:218.
       "that the many societies . . .": *Jewish Chronicle*, March 18, 1882.
       "On the 3rd . . .": Oliphant, *Memoir*, 2:219.
       "It is true that I . . .": Quoted in *Jewish Chronicle*, April 28, 1882.

120   "a committee whose task . . .": Ibid., May 5, 1882.
       "are arriving here almost daily . . .": Ibid., May 26, 1882.

120   "We have organized ... brought to Jaffa." Chissin, *Palestine Diary*, pp. 33–34.

121   "When, therefore ... to settle in Palestine." *Jewish Chronicle*, June 2, 1882.

121-24   Khissin's journey: Chissin, *Palestine Diary*, pp. 265–66, 34–35, 36–53.

124-25   Netter's letter on Palestine: *Jewish Chronicle*, March 24, 1882.

125   Rebuttal about Mikveh Israel: Ibid., March 31, 1882.

       Schafier and twenty-eight orphans: Ibid., March 3, 1882.

126   "At about nine o'clock ...": Chissin, *Palestine Diary*, pp. 75–76.

       "About ten days ago ...": Ibid., p. 83.

       "It is believed ...": *Jewish Chronicle*, October 13, 1882.

       "concern himself with the settling ...": Chissin, *Palestine Diary*, p. 84.

126-27   Baron de Rothschild's visitors: See Simon Schama, *Two Rothschilds and the Land of Israel* (New York, 1978), pp. 52–63.

16. RETURNERS TO THE SOIL, II: THE UNITED STATES

Page

128   "establish a class ...": Abraham Menes, "Die Am Oylom Bavegung," in E. Tcherikower, ed., *Geshikhte fun der Yiddisher Arbeter-Bavegung in die Fareynikte Shtatn*, 2 vols. (New York, 1945), p. 210. Translated by the author.

128-29   Vineland colony: Joseph Brandes, *Immigrants to Freedom: Jewish Communities in Rural New Jersey Since 1882* (Philadelphia, 1971), pp. 50–56.

129   Julius Goldman's report: Hebrew Emigrant Aid Society of the United States, *Report on the Colonization of Russian Refugees in the West* (New York, 1882). "die the natural death ...": *Jewish Chronicle*, July 7, 1882.

129-30   Demise of the Hebrew Emigrant Aid Society: Gilbert Osofsky, "The Hebrew Emigrant Aid Society of the United States (1881–1883)," *Publications of the American Jewish Historical Society*, vol. 49 (1960), p. 184.

130   Michael Heilprin: See Gustav Pollack, *Michael Heilprin and His Sons* (New York, 1912).

       "worked for the immigrants ...": Abraham Cahan, *Bletter fun mein Leben*, 5 vols. (New York, 1926–1931), 2:135. Translated by the author.

131-32   "Our long wanderings ... for the week is assigned." Abraham Menes, "Am Oylom," pp. 215–16.

132   "a lot of trouble ... of the other members." Cahan, *Bletter*, 2:297–303.

133   "Vast oceanic movements ...": "Currents," in Morris U. Schappes, ed., *Emma Lazarus: Selections from Her Poetry and Prose* (New York, 1967), p. 51.

17. MOTHER OF EXILES

Page

134   "This Liberty will not be ...": James B. Bell and Richard I. Abrahams, *In Search of Liberty* (New York, 1984), p. 25.

135   "The $250,000 ...": Ibid., p. 40.

       "I am a young man ...": Ibid., pp. 40–41.

136   "O France, the beautiful ...": In Marvin Trachtenberg, *The Statue of Liberty* (New York, 1986), p. 220.

136-37   "The New Colossus": In Morris U. Schappes, ed., *Emma Lazarus: Selections from Her Poetry and Prose* (New York, 1967), p. 48.

18. RUSSIA, 1887–1891: EXCLUSION AND EXPULSION

Page

141-42   Pahlen Commission: S. M. Dubnow, *History of the Jews in Russia and Poland*, 3 vols. (Philadelphia, 1916), 2:336ff; and Louis Greenberg, *The Jews in Russia*, 2 vols. (New Haven, 1944–1951), 2:25–28.

142   "Why do they so gladly . . .": Salo W. Baron, *The Russian Jew Under Tsars and Soviets* (New York, 1964), p. 54.

142-43   Military service and *numerus clausus:* See Greenberg, *Jews in Russia*, 2:34–39.

143   "We travelled . . .": Sholom Aleichem, "Gy-Ma-Na-Si-A," in *Favorite Tales of Sholom Aleichem*, trans. Julius and Frances Butwin (New York, 1983), pp. 613–26.

      "All my inclinations . . .": Chaim Weizmann, *Trial and Error* (New York, 1949), pp. 29–30.

145   Edicts of March 28–29, 1881: Dubnow, *History*, 2:398.

146   "Under Yourkoffsky's personal supervision . . .": Harold Frederic, *The New Exodus: A Study of Israel in Russia* (London, 1892), p. 200.

146-47   Testimony of "H.P.": J. B. Weber and Dr. Walter Kempster, *Letter from the Secretary of the Treasury, Transmitting a Report of the Commissioners of Immigration upon the Causes Which Incite Immigration to the United States* (Washington, 1892). The present text is retranslated by the author from a French version of this report, *La Situation des Juifs en Russie* (Paris, 1892), pp. 27–28.

147   "As Moscow is the heart . . .": Frederic, *New Exodus*, p. 196.

147-48   Israel Deyel's letter: Ibid., pp. 286–89.

19. IN THE NEW CURRENT

Page

149   "The measures now being enforced . . .": Baron Maurice de Hirsch, in *The Forum*, August 1891, p. 627.

149-50   Baron de Hirsch: See Samuel J. Lee, *Moses of the New World: The Work of Baron de Hirsch* (New York, 1970).

150   Jewish colonization in Argentina: See Robert Weisbrot, *The Jews of Argentina* (Philadelphia, 1979), pp. 42–49; and Howard M. Sachar, *Diaspora* (New York, 1985), pp. 279–81.

150-51   The Jewish Colonization Association: See S. M. Dubnow, *History of the Jews in Russia and Poland*, 3 vols. (Philadelphia, 1916), 2:414–21.

151   " 'America' was in everybody's mouth . . .": Mary Antin, *From Plotzk to Boston* (Boston, 1899), pp. 11–12.

      "Next year—in America": Mary Antin, *The Promised Land* (Boston, 1912), p. 141.

      "bringing their trouble . . .": Ibid., p. 140.

152   "The Palestine movement . . .": *The American Hebrew*, July 24, 1891.

      "Mechanically . . .": Harold Frederic, *The New Exodus: A Study of Israel in Russia* (London, 1892), p. 271.

      "There are Russian soldiers . . .": Ibid.

153   "a searching examination . . .": Antin, *Promised Land*, p. 170.

153-59   The itinerary: The two interweaving accounts are from Antin, *From Plotzk*, pp. 35–79, and Frederic, *New Exodus*, pp. 270–79.

20. REBUILDING THE GATE

Page
160   "What followed was slow torture . . . at an END." Mary Antin, *From Plotzk to Boston* (Boston, 1899), pp. 79–80.

160-61 "The last day of our journey . . . and young children." Emma Goldman, *Living My Life*, 2 vols. (New York, 1931), 1:11–12.

163   "ramshackle pavilion": Willard A. Heaps, *The Story of Ellis Island* (New York, 1967), p. 6.

"As the vessels proceed . . . immigrants are sent." *The New York Times*, January 31, 1897. Reprinted in Allon Schoener, ed., *Portal to America: The Lower East Side 1870–1925* (New York, 1967), p. 21.

"ascend to the second story . . .": Julian Ralph, "Landing of the Immigrants," *Harper's Weekly*, October 24, 1891. Reprinted in Barbara Benton, *Ellis Island: A Pictorial History* (New York, 1985), p. 38.

163-64 "If any immigrant fails . . . for her to land." *The New York Times*, January 31, 1897.

164   "with an unfolded telegram . . .": Abraham Cahan, *Yekl: A Tale of the New York Ghetto* (New York, 1896: reprint, 1970), pp. 33–34.

The New York Times and *Harper's Weekly* articles: As cited above.

21. JEWISH NEW WORLDS IN THE 1890s

Page
165   "cries of joy . . .": Abraham Cahan, *The Rise of David Levinsky* (New York, 1917), p. 90.

"My first visit . . .": Abraham Cahan, *Bletter fun mein Leben*, 5 vols. (New York, 1926–1931), 2:72. Translated by the author.

166   "When I first arrived . . .": Ibid., 2:74–75.

167   "Chicago, especially the West Side . . . to or from business." Quoted in Louis Wirth, *The Ghetto* (Chicago, 1928), pp. 180–81.

167-68 "In all but the severest weather . . .": Edmund I. James, ed., *The Immigrant Jew in America* (New York, 1906), p. 59.

169   Petticoat Lane: Israel Zangwill, *Children of the Ghetto* (Philadelphia, 1892; New York, 1899), pp. xvi–xvii.

170   "Aye, mon . . .": Lloyd P. Gartner, *The Jewish Immigrant in England, 1870–1914* (London, 1960), p. 60.

Grand Rabbi Henry Joseph: Robert Weisbrot, *The Jews of Argentina* (Philadelphia, 1979), pp. 36–37, 45–48.

170-71 "the gauchos around there . . . We learned quickly." Ibid., pp. 50–51.

171   Shmilekl the Gaucho: Ibid., p. 51.

"The Baron's wish . . . to pay their debts." Chaim Chissin, *A Palestine Diary: Memoirs of a Bilu Pioneer, 1882–87* (New York, 1976), pp. 215–17.

172   "For a poor village . . .": Raphael Patai, ed., *The Complete Diaries of Theodor Herzl*, trans. Harry Zohn, 5 vols. (New York, 1960), 2:740.

"Were I to sum up . . .": Ibid., 2:581.

22. RUMANIA, RUMANIA

Page
174   Benjamin Franklin Peixotto: Cyrus Adler and Aaron M. Margalith, *With Firmness in the Right: American Diplomatic Action Affecting Jews, 1840–1945* (New York, 1946), pp. 100–110.

174   "There is little conception in America . . .": Ibid., p. 113.

176   "They wear long sandals . . .": Quoted in Joseph Kissman, "Die Yiddishe Emigratzye fun Rumenia bis der ershter Velt-Milkhome," *YIVO Bletter*, vol. 19, no. 2 (March-April 1942), p. 29. Translated by the author.
Names of groups: Ibid., p. 31.

176-77   "Mama, where . . .": Ibid., pp. 30–31.

177   "We were and are . . .": Ibid., p. 31.

177-80   Story of The Barlad Wayfarers: Jacob Finkelstein, "Zikhroynes fun a Fusgeyer fun Rumenia keyn America," *YIVO Bletter*, vol. 26, no. 1 (September-October 1945); pp. 105–28. Translated by the author.

179   "To the distinguished directors . . .": In Joseph Kissman, "Materialn vegen der Yiddisher Emigratzye fun Rumenia," *YIVO Bletter*, vol. 20, no. 2 (November-December 1942), pp. 280–81. Translated by the author.

23. THE HEBREW IMMIGRANT AID SOCIETY

Page

181-82   "The Bureau of Immigration . . . an immense spider web." *The New York Times*, December 3, 1900. Reprinted in Allon Schoener, ed., *Portal to America: The Lower East Side 1870–1925* (New York, 1967), pp. 22–23.

182   "all idiots, imbeciles . . .": Willard A. Heaps, *The Story of Ellis Island* (New York, 1967), p. 73.

183-84   The twenty-nine questions: Sample questionnaire in ibid., pp. 30–31.

185   White appealed only twice: John L. Bernstein, "HIAS Then and Now." *Rescue, Information Bulletin of HIAS*, July-August 1944, p. 5.
"Few of the European Jews . . .": United Hebrew Charities, *Fourteenth Annual Report, 1888*.
"These people are dazzled . . .": United Hebrew Charities, *Twentieth Annual Report, 1894*.
Creation of Hebrew Sheltering House Association: *The American Hebrew*, November 23, 1889.

185-86   "The *Hachnosses Orchim* . . . before a Russian official." Quoted in Mark Wischnitzer, *Visas to Freedom: The History of HIAS* (New York, 1956), p. 35.

186   Henry Rice speech, October 1901: *The American Hebrew*, November 1, 1901.
"It is time . . .": Ibid., October 25, 1902.

187   "In carrying out the plans . . .": Quoted in *The American Hebrew*, December 26, 1902.
"that terror of the immigrant . . .": *The New York Times*, December 3, 1900.
"Is it surprising . . .": Henry Pratt Fairchild, *Immigration* (New York, 1913), p. 186.

187-88   The meeting of the Voliner Zhitomirer Aid Society: John L. Bernstein, "HIAS Then and Now," p. 5.

188   "In order to arrange that . . .": Ibid.
"The Hebrew Emigration Aid Society . . .": *The American Hebrew*, January 16, 1903.

189   "A petition . . .": Ibid.
"spoke against the attempt . . .": Ibid., January 23, 1903.

24. CITIES OF SLAUGHTER, I: KISHINEV

Page

195   "Moldavians in tall . . .": Quoted in Henri Troyat, *Pushkin* (New York, 1970), p. 175.

195   "Its leading boulevard . . . in modern times." Michael Davitt, *Within the Pale: The True Story of Anti-Semitic Persecution in Russia* (New York, 1903), pp. 158–59.

196   "on a level . . . average Russian Mujik." Ibid., pp. 92–93.
      "The recent ritual murders . . .": Quoted in ibid., p. 53.

197   "to the police, soldiers . . . Disseminators of Socialism." Ibid., p. 98.
      "a shocking ritual murder . . .": Quoted in *Jewish Chronicle*, March 27, 1903.

198   "There in a fruit garden . . . been sewn up." Ibid., April 17, 1903.
      "bloody punishment": S. M. Dubnow, *History of the Jews in Russia and Poland*, 3 vols. (Philadelphia, 1916), 3:71–72.

199   "visited the Governor . . . propaganda of socialism." Davitt, *Within the Pale*, pp. 123–24.
      "band of strangers . . .": Ibid., p. 124.
      "Easter came . . . center of the town." *Jewish Chronicle*, May 8, 1903.

200   "Thirty bands . . .": Davitt, *Within the Pale*, p. 125.
      "In half an hour . . .": *Jewish Chronicle*, May 8, 1903.

200-02   "during the five hours . . . as stated by Joseph." Davitt, *Within the Pale*, pp. 127–67.

25. IN THE WAKE OF KISHINEV

Page

213   "Arise and go now . . .": Ch. N. Bialik, "B'Ir Ha'Haregah," *Shirim* (Tel Aviv, 1960), p. 370. Translated by the author.
      "I understood the horror . . .": Quoted in Cyrus Adler, ed., *The Voice of America on Kishineff* (Philadelphia, 1904), p. 241.

214   "Apart from the desperate . . .": Michael Davitt, *Within the Pale: The True Story of Anti-Semitic Persecution in Russia* (New York, 1903), p. 170.
      "See all this . . .": Bialik, "B'Ir Ha'Haregah," p. 371.

214-15   Hilfsverein and Berlin conference, June 1903: *The American Hebrew*, July 10, 1903.

216   "an immense body of persons . . .": Quoted in Ronald Sanders, *The High Walls of Jerusalem* (New York, 1984), p. 118.

217   "The President inspected . . .": *The American Hebrew*, September 11, 1903.

217-18   "The Hebrew Immigrant Aid Society . . .": Ibid., July 1, 1904.

218   "One of the pleasantest . . .": Ibid., April 15, 1904.

26. CITIES OF SLAUGHTER, II: 1905

Page

219   "This is not the time . . .": Quoted in S. M. Dubnow, *History of the Jews in Russia and Poland*, 3 vols. (Philadelphia, 1916), 3:94.

219-20   "Corporal of the 7th Company . . . obliged to do so?" *Jewish Chronicle*, May 19, 1905.

220-21   "The fall of Port Arthur . . .": Ibid., January 6, 1905.

221   "has provoked riots . . .": Ibid.
      David Soskice interview: Ibid., January 27, 1905.

221-22   "The anti-Semites, headed by . . .": Ibid., February 10, 1905.

222   "Slay the students . . . Down with the Constitution!" Dubnow, *History*, 3:114.

222   "As the Russian celebration . . . the maintenance of order." *Jewish Chronicle*, April 28, 1905.

222-23   "The disturbances here on Monday . . .": Ibid., May 12, 1905.
Zhitomir reports: Ibid.

223   *"pogrom"*: *The Times* (London), March 17, 1882; *Jewish Chronicle*, March 17, 1882. See entry on "pogrom" in Oxford English Dictionary.

224   "The whole country was jubilant . . .": Arnold Margolin, *From a Political Diary: Russia, the Ukraine, and America, 1905-1945* (New York, 1946), p. 8.
"It produced a great outburst . . . Jewish provocation." *Jewish Chronicle*, November 10, 1905.

224-25   "In connection with the manifesto . . .": Dubnow, *History*, 3:128.

27. WANDERING SCHOLARS, I: SHOLOM ALEICHEM

Page
226   "Life returned to normality . . .": Marie Waife-Goldberg, *My Father, Sholom Aleichem* (New York, 1968), pp. 161-62.
"My, my . . . of every kind." "Shprintze," in *Favorite Tales of Sholom Aleichem*, trans. Julius and Frances Butwin (New York, 1983), p. 533.

226-27   "whole village . . . suffer for it.": "Get Thee Out," in ibid., pp. 650-51.

227   "with valises, sacks . . .": Sholom Aleichem, *In the Storm*, trans. Aliza Shevrin (New York, 1984), pp. 215-16.
"For my father . . .": Waife-Goldberg, *My Father*, p. 164.

227-28   "Hey, we're going . . . getting close to America." "Mottel Peyssi dem Chazns," in Sholom Aleichem, *Oysgeveylte Shriftn* (Bucharest, 1957), pp. 111-31. Translated by the author.

228   "Brody, in Austrian Galicia . . . streets of Brody." Waife-Goldberg, *My Father*, pp. 167-68.

229   "A nice city . . .": "Mottel," p. 131.
"They spoke Yiddish . . .": Waife-Goldberg, *My Father*, p. 167.
"But their language . . . without pillows?" "Mottel," pp. 131, 133.
"We packed up . . .": Waife-Goldberg, *My Father*, p. 170.

229-34   Mottel's travels: "Mottel," pp. 140-238.

234   "Jewish Mark Twain": Waife-Goldberg, *My Father*, p. 187.

28. GALVESTON

Page
235   American Jewish Committee: See Naomi W. Cohen, *Not Free to Desist: The American Jewish Committee 1906-1966* (Philadelphia, 1972).
New York "Kehillah": See Arthur A. Goren, *New York Jews and the Quest for Community: The Kehillah Experiment, 1908-1922* (New York, 1970).

235-36   Jacob H. Schiff: See Cyrus Adler, *Jacob H. Schiff: His Life and Letters*, 2 vols. (New York, 1928).

237   "New Orleans, Charleston, Savannah . . .": Ibid., 2:96.

237-39   Schiff, Sargent, Zangwill and the two letters: Ibid., 2:96-99.

239   "On a misty summer day . . .": Quoted in Mark Wischnitzer, *To Dwell in Safety: The Story of Jewish Migration Since 1800* (Philadelphia, 1948), p. 126.
"the euthanasia . . .": New York *Herald*, January 9, 1907.

29. WANDERING SCHOLARS, II: ALEXANDER HARKAVY

Page
242-48   Harkavy's itinerary and interviews: Alexander Harkavy's manuscript "Diary of a Visit to Europe in the Interests of Jewish Emigration, 1906-07," in the collection of the American Jewish Historical Society, Waltham, Massachusetts.

30. MR. SCHIFF STEPS IN

Page
249-51   Harkavy, the Russian immigrants, and the Duma offer: John L. Bernstein, "HIAS Then and Now," *Rescue, Information Bulletin of HIAS*, July–August 1944, p. 5.
252-53   "cease to care . . . and shower baths." *The American Hebrew*, April 19, 1907.
253   "At the information bureau . . .": Ibid., January 31, 1908.
    "pressing need . . .": Ibid., May 8, 1908.
254-57   Waldman's account: Morris D. Waldman, *Nor by Power* (New York, 1953), pp. 348-51.

31. THE HEBREW SHELTERING AND IMMIGRANT AID SOCIETY

Page
258   "At a meeting . . .": *The American Hebrew*, February 21, 1908.
258-59   "714 immigrants guided . . .": *Der Yiddisher Emigrant*, August 1908.
259   "is not, properly speaking . . .": *The American Hebrew*, June 5, 1908.
    "We want your help . . . overlooked by the wealthy." Ibid., December 25, 1908.
260   "American Jewish Society . . . anyone until now." *Forverts (The Jewish Daily Forward)*, January 10, 1909. Translated by the author.
260-61   "The New Emigrant Society": Ibid., January 12, 1909.
261-63   "The annual meeting . . . for which they had organized." *The American Hebrew*, January 15, 1909.
263   "But the Hebrew Immigrant Aid Society . . .": *Forverts*, March 20, 1909.
    "Sheltering House and Immigrant Aid . . . Council of Jewish Women." *The American Hebrew*, April 2, 1909.

32. THE FAILURE OF RUSSIAN LIBERALISM

Page
267-68   "In 1895 . . .": Vladimir Nabokov, *Speak, Memory* (New York, 1966), pp. 174-75.
268   "This was . . .": Shmarya Levin, *Forward from Exile*, trans. and ed. Maurice Samuel (Philadelphia, 1967), pp. 415-16.
    "How was it possible . . .": Ibid., p. 377.
    "*Pogromshchiki!*" Louis Greenberg, *The Jews in Russia*, 2 vols. (New Haven, 1944-1951), 2:79.
    "The deputies . . .": Levin, *Forward from Exile*, p. 417.
269   "What can we do with them? . . .": Michael Davitt, *Within the Pale: The True Story of Anti-Semitic Persecution in Russia* (New York, 1903), pp. 65-66.

269-70 "Throughout all Europe . . .": From complete English text of the *Protocols* in Herman Bernstein, *The Truth About "The Protocols of Zion"* (New York, 1935: reprint, 1971), p. 313.

270 "Our year 1905 . . .": Norman Cohn, *Warrant for Genocide* (New York, 1967), p. 115.

"the secret archives . . .": Ibid., p. 68.

271 "Did not the ass . . .": Bernstein, *The Truth*, p. 366.

"Drop the *Protocols* . . .": Cohn, *Warrant*, p. 115.

271-72 "Orthodox Christians! . . .": Maurice Samuel, *Blood Accusation: The Strange History of the Beiliss Case* (New York, 1966), p. 17.

273 "One can point . . .": Ibid., p. 230.

"of practically illiterate . . .": Ibid.

The two verdicts: Ibid., pp. 248–49.

33. IMMIGRATION ON THE EVE

Page

274 "Charged with the duty . . .": *Jewish Immigration Bulletin (HIAS Monthly Report)*, November 1913.

275 "The Hachnosses-Orchim . . . from all parts of the country." John Foster Carr, *Vegveyser fun die Fereynigte Shtatn far dem Yiddishen Immigrant* (New York, 1912), p. 8. Translated by the author.

"The work of the Society . . .": HIAS, *Annual Report*, 1914, p. 8.

276-78 Ellis Island Committee Report: HIAS, *Annual Report*, 1913, pp. 21–24.

279 "Radical departure . . .": Mark Wischnitzer, *Visas to Freedom: The History of HIAS* (New York, 1956), p. 56.

281 "not to permit the spirit . . .": Ibid., p. 57.

34. WAR AND THE JEWS OF EASTERN EUROPE, I: 1914–1915

Page

282 "When the war broke out . . .": American Jewish Committee, *The Jews in the Eastern War Zone* (New York, 1916), p. 7.

282-83 "We were born and grew up . . .": Quoted in Louis Greenberg, *The Jews in Russia*, 2 vols. (New Haven, 1944–1951), 2:94.

283 "one of whose legs . . .": The National Workmen's Committee on Jewish Rights, *The War and the Jews in Russia* (New York, 1916), p. 78.

284 "Do not let yourselves . . .": Lucjan Dobroszycky and Barbara Kirshenblatt-Gimblett, *Image Before My Eyes: A Photographic History of Jewish Life in Poland, 1864–1939* (New York, 1977), p. 115.

"True, all the peoples . . .": *Jews in the Eastern War Zone*, p. 8.

"In the German newspapers . . .": *War and the Jews in Russia*, p. 56.

284-85 "the success of the slander . . . could not." Ibid., p. 50.

285 "shocking treachery . . .": Greenberg, *Jews in Russia*, 2:99.

285-86 "the Poles of the town . . . hostages were released." *Jews in the Eastern War Zone*, pp. 41–42.

286 "denounced the Jews as German sympathizers . . . and shops plundered." Ibid., p. 43.

"whose right cheek . . .": Isidore Hershfield's Report, *Jewish Immigration Bulletin (HIAS Monthly Report)*, June-July 1916, p. 15.

"the progress of the war . . .": *War and the Jews in Russia*, p. 54.

287   "The Supreme Commander-in-Chief . . .": Ibid., p. 55.

"Fire! Fire! . . .": Don Gussow, *Chaia Sonia: A Family's Odyssey, Russian Style* (New York, 1980), pp. 24, 25.

"At the present moment . . .": *War and the Jews in Russia*, p. 64.

288   "Scarcely had I reached Riga . . .": Ibid., p. 77.

35. WAR AND THE JEWS OF EASTERN EUROPE, II: ISIDORE HERSHFIELD'S MISSION

Page

289-90   Mrs. Greenwood: *Jewish Immigration Bulletin (HIAS Monthly Report)*, November 1915, pp. 5-6.

290   "Shortly after the war broke out . . .": Ibid., p. 6.

291-94   Hershfield's journey and report, ibid., June-July 1916, pp. 6-16.

36. 1917

Page

295   "All the limitations . . .": S. Ettinger, "The Jews in Russia at the Outbreak of the Revolution," in Lionel Kochan, ed., *The Jews in Soviet Russia Since 1917* (Oxford, 1978), p. 15.

296   "I am afraid England . . .": Quoted in Zosa Szajkowski, *Jews, Wars and Communism*, 2 vols. (New York, 1972-1974), 1:13.

"The Jews support Germany . . .": Ibid., 1:4.

"No matter how terrible . . .": Ibid., 1:6.

"That which has long . . . AT AN END." Ronald Sanders, *The Downtown Jews* (New York, 1987), pp. 434-35.

297   "largely anti-Russian, and . . .": Ronald Sanders, *The High Walls of Jerusalem* (New York, 1984), p. 325.

"it is no longer a capitalist war . . .": Sanders, *Downtown Jews*, p. 435.

"I am a German by birth . . .": Szajkowski, *Jews, Wars and Communism*, 1:132.

"Whoever witnessed that spectacle . . .": HIAS, *Annual Report*, 1917.

298-99   "From all corners . . . against her enemies." Nahum Sokolow, *History of Zionism*, 2 vols. (London, 1919; reprint, 2 vols. in one, New York, 1969), 2:40-41.

299   Balfour Declaration: See, e.g., Sanders, *High Walls*, p. xvii.

300   "definitely reactionary": Salo W. Baron, *The Russian Jew Under Tsars and Soviets* (New York, 1964), p. 205.

"the removal . . .": Ibid., p. 206.

37. INTERLUDE IN YOKOHAMA

Page

303-04   "A miracle then happened . . . the Chinese section of Yokohama." HIAS, *Annual Report*, 1917.

304-05   "I have lived in Yokohama . . .": *Jewish Immigration Bulletin (HIAS Monthly Report)*, December 1917, p. 15.

305-07   Mason's mission: Samuel Mason, "Our Mission to the Far East," ibid., September 1918, pp. 10-16.

307-09   Ceremony of February 11, 1918: Ibid., May 1918, pp. 5–7.

309   Yokohama Seder: Mark Wischnitzer, *Visas to Freedom: The History of HIAS* (New York, 1956), p. 85.

38. THE LEMBERG POGROM

Page

311-12   Nineteenth-century Lemberg: See Ezra Mendelsohn, "From Assimilation to Zionism in Lvov: The Case of Alfred Nossig," in *The Slavonic and East European Review*, October 1971, pp. 521–34; and Mendelsohn, "Jewish Assimilation in Lvov: The Case of Wilhelm Feldman," in *Slavic Review*, December 1969, pp. 577–90.

313   "What a strange picture . . .": Rosa Bailly, *A City Fights for Freedom: The Rising of Lwów in 1918–1919*, trans. from the French by Samuel S. B. Taylor (London, 1956), p. 79.

313-14   "TO THE PEOPLE OF LVIV": M. Stachiv and J. Sztendera, *Western Ukraine at the Turning-Point of Europe's History, 1918–23*, 2 vols. (New York, 1969), 1:109.

314   "What would the Jews . . .": Bailly, *A City*, p. 102.

314-15   "TO THE JEWISH POPULATION . . .": Joseph Bendow [Joseph Tenenbaum], *Der Lemberger Judenpogrom, Nov. 1918–Jan. 1919* (Vienna, 1919), p. 14. Translated by the author.

315   "the most popular organ . . .": Ibid., p. 15.

      "supplied with arms . . .": Bailly, *A City*, p. 102.

315-16   "AGREEMENT . . .": Bendow, *Judenpogrom*, pp. 18–19.

316   "Maczynski was quite worried . . .": Bailly, *A City*, p. 235.

      "New kinds of heroes . . .": Quoted in Bendow, *Judenpogrom*, p. 20.

316-17   "The Neutrals": Ibid.

317   "pogrom idea": Ibid., pp. 19, 21.

      "were promised three days . . .": *Report by Sir Stuart Samuel on His Mission to Poland, Presented to Parliament by Command of His Majesty* (London, 1920), p. 9.

      "General Roja's coming . . . Day of Reckoning": Ibid., p. 31.

      "streets gay with bunting . . . soldiers and civilians." Bailly, *A City*, pp. 311–312.

318-19   "On November 22 . . . today you have to die." Bendow, *Judenpogrom* pp. 32–34.

319   "a body of soldiers came . . . by Polish soldiers." *Report by Sir Stuart Samuel*, pp. 9–10.

      "It must be borne in mind . . .": Bailly, *A City*, p. 316.

      "The synagogue was burned . . . of the Jewish shops." *Report by Sir Stuart Samuel*, pp. 9, 32.

319-20   "On Thursday, November 28 . . .": Joseph Tenenbaum, *In Search of a Lost People* (New York, 1948), p. 13.

39. POLAND AFTER LEMBERG: AN ITINERARY

Page

321-25   Israel Cohen in Poland: "Diary of a Mission to Poland," in Israel Cohen, *Travels in Jewry* (New York, 1953), pp. 48–81.

325-27   Israel Cohen in Lemberg: "The Lemberg Pogrom," in ibid., pp. 82–92.

40. THE UKRAINIAN HOLOCAUST, I:
FROM NATIONAL UPRISING TO POGROM

Page

328   "As a natural result . . .": Arnold Margolin, *From a Political Diary: Russia, the Ukraine, and America, 1905-1945* (New York, 1946), p. 24.

330   "Notwithstanding these bad omens . . . to their previous promises." Ibid., pp. 20, 28.

331   "after the Ukrainian parties . . .": Ibid., p. 32.
        "illegal commerce and speculation flourished": Quoted in W. E. D. Allen, *The Ukraine: A History* (Cambridge, 1940), p. 297.

332-33   "The [Ukrainian] farmers . . . akin to Americans." Margolin, *Political Diary*, p. 24.

333   "personal-national autonomy . . . national life." Salo W. Baron, *The Russian Jew Under Tsars and Soviets* (New York, 1964), p. 218.
        "suspicious of the entire Jewish population . . .": Elias Heifetz, *The Slaughter of the Jews in the Ukraine in 1919* (New York, 1921), p. 8.
        "Jews were frequently . . .": Quoted in Allen, *The Ukraine*, p. 297.

334   "At this time . . . hate of our people." Heifetz, *Slaughter*, p. 15.
        "The well-being of the population . . .": Ibid., p. 17
        "Even the authorized trading . . .": Quoted in Allen, *Ukraine*, p. 297.

334-35   "of exaggerated reports . . .": Heifetz, *Slaughter*, p. 8.

335   "the stormy surge . . .": Abraham Revutsky, *In die Shvere Teg oyf Ukraina* (Berlin, 1924), p. 316. Translated by the author.

335-36   "On January 2 . . . the massacre began." Comité des Délégations Juives, Paris, *The Pogroms in the Ukraine* (Paris, 1927), p. 132.

336   "supporters of the Soviets . . .": Ibid., p. 147.

336-38   The pogrom at Zhitomir: Ibid., pp. 148-62.

41. THE UKRAINIAN HOLOCAUST, II:
FROM POGROM TO ANNIHILATION

Page

339-43   The meeting in Revutsky's room: Comité des Délégations Juives, Paris, *The Pogroms in the Ukraine* (Paris, 1927), pp. 173-75.

343-46   Semosenko at Proskurov: Ibid., pp. 178-87.

42. IN THE EYES OF THE CIVILIZED WORLD

Page

347   "criminal elements . . .": Arnold Margolin, *The Jews of Eastern Europe* (New York, 1926), p. 143.

348   "It was recognized . . .": David Lloyd George, *Memoirs of the Peace Conference*, 2 vols. (New Haven, 1939), 2:881.

348-49   "It is to be borne in mind . . .": Charles Reznikoff, ed., *Louis Marshall, Champion of Liberty: Selected Papers and Addresses*, 2 vols. (Philadelphia, 1957), 2:536.

349-50   "Within the meaning . . . Sundays or other holy days." Nathan Feinberg, *La Question des minorités à la Conférence de la Paix de 1919-1920 et l'action juive en faveur de la protection internationale des minorités* (Paris, 1929), p. 150.

350   "any interference . . .": Lloyd George, *Peace Conference*, 2:884.
350-51   "A Jewish deputation . . .": *Jewish Chronicle*, February 28, 1919.
351   "How do you account for . . .": Ibid., May 30, 1919.
          "Poland accepts . . .": Lloyd George, *Peace Conference*, 2:882.
351-52   "Polish nationals . . ." and Articles 10 and 11: Oscar Janowsky, *The Jews and Minority Rights, 1898-1919* (New York, 1966), p. 176.
352   "The information at the disposal . . .": Ibid., p. 183.
          The Ukrainian delegation: See Arnold Margolin, *From a Political Diary: Russia, the Ukraine, and America, 1905-1945* (New York, 1946), ch. 4.
353   "The Black Hundreds, Bolsheviki . . .": Margolin, *Jews of Eastern Europe*, pp. 144-45.
          "Why do you stand up . . .": William Henry Chamberlin, *The Russian Revolution*, 2 vols. (New York, 1965), 2:217.
354   "The assassination of the Ataman Grigoriev . . .": Elias Heifetz, *The Slaughter of the Jews in the Ukraine in 1919* (New York, 1921), pp. 71-72.
354-55   "Our free but not yet . . .": Comité des Délégations Juives, Paris, *The Pogroms in the Ukraine* (Paris, 1927), pp. 214-16.
355-56   "willing to grant . . . prevailing in Poland." *Jewish Chronicle*, May 16, 1919.
356-57   "I had not been with Denikin . . . unreasoning hatred." John Ernest Hodgson, *With Denikin's Armies* (London, 1932), pp. 54-63.
357-58   "In the first three days . . .": Norman Cohn, *Warrant for Genocide* (New York, 1967), p. 123.

43. WANDERING SCHOLARS, III: CROSSING THE ZBRUCZ

Page
359   "We ran all the way . . .": Quoted in Norman Davies, *White Eagle, Red Star: The Polish-Soviet War, 1919-1920* (London, 1972), p. 105.
359-60   Isaac Babel: All quotations from Babel in this chapter are from I. Babel, *Izbrannoye* (Moscow, 1966), translated by the author. The quotations on these two pages are from *Konarmiya (Red Cavalry)*—"Peryekhod chyerez Zbrucz," p. 27; "Berestechko," pp. 91-92; and "Gedali," p. 51.
360-61   "The Bolsheviks have captured . . . spontaneous antipathy." Lord D'Abernon, *The Eighteenth Decisive Battle of World History* (London, 1931), pp. 50-52.
361-62   "He describes the Russian . . . to do with England!" Ibid., p. 75.
362   "One of the most surprising . . . particularly feared." Ibid., pp. 107-8.
          "A stooping youth . . .": "Afonka Bida," in *Konarmiya*, in *Izbrannoye*, pp. 101-2.
363   "This fantastic story . . .": Arthur L. Goodhart, *Poland and the Minority Races* (London and New York, 1920), p. 90.
          "The Poles are afraid . . .": "Zamoste," in *Konarmiya*, in *Izbrannoye*, pp. 131-132.

44. THE REFUGEES OF 1920

Page
367   "It is doubtful . . .": William R. Grove, *War's Aftermath: US Relief Organization in Poland* (New York, 1940), p. 79.
          "Meanwhile . . .": Quoted in ibid., p. 74.

368   "Brest is a city . . . raging terribly." Boris D. Bogen, *Activities of the Joint Distribution Committee in Poland, February 1, 1920–July 1, 1920* (New York, 1920), p. 70.

369   "With the arrival . . .": Grove, *War's Aftermath*, p. 188.

369-70   "This morning . . .": Arthur L. Goodhart, *Poland and the Minority Races* (London and New York, 1920), p. 27.

370   "On the 20th of March . . .": Grove, *War's Aftermath*, p. 73.

370-71   "During the afternoon . . . perfectly well." Goodhart, *Minority Races*, pp. 39–40.

371-72   "Mr. 'A' wrote to us . . .": HIAS, *Annual Report*, 1920.

372-75   Kamaiky's mission and report: *Jewish Immigration Bulletin (HIAS Monthly Report)*, October 1920.

375-76   "Many immigrants . . .": HIAS, *Annual Report*, 1920.

376   "The influx . . .": *Jewish Chronicle*, September 17, 1920.

376-78   The Gussow family emigration: Don Gussow, *Chaia Sonia: A Family's Odyssey, Russian Style* (New York, 1980), pp. 173–206, 213–19.

378-79   Moses and Minke Gingold: From Gingold family recollections and documents. My thanks to Dr. Sol Gingold for providing a copy of the Glosser affidavit.

45. CLOSING THE GATES

Page

380   Palmer raids: Robert K. Murray, *Red Scare: A Study of National Hysteria* (New York, 1954), ch. 13.

381   "Reds Attempt . . . today." *The New York Times*, August 16, 1920.
       "There is a super-capitalism . . .": Dearborn *Independent*, May 22, 1920.

382   "One of the Commissioners . . .": *The New York Times*, August 17, 1920.

382-83   "Would Bar All Aliens . . .": Ibid., December 2, 1920.

383   "This talk about . . .": Ibid., December 5, 1920.
       "Mr. Siegel said . . .": Ibid., December 8, 1920.
       "The fact is . . .": Ibid., December 10, 1920.

384   "declared that unless . . .": Ibid., January 4, 1921.
       "an insult to the great . . .": Ibid., January 5, 1921.
       "the present inrush was not . . .": Ibid., January 4, 1921.

384-85   John L. Bernstein's testimony: *Jewish Immigration Bulletin (HIAS Monthly Report)*, January 1921.

386   Dillingham's report: Edith Abbott, *Immigration: Select Documents and Case Records* (Chicago, 1924), p. 237.
       "That the number of aliens . . .": Ibid., p. 240

46. ORGANIZING EMIGRATION

Page

388   "I am informed . . .": *The New York Times*, June 6, 1921.

388-89   HIAS purchase of Astor Library: *Jewish Immigration Bulletin (HIAS Monthly Report)*, November 1920.

390-92   Brussels conference: Jewish Colonization Association, "Compte-Rendu de la Conférence de Bruxelles (7 et 8 juin 1921)." Typescript at Jewish Division, New York Public Library. Translated by the author.

393   "The emigration conference . . .": *Jewish Chronicle*, October 7, 1921.
Emigdirect: Vereinigtes Komitee fur Jüdische Auswanderung, "Emigdirekt," *Entstehung und Tätigkeit, 1921–1925* (Berlin, 1926).

47. BRITISH PALESTINE

Page
394   "freedom of immigration," and ". . . 80,000 Jews annually." Ronald Sanders, *The High Walls of Jerusalem* (New York, 1984), pp. 559, 643.
395   "as of right" and "economic capacity": See ibid., p. 658.
Arab influx: See Joan Peters, *From Time Immemorial* (New York, 1984), especially chs. 12–13.
396   "Since I had been accepted . . .": "Golda Meyerson of Milwaukee Makes Aliyah (1921)," in Levi Soshuk and Azriel Eisenberg, eds., *Momentous Century: Personal and Eyewitness Accounts of the Rise of the Jewish Homeland and State, 1875–1978* (New York, 1984), p. 142.

48. A POLISH MINORITY

Page
398   "After dinner . . .": Arthur L. Goodhart, *Poland and the Minority Races* (London and New York, 1920), p. 40.
"it accused the Zionists . . .": *Jewish Chronicle*, March 18, 1921.
399   "In the afternoon . . .": Goodhart, *Minority Races*, p. 25.
"He was a most venerable-looking . . .": Ibid., pp. 20–21.
399-400   "A soldier made a shameful attack . . .": *Jewish Chronicle*, August 6, 1920.
400   "Later in the morning . . .": Goodhart, *Minority Races*, p. 21.
"a Committee from the Zionist organization . . .": Ibid., p. 24.
411   Polish Zionism: See Ezra Mendelsohn, *Zionism in Poland: The Formative Years, 1915–1926* (New Haven, 1981).
"From the fifth grade on . . .": Quoted in Celia Heller, *On the Edge of Destruction* (New York, 1977), p. 112.
"They took the same position . . .": Goodhart, *Minority Races*, p. 25.
412   "Jewry . . .": Quoted in Bernard K. Johnpoll, *The Politics of Futility: The General Jewish Workers Bund of Poland, 1917–1943* (Ithaca, 1967), pp. 130–31.
"the present regime . . .": Ibid., p. 153.
413-15   Israel Cohen in Lwów: Israel Cohen, *Travels in Jewry* (New York, 1953), pp. 123–27.

49. GERMANY SUCCUMBS

Page
419   "From time immemorial . . .": *Jewish Chronicle*, February 17, 1922.
"The Supreme Command . . .": Ibid., November 4, 1921.
420   "For very many people . . .": Count Harry Kessler, *Walther Rathenau: His Life and Work* (New York, 1969), p. 280.
"Rathenau had very close . . .": Norman Cohn, *Warrant for Genocide* (New York, 1967), pp. 145–46.
"that Rathenau had himself confessed . . .": Ibid., p. 146.
"Three hundred men . . .": Kessler, *Rathenau*, p. 121.

421 "Behind the murderers . . .": Cohn, *Warrant*, p. 147.

"designates not only the religion . . .": Quoted in Jacob Katz, *From Prejudice to Destruction: Anti-Semitism, 1700–1933* (Cambridge, Mass., 1980), p. 178.

421-22 "Strange sight! . . .": Kessler, *Rathenau*, p. 36.

422 "the tragedy of the Aryan race . . .": Ibid., pp. 36–37.

"Probably the Aryan was . . .": Adolf Hitler, *Mein Kampf*, trans. Ralph Manheim (Boston, 1943), p. 304.

"With satanic joy . . .": Ibid., p. 325.

"the best proof . . . ultimate final aims." Ibid., pp. 307–8.

423 "I gradually became aware . . .": Ibid., p. 61.

"The most frightful example . . .": Ibid., p. 326.

"A Germanic State . . .": Ibid., p. 329.

423-24 "On the nights of March 9th and 10th . . .": Quoted in American Jewish Committee, *The Jews in Nazi Germany* (New York, 1933), p. 21.

424 "In every local section . . . called to battle." Walther Hofer, ed., *Der Nationalsozialismus: Dokumente, 1933–1945* (Frankfurt a. M., 1957), pp. 282–83. Translated by the author.

424-26 Scenes of the boycott: Lion Feuchtwanger, *The Oppermanns* (New York, 1983), pp. 257–258, 261, 265.

426 "In the main . . .": Konrad Heiden, *Der Fuehrer* (New York, 1944), 655–56.

426-27 "a special department . . .": Mark Wischinitzer, *To Dwell in Safety: The Story of Jewish Migration Since 1800* (Philadelphia, 1948), p. 336.

427 "in the last analysis . . . must not be." Heiden, *Fuehrer*, p. 588.

50. JEWISH REFUGEES, 1933–1937

Page
428 "The center of gravity . . .": HIAS, *Annual Report*, 1933, p. 7.

The Seven Deadly Sins: See Ronald Sanders, *The Days Grow Short: The Life and Music of Kurt Weill* (New York, 1985), pp. 197–202.

429 HIAS letter to Roosevelt: Mark Wischnitzer, *Visas to Freedom: The History of HIAS* (New York, 1956), pp. 137–38.

430 "We have no wish . . .": Quoted in Norman Bentwich, *The Refugees from Germany: April 1933 to December 1935* (London, 1936), p. 58.

"MacDonald was physically impressive . . .": Norman Bentwich, *My 77 Years* (Philadelphia, 1961), pp. 130–31. See also Michael R. Marrus, *The Unwanted: European Refugees in the Twentieth Century* (New York and Oxford, 1985), pp. 161–65.

431 "A citizen of the Reich . . .": Walther Hofer, ed., *Der Nationalsozialismus: Dokumente, 1933–1945* (Frankfurt a. M., 1957), p. 284. Translated by the author.

431-32 MacDonald's letter of resignation: Reprinted in Bentwich, *Refugees from Germany*, pp. 219–28.

432 "The daily grace . . .": Ibid., p. 156.

432-33 "While Jewish organizations abroad . . .": *Jewish Chronicle*, January 17, 1936.

433 "Schacht vs. Goebbels . . .": Ibid., February 14, 1936.

"The signs '*Juden unerwünscht*' . . .": William L. Shirer, *The Rise and Fall of the Third Reich* (New York, 1960), pp. 232–33.

433-34 "constructively with the larger . . .": Bentwich, *77 Years*, p. 132.

434 "all citizens in Poland . . . only brutalize the nation": Ezra Mendelsohn, *The Jews of East Central Europe Between the World Wars* (Bloomington, 1983), p. 72.

434-35   "The Jews . . . in furthering Jewish emigration." Quoted in *Jewish Chronicle*, August 21, 1936.

435   Madagascar: See Michael R. Marrus and Robert O. Paxton, *Vichy France and the Jews* (New York, 1981), p. 61.

51. FROM THE *ANSCHLUSS* TO EVIAN, MARCH–JULY 1938

Page

436   "If Providence . . .": William L. Shirer, *The Rise and Fall of the Third Reich* (New York, 1960), p. 347.
"For the first few weeks . . .": Ibid., p. 351.

436-37   "The plight of the Jews in Austria . . .": Quoted in Deborah E. Lipstadt, *Beyond Belief: The American Press and the Coming of the Holocaust, 1933-1945* (New York, 1986), p. 87.

437   "It all went like an assembly line . . . unthinkable in Berlin." Eichmann trial testimony, quoted in Gideon Hausner, *Justice in Jerusalem* (New York, 1968), pp. 38–40.

437-38   "Thousands of Jews . . .": Israel Cohen, *Travels in Jewry* (New York, 1953), p. 42.

438   "The Jews of the world . . .": *Jewish Chronicle*, March 18, 1938.
"The government has become . . .": *The New York Times*, March 25, 1938.
"with conditions as they are . . . our immigration quotas." Quoted in David S. Wyman, *Paper Walls: America and the Refugee Crisis, 1938-1941* (New York, 1985), p. 47.

438-39   "violate the immigration policies . . .": Ibid., pp. 46–47.

439   "it should be understood . . .": *The New York Times*, March 25, 1938.
"a notorious opponent . . .": Arthur Ruppin, *Memoirs, Diaries, Letters* (New York, 1971), p. 293.
"would naturally prefer . . .": Arthur D. Morse, *While Six Million Died: A Chronicle of American Apathy* (New York, 1968), p. 211.

439-40   "Our American cousins . . .": *Jewish Chronicle*, July 15, 1938.

440-42   Evian Conference: *Actes du Comité Intergouvernemental, Evian, du 6 au 15 juillet 1938*. Translated by the author.

442   "It was always a moot point . . .": *Jewish Chronicle*, July 15, 1938.
"The published outcome . . .": Norman Bentwich, *My 77 Years* (Philadelphia, 1961), p. 148.

443   "The conference was poorly prepared . . .": Ruppin, *Memoirs*, p. 293.
"Evian is the first . . .": *Jewish Chronicle*, July 15, 1938.
"within six years": Ibid.

52. THE NIGHT OF BROKEN GLASS

Page

444   "Editorial opinion . . .": *The New York Times*, September 21, 1938.

445   "The government of the United States . . .": Ibid., September 28, 1938.
"that it is not the business . . .": Ibid., September 21, 1938.
"With ruthless precision . . .": *Jewish Chronicle*, April 29, 1938.

445-46   "The persistent 'dumping' . . .": Ibid., September 2, 1938.

446-47 "On October 27, 1938 . . .": Zindel Grynszpan's account was given at the fourteenth session of the trial in Jerusalem of Adolf Eichmann, April 25, 1961. It is reprinted in translation in, among other places: Martin Gilbert, *The Holocaust* (New York, 1985), pp. 67-68; and Rita Thalmann and Emmanuel Feinermann, *Crystal Night* (New York, 1974), pp. 35-36. I have conflated those two texts.

447 "Dear Herschel . . .": Thalmann and Feinermann, *Crystal Night*, p. 33.
"The SA should be allowed . . .": Ibid., p. 58.

448 "Despite authoritative warnings . . .": *The New York Times*, November 10, 1938.
"At 3:00 A.M. on November 10 . . .": Walther Hofer, ed., *Der Nazionalsozialismus: Dokumente, 1933-1945* (Frankfurt a.M., 1957), pp. 291-92. Translated by the author.

449 "Towards noon . . .": Thalmann and Feinermann, *Crystal Night*, pp. 75-76.
"The scope of the destruction . . .": Hofer, *Dokumente*, pp. 292-93.

53. THE NEW REFUGEE CRISIS

Page
451 "The news of the past few days . . .": *The New York Times*, November 16, 1938.
"technically . . . not a recall . . .": Ibid., November 15, 1938.

451-52 "In these circumstances . . .": Ibid.

452 "a society of émigrés . . .": Ibid., August 22, 1938.

453 "The Evian refugee conference's . . .": Ibid., November 20, 1938.

453-54 "It was officially announced tonight . . .": Ibid., December 13, 1938.

454 "asking the world to pay . . .": Henry L. Feingold, *The Politics of Rescue: The Roosevelt Administration and the Holocaust, 1938-1945* (New Brunswick, 1970), p. 52.
"adopted a resolution . . .": *The New York Times*, January 17, 1939.

455 "The British Cabinet . . .": Ibid., November 17, 1938.
"it may be years . . .": Ibid., November 22, 1938.

455-56 "It is generally recognized . . .": Ibid.

456 "an exceptionally large number": Ibid.
"A ten-coach train . . .": Ibid., December 10, 1938.

456-58 Roosevelt's November 18, 1938 press conference and comments by Congressmen: *The New York Times*, November 19, 1938.

54. THE COURSE OF THE *ST. LOUIS*

Page
459 Hitler's Reichstag speech of January 30, 1939: *The New York Times*, January 31, 1939.
"sinister flourish": *The Times* (London), January 31, 1939.

459-60 "The suggestion . . .": *Jewish Chronicle*, February 3, 1939.

460 "basis of the program . . .": Henry L. Feingold, *The Politics of Rescue: The Roosevelt Administration and the Holocaust, 1938-1945* (New Brunswick, 1970), p. 64.

460-61 "Denouncing the dictators . . .": *The New York Times*, March 20, 1939.

461 *Fortune* poll of April 1939: Arthur D. Morse, *While Six Million Died: A Chronicle of American Apathy* (New York, 1968), p. 261.

461   "We feel it necessary . . .": Michael J. Cohen, *Churchill and the Jews* (London, 1985), p. 181.

461-62   "The dignity of the occasion . . .": Chaim Weizmann, *Trial and Error* (New York, 1949), p. 402.

462   Churchill's speech against the 1939 White Paper: Cohen, *Churchill and the Jews*, pp. 182–83.

463   "a mere tool . . .": *The New York Times*, January 6, 1939.
       "Jew Deal." "Rosenfeld": Described critically in League of American Writers, *We Hold These Truths . . .* (New York, 1939), p. 14.
       "President Roosevelt pointed out . . .": *The New York Times*, November 19, 1938.
       "President Roosevelt's criticism . . .": Ibid., November 17, 1938.

463-64   "The President told me . . .": *Jewish Chronicle*, October 28, 1938.

464   "a good deal of dismay . . .": Peter Grose, *Israel in the Mind of America* (New York, 1983), p. 138.
       "If it was necessary . . .": Cohen, *Churchill and the Jews*, p. 181.

464-65   "The situation of the Jews . . .": *The New York Times*, May 18, 1939.

465   "We shall fight with Great Britain . . .": See, e.g., Ronald Sanders, *The High Walls of Jerusalem* (New York, 1984), p. 664.

465-67   The *St. Louis:* See Gordon Thomas and Max Morgan Witts, *Voyage of the Damned* (New York, 1974); Arthur D. Morse, *While Six Million Died*, pp. 270–88; and contemporary newspaper accounts.

467   "The chief Alderman . . .": *Jewish Chronicle*, June 23, 1939.

55. THE FALL OF POLAND

Page
472   "First intimations . . .": *The New York Times*, September 12, 1939.

472-73   "You must distinguish . . .": Léon Poliakov, *Harvest of Hate* (New York, 1986), p. 34.

473   "In his Reichstag speech . . .": *Jewish Chronicle*, October 13, 1939.
       "2,000 Vienna Jews . . .": Ibid., October 27, 1939.

473-74   "The determination of the Nazis . . .": Ibid., November 10, 1939.

474-75   The White House conference of the Intergovernmental Committee: *The New York Times*, October 18, 1939.

475   "The famous French author . . .": *Jewish Chronicle*, November 10, 1939.
       "The French authorities . . .": Ibid., November 24, 1939.

475-76   "It is officially announced . . .": Ibid.

476   "a program for the mass settlement . . .": *The New York Times*, October 18, 1939.
       "The campaign of extermination . . .": *Jewish Chronicle*, December 1, 1939.

476-77   "Particulars of the conditions . . .": Ibid., December 15, 1939.

477   "has published an article . . . within a short time." Ibid., January 12, 1940.

56. THE COLLAPSE OF WESTERN EUROPE

Page
478   "It has been reported . . .": *The New York Times*, March 3, 1940.

478-79   "The only country . . .": *Jewish Chronicle*, May 31, 1940.

479   "Disquiet about Britain's 'Fifth Column' . . .": Quoted in Peter and Leni Gill-
man, *"Collar the Lot": How Britain Interned and Expelled Its Wartime Refugees* (London, 1980), p. 78.

"subject to oppression . . .": Ibid., p. 43. Figures are in this book and in Bernard Wasserstein, *Britain and the Jews of Europe, 1939–1945* (London, 1979),
p. 85.

480-81   "The hot sunshine . . .": *The New York Times*, May 11, 1940.

482-83   The dumping of Jews in Unoccupied France: See Michael R. Marrus and Robert O. Paxton, *Vichy France and the Jews* (New York, 1981), pp. 10–11.

483   "after the conclusion of peace . . .": Ibid., p. 10.

"Attached . . .": Léon Poliakov, *Harvest of Hate* (New York, 1986), p. 46.

"great effort to provide . . .": Gideon Hausner, *Justice in Jerusalem* (New
York, 1968), p. 63.

484   "Apparently nobody wants to know . . . because we were Jews." Hannah Arendt, "We Refugees," *Menorah Journal*, Winter 1943, p. 70.

484-85   "I was five weeks in Gurs . . .": Letter to the Editor, *Midstream*, September
1962, p. 87.

485   Arendt's emigration: See Elisabeth Young-Bruehl, *Hannah Arendt: For Love
of the World* (New Haven, 1982), pp. 148, 163.

57. REFUGEES OR SPIES?

Page
486   "the paltriest kitchen-maid . . .": Bernard Wasserstein, *Britain and the Jews
of Europe, 1939–1945* (London, 1979), p. 88.

487   "because of the danger . . .": *Jewish Chronicle* June 21, 1940.

"subjugated and starving . . .": Winston S. Churchill, *The Second World War*,
Vol. 2, *Their Finest Hour* (Boston, 1949), p. 118.

"The French had been more hospitable . . .": Quoted in Heinz Pol, "Spies
Among Refugees," *The Nation*, August 31, 1940.

487-88   "already started to organize . . .": Quoted in David S. Wyman, *Paper Walls:
America and the Refugee Crisis, 1938–1941* (New York, 1985), p. 185.

488   "Factories sabotaged . . .": *American Magazine*, August 1940.

"When all allowance . . .": *The New York Times*, August 21, 1940.

Confessions of a Nazi Spy: See *The New York Times*, Sunday, June 2, 1940,
sect. 2.

489   "Dies Asks U.S. Ban . . .": Ibid., August 27, 1940.

490   "In the Department . . .": Fred L. Israel, ed., *The War Diary of Breckenridge
Long: Selections from the Years 1939–1944* (Lincoln, Neb., 1966), pp. 94–95.

490-91   "Still engaged in preparation . . . right into the United States." Ibid., pp. 101,
108.

491   "We can . . .": Quoted in Wyman, *Paper Walls*, p. 173.

"The American Consulate in Lisbon . . .": *The New York Times*, June 20, 1940.

491-93   *Quanza* episode: *War Diary of Breckenridge Long*, pp. 130–31.

58. THE BARRIERS STRENGTHEN

Page
494   "Refugee Ship Off Palestine . . .": *The New York Times*, November 26, 1940.

495   Aliyah Bet: See William R. Perl, *Operation Action* (New York, 1983); and Ye-

huda Bauer, *American Jewry and the Holocaust: The American Jewish Joint Distribution Committee, 1939–1945* (Detroit, 1981).

495-96 "Illegal immigration into Palestine . . .": Quoted in Bauer, *American Jewry and the Holocaust*, p. 134.

496 "Summing up the immigration situation . . .": *Jewish Chronicle*, January 3, 1941.

"According to German sources . . .": Ibid.

"who, for sentiment or for sympathy . . .": Fred L. Israel, ed., *The War Diary of Breckenridge Long: Selections from the Years 1939–1944* (Lincoln, Neb., 1966), p. 133.

497-98 "Yesterday . . . a little sarcastic.": Ibid., 151–52.

498 Alsop and Kintner on Long: "Capital Parade," *Washington Post*, November 25, 1942.

498-99 "This morning . . . into a fight." *War Diary of Breckenridge Long*, p. 156.

499 "Delays War Haven . . .": *The New York Times*, December 15, 1940.

499-500 "Like the experiment of prohibition . . .": Westbrook Pegler, "Fair Enough," *Washington Post*, December 18, 1940.

500 "to be joined up with . . .": *War Diary of Breckenridge Long*, p. 162.

59. THE DESCENT INTO UNTRAMMELED SLAUGHTER

Page

501-02 "It is estimated . . . what conquest would mean." *Jewish Chronicle*, June 27, 1941.

502 "The last Soviet column . . .": Joseph Tenenbaum, *In Search of a Lost People* (New York, 1948), pp. 114–15. Tenenbaum, who had settled in the United States after living in Lemberg through the 1918–19 pogroms, revisited the city at the end of World War II and wrote this account after interviews with eyewitnesses.

503 "Massacres of thousands of Jews . . .": *The New York Times*, October 26, 1941.

"Three days after . . .": Tenenbaum, *In Search*, p. 116.

503-04 "The extermination of the Jews . . .": *Jewish Chronicle*, August 15, 1941.

504 "The butcheries in France . . .": Churchill statement quoted in *The New York Times*, October 26, 1941.

504-05 "In view of the increasing number . . . to enter the United States." Ibid., June 19, 1941.

505 "No Ban on Refugees . . .": Ibid., June 26, 1941.

505-06 "We are aware of the situation . . .": *Jewish Chronicle*, August 8, 1941.

506-07 "Personally . . . our policies and practices." Fred L. Israel, ed., *The War Diary of Breckenridge Long: Selections from the Years 1939–1944* (Lincoln, Neb., 1966), pp. 205-6.

507 "At the request of the President . . .": Ibid., pp. 216–17.

508 Rankin's accusation: *Jewish Chronicle*, July 11, 1941.

"He has told more than one . . .": *Life*, August 11, 1941, p. 65.

"the three most important groups . . .": *The New York Times*, September 12, 1941.

"that a small group . . .": Ibid., September 10, 1941.

"The Attorney General agrees . . .": *War Diary of Breckenridge Long*, p. 217.

509 HICEM's work: HIAS, *Annual Report*, 1941.

"All Jewish emigration . . .": *Jewish Chronicle*, November 14, 1941.

60. RESPONDING TO THE INCONCEIVABLE

Page

510   "The only thing now . . .": Quoted in C. L. Sulzberger, *The American Heritage Picture History of World War II* (New York, 1966), p. 149.

511   "The Nazis' rage . . .": *Jewish Chronicle*, January 24, 1941.
       "The war in Russia . . .": Ibid., June 26, 1942.

512   *Daily Telegraph* reports of June 25 and 30, 1942: Quoted in Walter Laqueur, *The Terrible Secret* (New York, 1982), p. 74.
       "gave figures of the massed slaughter . . .": *The Times* (London), June 30, 1942.
       Zygielbojm versus Schwarzbart: Laqueur, *Terrible Secret*, pp. 75–76, esp. fn.

513   "No figures are available . . .": *The New York Times*, July 4, 1942.
       "The dastardly threat . . .": Rabbi Louis I. Newman at Temple Rodeph Shalom, New York, in ibid., June 21, 1942.

513-14 July 22, 1942, meeting at Madison Square Garden: *The New York Times*, July 23, 1942.

515   "earmarks of war rumor . . .": David S. Wyman. *The Abandonment of the Jews: America and the Holocaust, 1941–1945* (New York, 1984), p. 43.
       "Received alarming report . . .": Laqueur, *Terrible Secret*, p. 77.
       "the legation's comments . . .": Wyman, *Abandonment*, p. 44.

516   "I regret to tell you . . .": Ibid., p. 51.

516-17 Report of Polish National Council: *The New York Times*, November 25, 1942.

517   "had learned through sources . . .": Ibid.

61. A CHOICE WITHOUT PRECEDENT

Page

518   The Archbishop of Canterbury's letter: *The Times* (London), December 5, 1942.
       "At one time . . .": David S. Wyman, *The Abandonment of the Jews: America and the Holocaust, 1941–1945* (New York, 1984), p. 53.

519   "Last week I was asked . . .": Bernard Wasserstein, *Britain and the Jews of Europe, 1939–1945* (London, 1979), p. 171.
       "that he was profoundly shocked . . .": Wyman, *Abandonment*, p. 73.

519-20 Eden and the United Nations statement: *The New York Times*, December 18, 1942.

520   The ensuing scene in the House of Commons: Wasserstein, *Britain and the Jews*, pp. 173–74.
       "There is a school of thought . . .": Winston S. Churchill, *The Second World War*, vol. 4, *The Hinge of Fate* (Boston, 1950), p. 685.

520-21 The questioning of Eden in Parliament: *The Times* (London), December 22, 1942; *Jewish Chronicle*, December 25, 1942; Wasserstein, *Britain and the Jews*, p. 178.

521   "While His Majesty's Government might . . .": *The Times* (London), November 25, 1942.
       "war by refugee": This concept was popularized in an article by Samuel Lubell, "War By Refugee," *Saturday Evening Post*, March 29, 1941.

522   "That, in view of the massacres . . .": *The Times* (London), February 11, 1943.
       "The Rumanian Government . . .": *The New York Times*, February 13, 1943.

522-23 January 20, 1943, Foreign Office Memorandum: Wasserstein, *Britain and the Jews*, p. 184.

523-24   Sir William Beveridge: "The Massacre of the Jews," in the Sunday *Observer*, February 7, 1943.

524   "that the whole problem . . .": Quoted in Wyman, *Abandonment*, p. 97.

62. MOUNTING PUBLIC PRESSURE

Page

525-26   "For Sale to Humanity . . .": *The New York Times*, February 16, 1943.

526-28   The March 1, 1943, rally at Madison Square Garden: Ibid., March 2, 1943.

529   The State Department letter of February 25, 1943: *Documents on American Foreign Relations*, vol. 5, 1942-1943, pp. 289-90.

530   "We Will Never Die": *The New York Times*, March 10, 1943.

530-31   "The People Have Spoken . . .": Ibid., March 10, 1943.

531   "The question of the plight . . .": *The New York Times*, March 24, 1943.

63. VEXED BERMUDA

Page

532   "The Anglo-American conference . . .": *The New York Times*, April 19, 1943.

532-33   "The 'Bermuda Conference' on Refugees . . .": Fred L. Israel, ed., *The War Diary of Breckenridge Long: Selections from the Years 1939-1944* (Lincoln, Neb., 1966), p. 307.

533   "dead hand . . . positions of yesterday." *The New York Times*, April 13, 1943.

534   "The limits of achievement . . .": Ibid., April 20, 1943.

        "Movement of refugees . . .": Ibid., April 22, 1943.

        "Refugee Transfer . . .": Ibid., April 23, 1943.

        "Armored cars and trucks . . .": Ibid.

535   "shame . . . possible embarrassment." Ibid., April 29, 1943.

        "My companions of the Warsaw Ghetto . . .": Ibid., June 4, 1943.

536-37   "Never Again . . .": *Jewish Chronicle*, May 28, 1943.

64. THE MOVE TOWARD RESCUE ACTION

Page

538-39   "The refugee question . . .": Fred L. Israel, ed., *The War Diary of Breckenridge Long: Selections from the Years 1939-1944* (Lincoln, Neb., 1966), p. 316.

539-40   Twelve-point program: *The New York Times*, August 12, 1943.

541   "The American Jewish Conference . . .": Ibid., September 2, 1943.

542   "dissent from concurrence . . .": Ibid.

        "the helpful contributions . . .": Ibid., September 12, 1943.

        "It can be done! . . .": Ibid., October 21, 1943.

        "advise the British Government . . .": Ibid., November 1, 1943.

543   "Statement on Atrocities . . .": Ibid., November 2, 1943.

543-44   "My Uncle Abraham Reports": Ibid., November 5, 1943.

544   "The Conference . . .": Ibid., November 19, 1943.

        Senate-House rescue resolution: Henry L. Feingold, *The Politics of Rescue: The Roosevelt Administration and the Holocaust, 1938-1945* (New Brunswick, 1970), p. 223.

544-45   "The attack on British policy . . . to enter Palestine." *The New York Times*, November 20, 1945.

545-46   "Speaking as co-chairman .. to remain secret." Ibid., December 3, 1943.

546-47   "We did every legitimate thing . . . by the Hitler regime." Ibid., December 11, 1943.

547   "I made a statement . . .": *War Diary of Breckenridge Long*, p. 334.

"to natives . . .": *Documents on American Foreign Relations*, vol. 5, 1942–1943, pp. 289–90.

Emanuel Celler's remarks: *The New York Times*, December 12, 1943.

"The Jewish agitation . . .": *War Diary of Breckenridge Long*, p. 335.

65. THE WAR REFUGEE BOARD

Page
549   "the difficulties of disposing . . .": David S. Wyman, *The Abandonment of the Jews: America and the Holocaust, 1941–1945* (New York, 1984), p. 182.

"Report to the Secretary . . .": Arthur D. Morse, *While Six Million Died: A Chronicle of American Apathy* (New York, 1968), p. 89.

549-50   "to take all measures . . . rendered to war refugees." *Rescue, Information Bulletin of HIAS*, February 1944, p. 6.

550-51   "a certain amount of invidious comparison . . .": *Jewish Chronicle*, February 11, 1944.

551   Senate Palestine resolution proposal: *The New York Times*, March 29, 1944.

"the situation in the Moslem world . . .": Arthur Krock in ibid., March 8, 1944.

552   "The President has authorized us . . .": Ibid., March 10, 1944.

553   "In one of the blackest crimes . . . to convict the guilty." Ibid., March 25, 1944.

553-54   "stacked up . . . relatively small number." Ibid., March 29, 1944.

554   "Foreign Secretary Anthony Eden . . .": Ibid., March 31, 1944.

66. FINAL EFFORTS

Page
555-56   "to be placed . . .": *The New York Times*, June 10, 1944. See Ruth Gruber, *Haven* (New York, 1984), for the story of the Oswego refugees.

556   "there will be nothing but gratitude . . .": *Jewish Chronicle*, June 16, 1944.

556-57   Ira Hirschmann: See his book, *Caution to the Winds* (New York, 1962).

557   "a go-getter . . .": Bernard Wasserstein, *Britain and the Jews of Europe, 1939–1945* (London, 1979), p. 328.

557-58   "The Germans' march into Hungary . . .": *Jewish Chronicle*, March 24, 1944.

558   "Only a miracle . . .": Ibid., April 7, 1944.

"The deportation . . .": Ibid., July 14, 1944.

558-60   Joel Brand: See Alex Weissberg, *Desperate Mission: Joel Brand's Story* (New York, 1958).

559   "Everyone with whom I have talked . . .": Wasserstein, *Britain and the Jews*, p. 251.

"arrived in circumstances so suspect . . .": Ibid., p. 256.

"I would not take it seriously": Ibid., p. 259.

559-60   "This fantastic and revolting offer . . .": *Jewish Chronicle*, July 21, 1944.

560   "According to a report . . . much larger." Wasserstein, *Britain and the Jews*, p. 264.

560-61   "temporary havens . . . a practical impossibility." Ibid., p. 266.

561   "The State Department made clear . . .": *The New York Times*, August 18, 1944.

561-62   "It is not contemplated . . .": David S. Wyman, *The Abandonment of the Jews: America and the Holocaust, 1941–1945* (New York, 1984), p. 291. The unlikelihood of the bombing proposals' ever having reached Roosevelt is in a note on p. 410 of Wyman's book.

562-63   Raoul Wallenberg: See John Bierman, *Righteous Gentile: The Story of Raoul Wallenberg, Unsung Hero of the Holocaust* (New York, 1981).

67. DISPLACED PERSONS

Page

567   "German civilians . . .": *The New York Times*, April 18, 1945.

568   "As we entered the camp . . .": Richard Crossman, *Palestine Mission* (New York, 1947), p. 11.

568-69   "About ten miles . . .": Oscar Pinkus, *A Choice of Masks* (Englewood Cliffs, N.J., 1969), pp. 35–36.

569   "Generally speaking . . .": "Report of Earl G. Harrison," Appendix B in Leonard Dinnerstein, *America and the Survivors of the Holocaust* (New York, 1982), p. 292.

"Some of these centers . . .": Crossman, *Palestine Mission*, p. 77.

570   "from the Jewish transit camps . . .": *Jewish Chronicle*, September 28, 1945.

"morally wrong and politically indefensible . . .": Dinnerstein, *America and the Survivors*, p. 78.

571   "the view that all . . .": Ibid., p. 80.

571-72   "There were housed . . . and nothing else." Crossman, *Palestine Mission*, pp. 80–81.

572   "(a) that 100,000 certificates . . .": *Jewish Chronicle*, August 30, 1946.

"because they don't want . . .": Ibid., June 14, 1946.

573   Gallup Poll: Dinnerstein, *America and the Survivors*, p. 114.

"Of the 39,000 . . .": HIAS, *Annual Report*, 1946, p. 9.

68. WASHINGTON AND JERUSALEM

Page

575-76   "More than 700 persons a day . . .": *Jewish Chronicle*, August 30, 1946.

576-77   "Even while fighting was still . . . some other point." Levi Soshuk and Azriel Eisenberg, eds., *Momentous Century: Personal and Eyewitness Accounts of the Rise of the Jewish Homeland and State, 1875–1978* (New York, 1984), pp. 236–40.

578   "A faint light . . . the longed-for shore?" Ibid., p. 245.

579   "also expressed his support . . .": *Jewish Chronicle*, October 11, 1946.

"that the Mandate should be terminated . . .": Walter Laqueur, ed., *The Israel-Arab Reader: A Documentary History of the Middle East Conflict* (New York, 1968), p. 108.

UN Resolution, November 29, 1947: Ibid., pp. 114–15.

580   "If we are to remain . . .": *Life*, September 23, 1946.

581   "Who are these people? . . .": Leonard Dinnerstein, *America and the Survivors of the Holocaust* (New York, 1982), p. 129.

"Weren't the DPs *Jews?* . . .": Ibid., p. 133.

"have the effect of abrogating . . .": Ibid., p. 142.

581-82   "will be open to the immigration of Jews . . .": Laqueur, *Israel-Arab Reader*, p. 127.

582   The Eliahu Epstein–George C. Marshall exchange of letters: Soshuk and Eisenberg, *Momentous Century*, pp. 263, 266.

583   "The bad points of the bill . . .": *The New York Times*, June 26, 1948.
"The DP Act of 1948 . . .": HIAS, *Annual Report*, 1948, p. 5.

69. PASSAGES FROM POSTWAR EUROPE

Page
584   "On Saturday, October 30 . . .": *Rescue, Information Bulletin of HIAS*, October-November 1948, p. 1.
584-85 "Even before contact is made . . . on their trip." HIAS, *Annual Report*, 1947, p. 18.
585-86 "A group of DPs . . . 'I think we're home.' " *Rescue*, June 1949, p. 1.
586   "Despite the fact . . .": Ibid., June-July 1950, p. 1.
587   "we are one and all immigrants . . .": Mark Wischnitzer, *Visas to Freedom: The History of HIAS* (New York, 1956), p. 254.
588-89 "It is stated occasionally . . . required by the law." HIAS, *Annual report*, 1948, pp. 6–7.
589   "When in the summer of 1952 . . .": Wischnitzer, *Visas*, p. 261.
589-90 "About 22 months ago . . .": Ibid., p. 268.

70. THE END OF JEWISH EASTERN EUROPE

Page
592   "Communist newspapers . . .": *The New York Times*, October 11, 1956.
593   " 'extraordinary measures' . . .": Ibid., November 9, 1956.
594-95 Miksa Frankel's narrative: *Rescue, Information Bulletin of HIAS*, Summer 1957, p. 3.
595   "*our* Jews over *their* Arabs": Norman Davies, *God's Playground: A History of Poland*, 2 vols. (New York, 1982), 2:588.
596-97 "In rapid retribution . . . of anti-Semitism." *The New York Times*, March 13, 1968.
597   "At no time in his address . . . the only fatherland." Ibid., March 20, 1968.
598   "As an immediate reaction . . .": HIAS, *Annual Report*, 1968, p. 5
"from September to November 1969 . . .": Ibid., 1969, p. 5.

71. SOVIET JEWS

Page
599   "if possible, to penetrate . . .": Elie Wiesel, *The Jews of Silence*, trans. Neal Kozodoy (New York, 1966), p. vii.
"Do you know . . .": Ibid., p. 10.
600   "About a hundred *hasidim* . . .": Ibid., p. 24.
601   "Where did they all come from? . . .": Ibid., p. 44.
Alla Rusinek: "How They Taught Me I Was a Jew," by Alla Rusinek. Reprinted from *The New York Times*, in Richard Cohen, ed., *Let My People Go* (New York, 1971), pp. 50–52.
601-02 "A packed congregation . . .": *Jewish Chronicle*, September 27, 1968.
602   "An estimated 12,000 people . . .": Ibid., October 18, 1968.

602   "The freedom to emigrate . . .": Quoted in Lionel Kochan, ed., *The Jews in Soviet Russia Since 1917* (Oxford, 1978), p. 349.

603   "It is known that . . .": Ibid., p. 351.
       "Reports that Soviet Jews . . .": *Jewish Chronicle*, January 6, 1967.
       "I do not wish to be a citizen . . .": Cohen, *Let My People Go*, p. 35.

604   *Khronika* and *Iskhod:* Kochan, *Jews in Soviet Russia*, p. 350.
       Dragunsky, Kosygin: Ibid., p. 355.

604-05 "New Surge of Emigration . . .": *The New York Times*, November 6, 1971.

606   "More Than Half . . .": Ibid., December 12, 1976.

607   "the next phase of their journey . . .": Emanuel Litvinoff, "Crossroads to Freedom," in *Insight: Soviet Jews*, February 1977.
       "Here they stay . . .": HIAS, *Annual Report*, 1976, p. 18.

608   "A research study . . .": *The New York Times*, August 12, 1979.
       "Whither emigrate? . . . ": Chaim Chissin, *A Palestine Diary: Memoirs of a Bilu Pioneer, 1882-87* (New York, 1976), p. 263.
       "Many of our unhappy brethren . . .": *Jewish Chronicle*, April 21, 1882.
       "the utter sacredness and necessity . . .": Zosa Szajkowski, "Materialn vegen der Yiddisher Emigratzye keyn America in 1881-1882," *YIVO Bletter*, vol. 19 (March-April, 1942), p. 277. Translated by the author.

AFTERWORD

Page
609   Literature of accusation: Of the books on this theme, the strongest indictments of Roosevelt and his administration are: David S. Wyman, *The Abandonment of the Jews* (New York, 1984), and Arthur D. Morse, *While Six Million Died* (New York, 1968); and, less strongly, David S. Wyman, *Paper Walls* (Amherst, 1968), Henry L. Feingold, *The Politics of Rescue* (New Brunswick, 1970), and Saul S. Friedman, *No Haven for the Oppressed* (Detroit, 1971).
       A similar, though less strident, approach to the role of the British government is in Bernard Wasserstein, *Britain and the Jews of Europe 1939-1945* (Oxford, 1979), and Michael J. Cohen, *Churchill and the Jews* (London, 1985), which surveys the theme through Churchill's entire career. The role of Canada is dealt with in Irving Abella and Harold Troper, *None Is Too Many* (New York, 1983). That of all the Allied Powers is treated in Martin Gilbert, *Auschwitz and the Allies* (New York, 1981).
       The treatment of Nazi persecutions by the American press is surveyed in Deborah E. Lipstadt, *Beyond Belief* (New York, 1986). The responses of the American Jewish community are analyzed in *American Jewry During the Holocaust*, a report by the American Jewish Commission on the Holocaust, issued in 1984. The problem of when and how information about the slaughter reached the West is dealt with in Walter Laqueur, *The Terrible Secret* (London, 1980).

Acknowledgments

This book was made possible by a generous grant from HIAS (United Hias Service, Inc.), with funds provided by Elliot and Louis Liskin in memory of their parents, Joseph and Ida Liskin. The arrangement was made through the good offices of George Jaffin, distinguished lawyer and philanthropist, and Edwin Shapiro, former president of HIAS. My gratitude to all these parties is reflected in the dedication at the beginning.

I am also grateful to Irving Goodman and to my literary agent, Georges Borchardt, who formed the final and decisive links in the chain that brought HIAS and myself together.

The research for this book was done in various places, but I particularly want to thank the staff of the Jewish Division of the New York Public Library, who bore the burden of my inquiries and my presence during more than two years. I am also grateful to the Butler Library, Columbia University—especially its quiet and comfortable microfilm reading room—to the library and archives of the YIVO Institute for Jewish Research, to the Leo Baeck Institute, and to the American Jewish Historical Society and its director, Bernard Wax. Last but not least, HIAS made its archives available to me, and I am grateful to Brenda Schaefer for her patience and kindness in guiding me through them, as well as for her help in many other respects.

I also want to thank my editor, Marian S. Wood, for her astute comments and help all along the way.

And above all, eternal gratitude goes to my wife, Beverly Sanders, who sustained me through sickness and health throughout this project, as always, and who, as a skilled editor, provided constant and invaluable advice.

Index

649